Assembling Alternatives

Assembling Alternatives

Reading Postmodern Poetries Transnationally

Edited by Romana Huk

Wesleyan University Press
Middletown, Connecticut

Published by Wesleyan University Press, Middletown, CT 06459

Printed in the United States of America
5 4 3 2 1

Library of Congress Cataloging-in-Publication Data
Assembling alternatives: reading postmodern poetries transnationally /
edited by Romana Huk.
p. cm.
Includes bibliographical references.
ISBN 0-8195-6539-3 (alk. paper)—ISBN 0-8195-6540-7 (pbk.: alk. paper)
1. American poetry—20th century—History and criticism. 2. Postmodernism (Literature)—United States. 3. English poetry—20th century—History and criticism. 4. Commonwealth poetry—20th century—History and criticism. 5. Postmodernism (Literature)—Great Britain. 6. Postmodernism (Literature)—Australia. 7. Postmodernism (Literature)—Ireland. 8. Postmodernism (Literature)—Canada. 9. Poetics. I. Huk, Romana, 1959–

PS310.P63A87 2003
811'.5409113—dc21 2002154344

Contents

II *Intranational divides and intracultural differences*

III *In practice / polemics*

Acknowledgments

The conference that generated not only this book but subsequent exchanges between the poetry communities it hosted would not have been possible without the generous support it received from numerous organizations, departments and offices on campus at the University of New Hampshire. I would like to gratefully acknowledge the help of the UNH Center for the Humanities, the Vice President's Office for Academic Affairs, the Vice President's Office for Research, the College of Liberal Arts, the Department of English, the Parents' Association, the Class of '54, and the Writers' Series (coordinated by the poet Charles Simic). I would also like to thank the Canadian Consulate/Boston and the Irish Arts Council.

Equally importantly, I would like to thank all those participants who came to *Assembling Alternatives* but whose work is not represented in this book. Without them the event would not have been what is was—and this book would simply "not have been."

Special thanks to Victoria Stec, who worked diligently with me during the last stages of preparing the manuscript and checking the copyediting, and to Tom Butler for his second pair of eyes on final proofs. Very special thanks to Peter Holland, my husband, for innumerable bits of advice; I dedicate my 1/25 of this book to him.

And finally, many thanks to those small presses who do not appear below in our formal acknowledgments but whose friendship with our essayists (indeed, in some cases they *are* our essayists!) tacitly allowed us to quote from their publications.

All quotes in Alison Mark's essay from Charles Bernstein, *A Poetics,* copyright © 1992 by Charles Bernstein, appear by permission from Harvard University Press. All quotes from Veronica Forrest-Thomson's *Collected Poems* are reprinted by kind permission of Anthony Barnett.

Peter Middleton is grateful to Allen Fisher for permission to quote from *Brixton Fractals* (Aloes Books, republished by Tsunami, Vancouver) and from his work in *Future Exiles*.

Keith Tuma thanks cris cheek for lines quoted from "Stranger" and "Distance No Object."

In Don Wellman's essay: "Letter Sycorax" by Kamau Brathwaite, from *MiddlePassages,* copyright © 1993 by Kamau Brathwaite. Reprinted by permission of New Directions Publishing Corp. Excerpts from *The School of Udhra,* copyright © 1993 by Nathaniel Mackey. Reprinted by permission of CITY LIGHTS BOOKS. Excerpts from *The Maximus Poems: Volume Three.*

Edited/translated by George Butterick. Copyright © 1983 by the Estate of Charles Olson and The Regents of the University of California and copyright © 1975 by the Estate of Charles Olson.

Kathleen Crown wishes to thank Ed Roberson and Tracie Morris for allowing her to quote from copyright material.

cris cheek would like to thank Bill Grifiths for permission to quote from *War w/Windsor* (Pirate Press, 1974) and Tom Leonard and Galloping Dog Press and Jonathan Cape for lines quoted from *Ghostie Men* and *Nora's Place,* all poems © Tom Leonard.

Nancy Gish is grateful to Emily Todd for permission to quote from her interview with Liz Lochhead in *Verse* 8:3/9:1 and to Polygon Press for their permission to quote from *Dreaming Frankenstein* (1984) by Liz Lochhead. Excerpts from "The Queen of Sheba" by Kathleen Jamie, *Mr. & Mrs. Scotland Are Dead: Poems 1980–1984,* Bloodaxe Books, 2002.

Linda Kinnahan is grateful to Reality Street Editions for permission to quote from Denise Riley's *Mop Mop Georgette* (1993) and to Kathleen Fraser for lines quoted from her prose.

Susan Rudy would like to thank Jeff Derksen, Daphne Marlatt and Fred Wah for permission to quote from copyright material.

In John Wilkinson's essay: "Emotions of Normal People" by Charles Bernstein, *Dark City,* Los Angeles: Sun and Moon Press, 1994: used with the permission of the author. "Billie" and "February" copyright © 1986 by John Wieners. Reprinted from SELECTED POEMS: 1958–1984 with the permission of Black Sparrow Press.

Bob Perelman is grateful to Rachel Blau DuPlessis for permission to quote from *The Pink Guitar* (New York: Routledge, Chapman and Hall, Inc., 1990); and to the University of California Press for permission to quote from Charles Olson's *The Maximus Poems* (Berkeley, 1983).

Rod Mengham would like to thank J. H. Prynne for permission to quote from his poem "Her Weasels Wild Returning."

Preface

Readers will quickly notice that this book is somewhat unusual, visually speaking. I don't mean by this to refer directly to the interesting format of John Cayley's chapter, for example, or to the generic play of M. NourbeSe Philip's "Interview," though many such examples of innovation occur throughout this collection. I refer instead to systematic choices made in producing the book as a whole—and what I mean, more generally, is the choice *not* to systematize. In other words, and unlike almost any other collection of essays currently in print, this volume has not been subject to a "regularization" of punctuation usage, spelling, and other kinds of grammatical/elemental presentation. Our editors at Wesleyan University Press have been unusually understanding about the need for a book such as this—focused as it is on the differences as well as similarities between national traditions in avant-garde writing—to foreground differences in usage rather than level them or "Americanize" the work of our Canadian, Australian, Irish and British contributors; such processes would be counterproductive to our purposes. Free of them, all kinds of interesting distinctions in the writing appear, however subtly, as well as noteworthy crossovers and mergers. (To offer, rather lightheartedly, just one example, readers might enjoy looking for the paragraph in Peter Middleton's essay where 'favour' and 'favorite' both can be found, suggesting the transatlantic nature of this essayist's reading/writing habits.) It is perhaps quirky of me to insist that Wesleyan's fine copyeditors stay their pencils and allow such seeming "inconsistencies" to remain, but I do so in part to question the unexamined value placed on such consistency in a book like this. *Why* nurse the assumption that the collection most carefully rendered "consistent" across the work of international contributions is the book best produced? We have, most carefully, produced a book that honors differences, even the most minute, in writing (though I have gone so far as to correct typos and seek consistency *within* essays; that may well announce certain failings of my own in this venture). The result is as profound as readers wish to make it: they may see it as supportive of those essays in this book that ask complex questions about the material history of the text; or, at the simplest level, they may simply enjoy seeing unfamiliar spellings and marks and hearing the differing rhythm of clause-building in work written outside their own varying traditions. In my own case, I notice and enjoy the often differing sense of where commas go in particularly writing from overseas, or other traditions' lack of familiarity with those places where we in the States have been systematically replacing nearly every "which" with a "that." I have tried, by leaving in even the different quotation marks—the "inverted commas"—that "British English" is recognizable for producing, to call attention to a number of less visible differences, as well as to ask readers to think about the equally interesting variations that occur in the work of our Australian and Canadian and Irish contributors. Capitalizations, for example, say a good deal; I find it significant that terms used ubiquitously by all of our contributors—such as, say, "Language poetry"—will be differently capped or not capped from essay to essay. Readers must be aware, however, that essayists were *not* aware, as they were finishing revisions for the book, that these differences would be allowed to stand. Therefore, as in most other circumstances that we must live with, both intentionality and inadvertency remain less readable here than one might like them to be—given that, in this case, essayists who might be *au fait* with American usage may well have translated themselves in advance for our American publisher.

Still, and in any case, here is the text—close to as it was when I received it, with only small bits of help from me for the sake of clarity and accuracy.

Romana Huk

Romana Huk

Introduction

In August of 1996, when the international conference/festival from which this collection takes its title was convened, the problems of reading inflections of "postmodern" practice in poetry across national boundaries had barely been touched as a topic of debate.[1] Many of the hundred-plus leading avant-garde poets and critics in attendance had little acquaintance with others outside their own or, at best, their neighboring traditions, even if most had some knowledge of American work or had some opinion about its influence as the dominating architect/anthologizer of "Language poetry," that amorphous field of writing for which the term is now internationally if loosely used to join together poets working in interaction with postmodern or poststructuralist theories of language. Of the countries represented most fully—the U.S., U.K., Canada and Ireland (as well as Australia, by virtue of the appearance of several of its key critics)—only the first could boast of prolific production in the way of an avant-garde poetics, as well as of having turned heads at big presses and within academe; however, the very success and energy that characterize the American scene have also been fueling the centripetal force of its attentions and movements. My initial desires when dreaming up the conference included simply introducing the British and Irish poets whose work I was coming to know while on sabbatical in London to their American and Canadian counterparts. I had only begun at that point to suspect that the little flurries of antagonism between traditions and parodies of one another that I had seen were symptoms of larger problems—even larger than simple size-envy or post-post-colonial complexes—that upon examination could not only change the seamless way we read such practice across national boundaries, but also suggest how assumptions about what constitutes "radical" departure in each imagined community might be *re*-read from within.[2] In the years that have followed the conference, during which time this book has itself gone through several permutations and re-sortings of relevant issues, the matters with which we were dealing have come into what I find to be rather startling new focus. I will try to explain them as I see them; not all in this book would agree with my assessments, nor many inflect the issues along my lines, but I ask that readers regard this introduction as being an essay by yet an/other reader, and not as one seeking to define the trajectory of this book.

I

The very idea of starting up from the concept of "nation" is controversial, but I do so on purpose in order to redress the universalizing tendencies of not only postmodern poetics but also of the theories from which they take their inspiration. The latter's panoramic view of linguistic dynamics lends itself to imaginations of a global avant-garde community, and it of course makes sense that a marginalized practice *would* imagine itself part of something larger, and its likeness elsewhere—a habit fairly standard in avant-garde movements since the beginning of the last century. Even mid- to late-twentieth-century discourses on cultural relativisms, and their differing inscriptions of identity formation as well as power relations in the languages of their historical communities—regulated and perpetually re-envisioned as "national" ones—have continued to be read comfortably alongside unspoken assumptions in postmodern poetics that its overall project does or should transcend such boundaries. The contradictions inherent in the millennial world of theorizing are such that even the field most crucially informed by sophisticated readings of nation-specific mythologies and their impact on culture—post-colonial studies—has only in the last few years begun to combine post-national visions such as those of a "black Atlantic" with consideration of the more sobering prophecies of thinkers who have warned that the dangers of overweening theorization outstripping specific cultural study have required new attention since the early 1990s.[3] Exposing the artificiality of national boundaries around "multicultural" terrains has meant slighting the site-specific inflection of cultural difference that national imaginaries silently conduct. As a result, the phrase "crossing cultures" in the fields of cultural and literary studies is still often assumed to refer solely to the transmission across or transgression of ethnic or racial boundaries in cultural practice—so much so that even our press's readers for this volume negated its original subtitle, "reading postmodern poetries cross-culturally," arguing that we hadn't enough essays specifically focused on those issues. But the project of the book—despite its acquisition of a new subtitle—remains the same: to consider how the abstract identification/construction of "nation" creates deep cultural boundaries, even between seemingly seamless racial communities, such as the largely white community that has taken part in constructing the dominant avant-garde aesthetic; grounded in European post-structuralist theory, it recognizably links art communities in North America with their British, Irish and Australian counterparts (as well as with other non-Anglophone constituencies not treated in this book). We also attempt to critique the supposedly colorblind universalisms that emerge, ironically, from such matrices of Euro-North American "alternative" poetics by including essays that come into dialogue with them from the perspective of crucially differing, "other"-cultural postmodern philosophies. But our focus is primarily on probing the very center to those aesthetics which does not hold—which reveals itself as nationally inflected in each of its differing "states" or sites of production.

Introducing us to the problem from the purview of North American poetics, Canadian writer Jeff Derksen argues in the first essay of this book that "[a]ny commonly shared poetics of difference must assume an unquestioned linguistic or contextual norm"—an untenable situation not only for Canadian poets writing from orienting national constructs of identity that differ from those of their more influential neighbor, as well as for the differently raced or postcolonial poets also discussed in the following pages, but for every writer who took part in the 1996 conference. As Irish poet Trevor Joyce recalls at the outset of his essay, some American critics had difficulty at the conference in seeing what was radical or "alternative" about the work performed by poets from other countries during the fifty-plus readings that took place in its "festival" alter-hours; he also recalls that his countryman Billy Mills critiqued the conference's proceedings because they seemed, from an Irish perspective, to be constructing a notion of the avant-garde "purely in American terms"—an observation I had to absorb and think through a good while, having been caught out as the organizer, and as an American, by the very problem I was hoping to expose, despite the transatlantic (largely British) foci in my own work.

Attempting to reassess one's own positions in these matters is difficult because poststructuralist forms of linguistic theorizing have themselves tended to dislocate speakers from individual contexts as well as words and images from their comfortable homes in accommodating discourses at the same time that they assume the need for detailed critique of such structures in culture. Perhaps as a consequence of their conflicted approach to identity and history, strategies of experimenting with and newly deploying (as well as commenting on) language in avant-garde poetics have rarely taken stock of the number of ways in which powerful and still operative *national* narratives of identity and progress inform both their methods and their results. In the United States, for example, the same body of avant-garde poetic theory that, especially at the start, demanded the death of the particular subject on the one hand and demanded the assessment of particularity, of "heterogeneous and anomalous elements rather than homogenizing ones" on the other, demonstrating these contradictions even as it perpetuated others inherent in American philosophy. Responsible for so many exhilarating new practices in poetry, that body of theory is also responsible for homogenizing America once again in the very mold of its traditional, oxymoronic image of the "melting pot," where the differences between groups and selves in history is erased by a vision of utopian democracy that never critiques its conceptualization as being culture-specific with an historical, political project. That self-replicating project creeps continually into avant-garde ones, inadvertently, in statements as seemingly inarguable as Charles Bernstein's recent reiteration that "for writing, or reading, to assume—and consequently 'express' or 'project'—a national identity is as problematic as for writing to assume a self or group identity."[4] Considered sceptically, the only alteration in such new formulations that continue to obviate historical difference seems to be that the overt nationalism of the earlier mythos is elided. And not assessing the differences *between* national imaginaries further complicates any attempt to situate one's own views in the course of post-millennial conversations about the state of the art worldwide. Splits such as the one Barrett Watten describes in his essay between American poets' self-canceling tendencies and what Peter Middleton describes as British poets' self-exilic ones, for example, often lead to arguments about which is the "better" or more advanced avant-garde practice, while considerations of what sort of tradition the work is departing from—in which context it is "radical in relation," as Australian critic Philip Mead puts it in his essay—as well as the extent to which it is unconsciously caught up in that tradition remain unexplored.

The argument of this book is, then, that understanding the embedded nature of one's own formative assumptions in the articulation of an avant-garde poetics is difficult unless an attempt to read others' versions of "the radical" is made, and through that encounter with otherness one's own construction of "innovation" is reassessed. This is the kind of work waiting for readers of the present collection. It begins with a "Part I" dedicated to reassessing the avant-garde activity of these representative English-speaking countries when each is juxtaposed with others assumed to be engaged in the same project.[5] Part II takes the same concerns into intranational cultural spaces, those divided by race, class and gender as well as intranational *national* differences, such as those dividing Scottish from other "U.K." poets; the issues that arise there sketch in a diagram of the ways in which Language poetics can be inadvertently used to perpetuate exclusive practice within a culturally diverse context. Part III is more loosely configured as one reserved for discussion of new directions in radical practice, as well as for some polemical arguments about the same that arose at the '96 conference. This section begins by considering the ways in which the performance of writing, and writing for performance—perhaps the most importantly retheorized elements in recent avant-garde practice—have either served to crystallize the issues surrounding contextual differences in (and literal "place" of) writing, or have taken writers into cybertextual spaces. The remaining five arguments in the section espouse such projects as connecting earlier avant-garde poetics' foci on the material text to a newly conceived version of "cultural practice," or reconsidering these poetries' political work alongside mainstream millennial trends and revisiting the effect(iveness) of their resistance to accessibility—even constructing an "after-avant-gardism" in terms of movement from parataxis to startling new kinds of cohesion. Either by way of polemical generalizing, or by closely reading an exemplary poet's work to make their points, each of these essayists engage with questions about how at this point, more than thirty years into the avant-garde "Language" project, its formal choices might change or be re-read; they divide, at times explosively, over the answers, given their differing national/cultural and gendered positionings.

It may seem from my descriptions of it that this book is far too focused on the *problems* of reading these poetries from a distance, rather than the positive results of doing the same, but the essays themselves will rectify any such impression. My assumption is that what has been called experimental or avant-garde or radical or postmodern poetry has so convincingly demonstrated its strengths in recent years that it can and must bear internal critique, especially now as millennial temptations to eulogize it and its accomplishments—often by anthologizing and narrating its "progress" in vast tomes—endanger new-century continuance of what, in (its own) theory, should always remain a problematized, revisionary, self-reflexive practice.[6]

II

For those unfamiliar with the history of what Americans dubbed L=A=N=G=U=A=G=E poetry in the 1970s, the first essay in this book by Jeff Derksen will be the place to start—not least because, in the spirit of the collection as a whole, that story is retold from a Canadian perspective and it emphasizes "the effect of cultural nationalism on the reception of poetry as well as the antagonism created by language writing's self-definition as an 'American' poetic movement.'"[7] Given the sociotemporal matrix of its emergence—during the Vietnam War and the civil rights era, a fact that Barrett Watten returns to in his essay as he discusses the context-sensitive nature of the movement at its outset (as opposed to what he sees as its current disconnection from culture)—Derksen argues that its genesis "foregrounds the role of the nation in cultural production" in a way that has been helpful to Canadian writers of radical work as they attempt to induce a response that would emerge differently (and therefore tellingly) from that in the United States. Obviously distanced from as well as influenced by a burgeoning Canadian cultural nationalism that repels American influences in the arts, the culture-specific work of avant-garde poets in Vancouver, which Derksen discusses as an example, draws upon a reading of American Language work as *national* writing whose methods cannot be directly applied elsewhere but reward recontextualization. "Language writing does not circulate across national borders as a siteless transnational avant-garde," Derksen argues, initiating the key polemic that runs in many inflections throughout the essays to follow in this book. Yet he is keen to suggest that awareness of positionings outside dominant ones—such as those in the U.S.—as well as outside "transparent internationalisms," which Watten also warns us have taken over from what he sees to have been the locatedness of early Language interventions, allows for a "locating [of] language writing in a transnational field of relations" where it is both specific to local crises in the production of meaning and able to address the effects of a world system.

Miriam Nichols goes on to discuss the work of young writers such as Derksen in the Canadian sphere as being importantly and differently focused on this kind of dialectal viewing of one's local space in a global context because national borders signify so differently in Canadian mythologies of identity. As Linda Hutcheon has also famously argued, Canada's cobbling together of what she terms an "archipelago" of separate spaces, each with their own ethnic or otherwise intranational autonomy, leaves little horizon for the imagination of national identity.[8] There is no sense of connective ancient past, or American-style "drama of a founding revolution," as Nichols puts it, with its spin-off conceptualizations of progress from radical departure continued in idealized images of the pilgrim/immigrant and the discoverer/poet. "When [the American poet, Ron] Silliman imagines 'A small man / (neither warrior nor monk) . . . lean[ing] over a desk in an attempt / to imagine the world'," Nichols argues, "he renovates a rhetorical gesture that can be traced back through Olson, Pound and Whitman to Jonathan Winthrop and the Puritan 'City on a Hill.'" Canadian writers—unless they are highly visible, as are Margaret Atwood or D. G. Jones—seem to lack the sense of public address Nichols perceives in American Language poetry; she describes Derksen's "tourist-like indifference to borders" as the stance of the shopper rather than the citizen or the revolutionary, whose Canadian resistance takes the form of errancy and irony rather than critical admonition, and whose "avoidance of the national" differs quite crucially from Charles Bernstein's. And yet Irish or British or Australian writers might argue that her description of such impossibly displaced borders sounds remarkably *like* Bernstein's conceptualization of what he calls "the impossibility of America" (given the "multiplicity of Americas that make U.S. culture as vital as it is"[9]). When she suggests that Canada "has never had a nationally recognized political imaginary" and, through reference to Robert Kroetsch's essays, that Canada is a postmodern country whose "very falling-apart of [its] story is what holds its story together," she constructs a model of identity/positioning for the poet that echoes Bernstein's in that it is released from historical constraints on linguistic imagination; it involves, as Bernstein describes it in the U.S., "replacement of the national and geographically centered category of English . . . poetry not with the equally essentialist category of American poetry but with a field of potentialities, a virtual America that we approach but never possess."[10]

Connecting up his own readings of young "post-1989" poets from Canada as well as the States, American critic Steve Evans provides yet another view of poetic relations by charting the social history of changed sensibilities which he argues has made new writing in both countries take a new course, off the tack of its precursors in Language poetics. Evans's assessment of North American poetry of the new generation is that theirs is a "returned emphasis on poetic practice as opposed to theoretical discourse." New emphases on ethics, action and community sync, some may think strangely, with first-generation Language poet Bob Perelman's suggestion in our final section of this book that there must be a new "socialized texture" to avant-garde work; but Evans's essay asserts discontinuity rather than continuity in this project, and his return to the use of collective pronouns marks the new generation's departure from departure: "'we have to decide to enunciate our "we," our community, in order to enter history,'" he writes, quoting the philosopher Jean-Luc Nancy; in Evans's view this must happen"[i]n the wake of, and in deliberate contrast to, the self-assertive, auto-exegetical, and reciprocally evaluative conduct of the language-centered writers." He claims with such a remark that postmodernism has managed only an updated version of modern, transcendent, egoistic work, while current work attempts a return to the pronominal status of a humbler, self-historicizing collective form; yet quite interestingly he will not articulate the new movement's "manifesto" because, as he writes, "[i]t is action that articulates community, these poets seem to be saying, and action—as it transforms conditions—outpaces the terms of its own recognition." An important new conception of how poetics intersect with history is coming into form in this essay as it attempts to struggle past certain inherited contradictions in theory and practice—as it attempts to make life liveable, as his epigraph from Oppen has it. As with performance work, the new poetries seem to suggest that *something* exceeds the old focus on language operations—"suffering," for one thing, as Evans suggests—and requires attending to. And yet that something, as well as newly devised methods of approaching it, differs from context to context; if this essay included work by some of the new young British poets, for example, that "we" would not hold together a community in agreement.[11]

Until the effects of "distance," as Keith Tuma's essay figures it, in seeing one's own projects are taken into account, the readings and implicit (sometimes explicit) judgments of other-national explorations of postmodern thought in poetic form will, ironically, continue to isolate traditions rather than allow for the reading back of difference. The American/British axis of influence tends to be especially prone to such dismissals and antagonisms; the close relationship of the two traditions, despite America's turnabout at the height of its own nationalizing departure from British sway, seems to promote even deeper contempt on either part for what is perceived as lack of sophistication in the other's work—whether it be described as being due to residual "traditionalism" or jejeune naïveté[12]—perhaps because shared assumptions of fundamental sameness preclude respect for differences. Tuma's invaluable and judicious explication of some of the transatlantic disagreements that have arisen, as well as the attempts to spawn "a transnational or international discourse about poetry," which his essay expresses sympathy with, seems to resign itself for the moment to an era in which the major spokespeople are "busy gathering the world into [their] definitions." We are all vulnerable to such oxymoronically destructive community building; even Tuma in this admirably balanced treatment of the issues reproduces yet again the familiar trope of progression in which British and Irish poetries "lag behind" American ones in many respects, when what we require is a sense of differing trajectories of movement—what *has* been happening in other contexts rather than what has *not*.

Alison Mark's study of the American reception of Veronica Forrest-Thomson's notes toward an avant-garde poetics sets up this discussion as it follows in this section, because her careful comparison of Charles Bernstein's importation of Forrest-Thomson's ideas from *Poetic Artifice* (1978) into his own *Artifice of Absorption* (1987; also in *A Poetics,* 1992)—something that, to his credit, no one had thought to do before, despite the fact that her articulation of principles should be read on a continuum with Marjorie Perloff's groundbreaking book, *Radical Artifice* (1991)—highlights the differing conceptions of "community," "audience" and "radicality" that undergird a number of discrepancies between the formal dispositions of American and British avant-garde work. Although several crucial theorists such as Jonathan Culler (who became her husband) were indebted to Forrest-Thomson for her sophisticated rethinkings of the place of artifice in investigations of "the real" in any Wittgensteinian or postmodern linguistic landscape, the differences between her formulations and, say, American ones are telling. Whereas, for example, Forrest-Thomson—whose lineage of linguistically innovative poets begins with Donne—retains a line between semantic elements (what Bernstein calls "only those elements to which a / relatively fixed connotative or denotative meaning / can be ascribed"[13]) and nonmeaningful or contributing elements, Bernstein faults her for assuming that *anything* is nonmeaningful. In other words, whereas she suggests that some things are communally meaningful and others—like sound—are indeterminate, placing the latter in the category of the discontinuous as opposed to the continuous with conventional lines of meaning, Bernstein negates the distinction and assumes, according to poststructuralist principles, that all units of meaning are signs borne out of linguistic imaginings and should be treated alike. His is a recognizably American revolutionary departure from what is perceived as typically British hierarchical methods of categorizing and codifying; it makes allowance for greater departure from communal ways of habitual meaning—or for inaccessibility, if one so reads the relegation of signs to the semantic level of sounds—in American poetics, whereas Forrest-Thomson's application of her theories in her own poetry retains a discursiveness some Americans find to be too "traditional" because it attempts to maintain a relationship between the continuous and the discontinuous, and does not as often value the option of breaking language down into deconstructed fragments, as American work was at the time becoming notorious for doing. The emphasis in British experiment has tended to be on the critique of historical discourse rather than of language *qua* language, as code or tool; socially oriented rather than individually oriented, and less abstract (or theoretical) or idealistic and universal in application, British work often enacts a different kind of politics—one also based in post-Marxist philosophy, though on a version less "poetically" or figuratively transformed.[14] Embracing some, but not all, of Language writing's formal imperatives within an only seemingly more traditional line, innovative British work might seem to Americans at times as mere application of Language poetics when in reality it often moves from a different starting point, and with a different project in mind.

And yet Peter Middleton in his essay for this section explores similarly contradictory, if very different, constructs of individualism operating in tension with such discursiveness in British writing that ironically impede the collection and dissemination of ideas and small press work in the U.K. Working back through cultural theorists such as Marilyn Strathern, Middleton traces ideologies of exile in English culture that, unlike American ideologies of the individual revolutionary, he argues, are more "autonomous of relationship" and therefore less admissive of collective and critical movements such as those that spawned either the "New American Poetry" or the Language movement. Differing trajectories of postwar nationalistic sentiment of course play their part in Middleton's argument; "[w]here Ron Silliman imagines that an American poetry will be bold, innovative and cosmopolitan," he writes, British poets are "afraid that Britishness is equivalent to nostalgia for settled traditions" or, worse, nostalgia for imperialism's heyday, patrician modes and their moral superiority. "The proliferation of discourses of exile, fragmentation and individuality in recent British poetics suggests that poetic community has been almost unimaginable during [the Thatcherite] period when society was declared dead, and no alternative was acknowledged possible." It may have been that such conditions provoked suspicion of the envisionings of American Language poetics which, as Keith Tuma writes, have been "prone to utopian, declamatory modes of appropriating discourses of possibility" gleaned from Emersonian as well as Marxist and other ideological systems of thinking. Their discursive conglomeration of visions of democratic access to the dismantled "means of production" in deconstructed language the British mistrusted, Middleton suggests, for claiming to offer an "alternative to the consumerist dumbing down produced by strategies of capitalist exchange" when their model of the reader as active participant in the production of meaning seemed "merely a homology of the manipulation of consumer choice." In this essay both American and British visions of poetry's political effectiveness are connected quite ironically to the very structures of political imagining that they hope to transcend in their respective national labyrinths.

Comparisons of avant-garde Irish work with that of British and North American work reveal further differences between anglophone traditions. As well as something about reading them: that "nation" is indeed writ large, or projected onto poetries belonging to countries whose identity is less stable or "post-colonial." In view of prevailing tendencies to downplay the critical nature of national positioning, it is curious to find that non-Irish critics who have been writing about avant-garde Irish poetry in the several years since the conference have tended to remark upon the fact that a number of Irish poets have taken interludes of living outside the country.[15] The fact is normally emphasized in order to depict the Irish context as one particularly hazardous to the health of poetic innovation, as well as explain why it has taken so long for readers outside Ireland to become aware of its tradition of "New Writing."[16] Yet it is also true, as Trevor Joyce makes clear in his essay for this section, that starting points for imagining postmodern forms for poetry are vastly different in his literary context where political conditions have produced polarizing rather than liberal/liberalizing national effects since the '60s, and where figures such as Yeats and Kavanaugh rather than Williams or MacDiarmid or Bunting have dominated in the project of articulating a post-colonial Ireland—causing it to sometimes still seem that "radical content is permissible only through conventional 'form.'" Both the Irish tendency toward exile *and* its works' tendency to evade immediate detection as "Language"-affiliated might be more helpfully explored by investigating the specific—and more overt, but no more powerful—constructs of identity that "nationality" poses in this context. One might begin by remembering that the most important precursor to postmodern work in Ireland, Samuel Beckett, was also peripatetic, but nonetheless an explorer of a relation to national identity profoundly different from that of writers in the "New World" in its Joycean awareness of its post-colonial, linguistic entrapment, its understanding that the contours of national culture shape the very avenues of experiment and departure—the latter producing Icarus-like acts of fruitless hubris if, like James Joyce's Stephen Dedalus, one attempts to fly too high above those who have invented one's available constructions for escape. Therefore, while built on Beckett's call to acknowledge "the breakdown of the object . . . [and] rupture of the lines of communication," which Trevor Joyce recalls as seeming as relevant in the '70s as they were in the '30s when they were first written, Irish avant-gardism has nonetheless remained less credulous of the advantages to be gained in wholly breaking from its culture's mainstream concerns and forms than its counterparts in other countries have tended to be. This is evidenced by the haunting lyricism in the work of Joyce himself or of his colleagues Randolph Healy, Maurice Scully, Billy Mills, Geoffrey Squires, and even in the more formally disjunctive work of Catherine Walsh and Sean ó hUigín —as well as by the common interest in translation from pre-modern Irish language poetry that Joyce attributes to himself, Maurice Scully, and Michael Smith. Such characteristics importantly link Irish work with black British writing, which also retains or engages with elements of discontinued, pre-colonial or colonial narratives and their silencings in history. The project of theorizing exploded identity and its linguistic debris is less evident in these poetries whose sense of nationhood is not that of an artificial and "impossible" boundary or constraint upon a burgeoning multiplicity, but of an engineered and very real construct whose historical effects both demand investigation and compromise the creation of a politically viable form of resisting other imperial impositions of identity.

Australian critic Philip Mead also makes clear in his essay for this section that nations outside imperialistic centers for progress are more aware of theirs as a liminal space into which powerful, "central" ideas are imported—an awareness that affords other sorts of strengths insofar as it precludes the reading of nationality as transparent or irrelevant. Australians knew, at some level, that they "were exchanging one imperialism for another" when they turned to America at midcentury for writing models to take them beyond those (British) New Critical ones that had dominated their literary world up until that point; theirs was an agonistic back-and-forth of allegiance and allergy, an "entanglement of a (national) poetry and poetics in both the emancipatory and imperialistic meanings of postmodern American culture." The internal contradictions of "the North American poetic tradition" as Mead refers to it also were not "lost in translation"; "[e]xternal to that poetic tradition, the liberatory, utopian space of American poetry was (and is) in acute ironic tension with national and international movements of political dissidence that are rhetorically founded on resistance to the threat of colonizing American values and U.S. global imperialism." Mead argues that the threat of too simplistic postcolonial response includes "reverse appropriations of old empire," which occur in the work of Derek Walcott, Seamus Heaney, Les Murray and others, and involve writing in the "vigorous vernaculars of these ex-colonials, welcomed eagerly by the metropolitan center, [to] revivify the sick heart of empire"; confronting the legacy of such work has motivated the new generation of Australian avant-gardists, whose acquaintance with poststructuralist theory (which was "hardly available" to them in the 1970s, when Anglo-American experimentalists were translating it into poetic practice) has produced a more self-reflexive response that is "postmodern" in ways Mead describes as being palpably different from that of the Americans whose influence was so critical before and during the time of its formation.[17] Less prone to asyntactic play, self-cancellation and the dismantling of meaning, Australian work (such as the swiftly changing projects of John Kinsella) is, Mead argues, more invested in "heteroglossia" and in exploring hybrid positionings for the writer, which "both generate and un[do] the tragedy of [the grammatical level's] rhetorical meanings" and therefore "the fate of the self in the contemporary world." In this respect linked to what both David Marriott and Lisa Robertson describe in the third part of this book, respectively, as the necessity to retain the differently inflected positioning of the writing subject in other-raced and women's work, Mead's argument raises questions about the relationships *between* categories such as nation and gender and race as discourses of locationality versus erasure, allowing us to make a transition from the issues informing Part I to those that begin to develop in Part II.

III

If reading across national boundaries foregrounds their shaping properties through a look at them from without, reading across intranational varieties of boundaries, and across related "margins" internationally, foregrounds the same national boundaries through a look at them from without *and* within. It zeroes in on the locatable (rather than stereoptypically "postmodern"—i.e., indeterminate) positioning of those whose difference makes for obstruction before our newest "window on the world," the one that now makes peculiar subject-standpoints transparent in order to give out on postmodern views of *language,* in much the same way that Victorian readers famously looked through that particular window of words onto supposedly objective views of the "real." As postcolonial and feminist theorists have argued, the author who died in post-Barthesian writing is one whose lines merge seamlessly with the dominant discursive contours of (western) culture, but not all gaze on language from the same central positioning; "[t]hey see it as postmodern," Caribbean/Canadian M. NourbeSe Philip writes with regard to critics' views of the linguistic strategies in her work, objecting to such identification of her project as she explains it in the first essay of this section. The similarly hostile response that Scottish writer Robin Purves keyed onto an electronic avant-garde poetry chat-line when confronted by American notions of a transnational vision for postmodern work is related to the same argument.[18] The thin but crucial line of connection between differently raced, gendered and "intranational national" contingents in avant-garde work can be traced along their differing trajectories of thought on issues of poetic content, linguistic history, and the positioning of their own discursively constructed selfhood over and against that of the national/dominant one currently critiqued in theory, which ironically essentializes it in each venue as the "going" one for all.

When describing the kind of work he finds valuable, Charles Bernstein writes that it "tends to be preoccupied with finding the possibilities for articulation of meanings that are too often denied or repressed by a (multinational) culture that we are always being subjected to, and that we are indeed subjects of, and which, moreover, can be understood as its nowhere explicated subject: Poetry which is political not primarily in its subject matter, or representation of political causes, however valuable that may be, but in the form and structure and style of the poems, and in the attitude toward language."[19] Lynn Keller and others at the conference argued against this line of demarcation being drawn between poems called "avant-garde" and poems called "mainstream" without attention being paid to their conceptual (if not formal) affinities with Language work.[20] But the problem with such a template for raced/postcolonial writers in particular is that it subordinates the memory of specific, and other, "subject matter" or difference that is not readily available to that "*multi*-nationally" assumed subject, and supposes that formal departures are the sufficient mode for articulation of the suppressed when such departures can only be understood if one assumes a common structural starting point and shared "imaginary." As David Marriott—perhaps the the only black poet in Britain at the time of the conference to be readily identified with experimental projects—has argued in psychoanalytic terms, the American theoretical injunction to disperse particular strands of raced memory, as well as psychological affect, encourages a sublimation of the differences in traumatic experience associated with coming into language; what is left is the "surface sheen" of plucked signifiers owned equally—democratically—by all and none. Yet the fact that so few other black poets have chosen to work within avant-garde circles in the U.K. suggests that the problems of reading across intranational raced lines are shared between countries. I first became very aware of them when I looked out over the "assembly" we had gathered for the '96 conference, which was startlingly white; despite the fact that several important writers such as Nathaniel Mackey and Harryette Mullen had planned to be there, but could not in the end, the nonrepresentative nature of our group seemed to point up real, practical problems—problems that our theories concerning the similarity of all comers to the Language/avant-garde "textual project" would deny are there.[21] Don Wellman remembers in the second essay of this section that no one argued at the conference about the ways in which the language of experiment "should be brought to bear on cultural revolution"; it is yet another irony of avant-gardism that its political investment in critiquing and changing culture discourages the splintering-off of groups that might contribute to that project as well as, perhaps, provide for ongoing internal critique of avant-garde aesthetics themselves. Though those related groups differ a good deal from one national context to another—as a comparison of, say, African American Nathaniel Mackey's and black British David Marriott's writings in poetics might show—Wellman attempts to read raced writing as being conjoined by a kind of "intercultural textuality" that marks its resistance through what he describes as an "opacity of hybrid forms." As a linguistic construct, it counters the essentializing propulsion of other versions of unifying visions of extra-nationalized racial affinity at the same time that it depends upon an historical, if all-but extra-discursive, irreducibility that cannot be submerged within that "nowhere explicated" text that composes the "multinational subjectivity" described by Bernstein.

The emphasis on revisiting history in new black writing and postcolonial theory is a constant; as Philip puts it in her essay, "Interview with an Empire," history is not as dead for her as it is for Baudrillard and other enabling theorists of postmodernism because her "distrust" of language is also an "historical distrust." Her view of national constructs as "spaces" already written on (or not) by discourses of race is of particular relevance to the key issues in this volume. The idea that one cannot be "seen" the same way or write to the same effect across differing spaces suggests that work done on either side of the "black Atlantic," as Paul Gilroy has named it, will vary not only in its interpretation by readers but also (and consequently) in strategies used to depart from constructions of black selfhood as accumulated (and suppressed) differently in each such context. Therefore the importance of the body in black performance has not only to do with its role in oral traditions, and but also with its being, ironically, the physical sign of historical presence predicated on symbolic loss, evidence of a continuous if dispersed line of raced experience that teaches us much about differences between venues of national enculturation because it has been variously inflected and distorted in differing linguistic contexts that have irremediably blurred all inscriptions of it. Like David Marriott, who has written about her work in ways that reveal the projects of his own,[22] Philip is not focusing so much on the workings of language as on the workings of memory in it, or without it; "[t]he challenge for me is to write from that place of loss. Of nothing if you will. To make poetry out of silence." The form of her essay—with its tragicomical title reminiscent of the recent Tom Cruise blockbuster "Interview with the Vampire"—dramatizes or performs the fact that her writing can exist only in dialogue with that which would, in a figurative sense, kill it in order to live, as empires/vampires do, and as dominating identities must in defining themselves against while simultaneously erasing the "other." Working within the language that was "never intended or developed with me or my kind in mind," Philip must subject it—even as it constructs her as subject—to a "transformative process" through which emerges work that is formally more like that of her North American counterparts than like David Marriott's but similarly charged with affect, with the history of traumatic entry into a system of complex signs and mis-signalings that she figures as an abusive collective parent who is both engendering and genocidal.

In interesting juxtaposition with Philip's argument, Kathleen Crown in her essay on African-American poets Ed Roberson, Harryette Mullen and Tracie Morris suggests that unlike white writers in postmodern modes who have set out to question mythologies of the "private voice," black poets who feel themselves engaged in similar projects have also and equally problematized the *public* voice. That voice is the same one that Miriam Nichols hears still in American Language writing, the voice of theory as it promotes a systemic view of the workings of language, the voice of any representative poetics, and *all* voices addressing an audience one assumes to be in a similar position/value system/historical moment/memory world to oneself. By creating what Crown calls "sonic interventions," African-American writers insert a bodily presence of difference between that public voice and its audience that is, supposedly, seamlessly connected along the same discursive lines; in doing so, they hold with Bernstein's notions about the semantic nature of each fragment of articulation at the same time that they torque the significatory with lyric affect in order to work from/with/on the rhythms that, as Wellman argues, poets like Brathwaite have marked by color. Changing the material focus in poetry from the "fundamental building blocks of sense" in language[23] to the "*sound* of Caliban," as Houston Baker puts it (my emphasis), these writers engage in a practice informed by what Crown defines, after Baker, as "supraliteracy": a "maroon or guerilla action carried out within linguistic territories of the erstwhile masters." It is, as Crown cautions us, "not simply one of recalling the sounds of oral language into our visual practices of reading and writing, but of understanding how sound is already at work in both expanding and solidifying our present modes of literacy, which are most centrally our means of access to knowledge." Like Mark, but from the perspective of intra- rather than international difference, Crown explores the influence that seemingly nonrational and nondiscursive elements of speech can bring to bear on rational public discourse—and in doing so, she hopes to deeply disturb the dualities of voice/sign, orality/writing upon which certain assumptions in postmodern poetics have been grown.

Without question, recent theories concerning the body's opposition to or interference with the text, as well as those concerning the body's centrality in raced experimentation, have placed new pressures on writers whose work has to date tended to focus exclusively on language as code or intertext. As younger writers such as Miles Champion have put it, there have always been tensions between those who will not acknowledge a "person" behind the poem and those who do; but recently many feel compelled, despite allegiances they might have to early Language poetry principles, to either explore the notion of "presence" or find new ways to reject it as they rethink the role of performance in their work.[24] The emphasis in, for example, cris cheek's and Caroline Bergvall's work (what Bergvall in the next section refers to as "writing for performance") is to reveal language's involvement in the body's space of movement, and vice versa—spaces in which the body negotiates with the Wittgensteinian, linguistically delimited world as "read." Noted for their eroticism—evident in cheek's essay's focus on the tongue, for example, as the sensual organ that is "indexical of the body of language which it produces and of the body which produces it"—both cheek and Bergvall perform the desirous deployments of language, feeling their way through and often resisting that textual world and its intellectual history by taking Barthesian pleasure in allowing layers of constraint to slip off and discourses to slide into one another, exposed in a kind of textual intercourse that is "framed" by its connection/aversion to arenas of basic instincts. The creator of the recording entity *Sound & Language,* cheek explores sound or "voice" as bodily production often torturously channeled by words; as Keith Tuma suggested at the outset of his essay in this book's first section, he does so by experimenting with the distances that separate sound's intimacy as generated within the body from its movement through not only cyberspace but also, in live performance, through hand-held deflectors, musical instruments and other kinds of "remote controls" (walkie-talkie displacements, for example, in addition to computer displacements like the one Tuma describes). His responses involve grounding in present locality—whether it be Madagascar or London—the sonic experiment that Crown describes in "displaced," or differently memoried raced writing, and that Australian performance poet Hazel Smith spoke of at the conference as enabled by technological mediation as analogy for social construction. Beginning his essay autobiographically with an exposition of his own initial range of registers and class encounters, cheek moves on to welcome the "dispossession and deterritorialization" that has come with the proliferation of "Englishes" accomplished through "rewriting the sonic terrains of poetries" in black British and other postcolonial and/or devolving arenas; our readers might compare his optimistic take on what is accomplished through such cross-cultural "re-writings" with Don Wellman's rather different view offered earlier in Part II. Understanding speech as choreography, in other words, or orchestration of habits of stance/gesture in specific contexts and words spoken on both programmatic as well as more abstractly communicative, musical levels, cheek destabilizes language as "code" to consider language as "usage," different in every contact zone. Riffing on Derridean returns of the written to the spoken, cheek espouses a "live writing" that crosses disciplinary and discursive boundaries, arguing that "cross-art-form terrains of linguistic communication ought to be taken into consideration more often."

One might argue that the real argument that emerges between these ways of looking at sound, language, performance and perhaps even "emergent subjectivities" spins on the axis of views of history and what role the historical plays in the postmodern landscape.[25] It is a pity that no essay in this text attends to the differences between "knowledges" accessed by raced writing in the States and that of postcolonial figures at work in the U.K.; it is surprisingly difficult to either find or commission work on the topic.[26] But it is quite interesting to consider, for instance, that while Harryette Mullen's emphases on redefining both selves and community—the latter having long been an elided or notional rather than a working construct in avant-garde poetics, even one actively shunned due to, again, dominating constructions of it as coercive or cooptive—link her to black writers on the other side of the Atlantic, the fact that for her, as an African American, historical (or pre-U.S. national) raced traditions are something she reads about rather than experiences or remembers will make her practice differ significantly from those whose roots in the U.K. date back only fifty years, to the great waves of immigration that began in the late 1940s, and whose memory of cultural displacement is immediate and transformative of any initiating conceptions of self in the regard of both nation and audience.[27]

As Nancy Gish argues, such differing conceptions even among those supposed to be equal members of "The United Kingdom" force us into reading innovation from particularized angles that are attentive to very different points of departure and their equally different results. Her essay on the work of Scottish poets dovetails interestingly with Philip's as it suggests that history, again, has ceded/seeded those points or non-points of departure for the nationally as well as racially marginalized subject, and that in Scotland, English censorship of the native tongue and self-rule has long prevented the comfortable sense of integrated "subjecthood" and self-determination—i.e., the "subject" of deconstruction in modern western theory. Yet, and perhaps as a consequence of having existed in a less violent or revolutionary relationship than has Ireland to its dominator, as well as having long and successfully participated in the innovations and economic rewards of industry in the kingdom, Scottish nationalism has developed out of its own particular cultural roots what Gish describes as a polyvocal rather than univocal position of opposition. Its model of the self as riven by empowering internal divisiveness—a familiar Scottish construct of "Caledonian antisyzygy," most famously deployed early in this century by the important modernist poet and nationalist Hugh MacDiarmid but also, Gish argues, evident in mainstream work such as Robert Louis Stevenson's *Dr. Jekyll and Mr. Hyde*—follows, or perhaps predates, such national constructs. But in either case, it suggests that for these poets the postmodern project of fracturing models of the poetic subject will require a different sort of critique from that employed by universalized Language poetry practice—the sort that Robin Purves, as was mentioned earlier, rejected for the project of Scottish experimentalist Tom Leonard. In distant but interesting relation to writers coming out of creolized traditions who must choose which written language they take to *represent* rather than deliver their own "voice," Scottish poets must, Gish argues, choose a dialect from among a range of oral, intoned and written differences in

Scottish versus English language—all of which "secede," as she puts it, from the dominant paradigm through acknowledgment of internal discursive byways that intersect in construction of the self. Such relations between divided-national, social, raced and sexual positionings are later explored in her essay through focus on the half-Nigerian, half-Scottish lesbian poet Jackie Kay, adopted by white Scottish parents of higher class than her poor white mother. Gish argues, much as Lynn Keller and others not included in this volume had, importantly, at the conference, that the seemingly "mainstream" character of some of the forms used in Kay's work is too-simplistically read given the *content* of the poems—content that pastes in mainstream discourses as *context,* and that refuses the contentment of self-identification but continually seeks to understand *self-positioning* (a very different thing) amid competing languages of race, class, nationality and sexuality that surround her and that construct her own inner nexus of identificatory desires. Kay's "autobiographical" works—such as *The Adoption Papers*—often seek no certain origin from which to begin a narrative but spin a web of languages that have made her what she is: "character-ized" in their contradictions at a very locatable juncture of discursive binding. Languages of nationality get in the way of even revolutionary lesbian love in this poetry; and though one might argue that language-qua-language receives less investigation in Kay's work as a whole than it does in other more recognizably "linguistically innovative" projects, discussion of its strategies draws attention to the fact that, in those latter, radically disjunctive projects, historical trajectories for an author's positioning in language—here delivered by semicoherent narrative means—often get dissected so that the very specific discursive location of a figure like Kay is in danger of being lost in larger homogenizing political, cultural and linguistic matrices.

And such attention draws us back also to ongoing arguments—in Language poetics particularly but also in all of the avant-garde traditions discussed here—concerning differences between male and female orientations toward subjectivity and form, given that women have, as Linda Kinnahan writes in the next essay in this section, often worked in "hybrid" modes somewhere between discursive feminist politicking (one version of "group" expression discouraged by Language poetics), exploratory "self"-expression, and linguistic innovation/disruption. Writing about both American and British women working in avant-garde modes, Kinnahan discusses the transparently masculine aesthetic within which both are forced to operate in order to find a place on the literary map, even if it is under what she describes, in Marianne DeKoven's words, as avant-gardism's "tiny firmament." That means, as it means for postcolonial writers, accepting postmodernist theory's generalized models of the self and community in order to reject them in work that focuses on analyses of language from non-specific starting points; this because, as Kinnahan writes, "[t]he 'I' in experimental women's writing continues to raise flags within (or be ignored within) reading communities hostile to, indifferent to, or unaware of feminist concerns with language." Quoting from work by British poet Wendy Mulford, Kinnahan asks "whether the voice identified as feminine will always carry traces, within postmodern discourse, of what this discourse would consider the 'error' of lyric, a feminized/feminine expressivity to be 'cut out.'" Harryette Mullen's engagement in "lyric hybridity" links up with Mulford's thoughts on practice, both of them (if to differing degrees) guarding the option of using lyric affect (indeed the "error" of choosing it in postmodern aesthetics) to demonstrate a differently positioned and therefore differently sentient being at work in the work—"present" in the sense that has been so problematized in avant-garde writing, meaning historically and physically placed in the midst of linguistic critique and not in the transcendent position of the (male) post-modern theorist or poet. Indeed, the relations between Gish's and Kinnahan's projects, as well as not only Crown's argument concerning the conflict between political/community action and aesthetic imperatives in Mullen's work but also Philip's argument concerning the potential erasure of historical, silenced experience and its legacy in raced linguistic experiment, underline the connections between national, raced and gendered differences in poetic experimentation in terms of their contextual/historical approaches to language. At the same time, perceiving these apparent relations forces us to begin to "re-historicize" the very specific ground from which the principal tenets of postmodern poetry sprang, and in time, perhaps, supplement our discussions of the gender politics involved with analyses of the *differences* within those politics given differing nationalities and therefore differing political spaces that both support and exclude them.

Taking another tack, Canadian writer Susan Rudy offers what might indeed be a nationally inflected view of the efficacy of methods of "border crossing"—sexual, racial, national—that have been employed by poets attempting to redefine the space of selfhood. She takes up the question of whether crossing is positive or even a possibility, opposing the models of doing so that suggest one can move from one integrated "state" (whether personal or political) into another. Qualifying Judith Butler and Biddy Martin's assertion that "every identification presumes a crossing of sorts," Rudy argues that we are always already in spaces inflected by other-cultural sources, and that identificatory desire draws us to intersections where "no one kn[ows] for sure" how to place us. Drawing on the work of Canadian writers as different as Jeff Derksen, Fred Wah, and Daphne Marlatt, she suggests that being "present" is really the same as crossing—is, as Derksen is in what she describes as the overdetermined microcosm of works like *Dwell* (1993), to simply maintain sitedness in order to make those intersections available. It is to attempt to translate "what you're actually experiencing," as the more culturally complicated Marlatt puts it, into new languages, none of which will accommodate (as indeed her "original" one also cannot) what she, as an Australian-cum-Malaysian-cum-Canadian writer, and a once-heterosexual mother-cum-lesbian, might know or begin to articulate. Somewhere in that "culturally constructed invisibility" that is her fraught "here" are the crossed lines that are also "there"—lines that are akin to the hyphen in Wah's Chinese/Swedish/Canadian identity, which, Rudy writes, connect him to a postmodern version of multiplied selfhood instead of "crossing [him], in all of [his] complexity, out."

By contemplating Canadian writer Gail Scott's strategies for narrating beyond "millennial states of mind"—by which she means the discourse of "contained communities" created by those who "pretend to be outside that which they narrate" and address themselves to those they "suppose not to live there"—Carla Harryman suggests another avenue toward intercourse between "erotic personalities" and sites of otherness, whether they be "pediments" (monuments of the past, including people, texts) or places. "The work of André Breton might serve as a site, analogous to some local architecture, that such a personality might situate herself in relation to . . . someplace else, a city, Montreal." The erotic personality as Harryman describes it through Ernst Bloch's writings is, despite his disclaimer in the quoted epigraph to her essay, related in part to the "narcissistic" one that British avant-gardist and theorist Denise Riley has described at work in her writing, and that Lisa Robertson, in her essay for the next section, rescues from critique by John Wilkinson; both are engaged in a process of self-identification through, as Robertson describes it, "a formative cathexis of the subject with an outer milieu. . . . Libidinal drives, a nexus of recognitions and desires, [animate] the supple sociality of a self produced by its own desire for, and in, the world." Harryman's use of Bloch's construct of the erotic personality introduces the element of hopefulness, a "lusting after the anticipatory terrain" of the uncontained "state," in which people live and participate with an eye toward the future outside the text rather than remain outside from the start, caught in fearful narratives about places and people, like the learned response to "scary urban environment with Queers and Québecois" Harryman describes for those of a "millennial state of mind" contemplating Montreal. "It doesn't really matter where any one of us lives. [The millennial narrative] feeds off perfection and plague, leaving a place, a stage, a contained community between what is said to be desired and said to be too frightening to think about." Through her own imaginative interaction with Scott's text, its interactions with André Breton, his *Nadja,* and a particular Montreal community made up of a series of portraits of women in the course of this novel, Harryman suggests in part that Canadian writing's less stringent division between modern and postmodern aesthetics allows for this text's active, "carnivalesque" interplay of pediments and "sky," or horizon, as her title has it; "her very contemporary feminism [is able to] talk back to history without foreclosing the forward-looking, anticipatory possibilities of imaginative investments."

But as Australian critic Ann Vickery warned through her paper delivered at the conference, erotic or desiring crossings and collaborations *can* function dangerously closely to those powermongering dynamics now made familiar in psychoanalytic theory. The trope of travelogue, for example, that Canadian poets Marlatt and Betsy Warland use in *Double Negative*—a collaborative work that sets out to "imagine-a-nation" from lesbian starting points by figuratively re-exploring the masculine space of the Australian outback—could be seen as a cloak for a bit of North American pioneering rather than "engagement" with another culture. Seeing that outback which, in its conventional depictions as "otherness and negativity . . . uncannily echoes those of lesbian alterity," the collaborative speakers of this work plant an intracultural project on an international jaunt by imagining a foreign space for the investigation of unwritten aspects of self. The collaborators themselves understand the dangers involved: "an act of freedom may well be, from another perspective, an act of conquest or commodification"—in other words, as Vickery went on to say, "a paradox of tourism exists [in such a strategy] in that while the tourist attempts to find a nostalgic 'out there' . . . often the local culture becomes consumed or altered to cater for particular needs." Though it is true, as American poets Lyn Hejinian and Carla Harryman argue in their collaboration, *The Wide Road,* that "there are ways of crossing distinctions . . . which create a liberated space through the blurring of identity—a blurring which collaboration emphasizes," I would argue that such blurring widens the possibilities for self-identification but not *self-critique* through perception of self (as constructed by one's sitedness, as specifically located in historical/national discursive systems and not as that "alter ego" of the same in postmodern theory, the amorphous or erased self) from the purview of the cultural or national other. As a result, the very erotics of identification that offer such promising new ways—described convincingly in Harryman's essay for this section—of thinking about self-reassembly in our postdeconstructive moment can preempt any real "congress" if intra/intercultural exchange is limited to ironic expansions of constructs of self-fulfillment.

IV

The last section of this book contains eight essays that disrupt any attempt to do what, in the years following the conference, might be seen as worrisome acts of memorializing—i.e., a summation of the accomplishments of the last thirty or forty years of avant-garde writing, given the millennial moment's artificial sense of an ending that tempts us to engage in organization of the past. Certainly I would not wish to cast aspersions on the breakthrough efforts of anthologizers like Jerome Rothenberg and Pierre Joris, whose monumental compilation of alternative *Poems for the Millennium* has done its own disruptive work in *fin de siècle* conversations about poetry across mainstream lines; but I would suggest that its collection must be accompanied by collections like ours that redraw the differences between the spaces from which these poets write, and discourage universalized ways of reading their work that elide those differences. Toward *that* end, or nonending, this third section bristles at times with disagreement about borders of all kinds in the past, present and future of avant-garde writing.

It begins with the seismic challenges that electronic as well as performance writing have brought to discussions of that future—tying itself, as the use of that latter term will signal here, to essays in the preceding part of this book. In addition to the relationship between words and sound, experimental poetry has from the outset been concerned with the strange relation between words and space. Particularly the notion that, as Wittgenstein famously put it, the limits of language are the limits of our world, demarcating the artifice we make of space—personal, cultural, national—as we move intelligently/intelligibly through it using meaningful signposts of words and sound. The first two essays of this section not only investigate the growing importance of performance as a whole in avant-garde writing, but also update talk about the kinds of spaces now available for the "installation" or performance of work within those Wittgensteinian limits in poetry—such as ones structured around new conceptions of cybertext as virtual space, alongside ones evolving through what in Caroline Bergvall's terminology we have come to call "writing for performance." It often involves new technologies as construction equipment, one might say—equipment that both fashions new spaces and comes with its own inescapable programming possibilities and epistemologies, ways of reading (or "literacy" as John Cayley explains it in his essay for this section). Such new "languages" coming into being in performance works create interesting new connections between them, and across cultures and national boundaries, even as they illustrate their differences; again, as the Australian performance poet Hazel Smith said in her paper for the conference, the strengths of the "new sonic poetries" issue in part from their tendency, given their technological language, toward cultural hybridity and therefore another kind of capability to alter the sound of "the private voice" even as one speaks. She herself is "dedicated to a sonic poetry which emphasizes a female perspective, female uses of language, and a female voice," and describes her work and that of other women working in Australia as engaging in a "'feminist performance linguistics,' because it brings together musicality, performance and linguistic experimentation, a convergence which seems to [her to be] particularly strong in Australia." Its practice generates new studies of lyric subjectivity and reconstructions of the same that can emerge from "highly semantic" deployments of nonromanticized or nonessentialized sounds; such emphases on investigative semantics rather than the a-syntacticality of earlier Language experiments in poetry are in sync with other kinds of newly reconstructive strategies not only in feminist and raced writing but also across the board in avant-garde work.

Also at the conference to map out new forms and semantic terrains in the related realm of electronic space were important thinkers like Jim Rosenberg, who offered a view of what an electronic "prosody" might look like, and Loss Pequeño Glazier, assembler of the Electronic Poetry Center (EPC) at the State University of New York at Buffalo—an invaluable, vast resource that is also home to the largest of the American poetry internet chat-lines. Glazier lamented in his talk the lack of "a single multi-platform program for the computer generation," which would allow writers across the world to access one another's work despite the fact that they may be produced on differing operating systems. He also mused about the lack of an adequate vocabulary for discussing "e-poetries"—or even agreement as to what they are. They are not, Glazier asserts, anything that can be printed out on regular pages or reproduced in other media; they can only be "innovative poetic practices in various digital media, that is, writing/programming that engages the procedures of poetry to investigate the materiality of language" through the employment of hyperlinks, kinetic elements and other such ways of moving in electronic space. By broadening that awareness to include the differences in such usage that occur in differing national arenas, he argues, critical discussion might query the tendency for U.S. viewpoints to dominate the conversation on e-poetry. Toward that end, Glazier very helpfully offered his audience swift glimpses into numerous communities at work in other places well beyond those featured at the conference, such as France, Mexico, Brazil and Norway, seconding Hazel Smith's suggestion that poetries operating within new technologies are more readily shared and more readily inspire intercultural collaboration.

Certainly the presence of Canadian-cum-British writer John Cayley on the electronic scene/screen has challenged the notion that U.S. viewpoints and practices dominate the conversation in this field of work. Well-known for his interest in Chinese poetries—an interest shared by other major players in British and Irish avant-gardism such as J. H. Prynne and Trevor Joyce[28]—Cayley's practice seems to be infused with the vision of languages as varying systems of "characters," whose metaphorical dimensionality as signs and historical signposts he investigates in the space he makes multidimensional on screen by adding elements like timed movement of words and letters. In his treatment of the electronic sphere in poetry, Cayley begins to do as Glazier suggests someone must: draw a theoretical outline around the activity that has become e-poetry/performance and understand its place in that movement of "avant-gardes" throughout this century that has ignored or downplayed it as a lesser actor on its front. Like Bergvall, whom Glazier appreciates for her awareness of the centrality of the poet's media and the part it has *always* played in the "performance" of presenting poems, Cayley is aware of contradictions at work in the disparaging of electronic poetry for such things as its reliance on certain kinds of programming, and demonstrates with the form of his essay his perception of our continuingly romantic notion of writing's separation from its technologies—its "programmatology." At the conference, Canadian poet Steve McCaffery's revisionist reading of Jacques Derrida's *Of Grammatology*—in which he "complicate[d] any claims to a logocentric subservience of writing to speech in western history"—served as an intriguing complement to Cayley's essay in its *re*-deconstruction of such notions. Mapping increments in writing's history that categorical readings like Derrida's must suppress, he revealed a written tradition distinct from the oral one with its "metaphysics of presence"; it hinged in part on his argument that *scriptio continua*—connected-up writing "experienced as letters becoming words" because the reader must wrest them out of its "prosemantic continuum" without word separations—actually replaced interpunctual writing, and remains as evidence of writing's early awareness of its "stubborn materiality," its berth in dead letters. [29]

We have done our best to reproduce Cayley's essay's visual complexity, written for an electronic medium, in the necessarily monodimensional form of our pages. Here it appears as a dually apportioned space whose marginal commentary writ large represents the loosely floating, atmospheric admonitions of an entropic conventional wisdom subverted by the very thing it demonizes: careful, calculating, numbered thinking about poetic "technology." Somewhat surprisingly, the "arch-conservative counter-current" running down the right side of each page is from Heidegger's metaphysics of poetry, "What are poets for?" in *Poetry, Language, Thought*. That text, as Cayley explains in a footnote, "claims that [poetry] can (in exceptional circumstances) transcend (even) its (traditional) technologies and (the evil of) technology itself." In a quasi-aleatory gesture, Cayley traces in isolated, outlined letters a response within the marginalized Heideggerian text: "technology calculation numbers" travel through its diatribe, so that Heidegger's repeated questions receive this as an answer as well as the sophisticated outline of thought (numbered to make a point) emerging to its "left." In other words, Cayley not only demonstrates that even a thinker as influential as Heidegger has been for avant-garde writing inadvertently adheres to some of those romantic notions of writing's separation from its media, but also suggests that poetic thinking—Heidegger's and everyone else's—depends on "numbers," calculation, and, if not metrical feet anymore, then aleatory processes and other ways of shaping material. He reinterprets such numbers—for Heidegger "the sign of artless calculation"—as "the basis of all artistic formalism." Cayley goes well beyond such assertions to explore the idea that what electronic media actually offer is a form for changing conceptions of literacy and literary space, just as codexspace at its advent allowed for the internalization of literacy; in other words, such media "may well allow the internalization of textualities or modes of verbal culture which have been characterized in recent critical theory," such as those that incorporate the dynamics of intertextuality and the problematization of unitary identity for both author and reader. Certainly they allow for "cyborg authorship" and sped-up aleatory procedures, as well as—perhaps—an effective arena for the interactiveness (rather than mere consumption) on the part of readers that Language poetry principles have long called for in quasi-Marxist terms. They even offer what he calls "a potential form of pure literacy [as opposed to texts that imply speech or verbal performance] with a (currently limited) capacity to, itself, perform" given its ability to generate procedural and chance modulated work in "real time"—another answer to the problems of performing Language writing that might be related to Smith's, but with a more rigorous focus on language and its author as "programmer of" rather than voice behind the text.

Caroline Bergvall's starting point for "writing for performance" might be spotted somewhere between cheek's in Part II and Cayley's above—between, that is, a kind of adaptive bodily presence or redefined subjectivity and "pure literacy." Like Cayley, her focus is the *page*—or rather the assertion that the text exceeds its space, is *not* the page. Her work and her pioneering of the Performance Writing program at Dartington College of Arts (Devon, England) have from the start depended upon an understanding of that fundamental irony: writing is highly spatialized. The beginning of her essay pays homage to Francis Ponge for "choos[ing] to situate his writing at the level of the page (site of production) rather than at that of the book (site of consumption)"; the making of what Gérard Genette has called the "pre(-text)" is included in his bought text, revealing what Bergvall describes as "the many dissociative operations linked to the genesis of a literary text"—that "processual stage's messy, near-corporeal jostling and intertextual sweating out of information." In her own work these concerns often take the form of localizing the same text to differing venues of publication or enactment; such practice suggests that a text is both itself and the space beyond it—is always, in a sense, an installation. Although the relationship between her performance work and that of John Cayley's illuminates the connection between electronic and other kinds of performance—both "spatialize" the text, and "link" it to extratextual materials available simultaneously below the level of the page or screen—there is in Bergvall's work a reluctance to erase the situatedness of the author that impacts strongly on her views concerning the ready "translation" of avant-garde practices across national or cultural boundaries. Despite the fact that she herself works from a seemingly fluid background of Norwegian and French as well as English (and, increasingly, American) cultural influences, she resists models of reading that collapse authorial difference in the "author function" by maintaining that while signatures cannot authenticate or make present the personage of the author, "a remnant, a remainder and a testimony to both a living past and a set of irreducible and ineliminable corporeal traces" exist in every writing. Her arguments further illuminate the importance of performance to many of the black British writers that Wellman, Crown and others discuss in their essays for this volume; their objections to postmodern tendencies to subordinate difference to the operations of language may be read in their emphases on performance in their work, though their practice of course also often links back much more potently to the "living past" of various oral traditions. The need to "rehistoricize" and resituate both the written and the unwritten in the late or post-postmodern landscape is evident in the growing importance of writing for performance in the avant-garde field; as Bergvall puts it, "modern and postmodern writing has developed a keen understanding of the performance of writing as one that allocates them particular and uncommodifiable points of fixture at specific (textualized) occurrences. It is the paradox of Barthes' degree-zero that it can be read as seeking to dehistoricize and overmotivate the arbitrary sign." Her essay provides us with a short-list of artists across Europe and North America whose work is seeking to change our view of where we are when we write and where we are when we read—provocations that are key to understanding the problems of reading transnationally.

It is exactly that problem of the "overmotivated arbitrary sign" that David Marriott takes up in his essay, which follows Bergvall's and moves us from issues of performance work to raced concerns. These find connection to Bergvall's in their attention to the *locatedness* of the subject wielding such signs, and in this essay, as in Philip's earlier, our focus becomes the historical positioning of silences incurred through practice that "disavows" the trauma of unequal entry into language. In his psychoanalytic diagnoses of what he, as a British writer, understands to have happened at L=A=N=G=U=A=G=E poetry's inception and in some versions of its subsequent practice, Marriott suggests that the "disavowal of heteronomous speaking subjects" in favor of a "fetishization of the signifier . . . exclude[d] its own historical-political inscription" in a nation whose mythologization of its unity in melting-pot metaphors continues, as I argued earlier, even into the present day. Read from the angle of our larger project in this book, the essay constitutes a critique of American constructions of "the individual" in a system that co-opts difference; relating this to the at times "circular logic" of Language poetics, where "indeterminacy is meant to be enabling as a non-commodified basis for communication (even though the theorists reject this term). . .[and though] the reader is constituted as an affect without ideational autonomy," Marriott describes the psychological processes of phobic speech, in which acknowledgment of the loss of the heterogeneous is guarded against, as being tailored to a national as well as aesthetic project. His response to the *theory* behind Language work—and it is important to interject here that the practice has never fully adhered to the theory, but British readers in particular have tended to read it as if it did, as if they were continually reading from its discursive "outside," as Derksen describes it—

demonstrates his recognizably different assumptions about both revolutionary aesthetics and residual constructions of "the individual," the latter of which still inform national inflections of postmodern thinking, as his essay both purposefully and inadvertently proves. The last words of this highly theoretical piece which avoids bringing in issues of race too specifically are nonetheless very powerful in their innuendo; it *is* a "time when representation and historical events are becoming increasingly dislocated, if not segregated"—and the specific national history that those words conjure up suggest that in Marriott's view such influences need re-evaluation alongside other historical players in the theater of postmodern thought.

Barrett Watten's essay begins, if not fully, to answer Marriott by rereading the history of Language poetics, evaluating the materials and formal strategies that have congealed into a dominant avant-garde aesthetic but which may have outlived the imperatives of the cultural moment from which their project sprang. He begins by reminding readers that American L=A=N=G=U=A=G=E writers *were,* at the outset, "all but obdurately particularist" in their reactions to, and situation in, their own cultural moment, thereby attempting to counter 1990s allegations that Language writing has resisted historicization and situation (as well as accountability) in terms of authorial identification. Watten goes on to suggest that it *did* indeed respond, not only to topical events such as the Vietnam War but also to philosophical calls to action, such as Barthes' contextual, 1968 call for the "Text" to supercede the "Work"—to make poetry that exceeds the boundaries of the literary work to become a signifying practice that defers utopian action but that is also, as Barthes described it, "a social space that leaves no language safe, outside, nor any subject of the enunciation in position as judge, master, analyst, confessor, decoder." Such a text is a cultural construction that is simultaneously productive of the new meaning it represents, Watten argues; the problem with recent Language writing in his view is that it has simply "reproduced an unstated and normative hierarchy of formal values" from that initiating movement, "effacing cultural motives and meaning" from it and "leading to a 'lingua franca' of decontextualized textuality." He suggests that to become responsible again writing must, at this stage, move from that "material text" to, as his title has it, a "cultural poetics" that responds to its own context and "open[s] out to a much larger and more representative range of cultural meanings." Yet in his attempt to read *across* national cultures, Watten encountered, at the 1996 conference, the difficulties of creating dialogue with a tradition that in many respects shares one's own concerns but defines the ways and means (and sometimes even ends) differently. For example, many of the British poets and critics present took exception to his view that, as he puts it in his essay for this book, their realm continues to experience "a general horror of mass culture in the tradition of repressive pastoralism" that functions in alignment with what he diagnoses as their residual "post-Eliot modernism."

This reading of the British scene since the war has also been put forward in various permutations by other Americans, such as Charles Bernstein (whose full view of it takes into account more provincial writers than does Watten's) and Keith Tuma (whose book-length study of British poetries reiterates the perceived or supposed differences between urban, Language-influenced poets in London and "neo-modernists" writing in Cambridge).[30] I would suggest that Watten and all involved may be somewhat guilty of the same sort of reductive reading that he reveals others—and particularly foreign-nationals—as having done of the original L=A=N=G=U=A=G=E movement and its legacy; this debate demonstrates more forcefully than I am able to here how necessary it is to attend to the issues raised in this book.

J. H. Prynne's work, for example—though at the heart of the "Cambridge School" described as most guilty of "repressive pastoralism" or "patrician" attitudes toward language by Watten, Bernstein and Tuma (and indeed some Londoners)—stands to be rather violently misread if such judgments precede the act, as Rod Mengham's essay further on in this section makes clear. From another angle, and through his reading of American poet John Wieners over and against American avant-gardism in general, John Wilkinson also confronts Watten's reading of U.K. work by reciprocating that, to him, "much accomplished American poetry of the eighties sounded and looked like the epic of hypertrophic consciousness" in its "access to all areas" (across, for example, class and race in colloquial reference) through which it "consumed indifferently." A practicing social psychologist, Wilkinson uses the language of his trade to describe the differences he sees between, on the one hand, Wiener's work, which he reads as "wrested from the disintegrative attacks of schizophrenia" but nonetheless protective of a specific, oppressed identity through its situatedness in a particular gay/transvestite literary milieu and its anxious, lyric control over discursive elements, and, on the other hand, 1980s Language work, which he reads as being *more* "schizoid in its blank control," and in its use of what were by then formulaic formal moves toward "death-of-the-author" disjuncture, which he relates to national/cultural schizophrenia as evidenced in the workplace through "competence in a formulaic language erasing the situatedness of a writer." (In his essay, Watten described the same in poetry as "normative formal values" in a "decontextualized textuality.") "The irony is that play with a formulaic repertoire by a person with schizophrenia may be more controlled by intention than the formulaic verse of the amateur poet"; by making such statements, Wilkinson reveals his own cultural propensities to value lyric control and not discount intentionality, an issue he also takes up in the essay—answering some of the American critiques of that position as described in Tuma's essay in this book's first section. The problems of reading across national cultures are dealt with very openly in this piece; Wilkinson writes that "[t]o read a poem in English from another culture and time facilitates my own projections." His essay should be read in counterpoint to those who minimize the difficulty of "cross-over," to recall Susan Rudy's phrasing from her essay in the second section of this book; readers will by now have recognized that certain arguments like hers, Harryman's, cheek's and others' contribute to the optimistic reading of transnational drives and border crossings of various kinds described in our collection, while essays like Wilkinson's give us pause. Given that he reads postmodern poetry as both investigating and participating in social and psychological pathology, we understand the implications of his playful statement that "the perils of misdiagnosis of schizophrenics through ignorance of a patient's cultural and linguistic matrix is well-known." If a poet persists (as Bernstein has accused the British of doing) in pursuing "unobtainable lyric"[31] in an attempt to investigate the new trauma of the subject, is that poet less or more mad—or avant-garde—than those who don't? How easy is it to cross a cultural line—whether national or intranational, such as other-sexual—without understanding the new context and situation that presents itself well enough to guess what a text's mode of resistance is, what it is operating against? Wilkinson's reading of American avant-gardism suggests that the difficulty Americans have in appreciating British avant-gardism is quite mutual. And arguing for the "healthiness" of a "situated if transcursive reintegration" of poetic speakers, he argues implicitly against the sort of "multipl[ying of] pronouns, or part-people whose intersection and interaction develop a populace" that goes on in the optimistic crossings and samplings that others of our essayists envision on the poetic horizon.

Bob Perelman's well-known work on the next step for avant-gardism rhymes in some ways with both of the foregoing essays but departs radically as well, given his recent and very controversial support for a return to greater accessibility in innovative writing. His book-length study of what he calls *The Marginalization of Poetry*[32] appeared not long after the 1996 conference; debate sessions were arranged in New York and other centers of avant-garde writing to discuss that text, from which his essay for the present collection might be thought of as having been (pre)excerpted. Originally entitled "The Familiar" (its title now demonstrating the effects of those later debate sessions), Perelman's essay is predicated on the assumption that "contact with familiar social structures in language is a crucial element for politically and poetically ambitious writing"—a notion one might remember from Veronica Forrest-Thomson's articulation of an avant-garde poetics back in the 1970s (see Mark's essay in Part I and my discussion of it above, pp. 8–9). In other words, "the new emerges from the familiar"; there must be an act of identification (or series of shifting provisional identifications) for change to actually take place. He notes that there has been a decrease in fragmentation and increase in narrative structure—even "complete sentences"—in recent avant-garde American work, though he admits this assessment depends on whom one reads. "The texture of the writing is [therefore] more socialized," he writes—a conceptualization quite different from Watten's "contextualization" or Wilkinson's "situation"—distinguishing what has become "foundational" in poetics from the everyday, contextual experience of linguistic negotiation with which readers are "familiar":

> [C]rude generalizations . . . have assumed dogmatic profiles. . . . Among these dogmatic terms are transparency; habit; coherence of person, subject, voice; narrative; grammaticalness: the case against such things has assumed foundational status for a whole range of anti-foundational writing and critique. These real sources of social—and hence poetic—relevance are being overlooked—at least, in our poetics; in practice we use them all the time.

This last point connects Perelman's view of the necessary future for avant-garde poetry to that of Evans in the first section of our book, even though Perelman is a founding member of the original L=A=N=G=U=A=G=E movement that Evans rejects. The issues that Perelman and Evans raise return us yet again to the problems of reading radical writings—even if they *are* in/about a shared language, and written in a globalizing economy with its virtual media-driven/mediated world—across differing national contexts, given their peculiar realms of the "familiar," histories of collective action, and opaque memory, texts that eternally return for rewriting and opposition. The tension between "provinciality" and necessarily elliptical "globalism" or "universalism" has never been so high in the avant-garde field, as is evidenced by its presence in the writings of each of the generations presently engaged in imagining its future.

One can read the recent work of J. H. Prynne, that enormously influential writer in the U.K., as responding in rather different, more critical terms to visions of "globalism" as well as to the problem of what comes "after avant-gardism," as Rod Mengham's title for his essay has it. Mengham, also a poet in Cambridge (as well as one of Prynne's publishers), reads a recent work by this notoriously difficult poet in his essay in order to suggest that there are new directions discernible in it—ones that take the avant-garde's signature "disjunctiveness" into a different phase of experiment—and along the way explains and dispels some of the allegations that American critics in particular have tended to level against this body of work. Mengham describes the earlier, hallmark poems of Prynne's as ones in which "discursive heterogeneity had always been posed with reference to at least the last remaining traces of an ebullient colloquialism, drawing into itself and illuminating with an extraordinary vividness the vectors of a social politics"; the evident routines of a speaking voice, however controlled by the trajectories of other discursive projects, was signaled by the "resonance of lyric" available in the work as well as "a gleefully impacted slang." As Edward Larrissy has commented, British avant-gardism has been far more focused on the historical dynamic between individual and social discourse than it has on the erasure of the subject or its ontology within language as a system[33]; arguments about the "metaphysics of presence" or "regressiveness of lyric" in these poems (again, see Tuma's essay for an account of one such debate) disregard the differences in context, goals and definition of "the radical" between avant-garde traditions. Even patterns of internal critique differ on either side of the ocean; while Steve Evans in our first section of essays argues that the new generation of American and Canadian poets has rebelled against their Language predecessors by "refus[ing] to subordinate the social to the linguistic," and by returning to lyric forms and direct address, it is interesting to see that Prynne, in Mengham's reading, seems to have moved to another place. In *Her Weasels Wild Returning,* a poem that, Mengham writes, "announces in its title the necessity to reflect on the ambiguities of return, on flight to and from a wild, uninvested, unhoused condition," Prynne seems to attempt, whether in good or bad faith, to depart from the disjointed routines of a speaking voice in order to envision the language of that space "returned to" after postmodernism's critique of it, a space that must "deterritorialize both masculine and feminine" (as representatives of extremes of "mutual incomprehension") or "equalize them." Distinguishing the effect of its stylistic unity, in which all the usual competing discourses of avant-garde montage become instead "systematically imbricated with each other," Mengham suggests that "*Weasels* seems to point in a direction beyond avant-gardism," into that space defused of historical power-lines that avant-garde poetry seems to wish to create. That the motif of air travel between cultures in the poem is presented as near-farce—a jet-plane crossing of borders as meaningless as tourism in the business of national/ cultural exchange—might be worrying to readers of this book; the poem seems to raise a number of the questions we are asking here about what it might actually mean now to speak "in collective terms" and to one another over such vanishing "(border)lines." It may be offering in new form that old bit of wisdom some of us recall from our reading of fairy tales: "Be careful what you ask for—you may get it."

And finally Canadian writer Lisa Robertson responds to all four of the (male) writers above by undermining any new view of "after-avant-gardism," given the sexual (and cultural) biases that she feels still uphold certain formal proscriptions, and make any fantasy about the "deterritorialization [of] both masculine and feminine" influences in language unimaginable. Her feminist critique of some of the same foci on the materiality of the linguistic fragment in American poetics that Watten, Perelman and Wilkinson also critique in their various ways takes a turn on them as well; her essay becomes one of reading the most privileged avant-garde procedures as gendered and exclusive of feminine methods of achieving similar conceptual ends. Thus she takes Wilkinson to task for, as I mentioned earlier, his suggestion in a (largely positive) review of Denise Riley's work that her slightly *too* self-focused (as opposed to schizophrenic) "narcissistic fidgeting" between self-identifications bears "no saving grace."[34] Wondering over what she as a Canadian hears as an unfamiliar, moralizing tone in Wilkinson's British voice, she begins by asking him "for enunciative mobility not therapeutic redemption," going on to suggest that

> [t]he reflexivities of Riley's poems index variant identificatory economies, economies vigilant in their enacted critique of the enculturation of femininity as a signifier for nature, managerial adeptness, familial morality and material availability. Riley's sardony preserves the duplicity, the netherness, the *not-me* of the narcissistic identification.

Taking her critique back to Rousseau and the eighteenth-century's "heightened gothic sensibility for the fragment," as well as its referencing of women within a symbolic materiality (as maternal/sexual body, as nation, etc.), Robertson suggests that current fetishizations of the paratactic fragment in avant-garde poetry have thus far "buttresse[d] foundational opacities which also encrypt symbolically maintained metaphysics of difference. . . . Women provide a material source and mute symbol for the political state *and* revolutionary pedagogies and methods" (my emphasis). How does a woman innovate with such materials? "The moral of the story is clear. The good poet enters the bordello for research purposes only. She's a social worker." Bringing our book full circle by reminding readers that any broad discussion of "avant-gardism and after" must begin with critiques of it from the perspectives of such intracultural as well as intercultural and international debates, Robertson offers a "performative" avant-gardism, one alerted to the whole of the repertoire, observance becoming enactment and re(ad)dress. She's aware that "[t]he specific uses or skeptical misuses and tactical negotiations of such techniques on their enunciative stages, configure and produce a political imaginary."And by investigating the opposition to various rhetorics of identification and narrative affect in avant-garde writing, Robertson reveals her view of the hidden boundaries of "post-modern" practice and dates them at more than two hundred years old. "The new is not a limit, but a transitive agency. To greet the flicker of becoming, we need skeptical suppleness, a tactical shimmering."

As Charles Bernstein suggested very recently, on a note that matches up with what Barrett Watten, Caroline Bergvall, Peter Middleton, Jeff Derksen, Philip Mead and a number of others have, from their differing angles, argued here, "the problem [of writing an avant-garde poetry] is how to pursue affinities [between poets] while resisting unities. . . . And that means enacting poetry's contemporaneity—the willingness of poets and ability of poems to act on and in the present social and cultural circumstances. . . ."[35] Bernstein is addressing his thoughts to a "poetics of the Americas," while our writers here are addressing the same problems within an international community of poets and are therefore, perhaps, more willing to think through what Bernstein suggests we should not specify: "the nature of th[e] collectivity" from which they write—their differing histories with their formative and differently limiting mythologies. Yet it is in many ways only because Charles Bernstein and a host of others have done such a powerful job of arguing for "the common ground of linguistic exploration"[36] that a book like this one can provide the "other" side of that argument; I therefore want to end my own comments here by saluting them (veering sonically toward the French form of toasting—*salut*—rather than the military gesture implied) as well as all of the writers whose work is to be found in the pages that follow. For readers who wish to pursue these issues in related books and journals, our essayists have compiled a bibliography of relevant texts which can be found at the end of this book in "Further Readings."

Notes

1. *Assembling Alternatives: An International Poetry Conference/Festival,* August 29–September 2, New England Center, University of New Hampshire. Organizer: Romana Huk; graduate student assistant: Laurie Quinn. Funding sources included many offices on campus, primarily the Center for the Humanities, as well as the Canadian Consulate and the Irish Arts Council. Interestingly, it was more difficult to find funding from American and British national sources for the arts.
2. At this point I should also acknowledge the very key role that Peter Middleton and Peter Nicholls' conference at the University of Southampton in 1994 ("Writing at the Limits") played in my own formulations; they should be credited with starting new conversations between several leading British and American poets brought together to argue through differences as well as compare their art.
3. See, for example, Edward Said, *Culture and Imperialism* (New York: A. A. Knopf, 1993), p. 60.
4. Quotes are from Charles Bernstein, "Poetics of the Americas," in *My Way: Speeches and Poems* (Chicago and London: The University of Chicago Press, 1999), pp. 114–15. I choose Bernstein's ideas to work from because they are among the most visible in American poetics, having appeared from academic presses as ascendant as Harvard and Chicago. The concept critiqued here is more complex than my treatment on this page suggests, and I return to it at the end of the introduction in homage because in this '99 incarnation it has taken on new inflections that are genuinely helpful rather than continuingly diversionary. Bernstein was a very important participant at the conference, and though no contribution appears from him in this volume, the frequency of my engagement with his ideas in introducing it suggests the same.
5. Of course not all the poetries discussed in the book are from simply English-speaking contexts; certainly Ireland, Canada, and parts of the U.K. and former Commonwealth have at their root or in their oral or national traditions another

tongue. Language is, however, defined in part by national boundaries and nationalized curricula and, as a number of the essays in this book argue, it encodes differing dispositions toward everything from individual versus social identity to radical departure in the arts.

6. Among the major anthologies that have appeared in the last decade are *From the Other Side of the Century: A New American Poetry 1960–1990,* Douglas Messerli, ed. (Los Angeles: Sun & Moon Press, 1994); *Postmodern American Poetry,* Paul Hoover, ed. (New York and London: Norton, 1994); *Conductors of Chaos,* Iain Sinclair, ed. (London: Picador Press, 1996); *Poems for the Millennium, Volume Two: From Postwar to Millennium,* Jerome Rothenberg, Pierre Joris, eds. (Berkeley, Los Angeles, London: University of California Press, 1998); and our own press's *Other: British and Irish Poetry Since 1970,* Richard Caddel and Peter Quartermain, eds. (Middletown, CT: Wesleyan University Press, 1999).
7. All quotes not otherwise identified should be assumed taken from the essay being discussed (in this case, Derksen's). The "L=A=N=G=U=A=G=E" movement acquired its name in part from the New York–based *L=A=N=G=U=A=G=E* magazine (four volumes between 1978 and 1981), selections from which were gathered by Charles Bernstein and Bruce Andrews into *The L=A=N=G=U=A=G=E Book* from the University of Southern Illinois Press, and was referred to as such in the California Bay Area–based *Poetics Journal* edited by Lyn Hejinian and Barrett Watten (ten issues since 1982). Steve Evans in his essay in this book's first section also recounts the history of the movement's beginning.
8. See Hutcheon's section, "Crypto-Ethnicity," which makes up part of the forum entitled "Four Views on Ethnicity" in *PMLA* 113: 1 (January 1998): 28–33; see also her book *The Canadian Postmodern: A Study of Contemporary English-Canadian Fiction* (Toronto and New York: Oxford University Press, 1988).
9. Bernstein, p. 114.
10. Bernstein, p. 117.
11. I am thinking here of one of the most influential young poets who until recently was working in London and running a reading/performance venue with Caroline Bergvall: Miles Champion. His work, though in part published by a press as mainstream as Carcanet (edited by Michael Schmidt), is deeply informed by early Language poetics, which have to date been so problematized in the U.K. that adherence to them is in itself a form of departure for some. See David Marriott's very different assessment, however, of not only the bankruptcy of Language poetics but also its relation to history.
12. Bob Perelman responded to a panel of British writers such as Drew Milne and David Marriott at the mini-conference "Writing at the Limits" (see note 2 above) by saying that their deeply critical reading of the Language revolution made him feel as though he and his fellow instigators were being accused of having been "jejeune" in their conception of its premises. Other British writers have made similar analyses, often with their critique focused on what they consider to be a cosmetic and ill-applied use of Marxist principles to achieve an ascendancy of individualized readers' responses over dominant codes of meaning production.
13. Charles Bernstein, *Artifice of Absorption* (Philadelphia: Singing Horse Press/Paper Air, 1987), p. 8.

14. A number of the essays in this book retell the story of developing a Marxist model for reading in North American avant-gardism; in short, it involves creating an homology between the act of reading (making meaning) and the act of producing goods and capital. Many British poets have found this homology suspect; it has been most famously critiqued by Rod Mengham in *Textual Practice* [no title; 3:1 (Spring 1989): 115–124], and that critique has most famously been responded to by Marjorie Perloff in the opening to chapter 6 of *Radical Artifice*.
15. I am thinking here, for example, of Peter Quartermain in his introduction to a selection of British and Irish poets in *West Coast Line: A Journal of Contemporary Writing and Criticism* 17:29/2 (Fall 1995) and Robert Archambeau in his various writings on Irish poetry (see in particular *Another Ireland: An Essay* (Bray: Wild Honey Press, 1997).
16. Trevor Joyce describes this tradition and the press by that name—one that published work by Beckett among other famous twentieth-century avant-gardists—in his essay in Part I.
17. As Mead explains, the post-colonial relation between Australia and the U.K. "cauterizes" the former's ability to read the latter's experimental breakthroughs—another instance of nationhood precluding the conceptualization of a truly transnational millennial circulatory system for poetics.
18. For more on Purves's response, see Keith Tuma's essay in Part I, pp. 143–144.
19. Bernstein, *My Way*, p. 107.
20. Keller's very fine reading of Alice Fulton's work at the conference [published subsequently in *American Literature*; see Gish, endnote 1, p. 270] was very critical of the organization of the event and its exclusion of supposed "mainstreamers" like Fulton. She saw the boundaries I drew as being indicative of the "fundamentally binary" configuration at work in contemporary American poetry. She suggested that while the conference "diversified the alternative" somewhat, "for instance, through its inclusion of a younger generation of Language-influenced writers . . . it left intact experimentalism's monolithic Other, the 'mainstream,' whose characterization as theory-phobic and invested in 'natural speech' and unproblematized personal expression is often unfair and inaccurate." A generous and attentive reader of a wide range of work, Keller suggested in her paper that such "them and us" thinking seems peculiarly strong in the States, where the institutionalization of poetry writing programs plays a major part in oppositional map-drawing.
21. See, for example, the discussion between African-American poet Erica Hunt and Bruce Andrews, one of the founding members of the L=A=N=G=U=A=G=E revolution, in the latter's *Paradise & Method: Poetics and Praxis* (Evanston, IL: Northwestern University Press, 1996), pp. 62–63, particularly. There Hunt suggests that some groups may have differing oppositional strategies designed to reach their different sets of readers, which are still "analogous to a more textual project"; Andrews rejects the idea that any project should be "less textual," explaining that "if the fundamental building blocks of sense [which] reside at a lower level in the fundamental structure of the sign. . .[are] not addressed first, the power of the work to address the nature of the social order evaporates." Statements like this seem to wish to separate the political project of the avant-garde from the less politically-effective practice of others; they suggest a de-racialized starting point for all, at the

level of fundamental linguistic operations, but in actual effect eliminate many raced writers' work from the list of the "unevaporated." See Marriott, p. 337.

22. See especially Marriott's essay "Figures of Silence and Orality in the Poetry of M. Nourbese Philip" in *Framing the Word: Gender and Genre in Caribbean Women's Writing,* Joan Anim-Addo, ed. (London: Whiting and Birch, Ltd., 1996), pp. 72–85.
23. See note 21 above.
24. I am loosely referring to material Champion brought along to speak from during a panel discussion at a degree show of work at Dartington College of Arts (June 1999), where Caroline Bergvall was at the time directing the program in Performance Writing.
25. For a fine, Foucauldian discussion of differing conceptions of history at work in postmodern versus postcolonial art in the U.K., see Gilane Tawadros's essay "Beyond the Boundary: The Work of Three Black Women Artists in Britain," in *Black British Cultural Studies: A Reader,* Houston A. Baker, Manthia Diawara, and Ruth A. Lindeborg, eds. (Chicago and London: The University of Chicago Press, 1996).
26. Readers might wish to pursue my own work on this topic; see, for example, "In anOther's Pocket: The Address of the 'Pocket Epic' in Postmodern Black British Poetry," *The Yale Journal of Criticism* 13: 1 (Spring 2000): 23–47 (a special issue on "Pocket Epics: British Poetry After Modernism" edited by Nigel Alderman and C. D. Blanton), or "The Progress of the Avant-Garde: Reading/Writing Race and Culture According to Universal Systems of Value," in *Poetry and Contemporary Culture,* Jonathan Allison and Andrew Roberts, eds. (Edinburgh: Edinburgh University Press, 2002), pp. 141–64.
27. See the interview between Mullen and several Canadian poets compiled by Louis Cabri, "Harryette Mullen: In Calgary, Alberta," *Boo* 7 (July 1996): 2, effectively, of the unpaginated magazine.
28. Prynne has edited an issue of *Parataxis* focused on recent Chinese poets; Joyce has taught courses in classical Chinese poetry. This kind of interest seems less a hangover one from romantic Poundian interests in the transhistorical Chinese "ideogram" and more one that approaches such otherness as Steve McCaffery does in his historical investigations of his own English language and its changes in appearance given its use as various sorts of cultural inscription. (See McCaffery's essay that was delivered at *Assembling Alternatives* in his new collection described in the note below).
29. Steve MacCaffery's paper for the 1996 conference appears in his newest collection of essays, *Prior to Meaning* (Evanston, IL: Northwestern University Press, 2001). Its title in its original form was: "Between Verbi Voco and Visual: Some Precursors of Grammatology—Scriptio Continua, Mercurius van Helmont, Joshua Steele, Peter Walkden Fogg and that Precarius Binary of Speech/Writing."
30. Charles Bernstein, "Leaking Truth: British Poetry in the '90s," *Sulfur* 35 (Fall 1994): 204–212; see also Keith Tuma's *Fishing by Obstinate Isles: Modern and Postmodern British Poetry and American Readers* (Evanston, IL: Northwestern University Press, 1998).
31. See the debate raised in Keith Tuma's essay in Part I.
32. Bob Perelman, *The Marginalization of Poetry: Language Writing and Literary History* (Princeton: Princeton University Press, 1996).

33. See Edward Larrissy's essay, "Poets of *A Various Art*: J. H. Prynne, Veronica Forrest-Thomson, Andrew Crozier," in *Contemporary British Poetry: Essays in Theory and Criticism,* James Acheson and Romana Huk, eds. (Albany: State University of New York Press, 1996), pp. 63–64, especially.
34. See Robertson's note to Wilkinson's review in *Parataxis*.
35. Charles Bernstein, *My Way,* p. 116.
36. Charles Bernstein, *My Way,* p. 120.

Part I

International inflections / histories / comparisons

Jeff Derksen

Where Have All the Equal Signs Gone?

Inside/Outside the L=A=N=G=U=A=G=E Site

The critical discursive exterior that has partially defined language writing reads very much like a discovery narrative that, once having sighted the "new," seeks to explain its wonders to the citizens back at home. From early sightings such as Lee Bartlett's "What Is 'Language Poetry'?" and Marjorie Perloff's "The Word as Such: L=A=N=G=U=A=G=E Poetry in the Eighties"—which updates Bartlett's title with its opening sentence, "But is it poetry?"—the impulse has been to explain and contextualize this poetic movement and its poetry to an institutional audience in order to make it, literally, readable. These two early readings do not function as colonizing acts that absorb language writing into existing institutional frames; rather, language writing is seized as an already coherent challenge to the institutional reception and production of poetry within the U.S. As the writers associated with the language writing site had seized the means of representation and detailed the modes and relations of production of their poetics—both in terms of the political economy of poetry and in terms of a specific poetics with an aesthetic history and ideological intentions—a tension and a lag time existed between the self-determined formation and function of this politicized community and the discursive outside that was trying to, in a sense, bring them home.[1]

This tension within and belatedness of the critical readings of the language writers' work often engage theories of production, reception and contextualization that conflict with the poetics the writers themselves had developed.[2] Thus two initial crises are agitated and addressed by language writing: the complacent state of official verse in the U.S. and the lack of a critical practice beyond interpretation which views the text as authorial intention and as the mark of a unique subjectivity in time. The paradigm of the historical avant-garde is both the most readily available and ready-made frame to move readings of the language writers into the theoretical and social discourses the work itself engages. Yet, the historical avant-garde is ultimately too historically bound to address the fundamental challenges that the language writers present to the production and social role of poetry in a public sphere that was rapidly changing as a result of social disinvestment and the reorganization of the relations of culture and politics in America due to the pressures of globalization and neoliberalism. For the language writers, this negation of bourgeois aesthetics was also a struggle based on an analysis of the writers' "positionality" or social situatedness. As Ron Silliman suggests: "The function of a truly political writing is to, first, comprehend its position (most explicitly, that of its audience) & to bring forth these 'new' meanings according to a deliberately political program. Let us undermine the bourgeoisie" ("IF BY WRITING" 168). Nonetheless, the relationship between language writing and the historical avant-garde's negation of bourgeois aesthetics was grafted onto the language writers' project as the primary framework through which to situate their production. This critical placement of the language writers upholds Walter Kalaidjian's view that ". . . any textual praxis that would lay claims to powers of cultural critique is inescapably tied to the mixed status and fate of the historical avant-gardes" (7).

This tension between inside and outside, between the reiterative act of community or formation (a historically situated and determined site of production) and a forceful, if mistakenly totalized discursive exterior, provides a potent methodological frame through which to read language writing. Yet, foregrounding an institutional frame as a determinant in the reception and self-configuration of the language poets is not adequate to register their impulse for change within the social imaginary nor their intention to engage forcefully with changes within the world system—both dynamics that the language writers registered primarily at a national level. Language writing did not aim exclusively at academic reception and canon revision, but rather at the transformation of a social subject through language and through a model of productive consumption for reading. Seizing the structuralist homology of language and social order, language writing proposed to locate the subjective within the structural by refiguring the reader in a more equitable relation of (textual, and by extension, social) meaning production. The commodification of everything—including the process of reading—and the deepening alienation brought on by the processes of global capitalism led the language writers to target language and reading as the sites of engagement. Language writing at no point accepted the reflect or deflect model of the function of the cultural within globalization. Rather, to paraphrase Louis Zukofsky on poetics, the language writers' stance toward social relations within globalization is, upper limit, utopic transformation via a transformed productive reader or, lower limit, anger.[3]

Without stalling at the anxieties of what language writing might be—

whether it is a radical poetic movement articulated to larger social struggles or complicit in the reproduction of the symptoms of globalism, whether the movement constitutes a group and, if so, whether the group formation functions as a trademark to enable a swifter accumulation of cultural capital within the academy (all earlier stages of the reception of the language writers)—I will outline the shifting and diverse ways that language writing is imagined by a discursive exterior alongside its formulation by practitioners within the site. Even the naming of this movement (or site) carries an antagonism between discursive exterior and productive site that results first in the equal signs between the materialized letters (adopted from *L=A=N=G=U=A=G=E* magazine) dropping away to leave the less materialized, more generic name, "language poets." This moniker was further distanced and ironized to the "so-called language poets," or Ron Silliman's inversion, "language poets, so-called" ("Dysfunction"). The "so-called" in the language writers' case blocks a homogenous group definition from forming into a single heroic identity—"this is the deconstruction of team," as Bernstein says (*Content's Dream* 347).

This nervous naming also establishes the connection and influence of the Russian Formalists. Osip Brik's aggressive defense of the Formalists in 1923 was titled "The So-Called Formal Method." Brik used his title ironically as well, designating what he felt the Formalists' project had been reduced to, not what it was in practice and potential. Brik's use of "so-called" drew attention to a discursive outside which was in ideological conflict with the Formalists rather than to an internal fragmentation of the Formalists. In the language writers' case, the qualifying "so-called" blocks the outside imposition of a homogenous group definition and signifies an internal tension where the movement at times presents itself as a loosely structured formation, yet one which defined its borders through cohesive nationally framed anthologies where those not included (but perhaps who could be understood to be "so-called" language writers) are banished to exhaustive lists in the introduction.[4]

Past the ambiguity and hesitation in naming, the internal defining process of the language writers is neither singular nor uncontested, and it continues to be contestatory around both aesthetic and ideological issues and the status of the group as such. It is not a site that presents itself as internally seamless, but more as a central, collaboratively organized constellation of urban writers (with fringe or marginal associate members) who share similar approaches to language and readerly production due to their reaction to social and aesthetic determinants. Bob Perelman indicates the commonalities:

> But there was a loose set of goals, procedures, habits, and verbal textures: breaking with the automatism of the poetic "I" and its naturalized voice; foregrounding textuality and formal devices; using or alluding to Marxist or poststructuralist theory in order to open the present to critique and change. (*Marginalization* 12–13)

The internal definitions by practitioners are not less determined than others and should not be understood as somehow more. Yet, neither have language poetry's institutional readings produced an external consensus about the formation's place within the cultural field or the validity of its strategies in the social. Rather, both the interlocked inside/outside processes of reception and production (reception of the writing, but production of an understanding of the language writers as a formation) are contingent, and reflect overlapping frameworks embedded in the interface of poetics and social determinants, recording how a poetics that is self-consciously aesthetic and social can be iterated. The gaps, misconnections and elisions in this process foreground the continuing crisis that literary criticism imagines itself in and reveal the absence of a methodology that can correlate the formal level of poetry with social structures in other than a reflective manner. So, while the language writers can be figured, in an institutionally situated reading, as a challenge to canon formation or an affront to the "workshop poem," they are more productively read as being in excess of a discourse of poetry that does not adequately relate the text within a larger cultural field or within the discourses of the social. At this moment, in the presentness of globalization and theories of its formation and effects, does the culture-ideology of consumerism and the interrelatedness of the economic and the cultural of globalization reframe the potential of the language writers? This is not a retro-fitting revisit to the closed factory, but a rearticulation based on cultural poetics to read beyond the national framework (but not to disarticulate from it) and to read beyond the reflect or deflect paradigms for the cultural within globalization. Meanings and devices may have their homecomings, but how to read their presentness?

This reframing of the language poets begins at the national. The tension of the discourse of nationalism and the nation is a primary framework for the understanding of language writing—both as a site and in terms of its production. While the language writers were framed within the accepted paradigm of the avant-garde in terms of cultural critique and as being an urban movement, they were not linked to the internationalism of the historical avant-garde. Yet, the language writers do appear to be classically transnational in many ways: in their rearticulation and recontextualizing of Russian Formalism; in their translation projects with contemporary Russian and French poets and their dialogues with Canadian and British writers; in their connection to the emergence of the so-called "Chinese Language Poets"; and in their relationship to "continental" theory.[5] Likewise, on the level of semantic content, the language writers are not limited to representation of a national culture and icons, nor contained by a parochial localism or mildly fetishistic urbanism. On the semantic level, the language writers opened American poetry up to a much wider vocabulary and semantic content than the official verse culture at a time when the national poetry was seen as "a poetics of accommodation" (von Hallberg) complacent and capitulating to dominant cultural modes of representation.[6]

Understanding the reception of the language writers, and why a frame of the historical avant-garde was a near necessity to situate their poetics—in the way that George Hartley and Linda Reinfeld apply it to materialize the language writers as historical and not as an aberration—requires a reading of official verse at that time to illustrate the gap between the two practices.

The institutional and nationalistic frameworks of reception that the language writers themselves and others have used to conceptualize their work at times disarticulates this formation from a place within the cultural that is understood to be constitutive of the social. Within the critical mapping of their work, the sites where the effects of language writing materialize are *primarily* national and *secondarily* institutional. In their principles of anthologizing their work and in locating social determinants to their ideological relation to aesthetics, the language writers are predominantly nationalistic. This is a double bind, as their critique is of the American nation-state (or perhaps more precisely of the state, but not of the nation). Inevitably, they are articulated to the site of their critique by their engagement with it. The textual production and publishing of the language writers could be read, however, within Immanuel Wallerstein's paradigm of an antisystemic cultural formation (191–94): a movement which consciously counters a system that seeks to interpellate a subject within a particular set of relations. These relations, for the language writers, are the social relations of the U.S. and, by extension, globalization—particularly if globalization is figured as an extension of "Americanization" in the world system. This antisystemic gesture is both speculative and discursive, engaging with the logics of globalization rather than at, in the lonely hour, the site of the local. In this antisystemic intention, language writing is also a situated response to a national crisis—the oscillations of language writing address institutional effects, national sites and structures of feeling, and global discourses and logics.

From So-Called to Neo: The Frame of the Avant-Garde

> *. . . there was never any self-consciously organized group known as the language writers or poets—not even a fixed name.*
>
> —Bob Perelman, *The Marginalization of Poetry*

> *I have cited Grenier's "I HATE SPEECH!" proclamation . . . so often that I have been accused, no doubt correctly, of constructing a myth of origin for language poetry out of these three words.*
>
> —Ron Silliman, *Poetics Journal* 10

Robert Grenier's statement, "I HATE SPEECH," in the premier issue of *This* magazine (1971), is designated as the originary statement for the language writers (Perelman, *Marginalization;* Reinfeld, Silliman, *New Sentence*).[7] However, at this moment, this upper-cased challenge (sharing that typographical similarity with Charles Olson's exclamations throughout "Projective Verse") serves more as a departure point than a point of origin. Grenier's pronouncement—or rather the valorization of Grenier's statement as the moment of origination—determines the language writers as an historical avant-garde, gaining its originality in splitting from the poetics of the previous avant-garde, the New American Poetry. It obviously initiates an attack on voice-based poetry, and by extension the solidified subject and transparency of language.

Yet breaks from previous avant-garde formations are not without entanglements. Historically, theories of the avant-garde have emphasized the completeness of the split from the past, building a trope of originality, as Rosalind Krauss has argued: "More than a rejection or a dissolution of the past, avant-garde originality is conceived as a literal origin, a beginning from ground zero, a birth" ("Originality" 53). Yet New American Poetry cannot be reduced merely to a speech-based poetics, and language writing's relation to it is not only an antagonistic struggle over cultural capital and positions in the field of cultural production as Pierre Bourdieu's field theory generically suggests. Read through Bourdieu, Grenier's statement initiates not a breach, but a struggle over positions and a "space of possibilities":

> But through the stakes of the struggle between the dominants and the challengers . . . these strategies also depend on the state of the legitimate problematic, that is, the space of possibilities inherited from previous struggles, which tends to define the space of possible position-takings and thus orient the search for solutions and, as a result, the evolution of production. (*Cultural Production* 183–84)

Through, as Ron Silliman notes, "not so much a break as an interpretation, a foregrounding of concerns already active within New American poetry" ("Dysfunction" 173), language writing materializes as a continuation of the problematic of poetry and the social sphere, poetry and the institution, and of poetry's address to the nation at a time of national and global shifts in the production of meaning brought on by new relations of production and technological change. That this sense of national address on the commodification of the public sphere and of language itself is evident in Olson's *The Maximus Poems* articulates the language writers to a larger national political project at the level of address, rather than an absolute rupture of this previous avant-garde.

The language writers can be placed into a more social model of the avant-garde and not one defined by ruptures of previous aesthetics. As Andreas Huyssen writes: "no other single factor has influenced the emergence of the new avant-garde art as much as technology, which not only fueled the artists' imaginations . . . but penetrated the core of the work itself" (9). Here the technological imagination of the language writers is the emergent *technoscape* (Appadurai 33–37) and the form of globalization it enables. As Walter Kalaidjian suggests, advanced capitalism's mode of consumption, linked to Fordist modes of production, required a shift in the production of oppositional culture as well (11)—a shift whose strategies would not fit into definitions of the function of the historical avant-garde. The language writing project is more usefully analyzed in the relationship to the shift in modes of production with its resultant shift to the culture-ideology of consumerism of globalization rather than a positions war with a previous avant-garde. Further, as I suggested earlier, Bourdieu's field concept is itself altered by the relation of the economic and the cultural within globalization; the concept of position-taking within a cultural field has to be refigured as a position-taking within the culture-ideology of consumerism and therefore of the relations of globalization. The semi-autonomous relations of the cultural field are now shot through with the logics of globalization and any analysis of the field is fundamentally altered.

There is a point when the structural economic homologies of Bourdieu can be reenacted into the logic of capital. Consider this reading of the language writers' institutional position from Kalaidjian's excellent reading in cultural poetics, *American Culture Between the Wars*: "Signs of such a takeover [similar to the New American Poetry] of the Language enterprise are already abundant. But it remains to be seen how these writers will negotiate the institutional pressures that often absorb emergent ventures on the margins of today's culture industry" (189). *Takeover, enterprise,* and *venture* are drawn from a vocabulary ideologically grating to the politicized aesthetics of the language writers, who sought to return language and the production of meaning "back" from commodification—to "rescue" the word and the reader, in Linda Reinfeld's terms. For my purposes (and at this moment) such a frame for understanding an avant-garde formation carries over the prevalent cultural discourse for the cultural within globalization—that is, culture must be understood on economic terms, even if homologously. In contrast, some of the *speculative* power (and I use this term speculatively but not so cautiously) of the language writers was in their insistence on the direct transmission or link of the micro-aesthetic to the macro-ideological. The strength of, particularly, their earlier statements springs from their insistence on the cultural's structural and subjective effects against the logics of capitalism. To read this in the present moment of globalization is an insistence against the foregone capitulation of the cultural to the economic.

There is a convergence of internal configuring and external definitions of language writing as an aesthetic breach and a challenge to canon formation initiated by Silliman's view of the role of the institution in the reception of poetry and in canon formation. In "Negative Solidarity: Revisionism and 'New American' Poetics," Silliman reinforces the language writers' position as a classical avant-garde:

> Like other avant-garde movements, "language poetry" began by identifying its own distinctness, criticizing the naive assumptions of a speech-based poetics. But unlike many of its modernist ancestors, "language poetry" also drew positive connections between itself and the work of preceding generations. . . . (170–71)

Silliman here rejects the kind of heroic position of absolute "originality" that Krauss debunks as a myth of the avant-garde, but for a writer whose theoretical formations of the language writers' project have been based on a marxist critique of alienation and relations of production, this is a turn away from a more broad social project. In "The Political Economy of Poetry" (*New Sentence* 20–31) we can see the marxist basis of Silliman's argument against the academy through a structural homology of poetry and society:

> This struggle [Poetry in America] is as much one between audiences as it is between poets (or, to be more precise, it is one between social formations, including, but never limited to, economic classes, from which audiences are composed around individual authors). It is class war—and more—conducted through the normal social mechanisms of verse. (31)

There is a productive ambiguity here in this quotation. The class war waged in poetry can also be seen as a deflection from the class war being waged in society, but instead is transposed onto the cultural field of poetry. In this homology, poetry does not stand in for the social, but is a site where the antagonisms of the social become visible and contested.

However, Silliman drifts from this position into unproductive reductions. Firstly, he contends that the two generations of the American avant-garde "have defined themselves as opposed to the bland confessional narratives of workshop verse" ("Negative Solidarity" 171). Silliman's definition is social only if the homology of poetry as the site of class warfare—the site through which "to undermine the bourgeoisie"—is still operative. Otherwise, it is a reduction of politicized avant-gardes to aesthetic badgering in the Fordist creative writing programs of American universities. In another curious materialization of social relations within the cultural field of poetry, Silliman argues: "Academic colonization is poetry's fundamental social problem precisely because it incorporates the politics of culture into a process that can be determined institutionally" ("Negative Solidarity" 175). The discourse of colonization is troubling applied to the relationship of poetry to the academy, for it implies a homology between how poetry is received institutionally and how nations are dominated. Yet it underscores the homological relations that Silliman sees with the academy. Despite this, Silliman's trajectory for the possibilities of language writing appears to have shifted in two stages: first, from a speculative poetics utilizing the homology of language and social order to a more institutional critique based on the homology of the relations of reading and the relations of production; and second, to poetry's possible intervention in the ideological state apparatus of the academy and the national poetry canon.

Staking a less homologous role, yet a rearticulatory one, for poetry in the institution, Alan Golding has persuasively written that the movement of language writing into the academy may in fact lead to an alteration of the academy, that the poetics of the language writers might not be so readily absorbed or neutralized. "Language poetry," Golding writes, "seeks to affect how the ideological state apparatuses mediating American poetry shape poetry readers as social subjects; it seeks to broaden the range and nature of subject positions the American poetry 'establishment' makes available" (170). This institutional strategy involves, in Golding's terms, a complicit resistance from inside the institution.

Golding is able to reconcile both an institutional and a social function for poetry by designating the academy as an ideological state apparatus (ISA), as Silliman also does. This slide into institutional sites then is not a foregone defeat, complacent positioning, nor market buy-out because Golding crucially opens the ISA to rearticulation. Otherwise, it is dour (even globalistic) to imagine that the effects of cultural production, of poetry, are wholly determined by its institutional placement, and it may be the ideological effect of the academy as an ISA to produce the belief that the institution is the sole site of value and effect for poetry. Conceptual art's model of intervention into institutions is applicable here in order to chart how cultural production circulates within and rearticulates sites. Conceptual artist Joseph Kosuth pushed for art's ability "to critique the institution while simultaneously provid[ing] an alternative to it" (253). Yet, even when the institution figured as an ideological state apparatus, it could be argued (as Kosuth himself has), that institutional critique turned conceptual art's interventions too inward, resulting merely in commodifying its own institutional interventions and opening the market to conceptual art.

More recently, Hal Foster provides three claims for institutional critique as a movement from the historical avant-garde and from the neo-avant-garde:

> *1) the institution of art is grasped as such not with the historical avant-garde but with the neo-avant-garde; 2) the neo-avant-garde at its best addresses this institution with a creative analysis at once specific and deconstructive (not a nihilistic attack at once abstract and anarchistic, as often with the historical avant-garde); and 3) rather than cancel the historical avant-garde, the neo-avant-garde enacts its project for the first time—a first time that, again, is theoretically endless.* (*Return* 20)

Clearly, the language writers are a neo-avant-garde formation in their understanding ("grasping") of the political economy of poetry, the formation of the cultural field, and their reaction to institutions of reception. However, on

Foster's third point, the language writers do not enact themselves for the first time endlessly, but rather work with different strands of the previous national and transnational avant-gardes (New American Poetry and Russian Formalism, for example). However, the devices and stances of these previous avant-gardes are retooled and recontextualized to present social relations. Within the relations of globalization, such institutional critiques and resistances can be met with "flexible" accommodation through which the "oppositional" art form gains cultural capital from the very institution that was the focus of intervention. As with conceptual art, the oppositional gesture becomes absorbed within the culture-ideology of consumption. Or, as appears to be the case more and more, oppositionality is configured only aesthetically in a return to the model of the historical avant-garde. Or more bleakly, in the spatiotemporal arrangement of globalization, resistance is in the past, get with the present (globalization dot com).

Is language writings' institutional intervention belatedly following the neo-avant-gardist path of conceptual art? Or can the institutional interface of the language writers be rethought in a set of overdetermined and complex relations, as Silliman tries to do it? In such relations, the institution as a site does effectively contain an anti-institutional practice, a practice aimed at expanding the boundaries of texts that matter. Yet, even if access to such ideological sites can be gained, institutional interventions and canon reformation may not be easily accomplished because the canon, as John Guillory argues, is both "the inevitable embodiment of hegemonic values" and a record that relies on the "history of consumption, the history of judgment of cultural products" (20). That is, the canon is historical and deeply diachronic, reflecting the hegemonic values of society rather than the interventions of the cultural field. This history of consumption and judgment is ultimately based on representation. Curiously, what is defined as the nonrepresentational aspect of language writing—but what could perhaps be better termed its hyper-referentiality[8]—may also work to narrow access to institutions. The process I am describing is both a limiting of access and a stripping away of the social relations embedded in and presented by the text. It is through this movement of rejection and absorption that the academy reproduces itself and hegemonic cultural values. Thus "academic colonization" is not so much a colonizing act, but a mimetic process through which relations are reproduced. Yet, is it productive to locate the institutional settings of culture as the hegemonic formation to be resisted? These politics are effective only if, through a homology, the institution stands in for society or social relations and, thus, contains effects. Seen as an ISA, institutions become sites that can be rearticulated to yield a resultant social effect. Seen as semi-autonomous fields, these sites are only repositories of cultural capital.

Language Writing Versus the Commodity as Such

To critique modes of cultural consumption and the relations of meaning production, the language writers began with a marxist homology of language and social structure and the role of cultural consumption in the reproduction of the relations of production. The texts most frequently cited as laying the foundation of this ideological/aesthetic stance toward language are Charles Bernstein's "The Dollar Value of Poetry" (*Content's Dream* 57–60) and Silliman's "Disappearance of the Word, Appearance of the World," *(New Sentence* 7–18) with important theoretical contributions from Steve McCaffery (*North*). Bernstein and Silliman use Marx's construct of commodity fetishism to illuminate how the production of social meaning is separated from its "human makers." For Silliman, "Under the sway of the commodity fetish, language itself appears to become transparent, a mere vessel for the transfer of ostensibly autonomous referents" (*New Sentence* 11). For Bernstein, experience is eclipsed by the commodity: "What purports to be an experience is transformed into the blank stare of the commodity" (*Content's Dream* 59). This reading of Marx politicizes Shklovsky's famous purpose of art where "in order to return sensation to our limbs, in order to make us feel objects, to make the stone stony, man [sic] has been given the tool of art" (6), but with an emphasis on meaning's place within ideology and without Shklovsky's ocularcentrism—his emphasis on vision as the sense through which to return to the "real." A key difference is that Shklovsky sought to make the "world" visible and tangible while the language writers seek to make ideology visible. Following Louis Althusser, Bernstein and Silliman emphasize the materiality and material effects of ideology rather than invoke ideology as imaginary relations to real conditions. "Whereas for modernists," comments Michael Davidson, "the defamiliarization of words implies a desire for a realm of pure literariness, for Language-writers defamiliarization involves the interrogation of discursive and ideological structures" (18). Defamiliarization returns as a device to reveal the global articulations and relationships which are "misrecognized" within the ideology of globalization.

Lyn Hejinian, in her influential essay "The Rejection of Closure," expands the aesthetic heritage of the further Russian Formalists by locating a social function for poetic devices. Hejinian locates the effect within the cultural field, but also articulates the textual effect into an ideological formation:

> The "open text," by definition, is open to the world and particularly to the reader. It invites participation, rejects the authority of the writer over the reader, and thus, by analogy, the authority implicit in other (social, economic, cultural) hierarchies. . . . ("Rejection" 135)

The text resists the "ultimately impossible fixity" of meaning and, through a homology, speculates on meaning formation within the social. Let me flip this around. Where Ernesto Laclau is able to develop a model of the fixity of society from the social via hegemonic forces (and the ideological effect of a hegemonic formation) by textualizing society (*New Reflections* 89–92), Hejinian and the language writers formulate a poetics by socializing the text. In the poetics of the language writers, the homology of language and social form privileges an effect for poetry based on a structural resemblance across the field of language. For the early theorizing of the language writers, this homology was binding, with the functions of capitalist society deeply embedded into all levels of language. At the level of the word: "Words not only find themselves attached to commodities, they become commodities and, as such, take on the 'mystical' and 'mysterious character' Marx identified as the commodity fetish" (Silliman *New Sentence* 8). At the morphological level: "Grammar as repressive mechanism, regulates free circulation of meaning (the repression of polysemeity into monosemeity and guided towards a sense of meaning as accumulated, as surplus value of signification)" (McCaffery "Notebooks" 160). In this aspect, the language writers reject the distinction between discursive and nondiscursive as Laclau also does (*Hegemony* 104–14). This enacts a reverse homology based on the determination of language by the relations of production within the corresponding stages of capitalism. The homology possible after the "textual turn" (Foster *Return* 71–98) or the "descent into discourse" (Palmer *Descent* 3–47) is that, broadly, society is structured as a language. For the language writers, this was forcefully reversed (but not split): language and the society are structurally bound and therefore normative syntax, genre expectations, and even the word are the hegemonic forces that fix language into a reflection of repressive social relations. So the Law of Grammar becomes, for McCaffery, similar to the Law in Althusser's hailing of an always already subject (*Lenin* 170–77).

Hejinian's model of an open text and the rejection of closure refigure the reading subject. The opened text is the structural shift that allows the model of the productive reader to counter the alienating effect of commodified language. Briefly put, structurally opened texts allow the reader to construct meaning as a nonalienated producer in a similar (or homologous) position as the writer. As with the cultural studies project, subjective agency is located in the reader/consumer as the producer of contextual or localized meanings. Once freed from the repressive mode of meaning production as merely decoding fixed meanings and given access to what Hartley refers to as "egalitarian relations of production" (26), the reader is able, through the effectivity of devices, to read ideology, to see it materialized both within language and within the text as a cultural ideological apparatus (CIA). Hartley extends this by arguing, " . . . furthermore that the conception of reading as the constitution of its object—in other words, the writing of that object—points to a conception of literary practice not just as the object of criticism but as a mode of intervention in ideological struggle" (27). However, unlike cultural studies, where this shift to readerly/consumer agency recodes and redeploys the meanings of (mass) cultural products within particular sites and cultural formations, in language writing there is a more constricted agency but, conversely, wider imagined effects. It is the open text which allows the reader to enter into the overdetermined field of language and reproduce it. Conversely, a closed text would propose (or enact) a simple decoding of the fixed meanings of the writerly production. As Hejinian writes: " . . . we can say that the 'closed text' is one in which all the elements of the work are directed toward a single reading of the work. Each element confirms that reading and delivers the text from any lurking ambiguity" ("Rejection" 134n.). The rearticulation of the Russian Formalists brings forward a radicality in the effectivity of the device in that "each element" can also deliver the open text towards ambiguity and nonfixity.

While the text is produced anew within these altered relations of production, the text itself is not the object of recovery or rescue. Rather the text is a *force* that initiates the process of the production of a *productive reader*. The productive reader's agency is enacted by the instrumental open text. It is the reading subject who is constructed here: a reader who is able to read ideology. Bruce Andrews outlines the problematic: "The task, beyond coding and decoding particular messages, is also one that raises the question. 'What is this code?' 'How is it that these codes are constructed?'" ("Total Equals What" 55). The principal push is from recoding a text to understanding its social determination and the limits of a political imaginary. The praxis, in this extension, is " . . . one that implicitly recognizes the possibilities of constructing and reconstructing a society" because language and writing are not determined in a base-superstructure model; rather, "writing and language are both active and they are constitutive of this social body" ("Total Equals What" 59). It is praxis that lifts this poststructuralist commonality beyond the usual equity or transposition of the reader and the writer.

In his monumental book, *The American Poetry Wax Museum,* Jed Rasula claims that: "Language poetry's most conspicuous contribution to a discussion of politics and poetic value has been an examination of the sublimated political asymmetries of the reader/writer relationship" (406). Yet, this denies the extension to praxis in the social as Andrews imagines it. Not because Rasula views this as a contribution within poetics, but because he structures it as only refiguring the reader/writer relationship rather than the reader's relationship to ideology and therefore social relations. In terms of cultural studies' imaging of a productive consumption with its potentially radical recodings, the language writers seek the transformation *of the reader* rather than the transformation *of uses* of the cultural product. In the relationship between marxian theory and aesthetics, Andrew Ross describes a "shift from the humanist insistence on the priority of delivering the individual from the alienated situation of the commodity existence, to the emphasis on the priority of analyzing the rationality of systematic discourses" ("*Commodity Form*" 366). This shift, or trajectory, can be productively applied to language writing.

Yet, Steve McCaffery critiques this "shift from sign consumption to sign production" (*North* 14) , implying that the productive model of consumption is overly prescriptive by asking, "[i]f semantic productivity sees a complete freedom in relating to texts, one would be forced to ask why freedom here *must* be constrained by a need to produce" (*North* 157). In the place of productive consumption, McCaffery proposes a model of general economy: "The text returns a use-value by offering itself as unexchangable, outside the logic of the commodity, thereby opening ambivalently to both semantic loss and productional recovery" (*North* 20). This line of inquiry is not answered within language writing; perhaps not because it alters the triad of production, subjectivity and agency, but because it challenges the pedagogical nature of the productive reader and looks outside of a productive model of oppositional culture.

Extra-National Equal Signs: Culture and Foreign Policy

> But do we at least agree
> that the human body is paradise
> and that the United States
> of America is not?
>
> —Bob Perelman, *Captive Audience*

The language writers have been read by their discursive exterior as an exclusively aesthetic or national phenomenon, or as engaging with a siteless capitalism. However, the language writers, by moving poetics into the problematic of culture, link the materiality of language (that is, language as a site where ideology is materialized and not language as materially plastic) and the material conditions of its production. The next step is to define a poetics with the ability to move from the material condition of poetry's production at the local and national level to a geopolitical and geocultural level.

In this direction, a more recent internal definition on the part of some language writers establishes a relationship between their poetics and the crisis in public meaning caused in America by the Vietnam war. This is a movement in the internal definition of the language writers from the materiality of language—"from writing as meta-sign to writing as writing" (*North* 146), as McCaffery designates it—to the production of meaning via the productive reader, and further to an exteriorization of a politicized aesthetics in dialectical relationship with social conditions. In the introduction to the "Language Sampler" in the *Paris Review* (no. 86 1982), Charles Bernstein notes that the tone of "anger" in the selected Perelman poem, as well as the "quieter distress" in Susan Howe's work, "is not, of course, a formal dimension but a reaction, in part, to the events of the current period, including a barbaric U.S. military and social policy" (*Content's Dream* 242). This invocation of larger social relations is made more specific in Marjorie Perloff's initial sighting of the language writers: "Both in San Francisco and New York, the Language movement arose as an essentially Marxist critique of contemporary American capitalist society on behalf of young poets who came to age in the wake of the Vietnam War and Watergate" (*Dance* 233). More recently, in an essay on Bruce Andrews' work, Peter Quartermain draws the line from poetic production to the domestic and foreign politics of the U.S.: "Like most of the first generation Language Writers . . . Andrews was a teenager and then at college during the Viet Nam War, a circumstance which points to the political element in his writing" ("Getting Ready" 162). Posing the domestic effects of the international politics, Quartermain gives a broad context for the politicization of Andrews' work; but how such determinants are materialized into cultural practice is not explicated. The "Vietnam War" then stands as a backdrop for the production of language writing.

In the collaboratively written *Leningrad* (Michael Davidson, Lyn Hejinian, Ron Silliman and Barrett Watten) the authors specify that, with a crisis in the national culture, a parallel crisis of public meaning arose as the galvanizing aspect of this community and that "[t]he impact of the Vietnam war on one generation of American intellectuals cannot, and should not be discounted" (10). In response to an interview question from Andrew Ross, Watten responds more directly on the influence of the Vietnam war, expanding on what Quartermain raises:

> The central problem of reference in this writing may be seen in a context as directly related to the administration of information about the War on the part of the government and media that elicited, from intellectuals-in-the-making, a radical denial of consent for the conduct of the War. . . . There was a denial of "national" culture in all aspects. . . . The formation of radical tendencies in the arts discussed above occurred directly as a refusal of the larger context, but at the same time it was a response to the crisis of meaning at that level. ("Reinventing Community" 197–98)

Watten links the "national crisis of Vietnam" to an investigation of the language of subject formation and social identities, a distrust of historical representation, and the crisis of meaning.

This framing of the aesthetics of the language writers as a determined response to an internal crisis caused by American foreign policy (and the function of the U.S. within the world system) foregrounds the role of the nation in cultural production—even if the response is entirely negative, as Watten's quotation marks around nation indicate. Do these gestures of resistance to a national culture by the language writers then get read as a more critical form of cultural nationalism to counter the retrograde nationalism of imperialism? Is there a sense of national address, such as is found in Charles Olson's Miltonic project of "the initiation / of another kind of nation,"[9] or can the poetics of the language writers be read outside of the frame of national narration as a non-narrative site of resistance within the teleology of a nation? What Watten and others are identifying here is the relationship between nation and culture, but also how the interpellation of a national subject occurs through the cultural and how this then extends beyond the boundaries of the nation and into the world system. Laura Kipnis is precise in this set of articulations:

> So the aesthetic discourse becomes first a strategic political instrument and a site on which foreign policy . . . becomes assimilated to subjectivity: foreign policy becomes a lived relation of perception and knowledge that is exercised in the practice of the aesthetic judgment. (210)

Kipnis, in an Althusserian manner, covers the constitution of a national subject through the interiorization of an ideological aesthetic and national discourses. But beyond a powerful interpellation or determination, Kipnis locates this internalized "foreign policy" as part of culture by making it a lived relation. This adept definition locates the cultural as a prime site of antisystemic rearticulation. It is this formulation, this set of articulations which allows the language writers to be simultaneously national (as a critique) and extra-national and able to extend their critique to the world system and globalization.

Devices Across the Border, or, The Rejection of Institutional Closure

> Forget it forget it write about US.
>
> —Dorothy Trujillo Lusk, *Redactive.*

> I was a formal device
> before I was born.
>
> —Kevin Davies, *Comp.*

An analysis of the reception of language writing in Canada, both institutionally and within writing communities, foregrounds the effect of cultural nationalism on the reception of poetry as well as the antagonism created by language writing's self-definition as an American poetic movement emerging in reaction to changes in public meaning in the U.S. Language writing does not circulate across national borders as a siteless transnational avant-garde; instead it becomes a situated response to a particular national crisis, a crisis which is more emphatically a crisis created within and enabled by the world system. Yet, the circulation of culture opens cultural production up to other situated uses, other recontextualizations and rearticulations.

In Canada, the relationship of theory to so-called radical texts defines an outer horizon of intelligibility that language writing and others with shared aesthetic-ideological textual tactics fall outside of. In effect, alternative canon formation or canon revision appropriates a discourse of radicality while narrowly limiting what is deemed meaningful. As Bourdieu writes, "[t]he work of art is an object which exists only by virtue of the (collective) belief which knows and acknowledges it as a work of art" (35), and as works of art are manifestations of its field of production, it is at the boundary of the field where struggle for entry and the delimiting of territory take place (42–43). Politicized texts that contest normative representation within language and within a politics of recognition, or texts that look for effects outside of a subscribed agency, are refigured as "difficult"—which shifts them into being language puzzles to be decoded by an individuated reader. Or such texts are designated "experimental," leaving them within an aesthetic realm unaffected by social determinants. This depoliticizing of texts enacts a national boundary of intelligibility by failing to engage with the material determinations of these texts. An official national literature thus tends to elide history (as a determinant) from its readings in order to form an archive of texts that can be recognized under the sign of a nation.

The result of this delimiting—of effect and of positions—has dampened and depoliticized the effect of language writing within Canadian institutions. Aside from the barriers inherent to institutional interventions, there is—for a poetic movement that has defined itself as "American," particularly in its anthologies—the still-strong veil of Canadian cultural nationalism to pierce. In terms of Canada's place within the world system, it may appear that cultural nationalism has been disrupted or renegotiated through international trade pacts such as NAFTA and the eroding of barriers to transnational economic and cultural trade, even in the face of U.S. protectionism. However, in the arts, there was a strong lobby against NAFTA and in favor of taking culture "off the table" as a negotiable commodity, recognizing that the American culture industry would override its smaller Canadian counterpart. Retrospectively, this was a resistance to the becoming economic of the cultural and the attempt to alter the configuration of the cultural in globalism and not old-time Canadian cultural nationalism. Despite the remapping of culture and nation by challenges to official multiculturalism in Canada and despite the partial withdrawal of state cultural funding, cultural nationalism remains a primary framework not only for the production of culture in Canada, but also in the reception of culture. To see a presence and an effect of language writing in Canada, focus must shift from official sites to formations of writers and little magazines. This shift sidesteps the invocation of the institution as the primary site for the effect of poetry.

One such rearticulation of the language writers—where similar devices and tactics of language writing were redeployed by a group of emergent poets in the mid-eighties in Vancouver—exceeds both their internal and external definitions. Within this emergent cultural formation, the language writers figured not only as a response to a crisis in the production of American poetry nor as a uniquely American articulation, but as a politicized poetic methodology adaptable to the particular crisis in the public sphere in Vancouver. This recirculation of the politics and tactics of the language writers opens the problematic of the circulation of culture and of the narrowness of the imagined influence and effects of language writing as a national formation.

The materialization and rearticulation of the language writers is most readable in the scene of Vancouver writers who emerged through self-produced magazines and chapbooks around the mid-eighties. This then-emergent cultural formation had its own "institutional" or supplemental site in the artist-run Kootenay School of Writing (KSW) and parallel gallery, Artspeak. By organizing the New Poetics Colloquium in 1985 (the first large-scale international gathering of the language writers), KSW was associated with and made nearly synonymous with language poetry by a discursive exterior that used cultural nationalism to frame the poetics. This frame had already been utilized in the reception of the early-sixties TISH poets as they took up and modified New American poetry for their own investigations of place, history and poetic practice.

For the emergent formation of writers and artists in Vancouver—whose poetics are hybrids of at least the more innovative and rearticulatory aspects of Canadian literature, the language writers and contemporary visual arts—this prefabricated frame produced predictable external discursive definitions. From accusations that "language-centred writers" were "retreat[ing] into expressive Kabalas [that] killed New American poetry" and that will now "probably destroy what little audience poetry has left" (Fawcett 101) to more nuanced readings recognizing a paradigm of a Canadian avant-garde in TISH (Bowering), these external definitions have failed to link these poetics to present structures of feeling in Vancouver that would provide a more articulated social field in which this work could be situated. To do so would move past defining this community of writers—who have been producing work for almost two decades now—as a formation that is a continuation and opposition to a sixties avant-garde, as a breach of cultural nationalism, or as an extension (or branch plant) of language writing. A cultural poetics would enable these poetics to be placed in a field of relations to take into account the changes in the public sphere in Vancouver in the mid-eighties (precipitated by the hosting of Expo 86); the high unemployment level which created an economics of the community; the effects of globalization through the implementation of Thatcherist policies by the provincial government; and a homology of poetics to economics. This homology would expand on a poetics that utilized the general economic aspects of language, the excess of language, at a time when governmental restraint was radically altering the relationship of the social sphere to education, union organization, culture in general, and working-class culture in specific. That is, these determinations in the cultural and political sphere resulted in a poetics of excess during a time of restraint and of a poetics articulation at a time when the local governments didn't even make the nouns, but only burnt the connections, to paraphrase Perelman's poem "Person": "all without a verb / because capitalism makes the nouns / and burns the connections" (*First World* 51). In this instance, the local was not the last line of defence against globalization, but the very structure which enhanced globalization, bypassing national regulations and policies to attach itself to globalism's scapes. The writers and artists around KSW and other artist-run centres in Vancouver could be seen as a moment of collectivity at a time when the individual and individual interest was being promoted and enacted by the federal and provincial governments, when neoliberalism was solidifying as a dominant discourse.

By turning lastly to other writing communities as a discursive exterior for language writing, I am emphasizing that institutions should not be privileged as a dominant site or set of discourses. The academy, along with other social institutions that give an official shape to poetic production, is not buffered from its own discursive outside. A discursive exterior is felt not only in how it articulates a poetic movement, but also in how poetry's social effect might be registered. There is a discursive impasse as poetics move into the social sphere; narratives and critiques of cultural production tend to hinge on the massification of effects and, as a result, poetry's cultural capital has not been bullish. However, a cultural poetics that could move from the micro-aesthetics of the text to the macro-ideology of nation states and of a geoculture could locate the effects of poetry at the field of its own production, at an institutional level, and in the social sphere.

Acknowledgments

The author wishes to acknowledge the support of The Social Sciences and Humanities Research Council of Canada and The Killam Trust. Additional thanks to Romana Huk and Louis Cabri.

Notes

1. This early self-constructing self-critique was done in magazines (most notably *L=A=N=G=U=A=G=E* and *Poetics Journal*) and in talks series. Much of this work has been collected in *The L=A=N=G=U=A=G=E Book* (eds. Bruce Andrews and Charles Bernstein. Carbondale and Edwardsville: Southern Illinois University Press, 1984) and in individual writers' collected essays, such as Charles Bernstein's *Content's Dream: Essays 1975–1984* (Los Angeles: Sun & Moon, 1986); Ron Silliman's *The New Sentence* (New York: Roof, 1987); Steve McCaffery's *North of Intention: Critical Writing 1973–1980* (New York/Toronto: Roof/Underwhich, 1986); Alan Davies' *Signage* (New York: Roof, 1987); and Bruce Andrews' belated *Paradise and Method: Poetics & Praxis* (Evanston: Northwestern University Press, 1996). To break the male pantheon of this list, see *Poetics Journal* 4, "Women & Language" (1984).
2. Fredric Jameson's reading of Perelman's "China" (in "The Cultural Logic of Late Capitalism," *Postmodernism, Or, The Cultural Logic of Late Capitalism*. Durham: Duke University Press, 1991) as a symptom of late capitalism has generated some continued debate, from an array of positions. See also George Hartley, "Jameson's Perelman: Reification and the Material Signifier," *Textual Politics and the Language Poets* (Bloomington: University of Indiana Press, 1989): 42–51; Gayatri Chakravorty Spivak, *A Critique of Postcolonial Reason: Toward a History of the Vanishing Present* (Cambridge, Mass.: Harvard University Press, 2000): 330–336; Bob Perelman, *The Marginalization of Poetry: Language Writing and Literary History* (Princeton: Princeton University Press, 1996): 59–78. My favourite intervention into this discussion is again from Perelman himself, from his poem "Movie" in *Captive Audience* (Great Barrington, Mass.: The Figures, 1994):

   > . . . I
   > call it the schizophrenic
   > theory, Bob, if we can
   > make the reader believe that
   > any word can come next . . ."
   > where any word refers to
   > the nuclear bombs Nixon wanted
   > to have Vietnam believe
   > he was willing to drop on them
   > if they didn't stop defending
   > themselves. . . . (55–56)

   This is also an example of the language writers' unwillingness to let a discursive exterior control their representation.
3. Famously, from *"A"* 12 (Berkeley: University of California Press, 1978), Louis Zukofsky regarding his poetics:

An integral
Lower limit speech
Upper limit music (138)

4. Not to overly single out Silliman for criticism, but he is the master of the list of who got left out but who could have been included. See, for example, his introduction to *In the American Tree* (Orono: National Poetry Foundation, 1986); he supplies an aditional seventy-nine names of writers who could be considered part of the language writers' nexus. See as well his introduction to *The Art of Practise: Forty-Five Contemporary Poets* (eds. Peter Ganick and Dennis Barone; Great Barrington, Mass.: Potes & Poets Press, 1994) for another list. This listing tendecy is also found in Perloff's essays, where she tends to note emerging writers. Curiously these lists tend to be extra-national, an eruption into the nationalistic frame of the language writers, giving the names of writers in other countries who are affiliated but not included. In fact, it is in the process of anthologizing that the language writers have been the most vigilante in their border defences, despite the listings. The inexplicable exclusion of Steve McCaffery from *In the American Tree* fundamentally misrepresents the language writers. Curiously, Alan Davies, another Canadian, is included in the anthology; however, Davies has lived in the U.S. for many years. It appears that it is a matter of geography then, rather than nationality. For McCaffery cannot be considered "Canadian" because of his inclusion in a Canadian literary canon. *In the American Tree* is organized geographically, with sections of "East" and "West," suggesting a kind of localism or, conversely, national coverage. The tensions in the anthologizing of the language writers involve a national tension, a geographical tension, and (as always) a tension of inclusion and exclusion. The formal innovation of the poetry is not carried over to the form of anthologies: they tend to be normatively organized with no challenge to literary models of poetry formations.
5. Raymond Williams, in his reading of the avant-garde as a modernist phenomenon, emphasizes the internationalism of the historical avant-garde. "The true social bases of the early avant-garde were at once cosmopolitan and metropolitan. There was rapid transfer and interaction between different countries and different capitals, and the deep mode of the whole movement, as in Modernism, was precisely this mobility across frontiers: frontiers which were among the most obvious elements of the old order which had to be rejected, even when native folk sources were being included as elements or as inspiration of the new art" ("The Politics of the Avant-Garde," *The Politics of Modernism: Against the New Conformists*. London: Verso, 1989: 59).
6. For instance, see Rae Armantrout's hilarious review of *The Morrow Anthology of Younger American Poets*. Armantrout summarizes the content of the anthology: "Thus we see the 'typical younger American poet' is outdoors in an 'abandoned' location doing physical labour with a sharp implement" (*Poetics Journal* 6: 142).
7. Recently, Barret Watten has challenged Grenier's statement as the originary moment of language writing. But, rather than dispute the logic of an originary moment and its avant-gardist limitations and historical abruptness, Watten proposes an alternative originary moment: the Clark Coolidge poem "MADE THOUGHT" from the same issue of *This* magazine (Issue 1, Winter 1977). So the originary site

of language writing has been shifted a few pages in the same magazine. I'll propose the originary moment of the end of the language movement: August 1985 in Vancouver. The New Poetics Colloquium organized by the Kootenay School of Writing (the first major gathering of the language writers) clearly showed they did not have enough unity.

8. For a continuation of this grappling over terms and representations of "so-called language writing" and the devices it set in circulation, see my introduction to "Disgust & Overdetermination: a poetics issue," *Open Letter* 10/1 (Winter 1998).

9. These are the closing lines of the penultimate poem of *The Maximus Poems,* edited by Charles Boer and George F. Butterick (New York: Viking Press, 1975, not paginated), which come just before the closing lines, "my wife my car my color and myself" (635). This instance of closure is opened up by its relationship to Samson's final speech in Milton's "Samson Agonistes" in *Complete Poems and Major Prose,* edited by Merritt Y. Hughes (New York: Macmillan, 1957):

   "Happ'n what may, of me expect to hear
   Nothing dishonorable, impure, unworthy
   Our God, our Law, my nation, or myself;
   The last of me or I cannot warrant" (ll. 1423–26)

   Olson here has constructed himself as a Miltonic figure. A poet who addressed his nation and who attempted to create a nation of readers ("fit though few"). The previous pages of *The Maximus Poems* further build on this connection. Olson writes: "but now I am a poet / who thinks more than writes. . . ." I read this as an allusion to both Milton's and Olson's emphasis on praxis—both social and textual. Olson then has moved from an address to his nation as "I, Maximus of Gloucester" to a somewhat despondent poet who is no longer writing. This parallels Milton's construction as a split figure: the political and spiritual writer and the Restoration-defeated revolutionary writer. This intertextual connection opens a different field to view Olson in—one that emphasizes his role as a national poet who sought to address his nation at a particular historical juncture (post-war America for Olson, revolutionary and Restoration England for Milton) through an epic poem. And both poets sought out a new form for their national epics: Olson's postmodernism on the cusp of the modernist intrigue with the relation of the one to the many utilized an open field composition, drawing on (like Pound) discourses and images from a huge temporal and cultural range; Milton, for his part, used his blank verse for *Paradise Lost* (and likewise we see Spenser create a unique verse form for his national poem, *The Faerie Queene*). Olson in some ways inserts himself into literary history through Milton, but he also, like Milton, projects himself as a national poet.

Works Cited

Althusser, Louis. *Lenin and Philosophy and Other Essays*. Trans. Ben Brewster. New York and London: Monthly Review Press, 1971.

Andrews, Bruce, and Charles Bernstein, eds. *The L=A=N=G=U=A=G=E Book*. Poetics of the New Series. Carbondale and Edwardsville: Southern Illinois University Press, 1984.

———. "Total Equals What: Poetics and Praxis." *Poetics Journal* 6 (1986): 48–61.

Appadurai, Arjun. Modernity at Large: Cultural Dimensions of the Global. *Public Worlds* 1. Minneapolis: University of Minnesota Press, 1996.

Bartlett, Lee. "What Is 'Language Poetry'?" *Critical Inquiry* 12 (Summer 1986): 741–51.

Bernstein, Charles. *Contents Dream: Essays 1975–1984*. Los Angeles: Sun & Moon, 1986.

Bourdieu, Pierre. *The Field of Cultural Production: Essays on Art and Literature*. Ed. and trans. Randal Johnson. New York: Columbia University Press, 1993.

Bowering, George. "Vancouver as Postmodern Poetry." *Vancouver: Representing the Postmodern City*. Ed. Paul Delaney. Vancouver: Arsenal/Pulp, 1994, 121–43.

Brik, Osip. "The So-Called Formal Method." Trans. Anne Shukman. *Russian Poetics in Translation,* no. 4 (1977): unpaginated.

Davidson, Michael. *Ghostlier Demarcations: Modern Poetry and the Material World*. Berkeley: University of California Press, 1997.

Davidson, Michael, and Lyn Hejinian, Ron Silliman, and Barrett Watten. *Leningrad: American Writers in the Soviet Union*. San Francisco: Mercury House, 1991.

Davies, Kevin. *Comp*. Washington, D.C.: Edge, 2000.

Fawcett, Brian. *Unusual Circumstances and Interesting Times, And Other Impolite Interventions*. Vancouver: New Star, 1991.

Foster, Hal. *The Return of the Real: The Avant-Garde at the End of the Century*. Cambridge Mass.: MIT Press, 1996.

Golding, Alan. *From Outlaw to Classic: Canons in American Poetry*. Madison: University of Wisconsin Press, 1995.

Guillory, John. *Cultural Capital: The Problem of Literary Canon Formation*. Chicago: University of Chicago Press, 1993.

Hartley, George. *Textual Politics and the Language Poets*. Bloomington: University of Indiana Press, 1989.

Hejinian, Lyn. "The Rejection of Closure." *Poetics Journal* 4 (1984): 134–43.

Huyssen, Andreas. *After the Great Divide: Modernism, Mass Culture, Postmodernism*. Theories of Representation and Difference Series. Bloomington: University of Indiana Press, 1986.

Jameson, Fredric. *Postmodernism, Or, The Cultural Logic of Late Capitalism*. Durham: Duke University Press, 1991.

Kalaidjian, Walter. *American Culture Between the Wars: Revisionary Modernism & Postmodern Critique*. New York: Columbia University Press, 1993.

Kipnis, Laura. *Ecstacy Unlimited: On Sex, Capital, Gender and Aesthetics*. Minneapolis: University of Minnesota Press, 1993.

Kosuth, Joseph. *Art After Philosophy and After: Collected Writings 1966–1990*. Ed. Gabriele Guerico. Cambridge Mass.: MIT Press, 1991.

Krauss, Rosalind. "The Originality of the Avant Garde: a Postmodernist Repetition." *October* 18 (1981): 47–66.

Laclau, Ernesto and Chantal Mouffe. *Hegemony and Socialist Strategy: Towards a Radical Democratic Politics*. London: Verso, 1987.

——. *New Reflections on the Revolution of Our Time*. Phronesis Series. London: Verso, 1990.

Lusk, Trujillo. *Redactive*. Vancouver: Talonbooks, 1990.

McCaffery, Steve. "From the Notebooks." *The L=A=N=G=U=A=G=E Book*. Poetics of the New Series. Eds. Bruce Andrews and Charles Bernstein. Carbondale and Edwardsville: Southern Illinois University Press, 1984, 159–61.

——. *North of Intention: Critical Writings 1973–1986*. Toronto: Nightwood; New York: Roof, 1986.

Palmer, Bryan D. *The Descent into Discourse: The Reification of Language and the Writing of Social History*. Philadelphia: Temple University Press, 1990.

——. *Solidarity: The Rise & Fall of an Opposition in British Columbia*. Vancouver: New Star, 1987.

Perelman, Bob. *Captive Audience*. New York: The Figures, 1988.

——. *The First World*. New York: Roof Books, 1986.

——. *The Marginalization of Poetry: Language Writing and Literary History*. Princeton: Princeton University Press, 1996.

Perloff, Marjorie. *The Dance of the Intellect: Studies in the Poetry of the Pound Tradition.* Cambridge: Cambridge University Press, 1985.

——. "The Word as Such: L=A=N=G=U=A=G=E Poetry in the Eighties." *American Poetry Review* 13.3 (May/June 1984): 15–23.

Quartermain, Peter. *Disjunctive Poetics: From Gertrude Stein and Louis Zukofsky to Susan Howe*. Cambridge Studies in American Literature and Culture. Cambridge: Cambridge University Press, 1992.

——. "Getting Ready to Have Been Frightened: How I Read Bruce Andrews." *Aerial* 9. 1999: 161–182.

Rasula, Jed. *The American Poetry Wax Museum: Reality Effects 1940–1990*. Urbana, Ill.: National Council of Teachers of English, 1996.

Ross, Andrew. "The New Sentence and the Commodity Form: Recent American Writing." *Marxism and the Interpretation of Culture*. Eds. Cary Nelson and Lawrence Grossberg. Urbana: University of Illinois Press, 1988, 361–80.

——. "Reinventing Community: A Symposium on/with Language Poets." *Aerial* 8 (1995): 188–99.

Shklovsky, Viktor. *Theory of Prose*. Trans. Benjamin Sher. Elmwood Park: Dalkey Archive Press, 1990.

Silliman, Ron. "Canons and Institutions: New Hope for the Disappeared." *The Politics of Poetic Form: Poetry and Public Policy*. Ed. Charles Bernstein. New York: Roof Books, 1990, 149–174.

——. "The Dysfunction of Criticism: Poets and the Critical Tradition of the Anti-Academy." *Poetics Journal* 10 (1998): 179–94.

———. "IF BY 'WRITING' WE MEAN LITERATURE (if by 'literature' we mean poetry *(if . . .))*. . . . ." *The L=A=N=G=U=A=G=E Book.* Poetics of the New Series. Eds. Bruce Andrews and Charles Bernstein. Carbondale and Edwardsville: Southern Illinois University Press, 1984, 167–68.

———. "Negative Solidarity: Revisionism and 'New American' Poetics." *Sulfur* 22 (Spring 1988): 169–75.

———. *The New Sentence.* New York: Roof, 1987.

———. *Tjanting.* Berkeley: The Figures, 1981.

von Hallberg, Robert. *American Poetry and Culture, 1945–1980.* Cambridge, Mass.: Harvard University Press, 1985.

Wallerstein, Immanuel. *Geopolitics and Geoculture: Essays on the Changing World-System. Studies in Modern Capitalism.* Cambridge: Cambridge University Press: 1991.

Watten, Barrett. "The Bride of the Assembly Line: From Material Text to Cultural Poetics." *Impercipient Lecture Series,* Vol. 1 no. 8 (Oct. 1997).

———. *Total Syntax.* Poetics of the New Series. Carbondale: University of Southern Illinois Press, 1985.

Miriam Nichols

A/Politics of Contemporary Anglo-Canadian Poetries

The Toronto Research Group and the Kootenay School of Writing

I

Canada has never had a commonly acknowledged political imaginary. This is not to deny a long history of various political, economic, and cultural nationalisms,[1] but Canadian nationalism has always had to compete with British and American influences, incompatible regional interests, provincial-federal power struggles, and a colonized economy. In their primer on Canada's political economy (*The Political Economy of Canada,* 1992), Michael Howlett and M. Ramesh argue that the major institutional contributors to public policy are structurally fragmented: the state must contend with jurisdictional divisions and an electoral system that exacerbates regional disparities; the business community is divided between large and small, domestic and international corporations, as well as sectoral interests; labor in Canada has a history of divisions between national and international, public and private affiliations, and consequently a decentered collective bargaining record. This fragmentation contributes to the difficulty of ameliorating Canada's historical dependence on a resource-based economy and hence on foreign investment and international markets. In *Open for Business: The Roots of Foreign Ownership in Canada* (1989), Gordon Laxer challenges the idea that this economic dependency developed inevitably from Canada's position as a late-blooming industrial nation next door to an economic superpower. He argues instead that ethno-nationalist divisions between French and English agrarians and workers at crucial points in the development of the country led to the failure of national populist agendas that might have brought more independence. Now that

Canada's branch plant economy has become entrenched, however, Laxer suggests that it will be difficult to change. Howlett and Ramesh agree with Laxer on this latter point, and they suggest that Canada now faces the possibility of resource depletion and the economic effects of globalization—trade agreements that further reduce the possibility of national economic planning—without a coherent strategy. They conclude that neither the right nor the left will be able to implement its agenda unless the internal divisions of one or more of the players can be overcome.[2] At issue, finally, is the state's ability to respond to democratic direction. What Laxer, Howlett and Ramesh express as political economy, a poet might register as the "angular avenues / of the city / of diminished expectation" (Culley 84).

Canadian writing, like writing anywhere, is marked—not determined—by its social context. In the 1960s and '70s, practitioners of thematic criticism, like Margaret Atwood and D.G. Jones, worked to bolster national self-awareness with unifying meta-narratives; at the same time, more radical nationalists, such as Robin Mathews, argued the validity of existing Canadian traditions, and worked for the legitimation (rather than construction) of a national self, which Mathews presented as under siege by American cultural imperialists and by Canadians sympathetic to American liberalism. Opposing both of these positions, postmoderns like Robert Kroetsch and George Bowering wrote the local as a deconstruction of British, European, and American nation-stories. In these conflicting constructions, Canada's public self was, and continues to be, understood as problematic: it is either in need of definition, or embattled, or simply undefineable.[3] The language writers I want to talk about practice poetries that are genealogically closest to the postmodern, and sensitive to the colonized status of Canada's economy. While they combine political attunement with formal investigation, they are less concerned with critiquing institutionalized politics than with economic determination and transnational issues. In Steve McCaffery's phrasing, "Capital, Reason, Philosophy and History" are the targets, and from this perspective, the Canadian state is a symptom rather than the cause of—or solution to—systemic problems in these regimes.

Now some qualifications. First, the Toronto Research Group (TRG) and the Kootenay School of Writing (KSW) poets make use of postmodern epistemology and deconstructions of the Cartesian subject as do writers elsewhere, but this shared contemporaneity doesn't quite account for the traces of a colonial history that mark their work or the display of indifferent-to-hostile attitudes toward nationalism. Secondly, I am not implying necessary similarity in point of view between these writers, nor do they represent anyone; in relation to the academic mainstream with its emphasis on fiction and central Canada, they are as Who's to Horton. However, they do share the sociality of living in a country where the powers of the private, corporate sector and foreign ownership have historically overshadowed those of the public, and to the extent that they illuminate this condition they speak to a commonality that others from both margin and center may respond to differently—with anxiety about national identity, for instance. Finally, my qualification of this writing as Anglo, while vulnerable to counter-example, is meant to distinguish my topic as writing positioned within British and European cultural traditions, albeit critically. I confess here, too, that I want to stretch the adjective to imply "mainstream" and "masculinist,"[4] my purpose being to exclude identity politics from the present discussion as requiring a different analysis, even if said politics are practiced by Anglo feminists. The Canadian state may be usefully constructed as powerful if the purpose is to mobilize ethnic, racial, sexual, or gender-defined groups for specific political reasons. As exemplified by the Japanese redress movement, the legal struggles of gay activists, or the many First Nations treaty negotiations currently in process, political remedies for local injustices can be an essential and achievable aim. My topic, however, is limited to writing which is embedded in mainstream culture as its negative and nemesis. From this position of complicity, economic determiners or transnational cultural practices, including those which feminists have identified as patriarchal, may seem more powerful than political processes at home. Both points of view express a not so distant colonial history, but from different angles.

What I am calling a/politics in the work of bp Nichol and Steve McCaffery (TRG),[5] and Jeff Derksen, Lisa Robertson, Peter Culley, and Deanna Ferguson (KSW)[6] is thus a writing that is politicized, and sometimes intensely so, and marked by its Canadian context, but not a writing oriented to institutional politics.[7] One of the traces of this a/politics is the rejection of nationalist engagements in favor of a local–global split.[8] In this split, the local may be transvalued over the international, or presented as inadequate to the large forces that threaten to overwhelm it. Alternatively, it may appear as already commodified and hence the site of permanent alienation. In both cases, the writing remarks upon and is marked by its attention to transnational economic considerations. This attention may be both direct and abstract, as in Steve McCaffery's work on a general economy of writing that broadly challenges the commodifying effects of capitalism—"exchangist" thinking in economics, philosophy, politics, linguistics—or it may take more oblique forms. Nature, for instance, has always figured importantly in mainstream Anglo-Canadian writing where it has been variously depicted as hostile, sublime, mysterious, seductive, or redemptive; an empty space, the middle of nowhere, a place of terror, beauty, death, silence, or pure potentiality. All these figurations of nature present the land, and sometimes the aboriginal inhabitants, as ahistorical and hence available for discovery, narration, development, or conquest. They also recall a very old European dream of the end of history, expressed in golden-age or new-world fantasies about utopian plenitude, or in tales of apocalyptic destruction.[9] In a Canadian context, these European nature narratives complement, rather than contradict, the commercial view of the country as a vast warehouse of exploitable resources. Among the various tasks that engage younger writers like Jeff Derksen, Lisa Robertson, Peter Culley, and Deanna Ferguson is the rewriting of nature as a social artifice, commodity, or commercial landscaping-over of indigenous or minoritarian histories. As Derksen says of his project, "I make it *old* here" (32).

Making it old, or making it global are not, of course, practices exclusive to Canadian language writers, nor can these writers be distinguished beyond counter-example from their counterparts who live elsewhere. Rather they differ from writers whose work *is* marked by nationalism, especially writers from the United States, since of the two nations from which Canada has historically distinguished itself (the U.K. and the U.S.), the U.S. is most immediately present to Canadians. When Derksen "make[s] it old," for instance, he comments ironically on Pound's "make it new"—and on the American fascination with newness and generational change—while at the same time deconstructing nationalist rhetoric in Canada by uncovering the imperial origins of that rhetoric. Similarly antagonistic to national narratives, Deanna Ferguson, in her treatment of Anglo-Canadian settler literature in *Rough Bush* (1996), sweeps aside pioneering sagas that have been fundamental to Canadian nationalism. Or there is Steve McCaffery's general economy, which is deconstructive of identity in all regimes, and yet ironically marked as "north of intention." These writers, and the others I have named above, practice a Canadian *différance* which offers a negative, relational identity: it is anti-nationalist with respect to the rhetoric of their own country, but also un-American, and not-British.

II

The reports of the Toronto Research Group, issued between 1972 and 1983 by Nichol and McCaffery, display a broadly defined postmodernism as the common ground worked out between them. What the two seem to have shared was a scepticism of realist epistemologies and narrative forms; a distrust of writerly authority and of the speech-writing dichotomy; an insistence on the materiality of the text as sound, grapheme, and book-machine (book-as-object); a commitment to processual over static form; an interest in "low" art forms, like the comic book; and a faith that "word order = world order" (*RG* 99). Given these assumptions, their writing functions as a general critique of western rationalism, but the manner in which they inflect the ground they share distinguishes them from each other, and points to the geo-historical context of the writing.

Nichol's best known work to date, *The Martyrology,* does not announce itself as political in the narrow sense of the term, but rather ethical and existential.

In this multivolumed poem, the poet assumes the role of witness to the antic creativity of an embodied Logos; he attends the continual presencing of word-things, as well as the processive coming-to-be of a lower case "i," within the play of a vast, "letteral" world that the diminutive subject does not control or fully comprehend. The sacrificial component of Nichol's poetic, as indicated in the title of the poem, consists of the subordination of the will to the play of the Word. While this sacrifice of the will might be read as part of a postmodern quarrel with authorial intention, Nichol writes the polemic distinctively as a trope of religious service—a martyrology—where the lower case first person (a very small local unit) submits to the play of a Logos (a very large global field) that transcends it. This trope carries a trace of colonial passive-aggression: we are adrift without history or tradition in a great, mysterious space, dwarfed by the forces of nature ("letteral" nature, in Nichol's case). Read in this context, rather than in that of textualist deconstructions of the author, the passivity of the poet's first-person voice suggests complicity, as much as argument, with the imperialist view of the land as empty and Other.

This colonial marking of the poetry is much clearer in the cosmogony that forms the pre-text of *The Martyrology*. In an introduction to her selection of poems from Nichol's otherwise unpublished "Plunkett Papers," Irene Niechoda points to "the slippage between Plunkett and heaven / Cloud-town, personal genealogy and cosmic myth, *'istorin* and history" (66). Plunkett is a real town "south east from Saskatoon on highway 14," Nichol says, and home to his grandparents (Niechoda 66). He is thus able to trace his genealogy to Plunkett, but after that, personal history turns into myth. The Plunkett papers combine Judaic, Egyptian and Hopi creation stories and include a creator-god Nichol calls Cloud-hidden. Plunkett comes to be when Cloud-hidden says "plunk it there" (76). The Plunkett story—and I cannot convey the complexity of it in a sketch—includes two important moves. First, the myths are not handled as functioning cultural narratives but as positioners; they place the poet as suppliant in relation to a Living Logos of unrecoverable origin: Cloud-hidden is a name for the mythic source of the letteral, languaged world, and he is operationally transcendent in relation to the human will. Secondly, the Plunkett tale mythologizes a new beginning in a land without history, and this dehistoricizing of place persists in *The Martyrology* itself. As Nichol writes later, in Book Three, ". . . in this new world / we lack a sense of history / a real sense of time / claim our father's father's father as our heritage / & press no further" (n.pag.). The story of a distant and mysterious power plunking a town down in the middle of nowhere is part of a colonial narrative or landscaping-over of indigenous histories, and it clears the way for the existential confrontations which later surface in *The Martyrology*. Thrown into a particled language field on which he claims no historical leverage, the poet is left alone to ponder the mysteries of life and death. In *Gifts* (Book Seven of *The Martyrology,* published posthumously, 1990), Nichol writes that, "the language comes alive as you come alive and the real mysteries remain" (n.pag.). Elided from the explicit consciousness revealed in the poem is the recognition that the site of the "mysteries" has been cleared of history—that the "mysteries" of life and death are historically mediated. Certainly Nichol's stunning materializations of language derive from a postmodern agenda, and offer a rich source for the meditations of future writers and readers, but the tropes he favors in *The Martyrology* can also be read as uncannily resonant with Canada's colonial past. Moreover, the diminished, lower-case subjectivity Nichol allows for, while suggestive of an ethics of mutual constitution and communal interdependency ("i" has a relational identity), does not play itself out at the civic or political levels. The poet's "i" seeks community, but in a lexicon that moves either to the domestic (family and friends) or mythic: the Logos speaks the language of "scrapture" (Nichol's word) rather than history, and the effect is to veil the political meanings of the text.

Like Nichol, Steve McCaffery works with the materiality of the language, but he offers a hydraulic, rather than a biological model of form, and hence a writing that moves further toward a deconstruction of the humanist subject than does that of Nichol. In "Writing as a General Economy" (1985), one of his most important and familiar statements of poetics, McCaffery locates his work in a challenge to "a writing of use value" (203) through the release of the graphic, phonic, and gestural components of language (204). McCaffery cites Bataille in this essay, in support of a writing of "unmasterable excess, inevitable expenditure and a thoroughly non-productive outlay" (209), which performs a disruption of restricted economies like the above named "Capital, Reason, Philosophy and History" (203). He is also careful to make clear that the general is not an alternative to the restricted, but rather "[i]n most cases . . . a suppressed or ignored presence within the scene of writing that tends to emerge by way of rupture within the restricted" (203). The relationship between the restricted economies of state institutions and the general economy McCaffery outlines is thus chronically agonistic rather than revisionary or constructive and registers the poet's distrust of rationalist interventions in cultural or political institutions.

Another important figure of this writing of expenditure is the nomad. McCaffery says of such writing that "the semantic mechanism is rendered nomadic, meaning wanders from one term to another" ("WGE" 206). The trope is Deleuzean and more widely available in the rhizomatic structure of poems like "Effect of Cellophane" (in *The Black Debt,* 1989) and *Theory of Sediment* (1991). In a re-thinking of form that seems particularly congenial to McCaffery's textual practices, Deleuze distinguishes nomadic territory as a "local absolute" rather than "relative global" space (54); the former is a "nonlimited locality" without boundaries, points, or horizons, and the latter is divisible space in which one passes from point to point. Similarly, McCaffery speaks of a writing that includes "escape lines, seme grids, opacity vectors, finesses of final sedentary leanings, initial waves against all polar signs" (*TS* 18–19). In the title piece of *Theory of Sediment,* for instance, he writes: "Sedimentary elements have the quality of residue from the higher hills of the seventeenth allegory in the poem about the carriage derailing between more conversations about the game" (107). This sentence seems to offer information about the titular "theory"—a "theory" of the material text, perhaps, figured as phonic or graphemic "residues" washed down from the "higher hills" of allegory. But the sentence enacts the "derailing" it talks about, moving off into "more conversations about the game," where carriage, conversations, and game might be construed as allegories of writing and hence the very allegorical hills that were apparently left behind. The point is that the sentence doesn't go anywhere (travel from point to point); it simply reinscribes itself, fills the page so that there is no empty space—*no lack.*

In contrast to Nichol, then, McCaffery presents a full, rather than empty, space, thus drawing out the violence of various restricted economies that impose direction or containment on social energy. These restricted economies would include narrative reterritorializations of linguistic flows, capitalist economics ("exchangism"), and the literal settling of North America to the detriment of nomadic peoples.[10] Like Nichol, however, McCaffery rejects the wilful subject as an agent of change; his anti-institutional, anti-rationalist stance means the practice of a poetry that always courts the repressed other of the current state of things, and that displaces the will with desiring production and the permanent revolution of constant becoming. As McCaffery writes in "Teachable Texts" (*The Cheat of Words,* 1996), he is continually "Hoping that poetry / is the politics that stays politics" (102). In other words, he rejects the language of nationalism and institutional politics, and not only in his poetry. The essays in *North of Intention* (1986), and the prose collaborations with Nichol now published in *Rational Geomancy* (1992), reveal a critical approach to poetics that seems to be genealogical and transnational, rather than geo-historical. What engages McCaffery is the creative-disruptive potential of poetic language—not the establishment of national differences. Why, then, "north of intention"?

A primary contrast to the poetic practices of both Nichol and McCaffery, and a comparison that McCaffery seems to invite with his comments on Ron Silliman in "Writing as a General Economy," is Silliman's work of the late '70s and '80s as exemplified in formal innovations like the "new sentence."[11] McCaffery suggests that Silliman restricts the "free-play of signification" ("WGE" 212) between sentences by re-establishing closure at the higher formal level of the poem as a whole. This critical observation seems to be confirmed obliquely by Silliman's own comments about his work. Interviewed in

The Difficulties (1985), Silliman says that in *Tjanting* (1981) he wanted to see "what class struggle [would] look like, viewed as a form" (35). But read as a homologue of political space, the poem reterritorializes linguistic play, and not only in *Tjanting*. In *What* (1988), for instance, the sentence is indeed a unit of measure as Silliman claims in *The New Sentence,* and the poem proceeds by accumulating these disjunctive minims, one by one. At the end of the poem, however, the "ones" add up to a wonderfully complex, multileveled world, composed of logically unrelated, but formally equal units. The poem is thus readable as a political space to which each separate "one" contributes equally—a radically democratic space, in other words.

This idea that American language writing might be read as a political homologue finds explicit expression in Lyn Hejinian's "The Rejection of Closure"; the open text "invites participation," Hejinian says, "rejects the authority of the writer over the reader and thus, by analogy, the authority implicit in other (social, economic, cultural) hierarchies" (272). My citations are from the 1980s and the claims to liberation of a reader-oriented writing were challenged then—by McCaffery as early as 1976[12]—but my point is simply that engagement with political forms that are national in scope has been available as a serious option for radical American poets, at least until the present decade when the Scylla of balkanization[13] and Charybdis of global economics have beset everyone's ship of state. When Silliman imagines "A small man / (neither warrior nor monk) . . . lean[ing] over a desk in an attempt / to imagine the world" (*What* 126), he renovates a rhetorical gesture that can be traced back through Olson, Pound, and Whitman to Jonathan Winthrop and the Puritan "City on a Hill." When Charles Bernstein launches a meditation on the genealogy of the contemporary writerly text in his important "Artifice of Absorption" (1992), he crosses national and historical boundaries, and offers a vocabulary that is as useful for describing the work of Canadians as it is that of Americans; however, when he writes in "Comedy and the Poetics of Political Form" (from *The Politics of Poetic Form,* 1990) that "convention and authority can, and ought, serve at the will of the polis and not by the Divine right of kings or the economic might of Capital" (239), he speaks in the admonitory voice of an enfranchised American citizen who can still imagine a *polis* sufficiently unified to oust kings and bring the captains of industry to heel. Such a *polis* need not exist to live on as a regulating concept for American writers.

There are subtler distinctions, too. McCaffery presents his writing in terms of excess. Bruce Andrews, whose "politics . . . of both the Sign & Social Context" (28) rivals McCaffery's "Capital, Reason, Philosophy and History" in scope, understands radical writing as social analysis and ideology critique. In his "Poetry as Explanation, Poetry as Praxis" (1990), Andrews advocates the "contesting" of institutionalized writing and suggests a Bakhtinian "dialog with one's own future and an address to the external world" (32). But behind the contest and address, the analysis, the critique, or the dialogue, there is surely a concerned citizen. Or Silliman, again, in his contribution to *The Politics of Poetic Form,* refers to the corruption of institutional politics in the U.S., and concludes that the radical must choose one of three options: abandon the political process, wait for a revolution that will never come, or try for change at a cultural, rather than political, level where gains may be easily lost (160). The distrust of institutional politics, which Silliman expresses here, may well intensify for American writers as economic globalization renders all national political organizations less autonomous, and more vulnerable to unhappy compromises. Yet in 1990, Silliman writes his misgivings in terms of the *corruption* of the Democratic party, rather than as a lack of faith in rational intervention as such, or in the state's *ability* to respond to direction.

In contrast, Nichol and McCaffery, wandering saint and profligate sinner, are *un*worldly: they resist dominant social systems through errancy rather than critical admonition, analysis, or dialogue. Or to switch metaphors, they are subversive because they just won't work on the farm. Both adopt the role of nomad rather than citizen, and both orient themselves to levels of engagement other than the national—Nichol to the existential wayfarer; McCaffery to transnational concerns. It is perhaps a Canadian irony that this abandonment of institutionalized politics makes good sense in the geo-historical context of the doubtful autonomy of the Canadian state.

III

The younger poets who have drawn from the energy of the Kootenay School often seem closer than Nichol and McCaffery in their practices to the politics which Andrews identifies and which Bernstein has described as the unveiling of "instruments of power" in what appears to be "neutral or given" ("WM" 588). But in their choice of genres (travel literature, pastoral, landscape art), and in their poses (*flâneur,* profligate, saboteur, minor artist) they differ from their American models. In *Dwell* (1993), Jeff Derksen characterizes resistance to the economic imperative in Canada to "Sell abroad or go under" (3, 26) as "A strike that tries to 'inconvenience the public as little as possible'" (4). Borders, he says, soon "will mean nothing / more than knowing where to cut your lawn" (2), and nature has been produced as "The late fall beauty / of an Outstanding / Development Opportunity" (28). The subject of these poems is at once complicit, ironic, horror-struck, and resistant: "I won't say the imperialism placated me," Derksen writes, "but that / the stroking of the consumer goods really calmed me / down" (7). Unlike Nichol's lower case "i," which is formed through alterity and integrated in the bio-social matrix from which it derives, Derksen's "I" has been produced as a commodity. "If I am alienated from the production of me," he jokes, "then I am / in a commodity relation with myself, hence big / bargains" (72). The principle target of Derksen's wit is transnational capital, rather than the structure of the state, and in the global marketplace, the subject is a *flâneur,* or perhaps a shopper, but not a citizen. Constructing the "I" as a tourist in one series in the book, Derksen speaks of being "poised between participant and observant" (32). This posture is chronic, rather than temporary. Whether home is in Alberta or Andalucía, it is always part of the same "common market." What Derksen offers in *Dwell* is "A special view / of history / through development" (46), where the reference to Charles Olson underlines the difference between the Black Mountain push for local authenticity and participation ("polis / is eyes") and Derksen's darker view of European history in North America as the economic colonization of the local and indigenous.

In *Dwell* Derksen begins to rehistoricize scenic and social terrain that has been landscaped for market. In a different way, Lisa Robertson also contributes to this project of "making it old" through her renovation of pastoral conventions in *XEclogue.* "I needed to pry loose Liberty from an impacted marriage with the soil" (n.pag.) she says in her "Prologue." Robertson rewrites the pastoral alignment of nature with abundance, freedom from toil, and antinomian self-rule as profligacy, ornament, and excess: "sluttish thickets and rivulets of green," or "bitchy, sybaritic, flickers of leaf" ("Eclogue One: Honour," n.pag.). Her revision of the bucolic as a sexual, textual scene of decadence and naughty pleasure rather than rustic innocence thus resonates ironically with the mainstream landscaping of Canada as a country of untouched wilderness zones, as these have been produced not only by numerous poets and literary critics, but by British Columbia's municipal and provincial tourist bureaus, which have for years invited the world to come to "super natural B.C." and bring its wallet. Redecorated as a bordello of the imagination in *XEclogue,* Robertson's pastoral has a complex cultural history that belongs in distinctive ways to British Columbia, as tourist destination and exploitable resource; to Canada, as the imperial myth of an empty, ahistorical, and available land; and to the Euro-centered world, as golden-age or millennial mythology. Robertson's overly lush textscapes expose the artifice of the pastoral, and by extension the constructed status of "nature" in other narratives, but they also resist the installation, in a still-moving word-world, of the proper and of property.

In the *Eclogues,* an obvious source text for Robertson, Virgil juxtaposes golden-age poems with those that reference the historical brutalities of conquest: the poems were written at a time of civil war which saw Julius Caesar expropriate land from rural Italians in order to reward his troops. Colonization suggests a parallel theme. Robertson addresses this issue of property in an assault on boundaries as such. Sentences overstuffed with adjectives, a sexualized vocabulary, and synaesthetic deterritorializations constitute a breaching of conceptual borders, and hence, by deconstructive logic,[14] borders of all kinds. In a sentence like "Nancy straps the audible sulk of a method to her hips" (n.pag.), not only does the term "method" take on the tangibility of a dildo (and deliver a rude poke at methodologies), but the phrase "audible sulk" fuses sound with attitude or mood.

The critical force of *XEclogue* thus is directed not just at dysfunctional political institutions, or particular social injustices, but at the much broader target of knowledge in general. Rather than the traditional shepherd's calendar of seasonal events, the poem concludes with an "incendiary calendar" which has all the bucolic sweetness of a hand-grenade—ready to be lobbed at the taxonomies on which knowledge is founded. Hence there is a "Day of the Theoretician of the Animals," a "Day of Prepositions," a "Day of the Dream of Justice" and many more days that defy conventional systems of classification ("Eclogue Ten: Utopia," n.pag.). Deterritorializing, desirous production displaces the idealism of the conventional pastoral, yet Robertson remains faithful in an ironic way to the antinomian element in golden-age myths. Although in a manner quite unlike Derksen's cool *flâneur,* her flushed first-person narrator and cast of characters (Lady M, Nancy, the Roaring Boys) also position themselves as deconstructive of states and borders.

Deanna Ferguson brings entirely different strategies to political engagements that are, however, similarly broad. In *The Relative Minor* (1993), her first full-length collection of poems, Ferguson includes an untitled preamble that serves as a prologue, where the phrase "documentary, dumb-in-the-mouthe" and the imperative, "Pose as a rupcha" (9), indicate something of her strategy. The documenting of mainstream culture in such a way as to disrupt its transmission is an aim of the book. In "Received Standard," for instance, Ferguson aligns grammatical convention and modernist aesthetics with class oppression and state terrorism. The "uniformly grammatical" and a "straight gauge / education" draw the remark, "You serve everything in tin cups?" (30). Plato and Pound appear in a passage about the practice of eugenics during World War II: "1941 deferred eugenics / to Plato in the sense that Pound developed / pervading stress on the concrete. No / superfluous word or weeding out. . ." (32). Ferguson responds to such "standards" by using language like a prophylactic. The metaphor is hers. "Instruct Obstruct" consists of truncated instructions for what sounds like the use of a diaphragm:

> Men and women are taught proper use
> Soft, rubber, dome, mouth.
>
> Place in place the back of. Spring.
> Holding up against swimming. Beyond escaping. (*RM* 69)

What is to be guarded against is impregnation by conventional logics, until conventions, like exhausted sperm, give up: "Because has a limited life," Ferguson says in this poem (69).

"Sidewinder," a piece consisting of phrases separated by two "does not equal" signs, exemplifies Ferguson's obstructive tactics. Phrases like "mower model palsied for ≠≠cake has never missed my chain jerk every" (46) block the exchangeability of meaning and imply a similar obstruction of "exchangism" (McCaffery's sense) in other regimes as well. Unless words are used in recognizable grammatical patterns, they "do not equal" each other as units of currency in the transfer of information. And if a currency does not circulate—well, the metaphor is easy enough to extend to the social and economic spheres. Similarly, Ferguson's "dictionary" poem, an untitled piece which glosses the words in "Sidewinder" in the manner of a dictionary, is comically disruptive. Ferguson offers definitions for an idiosyncratic selection of words which she has solemnly alphabetized. Dictionaries are crucial, enabling documents in the circulation of knowledge, and standard-making bastions of reliability. Ferguson's definitions are sometimes conventional, sometimes not. The point is sabotage. Hence "fealty" means "faithfulness allegiance," and "harbinger" "indicates what is to come," but "loofa" is a "humorous treatment of a very serious situation" and "lyric" means "the principle that at a fixed temperature the pressure of a confined idea varies inversely with its volume" (58, 59).

As these poems suggest, Ferguson pushes back against idealisms that persist in the culture; she also "do the men in different voices" (*RM* 29). "Perth Bless," for instance, is an intra-linguistic sound translation of Louis Zukofsky's "Perch Less." The latter is a short lyric of two stanzas, in which Zukofsky skilfully plays off some of the most hackneyed of lyrical arrangements—youth, nature, light, flight, and the joy of life. Urging his bird to "perch less," and his boy to "Butt age," the poet affirms that "Foolishness is joy" (131, 132). Ferguson will have none of it. "Been bird / Splatter hopes" she says, and "No butt thing as / Sublime" (82). The humanist link between nature and spirit that lingers like a perfume in the Zukofsky poem, hits the ground like too-tangible bird droppings in Ferguson's translation. Moreover, Zukofsky's "Butt age, boy" becomes "Clit day, Joe" in a move that not only draws attention to the gender of the generic "youth" Zukofsky celebrates, but also displaces the discrete *joie de vivre* of lyric convention with a much blunter sexuality. "Perth Bless" ends comically with the line, "Foolishness is lopped" (82).

In the titular sequence from *Rough Bush* (1996), Ferguson applies more of this *attitude* to the most canonical of Canadian texts. The sequence is drawn from Douglas Daymond and Leslie Monkman's *Literature in Canada* (1978), a two-volume teaching-anthology that collects mainstream Canadian literature, from Jacques Cartier's account of voyages made between 1534 and 1541, to the work of contemporaries like Tom Wayman and Susan Musgrave. Ferguson leans toward the older texts in the collection—texts that reflect the standards of their times, and unabashedly promote the imperial enterprise with an arrogance that jars contemporary ears. In the Cartier excerpt, for instance, the explorer records a meeting with "savages" in which he and his men trade "hatchets, knives, beads and other wares" for everything the tribe owns, "so that nothing was left to them but their naked bodies" (3). Cartier dismisses the furs he gets for these trinkets as "of little value" but notices the fertility of the land with some interest, and the docility of the inhabitants, remarking that they should be easy to convert to Christianity. "I'm fine, but I'm rather / inclined to believe as I run" (n.pag.), Ferguson remarks.

Other source texts for *Rough Bush,* notably Susanna Moodie's *Roughing It in the Bush* (1852), from which Ferguson takes her title, and Isabella Valency Crawford's *Malcolm's Katie* (1884), include passages that present just the kind of landscaping that promotes the colonial agenda by clearing the land of history. For instance, Moodie initially responds to the country in language that belongs to British and European romanticism: nature is sublime, and the aboriginal inhabitants are noble savages. When it comes to establishing a farm, however, literary nature evaporates into backbreaking labor, bad weather, and blackflies. In a process which enacts a kind of reverse colonization, Ferguson recombines words and phrases from *Roughing It* in such a way as to offer the reader a textual "rough bush" with no through passage in the way of linear syntactic paths or meaningful clearings. Where her sources interpret experience in terms of the conventional pieties of literature and religion, she returns their tales to the materialities of life, labor, and language (Foucault's triplet). In a piece drawn from *Malcolm's Katie,* the latter a long melodramatic poem in which true love conquers all and nature goes along for the ride, Ferguson translates the lines "'Arise, be not dismayed, arise and look; / If he shall perish, 'twill be as a god, / For he will die to save his enemy'" (300), as "Be not dismayed, arise and look, / for if soul splits from sound, 'twill / be twice as good" (n.pag.). And in a poem beginning "Nature, that no right / withered wind-breathed / house of ill," nature sublime and other becomes a nature breeding flies and the "fetid weft / of ice-rimmed mist" (n.pag.). As in *The Relative Minor,* Ferguson directs the critical energy of *Rough Bush* against "received standards"—this time, those that have been fundamental to Anglo-centered, cultural nationalism. In this Canada, Ferguson is a saboteur.

Peter Culley, on the other hand, takes up the deceptively innocuous role of minor landscape artist, and uncrowned poet laureate of Hammertown, otherwise known as Nanaimo, a harbour town on Vancouver Island. Yet in *The Climax Forest* (1995), the landscapes are cyborgs, made of competing nature narratives and current technologies welded to the flora and fauna around Culley's Nanaimo home. *The Climax Forest* offers a compendium of landscapes, in which nature is variously depicted as a wilderness ("When two races meet / they act like two species of animals, / they fight, eat each other, bring diseases to each other . . ." 41); a gothic sublimity ("the irredeemable natural world in / whose dark caves he was encompassed" 51); a natural history in which the two terms contaminate each other; a garden ("some great / nodding blossom" 65); or nightmare inversion of bucolic bliss with "Freud as Freddy Kruger,"[15] a landscape of "sulphurous mud," and the poet hilariously standing "On the shore / in a sweet peace / Watch[ing] the little fish's [sic] bathe / in the clear stream" (81). Culley's Hammertown "is a zone / Of permanent permission, where / the damp exhausted firework of *polis* / Bobs to the surface of a tainted puddle, / where cattle from untasted fields do / Bitterly return, their lowing ting'd / with unhealthy intelligence" (90–1). The commercial interests that have "permanent permission" in this small town finally produce a thing of Terminator-like qualities:

A caravan
    of bright yellow trucks,
Jostling like bland mugged thugs
    along a granulate roadway
Of broken bottles, bristling
    with crab claws, with arms like
Monstrous barbed
    dog cocks, depositing
Layer after layer of
    sulphurous spoor
Into a vale of rubber smoke . . . (92)

The only apparent opposition to the commercial forces indicated by the yellow trucks takes the form of one determined woodpecker:

The woodpecker
    rears back
And slams
    its full weight, all the power
In its teeny shoulders—
    PECK!
Into the unyielding spruce—
    PECK!
PECK!
    PECK!
and works it right out
    and slams it right out

and clears it right out
    and erases the blackboard
and erases the tape
    and pops the lid off
and tears the roof off
    and boils it right down
from an oil tanker
    to a teaspoon . . . (91–92)

Although the woodpecker (libidinal force?) is pictured as triumphant over the spruce tree/tanker, the absurdity of the confrontation emphasises the disproportion between 'borg and resisting bio-unit. Only in Culley's appeal to geological time—to the "continental plate" or "iron mountains"—does there seem to be an imaginable end to this landscaping gone wrong. "The Iron Mountains" is the last poem of the collection, and in it "the nameless city" is "shattered somehow / into jagged and icy / shards of light, spinning / and careening / into the darkness" (109–10). But this is a vision of human annihilation.

Culley's "shattered *somehow*" (my italics) suggests a rejection of rational means of intervention in a political economy that now more than ever seems to be spinning out of the reach of the polity. In their concern with the very visible effects of the market, rather than with an errant state, or in their sybaritic responses to social and grammatical decorum, or in their tourist-like indifference to borders, or in their guerrilla-like resistance to overwhelmingly large, transnational social and economic forces, these Canadian language poets differ from those among their American counterparts who continue to reference a faulty *polis* and offer improvements, or who claim the hortatory rights of citizenship. This difference is both cultural and material—an old difference between Puritan settler and economic-immigrant rhetoric, a more contemporary difference between a large, influential economy and a small, open one—although it seems to be dissolving fast as the incompatibility of democratic political systems with transnational markets becomes everyone's concern. The rhetoric of democracy, even radical democracy, has become much less plausible, and it is much more difficult to imagine intervention in a global market than it is in a coercive or corrupt political regime that can at least be held up for censure. Whether the market will self-destruct,[16] or whether radicalism at the cultural level can ameliorate the often deleterious effects of the new global economy on the folks at home remains at issue. I am rather inclined, with Deanna Ferguson, to believe as I run, however absurd the gesture. In an early poem from *The Relative Minor,* Ferguson names the anxieties and aspirations that continue to haunt many contemporary poets and artists—

until all events speak for themselves
until representations know what it feels like
until positioning in the order is located
until orders of knowing suss up
until strata is axed as metaphor
until economic isn't always the organizer
fear, baby. (*RM* 19)

Notes

1. Here are two contrasting examples of the nationalist line: on the Canadian identity, philosopher George Grant writes:

   > The fact that the Canadians had consciously refused the break with their particular past [i.e., had refused the American revolution] meant that they had some roots with tradition, even though that tradition was the most modern in Europe up till the eighteenth century. Indeed, when one reads the speeches of those founders whom we celebrated in 1967, one is aware of their continual suspicion of the foundations of the American republic, and of their desire to build a political society with a clearer and firmer doctrine of the common good than that at the heart of the liberal democracy to the south. (68)

   The tradition that Grant regrets in this essay derives from the Christian humanism of Richard Hooker, as opposed to the modernity of Bacon, Hobbes, and Locke. This "red tory" line is represented in twentieth-century Canada by political and cultural figures such as Stephen Leacock, John Diefenbaker, Charles Taylor, George Grant and, more recently, David Orchard, contender for the Progressive Conservative party leadership.

   In contrast, Frank Davey has argued in *Surviving the Paraphrase* (1983), that "it is not unfair to say that the bulk of Canadian literature is regional before it is national—despite whatever claims Ontario or Toronto writers may make to represent a national vision" (10). Eleven years later, in "The Collapse of the Canadian Poetry Canon," Davey points to the coeval shattering of cultural nationalism in the identity politics of the 1980s and the eclipse of national economic planning by the new world order. Davey's own version of nationalism appears in the Preface to *Canadian Literary Power*: "*Canadian Literary Power,* and the power it may possess, is dedicated to the continuation of a national English-Canadian literary community. This is not a national community imagined in Toronto and constructed by authoritative national anthologists, or at another extreme a battlefield of mutually suspicious, self-aggrandizing cultural interests, but a polylogue of strong, locally produced institutions, discourses, and practices" (n.pag.).

2. See Chapter 12, "Conclusion: The Political Economy of Canadian Capitalism" in *The Political Economy of Canada* (253–259), for a summary of this argument about the weakness of the state.
3. Robert Kroetsch has argued cogently in various essays that Canada is not to be defined. In "Disunity as Unity: A Canadian Strategy" (*The Lovely Treachery of Words,* 1989), for instance, he suggests that Canada is a postmodern country (22), and says that the "very falling-apart of our story is what holds our story together" (21–22).
4. I don't want to be understood as insinuating that the writers I discuss here are soft on WASP conventions. Every one of them would rightly object to being so described because it is precisely the nexus of assumptions and practices associated with British and European traditions that they challenge. However, their strategies are deconstructive in relation to this still dominant culture, rather than strategically essential. They don't, for instance, use the term "woman" as a rallying point for political action, even though they might support such action in other ways. Instead, they are more inclined to handle gender as a social artifice to be deconstructed, and so with other mainstream social constructs. A deconstructive stance, however, requires *intimacy* with the discourse or discourses to be critiqued.
5. The TRG consisted of bp Nichol and Steve McCaffery. McCaffery provides an account of his meeting with Nichol in 1969 and of their collaborative work through the 1970s in his introduction to *Rational Geomancy: The Collected Research Reports of the Toronto Research Group 1973–1982* (1992). The original venue for the collaboration was a regular, TRG section in the journal *Open Letter* (edited by Frank Davey), and this section sometimes included "guest reports." McCaffery lists Howard Adelman, Barbara Caruso, Christopher Dewdney, Haroldo Gonzales, Julia Keeler, and Opal L. Nations as contributors (*RG* 16).
6. The KSW was established as a non-profit society in 1984, and has since provided a venue for new writing and a locus for a community of poets and artists. While membership is always in flux, and not necessarily coincident with writers associated with the School, a very partial list would include founding members Colin Browne, Jeff Derksen, Kathryn McLeod, Tom Wayman, and Calvin Wharton, and at different times, Lisa Robertson, Colin Smith, Dorothy Trujillo Lusk, Michael Barnholden, and Andrew Klobucar. Deanna Ferguson and Peter Culley are not KSW members, but both have been vital participants in a poetry scene that orbits the KSW. Ferguson, for instance, has worked with Michael Barnholden to publish Tsunami books, a small press that has brought out the work of many KSW alumni. Peter Culley acknowledges the importance to his work of this same local milieu in the many dedications to artists and writers in his *Climax Forest*.
7. Since this essay was written in 1996, Andrew Klobucar has published a short essay titled "The Wobbly Roots of the KSW" (1998), in which he aligns the politics of the school with an anarcho-syndicalist position aiming "not to reform capital, but overthrow it" (18). Klobucar explicitly dissociates the KSW from the "official" left of local labor organizations, which he characterizes as ineffectively "reformist" (16). It should be noted that Klobucar's essay, originally a conference paper, was erroneously published under the names of his fellow panelists as well as his own.

The piece appears in *Foundational Narratives,* attributed to Mike Barnholden, Andrew Klobucar, and Dorothy Trujillo Lusk.

8. See also Frank Davey's argument that in this local-global split, the local may be dimininshed to the personal. In *Post-National Arguments,* Davey reviews sixteen contemporary Anglophone novelists to conclude that "between the global field and their own immediate resources there is neither state nor polis. . . . Meaning here is constructed transnationally—world economics, universal beauty, humanism, Marxism—or else it collapses on the disillusioned individual . . ." (264).
9. In "The Canadian Writer and the American Literary Tradition," Kroetsch talks about a Canadian will toward silence and failure. He associates this impulse with a wilderness that is not a frontier to be conquered but a presence that "we want . . . to conquer us" (*LTW* 54). The other side of the Canadian version of new world mythology is the representation of nature as seductively destructive—an Otherness that lures the writer or artist toward death. On the thematics of this destructive "call of the wild" as a Canadian tradition in which Kroetsch participates, see Sherrill Grace's essay, "Kroetsch and the Semiotics of North" in the 1996 Kroetsch issue of *Open Letter* 9: 5–6 (Spring–Summer 1996): 13–24.
10. McCaffery makes the connection between a writing of expenditure and aboriginal practices in "Writing as a General Economy," where he cites the Kwakiutl potlatch as exemplary of a gift economy rather than one based on investment (220).
11. Silliman's influential and now well known proposition, published as an excerpt in *In the American Tree* (1986), and as *The New Sentence* (1987), was that the sentence might be treated as a unit of measure rather than a moment in the logic of a narrative. The new sentence cannot be integrated with others to form paragraphs or chapters.
12. Of the reader-writer relationship in language writing, McCaffery says that

> . . . Language writing proposes not only the unbinding of signs and referents and the polysemous development of the signifier, but also a closed Model Reader predetermined by the productional disposition he is compelled to adopt. She is constituted upon a series of prohibitions (you can't consume, you can't reproduce an identical message, you can't subvert a representation). Hence the emancipatory character of the reading becomes a mandatory liberation. . . . It is precisely their resistance to aberrant decodings that imposes a devastating qualification on the emancipatory scope of Language texts. ("Diminished Reference" 28)

Although this essay was published in *North of Intention* in 1986, it is dated 1976 in that volume.

13. I am thinking of the 1990s focus on cultural identity and limited constituencies, and the consequent difficulty of imagining a *polis* in the U.S. Interestingly, this is a problem raised by Erica Hunt in a discussion session with Bruce Andrews and others, recorded in *The Politics of Poetic Form.* Hunt distinguishes between "remaking identity and uncovering suppressed histories," and projects that are "more textual" (37); Andrews takes issue with the efficacy of identity politics.

14. See Derrida's *Aporias* for a deconstructive logic applied specifically to conceptual borders. In this text, Derrida deconstructs death as the gatekeeper concept of all concepts.
15. Freddy Kruger is the main attraction of the horror film series, *Nightmare on Elm Street.* He is a killer returned from the dead, distinguished by his burn-victim face and long, knives-for-fingernails, who reaches his adolescent victims by entering their dreams.
16. Klobucar, in the above named "Wobbly Roots of the KSW," raises this possibility (17).

Works Cited

Andrews, Bruce. "Poetry as Explanation, Poetry as Praxis" and "Discussion." *The Politics of Poetic Form*. Ed. Charles Bernstein. New York: Roof, 1990, 23–43.

Bernstein, Charles. "Artifice of Absorption." *A Poetics*. Cambridge: Harvard University Press, 1992, 9–89.

——. "Writing and Method." *In the American Tree*. Ed. Ron Silliman. Orono, Maine: National Poetry Foundation, 1986, 583–598.

Cartier, Jacques. "From *The Voyages of Jacques Cartier*." *Literature in Canada,* Vol. 1. Eds. Douglas Daymond and Leslie Monkman. Toronto: Gage Publishing, 1978, 1–3.

Crawford, Isabella Valency. *Malcolm's Katie*. In *Literature in Canada,* Vol. 1. Eds. Douglas Daymond and Leslie Monkman. Toronto: Gage Publishing, 1978, 267–301.

Culley, Peter. *The Climax Forest*. Vancouver: Leech Books, 1995.

Davey, Frank. *Canadian Literary Power*. The Writer as Critic Series IV. General Editor: Smaro Kamboureli. Edmonton: NeWest Press, 1994.

——. *Post-National Arguments: The Politics of the Anglophone-Canadian Novel Since 1967*. Toronto: University of Toronto Press, 1993.

——. *Surviving the Paraphrase*. Winnipeg: Turnstone Press, 1983.

Deleuze, Gilles and Felix Guattari. *Nomadology: The War Machine*. Trans. Brian Massumi. New York: Semiotext(e), 1986.

Derksen, Jeff. *Dwell*. Vancouver: Talonbooks, 1993.

Ferguson, Deanna. *The Relative Minor*. Vancouver: Tsunami, 1993.

——. *Rough Bush*. Buffalo, New York: Meow Press, 1996.

Grant, George. "Canadian Fate and Imperialism." *Technology and Empire*. Toronto: House of Anansi, 1969, 63–78.

Hejinian, Lynn. "The Rejection of Closure." *Writing/Talks*. Ed. Bob Perelman. Carbondale: Southern Illinois University Press, 1985, 270–291.

Howlett, Michael and M. Ramesh. *The Political Economy of Canada*. Toronto: McClelland & Stewart, 1992.

Klobucar, Andrew. "The Wobbly Roots of the KSW." In *Foundational Narratives*. Eds. Stephen Collis and Sharon-Ruth Alker. Burnaby: Simon Fraser Student Society

Printers, 1998, 14–19. [This essay erroneously appears under the authorship of Mike Barnholden, Andrew Klobucar, and Dorothy Trujillo Lusk.]

Kroetsch, Robert. "The Canadian Writer and American Literary Tradition." In *The Lovely Treachery of Words: Essays Selected and New*. Toronto, New York, Oxford: Oxford University Press, 1989, 53–57.

———. "Disunity as Unity: A Canadian Strategy." *Lovely Treachery*, 21–33.

Laxer, Gordon. *Open for Business: The Roots of Foreign Ownership in Canada*. Toronto: Oxford University Press, 1989.

McCaffery, Steve. *The Cheat of Words*. Toronto: ECW Press, 1996.

———. "Diminished Reference and the Model Reader." *North of Intention*. New York, Toronto: Roof/Nightwood, 1986, 13–29.

———, Ed. *Rational Geomancy: The Kids of the Book-Machine/The Collected Research Reports of the Toronto Research Group 1973–1982*. Vancouver: Talonbooks, 1992.

———. *Theory of Sediment*. Vancouver: Talonbooks, 1991.

———. "Writing as a General Economy." *North of Intention*, 201–221.

Nichol, bp. *The Martyrology: Books 3 & 4*. Toronto: Coach House, 1976.

———. *Gifts: The Martyrology Book[s] 7 &*. Toronto: Coach House, 1990.

———. "A Sorted 'Plunkett Papers.'" Ed. Irene Niechoda. In *West Coast Line*, No. 2 (Fall 1990): 65–82.

Niechoda, Irene. Introduction to "A Sorted 'Plunkett Papers,'" 65–68.

Robertson, Lisa. *XEclogue*. Vancouver: Tsunami Editions, 1993.

Silliman, Ron. "Canons and Institutions: New Hope for the Disappeared." *The Politics of Poetic Form*. Ed. Charles Bernstein. New York: Roof, 1990, 149–174.

———. "Interview [with Tom Beckett]." *The Difficulties*. Vol. 2, No. 2 (1985): 34–46.

Zukofsky, Louis. "Perch Less." In *Complete Short Poetry*. Baltimore and London: Johns Hopkins University Press, 1991, 131–132.

Steve Evans

The American Avant-Garde after 1989

Notes toward a History

A simple poetic undertaking: to see if life is livable, to make life livable. Without lying.
—George Oppen

There has been a continuous, because continuously risked and reinvented, avant-garde in American poetry since the opening decades of the twentieth century: independent, dissident, restless for aesthetic and social transformation, responsible for most of what is today considered significant in the nation's poetry. This avant-garde's distinctive demand—for the autonomy to compose a socially relevant poetic outside (and often in opposition to) the constraints of the capitalist market—has received as many historical inflections as there have been significant shifts in what some historians call "the short twentieth century."[1] Working with a modest and vulnerable but persistently renewed set of expressive means—the typically short-lived, privately funded, small-circulation magazine; the non-commercial, non-institutional publishing house; the low or zero-budget public performance—the generations emerging in the 1910s, 1930s, 1950s, and 1970s envisioned understandably different projects in light of their specific intersections with the large-scale forces that shaped the century.[2] If such terms as modernism, "Objectivism," the New American Poetry, and language-centered writing capture only in the vaguest profile the indescribably various set of successive poetic practices spanning four generations, they do nevertheless mark out a discrete series of actual historical accomplishments, a temporal trajectory that is at the same time a densely communicating web of interpersonal and intertextual relations; in short, though the word scandalizes superficial observers of the avant-garde, a *tradition*.[3]

The broad continuities of condition, stance, and impact that unite this tradition of poetic radicalism are often less visible than the local ruptures within it, for the simple reason that punctual events are more readily dramatized than abiding structures. Not surprisingly, these dramas of differentiation find an especially rich stock of affective and conceptual materials in the highly charged transition between generations. The break into modernity accomplished by the generation of Gertrude Stein and Ezra Pound was already a matter of intense and contradictory impulses, identifications, and anxieties, despite what amounted to the patent social-historical sanction these literary changes received from the simultaneous deep changes in other crucial spheres of life. Interestingly, it was not until certain of the language poets in the late 1970s and early 1980s took it upon themselves to spell out their poetic differences with the preceding generation of New Americanists that such a noisy—and largely one-sided—intergenerational dispute would again arise. The "Objectivists" in the 1930s had been more reticent about the differences of political commitment and personal *habitus* that unmistakably separated them from the first-wave, often fascist-leaning modernists like Pound: rather, they held fast to an unresolved but not unproductive dialectic between continuity of formal approach and discontinuity of ethico-political motivation. And the poets of the immediate post-war years had little need for intergenerational dispute, as the global synchronization of the war itself divided life—including literary life—into brutally clear categories of *before* and *after*.[4] In fact, that war-time generation's many assertions of transgenerational solidarity with radical modernism and "Objectivism" were themselves effectively polemical gestures in the more important battle against a conformist academy bent on poetic restoration.[5]

Dark Ages

The most recent transformation of the American avant-garde poetic tradition has taken place quietly in the years following 1989, largely if not exclusively through the agency of a new generation of poets. Born in the decade preceding 1968 and coming to consciousness in the rain of gunfire that killed presidents, civil rights leaders, and—in a ten year undeclared war that bankrupted the legitimacy of the government that conducted it but not before destroying countless lives on both sides—a staggering number of ordinary people, these poets entered adolescence just as the economic order of the post-war capitalist boom shuddered into global recession and for a second time in ten years the office of president was vacated under abnormal circumstances. Their secondary education coincided with the backlash social and economic programs of a resurgent conservative party, an artificially revived cold war, and the outbreak of a mortal sexually transmitted disease. Anti-imperial and socialist struggles in Latin America and the battle against apartheid in South Africa informed the political horizon of their college years, but a marked depoliticization of student populations and an increased orientation toward conventionally defined success were the more visible and typical tendencies of the period. The brokered conclusion of forty years of superpower nuclear standoff in the mid-1980s held nothing for drama to the unforeseen and utter collapse of the Soviet empire beginning in Eastern Europe in the autumn of 1989 and striking home in the summer of 1991.[6] The rapidity and enormity of this change called to mind Hegel's famous image, from his preface to the *Phenomenology of Spirit,* of a world dissolving bit by bit, until the "gradual crumbling that left unaltered the face of the world is cut short by a sunburst which, in one flash, illuminates the features of the new world" (7). However, in this case, the flash had nothing to illuminate but a no longer new, and anything but liberating, capitalism that immediately began dictating the meaning freedom would have for the former "second world," and by extension the entire globe: freedoms not of people, but of markets; not of unimpeded flows of informed popular discourse directed toward rethinking fundamental social structures, but of expert solutions imposed on paralyzed populations; not of engaged citizens in a regenerated civil society, but of predatory gangsters loosed into conditions of unbridled economic anarchy.[7]

Before intellectuals had time to finish their arguments as to the aptness of "late capitalism" as a periodizing term, the world became—to all effects and purposes—*only* capitalist. The first world stock markets soared, but in almost every other sphere of life a collective sinking feeling unmistakably set in,[8] and as early as the Gulf War in 1991 what had begun as a stunned silence turned into a summarily coerced one. Perhaps the earliest specifically poetic manifestation of the structure of feeling ascendant in this emergent set of conditions came in the form of Andrew Schelling and Benjamin Friedlander's magazine *Dark Ages Clasp the Daisy Root,* founded in the autumn of 1989 in a self-confessed mood of collapse, ruin, and disillusionment.[9] Crystallized in the journal's title was the thesis—widely intuited at the time[10]—that capitalism, unopposed, reverts to feudalism, closing the parenthesis around a two-century aberration (the Enlightenment) in millennia of hardship and domination. That subterranean and fugitive forms of solidarity and knowledge nevertheless persist is the argument of the title's remaining words, "clasp the daisy root." Though it would remain virtually imperceptible for at least another half-decade, an important change in radical poetic practice was already gripping down and taking root.

A Simple Poetic Undertaking

If a single question can be said to have synchronized the American poetic avant-garde between 1970 and 1989, it was surely the question "what is language?"

Inherited from Russian and Czech structuralism, as mediated by *Tel Quel* post-structuralism, and lent a palpable urgency by the circumstances in which it was posed (the Vietnam war; militant civil rights and liberation struggles), this question was in every way a *live* one, inspiring theory and practice, sparking debate and catching imaginations, changing the way many American poets wrote and read. In the eyes of some of the most active and accomplished writers of the era—eyes that had attentively passed over texts by Gertrude Stein and Ludwig Wittgenstein, Roman Jakobson and Robert Creeley, Louis Zukofsky and Roland Barthes—poetry was seen as a means to interrogate and intervene in "the discursive construction of social reality" (to use the period phrase).[11] This stance toward poetic composition retained its force well into the 1990s, holding the allegiance of its initial formulators, now middle-aged, and generalizing its appeal among young writers, graduate students, and—increasingly—tenured academics.[12] Many of the poems and arguments first articulated in forums defined by their mix of unruly independence, unstable authority, and passionate risk now commenced a second life as markers on a professional game board, and though this "institutional strategy" was an understandable outcome of real contradictions in the intellectual life of capitalist America, it was no less understandably viewed by many as a demoralizing capitulation to academic power.[13]

Nothing about the question "what is language?" jarred against its academic recontextualization: after all, modern linguistics—and the social theory predicated on it—had long struck a manifestly scientistic pose even in the work of a hero like Jakobson, friend and spirited celebrator of Khlebnikov and Mayakovsky.[14] Perhaps because they were harder to accommodate, more embarrassingly obvious and ethically intractable, another set of questions remained outside the academic economy. For instance, the question George Oppen had already posed in a mid-1960s notebook, when he imagined a "simple poetic undertaking: to see if life is livable, to make life livable. Without lying" (190). Or Bernadette Mayer's question of a decade later, in the desperate final line of "The Way to Keep Going in Antarctica": "If I suffered what else could I do." Neither the elder Objectivist, dispirited by his nation's refusal to let go its theocratic tenets and become a true democracy, nor the young New York School poet, as adventurous in her poetic explorations as the first Antarctic explorers had themselves been, could be charged with indifference to the linguistic basis of their common art. But their ethical and political questions—however immanent to linguistic and communicative contexts—did not admit of simple linguistic resolution or evasive formal-technical transposition. This refusal to subordinate the social to the linguistic distinguishes Mayer and Oppen from the project of language-centered writing, and it also explains their importance for the post-1989 generation. As one of the wittiest, and most politicized, members of that generation—the Canadian-born Kevin Davies—would say on the opening page of his 1995 chapbook, *Thunk*: "I knew I was a formal device before I was born. I wanted / a *bigger* prize, for having survived."

Survival: it is hard to imagine that the word has ever been so frequently uttered by inhabitants of a prosperous nation in peacetime as it has been in the American 1990s.[15] The social logics behind the hypersaturation of this sign are too numerous, and too contradictory, to be unraveled here, but it is possible to distinguish its use in relation to poetry from the spontaneous Social Darwinism of economic elites and the paranoid anti-federalism of some segments of the working class.[16] As a protest against false supercession, against the extinction of one of the oldest human art forms in the withering conditions of market-driven culture, against the incessant talk of its death, its marginality, its obsolescence, to say that poetry survives is to say that it remains a basic, and inalienable, possibility of human intelligence. Poet and editor Lisa Jarnot says as much—while adding the names of Allen Ginsberg and John Cage to those of Mayer and Oppen already mentioned—in speaking of her post-1989 contemporaries: "We are a generation critically aware that as Allen Ginsberg said in 1966, 'almost all our language has been taxed by war.' And perhaps what we share the most at this moment is an unspoken thought that John Cage is right when he tells us that language is something 'that you have to use in practical ways, for survival'" (Jarnot et al. 2).

An Impulse to Action

To belong to a biological generation, to share an historical horizon, to endure certain material conditions: important as these factors are, they remain inert data, powerless in themselves to constitute even rudimentary forms of collectivity, especially in the diffuse, discrepant social topography of the contemporary United States.[17] As the philosopher Jean-Luc Nancy observes: "'History' is not always and automatically historic. It has to be taken as an offer and to be decided. We no longer receive our sense from history—history no longer gives or enunciates sense. Rather we have to decide to enunciate our 'we,' our community, in order to enter history" (166).[18] In the wake of, and in deliberate contrast to, the self-assertive, auto-exegetical, and reciprocally-evaluative conduct of the language-centered writers, the scrupulous avoidance of certain inflated forms of framing discourse among the poets emerging after 1989 was anything but the sign of apathy that certain established avant-gardists mistook it for: rather, the intransigent refusal to self-identify registered a profound and warranted resistance to "entering history" under the terms presently on offer.[19] At the same time, this decision led in the direction of a returned emphasis on poetic practice as opposed to theoretical discourse. It is action that articulates community, these poets seemed to be saying, and action—as it transforms conditions—outpaces the terms of its own recognition.[20]

In its initial phase this activity took the form of a loosely coordinated swarm of small-circulation magazines like Friedlander and Schelling's *Dark Ages Clasp the Daisy Root* (Oakland); Jessica Grim and Melanie Neilson's *Big Allis* (New York); Jennifer Moxley's *The Impercipient* (Providence); Scott Bentley's *Letterbox* (Oakland); Robert Fitterman's *Object* (New York); Avery E.D. Burns's *Lyric&* (San Francisco); Sianne Ngai and Jessica Lowenthal's *Black Bread* (Providence); Dodie Bellamy and Kevin Killian's *Mirage#4/Period(ical)* (San Francisco); Elizabeth Fodaski's *Torque* (New York); and Brian Kim Stefans's *Arras* (New York); not to mention the more visible counterparts of these often furtive ventures such as Rod Smith's *Aerial* (Washington D.C.) and Peter Gizzi's *oblek* (New York and Providence), the twelfth and final issue of which gathered under the title *Writing from the New Coast* two volumes of poetry and poetics by younger writers.[21]

By the middle years of the decade, works first disseminated in these fugitive venues were being collected in chapbooks from the prolific Leave Books in Buffalo, with nearly a hundred titles between 1991 and 1995; in an excellent series from Situations press in New York, which between 1995 and 1997 brought out titles by Kevin Davies, Bill Luoma, Lisa Jarnot, Douglas Rothschild, Marcella Durand, Chris Stroffolino, and others; and in collections from Joel Kuszai's Meow press, which published Juliana Spahr, Peter Gizzi, and Jena Osman, as well as much of Ben Friedlander's work after the 1991 *Time Rations* (with O Books). Debut monographs also began to appear, most often under the aegis of avant-garde publishers from the previous generation. Rod Smith's *In Memory of My Theories* from O Books in Oakland, Lisa Jarnot's *Some Other Kind of Mission* from Burning Deck in Providence, and Juliana Spahr's *Response* from Sun & Moon in Los Angeles all appeared in 1996, as did Jennifer Moxley's *Imagination Verses,* an exception in this group for being published by Tender Buttons press, directed by a contemporary of the poets just named, Lee Ann Brown, whose own first volume, *Polyverse,* won a national competition in 1995.[22] In 1998, Bill Luoma, whose Situations chapbook *Western Love* and Figures chapbook *Swoon Rocket* both appeared in 1996, collected his prose under the title *Works & Days,* again with Geoff Young's The Figures press. And Kevin Davies's follow-up to his 1992 *Pause Button,* the then unpublished work tentatively titled "Karnal Bunt," was widely excerpted between 1995 and 1997 in Canadian and American magazines such as *Boo, The Impercipient, Raddle Moon,* and the *Exact Change Yearbook.*[23]

When Chris Stroffolino, Lisa Jarnot, and Leonard Schwartz set about assembling *An Anthology of New (American) Poets* for Talisman in late 1996 and 1997, they included most of the writers already mentioned—Davies and

Rothschild are two regrettable omissions—and added a number of others, including Mark McMorris, whose *The Black Reeds* came out in 1997; Peter Gizzi, whose *Periplum* appeared from Avec in 1992 and *Artificial Heart* from Burning Deck in 1998; Beth Anderson, whose *Impending Collision* appeared with the British rem*press (publishers also of Moxley's *Enlightenment Evidence* in 1996 and Jarnot's *Heliopolis* in 1998); Eleni Sikelianos, whose *to speak while dreaming* appeared from Selva in 1993; and Elizabeth Willis, whose *The Human Abstract* was selected in the National Poetry Series of 1994 and published the following year by Penguin. Hoa Nguyen, author of *Dark* (from Mike and Dale's in 1998); Renée Gladman, author of *Arlem* (from Idiom in 1996); and Judith Goldman, author of *adversities of outerlife* (from Object/poetscoop in 1996) are among the youngest contributors to the volume, born in 1967, 1971, and 1973 respectively.[24] Already with poets of their age one can observe an important shift in the horizon of poetic possibility as electronic publications rapidly pass from the status of technological oddity to easily accessible sites of alternative expression.[25]

The New Composition: Six Profiles

Composition is not there, it is going to be there and we are here.
—Gertrude Stein

What has emerged in the texts enumerated above is, as with all significant poetry, resistant to synopsis and paraphrase: the perceptions, emotions, linguistic combinations, intellectual positions, and social struggles articulated there belong to an imagination the integrity of which must be measured in terms of the singularity and necessity of its statements. By such standards the initial critical response, which has focused on a perceived rehabilitation of lyric forms, musical values, and direct address—all in tacit contrast to the previous generation's penchant for abstraction and hostility to lyric practice—is still far from coming to terms with the actual multiplicity of the new composition.[26] At the level of content, for instance, a renewed commitment to the articulation of suffering raises a number of serious and complicated questions; while at the level of composition, a commitment to what can be called the democracy of perception (with its origins in Whitman) continues to stimulate the discovery of new poetic forms, few of which have been critically charted.[27]

By way of embarking on this necessary, if hazardous, labor of specifying the stakes, stances, devices, and distinctions at work in post-1989 poetic composition, I want to turn now to a constellation of six poets who have known and recognized each other as contemporaries, and who have collaborated with one another, debated and disputed one another, changed one another's—and my own—thinking and writing: Kevin Davies, Lisa Jarnot, Bill Luoma, Rod Smith, Lee Ann Brown, and Jennifer Moxley.

As the metaphor of a "constellation" should suggest, this particular mapping of the poetic field is neither an entirely objective nor a remotely exhaustive one. It is, as criticism has little choice but to be in confronting the complex present of a vital and ongoing practice, implicated in values no external authority can vouch for, affective bonds no rigor can wholly neutralize, political convictions for which no consensus can be presupposed, and literary aspirations no republic of letters exists to ratify. Provisional and preliminary then, these profiles seek nothing more (nor less) than to render communicable something of the specificity and necessity, the stance and cadence, of certain texts—chosen from oeuvres elaborated over what already amounts to a decade or more—in which the complexity of contemporary experience has been given distinctive poetic expression.

Kevin Davies

Each high-definition, recombinable frame of Kevin Davies's poetry freezes with indelible linguistic precision a moment in the social process when "code happens" ("Overkill" 85). In this poetics of the *Pause Button,* a vividly contemporary counterpart of Walter Benjamin's practice of *dialectics at a standstill,* some frames simply mimic the grammar of social pathology: "Will fuck for books, no weirdoes" ("Throb") or "Depart from this area of / simulated passion *now*" (*Pause Button* 13). Others state the implicit rules governing social conduct: "'Hey Man' & the unthought are drinking buddies" ("Ephemera . . . " 44), or "Acting normal as a kind of overfunded performance art kids are encouraged to express themselves with" ("Throb"). Some frames deftly fuse manifest and latent messages while retaining the block syntax of pseudo-public utterance: "Clinton licks tender inner thigh of corporate crud agenda" ("Thunk"). Others pulverize that syntax, making the deep structure show through strategic deletions: "That's what happens / when you give a [ ] a [ ] & tell it to start shooting" (*Pause Button* 28), or "[Abject suffering homelessness] has its privileges" (*Pause Button* 69). There are frames that endow the haves with a vicious eloquence: "We contracted for the personal advantages of social entropy not endless replays of its symptoms" ("Ephemera . . . " 43), or "'If / they / grow / over / the / fence / we / *own* / them'" (*Pause Button* 12). Many more imagine a caustic form of have-not backtalk, a sort of post-Situationist vernacular for speaking truth to power and getting away with it: "If you're so smart / why are you a social worker" (*Pause Button* 20), "Hometowns are *reformist idiots*" (*Thunk*), or "America out of Milky Way now!" ("Throb" 66).

The medium in which these frames advance is a consciousness that mixes extremes, matching Flaubert for recessed impassivity one moment, Shelley for unleashed immediacy the next and Creeley for coloratura scaling of anguished self-reflexivity throughout. A mobile sum of semiotic excesses traversing devastated territory, weaving agilely between catatonics and fanatics, wise-guys and thugs, tempted by but never surrendering to the opiate of infotainment everywhere on hock, Davies's texts rehearse with an ever-renewed urgency the moment when spontaneous mind encounters structural determinacy—the great unthought term of the fantastic North American agora[28]—and train the attention with provocative insistence on the refusal to be human, the willful destruction of democratic potential, the assent voluntarily given to this or that unsurvivable proposition. The closing sequence of an assemblage published under the title "Throb (Claymation Kakistocracy, or)" in *Impercipient* 7 (1995) captures his stance with great economy:

> I love the look of humans when they sit or stand still & when they move around
>
> I love the look of them looking back & barking arbitrary commands, which I obey
>
> I love the fragrance of the grouping of incommensurate ego fantasias in the drone of winter
>
> I love the fuss of the not-quite of submission techniques
>
> I love to be an international unit of measure of the loading of the fissures in the communal membrane into silos on a prairie in a basement by a government of souls in trouble at a party with martinis for a long time
>
> Total sodomy. (67)

Like every other cell of Davies's composition, this one is a virtuoso display of poetic artifice: one notes the decaying arc of the declaration "I love" through its five-phrase inaugural repetitions; the way the ruse of a trans-species observing reason gets punctured in the relative clause concluding the second sentence ("commands, which I obey"); the lexical pseudo-lyricism of sentence three ("fragrance," "fantasias"), recording the drone in the budding grove of human hierarchy; the hectically pursued prepositional extensions of the fifth sentence describing with mock precision a subject impossibly situated; and the perverse kaleidoscope of allusions in the final line, evoking at a minimum language-writer Barrett Watten's critical volume *Total Syntax,* those unreproductive erotic acts still legally punishable in some American states, and the illicit coupling of Whitmanic and Derridean "dissemination" in the night of digitally-coded global capitalism.

The incisive work Davies does inside compositional cells, giving each utterance its distinctive play of pace and pause, tonal stance, lexical color, and rhythmic signature, is matched by his acrobatic ligature work, most visible in the highly emphatic handling of punctuation in *Pause Button* (1992). Where Charles Olson charged each parenthesis he opened with cognitive optimism and encyclopedic ambition, Davies makes his square brackets, whether filled or voided, into emblems of bad universality, demonstrating the actual relation of interchangeability underlying liberal individualism in its Western bureaucratic mode: "Easier to fill out a form that's already replaced you," he writes in "Duckwalkingaperimeter" (110). His em-dashes mark another form of interchangeability, an aesthetic one of provisional syntagms susceptible to reconstellation at a moment's notice in what he refers to as "a kind of conceptual art too ephemeral even to be documented" ("Duckwalkingaperimeter" 109). For though his poetics articulates itself as a series of breaks in the ideological flow—pauses that liberate the possibility of present tense thinking from the thrall of post-cognitive "Thunk"[29]—survival in Davies's poetry is closely associated with the staving off or negating of stasis, including the stases of the printed text.[30] As he puts it with characteristic dead-serious humor in "Meanstreak":

> The strong desire to *not know*
> with bilious certainty what's going to happen next, unlikely to gain a
>   majority but
> with a decent chance at grabbing some power in a coalition, is
> *only apparently* at odds with the need of humans to plan ahead to avoid
>   starvation. (61)

Lisa Jarnot

Reading *Some Other Kind of Mission* (1996) is like staring at a bruise you can't remember getting, after a night you can't recall the conclusion of, in a room you've never seen before. Lisa Jarnot gets this punished effect through terse rhythmic prose phrasing; a stammering, start-again looping of irreparably broken codes; and an art-brut approach to collage in which scrawled, struck-through, inked-over, amputated, circled, highlit, diagrammed, and mistyped texts form damaged palimpsests of mostly indecipherable messages. The social landscape of this non-progressive epic in which every fragment is equidistant from the same unrepresentable traumatic core has a run-down familiarity to it that is alternately banal and menacing: motels, grocery stores, gas stations, Kmarts and Sears, salad bars, bus routes, etc. Jarnot estranges these habitual sites of working-class American experience by inserting tokens of sexual exoticism and criminalized marginality into them (thus, among the persons of the poem we find "Lucky Pierre," a "Rough Trade Angel," a "Czechoslovakian Drag Queen"), as well as by systematic distortion of the already intermittent narratorial consciousness. Consider a typical prose block from the book's eighth section, which unfolds under the brusque assertion "I Sure as Fuck Would Know":

> He became attracted to china under willows after coffee in the pitch black clay. i had one dream last night after coffee in the pitch black clay having escaped from jail on the highway past the pitch of fields with peak crests in escape. the whole of terns, the eye of the bus ticket, the whole of the tern doubled back on the back of willows. representative of detraction, they extracted me from the clover, having been extracted from the dollars secret call. the kmart felling windows with a dust of sand the what museum. at the what museum in my dream the mcadanville lights they extracted from the sand. they extracted out the farm before the here it is at down the clay. they were terns, extracted from the sand, below and under after dream. i dreamt i took a bus to mexico to avoid the authorities who put me into christmas next to mao. before and after at the car port meet me playing candles in the window down the street. they have reached maturity in the darkness of the pitch black next to mao. shaving. he became attracted to china near the railroad tracks in the pitch black of the clay. i escaped on a bus to the river next to fear. mashed down on refusing the meshes of the afternoon. before and after at the car port shining tickets of the whole. peach crests, by the willows, on the back of, down to pitch. he meant the calls in dreams, crawfish in the eye of, net upon the bus. having crawled through the back of the pitch. at the back of making secrets and sand. running through the peach crest's unescape. at your wall of the museum in the pitch coordinate. (81)

Built of twenty-two sentences ranging in length from one word ("shaving") to thirty (the second sentence), with the majority falling at fifteen or so, this passage demonstrates Jarnot's distinctive ability to layer and cross-weave patterns at every level of her composition: syllabic (the /aek/ common to *attracted—black—back—detraction—extracted);* lexical (five uses of *dream* and its variants, eight of *pitch,* three of *tern* not counting its appearance in "afternoon"); phrasal ("He became attracted to . . . "); grammatical (prepositional phrases introduced by *next to* and *after);* rhythmic (getting caesural effects from stressed function words); and even ideological (the spliced cultural frames of a phrase like "into christmas next to mao"). This surcharging of the textual surface—in each discrete section and across the whole book ("tern," the name of a bird, appears on twenty or more pages, often more than once; an odd word like "meticule" catches the attention at every appearance)—results not in semantic depth, the promise of which must continually be sacrificed to the primary hermeticism of the project, but in the kind of structured enigma that motivates the search for meaning even while conveying the hopelessness of the hermeneutic (and by extension therapeutic) enterprise.

Jarnot quickly followed the publication of *Some Other Kind of Mission* with a chapbook-length serial poem entitled, after Jack London, *Sea Lyrics* (1996). Retaining the hypnotic phrasal rhythms and extending the lexical work of *Mission*—knowing just how the addition of a suffix ("spanishest" or "foreignest") or a count-adjective ("all" in "I have hardly noticed all the artificialist lagoons") or an inversion ("where winterless I am") will jolt the attention out of an encroaching rhythmic lull—*Sea Lyrics* dispenses with the graphic elements and breaks from the hermetic stance of the earlier book. Anchored by an omni-identificatory "I," this thirty-poem Lucretian catalog of the exposed and endangered life passed on bridges, lots, sidestreets, docks, by opossums, preachers, prawn, telemarketers, dogs, and detritus offers a less obstructed, more seductive reading experience, and its updated search for beatitude amidst the downcast and the outcast of San Francisco has already, and rightly, been recognized as an important mid-decade accomplishment.[31]

Bill Luoma

Bill Luoma's *Works & Days* (1998) shares with its Hesiodic namesake a number of important features. Both arise from experiences of devastating loss (Hesiod of his patrimony to a conniving brother; Luoma of his wife, the poet Helena Bennett, to cancer). Rather than narrating a single grand action, both texts cobble together sayings, tales, empirical observations, and flights of lyricism. Both mix naiveté of tone with a didactic aim, blending instruction in life's conduct with wonder at its contents. And both are texts that speak with what Hesiod calls "a sparing tongue" ("the best treasure a man can have is a sparing tongue, and the greatest pleasure one that moves orderly" [55]) and what contemporary linguist Basil Bernstein labels "a restricted code."[32] But for all their appearance of simplicity, Luoma's are eloquent and subtle texts—peopled, detailed, principled, humorous, and moving. In his wanderings from San Diego to New York and Providence ("My Trip to New York"), through the minor-league ballparks of the American south ("12 Peanuts & an Easton"), to San Francisco ("We Were in Burrito" and "The Replacements"), back to New York ("Auto Gobbler," "Tradition: An Allegory," and the "Ear Inn Reading Reports"), down to Philadelphia ("Illegal Park"), over to France ("The Annotated My Trip to NYC"), and eventually to Hawaii ("KPOI 97.5 The Rock You Live On"), Luoma follows a principle rendered explicit in a passage from "The Replacements" (where a lost metal cleat exercises all the motivating force of Lacan's *objet petit a*):

> At home I listen to a bird making a nest in my heater vent. I'll use the phone book to locate places that might satisfy my needs, but I don't phone them to nail down the particulars. I go there and see. The search becomes a project of wandering, with allowed rules that let you name things along the way that you're not searching for. Like the discovery of a new thrift store or the sighting of a person wearing a hat in a neighborhood you've never been in. This is the whole kind of lazy philosophy that describes my life. I assert

that getting lost is part of it. I embrace the inherent good in it. Fear is transformed into let's go into that thrift store. The bird continues to scrape the inside of the vent with twigs and grasses. (75)

In this particular updating of the Situationist *dérive* Luoma is for the most part alone: as in the other San Francisco-based text, "We Were in Burrito," an air of isolation and melancholy pervades. Almost everywhere else in the book, however, the project of "naming things along the way" is a collective one, involving a throng of strangers, acquaintances, and close friends, among the latter of whom the hilarious, idiosyncratic pair of Brian and Douglass stand paramount as slapstick muses forever in mid-routine:

O man there was this big huge guy. Did you see the big huge guy? Douglass asked us this when we got out of the liquor store. We had to get some scotch and I picked up a bottle that wasn't in the scanner's database. They had to do a time-consuming price check. While we were waiting Brian predicted that Douglass would be real proud of me for causing such a stir. (21)

Here the phenomenon of "time-consuming price checks" on commodities unrecognized by "the scanner's database" is brought to poetry with the precision of Hesiod telling Perses how and when to clip his fingernails or where and in which direction to stand when urinating, but the real focus of the passage is the magic of masculine admiration, capable of transmuting a boring dead-space in the life of consumerism into an act of quasi-heroic system jamming (a theme more concertedly pursued in "Astrophysics & You"). This is not to imply that Luoma shares Hesiod's—or even Jack Kerouac's—misogyny: no Pandora is loosed to explain the degeneration of men, except perhaps in an occasional aside by Douglass. In fact, the narrator's love of specific women—Helena, Margo, Kate, Juliana—and friendship with others—Jennifer, Cindy, Lisa, Marlene—is amply apparent in *Works & Days;* but unlike in the sumptuous and graphic "My Lover" poems (published in *Impercipient* 7 and *World* 53; 1995 and 1997 respectively) and the genre-stylized *Western Love* chapbook, this love does not form the principal compositional interest. That remains the interaction between men, expressively constrained, silly, cranky, heroic, sweet, as recorded in discrete paragraphs whose frame-by-frame progression recalls a slideshow[33] or the baseball box scores appearing on successive days in the newspaper.[34] In either analogy it is clear that these reports always derive their tone and function from being *for* someone (for Scott in "My Trip," or in the "KPOI" sequence for Charles who "never sees any of this so then this is for him"). Musing on Robert Creeley's "I Know a Man" in his annotations to "My Trip"—a work on whose opening page Creeley's "goddamn big car" is reduced to an irreparable and irretrievable state, the first of the many wrecks, breakdowns, and tow-aways strewn throughout *Works & Days*—Luoma explains his commitment to this form of poetic address:

I think Creeley had the right idea: it's "good" that the darkness surrounds us because it makes us form communities. Write poems for your friends to help keep them alive while you try to watch out where you're going reading the poems your friends write for you. Dharmok and Jilad at Tenagra. Ginsberg and Kerouac at the Sunflower. Kevin & Dug & Lisa in Nogo. I think that's the good the bad and the lovely of it.

ps your friends die anyway. (132)

As with Frank O'Hara, whose commitment to "personism" cannot be understood apart from its elegiac origins, what might seem glib or cliquish in Luoma's project is lent weight and dimension by the tragic-elegiac "darkness" that surrounds—and sometimes falls directly upon—his naive-seeming page. Writing across that pocket where, as Hesiod knew, "the gods keep hidden from men the means of life," Luoma affirms a community of life *and* death, works and idleness by day and perishing by night. His poems are befriending incitements to keep going, naming things along the way.

Rod Smith

Editor of *Aerial* magazine, publisher of Edge books, and manager of one of the truly indispensable independent bookstores in the United States—Bridge Street Books in Washington D.C.—Rod Smith is, most importantly, a poet whose work in aleatorical and procedural composition vitally extends the tradition of ego-bracketed, Zen-inflected anarchism inaugurated by John Cage and Jackson Mac Low in the immediately post-war decades.[35] From the early exploration of language as a Wittgensteinian "life-form" in *The Boy Poems* (1994); through the three interspliced serial works assembled in "A Grammar Manikin" (a twenty-page author-feature in *Object* 5 [1995]) and the seventeen works that make up his first monograph, *In Memory of My Theories* (1996); to the elegiac lyrics and savvy media critiques of *Protective Immediacy* (1997) and the Jasper Johnsian reflections of *The Lack (love poems, targets, flags)* (1997), Smith's impressive demonstration of range has kept an off-handed, self-effacing, stay-at-it workman's aura about it, that air of modesty in the midst of great daring common among genuine innovators.

Smith's texts—uniquely unstable syntheses of poetic indeterminacy, ethical decency, and political will-to-change—often crystallize around the contradiction between ephemerality and fixity, between the vanishing magnitudes of consciousness and the uncanny persistences of sign-assisted vision, between nature accepted in its chaotic indeterminacy and a sclerotic and often malign culture of reifying Midas-touches. His titles make frequent mention of states of diminished agency, often though not always with gendered connotations: males who have not yet acceded to their socially defined rights and responsibilities in *The Boy Poems*; the posable dummy of "A Grammar Manikin"; the categorical dispossession of phallic authority in *The Lack*; a mournful remembrance of dismantled thought-systems in *In Memory of My Theories*. Different evaluations attend these dispossessions: sometimes they are therapeutic, functioning as remedies to an unsustainable form of subjectivity (masculinity as symptom, mastery as unsustainable rationalist illusion); sometimes they offer comic relief to chronic determination and rigid designations; other times the reference is critical and the diminishment of human agency is judged in accordance with an utopic sense of what is possible as opposed to what is permitted.[36] Smith's formal gestures almost always involve second-degree transformations of found material in a perpetual diffusion and redistribution of already-existing signs. The ambient, "all-over" feel that results, especially in the longer works "Sieff," "For Loss," and the title sequence of *In Memory of My Theories,* is a function of his reduction or elimination of structuring repetition at lexical, semantic, or thematic levels. What repetition is retained—notably at the morphemic and phonemic levels of the text—is so tightly localized as to pass beneath the attentional threshold of many readers.

Juxtaposing discrepant source texts and experimenting with various degrees of authorial mediation from strict recomposition of predetermined lexical sets to relatively free improvisations, Smith's interpretation of collage privileges the purposely awkward combination, the collapsed or evaded pattern, the raised seam on a resolutely "non-poetic" surface, packed densities of linguistic intersection suddenly thinning into permeable membranes of direct address. The dozen-poem sequence "For Loss," for example, plays a series of forebodingly technical titles ("On the Calculation of Spherical Aberration Dependence" or "Rare-Earth Activated Harmonium Pulse") against wisp-light evocative phrasal fragments. Who would guess that the caption "Heterostructure Injection" would yield: "states / not / more / wish / to enter / people / always / fear / death / but // make / innovations. This is called the secret's innovation. / The great reason is plain / but the people / like by-paths" (51)? The nonrestrictive syntactic sequences, the words and word-clusters floating in semi-autonomy, the unanchored negative particle reversing what meanings do congeal, all endow (inject?) the text with a flickering agitation (heterostructure?) at odds with the intimations of tranquility in the lexical remnants from Lao Tzu's source text.[37]

The same device of making the conventional distinction between title and textual body into an opportunity to force two non-communicating registers into tense proximity is found alike in the early *Boy Poems* and in sequences from the recent *Protective Intimacy* like "The Era of Poets," as well as in a group employing well-known book titles ("The Responsibility of Intellectuals," etc.). Smith's sharing out of transparency-familiarity-dominance (concentrated in the titles) and opacity-defamiliarization-subversion (concentrated in the texts) suggests a condition in which the middle range of communicative competence has been violently elided: it is "for loss" of such a band of possibility that the hypertrophied scientific jargon of the Bell Laboratories stands in unmediated, indeed irreconcilable, relation to the "sufficient / bewildered / humility" of the text bodies (56). As Smith says in "Simon," one of the *Boy Poems:* "these alternatives cannot be harmonized." But their dissonance is, as his practice consistently shows, itself ample ground for a compelling and disclosing poetics.

Lee Ann Brown

At the close of *Crush* (1993), her early and influential Steinian anthem to irreducible erotic and poetic plurality, Lee Ann Brown writes: "I say these things not because they happen but because many things happen" (*Polyverse* 187). The remark makes a fitting caption to *Polyverse,* Brown's vast and various debut volume of nearly two hundred pages, more anthology in fact than monograph, where tightly economized anagrams for the Muses, nimble exercises in style, twice-heard hymns, giddy collaborations, cultivated verse gardens, long distance sentences (five pages from capital to period), and every sensually shaped stanza known to lyric form, are enlisted to break down poetry-impatient modern readers' resistance and open them to the pleasures of the art:

After Sappho

So many people
advised me against you.
How glad I am
we could not resist. (24)

Just consider the polyverted word-set of Brown's "Sestina Aylene," part of the section "Occasionally Named" in "Her Hearsay Hymnbook":

Beginning to pen a verse
I think of you—
what you must love
to do and do with ease:
Present a fruit or number
As from an empty

drawer. What's as empty
as the way we begin? Averse
to all Eve's droppers who number
our ways? Fact is, you
do much to ease
the why of Miss P. Love

or Funk: letter out. Love
letters love to be read as empty
poems or flowers named [heart's] ease,
the way a verse
faces to or on or in you,
for you can only then begin to number,

never delimiting that number
of ways in which you love
to make a poem. You
can tell a story of empty
necessity, a ring averse
to being filled too easily, to ease

simple closure. Easy
readings are possible but soon outnumber
even each other. A verse
demands a second love,
a torn page. Empty
breath slows through it, you

are surprised, you
read it slowly over, ease
into its second skin. Empty
fruits multiply and renumber
spaces to fill out love,
for ways to make a verse

not averse to being held a little longer. You
love to run and ease
into numbers of empty stays or stars. (74)

The direct address of one woman poet to another, the conversion of formal constraint to occasion for autotelic pleasure, the Zukofskian thinking-through of limited lexical sets are all typical of Brown's poetry, as is the thematic insistence on love, the incorporation of popular culture references, and the retention of ludic childhood practices (here, using the rebus image for "heart" in the text) as resources that nourish more sophisticated codes.

Brown's eclectic measures are often turned to descriptive purposes, from the ekphrasis of four flowers in "Cultivate" through the whole gritty, broke, overworked, pending condition of Manhattan bohemia in "Comfit" and "Daybook," to the book's many incidents of recollected or enacted eros (the opening line of "Demi-Queer Notion" for instance, "As I pinch my nipples & think of you"; or all of "Thang"; or a delicious translation of Paulus Silentarius that begins "Let's take off all our clothes, / Honey, and lie down / with our skins touching in every place possible"). Despite the premium on *sensed* as contrasted to merely *sensible* language a referential element nearly always lends her poems traction—the "little resistance" it takes, as she says in "Resistance Play," to make her "come / to terms" (135). One can say of Brown's "polyversal" word, as Zukofsky said of his "revolutionary" one, that "if it must revolve cannot escape having a reference. It is not infinite. Even the infinite is a term" ("An Objective" 16).

One of Brown's favorite wordplays involves swapping the Latin etymology of "sist" (from *sistere,* to set) for the Old Norse one from which we derive the word sister *(systir)* in words like "resistance" or "transistor." As Elaine Equi recently pointed out in the *Boston Review of Books,* Brown's poetic genealogy acknowledges "enthusiasm [as] the mother ('We are the daughters of enthusiasm'), excitement the sister ('Where are my excitement sisters')" (27). And while she devotes a lovely work in quatrains, "Sill Songs," to her biological sister Beth, more often Brown has in mind sisters by elective affinity, poets and musicians above all, with whom she collaborates in every meaning, and degree of action, implied by that word (letter sensitive as always, she long ago identified her initials in the second syllable of the word: col*lab*oration). If Stein (after whom Brown named her press Tender Buttons and under whose spell "Crush" was clearly written) is the mother of us all, and Bernadette Mayer the mother desirous "to please others in letters," even Frank O'Hara can get in, if ambivalently, on the engendering action:

> What's with these people
> boys or girls who tamp down
> the lyric impulse, the heart
> waiting in line, barefoot &
> illegal. Old-fashioned emotion
> is relegated to a loud radio
> void sometimes, but Frank O'Hara
> has faith in you & me even
> though or because we're girls.
> ("To Jennifer M." 67)

Jennifer Moxley

The first decade of Jennifer Moxley's poetry can be seen as an arc of successive formal integrations. Starting at zero-degree syntax with the pointillist lexical fields of *The First Division of Labour* (written 1989; published 1995), Moxley moved to syntactic ring-structures relying heavily on inversion and enjambment in *Enlightenment Evidence* (1996) before developing a disambiguated approach to the poetic line in *Imagination Verses* (1996) that gathers a wild velocity and semantic volume in the ten poems of *Wrong Life* (1999). The subjective stances of these works differ as well. At the start of her *oeuvre* stand the words "how given chorus / a she complete" (*First Division* 1): the subjectivity is collective, inexorably gendered,[38] and censored by existing historiographic practices ("the annotated vanishing"). If *First Division* is a reflection *on* history (and as such indebted to the work of Susan Howe), *Enlightenment Evidence* is a reflection *in* history, where Rosa Luxemburg's life—subject to numerous relative arrests before the absolute one of her assassination in 1919—is placed in a continuum-shattering dialectic with the present-day of Gulf War America. There are, naturally enough, elements of dialog here, and epistolary conventions of address deriving from Luxemburg's correspondence abound; but the more startling device involves a transhistorical doubling or fusion that effectively renders the first-person pronoun choral/plural. The weave of pronominal person and number in the following section is typical, as is the interrogation of what underground living—political, poetic—does to those whose untimely ideals drives them to it:

> you are proud in your underground
> anxious of audience
> rumor by rumor you live
> like a shifting star
> no one could ever accuse out of mystery,
> you are living through me like a storefront
> who heart on my sleeve receives
> the blows directly, holy
> I am not nor wanted and yet
> truth drips down some days
> and people rise up, not holy
> this lifeless body but hollowed
> and in the field of foreign ground
> from the murderous public river it shall
> rise up (21)

Choral and dialectical modes of address develop next into what Moxley, in her preface to *Imagination Verses,* refers to as an engagement with the "universal lyric 'I'" (x). As with the flagrant *literaturnost* of the book's design, the calculated anachronism of the generic "Verses" in the title, and the demonstrative embrace of that galaxy of emotive-linguistic excesses known in twentieth-century American poetry by the name of Hart Crane in the epigraph "What blame to us if the heart live on," Moxley puts the words "universal lyric 'I'" out there like a dare to the doxological avant-gardist who learned in the seventies to sneer at it as an "ideological construction." But that neither this facile rejection, nor any equally facile return to some prior state of supposed self-transparency is the point can be seen in the first line of the "Home World," the ode that opens *Imagination Verses*: "I will say what the register calls forth . . . " (3). The "I" conspicuously leads, but what it "will say" originates in "what the register calls forth," and that register is not only an utopically wide-horizoned experiential spectrum but also the unavoidable terminus of so many social relations in capitalism, the cash register, itself as much a concrete universal as the lyric "I" ever was.

Moxley, both in the early manifesto "Invective Verse" (1993) and the preface to *Imagination Verses,* envisions poetry as the negation or frustration of the limits society imposes on the expressive potential of subjects whether individual or collective. This negation is sometimes figured as explosive popular fury, as in "Ode to Protest," or as singular poetic task, as in "The Easter Lesson" of *Wrong Life,* which concludes in a ballade-like envoi where the conventional "prince" has become a poet:

> Poet, at the mid-point of our life's journey the vault will set a block to
>   entry,
> young in thought the world, despite these apparitions of grace, shall
>   abandon you
> to its discrepancies. Can you manage the small acts of sacrifice
> though they bleed the matter from your life? Can you doubt what you are
>   risking
> when, as the lynchpin of four thousand years, you choose to provide the
>   limits? (21)

Dante is the audible model for the lines, but a remark of Hegel's echoes here also: "Humans who want to be actual must be there, and to this end they must limit themselves. Those who are too fastidious toward the finite achieve nothing real at all, but remain in the realm of the abstract and peter out."[39] With this notion of the "limit" we come full circle to Kevin Davies's work, like Moxley's positioned at the limit, straining for transformation, and to the "simple poetic undertaking" Oppen proposed and each of the six poets I've discussed accept and distinctively interpret: "to see if life is livable, to make life livable. Without lying" (190).

Acknowledgment

For their generosity, lucidity, and hard work in organizing conferences that brought the ideal of international intellectual collaboration down to earth and into a lively interaction that the present article only begins to register, I would like here to offer my thanks to Romana Huk, Rod Mengham and Ian Patterson, Stephen Clark and Mark Ford, Robert Hampson and Alison Mark, and Michel Delville. I also owe a debt of gratitude to Espen Stueland and Richard Aarø of the Norwegian journal *Vagant* for commissioning and translating an earlier version of this article.

Notes

1. See Hobsbawm 5, et passim. Hobsbawm gives credit for the concept to Ivan Berend (xii).
2. Among those forces: modernization, class struggle, world war, global depression, genocide, cold war, anti-imperial and other liberation movements, technological innovation, ecological depletion. Such abstract words hardly begin to hint at the concrete repercussions of these forces in terms of human lives and human suffering.
3. The scandal arises in part from the fact that "tradition" in the sense of a binding pre-reflexive custom (pre-modern sense) is not at all the same thing as the reflexive (and selective) appropriation of prior historical action (modern sense). The German social theorist of art Peter Bürger's equation of "becoming historical" with the failure of the original avant-garde project and the inauthenticity of the post-war avant-gardes operates fully within the second, modern, sense of "tradition." His error, however, lies in ascribing to the "institution of art" a monopoly over historical meaning and tradition. Forceful alternatives to this position have been provided by British sociologist of culture Raymond Williams and, in the French context, by Pierre Bourdieu, both of whom acknowledge the potentially contestatory nature of popular and artistic "traditions."
4. Theodor Adorno's statements about the possibility of poetry—and indeed of any meaningful culture whatsoever—after Auschwitz have played an important role in focusing reflection on this historical divide.
5. One could cite countless examples; suffice it to recall John Ashbery's championing of Gertrude Stein, Robert Creeley's of Louis Zukofsky, Frank O'Hara's of Hart Crane, Robert Duncan's of H.D. Cary Nelson takes the full measure of the academic truncation of the modernist archive in *Repression and Recovery,* a passionate work that corroborates the long-standing testimony of these and countless other poets.
6. In China, the bloody suppression of a student-led democracy movement in August

of 1989 had signaled that Communist government's will to maintain autocratic political rule despite economic liberalization: there would be no Gorbachevian *glasnost* to accompany their brand of *perestroika*.

7. The young emigré writer Eugene Ostashevsky characterizes literary culture in 1990s Petersburg in the following terms: "The city's Baroque palaces and art nouveau mansions, late-nineteenth-century apartment buildings and classicist ministries are donning plastic shopsigns with names of Western brands and Russian corporations, the latter sounding quite savage to the Petersburg ear. The result is a vertiginous amalgam of past majesty and fast-food garishness, punctuated by remnants of Soviet squalor and general detritus. A palpable number of the intellectuals have left; mafia goons and their wanna-be's litter the landscape" (77).
8. In 1997, just as the global markets entered the first serious crisis of the new era, Hollywood director James Cameron succeeded in turning this popular sense of class-driven doom into its own form of economic miracle in the film *Titanic*. For an interesting account of that film's place in contemporary American social struggles, see Tom Frank's "*Titanic* et la lutte des classes: La guerre sociale racontée aux enfants."
9. See the editors' note following page 36: "Our plans for this magazine first took shape back in August, in a long conversation unwound through unlit streets back of Oakland. The sever of a difficult year had kept us from facing what we separately intuited as a collapse. Separately, we knew this collapse by its effect of disillusionment. An ethic of ruin in the ruins of the poem." Bill Luoma, Pam Rehm, Thad Ziolkowski, Peter Gizzi, Jennifer Moxley, Andrea Hollowell, Pat Reed, Jeff Gburek, and Helena Bennett are among the young writers Schelling and Friedlander published in the four-year run of their stapled magazine, along with older—if not at that time sufficiently appreciated—poets such as Alice Notley, Susan Howe, Robert Grenier, Larry Eigner, Ted Pearson, Stephen Rodefer, and Joanne Kyger.
10. Ridley Scott's *Blade Runner* had already made the argument credible in cinematic form by 1983.
11. The New York based magazine *L=A=N=G=U=A=G=E* (four volumes between 1978 and 1981) and Bay Area based *Poetics Journal* (10 issues since 1982) are only the most well-known of the many venues committed to some version of this axiom. Gil Ott's *Paper Air* (12 issues between 1976 and 1990) is an equally important, distinctively political, but less frequently mentioned, example.
12. Thus works written predominantly between 1975 and 1985, and initially anthologized in 1986–87 (Silliman; Messerli), began to attract academic attention in the late 1980s and early 1990s. By mid-decade, when a second wave of anthologization explicitly targeted the academic market (Weinberger; Hoover; Messerli), the "tendency" had given rise to an established and legitimated academic discourse with a clear institutional hierarchy of expertise, defined by figures like Marjorie Perloff, Charles Bernstein, Alan Golding, Michael Davidson, Rachel Blau Du Plessis, Hank Lazer, Bob Perelman, and Barrett Watten.
13. See the last chapter of Golding's fine monograph *From Outlaw to Classic*, "'Provisionally complicit resistance': Language Writing and the Institution(s) of Poetry" for an optimistic reading of this phenomenon, and Silliman's "Canons and Institutions: New Hope for the Disappeared" for a more skeptical, and I believe more

realistic, view. Silliman's sharply critical response to Bob Perelman's *The Marginalization of Poetry,* published in the *Impercipient Lecture Series,* is also worth consulting in this context.

14. Among the many relevant texts, see at least "On a Generation That Squandered Its Poets" (1931), collected in *Language in Literature* 273–300.
15. The poet Tina Darragh gives a fascinating genealogy of this word in post-Vietnam War America in her work *adv. fans-the 1968 series.*
16. To cite only two highly legible negative variants. Positive variants include all those expressions of popular intransigence against the injunction to disappear, whether class- or identity-based.
17. A diffuseness and discrepancy that coexists with, and partially explains, the hyper-coherence of the "culture"—referred to by Benjamin Barber simply as "McWorld"—dictated by the capital-intensive dominant media.
18. Translation very slightly modified. I comment at greater length on Nancy's remarks in "The Dynamics of Literary Change" 13–14.
19. In 1993, recalling W.B. Yeats's claim that the literary movements that endure are those that "hate great and lasting things," I hazarded—in the introduction to the "Technique" section of *Writing from the New Coast*—that a "hatred of Identity" was the strongest motivating force in the poetics emerging there (5).
20. To paraphrase Jacques Lacan: "[V]ery often, even most often, what is internal to what is called action is that it does not know itself" (qtd. in Eribon 211).
21. A few remarks are necessary to round out this very partial snapshot of the period. By 1990 few if any of the magazines associated with language-centered writing were still in existence, though most of the presses—Roof, Sun & Moon, The Figures, Burning Deck—remained active in spite of increasingly tenuous funding from state and federal agencies. Occupying more consecrated (and consecrating) positions in the field of experimental poetic practice were perfect-bound magazines such as Clayton Eshleman's long-standing *Sulfur,* Paul Hoover and Maxine Chernoff's *New American Writing,* and Brad Morrow's *Conjunctions.* Ed Foster's then fledgling *Talisman* magazine, the St. Marks Poetry Project's house organ, *The World,* and Cydney Chadwick's *Avec* all were at least potential places of publication for young poets. The polemically edited *apex of the M,* appearing between 1994 and 1998, sharply attacked the secular and avant-gardist bases of language poetry in the name of a spiritual poetic, though little work answering the editorial board's prescriptions was ever written. It was another magazine launched in Buffalo at the same time, *Chain,* that turned out to be—by virtue of Juliana Spahr and Jena Osman's inclusive and eclectic editorial policy—the more timely project. The editorial triumph of the period was arguably the *Exact Change Yearbook,* edited by Peter Gizzi and published by Damon Krukowski and Naomi Yang's Exact Change press in 1995. Projected as the first of an annually appearing series that sadly never materialized, the inaugural issue was a brilliantly anti-provincial blend of emergent and established, American and international writers.
22. The ensuing four-year delay in Sun & Moon's publication of the book would have been regrettable even if it had befallen an established writer: that it concerned a debut collection by one of the most promising poets of the new generation lends it an air of catastrophe. On a not entirely unrelated note, the encroachment of

publication- and prestige-conferring prize competitions within the avant-garde context, traditionally critical of devices long associated with the mainstream at its most transparently nepotistic and conformist, can be counted among the more dubious developments of the period under discussion.

23. To omit other writers associated, like Davies, with the Kootenay School of Writing in Vancouver—Lisa Robertson, Peter Culley, Nancy Shaw, Dan Farrell, Jeff Derksen all come immediately to mind—would be to lose an important dimension of this moment, in which the young British poet Miles Champion also figured importantly. The journals *Writing* and *Raddle Moon* are two indispensable reference points for KSW's energetic intervention into Canadian, and U.S., literary practice.
24. It must be mentioned that the Talisman anthology offers an extremely partial, indeed polemical, vision of the poetry emergent after 1989 in the United States. The exclusion of writers too closely associated with the project of language poetry (for example Robert Fitterman, Melanie Neilsen, or Brian Kim Stefans); unrepresentative selections from many of the writers included (for example, Benjamin Friedlander, Lee Ann Brown, and Bill Luoma); an unexamined retention of the nation as an organizing category (crystallized in the embarrassed parenthesis enclosing the word "American" in the volume's title); and a general failure to employ the anthology form as something distinct from that of, say, an ample magazine issue, all weaken the volume's claim to definitiveness.
25. The Electronic Poetry Center, launched on the internet by Charles Bernstein and Loss Pequeño Glazier at SUNY-Buffalo in 1994, provides the best overview of radical poetry on the web. It can be accessed at http://wings.buffalo.edu/epc. Among the many sites active in 1998, suffice it to mention Brian Kim Stefans's on-line version of *Arras*; Australian poet John Tranter's *Jacket*; Laura Moriarty's *non*; Kathy Lou Schultz's on-line version of *Lipstick 11*; Garrett Kallberg's *The Transcendental Friend*; Benjamin Friedlander and Graham Foust's *Lagniappe*; and the websites of Idiom and Meow presses.
26. In their ranging critical practices, Juliana Spahr, Chris Stroffolino, and Mark Wallace have all done much to advance this difficult task. Likewise, a host of recent magazines—Yedda Morrison and David Buuck's *Tripwire,* Lytle Shaw and Emilie Clark's *Shark,* Louis Cabri's *Philly Talks*—have provided crucial new forums for the broadening and complicating of the debates.
27. I have already cited the concluding line of Bernadette Mayer's "The Way to Keep Going in Antarctica": "If I suffered what else could I do." Another line from the same poem now becomes equally relevant, the imperative: "Look at very small things with your eyes."
28. Davies's work is thoroughly cognizant and critical of the post-NAFTA distributions of wealth and power in North America. "Karnal Bunt," the working title of his second collection, which was scheduled for publication by Edge Books in 1999, is named after a grain mould at the heart of a recent Canada-U.S. trade dispute (e-mail to the author, 21 March 1999).
29. The title of Davies's 1995 chapbook recalls a little known line of Frank O'Hara's: "interesting / that in Manhattan thunk is pronounced library" ("F.Y.I. #371b [Parallel Forces, Excerpted]," in *Poems Retrieved* 202).
30. Davies has described *Pause Button* as a "poem made up of the interruptions,

rewritings, and 'translations' of many poems & poem series, most of which were originally written or assembled for public readings." The same would appear to be the case for the work gathering toward "Karnal Bunt."

31. For more on *Sea Lyrics,* see Spahr 11–15.
32. Bernstein posits a distinction between "restricted" and "elaborated codes." The former are characterized by their condensation, context-dependence, embeddedness in affective social bonds, and particularism; the latter by their autonomy, reflexivity, rationality, and universalism. A tenet of Bernstein's sociolinguistics is that access to elaborated codes is unevenly distributed in class societies. See "Language and Socialization" 231 *et passim.*
33. In "The Annotated My Trip to NYC," a series of 101 brief commentaries occasioned by the collective translation of the work into French for Juliette Valery's Format Americain series, Luoma renders the analogy explicit: "These [paragraphs] are all slides by the way, slides that you would show to relatives after you get back from a trip. These slides are for Scott another San Diego friend who wanted me to send him some" (144).
34. As Luoma explains in "12 Peanuts & An Easton": "A box score is good in the morning for many reasons. For example, it's good to know how long games lasted, the umpires' names and how many double plays were turned. It's also good for small talk"—all of which applies, *mutatis mutandis,* to the genre-founding "reading reports" in the volume's latter half.
35. See the biographical entry on John Cage that Smith contributed to the *Dictionary of Literary Biography.* See also the fabricated dialogue between Ted Berrigan and John Cage published in *Tripwire* 2 (1998).
36. As in the substitution of the word "vicarious" for "various" in Smith's rewriting of Frank O'Hara's famous line, "grace to be born and live as variously as possible" (concluding epigraph on the colophon of *The Boy Poems*).
37. Smith explains his procedure in generating this series: "The vocabulary of the titles are from a Bell Laboratories Bibliography I found on the sidewalk in Georgetown. The vocabulary for the body of the poems is from an 1898 translation of Lao Tzu. Only transliteration I've seen, one or two english words for each chinese character so a lot of syntax drops out. Again, I was treating these texts as vocabulary, as though these were the only words I knew" (e-mail to the author, 25 August 1998).
38. The epigraph to *The First Division of Labour* is from Marx: " . . . there develops the division of labour, which was originally nothing but the division of labour in the sexual act."
39. *The Encyclopedia Logic* 92, 148.

Works Cited

Adorno, Theodor W. *Negative Dialectics.* Trans. E.B. Ashton. New York: Continuum, 1990.

——. "Cultural Criticism and Society." *Prisms*. 1967. Trans. Samuel and Shierry Weber. Cambridge: MIT Press, 1981.

Barber, Benjamin R. "Culture McWorld contre démocratie: Vers une société universelle de consommateurs." *Le Monde Diplomatique* 533 (1998): 14–15.

Bernstein, Basil. "Language and Socialization." *Linguistics at Large*. Ed. Noel Minnis. St. Albans, UK: Paladin, 1973. 225–42.

Bürger, Peter. *Theory of the Avant-Garde*. 1974; 1980. Trans. Michael Shaw. Minneapolis: University of Minnesota Press, 1984.

Bourdieu, Pierre. *The Rules of Art: Genesis and Structure of the Literary Field*. 1992. Trans. Susan Emanuel. Stanford: Stanford University Press, 1995.

Brown, Lee Ann. *Polyverse*. Los Angeles: Sun & Moon, 1999.

——. *Crush*. Buffalo: Leave, 1993.

Dark Ages Clasp the Daisy Root. Edited by Andrew Schelling and Benjamin Friedlander in Oakland, California, 1989–1993.

Darragh, Tina. *adv. fans—the 1968 series*. (Buffalo: Leave, 1995).

Davies, Kevin. *Karnal Bunt* [tentative title]. Washington, DC: Aerial / Edge, forthcoming. [Editor's note: In 2000, Edge Books produced Davies's *Comp.*]

——. *Thunk*. New York: Situations, 1995.

——. *Pause Button*. Vancouver: Tsunami, 1992.

——. "From *Overkill / a protoco*l." *Raddle Moon* 17 (1998): 80–89.

——. "From *Overkill / a protocol*." *Lingo* 8 (1998): 46–52.

——. "From *Throb (Claymation Kakistocracy, or)*." *Boo* 6 (n.d. [1995]): 8–9.

——. "From *Throb (Claymation Kakistocracy, or)*." *Impercipient* 7 (1995): 61–67.

——. "From *Duckwalkingaperimeter*." *Exact Change Yearbook* 1 (1995): 108–111.

——. "From *Meanstreak*." *Raddle Moon* 14 (1995): 57–63.

——. "From *Ephemeratatagalongonetceteradiosologoff*." *Impercipient* 5 (1994): 41–47.

Equi, Elaine. Introduction. "Poet's Sampler: Lee Ann Brown." *Boston Review* 23.5 (1998): 27.

Eribon, Didier. *Michel Foucault*. 1989. Trans. Betsy Wing. Cambridge: Harvard University Press, 1991.

Evans, Steve. "The Dynamics of Literary Change." *Impercipient Lecture Series* 1 (February 1997): 1–54.

——. Introduction to *Writing from the New Coast: Technique*. Ed. Juliana Spahr and Peter Gizzi. Providence: Oblek, 1993. 4–11.

Frank, Tom. "Titanic et la lutte des classes: La guerre sociale racontée aux enfants." *Le Monde Diplomatique* 533 (1998): 21.

Golding, Alan. *From Outlaw to Classic: Canons in American Poetry*. Madison: University of Wisconsin Press, 1995.

Hegel, G.W.F. *The Phenomenology of Spirit*. Trans. A.V. Miller. Oxford: Oxford University Press, 1977.

——. *The Encyclopedia Logic*. Trans. T.F. Geraets, W.A. Suchting, and H.S. Harris. Indianapolis: Hackett, 1991.

Hesiod. *Works and Days*. Trans. Hugh G. Eveyln-White. Loeb Classical Library 57: Hesiod, Homeric Hymns, Epic Cycle, Homerica. Cambridge: Harvard University Press, 1936. 3–65.

Hobsbawm, Eric. *The Age of Extremes: A History of the World, 1914–1991*. 1994. New York: Vintage, 1996.

Jakobson, Roman. *Language in Literature*. Edited Krystyna Pomorska and Stephen Rudy. Cambridge, MA and London: Belknap-Harvard University Press, 1987.

———. "On a Generation That Squandered Its Poets." *Language in Literature* 273–300.

———. "The Dominant." *Language in Literature* 41–46.

Jarnot, Lisa. *Sea Lyrics*. New York: Situations, 1996.

———. *Some Other Kind of Mission*. Providence: Burning Deck, 1996.

Jarnot, Lisa, Leonard Schwartz, and Chris Stroffolino, eds. *An Anthology of New (American) Poets*. Jersey City: Talisman, 1998.

Luoma, Bill. *Works & Days*. West Stockbridge and Great Barrington, MA: Hard Press / The Figures, 1998.

———. *Western Love*. New York: Situations, 1996.

———. *Swoon Rocket*. Great Barrington: The Figures, 1996.

———. *My Trip to New York City*. Great Barrington: The Figures, 1994.

———. "Poem (Face the arguments . . .)." *Impercipient* 7 (1995): 48–52.

Mayer, Bernadette. *Poetry*. New York: Kulchur, 1976.

Moxley, Jennifer. *Wrong Life*. Cambridge, UK: Equipage, 1999.

———. *Enlightenment Evidence*. Cambridge, UK: rem*press, 1996.

———. *Imagination Verses*. New York: Tender Buttons, 1996.

———. *The First Division of Labour*. Boston: Rosetta Chapbook, 1995.

———. "Invective Verse." *Writing from the New Coast: Technique*. Ed. Peter Gizzi and Juliana Spahr. Providence: Oblek, 1993. 182–83.

Nancy, Jean-Luc. "Finite History." 1990. *The Birth to Presence*. Trans. Brian Holmes et al. Stanford: Stanford University Press, 1993. 143–66.

Nelson, Cary. *Repression and Recovery: Modern American Poetry and the Politics of Cultural Memory, 1910–1945*. Madison: University of Wisconsin Press, 1989.

O'Hara, Frank. *Poems Retrieved*. Ed. Donald Allen. Bolinas, CA: Grey Fox, 1977.

Oppen, George. "'Meaning Is To Be Here': A Selection from the Daybook." *Conjunctions* 10 (1987): 186–208.

Ostashevsky, Eugene. "Dmitry Golynko-Volfson and New Petersburg Poetry." *Shark* 1 (1998): 74–84.

Silliman, Ron. "Canons and Institutions: New Hope for the Disappeared." *The Politics of Poetic Form*. Ed. Charles Bernstein. New York: Roof, 1990. 149–74.

———. "The Marginalization of Poetry by Bob Perelman." *Impercipient Lecture Series* 4 (May 1997): 1–12.

Smith, Rod. *Protective Immediacy (The Fire Works)*. Elmwood, CT: Potes & Poets, 1997.

———. *In Memory of My Theories*. Oakland: O Books, 1996.

———. *The Boy Poems*. Washington DC.: Buck Downs, 1994.

———. "John Cage." *Dictionary of Literary Biography*. Vol. 193: American Poets Since World War II, Sixth Series. Ed. Joseph Conte. Detroit: Gale, 1998. 33–45.

Spahr, Juliana. *Spiderwasp or Literary Criticism*. New York: Spectacular, 1998.

Stein, Gertrude. "Composition as Explanation." 1926. *Selected Writings*. Ed. and introd. Carl van Vechten. New York: Vintage, 1990.

Stroffolino, Chris. "The Inescapable Injustice of the Imagination: On the Recent Work of Jennifer Moxley. *Chicago Review* 43.2 (1997): 94–104.

Waldrop, Rosmarie. "The Ground is the Only Figure." *Impercipient Lecture Series* 3 (April 1997): 1–45.

Wallace, Mark. "A Reading of Against: Juliana Spahr as Poet, Editor, and Critic." *Tripwire* 1 (1998): 110–121.

Williams, Raymond. *Marxism and Culture*. Oxford: Oxford University Press, 1977.

———. *The Sociology of Culture*. 1981. Chicago: University of Chicago Press, 1995.

———. "The Politics of the Avant-Garde." *The Politics of Modernism: Against the New Conformists*. London: Verso, 1989. 49–63.

Zukofsky, Louis. "An Objective." *Prepositions: The Collected Critical Essays*. Expanded edition. Berkeley: University of California Press, 1981.

Alison Mark

Poetic Relations and Related Poetics

Veronica Forrest-Thomson and Charles Bernstein

The omission of Forrest-Thomson from so many accounts of Language writing seems extraordinary in the light of Charles Bernstein's recognition of the significance of her work in his long poem of poetics, *Artifice of Absorption* (Bernstein 1987, 22).[1] In my reinscription of Forrest-Thomson in the line of contemporary linguistically investigative poets—a term I now use following discussions at and subsequent to the Assembling Alternatives conference[2]—I will focus primarily on Bernstein's poem, and on Forrest-Thomson's major theoretical work *Poetic Artifice* (1978). The genealogy of linguistically investigative poets descends, for Forrest-Thomson, through Donne as much as Dada, and for Bernstein through the American linguistically investigative, formally active poetry of Dickinson, Zukofsky and Olson as well as the Europeans. Forrest-Thomson belongs to this line of investigative poets not only because of her poetic and theoretical virtuosity, but also for her interest in poetry's potential for the reimagination of language. As she says in *Poetic Artifice*: "The world is not something static, irredeemably given by a natural language. When language is reimagined the world expands with it" (1978, 20). Our relationship to language is intimately connected to, even constructs, our relationship with the world, and reimagining language involves an active participation in changing perception—an important concern of radically innovative poets.

My background theme here is the question of limitations, as raised by Wittgenstein in his proposition that: "*The limits of my language* mean the limits of my world" (his italics) (1985, 149 [5.6]). This statement from the *Tractatus* has been important not only for Forrest-Thomson's work, but also for that of successive experimental poets and theorists.[3] However, what their citations of this formulation tend to elide is the fact that Wittgenstein was specifically addressing himself to the limits of factual language—to the exclusion of ethics, metaphysics and, most significantly here, aesthetics. In fact, in the *Tractatus* Wittgenstein had actually assumed that "the structure of reality determines the structure of language." It was only much later in the *Philosophical Investigations* that he came to suggest "that it is really the other way round: our language determines our view of reality, because we see things through it" (Pears 1985, 13). It is thus the view of the later Wittgenstein, rather than the Wittgenstein of the *Tractatus,* which is most consonant with Forrest-Thomson's position, and that of subsequent investigative poets. In *Artifice of Absorption* one of the suggestions Bernstein makes is that "there are no limits that language cannot / reach" (1987, 55), though at another point he proposes that "The unreadable text is an outer limit for poetry" (47), and that poetry itself has both inner and outer limits (48), statements to which I will return.

A particular influence on Forrest-Thomson's work was Wittgenstein's hyphenated concept of the language-game. Language-games include not just the words utilized, but also, as she quotes in her poem "The Hyphen" (1990, 35), "the 'context in which we occur' / that teaches us our meaning", which forms part of what she calls in that poem a "state- / ment of our need to hyphenate"; to connect one element of language to another, not just to "a nonverbal situation existing outside language" (1978,18). The language-game consists of what Anthony Kenny calls "the words plus their behavioural surroundings"; that is, the human behavior which contextualizes the lexical units uttered (1975, 14). Kenny goes on to say: "In general the meaning of a word is not an object for which it stands, but rather its use in a language." The description of meaning as use which this involves suggests that the meaning of a word is defined by its relationship with other words, rather than by reference to the external world.

As Forrest-Thomson observes in *Poetic Artifice,* "Language is common to both the realm of poetry and to the domain of ordinary experience" (1978, 18); however, she also quotes the admonition in Wittgenstein's *Zettel* (and Bernstein quotes it from both): "Do not forget that a poem, even though it is composed in the language of information, is not used in the language-game of giving information" (Wittgenstein 1990b, 27 [160]; Forrest-Thomson 1978, x; Bernstein 1987, 9). Rather, as both Forrest-Thomson and Bernstein might agree, the poem is in the language-game of creating the possibility for new connections, not simply transmitting the already known. Hence any discussion of poetic language must direct attention to both continuity and discontinuity in language.

Forrest-Thomson's answer in *Poetic Artifice* to the problem of how to reconcile the two is that the same requirement is made of the reader as of the poet: the mastery of the capacity "to hold together, simultaneously, continuity and discontinuity in the requisite proportions" (1978, 21); the capacity to exercise what she called "suspended naturalisation".[4] Briefly, she defined naturalization as "the critical process" which makes:

> an attempt to reduce the strangeness of poetic language and poetic organisation by making it intelligible, by translating it into a statement about the non-verbal external world, by making the Artifice appear natural. (1978, xi)

The concept of suspended naturalization—the resistance to that urge to "reduce the strangeness"—undoubtedly owes its origins to Keats's concept of negative capability, "when man is capable of being in uncertainties, Mysteries, doubts, without any irritable reaching after fact & reason" (1952, 71). There is perhaps a more intimate relationship between the work of the Romantic poets—theory and practice—and that of radically innovative contemporary poetry than would at first appear or than many practitioners would accept; although, in a letter to me, Lyn Hejinian expresses very similar sentiments:

> It seems to me that a great deal of contemporary *American* poetry (the postmodern, rather than traditional poetry) is much more closely linked to English Romantic literature than is usually acknowledged, and I suspect that this is also the case (it seems to be, but I don't want to exaggerate my familiarity with *British* poetry) there too. In Forrest-Thomson's poetry the link seems very important, not in and of itself but as a point of origin, from which a splendid and dense body of work could radiate. (1995)[5]

In her preface to *Poetic Artifice* Forrest-Thomson says: "The question always is, how do poems work?" (1978, x). How they work—how they mean—as a primary issue, rather than what they mean. Two of the main areas on which she focuses in her attempt to answer this question are naturalization and the concept of "poetic artifice" itself.

Naturalization

In *Structuralist Poetics* Jonathan Culler says: "The best discussion of convention and naturalization in poetry is V. Forrest-Thomson, *Poetic Artifice*" (1975, 271, n19). A considerable portion of his own book is concerned with naturalization and forms of literary production in which central emphasis is placed on the position of the reader as the interpreter of what is written. Readers choose—particularly in the case of poetry—to engage with language which is distinctly different from the ordinary language of communication, and then seem driven to reduce its difference back to an assimilable narrative.

Bernstein, in *Artifice of Absorption,* says of Forrest-Thomson that:

> her terminology is intended to foreground artifice as much as possible & for this reason she wishes to cede as little as possible to the conventional semantic arena—a decision that makes her book, if flawed in this respect, so powerfully informative in the first place. (1987, 9)

Forrest-Thomson did not so much reject the semantic as wish to control the process of interpretation, keep it within the text, rather than resort immediately to the external world for the process of sense-making. This allows for a textual polysemy, making "many Naturalisations possible and none certain" (1978, 80).

Culler defines the role of a structuralist poetics as "the theory of the practice of reading" (259), and it is clear that the poetics of *Poetic Artifice* is equally concerned with this practice, and with that special form of reading called literary criticism. However, Forrest-Thomson stresses the extent to which the role of the reader parallels that of the writer (81), and thus also makes movements in the direction of a poetics of writing, particularly with reference to her own writing practice—gestures echoed and extended by Bernstein in his discussion of textual absorption and impermeability.

Poetic Artifice opens with the statement that:

> This book is an attempt to talk about the most distinctive yet elusive features of poetry: all the rhythmic, phonetic, verbal, and logical devices which make poetry different from prose and which we may group together under the heading of poetic artifice. (1978, ix)

Forrest-Thomson's intention was explicitly to develop and give an account of "ways of undertaking an internal naturalisation" (xii), as she called it, rather than an immediate external naturalization, or "unseemly rush from words to world" (xi). The method she chose was a revaluation of poetic artifice:

> Contemporary poetry has suffered from critics' disposition to make poetry above all a statement about the external world, and therefore it is now especially important somewhat to redress the balance, to stress the importance of artifice. . . . [I]t is only through artifice that poetry can challenge our ordinary linguistic orderings of the world, make us question the way we make sense of things, and induce us to consider its alternative linguistic orders as a new way of viewing the world.
>
> The best way to restore value to artifice is to find ways of discussing it which do not presuppose the subservience of form to extended meaning. And therefore my account of twentieth-century poetry offers a framework of concepts which allow us to dwell at length on the play of formal features and structure of relations internal to a poem. (xi)

The view of poetry as "a statement about the external world" is the epitome of what she called "bad", premature naturalization, or "extended meaning". The problem with premature naturalization is that it avoids the necessity of passing through the potentially transformatory different levels of organization within the poem: "In its anxiety to get at the 'meaning' *behind* the words it would overlook the meaning *of* the words" (163). The possibility of the "alternative linguistic orders" of poetry to which Forrest-Thomson refers depends upon the existence of established codes and orders of language. They depend, that is, on the inherently intertextual disposition of written language—indeed, as Culler suggests in *The Pursuit of Signs,* of "any verbal construct" (1981, 101).[6]

Forrest-Thomson prescribes in *Poetic Artifice* a process of reading in which the impulse to naturalize is resisted by a reader who attends to the techniques of poetic artifice. The resistance to naturalization is aided and guided by "levels of poetic language, such as phonetic and prosodic patterns, and spatial organisation" (1978, xi). Forrest-Thomson's focus is then on what Bernstein calls "antiabsorptive / techniques" (1987, 22). At various times she refers to these aspects of artifice or "levels of poetic language" as non-meaningful, non-verbal, or non-semantic. Shortly before her death, in her discussion with the French poet Michel Couturier at the 1975 Cambridge Poetry Festival, Forrest-Thomson referred to a less intransigent formulation: "semi-meaningful" levels of language (1975, 3). This certainly offers a more accurate reflection of her practice, even if "semi-meaningful" is still not a formulation with which Bernstein could concur, for in *Artifice of Absorption* he specifically and persuasively problematizes her designation of aspects of language as "non-meaningful" or "non-semantic" because:

> It
> seems to me she is wrong to designate the nonlexical,
> or more accurately, extralexical
> strata of the poem as "nonsemantic"; I would say
> that such elements as line breaks, acoustic
> patterns, syntax, etc., *are* meaningful rather than,
> as she has it, that they *contribute* to the meaning
> of the poem. For instance, there is no fixed
> threshold at which noise becomes phonically
> significant; the further back this threshold is
> pushed, the greater the resonance at the cutting
> edge. The semantic strata of a poem should not be
> understood as only those elements to which a
> relatively fixed connotative or denotative meaning
> can be ascribed, for this would restrict meaning to
> the exclusively recuperable elements of language—a

> restriction that if literally applied would make
> meaning impossible. After all, meaning occurs
> only in a context of conscious & nonconscious,
> recuperable & unrecoverable, dynamics. (1987, 8)

At the end of this section Bernstein implicitly subscribes to Wittgenstein's view that it is the context in which the words occur that indicates the meaning, though the reading of "context" is extended to include the unconscious and unrecoverable, the *pulsions* of language. Recuperability is clearly significant for, even if not equatable with, meaning, as Bernstein points out. However, I dispute the implicit identification between the nonconscious and the unrecoverable which I detect in Bernstein's syntactic parallelism; the "nonconscious" of a poem may actually be recoverable, by an acute reading of all the elements of poetic language—executed as Forrest-Thomson suggests in *Poetic Artifice*.

In effect, Bernstein's charge—like Forrest-Thomson's against William Empson (1978, xiv)—is that she does not carry her theory of artifice far enough. Indeed, Bernstein's footnote citing *Poetic Artifice* takes up the terms of her criticism of Empson, noting that:

> This remarkably precocious book carries Empson's criticism one step further than Empson was willing to go—into the realm of what Forrest-Thompson [sic] calls the "non-meaningful" levels of language, which she sees as the vital future for poetry. (1987, 66)

Her position, which Bernstein takes one step further by refusing to designate any aspect of language as "non-meaningful", is that she does not seek to avoid meaning entirely, but rather to shift the emphasis in reading—and indeed writing—poetry from the primacy of meaning. This constitutes a refutation of the view of meaning as an extractable "essence" of the poem, for as Bernstein observes: "the poem said in any / other way is not the poem" (1987, 11).

Forrest-Thomson's handling of naturalization (and its emphasis upon the need for suspended, in preference to premature, naturalization) is the key to understanding her attempts, as Suzanne Raitt puts it, "to capture the interaction between language and reality", and at the same time to challenge "the strait-jacket of meaning" (1990, 305). It is also the basis of Forrest-Thomson's readings of other poets, and her critique not only of more expansive readings, but also of the lack of attention paid by poets and critics alike to the importance of the features of artifice which can be employed to delay narrative assimilation—absorption—of texts, and thus to focus attention on the interplay of levels of linguistic organization "rather than to set them aside in an attempt to produce a statement about the world" (1978, xi).

Forrest-Thomson's articulation of the proper relation between interpretation and suspended naturalization is her suggested solution to the aesthetic problem of the attempt to transform experience into art—which is the other side of the extraordinarily powerful tendency (on the part of readers) to translate art into experience. For poetry, she said, "delaying tactics are its only resource" against the pressure of our constant naturalizing attempts to have art mirror life (1978, 81).

Artifice

In "The Separate Planet" she calls this critical term "the only which must have a capital letter" (Undated, 9–10). This is because for Forrest-Thomson "Artifice"—in a word—signifies the difference between poetic and other forms of language. She continues: "Artifice is the general term for the whole process by which poetry distances itself through technique from the world already given as natural in other languages." Artifice calls attention not only to itself, but to the constructedness of language, and how language constructs the world. It is *par excellence* the tool of self-reflexivity.

Frequently the titles of Forrest-Thomson's works on twentieth-century poetry and poetics underline this emphasis on artifice—titles such as "Rational Artifice" (1974), "Irrationality and Artifice" (1971a), "Necessary Artifice" (1973), and of course, *Poetic Artifice* (1978)—and the first section of Bernstein's poem is called "Meaning and Artifice". In Forrest-Thomson's theoretical work we can see the development of a poetics whose most complete statement is found in *Poetic Artifice,* but which implicitly resists the bifurcation of literature into theory and practice by embedding, arguing and demonstrating the theory in the body of her poems. Forrest-Thomson describes her own perception of the process in a "Note" to the collection *Language-Games:*

> There is the opportunity to turn theoretical debate and abstract statement into a means of technical experiment in the actual medium of poetry, to explore new formal possibilities while extending the range of material dealt with. This involves an assimilation, not merely of the ideas but of the speech-forms of the relevant areas of discourse and even their methods of typographical layout. (1990, 262)

This "assimilation" explains the significance of the—frequently unmodified—embedding of quotations, and aspects of typographical layout such as the use of footnotes. What Forrest-Thomson describes as "the opportunity to turn theoretical debate and abstract statement into a means of technical experiment in the actual medium of poetry" through a revaluation of poetic artifice is precisely the opportunity that is taken up by Bernstein in *Artifice of*

Absorption, in a similar resistance to the bifurcation of literature into theory and practice.

However, Bernstein's "absorption" and naturalization are not, of course, equivalent. In Forrest-Thomson's schema, texts do not "naturalize"—only the reader is capable of that; the reader whose active participation in the construction of the text has become such a fetishized orthodoxy of radically innovative poetics. In Bernstein's poetics the ability of texts themselves to "absorb" elements from other texts also becomes important. Absorption is the primary canonical mode; the mode of that tradition in poetry which performs most of the construction of the text on the reader's behalf, so that the reader becomes a consumer of commodified experience. Bernstein defines absorption through a chain of associations which holds some surprises:

> By *absorption* I mean engrossing, engulfing
> completely, engaging, arresting attention, reverie,
> attention-intensification, rhapsodic, spellbinding,
> mesmerizing, hypnotic, total, riveting,
> enthralling: belief, conviction, silence. (1987, 21)

The inclusion of silence is particularly interesting in the light of Forrest-Thomson's remarkable long poem "Cordelia, or 'A poem should not mean but be'" (1990, 104–9), in which she draws attention to, and attempts to elude the silencing of, the doubly marginalized female experimental poet. Bernstein's fairly representative catalogue of Romantic effects and affects in poetry gets a twist in its tail from the ideological implications of his last line, where "enthralling" leads grammatically through a colon to "belief, conviction, silence." Bernstein remarks that for Bruce Andrews "as for Perelman & Brossard, / the resistance to absorption is a / political act" (1987, 25–6). In spite of his appreciation of the possible reversals of polarity between absorption and impermeability depending on historical situation and readership, I suspect this is so for Bernstein, too. His insistence on the connection between poetics and politics (not a main feature of Forrest-Thomson's poetics) links his work to the preoccupations of the French *Tel Quel* poets.[7] As Marjorie Perloff has suggested (1981), radically innovative poets in America can be seen as working in the tradition of the French avant-garde (from which *Tel Quel* also sprang)—part of the twentieth-century contribution to the development of what Forrest-Thomson calls "the tradition of innovation" which she traces in *Poetic Artifice* (1978, 125). However, another line of inheritance from the British and American innovative traditions seems equally strong; and Perloff, sadly, has thus far overlooked Forrest-Thomson's contribution in her pursuit of "the French connection" (1981, vii), despite her own intense focus on artifice in her *Radical Artifice* (1991).

"Impermeability" is Bernstein's other coinage, which he defines at greater length, with more inventiveness, and with the addition of slang or vernacular expressions that counterpoint the critical terms. His repetition of "fanciful", calling to mind the Coleridgean distinction between fancy and imagination, is particularly worth noting:

> *Impermeability* suggests artifice, boredom,
> exaggeration, attention scattering, distraction,
> digression, interruptive, transgressive,
> undecorous, anticonventional, unintegrated, fractured,
> fragmented, fanciful, ornately stylized, rococo,
> baroque, structural, mannered, fanciful, ironic,
> iconic, schtick, camp, diffuse, decorative,
> repellent, inchoate, programmatic, didactic,
> theatrical, background muzak, amusing: skepticism,
> doubt, noise, resistance. (1987, 21–2)

We might expect Bernstein to focus on antiabsorption in terms of a radical poetics, but his argument is more subtle than a simple polarization, in spite of the contrasting list of synonyms. Absorptive and antiabsorptive are not articulated as contraries: "these terms / should not be understood as mutually exclusive, / morally coded, or even conceptually separable." Rather he configures them as "copresent / in any method of reading or writing, although / one or the other may be more obtrusive or evasive" (16).

In a phrase that echoes Forrest-Thomson's use of the word "prevent" in her "Sonnet" (1990, 91) in the line: "words were made to prevent us near" (that is, language comes both before and between us), Bernstein images the potential dynamics—a dialectic—of the interrelationship of absorption and its converse:

> the absorbed & unabsorbed cleave,
> since *cleave* means both to divide
> & to hold together. (1987, 16)

Indeed as his argument progresses, he identifies occasions on which antiabsorptive devices may paradoxically be used in the service of absorption; a performative instance is the following, in which Forrest-Thomson's terms can also be heard:

> There is, then, a considerable history
> of using antiabsorptive techniques
> (nontransparent or non-"naturalizing" elements)
> (artifice)

for absorptive
ends. This is an approach
I find myself peculiarly
attracted to, & which reflects my
ambiv*o*lence
about absorption & its converses. (1987, 37–8)

The varying line lengths focus attention on the two isolated words: "(artifice)"—which is also sealed in parentheses—and "ambiv*o*lence", with its idiosyncratic italicization of the "o". Recalling the dual meanings of *voler* in French (familiar from Cixous),[8] this invokes the senses of stealing and flying, in implicit apposition to that of value or valency (ambiv*a*lence). This clever coinage also carries a resonance of "vi*o*lence"—reinforcing the sense of textual disruption. The double juxtaposition of the two parenthetical elements not only serves as an illustration of an antiabsorptive technique but also enacts the double movement ("antiabsorptive techniques . . . for absorptive ends") implied by Bernstein's "ambiv*o*lence" where "absorption & its converses" are concerned.

Bernstein does not seek to create new critical categories into which texts can be divided. He is as much concerned with breaking down the distinctions between these terms which he has set up as with defining them:

To speak of a radically impervious text
is to speak oxymoronically—absorbency and repellency
are relative, contextual, & interpenetrating
terms, not new critical analytic categories.
The unreadable text is an outer limit for poetry . . . (1987, 47)

I will return shortly to the outer and inner limits of poetry, but the emphasis here is on thinking about these dynamics of absorption and impermeability, rather than assigning texts to one or the other, or in extracting meaning from their employment *per se*.

In the brief discussion which begins *Artifice of Absorption,* in which many of the terms are familiar from Forrest-Thomson's work, Bernstein attempts to define poem, meaning, reading, artifice, experience and reference in a minor miracle of compression. By invoking the poetic as a possible attribute of reading as well as writing, he raises both the long-standing problem of defining what a poem may be, and the question of the location of poetic meaning. At the same time he asserts the significance of the writer, in terms of her/his practice of artifice, and "specific design" for the reading of the piece as poem:

The reason it is difficult to talk about
the meaning of a poem—in a way that doesn't seem
frustratingly superficial or partial—is that by

> designating a text a poem, one suggests that its
> meanings are to be located in some "complex" be-
> yond an addition of devices & subject matters.
> A poetic *reading* can be given to any
> piece of writing; a "poem" may be understood as
> writing specifically designed to absorb, or inflate
> with, proactive—rather than reactive—styles of
> reading. "Artifice" is a measure of a poem's
> intractability to being read as the sum of its
> devices & subject matters. In this sense,
> "artifice" is the contradiction of "realism", with
> its insistence on presenting an unmediated
> (immediate) experience of facts, either of the
> "external" world of nature or the "internal" world
> of the mind; for example, naturalistic
> representation or phenomenological consciousness
> mapping. Facts in poetry are primarily
> factitious. (1987, 6)

If a theorist desires to retain any concept of the experience of poetry as inter-subjective, meaning cannot be relinquished. The concept of poetry as knowledge, as "epistemological / inquiry" (1987, 12), equally requires an insistence on meaning.[9] A powerful engagement with the question of how poems mean rather than what they mean makes Forrest-Thomson's poetics a vital part of the development of postmodern poetry in the tradition of innovation, as Bernstein is aware.

Bernstein recognizes that to view as liberatory the designation of aspects of poetic language as meaningless, is to cede ground that is far too important, and here his argument reconnects with Empson's—and Forrest-Thomson's—insistence on rationality. However it does so at a different level, within language itself:

> It is just my insistence
> that poetry be understood as epistemological
> inquiry; to cede meaning would be to undercut
> the power of poetry to reconnect us
> with modes of meaning given in language . . . (1987, 12)

Poems may not necessarily be written in the language-game of giving information, but the kinds of poem that interest both Forrest-Thomson and Bernstein—as the very existence of his poem of poetics bears witness—are written in the language of information. For both, the epistemological function of poetry is vital: both believe poetry has a function, hence the emphasis on how poems work. This places intelligibility high upon the list of desirable outcomes for their poems.

Bernstein offers an elegant formula for the inner and outer limits of poetry based on his conceptual schema of impermeability and absorption:

> Translating Zukofsky's formula for poetry
> (lower limit, speech; upper limit, music)
> I would suggest that
> poetry has as its outer limit, impermeability
> & as its inner limit, absorption. (1987, 48)

The line endings again epitomize the theme, connecting poetry to music and impermeability to absorption. All art may indeed constantly aspire to the condition of music; but for the art of speech, for poetry, a crucial aspect of its function—as "epistemological inquiry"—is sacrificed if it should achieve that desire.

Notes

1. This was re-published in a slightly revised version as "Artifice of Absorption", in Bernstein 1992, 9–89.
2. Particularly with Karen Mac Cormack, whom I acknowledge with thanks.
3. Forrest-Thomson quotes this statement in *Poetic Artifice* (1978, 20), and alludes to it in her "Note" to the collection *Language-Games* (1990, 261–63). Wittgenstein's proposition is cited, for example, by the poet Adrian Clarke (1995). It is a frequent reference in the work of anti-Realist novelists and theorists as well as poets (see Nash 1987, 232–34).
4. "Naturalisation" is the spelling which appears in *Poetic Artifice;* I have retained original spellings in direct quotations.
5. Elsewhere I have explored more fully the relationship between tradition and resistance, inherited paradigms and innovation, in the work of Forrest-Thomson and those whose work succeeds her own (e.g. Mark 1996).
6. I share Patrick ffrench's view that: "What the notion of intertextuality means is not only that a text is related to the totality of other texts as a network or series, but that the writing reorganises literature as a whole in traversing and transgressing it, reorganises also the text of identity (the subject) and of society (history). Intertextuality proposes a vision of literature as transformative of itself and of the world" (1993, 224).
7. This appears in his use of Marxist concepts and terminology and in the collection he edited in 1990.
8. Hélène Cixous also puns on "*voler*", suggesting that: "To fly/steal is woman's gesture, to steal into language to make it fly" (1986, 96). See also Herrmann 1979.
9. Forrest-Thomson's doctoral thesis was *Poetry as Knowledge: The Use of Science by Twentieth-Century Poets* (1971b).

Bibliography

Bernstein, Charles. 1987. *Artifice of Absorption*. Philadelphia: Singing Horse Press / Paper Air.

———. 1992. *A Poetics*. Cambridge, MA: Harvard University Press.

———, ed. 1990. *The Politics of Poetic Form: Poetry and Public Policy*. New York: Roof.

Cixous, Hélène and Catherine Clément. 1986. *The Newly Born Woman*. Trans. Betsy Wing. Manchester, U.K.: Manchester University Press.

Clarke, Adrian. 1995. "Equal, that is, to the Difference: Approaches to a Radical Poetic 1945–95." Paper. "Identity and Contemporary Poetry" Conference. Centre for English Studies, University of London. 11 May.

Culler, Jonathan. 1975. *Structuralist Poetics: Structuralism, Linguistics and the Study of Literature*. London: Routledge & Kegan Paul.

———. 1981. *The Pursuit of Signs: Semiotics, Literature, Deconstruction*. London: Routledge & Kegan Paul.

ffrench, Raymont Patrick. 1993. "A History of *Tel Quel:* The Logic of Literature." Diss. University of London.

Forrest-Thomson, Veronica. Undated. "The Separate Planet." Unpublished essay. Translated in Forrest-Thomson 1983.

———. 1971a. "Irrationality and Artifice: A Problem in Recent Poetics." *British Journal of Aesthetics* 2:123–33.

———. 1971b. *Poetry as Knowledge: The Use of Science by Twentieth-Century Poets*. Diss. University of Cambridge.

———. 1973. "Necessary Artifice: Form and Theory in the Poetry of *Tel Quel*." *Language and Style* 6:3–26.

———. 1974. "Rational Artifice: Some Remarks on the Poetry of William Empson." *Yearbook of English Studies* 4:225–38.

———. 1975. "Unrealism and Death in Contemporary Poetry." Poetry Forum discussion between Forrest-Thomson and Michel Couturier (with some interpolations by others). Cambridge Poetry Festival, 18 April. National Sound Archive, T6023WR-7359W.

———. 1978. *Poetic Artifice: A Theory of Twentieth-Century Poetry*. Manchester, U.K.: Manchester University Press.

———. 1983. "La Planète séparée: John Donne et William Empson." *John Donne*. Cahiers de l'Herne: Les Dossiers H. Paris: L'Age d'Homme. 231–44.

———. 1990. *Collected Poems and Translations*. Ed. Anthony Barnett. London: Allardyce, Barnett.

Herrmann, Claudine. 1979. *Les Voleuses de langue*. Paris: Des Femmes.

Hejinian, Lyn. 1995. Letter to Alison Mark. 22 January.

Keats, John. 1952. Letter to George and Tom Keats, 22 December 1817. *The Letters*. 4th ed. Oxford: Oxford University Press. 69–72.

Kenny, Anthony. 1975. *Wittgenstein*. Harmondsworth: Penguin.

Mark, Alison. 1996. "Reading Between the Lines: Language, Experience and Identity in the Work of Veronica Forrest-Thomson." Diss. University of London.

Nash, Christopher. 1987. *World-Games: The Tradition of Anti-Realist Revolt*. London: Methuen.

Pears, David. 1985. *Wittgenstein*. London: Fontana.

Perloff, Marjorie. 1981. *The Poetics of Indeterminacy: Rimbaud to Cage*. Princeton: Princeton University Press.

———. 1991. *Radical Artifice: Writing Poetry in the Age of Media*. Chicago: University of Chicago Press.

Raitt, Suzanne. 1990. "Veronica Forrest-Thomson: *Collected Poems and Translations*." *Women: A Cultural Review* 1:304–8.

Wittgenstein, Ludwig. 1985. *Tractatus Logico-Philosophicus*. London: Routledge & Kegan Paul.

———. 1990a. *Philosophical Investigations*. Trans. G.E.M. Anscombe. Oxford: Blackwell.

———. 1990b. *Zettel*. Ed. G.E.M. Anscombe and G.H. von Wright. Trans. G.E.M. Anscombe. Oxford: Blackwell.

Peter Middleton

Imagined Readerships and Poetic Innovation in U.K. Poetry

Contemporary British poetry presents an anachronistic facade. The great bulk of the poetry that is published by the main commercial publishers, reviewed in the newspapers, and distributed to ordinary bookstores, maintains a poetics that belongs to a premodernist era. Alongside but less visible to the ordinary reader, is a heterogeneous range of modernist, avant-garde, performance and political poetry that is largely kept out of sight by underfunding and deliberate exclusion, and usually vilified when its existence is noticed by mainstream reviewers. Narratives of heroic dissidence, terrorist poetics, unimaginative middle classes, or poetically dull barbarous yawps, depending on one's point of view, easily insist on themselves. Such stories may help to rally the avant-gardes or reassure the more conservative that they maintain continuity with tradition, but they also hinder recognition of the range and interdependencies of this work, and seriously distort the perceptions of readers from outside the U.K., whose access is already limited by the poor distribution of the more heterogeneous poetry through the ordinary channels of publication and publicity. It would help if we tried instead to think of these contemporary poetries as a series of heterogeneous universes rather than a single Manichean cosmos, because this would make much more apprehensible how each of these many poetries imagines its own and others' worlds in diverse ways. Quiet radicalism and thoughtful restoration of earlier poetic artifices might become more distinguishable. Much of what appears from the standpoint of hegemonic poetic norms to be reckless formal experiment might also be better understood as a sign of reformulated futures for the reception of poems whose degree of dissidence varies widely. These poems anticipate and so strive to create new community stages on which the poem can perform. Almost all readers can perceive that these innovative poems immediately incite a question: Is this really a poem? A consequent dismissal of the alleged pretender often follows from a failure to recognize that this question cannot be limited simply to a reified set of linguistic marks on sheets of paper. A poem is complexly extended through history, and therefore in space, time and subjectivity, in ways which are an intrinsic part of its being as a poem. Its meaning takes place during a multiplicity of temporally and spatially organized occasions. Some of the best recent poetry has developed from such meditations on the ethics and history of these basic conditions of public culture, which are not yet adequately matched by a sufficiently reflexive discursive debate about the structures of the field of poetry's performance, leaving the field open to a continuance of images and assumptions about collectivity which can hinder the fuller development of new strategies for the promulgation and interpretation of the diverse contemporary poetries in Great Britain and Northern Ireland. I shall call these simply British poetries, and not U.K. poetries, to follow most contemporary usage, despite the risk of political misrepresentation, for reasons that will be outlined in a moment.

"Remote, alienated, fractured" (*Conductors of Chaos* xvii). These are Iain Sinclair's terms for the poetry he likes and has chosen for a recent anthology of British poetry that has been largely neglected by the main commercial literary institutions.[1] They are not just Sinclair's invention; they are also part of the discourse of many contemporary poets, who favour similar self-descriptions, if less romantically disenchanted ones. Exile is a particularly favorite noun/adjective, used for both the title of the Picador collection of work by Brian Catling, Allen Fisher, and Bill Griffiths, *Future Exiles,* and in the introduction to the volume of poetry by Thomas A. Clark, Barry MacSweeney, and Chris Torrance, who apparently "each possess the authentic exilic perspective of hired guns in a range war" (*Tempers Of Hazard* ii). The exile as cowboy outside the social order of the town and ranch, shows by his hypermasculinity that his power only increases with isolation. This thoroughly American ideological figure of the mercenary who is able to use the machinery of death so skilfully, neatly encodes authorising affinities with American writing, alongside a characteristic recognition of and contempt for the marketplace, and an exaggerated insistence on the power of this poetry. In an interview for North and South publishers, Lee Harwood insists poetry is a solitary activity which aligns him with other poets who "step outside the mainstream" (Skelt, *Prospect* 63). Kelvin Corcoran, asked why he had never tried to edit a magazine, talks of himself as an internal exile, saying he can't imagine who would subscribe: "It'd be me, you and the milkman," he tells the interviewer (*Prospect* 165). His poems are "ghost conversations" with other poets as if the other poets were not fast enough on the draw. The poets in Denise Riley's collection *Poets on Writing* find life as a contemporary British poet solitary. Not all of them are as pained by isolation as John Hall, who stopped writing because his poetry lost the "continuities and momentum" ("Writing" 44) it needed, due to the demands of teaching and children, as well as a lack of wider support from readers and publishers. Peter Riley makes a virtue of solitude: "Poetry is a private act . . . it is left there on the page, abandoned by its creator, for those able or inclined to take it up and wheel it into their own gardens" ("Creative Moment" 113). Poetry makes good manure for the private culture of the garden, that marker of English attitudes to individuality, privacy, and nature. Hall was perhaps mistaken in believing that his lack of audience was the cause of his problems, since in Peter Riley's view this is the fate of all true poetry: "*There is no audience:* there is one reader at a time"(105). The remote, alienated poet may also be a specialist in fragmentation according to Michael Haslam, who praised Tony Lopez's book *Stress Management* by punning on the idiomatic and literal meanings of the word "shattered" to describe Lopez's innovative use of a disjunctive style. This poetry is "primed with real feeling, and feeling shattered is a speciality of his" (Lopez review 95). As these examples show, Sinclair's trinity of adjectives are expected to be an effective advertisement for the anthology, because they converge with already current images of decentred subjectivity, whose reference extends beyond the aesthetic into the political sphere as it was understood during the 1980s and early '90s.

This contemporary sampling of an older pattern of metaphors for artists who are avant-garde retains its latent spatial metaphors and discards any hint of communitarianism. Editors and poets carefully avoid any hint that poets might belong to groups and movements, share manifestoes, or emerge from a common class, education, sexuality, gender, or whiteness. Sinclair is insistent that the poets in his collection are "a quarrelsome bunch; dealing with them is like dipping an arm into a sack of vipers" (*Conductors* xviii). Since the viper or adder is the only indigenous poisonous snake, these are clearly very British creatures perhaps made angry by such close confinement. Eric Mottram, introducing his selection of poets for *The New British Poetry,* was careful to say that "they belong to no enclosure of school or movement" ("Treacherous Assault" 132) as if to avoid any viperishness that might be caused by such enclosure. As Drew Milne notes of the poets in Denise Riley's collection: "No one here wants to be guilty of being identified with a community" ("Cottage" 65). Andrew Duncan says that only outsiders ever talk of a Cambridge school of poetry: "The extreme loathing of the term 'Cambridge School' among its notional members is no doubt due to the fear that someone will say things and they will be taken for 'official secrets'"("Cambridge" 15). In more judicious terms Rod Mengham's paper for the Assembling Alternatives conference acutely describes a "challenged individualism" in J. H. Prynne's earlier poetry. Even the London poets who allowed themselves to be called *Floating Capital* are barely a school according to Adrian Clarke: "it is either fugitive and ephemeral or an obscure cumulation registered in glimpses liable unpredictably to bore, depress, provoke or excite" ("Underground" 15).

For English poets, national identities provide no viable image of community, both because of the lingering reactionary ideologies of patriotism, and because of the feebleness of federalism in the U.K. No one speaks of U.K. poetry the way Americans speak of American poetry. Even though "U.K." is the only inclusive term for the entire political territory of Northern Ireland, Wales, Scotland and England, their deliberately unclear constitutional position renders the nomenclature adjectivally impossible. No anthologist of U.K. poetry would be able to unselfconsciously parallel Ron Silliman's announcement of a "new moment in American writing" ("Language" xv) in his introduction to *In The American Tree*. The title *The New British Poetry* was a very self-conscious attempt to imitate Donald Allen's successful appeal to a renewed American cultural nationalism twenty-five years earlier that was effectively ignored by the editors themselves in their introductions. Ken Edwards comes closest and reveals the anxieties that surround any use of nationalism as a unifying identity when he says that the new poetry is "specifically British but non-parochial" ("Younger Poets" 267). Where Ron Silliman imagines that an American poetry will be bold, innovative and cosmopolitan, Edwards is afraid that Britishness is equivalent to nostalgia for settled traditions. His opposition between the parochial and the non-parochial draws upon a powerful image of Englishness embodied in the country village or parish, perhaps on the edge of a heathland, made up perhaps of thatched cottages, half-timbered houses and a manse or two, whose politics are handled by a parochial council and are inevitably very local in outlook (no wonder a Thatcher became the successor to a Heath). Even Drew Milne in his powerful call for a new "community of risk" ("Cottage" 59) amongst poets, is wary of attempts to factor into its constitution any form of appeal to national identity. His dismissal of recent academic writing as "accountant-led academic sameness and pedagogical tour guides for village idiots"(58) contrasted with "the impression of discrete cottage industries settling for honourable isolation as the aesthetics of agoraphobia"(60) shudders with that same fear of the muffling ideology of nostalgic Englishness heard widely in recent discussions by avant-garde poets. In the face of such dangerous absorption by the reactionary heritage, the poet must, in Nigel Wheale's words, refuse "to be covered by social or psychical description", or in Maggie O'Sullivan's, avoid "cliché-ridden rallying positions" ("Reader" 9). It really does seem, as John Wilkinson says, that "'we' has lost all possibility of adventure" ("Imperfect" 166). Poetic community cannot draw on national sentiments of the local imagined community as a way of generating and sustaining a network.

We should remember that the most influential theorist of the disappearance of the collective pronoun during much of the period in which these poets were writing was Margaret Thatcher, prime minister throughout the 1980s. In a notorious interview for a women's magazine she said: "There is no such thing as society. There are individual men and women and families" (Strathern 144)[2]. As well as abolishing society, she also abolished alternative visions of culture (saying repeatedly, "there is no alternative"), and developed a pervasive ideological discourse that shouldered aside others. She made, for example, the word "radical" unusable by the left for a while by appropriating it for her own policies. Her mastery of ideological discourse was astonishing, and so, as Hugo Young explains, "for want of an organized, politically credible alternative, the intellectual argument in favor of Thatcherite economics had carried the day . . . yet it could not be said that intellectuals, considered as a class, now rejected the post-war consensus in which most of them grew up" (*One of Us* 404). Intellectuals were hostile without being able to organise effective communities of resistance or even a viable political discourse, and were often simply drowned out in any public sphere by the skilful use which Thatcherism made of certain deeply held English convictions about individuality and society as axioms which entailed her monetarist and anti-socialist policies. The frustration that ensued put excessive torsion on the language of oppositional poetry and criticism of this time. Poets of the time were organised into networks, yet tended to lack conceptual resources for representing their activities both to themselves and to possible public spheres for their work.

To see how this worked, and why both left-wing poets and right-wing politicians would deny the existence of society or such metonymic counterparts as readerships and audiences, so that poets otherwise entirely opposed to Thatcherism could say that "there is no audience", we need to look more closely at existing ideologies of individuality. Marilyn Strathern's recent study of the English middle class genesis of some anthropological concepts of kinship identifies Thatcher's ideological claim that there is no such thing as society as merely a striking formulation of a deeply held middle class English belief about persons. Persons are believed to be individuals, and relationships between these individuals have "a conventional or artificial dimension" (*After Nature* 53), so a person is wholly distinguishable from her or his relations with others, and therefore from any social grouping, whether a poetic movement or society. Relationships are wholly extrinsic to individuals. Indeed the implication will always be that communities and societies are actually at odds with the natural diversity of individuals. The consequence is that the twentieth century English have believed that "relationships produced (individual) persons and that (individual) diversity led to productive relationships, such that individuals created individuals" (72), and such ideas have permeated their social theories, notably anthropological theories of kinship. Translate this into our specific context: the public activities of writers, like readings, discussion groups and magazines, produce individual poets, whose individuality enables them to produce distinctive, individual poems. Wheale describes the network of writers, publishers and readers who make up the small press world as capable of forming a "knowable community"

("Uttering" 10). To what extent has it been admissible that such a community might help determine the form of individual poems produced by those associated with it? Strathern says that for this English ideology, "individuals are not in themselves relationships", so if we translate this back into a poetics it could mean that a poem is always an autonomous text, whatever its extrinsic intertextual affinities with other poems and discourses. This would explain a collective inability of innovative U.K. poets to form persuasive images of their literary intersubjectivity, since English ideologies of sociality remain hegemonic throughout the "united" "kingdom". Margaret Thatcher could say that society didn't exist because social solidarities capable of effecting emancipatory social change had become very difficult to conceptualise in the face of this assertion of the solidity of individuals. Even individuality needs to be demonstrated, however, and so it is not surprising that in much of the poetry published by the commercial presses an autobiographical narrative, usually cast in the first person, expresses its observations in a lucid, expository manner that appears to be grounded in the control of this authorial individuality. Andrew Duncan actually calls this "total commodification of the artistic personality" resulting from "global Thatcherism" ("Cambridge" 12), but as I have been arguing, it is more specific to a particular culture than that. The least Thatcherite writer, Peter Riley, still insists that "truth passed through an author gains authenticity" ("Creative" 104).

Duncan's image of a blue planet points toward another reason why images of networks, collectivities and movements are so fraught with threat for these contemporary poets[3]. If the dominant ideological image of sociality is the market, then intersubjective cultural networks which promote other values may appear to their participants to be dangerously close to commodification if they seem too dependent on consumerist dynamics. The problem with poems is that they are not exactly like persons, because they do move from person to person forming part of the connection between them; and so this necessary alienability common to the circulation of all written texts seems to lay poetry open to the appropriation of the market which increasingly in Britain in the 1980s came to seem synonymous with government, public morality, and through the growing power of the multinationals, with the world. Avant-garde poets therefore turned to a deconstructed discourse of economic exchange, borrowing in part from a discourse already formulated in the U.S.A. by some Language writers, as a means for discussing the conditions under which poetry was produced and circulated. Since, as Keith Tuma pointed out in his paper for Assembling Alternatives, Language writing successfully both created new readership networks and intervened in existing ones, their poetic critique of commodification carried considerable authority.

Reading back through the journals in which Language writing was first discussed, and its relation to readerships and public debate were formulated, a

British reader is likely to be struck by the seemingly paradoxical concept of language at work. On the one hand it is reified and commoditized by capitalism, but on the other it remains the ground of our "commonness" (Bernstein, "Three" 22). The seeming contradiction is removed by advocating a poetics of resistance to instrumental uses of the medium of language, which will produce poems that outflank the market and help create new communities of readers and writers, capable of then moving into the political sphere. Poems can recover lost ethical potentials in language itself. To make this case, the Language writers had to oppose an earlier model of poetic community based on authenticity and individuality, and this led to something of a paradigm shift in American avant-garde poetry. Charles Bernstein spoke for many poets when he said in 1978 that continuing to write in the mode of the New American poets would be to merely "describe the conditions—of our alienation" ("Three" 21), without transforming them. It was not that the New American poets did not believe in commonality, they did; and their poetry, their magazines and their commitment to public readings, as well as their affinities with beat culture and the anti-war movement, all affirmed it. The change lay in a loss of belief in the use of certain poetic strategies to create a community. In 1972 an interviewer approvingly said to Robert Creeley, whose work constitutes a brilliant existential investigation of the conditions of the individual's alienation: "In your poems particularly prior to *Pieces* you tend to suppress the circumstances surrounding the poems, you tend to make your poems into general dramatic statements". In reply, Creeley mentions that one criticism he has taken seriously is that his poems are sometimes too personal, and says: "I wanted to strip away as much addenda as possible, to get it down to the nitty-gritty of the particular circumstance of feeling. I didn't want to argue that, o.k., that was true in Mallorca, but what would it be like in Boston? . . . I was trying to get not merely a 'universal' occasion but I was also trying to strip away all that kind of qualification" ("Tales" 107). The poem's absence of contingent detail was supposed to assist its passage into as wide a community as possible. Despite the prominence of American ideologies of individualism, the practice of both these American poetic movements suggests that individuality was not conceived as quite so autonomous of relationship, as in the English case. It would be interesting to see work similar to Strathern's carried out in the United States.

One reason for a pervasive unease with Language writing amongst the British poets was that they mistrusted its claim to offer an alternative to the consumerist dumbing down produced by the strategies of capitalist exchange. J. H. Prynne criticised Language poetry because although some of their texts "seem to promote inferred relations well outside the schedule" others seem merely to join the existing "market-economy" because making the reader an active participant in the production of meaning seems to him merely a homology of the manipulation of consumer choice: "Isn't it the classic freedom to eat cake, to diversify an assumed leisure and to choose out of a diversity which is precisely the commodity-spectacle of a predisposed array, clearwrapped in unitised portion-control?" (*Language Issue* n.pag.) he asks[4]. This would mean that the Language writing was no better than its heavily marketed dominant competitors in the mainstream, which the introduction to a 1980 anthology of English poetry published in France, *La Voix Off,* dismissed as "social climbing, entertainment and consumer product" ("Introduction" 1). Younger poets, according to the introduction of an issue of *Angel Exhaust* devoted to work by new writers, are all too ready to prepare their work for the market by making a fetish of their own authenticity, but because they also avoid poetic complexity they then paradoxically bleach out the very identity they are attempting to promote: "The self without ideas is inauthentic because cut off from the medium which nourishes it; it becomes merely a commodity" (Duncan, "Beaten" 2).

Commodification of poetry is not in itself the problem since both writers and readers want to promote the exchange of poetry, and this entails at least some momentary commodification at the point of transfer. The fear might seem to be that the poem itself undergoes an irrevocable transformation once taken into the market economy of commodity exchange. The real concern of this commodification critique is the fragmented state of the social relations of reception rather than the monetary conditions of distribution, prompted by the fear that the "knowable community" or imagined readership will be entirely absent or at best manipulated by hegemonic interpretative regimes. Such fears are understandable. Strathern says that within the culture of individuality "society becomes unimaginable as an associational dimension of people's affairs" because there are no longer any "analogies for relationships of commonality". The proliferation of discourses of exile, fragmentation and individuality in recent British poetics suggests that poetic community has been almost unimaginable during this period when society was declared dead, and no alternative was acknowledged possible. The problem with the discourse of opposition to commodification is that it easily entails an acceptance of the deeper ideology of individuality and the apparently indissociable values of originality, innovation, discovery and ethical responsibility. What is missing is any representation of the relations of reading, publication, circulation, debate and so forth, which any poem will undergo over time. I am not arguing that poets don't recognise the importance and existence of such networks. As both Linda Kinnahan and Keith Tuma pointed out at the conference that gave rise to this book, the recent anthologies of innovative poetry are evidence of the desire to create new networks and sustain existing associations. The problem has been to articulate them in tangible ways. John Hall thinks that viable activities of writing poetry take place in a "palpable" network of relations: "The palpability is expressed through forms of exchange, such as pay or requests or even the *palpable* exchange of pleasures" ("Writing" 47). His question—"what is the set of relations implied by the act of writing?" (46)—points to a widespread problem for the U.K. innovative poet: the difficulty of developing collective self-images that will assist the cognitive efforts necessary for the creation of a flourishing poetry scene.

Discourses of current poetics in the U.K. have foundered on these difficulties, which are made worse by what Jeff Derksen calls the lack of a method for tracing connections between poetic forms and social praxis. Poetry has often been more inventive than the public discourses that have promulgated it. Poets have responded to the dilemmas of obstructed public access and isolation with interesting poetic strategies for reimagining readerships, and in doing so, provided some of the most exciting developments in the poetry of the 1980s and early 1990s. As Rod Mengham says in his essay for this volume, since the 1960s Prynne's poetry has counterposed settlement and nomadism as images of community in order to rethink existing English ideas, and often aligned poet and reader with those nomads who gain an outside perspective on existing collectivities. Allen Fisher's work of the past decade began to depict a community of figures able to produce information and argument about the contemporary material world, based on models of science as an institution of disinterested enquiry. Denise Riley's recent poetry subtly reimagines psychoanalytic concepts in political terms. In each case the semantic performance of the poems includes a staging of their future use. The poetry therefore already invites a rethinking of the discourses of poetic community that are evident in the public discussions I cited at the opening of this essay.

One way to provide a figure for the imagined readership is to draw upon a familiar image of an ethically constituted intellectual community. Both Allen Fisher and J. H. Prynne have knowingly ensorcelled their poetry with science's many languages, not only as a means of adopting powerful explanatory discourses, but also as figures of a community of knowledge in action. Their underlying assumptions about science are shared by some recent historians of science. Steven Shapin, for example, argues that "the very power of science to hold knowledge as collective property *and* to focus doubt on bits of currently accepted knowledge is founded upon a degree and a quality of trust which are arguably unparalleled elsewhere in our culture" (*Social History* 417). Both Prynne and Fisher are chary of the dangers of a technocratic elite of experts which can produce its own poetic nonsense, as Prynne demonstrates in the "Plant Time Manifold Manuscripts" (1974), and to some extent in *News of Warring Clans* (1977). Fisher's poem "Bel Air", like other poems from *Brixton Fractals,* is a narrative that reads like the discursive equivalent of the photographic documentation of a Fluxus event, or an extended outdoor theatre piece. Its epistemological uncertainty is exacerbated by the recurrent use of technical scientific language to analyse physical events: "the children recognise the cloud shapes a / mathematician codes as corank one" ("Future" 94). The poem carefully distinguishes different categorisations, saying that "they see the dynamics / without knowing the internal parameters". The children know this means rain, without having to know the scientific concepts, but it is because of the internal parameters that rain will fall, demonstrating the pertinence of science. The trouble is that readers are like children. How many of these arty readers of poetry really know what a cloud corank one looks like? This is a poem that knows how little physics even its most dedicated readers are likely to have learned, and therefore the end of the poem tempts the reader with a quick fix, trying out the idea that ubiquitous surveillance "frees all concern about issues / of internal consciousness—violent / motions, unknown forces, tortuously / curved, even multiply-connected / geometry"(100). That's okay then, we don't need to worry about the internal consciousness of morality and the psyche, and can concentrate on material forces. The poem knows that this won't do. To take this attitude would be to give way to the comfortable ignorance induced by the State's endorsement of a culture of experts which helps circumscribe relations between such specialist communities and others. This passage in the poem is not merely cynical, however, because it also admits to uncertainty about the status of the scientific language which provokes a persistent hermeneutic unease. Similar moments of resistance to the language of scientific knowledge resurface again and again in the sequence. In "Boogie Break" we are told that "such technical language exhaust-fumed / reflection" (*Brixton Fractals* 67), as if this scientific discourse were a kind of inevitable pollution resulting from the culture of technology. How then can science provide an image of ethical responsibility for what Fisher elsewhere calls "the culture dreamed of"[5]?

Fisher attempts to provide one through a form of generic embodiment. He returns the language of science to generic types of individuals, and then shows them interacting and creating an incipient ethics of trust implicit in the dialogic ideal. In doing so he evokes one aspect of scientific research, which sociologists of science have called the "core sets": groups of experts who are the only ones capable of fully comprehending the experimental methods on which precise scientific knowledge rests, who have to find ways of communicating their knowledge to the wider culture through dialogue and trust[6]. In one of the poems from *Brixton Fractals,* "Black Bottom", a debate emerges between a Photographer, a Poet, a Mathematician and an Engineer about the continuity of form in a world of constant change. The Mathematician criticises poetry for the way "richness, connectance, and / interaction make instability" (64), claiming that local stability does exist. The Poet responds tartly by invoking a familiar criticism of the positivism of natural science, reminding the scientist of "the complexity of observation as / participation", and later reaffirming that "I am on an equal footing with what I see". To these claims the Mathematician responds with an extraordinary rebuttal: "I am not concerned . . . with / the successive destruction of individuals". What he means is that if the Poet's anti-positivist claim is right, then change alters not just that which is observed but the observer also, leading to the continual destruction of the observer of that moment. In what then could identity inhere? As far as the Poet is concerned, this is better than the Engineer's vision; but the poem insists upon the irresolution of this difference for which science provides a discourse all the characters accept, and which represents the activity of conceptual analysing of empirical phenomena as potentially significant political action. This is why much of what the characters actually do is to make formulations. The Burglar "reinterprets the state" ("Future" 92); the Painter represents "the struggle of objects for supremacy" (93) and then "matches the found pattern / of a star map / into a knitted pullover" (94); the Mathematician "took notes" (67) and "we call this knowledge" says the narrator. Neither art nor science emerge from these juxtapositions without challenge. The cumulative effect of the comedy, and the repeated admissions that even the narrative "I" is "a mere / phenomenal actualisation moved through a burning gap" ("Future" 104) as the poem "Birdland" expresses it, is to spin out uncertainty. Anticipating the reader's interpretative work has the effect of turning the reader into a mere phenomenal actualisation as well, yet the scientific register of the phrase proposes an image of a readership, already given partial dramatisation through the dialogues between the figures. Just as the scientist is both no more than a phenomenal actualisation predicted by science, and the creator of this science, so the writer and the poem are both no more than instances of discourse and creators of it. Individuality emerges within relationship which emerges from individuality.

The future of British poetry "probably lies in the direction Denise Riley is taking" according to Douglas Oliver, who insists that her poems "have got to reach the widest possible public because poetry itself needs that to happen". This blurb from the back cover of *Mop Mop Georgette* prompted a cautionary restraint in one of John Wilkinson's reviews of recent poetry. Although I take issue with his specific judgement in this essay, these reviews have provided an important model of how an intelligent, engaged reasoning with the practice and theory of recent British poetry can work with the details and the broad aims together. Yet in Wilkinson's review, as Kinnahan observes in her more extended discussion of his criticism of reflexivity in her essay for this volume, Wilkinson's criticism of reflexivity as narcissism comes surprisingly close to enforcing dominant masculine judgements on women's poetry. Wilkinson thinks that it is the narcissistic ego-ideal in Riley's poetry, its tendency to relinquish the struggle against narcissism and enjoy "the glide of the heart / out on a flood of ease" ("Illyrian Places" 59), which captivates her proponents like Oliver. There is another way to read this process, however, that recognizes the political perception in her work. In her poems "A Shortened Set" and "Laibach Lyrik: Slovenia 1991", Riley recognises the isolation of the individual poet which her contemporaries consider inevitable, and gives it a more psychoanalytic reading. Listening to the Yugoslavians negotiate their new, unwanted nationalist identities, she thinks of herself as a sentient observer, "a dark stand of trees, still, sealed black, outwardly silent but vibrantly / loud inside with others' gossip about itself, like 'the unconscious'" (*Mop Mop Georgette* 10). This poetically imagined self contains relationships within itself, in the manner which Strathern attributes to the Melanesian social groups whom she contrasts with the West, but diverges from ethnographic discourse by characteristically naming this the unconscious. By doing so the poem also cites and transmutes Freud's notorious difficulty in conceptualising sociality as anything more than a series of libidinally driven identifications prior to the differentiations of self-consciousness[7]. In "A Shortened Set" the narcissistic wound of the lyric complaint is imagined in political terms, first as a "perfectly democratic loneliness", and then as the "social democracy of loneliness" (social democratics split away from the Labour party, united with the Liberal party, and inadvertently helped keep Thatcher in power in the 1980s, so this political name implies a form of complacent sociality based on liberal individualism). Wilkinson reads this through the lens of an English ideology of individuation which shapes his interpretation of the psychoanalytic theory of identification. The result is that he somewhat mutes its political tones when he concludes that the problem these poems confront is this: "how is the wholeness of others to be apprehended and asserted when one's own provisional sense of wholeness depends upon the expropriation of parts of those others?" ("Illyrian Places" 61). This misses the reimagination of sociality in the image of a readership represented by a self "loud inside with others' gossip about itself, like 'the unconscious'". Wilkinson reads Riley's volume of poems as a mirror for studying her self-inventions because he conceives of all relations in psychoanalytic terms as forms of incorporating identification, and assumes that self-consciousness is specularity. Riley's poetry, however, presents self-consciousness in the image of gossip as a communicative network of relations between her poetry and potential readerships. She repeatedly invites a reader to answer back, to comment, to attribute a personal history to some mood. The poem will say "I'd thought / to ask around, what's lyric poetry?"—as if inviting the reader to explain, and as if asking around, chatting, gossiping, were where poetry is defined. In a sharp seizure of the reader's standoffishness, the poem says

Don't quote the 'we'
of pairs nor worse, of sentient
humanity, thanks.

That's attitudinising, in those
three lines. That's what I do.
Help me out of it, you
you sentient humanity.

("A Shortened Set," 22–23)

This is the problem for all these remote, alienated poets, seemingly offered only the extremes of self and humanity, and liable to fracture into irony and quotation, calling for the help of an imagined readership.

So with some relief we can surely agree that no, British poets need not be remote, alienated, fractured, in order to write good poetry. It is the actual conditions of circulation that are remote, alienated and fractured; the challenge is to distinguish between the necessary conditions of texts, and the contingent pressures of recent history in a large polity which is distantiating, alienates in order to control, and is fractured all the way from the unresolved political federalism to local structures of cultural funding. These have been bad times for presses, readings, grants, education and recognition. Poets have done much to resist these conditions. Small presses, little magazines, conferences, workshops, and even the unsung efforts of certain people who have persistently ensured that poets stay in touch with each other's work, have made an enormous difference. What has sometimes been lacking are the self-representations of poetry, readership, community, and political intervention that would facilitate these activities further. The conference out of which this collection emerged, and this collection itself, are signs that many people are now working towards concepts and discourses capable of sustaining and promulgating this important body of contemporary poetry in Britain, and encouraging new developments from within and without it.

Notes

1. "The work that I value is that which seems most remote, alienated, fractured. I don't claim to 'understand' it but I like having it around" (Sinclair xvii).
2. Various versions of this famous judgement exist, made around 1987, both in reported interviews and on the BBC. Strathern offers an interesting analysis of its

sociological implications. Thatcher is effectively saying that social relationships are increasingly hard to visualise.

3. Blue was the colour that symbolised Margaret Thatcher's Conservative Party, and it was used heavily throughout the decade as a foil to the red of the Labour Party, which had old associations with Communism that the Conservatives could play upon.
4. These citations are taken from a reprinted letter by J. H. Prynne, originally written to one of the Language writers, part of which appeared in a one-off magazine entitled *Language Issue* in which various British poets parodied Language writing under pseudonyms. There are no page numbers and no date given (but it appeared at some point during the first half of the 1990s). [Editor's note: The letter mentioned here and in Keith Tuma's essay, p. 152, has been reprinted in *The Gig* 7 (2002): 40–46.]
5. Allen Fisher, *Ideas of the Culture Dreamed of* (London: Spanner, 1982). Fisher's definition of "brend" is indicative of the problem of imagining sociality. Brend is subjective experience, and usually contrasted with art, because "in art the thing valued is separated from the valuing of it and turned into an object which is urged on other people. Individuals tend to overlook their brend" for the same reasons that the reification of great art is promulgated. The dreamed culture would make brend intersubjectively possible without such alienations.
6. See for example Harry Collins, "Expertise: Between the Scylla of Certainty and the New Age Charybdis", *Accountability in Research* vol. 5, 1997, pp. 127–135.
7. For a useful discussion of Freud's lack of a model of intersubjectivity, and its consequences for psychoanalysis, see Mikkel Borch-Jacobsen, *The Freudian Subject*, trans. Catherine Porter (London: Macmillan, 1989), pp. 202–203.

References

Allnutt, Gillian, Fred D'Aguiar, Ken Edwards, and Eric Mottram, eds. *The New British Poetry: 1968–1988*. London: Paladin, 1988.

Bernstein, Charles. "Three or Four Things I Know About Him", *L=A=N=G=U=A=G=E* Supplement No.3 (1981): 12–23.

Borch-Jacobsen, Mikkel. *The Freudian Subject*. Catherine Porter, trans. London: Macmillan, 1989.

Buck, Paul and Allen Fisher. "Introduction." *Voix-Off Angleterre*. Talence, France: Editions du Castor-Astral, 1980.

Clark, Thomas A., Barry Mac Sweeney, and Chris Torrance. *The Tempers Of Hazard*. London: Paladin, 1993.

Clarke, Adrian. "Underground Terminal". *Angel Exhaust* 8 (1992): 15–17.

Collins, Harry. "Expertise: Between the Scylla of Certainty and the New Age Charybdis." *Accountability in Research* vol. 5 (1997): 127–35.

Creeley, Robert. *Tales out of School: Selected Interviews*. Ann Arbor: University of Michigan Press, 1993.

Duncan, Andrew. "The Cambridge Leisure Centre: Traits." *Angel Exhaust* 8 (1992): 5–14.
Duncan, Andrew and Scott Thurston. "The Beaten Generation." *Angel Exhaust* 9 (1994): 1–5.
Edwards, Ken. "Some Younger Poets." In Allnutt et al.: 265–70.
Fisher, Allen. *Ideas of the Culture Dreamed of.* London: Spanner, 1982.
———. *Brixton Fractals: Gravity as a Consequence of Shape, First Set*. London: Aloes Books, 1985.
———. *Future Exiles: Three London Poets—Allen Fisher, Bill Griffiths, Brian Catling.* London: Paladin, 1992.
Hall, John. "Writing and Not Writing." In Denise Riley: 41–49.
Haslam, Michael. Review of Tony Lopez, *Stress Management* (Manuden, Herts: Boldface Press, 1994). *Angel Exhaust* 13 (1996): 95–98 .
Milne, Drew. "Cottage Industries and Agoraphobia Revisited: Further Notes on Risk." Review of Denise Riley, ed. *Poets on Writing*. In *Parataxis* 4 (1993): 58–69.
Mottram, Eric. "A Treacherous Assault on British Poetry." In Allnutt et al: 131–33.
O'Sullivan, Maggie. "To The Reader." In Maggie O'Sullivan, ed. *Out of Everywhere: Linguistically Innovative Poetry by Women in North America & the UK.* Saxmundham and London: Reality Street Editions, 1996.
Prynne, J. H. *Poems.* Edinburgh and London: Agneau 2, 1982.
———. Extract from letter to "Mr Hayles". *Language Issue* 1 (1993?): unpaginated.
Riley, Denise, ed. *Poets on Writing: Britain, 1970–1991.* London: Macmillan, 1992.
———. *Mop Mop Georgette: New and Selected Poems, 1986–1993.* London: Reality Street Editions, 1993.
Riley, Peter. "The Creative Moment of the Poem." In Denise Riley: 92–113.
Shapin, Steven. *A Social History of Truth: Civility and Science in Seventeenth-Century England.* Chicago: Chicago University Press, 1994.
Silliman, Ron. "Language, Realism, Poetry." In Ron Silliman, ed. *In the American Tree.* Orono, Maine: National Poetry Foundation, 1986.
Sinclair, Iain. "Introduction." *Conductors of Chaos: a poetry anthology.* London: Macmillan, 1996.
Skelt, Peterjon, ed. *Prospect into Breath: Interviews with North and South Writers.* Twickenham and Wakefield: North and South, 1991.
Strathern, Marilyn. *After Nature: English Kinship in the Late Twentieth Century.* Cambridge: Cambridge University Press, 1992.
Wheale, Nigel. "Uttering Poetry: Small-Press Publication." In Denise Riley: 9–20.
Wilkinson, John. "Imperfect Pitch." In Denise Riley: 154–72.
———. "Illyrian Places." Review of Denise Riley, *Mop Mop Georgette. Parataxis* 6 (1994): 58–69.
Young, Hugo. *One of Us: A Biography of Margaret Thatcher.* 2nd ed. London: Pan, 1993 [1991].

Keith Tuma

Slobbering Distance

American, British, and Irish Exploratory Poetries in a Global Era

If you look for it, you can find on the Web an odd little performance by cris cheek. Opening his mouth three times in the awkward slow motion of primitive internet video, calmly and rhythmically, like a goldfish almost, cheek's fifteen-second sequence reveals, word by word, each word a slip of paper in his mouth, a phrase: "distance no object." The video tongue of this English performance poet, glint in his eye, surely wags at us. But is it "distance [is] no object" we hope to read, as in "distance—no problem," a proposition concerning our shrinking worlds? Or does "distance" refer less geographically to some social or psychological space, here objectless, to auratic power reconfigured in cyberspace—distance *sans* destination, no arrival possible, just a melancholy liminality? One might very well wonder whether it is optimism concerning the communicative or aesthetic possibilities of the internet which is indicated, or if these three words imaged plump in the mouth instead ironically allude to while performing erasures of bodily presence and speech texture, utterance. Networked rather than localized, traversing boundaries with an ease unimaginable not so many years ago, cheek's sequence is theoretically available instantaneously and anywhere, even as the ways we have of understanding it and that availability are limited and I must remember that not just anybody is likely to stumble upon it without some prior knowledge of what one would like to call the community of exploratory poets, performers, and critics "put up" in the e-space where his author page is housed.[1] Happenstance hits by technologically empowered surfers might very well result in reactions very different from my knowing smile morphing into bemused smirk—depending on the site of the computer and the history of the computer-user suddenly confronted with this cheeky spectacle.

I want to read cheek's performance as tending toward ecstatic proposition, something akin to a futurist spasm announcing a new world and the irrelevance of the old, the avant-garde as it might have looked before avant-gardism was only theory, as compulsive disorder or desperate iteration, something as basic as "Look, Mom, no hands!" I want to read it as a manifesto for nomadic navigation toward some post-national future of cross-cultural and cross-artform engagement that we know little about and want to make. But the smirk comes with its obverse ironized reading tagging along, conscious that the word-image-film here cannot and will not give us what it promises: a world without distances, a dream anyway absurd and impossible and perhaps even dangerous enough to belong with curios like world government and universal language. Distance might be made more present in this performance, more tangible, even as the proposition refuses it. That cheek is not unaware of such potential ironies is suggested elsewhere by his poem "Stranger," where he writes, "Well, so everything is possible" and then adds sarcastically, "Now who's brought the cash?" (35). The promise of the moment up against materialities of various orders: words in the film-mouth will not slobber while everywhere we are slobbering, trying to figure out if we can figure out what to do and how we will know if anyone has noticed and what difference it might make.

The space between possible readings of cheek's text, between what one might call ironic and techno-arcadian inflections, is exactly the "space" now anxiously but also excitingly occupied by Anglophone poetries of the developed West, where virtual worlds are on the verge of transforming (if they haven't already done so) most of what we know as poetry and poetics. This is not the essay in which to discuss how all that is collapsing or emerging today in Ireland, Britain, and North America might elsewhere be dependent upon or oblivious to or awkwardly situated beside smothered locations left offline, resourced for labor, material, and goods. For the part of the Anglophone world I am concerned with, and more especially for the "exploratory poets" within it, the proposition that "distance [is] no object" raises and endlessly reiterates with increasing urgency speculation about globalization that is itself, like most theory these days, belated, futile perhaps, except as it might produce and reproduce the anxieties or excitement it means to address. What does or will globalization mean, some ask—as if that would be one or even a hundred things—symptoms, practices; as if one could stand outside the process and nod like an angel in a Wim Wenders film. Will globalization result in homogeneity, those notorious MacWorlds, synonymous with what some call Americanization, in a merging or partial or total erasure of manifold contexts and localities? How would this be different from what's always happened and happening in the destructive creation of cultures? Just faster? Will there be no THERE there soon—not even an American THERE perhaps, as we float off into some spinning ether of fantasy capital and capital image-texts? Could a nowhere of information leave us somehow wherever partly living in or dominated by a nospeech and no memory? How to go on? Now I remember! I'll go on forever: "I can remember when 'flesh too was once called ephemeral,'" John Wilkinson writes (3). Will globalization spawn difference rather than homogeneity, forcing identities and singularities "against all odds"? Or merely a survival strategy for all those seeking market niches for idiosyncratic cultural products and services? Maybe the etherbus will stop somewhere else altogether, or leave us sprouting like a billion pods infinitely connected and internally complex and in perpetual motion?

I wish I knew what globalization means or might mean, that's for sure, but I don't, and in that regard at least I am certainly not alone. As my daughter says lately, "You got it dude," to which I might add "and see what you can do with it." All I can point to, as if empirically, is the observation that, in the tiny, increasingly interwoven worlds of exploratory poetries, we are still some ways from hearing one another well enough to make either utopian or dystopian versions of the global—of the emergent cross-cultural mix—more than a curiosity or, worse, a rhetorical hammer. cheek's text-image is strangely empty, ambivalent as I take it up, it can be so easily batted about. It used to be that one would say that Americans were more prone to the utopian, declamatory mode of appropriating discourses of possibility, as one can still see for example in Charles Bernstein's recent efforts to name and sketch a transnational community of experimental poets joined in non-standard, oppositional, and "ideolectical" practice:

> The invention of an ideolectical English-language poetry of the Americas involves the replacement of the national and geographically centered category of English (or Spanish) poetry not with the equally essentialist category of American poetry but with a field of potentialities, a virtual America that we approach but never possess. English languages, set adrift from the sight/sound sensorium of the concrete experiences of the English people, are at their hearts uprooted and translated: nomadic in origin, absolutely particular in practice. Invention in this context is not a matter of choice: it is as necessary as the ground we walk on. ("Poetics of the Americas" 5)

The Emersonian echoes here (via Stanley Cavell) seek to describe lines of affinity and commonality uniting exploratory poetries across traditional boundaries, most of those involving the nation. Bernstein would describe a multinational, multicultural panoply of poetries joined in "cultural resistance" (11) not just throughout the Americas but also, we learn later in the essay, in England and Scotland as well—the representative poets in these locales being Maggie O'Sullivan, Tom Raworth, and Tom Leonard.

The umbrella that Bernstein is trying to hold here cannot, it seems, convince just everyone that it is time to come in out of the rain. Words from this same essay, excerpted and posted on a British-based poetics listserv which itself came into being partly as an effort to duplicate for international (mostly British and Australian) purposes what Bernstein himself had accomplished by starting a poetics listserv in Buffalo—that is, creating an online forum for exploratory poetry and poetics—fell just a little flat. They obviously irritated the Scot Robin Purves, who resisted the effort to gather his compatriot Tom Leonard into this transnational community. Part of Purves's hesitation involved his sense that Leonard's struggle as an oppositional Scots poet has more to do with the concrete than with virtual realities, that it has to do precisely with the nature of a Scottish audience whose geographic, national, and class identities were well known. It was clear that, to Purves, Bernstein's rhetoric seemed airy, verging upon an escapist fantasy from someplace else, and, worst of all, with designs on him. Or this is how I read what was pretty much simply a gesture of refusal.[2] While even a non-standard, "ideolectical" Leonard poem such as "Jist ti Let Yi No," which rewrites the famous William Carlos Williams poem in Glaswegian slang, is marked by a debt and a declared allegiance to an international avant-garde practice that has had some of its greatest successes in transforming poetry and culture in the United States, it makes no more sense to call it a generically "avant-garde" or "ideolectical" poem than it does to call it an American poem. In the passage above, Bernstein insists on an "absolute particularity in practice," which makes sense as a gesture respecting differences and localities, but then busies himself gathering the world into his definitions.[3] This will be—for some time, I suspect—the fate of even well-meaning efforts to spawn a transnational or international discourse about poetry, perhaps especially about "oppositional" poetry imagining that it has cultural and political work to do. Such discourse will be hugely ambitious and it will rankle.

What makes Purves a little nervous, of course, is the idea of belonging to a party or group somebody else is naming, and moreover naming from a position of power in the United States. There is no denying the clout of someone like Bernstein these days; the so-called "mainstream" poetry or "official verse culture" he and others set themselves against has been clobbered if not defeated in the United States, chased into its several holes in MFA programs and the Academy of American Poets. While this poetry survives in abundance and has its own virtues, the serious academic capital in the United States, insofar as there is anything by way of serious academic capital to be had by trafficking in poetry or poetics, is increasingly elsewhere. One might mention just a few examples: Bernstein himself has had or will soon have work published by The University of Chicago Press, Harvard University Press, and Oxford University Press. MIT Press has just produced a huge anthology edited by Steve McCaffery and Jed Rasula, 600 pages of "innovative writing" going back through the centuries and framed by an editorial discourse of arcane erudition and occasional pataphysical play. This anthology, like the recent two-volume University of California Press anthology edited by Jerome Rothenberg and Pierre Joris, *Poems for the Millennium,* makes the case for understanding recent exploratory practices as grounded in international traditions—centuries old in Rasula and McCaffery's book. In just the blink of an eye, it appears, the oppositional or the marginal can become the canonical, if the canonical can still be said to exist among such a proliferation of texts. English poets, Scottish poets, Irish poets might very well be forgiven for feeling the need to do what is possible in order not to be left behind by such impressive activity; they are obviously learning from it and beginning to produce comparable books, such as Clive Bush's recent critical tome on an accompanying anthology of Mottram-group poets.[4] (One notes, however, that this book authored by a British academic critic is produced by tiny Talus Books.) But while the situation is changing by the second, British and Irish exploratory poetry is only beginning to enter academic worlds.

If all of the exploratory poets at the Assembling Alternatives conference were bound by one thing, it would have been the sense that new or increased dialogue was desirable, but transnational or international communities of exploratory poets will be fools to imagine that new dialogue and community in or about poetry has much of a chance against international consumer culture—even if it does secure a global academic foothold. The British poet-critic D. S. Marriott names the global condition with a healthy realism when he reminds us that "This worldwide dominance of information technology and mass culture as spectacle has made the poetic work, whether conceived as a discrete record of personal experience or as an ongoing postmodern performativity or negative dialectic, extremely antiquated. Technologies of the word which allow marginal or medium publishing houses to continue circulating radical poetries and poetics seem almost quaint" (76). Indifference is global but also context-specific, produced by different national and local narratives, by specific institutional and economic realities. A generic avant-garde agonism—the desperate, brazen or stoic stake in some future—responds as it has for some time with statements such as Bernstein's suggestion that poetry "instructs us to count differently," that "poets don't have to be read, any more than trees have to be sat under, to transform poisonous societal emissions" (226). This is probably not so helpful. In doing the kind of work we need to continue to do in reimagining the institutions of poetry, and the ways in which poetry and performance might intersect with institutions and venues it has lately been isolated from, we are better off to remember with Bob Perelman that "in considering reading and the public sphere, some sense of number has to obtrude" (82). Such a pragmatic supplement to Bernstein's utopianism knows that even a dispersive poetic and critical practice such as Bernstein's own benefits, however slightly, from the more stable, slow, and ongoing mediations of institutions. One foothold is better than none if not enough. It has been our limited good fortune in the United States to have witnessed American exploratory poets such as the "language poets" able, slowly but surely, to engage segments of what is by British and Irish standards a large and stable university public. At the same time, exploratory poetry in Britain has had to invent institutions that we would do well to emulate in the United States, such as the performance writing and live writing programs at Dartington College of Arts, programs that resist the genre-bound categories still obtaining in too many institutions in the United States.

From the United States, it can sometimes seem that the struggles of exploratory poetry in Britain today duplicate the struggle of "language poetry" ten or fifteen years ago. Drew Milne's remarks of a few years ago noting a "hostility to traditional literary criticism and literary theory" among poets fueled by "a justifiable scorn shown to contemporary poetry by British academic literary critics" are still relevant. Exploratory poets in the States not so long ago were heard to mutter something like this to academics in order to get their ear: you are right to ignore this untheorized, suburban practice when we speak your language and it doesn't. What Milne hopes to stir up—a poetics, a discourse concerning innovative poetry—has been precariously but tenaciously in place for some time in the United States, first outside and then increasingly inside the academy, most recently moving outside academic spaces again. Exploratory poetry and the critical discourse that helps sustain it in Ireland lags behind Britain when it comes to making inroads in the university. Thus it lacks that sanction, for better or worse. To the extent that Irish poets such as Randolph Healy and Catherine Walsh have readers at all, they are almost entirely readers in Britain and the United States, while the Irish poets most read and sanctioned both at home and abroad have been poets who have traded on Irishness rather than "formal experiment." Michael Smith once described "the retardation of Irish society under the yoke of British imperialism" as having produced a situation where "the Irish poet's passport to success in London has always been his provision of local interest or colour; a regional voice, essentially diversionary" (156).

Let me try to make my one point in a slightly different way. The most impressive political work of that loosely affiliated group of recent American exploratory poets known as "language poets" had less to do with the politics of the sign than it had to do with the on-the-ground labor of sustaining networks of presses, distributors, and readers. As Hannah Weiner jokingly wrote in *Spoke,* the "language poets" seem to have known from the beginning that "they want[ed] the most publicity they can get" (7) and adjusted their tactics accordingly. They were opportunistic, if opportunism means using what was available by way of NEA grants and the like and building on that. But perhaps a still more crucial tactic was the pursuit of the legitimation offered by academic appointments and publications—the so-called "theory" advanced by language poets was instrumental here. I know that some in the American poetry world like to speak of this as "selling out," but I find it otherwise. By finding or occupying subdisciplinary and disciplinary niches already opened partly by predecessors among the New American poets in the expansive and hybrid American university, language poetry put itself in a position to challenge not just so-called "mainstream" poetry but also existing canons and critical methodologies, plugging itself into a "tradition of the new" that is far from solely American but perhaps exists as most American and most powerful when it is thought of as a tradition. Knowing that language poetry has had at least limited success in American universities, one reads with regret of what R. J. Ellis has called a "convention of critical silence" among alternative poets in Britain (74), or of what Milne calls "agoraphobia": "a patrician reluctance of small-press poets to write prose commentary on their own work or the work of others" (59); "hibernation strategies which envisage a futurity whose solace is retrospective" (28).

For all the gloom in these remarks by Ellis or Milne, the current situation of exploratory writing in England might well be viewed as encouraging, especially if one compares statements coming from elsewhere in the United Kingdom. In Scotland, according to Robert Crawford, the "infrastructure" necessary to support exploratory writing is altogether lacking. Crawford can only hope that "greater sympathy . . . be given to the predicament of a Scottish literary avant-garde" (30), which has been represented by one or several isolated writers—Hugh MacDiarmid, Ian Hamilton Finlay, Tom Leonard. Next to Milne's proposal for newly energized discourse as potential cure for defeatist resignation and public apathy, Crawford's essay seems timid, a near-total surrender. This is chastening for the American reader, as is knowledge of the situation of related poetries in Ireland, where one or two university-based critics like J. C. C. Mays and Alex Davis work nearly alone to keep modernist traditions such as those represented by the work of Thomas MacGreevy and Brian Coffey alive and in print while much of the Irish poetry world seems locked in a repetition compulsion chewing over the claims of the political on the one hand and the aesthetic on the other. If exploratory poetry in England struggles to gather its energies into active, communal discourse, to sustain just a few journals for such activity and to continue making small inroads into the university, similar poetries in Scotland and Ireland struggle merely to appear. Knowing of such differences really does bring distance "home" to an American reader.

Drew Milne's "community of risk" is meant to speak and apply to British communities, but it might be extended to include nascent transatlantic communities as well. It is predicated on a desire to resist a "conspiracy of expertise" or the "appearance of exclusivity," for this has too often, especially in Britain it would seem, been the "defeatist" response to wounds inflicted by a "culture industry." One post-Adornean justification for avant-garde "difficulty" and "hermeticism" has bred what Milne calls a "tyranny of expertise"; the task is instead to transform contemporary poetry's "vulnerability" into an avant-garde that is "open." In order to create a vital community or poetic practice, Milne thinks, British poets will have to become less wary of "direct statement" and less hostile to "collective criticism," willing even to risk "the embarrassment of manifestos." Pointing to the limited success of anthologies such as *A Various Art* (1987) and *The New British Poetry* (1988) in encouraging discourse, Milne writes that the goal must be to "clarify the challenge of such diverse projects, without blurring critical differences or denying the specific localities and experience which make such communities possible" (29). Charles Bernstein is quoted approvingly for having written of his and others' success in creating "communities of response" in the United States, and without obliterating the "conflicting" pathways of individual poets; this points to the status of the American example in Britain, as mentioned above. By way of contrast, Milne mentions the reluctance among English poets such as Peter Riley to acknowledge the existence of a "Cambridge School," a reluctance that must be somewhat painful for Milne given his professed desire to model critical exchange in his journal *Parataxis* after the exchange of letters among J. H. Prynne, Andrew Crozier, and Riley—all of them associated with Cambridge and the origins of such a purported "school"—in *The English Intelligencer.*

In his conference paper at Assembling Alternatives, Peter Middleton echoed Milne's concerns while demonstrating the deep roots of anti-collectivism and individualism in English ideology—I thought immediately of Wyndham Lewis's 1914 Vorticist manifesto proclaiming "an art of Individuals," Lewis's Stirnerian response to the enthusiasms of Italian Futurists. But it can't be merely specific national narratives or counternarratives that prevent collectivity in English or British poetry, but rather these in combination with real material limits as banal as the structure of education and publishing and the size of economies and art economies. Perhaps the English seem to be doing well in generating and supporting new poetries when compared to the Irish and Scots but not so well when compared to peers in the United States—where everything is happening, one hears some younger British poets utter lately—in part because, as simple as it sounds, North American economies are large enough to sustain more market niches in poetry.

I take it as an article of faith—exactly—that poetry can and will make its way and poets find their transnational affinities regardless of all the odds against them and it. One can read the work of the Irish poet Maurice Scully (or Billy Mills) and recognize affinities with American Objectivist practice as well as with the work of particular poets in the north of England who found Objectivism via Basil Bunting, via the visits of Robert Creeley, and by other means. Allen Fisher's debt to the Objectivist Louis Zukofsky is different from Mills' in Ireland or Richard Caddel's in Durham, less circumscribed by direct observation and *condensare.* Detailing such affinities and differences is important, but what I am suggesting here is that it is not enough for us—in this case for American readers—to know what is going on in this or that work, or from where it might or might not derive: we must also know what the work is likely to confront as it makes its way in its local worlds. To be attentive not only to the specificities of the work but also to its reception as that occurs in and changes across various locales—that would be the task of an informed transnational "community of risk."

How ready are Americans to hear, for instance, Robert Sheppard's words about his work co-editing an anthology of London poets, *Floating Capital* (1991)? Putting together this book, which found its publisher in Connecticut, Sheppard "was concerned that a crude form of cultural imperialism" did not "take hold." While "language poetry" had been important to some of the contributors to his anthology, Sheppard wrote, he wanted to "stress the British context for this work" (60). He was remembering the sixties and the seventies, when the perception that British exploratory poets were too much influenced by several among Donald Allen's New American poets had enraged and energized reactionary forces in Britain. How to avoid making one's work vulnerable to such predictable responses? Should one worry about them? To an American this might all seem merely anxiety, but we must be able at least to hear and understand it. Or, to offer another example, how might Americans hear Peter Riley when he insists that this same "American moment" in British poetry to which Sheppard refers was "over" by 1965; or that there is really no reason for British readers to read Ted Berrigan at all when the very different but British poet Gavin Ewart is homegrown and offers pretty much what can be found in Berrigan, a "species of deliberately wasteful or 'light' poetic which had a terrific bite at times" (15)? Are we sufficiently aware of the context of such remarks and of pertinent differences in the British poetry world? While everyone at Assembling Alternatives seemed to listen attentively, and networking went on more or less furiously, I left with the impression that I had come with: Americans typically know a whole lot less about contemporary British poetry than the British know about contemporary American poetry. We might in the United States acknowledge how self-obsessed we are or appear to be, and how even a declared internationalism might, when translated to British contexts, become entangled there in anxieties concerning American cultural imperialism. I name or include my own ignorance in these remarks.

It's not that I hope that a respect for distances, real or imagined, shrinking or even increasing, will result in some timidity or civility or a version of liberal tolerance or multinational pluralism. A "community of risk" must risk evaluation and contention. The caution with which Charles Bernstein has narrated his own forays into the British poetry world is exemplary, but I don't regret that, in the end, it wavers before preference and judgment. For example, several years ago in *Sulfur,* Bernstein reviewed *A Various Art* and *Floating Capital* together with *The New British Poetry* and *VerbiVisiVoco,* a Writers Forum collection of 112 poets:

> On a recent trip to England I was able to pick up additional material, only to realize how much more I had missed—how much the intense cultural differences between the U.S. and the U.K. make it easy, despite shared words and formal concerns, to miss crucial social and class contexts as well as unstated assumptions. Types of class antagonisms and gender prerogatives are played out in the alternative poetry scenes in the U.K. in ways that are more marked, and dispiriting, than in the U.S. (where class and "society" values nonetheless play a crucial legitimating function for official verse culture). Certainly it is striking how many current collections and anthologies of alternative British poetry include few or virtually no women. At the same time, a particular range of aesthetic procedures seems to be propped up by a patrician decorum and Oxbridge authoritativeness that barely covers over the thematic renunciation of these values. ("Leaking Truth" 205)

I prefer this to the softer if more ambitious coalition building on display in the more recent essay quoted above. Nothing is accomplished by allowing one's respect for the differences of a British context altogether to forestall declarations of interest. As Tom Raworth said to me once, "I don't want a square bicycle wheel just because it was made down the road." Americans can't abandon rigorous evaluation if British poetry is to be heard again in the United States. Bernstein's setting of the poets of *Floating Capital* "in sharp contrast" with those of *A Various Art,* his contrasting of the former's commitment to "open and new forms" and the latter's tenacious commitment to an "unobtainable lyric" and "pastoral (or postpastoral forms)" (206) may oversimplify but at least it does not waffle. At the same time one regrets an unnecessary static that can emerge from spurious attributions of sincerity or insincerity of motive, such as when Bernstein writes that the poets of *A Various Art* are only "ostensibly dedicated to alternative poetics" because they "display a corrosive dismissiveness toward exploratory works that are radically skeptical of the rhetorical grounding of both sprung and traditional lyricism" (206).

Similarly, if we examine one critique of language poetry associated with a few Cambridge poet-critics, we see that it concerns not poems but a few propositions extracted from a critical prose. Discussions of the politics of poetic form and of the role of the reader in language poetry are picked at for their naive optimism or unrigorous formulation, as British critics reject the notion that writing can be instrumental by virtue of its mode and the idea that specific poetic modes require of the reader more or less active hermeneutic roles. J. H. Prynne opts out of the utopian dimensions of Steve McCaffery's poetics—against the promise that language poetry's "de-referenced sign system" will leave the reader "free to opt for useful waste or wasteful utility" he poses the "classic freedom to eat cake" and the illusory freedoms of the supermarket as an apt analogue.[5] Anthony Mellors argues that particular phonic and typographic practices merely "represent the priority of the libidinal drives instead of actually effecting libidinal praxis" (86); D. S. Marriott more contentiously asserts that language poetry fetishizes the signifier and presents an "aesthetics of disavowal" which should be understood as "phobic" response to "the traumatic excess associated with referential markers of sexual and racial difference" in American culture (77). Some of these criticisms offer a contextualism in response to what is taken to be a formalism, but they give too little credit to the performative dimensions of "language poetry" poetics and can be guilty of reducing multiplicity and even incoherence in polemical writing on poetics to a few (discredited) propositions. It might be that several of the British readings of language poetry's manifestos, offered in the name of a contextualism, are not themselves sufficiently contextualized; until very recently, and with a few exceptions such as Peter Middleton and Ken Edwards, British poet-critics were not particularly attentive to the many varieties of poetic practice associated with "language poetry"—to the differences between the "new sentence" and other modes, for instance.

And the static emanating from Britain can indeed divide and obfuscate rather than open up discussion of real differences and productive evaluation. For all of his good intentions, his "community of risk," and his admiration for Bernstein's "community of response," Drew Milne's exchange of letters with Allen Fisher in *Parataxis* ends up demonstrating the difficulty of locating terms even to begin discussion with, revealing instead Fisher's understandable resistance to phrases like "the persistence of lyric." When Milne asks Fisher whether it is possible to speak of his procedures as combining "an Olsonian kind of open field together with procedures drawn from language poetry" (29), a hint of condescension is evident. Fisher responds by guessing that Milne didn't mean to be insulting and by offering a list differentiating amongst the American magazines and persons the "language poetry" group-label typically subsumes, indicating the poets and American precursors his own work might be said to have engaged. Such jockeying does not indicate a "community of risk" but rather a spasm of rhetorics and, sadly, it can be too typical of the acrimonious culture of criticism in Britain's small poetry journals. If Fisher is right not to stand for Milne's use of "language poetry" as a semi-scurrilous epithet, neither should Americans.

Still, I do not want to be critical of Milne's or any other discourse here, for it represents the start of something anyway. Static indicates transmission underway, which is more than we had not so long ago. "Distance no object" might be revised, right here and now. Slobber distance, we might say; make it both messy and real, desirable and a nuisance, prolific of enclaves and destructive of provincial ambitions. Let us slobber past all purities and excessive pride of place. Let us leave our own national anxieties at home while remembering that others have theirs we should try to learn something about. Let us keep distance alive as it's dying, if it is, but by all means without reifying it. The best plan is no plan, mostly, but simply to let what is already happening—or beginning to happen—go on, and without needing to make it go on in some systematic fashion. It's not that we can afford to be inactive or apathetic or to continue in some blissful darkness—far from it—but rather that any scheme for building community and dialogue might end up void of the critical contention actually needed to make and sustain poetic community—with stops and starts, with fits and tantrums, with real dialogue and mock manifestos both, e-events and a reading down the block. This is not a manifesto, but neither does it dismiss the need for them.

Notes

1. cris cheek's performance can be found at his author page at the Electronic Poetry Center of the University of Buffalo.
2. Robin Purves's comments were made on the Poetryetc listserv organized by John Kinsella; see the archives at poetryetc@listbot.com beginning on 9/22/98. Purves began by writing, "My first reaction to the quotation was to paste it over the peculiarly awful Scottish situation, successive headcases having tried to create a virtual Scottish poetry, succeeding, but bequeathing a field of virtualities almost entirely devoid of potential. . . . Nothing I have read of Tom Leonard's work leads me to believe that he'd have much or any truck with Bernstein's rhetoric." One assumes that one particular "headcase" Purves has in mind is Hugh MacDiarmid, whose "synthetic" Scots worked at some distance from the actual lived dialects of groups (and classes) in Scotland, which would seem to be of more interest to Leonard. See also my third footnote below.
3. Bernstein writes the following of "ideolectical" practice, contrasting it with the "dialectical": "Any comparison of ideolectical and dialectical poetry must confront this obvious contradiction: dialect, understood as nation language [Bernstein is discussing Kamau Brathwaite], has a centripetal force, regrouping often denigrated and dispirited language practices around a common center; ideolect, in contrast, suggests a centrifugal force moving away from normative practices without necessarily replacing them with a new center of gravity, at least defined by self or group. Furthermore, the social positions from which these practices emerge will often be quite distinct. Dialect poets may be regarded by the dominant literary culture as outsiders, but they are often also at the center of collective formations that are struggling to obtain self-respect and cultural legitimacy. Ideolect poets often eschew the center with which they may be associated by education or social position, to the point of refusing the collective identities with which they might otherwise be identified." "Poetics of the Americas" 7.
4. See Clive Bush, *Out of Dissent: A Study of Five Contemporary British Poets* and Clive Bush, ed., *Worlds of New Measure: An Anthology of Contemporary British Poets,* both books published by Talus Books in London in 1997.
5. Prynne's remarks were made originally in a letter to Steve McCaffery and were published in *Language Issue* #1, as addressed to "Ashley Hales."

Works Cited

Bernstein, Charles. "Comedy and the Poetics of Political Form." In *A Poetics*. Cambridge: Harvard University Press, 1992, 218–28.

———."Leaking Truth: British Poetry in the '90s," *Sulfur* 35 (Fall 1994): 204–12.

———. "Poetics of the Americas." *Modernism/Modernity* 3. 3 (September 1996): 1–23.

cheek, cris. *Stranger.* Lowestoft: Sound & Language, 1996.

Crawford, Robert. "Thoughts about a Scottish Literary Avant-Garde." *Gairfish* (1992): 26–31.

Ellis, R. J. "Mapping the U.K. Little Magazine Field." In Robert Hampson & Peter Barry, eds. *New British Poetries: The Scope of the Possible.* Manchester: Manchester University Press, 1993, 72–103

"Hales, Ashley" (J. H. Prynne). *Language Issue* #1, n.p., n.d.

Leonard, Tom. "The Proof of the Mince Pie." In *Intimate Voices* 1965–1983. Newcastle upon Tyne: Galloping Dog Press, 1984, 65–71.

Marriott, D. S. "Signs Taken for Signifiers: Language Writing, Fetishism and Disavowal." *fragmente* 6 (1995): 73–83. See the reprinted version in the present volume p. 338.

Mellors, Anthony. "Out of the American Tree: Language Writing and the Politics of Form." *fragmente* 6 (1995): 84–91.

Milne, Drew. "Agoraphobia, and the embarrassment of manifestos: notes toward a community of risk." *Parataxis* 3 (1993): 25–39.

———. "Cottage industries and agoraphobia revisited: further notes on risk." *Parataxis* 4 (Summer 1993): 58–69.

Perelman, Bob. *The Marginalization of Poetry: Language Writing and Literary History.* Princeton: Princeton University Press, 1996.

Sheppard, Robert. "Recognition and Discovery in the 1980s." *fragmente* 2 (Autumn 1990): 60- 61.

Smith, Michael. "The Contemporary Situation in Irish Poetry." In Douglas Dunn, ed., *Two Decades of Irish Writing: A Critical Survey*. Manchester: Carcanet, 1975, 154–65.

Riley, Peter. "Spitewinter Provocations: An Interview on the Condition of Poetry." *Reality Studios* 8 (1986): 1–17.

Weiner, Hannah. *Spoke.* Los Angeles: Sun & Moon, 1984.

Wilkinson, John. "Structure." *The Gig* 1 (November 1988):3.

My thanks to Nathaniel Dorward for assistance which helped make this essay possible.

Trevor Joyce

Irish Terrain

Alternate Planes of Cleavage

In the post-conference correspondence posted to the EPC (Electronic Poetry Center) website, Marjorie Perloff remarked: "It remains wholly unclear to me . . . what makes some of the people who read or performed 'linguistically innovative' or 'alternative'". While this is in many ways a fair point, I would suggest that it contains within itself some of the resolution of its own puzzlement: need it really be spelled out that in order to judge the degree to which work is 'alternative' or 'innovative', it must first be experienced within the context in which it has taken on its shape and meaning? From what base does it innovate? To what is it an alternative?

In my own paper, delivered at the beginning of the first full day of the conference, I attempted to anticipate this reaction, and to answer it, in relation to at least some of the Irish work there:

> When Romana Huk invited me here, she asked me how would I feel presenting my work, with its use of a comparatively standard syntax and narrative technique, in a forum made up largely of writers who had abandoned such supposed residues? . . . But every encounter must have an eye to the local terrain, and that in Ireland has been quite different from that in the U.S., though many of the same figures, particularly Pound, have been exemplary in both campaigns, so let me, without any claim to exhaustiveness, try to suggest a couple of factors which have determined or exemplified this difference.[1]

The point was echoed again on the final day of the conference in an altercation between Billy Mills and some of the North American poets present. Discussion had touched on whether the conference was representative of the variety of American alternative poetries. Billy intervened to point out its unrepresentativeness in a larger context: despite the declared focus in the conference program being "on four countries: Canada, Ireland, the U.K. and the

U.S.", the entire proceedings were almost wholly American-centered, he suggested, with the notion of the avant-garde being understood purely in American terms, and most specifically, in terms of Language poetry. The most pointed response came from Steve McCaffery: "Have you read these American poets you're talking about?" "Yes, but they haven't read me". Billy argued that British and Irish poetry was received there only in so far as it could be accommodated to U.S. models. The generous assembling of alternatives seemed threatened to polarize into assimilation or rejection.

While I am certainly not attempting here to isolate any "recognizably Irish quality," (to anticipate a later point), I do suggest that the planes of cleavage in Ireland may open quite differently from those in Britain, the U.S., Canada, or elsewhere, and, further, that those differences may be as interesting and productive as any similarities. Now, since it appears that one of the principal problems which bedevils 'alternative' poetry in every country is its exclusion from most general surveys, and hence the near-impossibility of getting information about it, I will attempt here to put on record, from my own perspective, some features of the local terrain to be negotiated by such poetry in Ireland.

In early '67, with Michael Smith, I co-founded New Writers' Press in Dublin, Ireland. The Press was dedicated to poetry and its name deliberately echoed Pound's call to 'make it new', which seemed highly relevant in the context of that time and place, which I have described elsewhere.[2]

> Yeats was securely installed at the summit of the Irish Parnassus. Immediately beneath him sprawled the other Twilighters. Up the slopes toiled Austin Clarke and Patrick Kavanagh, while Richard Murphy, Thomas Kinsella, and John Montague were safely through the foothills. There was a lower peak in the north of Ireland, a domestic K2 which had been settled by Louis MacNeice and John Hewitt.
>
> There was only one poetry press, the Dolmen, functioning in Ireland. Under Liam Miller it produced typographically beautiful editions. We admired it, but knew it wasn't going to cause any trouble to the existing order. In a pattern that will be familiar to those involved with women's writing, black writing, gay writing, and other such marginalia, the criteria by which Irish poetry was judged came from outside. The Irish article constituted a rustic variant of the metropolitan original, designed in London, and was distinguishable from it largely by its idiosyncratic subject matter: a rural setting, a spiritual folk, a primitive idyll. Further, this familiar marketable thing, the Irish poem, was invariably in the expressive mode: it took its theme from off the shelf, and told you, in lyric fashion, what the poet felt on the subject. (Joyce, "The Point of Innovation in Poetry", 20)

It's a complex and interesting question, why the '60s, so revolutionary in their impact elsewhere, should have produced such a conservative poetry in Ireland. Any answer must, I think, take account of the events in Northern Ireland whose increasing violence polarized Irish society from '68 on, and led even such a formally-aware poet as Thomas Kinsella to produce in "Butcher's Dozen" a piece of simplistic verse propaganda written in the immediate aftermath of Bloody Sunday. Significant also, I would suggest, was the nostalgia of many emigrant Irish, particularly the constituency of moneyed Irish-Americans, for the simplicities they fondly imagined to persist in Irish life. Their influence continues still in favouring a sort of airport-art variety of Irish poetry over any more troubling developments.

There were in the mid-'60s several magazines in Ireland which, under the direction of imaginative editors, had begun to publish work which broke the conventions. The best were *Poetry Ireland* under John Jordan, and *Arena* headed up by James Liddy. What New Writers' Press did was to channel this new writing under one recognized imprint, to surround it with a supporting context of criticism, and to offer young poets the chance of publication in book form, early enough to encourage them to innovate further. We also tried to present models of poetic innovation from other places and times.

The first volume issued by NWP contained a statement of editorial policy by Michael Smith, which indicated our intention to broaden rather than narrow the range of poetry available, with one necessary proviso:

> Most of the poets whose work will be included in this series are Irish and under thirty. Believing poets should be beyond the herd-instinct, they belong to no school, movement, club or clique. They are all serious poets—that is, human beings for whom writing poetry is, morally, a profoundly central activity, not a mere hobby or ornamental grace. (Smith, "Introduction to New Irish Poets" in *Sole Glum Trek*)

Over three decades, NWP made available innovative work by many contemporary Irish poets, including early or initial collections by several names now familiar in the Irish mainstream, but at the time we first published them, these writers were a welcome change from the previous orthodoxy. The problems with them arose later, when, having established some distinguishing trademark style which went down well with the Irish public, they fell into the rut of readings, interviews and television appearances, never reemerging to take another risk.

We also published non-Irish poets who were doing interesting things in English, including Jack Spicer, whose *Billy the Kid* we issued in '69,[3] and brought out a wide range of work in translation, including Vallejo, Ingeborg Bachmann, and the first volume entirely given over to Borges' poetry to be published in English anywhere in the world, so far as I am aware.

In '69 also we produced the first issue of *The Lace Curtain: A Magazine of Poetry And Criticism,* and issues 2 and 3 appeared the following year. This was intended as a general assault on Irish provincialism. As well as the work of our Irish contemporaries, we presented poetry by Kay Boyle, James Tate, Trakl,

Machado, and Gottfried Benn. The prose included Trotsky's analysis of the 1916 Easter Rising in Dublin.

By this time, we had started to have a discernible effect. A number of young poets emerged whose models were European or American, rather than Yeats or Auden, and we happily seized on what we saw of this as evidence of some success.

In the early '70s the Press entered on the second phase of its activity. Michael Smith had seen work by Brian Coffey in the pages of the *Irish University Review,* edited by Lorna Reynolds, and knew him as the editor of Denis Devlin's *Collected Poems.* He began a lengthy correspondence with Brian in early 1970, and with Brian's support, and expert direction, uncovered a number of Irish poets of the '30s whose overall, if only implicit, project seemed in significant ways continuous with ours. One of Brian's own lasting concerns was 'the elimination of the term irishness (sic) from the critical vocabulary' and he constantly urged Mike to use the Press towards that end; given its original aims, NWP needed little encouragement. Brian, however, could suggest the names and texts to support such a policy, which assisted Mike greatly in anthologizing the more interesting figures of the '30s, and also reinforced NWP's editorial focus through argument:

> The phrase: *recognizably Irish quality* is a bad one for either it refers to the purely physical effects of a biological kind and as such says nothing of interest about the poetry, or it sets up a very dubious criterion of a limiting kind almost certainly bound to bias the critical judgement which accepts it. . . . Poets work in words and how they work in words is the first object of a critic, not whether they are actually, nearly or remotely Irish. . . . (Coffey; personal letter to Michael Smith)

Under Brian's influence, NWP brought to light the work of an earlier generation of Irish experimentalists, who had begun their careers in the '30s, but whose work, not content to accept its provincial status, had subsequently been forgotten, with one notable exception, Samuel Beckett, though his fame was only grudgingly acknowledged in Ireland because of pressure from elsewhere. His poetry interested us with its lack of identifiably Irish furniture, its playfulness in terms of form and linguistic register, and its absolute avoidance of mastery, perhaps the most poisonous element in Yeats's legacy for his successors in Ireland.

One of the contacts made possible through Brian was Niall Montgomery. Niall designed the cover of the third *Lace Curtain* for us, but resisted our attempts to get from him for publication a collection of his own poetry. His few public readings were startling events. A small slim man in a three-piece pinstripe suit, with neat silver hair and carefully trimmed moustache, he gave extraordinary vocal performances against a background of shifting visual images, mixing and switching registers of language in wholly unexpected ways. They made all other readings of that period seem very tame. We eventually prevailed against his lack of literary ambition, and he gave us the text of *Terminal,* his selected poems, with permission to bring it out when we were ready. The reasons underlying Niall's lack of ambition for literary fame, which delayed the collection of his work, are obscure to me, but they seemed to centre around the apparent contradiction between his literary persona and the other parts of his life (he was a highly successful architect in Dublin), generating a sense that perhaps he had sacrificed the one for the other. This conflict continues still, with the resistance of Niall's family to the publication of his work, despite approaches by ourselves shortly after his death, and, most recently, by Christopher Cahill of the American Irish Historical Society. Once again, it appears, the genuinely innovative in Irish poetry is being repressed in favour of more 'respectable' imperatives.

> MANUAL PATHOLOGY in the traditional hang-nail
> manner
> cold tarred blazing of venetian blinds in the day-weary
> blind lids
> treble smell of piety lining the throat where the spine
> screeches
> how to invest in importance with the energy of rejected
> pleasures
> selling everywhere at a tremulous descant [4]

Niall was a significant figure in the more general Irish literary context, providing a link between Joyce and Beckett on the one hand, and the frequently hostile Flann O'Brien on the other. His generous support for us extended so far beyond the merely literary as to get jobs for both Gerry Smyth, a NWP poet, and myself during the '70s as he had done some decades earlier for Flann O'Brien.[5]

Up to this time the editorial policy of the Press had never really been made explicit, but the discovery of this body of experimental work clarified a number of issues, and made us suddenly aware that what we had been doing was continuous, in certain significant respects, with the work of Beckett and the Irish poets whose work he praised and supported in his early reviews.

Our contact with Beckett was by correspondence, and through the agency of Brian Coffey and Con Leventhal, but he made it clear repeatedly, both in comments passed on through Brian and directly, that he wholeheartedly supported our efforts.

Beckett encouraged us to take some of his critical pieces from the '30s, unpublished since their first pseudonymous appearance, and use them with his name attached. One of these provided us an introduction to an edition of

MacGreevy's *Collected Poems*, while we took another almost as a manifesto (Beckett, 58–63). The argument was clear and seemed to us as relevant in the '70s as it had been forty years earlier: it distinguished between those poets who had sensed "the breakdown of the object . . . rupture of the lines of communication", and those who had not. Beckett left little doubt that his sympathies lay with the former, among whom he names MacGreevy, Devlin, Coffey, and Montgomery. We took this as axiomatic and sought out the work of those who had some notion what to do given such rupture.

Brian Coffey had returned from a spell of teaching in the United States, and had settled first in London, and then in the south of England. Encouraged by NWP, he began to write again, almost prolifically, without diminution of the energy of his language or his formal inventiveness, although in almost total isolation. We published his *Selected Poems.* It was only at the New Hampshire conference that I realized that, due to his domicile in England, Brian was an exemplary figure not just for us, but for many British experimentalists also. The small press which he ran from London and Southampton, Advent Books, produced short print-runs of new work by many poets, often designed and printed by himself.

The fourth issue of *The Lace Curtain* constituted a comprehensive anthology of writing by and about these writers which highlighted their achievement, but the real success of NWP's reclamation of these forgotten experimentalists of the '30s lay not in any modification of the canon of twentieth-century Irish poetry, which has been superficial at best, but in making this work available to those fellow-poets both at home and abroad who could identify with its risks and achievements, and who could proceed from there in their own writing.

The only established Irish poet who has shown any inclination to stray from a successful formula has been Thomas Kinsella, who abandoned the constrained formalism of his early work, and began to incorporate in his poetry political and psychological materials, particularly from Jung, in a variety of manners. Among the younger writers outside of the NWP circle, Hugh Maxton was evidently interested in experimental techniques. Though his output was perhaps too small and intermittent for him to build up any considerable following, it deserves attention. In *Passage,* for example, Maxton "arranges extracts, translations, quotations and tabulations in a tally amounting to an active meditation on western humanity's lemming-like rush to self-destruction". It is "followed by 'surviving poems' to signify a vestigial lyricism not wholly contaminated by the privacies of an illusionistic personal style" (Maxton, cover note).

The last major discovery for the Press was the work of Geoffrey Squires, whose *Drowned Stones* we brought out in '75. Its abrupt transitions and juxtapositions of collage materials were much more radical and effective than in any other Irish poetry which had come to us. Squires continued developing new possibilities in his work, and his second volume from NWP, *Landscapes and*

Silences, had moved away from disjunctive techniques to construct new continuities in extended passages of meditation, similar in many ways to Beckett's late prose.

I have published elsewhere a history of the Press, complete with checklist of publications, so I'll not go into further detail here.[6] We produced few major volumes after the mid-'70s, and both Mike and myself felt confirmed in our isolation, and tired of trying to present a poetry of genuine risk to an apathetic readership. Mike turned to translation from the Spanish, and I to Chinese and Japanese models in my effort to produce a poetry I myself would want to read. We were both constrained to earn a living outside academia, and were effectively cut off from current developments in Britain and further afield.

When I attempted in New Hampshire to summarize the history of experimental poetry publishing in Ireland, I stopped here, with the lapse of New Writers' Press into a long sleep from the mid-'70s through the mid-'90s, troubled by occasional bursts of REM.[7] But at the Assembling Alternatives conference I met for the first time not only Geoffrey Squires, although NWP had already published two volumes of his work, but also Maurice Scully, Catherine Walsh, Billy Mills, and Randolph Healy, all of whom had been producing experimental poetry in Ireland for many years, without my ever having read them. My inadequate excuse for this is simply that their names are virtually unknown in Ireland, though I had, on one occasion, had them drawn to my attention. Along with James Hogan (another NWP poet, who published under the name Augustus Young) and myself, these had been mentioned by J.C.C. Mays in a ground-breaking article in 1990:

> Three writers discovered by New Writers' Press—Trevor Joyce, James Hogan ('Augustus Young') and Geoffrey Squires—struck me as the most original of their generation. . . . Yet Joyce and Squires have stopped publishing—and Hogan has gone away.
>
> . . . In more recent years, for example, a group of writers this time associated with *The Beau* made another attempt to pursue a kind of writing that was more than party tricks. . . . The result was a couple of books—an extraordinarily assured debut by Randolph Healy called *25 Poems,* some booklets by Billy Mills . . . and some exuberant, inventive collages by Maurice Scully. . . .
>
> . . . All they have in common with each other and across two generations is an impersonal interest in all poetic means available in the world at large, and a corresponding disinclination to settle for less than they might. (10–11)

Let me remark at this juncture that J.C.C. Mays (who currently holds the chair of English and American Literature at University College Dublin) is one of only two academics working in English studies in Ireland who have demonstrated in print any interest in or understanding of experimental Irish poetry. The other is Alex Davis, currently at University College Cork. That both are English says a great deal about the power of the (Celtic) Twilight zone.

Incidentally, in later correspondence with me, Jim Mays regretted forcefully his omission from his second group of poets of Catherine Walsh, whose work he had only since come to know and appreciate.

How had this more recent burst of activity come about? In the course of a recent conversation, "Maurice Scully recall[ed] that New Writers' Press introduced him to MacGreevy, Coffey and Devlin, whose work he found 'puzzling but intriguing'".[8] He himself started small-scale publishing in the early '70s with a brief series of poetry broadsheets, since he knew of no press likely to bring out the work he wanted to see published. He then edited the Trinity College magazine *Icarus* for a couple of years, and, after college, co-edited a journal called *The Belle* in Dublin in '79/80. In the early '80s under the imprint of The Beau Press, he published Randolph Healy's first volume, *25 Poems,* and also functioned briefly under the imprint of The Coelocanth Press.

As Maurice had become active just as NWP began to run out of steam, similarly in 1985, as Maurice withdrew from activity as a publisher, Billy Mills started hardPressed Poetry, joined a year later by Catherine Walsh. Aiming to publish themselves, initially, and other Irish poets who interested them, "plus non-Irish poets they felt should be read by the six or seven people in Ireland who were interested" (the words are Billy Mills'), they started in Dublin, and then moved on to Barcelona.

Billy and Catherine published sixteen volumes of poetry, including one by Tom Raworth, to celebrate his taking out an Irish passport.

David Lloyd was another Irish innovator, whose *Coupures* was published as a hardPressed volume. We first met David when, as a Cambridge undergraduate visiting his family in Ireland, he attended a NWP reading to mark the publication of my *Poems of Sweeny Peregrine* in '76. He was looking for a research topic, and we suggested to him that James Clarence Mangan would reward critical reappraisal as an avatar of sorts. David took up the suggestion, and his eventual reassessment of Mangan established that neglected figure as a nineteenth-century precursor of poetic experimentalism in Ireland. David's volume of essays on Irish culture, *Anomalous States,* has established him as one of the most influential literary and cultural critics dealing with Ireland, yet his work as an innovative poet is totally ignored.[9]

It is difficult to compare the Irish small-press scene with those in the U.K. and North America. Ireland in the '60s was a country drained by many decades of poverty and emigration. Its major literary figures were simultaneously occasions of pride and of shame—pride in their fame abroad, but shame either in the fact that many of the greatest had felt unwelcome here, or in the way their work flouted Irish norms. The habit of regarding publication and canonization as matters to be decided abroad, except in questions of nationality or religion, was deeply ingrained. There was no indigenous authority on matters of poetry, like the Poetry Society in England, where the mainstream could identify itself and be challenged; and since Irish universities maintained a lofty disdain of contemporary poetry, mainstream figures like Paul Durcan and Brendan Kennelly reached directly to a public audience for their poetry, their considerable success being measured in terms of entertainment value. Neither was there an established history of small-press alternatives to mainstream publishers, as in the U.S. As bookshops rarely if ever stocked alternative work from abroad, it was difficult to stay abreast of developments there. Literature in Ireland was a field of conflict, but it was the morality of works in the judgement of the Irish Censorship Board that made them controversial, and not their formal qualities.

Given the difficulties in getting books of experimental work under the present circumstances, Assembling Alternatives provided a great opportunity just to browse through acres of the stuff, getting a context for the papers and readings, and discovering things not mentioned elsewhere. A major find for me was the books of Tom Raworth, a writer with strong Irish connections whose work is highly suggestive given what passes for poetry in Ireland these days, but whose name is unknown to all but perhaps half a dozen readers here. Too often, perhaps, the champions of an alternative poetry in Ireland have been content to make that work known abroad, but have neglected to push it at home. New Writers' Press seems to have been the one, perverse and less than entirely successful, sustained attempt to bring innovative poetry before an Irish public.

Encountering such a range of poets, critics and editors suggested many new perspectives. I travelled by bus to the conference from Boston with Barbara Goddard, long-time member of the editorial board of *Tessera,* the Canadian feminist journal which brings together the politics of gender, language and nationality, all through formally innovative writing. That conversation focused for me some major questions as to why, in the parallel situation of Irish writing, Catherine Walsh is the only woman using such forms, and why she is so utterly marginalized, by poetry readers and feminists alike. It seems that in Ireland radical 'content' is permissible only through conventional 'form'.

For the first time, I heard informed and considered discussion of the possibilities offered by computer technology for the writing and presentation of poetry. I found the entire panel fascinating, but especially the presentation by Jim Rosenberg. I was lucky enough also to be able to buy from Joan Retallack the volume of conversations she had with John Cage just before his death, and Cage's mesostics made great sense in this context. This is the feature of the conference which has had most immediate and obvious effect in my own recent work, where I've used a computer spreadsheet to restructure my own 'conventional' text, then played the original and its transformations together in a complex weave (Joyce, *Syzygy*). It was here also that I first became aware of performance genuinely working as part of the texture of poetry, and I began to hope that some of the performers from the last night of AA could be got to Ireland soon, so that I could share the experience with others. I believe that the work of Niall Montgomery is much illuminated by being experienced alongside the work of cris cheek or Paul Dutton.

In Ireland, there are no second-generation Beats, or Black Mountain, or New York School to react to. There has really only been one literary movement here in this century. The Celtic Twilight achieved prominence partly because of its links with nationalist politics, and partly because of the quality of its major figure, Yeats. In consequence, pretty well all writers up to the '60s defined themselves in relation to this movement, either working from within it, as did Clarke and, to some extent, Kavanagh, or explicitly opposing it from outside, as did Beckett and his associates.[10] Beckett, though, was no polemicist in the manner of Pound or Carlos Williams or Olson. He quickly abandoned criticism and literary journalism to pursue his argument with Irish norms through the body of his poetry, prose and drama.

Also, in Ireland there has been minimal influence from 'creative writing' courses until the last ten years or so. Hence both mainstream and alternative poetries have, for better or worse, been unusually varied for such a small country.

The one major exception to this has been the Northern Irish school, where the influence of Hobsbaum deeply affected the development of poetry along the lines of the English 1950s. This alignment with the English mainstream had already been practiced by MacNeice. It was perfected by Heaney, Mahon, Longley, and others of their group, though Heaney, in particular, later included Kavanagh and Yeats among his models.

Neither, even, has the split between 'experimental' poetries and those of the mainstream always been as clean as one might expect. It is, for example, cause for surprise to me at least, that Walsh, Squires and Smith have a shared interest in the poetry of Austin Clarke, a frequent object of Beckett's disdain. A link to another, though internal, tradition is the common interest in translation from pre-modern Irish language poetry which can be found in Scully, Smith and in my own work.

It has been suggested by Billy Mills that one primary feature distinguishing the work of Walsh, Scully and Lloyd from that of the American Language poets lies in the refusal of the poets he named to grant language any priority in relation to the world, but rather to regard it as always fundamentally referential in whatever way.[11]

The effects of Assembling Alternatives are still resonating in Ireland. The next step was taken in Cork at the end of March '97, with a conference on Irish Experimental Poetry. It was organized to celebrate the thirtieth anniversary of New Writers' Press, and drew together, for a second time, Geoffrey Squires, Catherine Walsh, Billy Mills, Randolph Healy, Maurice Scully and myself, along with Judy Kravis, and Michael Smith. This was the first ever event of its kind in Ireland, and was so successful that it has become an annual fixture, now administered by Alex Davis. Scattered among the Irish participants at these events have been numerous others from the U.S., U.K. and Canada including cris cheek, Fanny Howe, Tom Raworth, Maggie O'Sullivan, Drew Milne, Karen MacCormack, Keith Tuma, Romana Huk, Harry Gilonis, Tony Baker, Ric Caddel, Susan Howe . . . the list goes on.

Another major development has been the success of Randolph Healy's Wild Honey Press, which is currently publishing the most exciting poetry appearing anywhere in Ireland.[12] It is a relief to see again an editor who is willing to bring out the work of contemporary Irish poets alongside the likes of Ron Silliman and Susan Schulz.

I have tried to argue that, without any native movement to oppose which could be taken at all seriously, Irish experimentalists have felt at liberty to appropriate "all poetic means available in the world at large", as Jim Mays put it. Perhaps the work of Irish innovators differs not just between themselves, but also in significant ways from what has happened in Britain, the U.S. and elsewhere. The fact that Heaney can be transported between continents with so little loss should not imply that those who have eschewed his facilities should be equally portable. Difficulties inevitably arise when specific explorations and achievements are lifted wholesale from their context, and interpreted in terms of another, external, agenda.[13]

The tug of Joyce, Beckett, and the other poets of the '30s has been strong enough to allow us to feel free of all hegemonies, whether from Britain, America, Europe or elsewhere, and to confirm to us that writing in Ireland can be radically innovative and independent without privileging any external authorities. We seek from nowhere the franchise to regard ourselves as innovators, or to provide a living alternative to those tendencies we find most intimately oppressive. We continue to read American, British, and other radical poetries with respect, sympathy, and sometimes with excitement. We look to have the same openness extended to us.

Notes

1. Joyce, "New Writers? Some Irish", unpublished.
2. For general perspectives on this period, see Michael Smith, Alex Davis, and Trevor Joyce's critical pieces. The volume *For the Birds* also contains an excellent bibliography of alternative Irish poetry. One aspect of 'experimentation' in Irish poetry not touched on by any of these sources is writing in the Irish language. Sean O'Riordan, who wrote only in Irish, appears to have been one of the most interesting

poets of the period, while Pearse Hutchinson, Michael Hartnett and Nuala Ní Dhomhnaill later did much of their work in Irish.

3. This had been brought to our attention by James Liddy, whose presence in California for much of each year linked him with the west coast gay scene, and gave us access to its poetry.
4. For details as originally published see Montgomery, 40. The version quoted here is as corrected by Niall Montgomery in the manuscript of *Terminal,* which is unpublished to this date.
5. Gerry still works at *The Irish Times,* and I only very recently left my job in Information Technology in the manufacturing industry to which Niall gained me access.
6. See Trevor Joyce, "New Writers' Press: The History of a Project" in *Modernism and Ireland: The Poetry of the 1930s,* Patricia Coughlin and Alex Davis, eds. (Cork: Cork University Press, 1995), pp. 276–306.
7. The most recent of these had seen the publication of Michael Smith, *Lost Genealogies;* Trevor Joyce, *stone floods;* and Geoffrey Squires, *Landscapes and Silences.*
8. Quoted by Keith Tuma and William Walsh in their introduction to the selection of five Irish poets in *Talisman: a journal of contemporary poetry and poetics* 18 (Fall 1998).
9. See David Lloyd's work listed in the Bibliography.
10. An interesting and somewhat isolated figure in this context is Louis MacNeice in that he, unlike Clarke and Kavanagh, was not swamped by Yeats's example, being rather a follower of Eliot himself. Hence, perhaps, the fact that he is able to write a critical study of Yeats, rather than merely sniping at him.
11. For a brief consideration of alternative Irish poetry in relation to Language poetry, see the Coda to Alex Davis, *Denis Devlin and Irish Poetic Modernism.*
12. Wild Honey books, like most other interesting small press publications from Ireland or Britain, can be obtained through Peter Riley (Books), 27 Sturton Street, Cambridge CB1 2QG, England.
13. This point is relevant not only to the questions raised by Perloff following AA, but also to the recent anthology edited by Ric Caddel and Peter Quartermain. Though five Irish poets are included, there is a remarkable gap between Coffey and Scully, Healy, Walsh and Mills, omitting the work of an entire generation of Irish experimentalists, and making it seem, to anyone not already familiar with the territory, that the more recent Irish innovators are responding to the British mainstream. I quote from Marjorie Perloff's comment on the book, circulated as part of its pre-publicity: "In the past two decades, British and Irish poetry have undergone a silent revolution. While the mainstream media present us with a 'Britain' still writing poetry under the sign of Philip Larkin or Ted Hughes, a number of strong oppositional voices have emerged, voices committed to a radical rethinking of the 'Movement' and its tepid aftermath. Ric Caddel and Peter Quartermain have produced an excellent anthology of this breakthrough poetry. No one interested in the 'turn' of poetry in the late twentieth century will want to miss it".

Bibliography

Archambeau, Robert. *Another Ireland.* Bray: Wild Honey Press, 1998.

Beckett, Samuel. "Recent Irish Poetry". *The Lace Curtain.* Dublin: New Writers' Press. Summer (1971): 58–63.

Cadell, Richard and Peter Quartermain. *OTHER: British and Irish Poetry since 1970.* Wesleyan University Press, 1998.

Coffey, Brian. Letter to Michael Smith. 8:ix:70.

Davis, Alex. *A Broken Line: Denis Devlin and Irish Poetic Modernism.* Dublin: University College Dublin Press, 2000.

Joyce, Trevor. "The Point of Innovation in Poetry". *For the Birds.* Ed., Harry Gilonis. Sutton: Mainstream Poetry Press, 1998, 18–26.

——. "New Writers' Press: The History of a Project". *Modernism and Ireland: The Poetry of the 1930s.* Cork: Cork University Press, 1995, 276–283.

——. "New Writers? Some Irish". Unpublished paper, 1996.

——. *stone floods.* Dublin: New Writers' Press, 1995.

——. *The Poems of Sweeney Peregrine.* Dublin: New Writers' Press, 1976.

Lloyd, David. *Anomalous States.* Dublin: The Lilliput Press, 1993.

——. *Nationalism and Minor Literature: James Clarence Mangan and the Emergence of Irish Cultural Nationalism.* Berkeley: University of California Press, 1987.

Maxton, Hugh. *Passage.* Bradford on Avon, 1985.

Mays, J.C.C. "Flourishing and Foul: Ideology, Six Poets and the Irish Building Industry." *The Irish Review* 8 (1990): 6–11.

Mills, Billy. "Other Places: 4 Irish Poets." *For the Birds.* Ed., Harry Gilonis. Sutton: Mainstream Poetry Press, 1998, 27–36.

Montgomery, Niall. "Blinds Somewhere Draw the Blinds." *The Lace Curtain* 4 (1971): 40–42.

Smith, Michael. "Introduction to New Irish Poets." *Sole Glum Trek.* By Trevor Joyce. Dublin: New Writers' Press: 1967.

——. *Lost Genealogies & Other Poems.* Dublin: New Writers' Press, 1993.

Squires, Geoffrey. *Landscapes & Silences.* Dublin: New Writers' Press, 1996.

Philip Mead

The American Model II

North and south, like east and west, belong to each other. The flow of imperial representations—West *to* East, North *to* South—is not uniform and predictable in reception, and may not even be unidirectional all of the time. As Stephen Greenblatt has remarked in the context of Indonesian villagers' uses of VCR technology, individuals and cultures on the receiving end of imperialisms have "fantastically powerful assimilative mechanisms, mechanisms that work like enzymes to change the ideological composition of foreign bodies" (4). In the analysis of cultural relations, we have learned from writers like James Clifford and Greenblatt how the *grands récits* always exist in relation to the *petites histoires*. This paper is concerned with some of the constitutive relations between the *grand récit* of US cultural imperialism (in Australia) and the *petite histoire* of radical writing since the 1960s. Australian literary discourse (particularly its subsets poetry and poetics)—an outpost and an independent settlement, postcolonial and metropolitan, a nowhere and a somewhere, a last frontier and a final resort—exists in specific and hybrid relations to the northern and global discourse of poetry and poetics. Radicality in poetic discourse, this paper argues, can't be read solely in terms of monocultural or singular historical contexts; it always exists in relation to other kinds of radical writing. The kind represented, for example, at the "Assembling Alternatives" conference in 1996. At the same time, to read radical poetries—even just Anglophone ones—as sharing some globalised genealogy and common project is to elide the specificities and tensions of cultural and political exchanges of (literary) language, especially incommensurabilities of cultural power. The questions that motivate this discussion, then, are how the (specifically Australian) poetic field is produced in its historical and political interchange with other (national and virtual) poetic fields and how that work of production relates to the complex and nationally/regionally specific "homology of language and social structure" (Derksen; 40). And lastly, given the various vectors and adaptations of the avant-garde in Australian poetic writing over the last thirty years, what kind of development does very recent work under that heading—an emergent (Australian) Language writing—represent?

The Fate of Freedom as an Export

The story of the influence of American poetry in Australia tends to alternate between first-person expressive accounts of authorial influence and broader narratives of political and cultural history. Whether inflected as personal or cultural, these narratives are all versions, structurally and thematically, of Freud's family romance: freedom emerges from the painful struggle with authority through growth and maturity.[1] Thus, at the level of the Australian poetic community and some of its repetitive narrativisations: stories about first reading Ginsberg, Duncan, Olson, O'Hara, Ashbery, Guest, Dorn, Berrigan, Rich (new authority figures to replace the English modernists and Movement poets); the ecstatic initial reception of Allen's *The New American Poetry* (a pure American product containing a new and richly heterogeneous poetic culture, complete with its own poetics); Australia as a New World nation with a breaking-off point like New England (however historically and ideologically different), but lacking dramatic expressions of political independence or founding figures of a democratic poetics (like Emerson, Whitman and Williams); England as the unthinkingly anglocentric and imperial mother (until around 1950); America as the postmodern step-father (after the mid-'60s).

Often the story emphasises local experience of cultural production and distribution: the earlier infiltration of Geoffrey Moore's (1954) *Penguin Book of Modern American Verse;* the Allen and Hall anthologies; stray issues of *Evergreen Review* that slipped past what were in the cold war era in Australia substantive censorship laws; a resistant strain of xenophobia (anti-Americanism) that expressed itself in immigration restrictions; the continuing colonisation of Australia by the copyright imperiums headquartered both in London and New York. Even today the copyright rules make it difficult and expensive to buy American books in Australia or to distribute Australian publications in the U.S. or the U.K., although the web is creating new and alternative possibilities of production and distribution for poetry and poetics (Wallace-Crabbe 43).[2] Bruce Dawe's account of his first contact with American poetry in the mid-1950s, for example, is the story of his encounter with a single book, the Geoffrey Moore anthology.[3] There is also a prehistory of U.S.-Australian poetic relations, going back to the nineteenth century (e.g., Charles Harpur and Emerson, Henry Kendall and Longfellow) and including publication and reviews of the Vorticist Ezra Pound in the [Sydney] *Bulletin* before 1914 as well as the efforts of 1920s and '30s radical national poets Frank Wilmot ("Furnley Maurice") and Bernard

O'Dowd to escape the dominant English models in favour of American exemplars—including Pound, but more particularly Whitman and Sandburg. These were largely ineffectual attempts to forge an alternative national poetic expression, one which foregrounded the social and political.[4]

Throughout the 1950s Hart Crane and Robert Lowell were variously incorporated into the work of poets like Francis Webb, Vincent Buckley and even James McAuley, but, excepting Webb, this was part of a dissident New Critical struggle against a dominant traditional/philological and Leavisite academic discourse of English Literature. Chris Wallace-Crabbe identifies the academic context of this brand of American import: "Among the immediate attractions of this American poetry [Marianne Moore, Stevens, Ransom, Lowell, Bishop, etc.] was the fact that it seemed not merely exotic but even mandarin" (47).

The most spectacular instance of American influence in Australian literary culture is defined by the group of postmodern or avant-garde writers, known as the Generation of '68, who emerge with the takeover of *Poetry Magazine* in 1971 and its transformation into *New Poetry*. It follows closely on the arrival in the early to mid-'60s of Donald Allen's once-banned anthology *The New American Poetry: 1945–1960* (1960) and Donald Hall's *Contemporary American Poetry* (published in London in 1962). This eruption of poetic energy in the early 1970s, which had already begun in the mid-1960s, was certainly catalysed by the importation of the New American poetry, but was probably also, simultaneously, an expression of a rising antagonism to the existing Australian tradition, distinctively native, but nevertheless inherited from and still in thrall to, "enfeebled English models . . . closely aligned with the conservative establishment that had dragged us into the shame of the Vietnam war" (Tranter, "Anaesthetics" 105). Olson, for example, according to Andrew Taylor, sounded more familiar than American, "something that broke with the hieratic literary speech of Australian poetry in order to sound like my own speech" (55). There were also, as Michael Wilding recognised, complex cultural and political factors at work, some of them global:

> Though the new writers [the Generation of '68] may not have consciously been concerned with expressing Australianism, though some would conceive of themselves as 'writers', as supra-nationals, the context in which they worked was Australian. Even at their most imitatively American, they demonstrated their Australianness in revealing the new domination of all areas of Australian cultural and economic life by the USA. Especially in the counter-culture. Indeed, this shift in emphasis to things American from things British is another framework in which to see the emergent new writing—a shift in the cultural centre for Australia created by the shift in the economic centre. (117)

This comment of Wilding's comes from one of a number of assessments of the advent of the new Australian writing that appeared in the late 1970s. The essays by Australian poets from a 1979 conference held at Macquarie University (Sydney) called "The American Model" (collected in Joan Kirkby's edited volume of the same name) is one of these assessments. They are an attempt to frame a widely representative critical response to the American influence of the '60s and '70s and to formalise its history. Kirkby's collection includes two critical essays by American poets Galway Kinnell and Louis Simpson who had visited Australia and attended the conference. The essays all deploy predominantly personalised and expressionist styles: what these Australian poets value in what they read as the antinomian, Adamic tradition of American poetry from Whitman on is perception and sensation, physicality of landscape representation, inwardness of subjectivity and (contradictorily) an awareness of self in social interaction, sophisticated formal innovation, the vulnerable human stance, and perhaps above all, ease of natural speech (Gilbert 351; Kirkby 2–3). This, in turn, is ratified by Kinnell's and Simpson's readings of Whitman, Poe and Williams.

It is an eclectic, uneven collection, uneasy about both its poetic and critical focus. Neither Simpson nor Kinnell, for instance, was associated with or even very sympathetic to the project of the *New American Poetry,* and none of the Australian poets or critics seems to have found a satisfactory language for what s/he is trying to express. The critical discourse of poetics in Australia, including these bio-historical narratives in Kirkby's collection, was a seriously underdeveloped one. Unlike its radical and heterogeneous object of study, the new Australian writing, it was a product of British- and New Criticism-derived academic critical discourse. Tranter is the contributor to the Kirkby volume who is most acutely sensitive to this problem. After censuring Christopher Pollnitz for a lame reading of Rae Desmond Jones's poem, "The Front Window," Tranter spends much of the remainder of his article in the attempt to suggest a flexible, poststructuralist framework for reading the work of the younger Australian poets. Tranter's proposal is too eccentrically reliant on elements of the aesthetic ideology and roped-in anthropology to be generally useful, but his instinct is correct: a postmodern critical discourse was lacking in Australia and what critical discourse was in circulation was inimical to innovative poetic practice. So to some extent, the Generation of '68 and, to a large extent, subsequent experimental and avant-garde poetries were either ignored or neutralised by the normative institutions of criticism in Australia. It is only with the advent of Language-influenced writing that a theoretically informed and flexible critical discourse on poetry and poetics has caught up with poetic practice.

A precursor to Kirkby's collection, also an expression of the mid- to late-'70s moment of critical consolidation, is Thomas Shapcott's trans-Pacific anthology *Contemporary American & Australian Poetry* from three years earlier (1976). This collection is a (roughly) chronological interleaving of Australian poets from A. D. Hope to Charles Buckmaster and American poets from Berryman to Daniel Halpern. In his introduction, Shapcott compares Australia with America in terms of *origins* and *assurance:* American poetry, assured about its past, has a longer tradition of discovery; Australian poets, less assured of their cultural traditions, are preoccupied with origins (xxiii). This project can be understood, then, in terms of Shapcott's thematic reading of the "New World cultures" of Australia and America in terms of landscape heritage and the voyager myth and in terms of his own personal experience of U.S. poetry and poetics (xxiii). Notwithstanding its greater cultural imaginativeness (the voyager myth), much of Shapcott's introduction reads like the essays in Kirkby's collection: the energy and grandness of modern American poetry have been put to good use by a poetic culture which is genetically different ("Australian poetry has consistently underplayed flamboyant gesture" [xxv]) but which has taken a leap forward in modernisation by its contact with America. Just as Shapcott had responded, in his 1970 anthology, *Australian Poetry Now,* to the early tremors of the seismic shift in Australian poetry which was already well under way, his *Contemporary American & Australian Poetry* seems like an attempt to catch up with that shift more substantively.[5]

One of the most important assessments of the American encounter from the perspective of the late '70s is John Tranter's anthology *The New Australian Poetry*. As its title suggests, it was a conscious reterritorialisation of Donald Allen's project. The collection was published in 1979, the year of the American model conference. Tranter's paper at the conference was a draft of his introduction for the anthology. The collection presents the work of twenty-four poets who "rose to public notice on the crest of a wave of poetry readings, 'underground' magazines, and a generally expressed antagonism to the established mainstream of poetry at that time, which they saw as too conservative" (xv). Tranter lists the factors that contributed to the advent of the New Australian poetry, from demographics (generationalism) to technology, but, as he argues,

> perhaps the strongest direct influence was from America, in the form of the new poetry that emerged there in the early 1960s. And here, the effect of two books was incalculable—Donald Allen's *The New American Poetry* (New York: Grove Press, 1960) and Donald Hall's *Contemporary American Poetry* (London: Penguin Books, 1962). They were big, various and completely new, and when they finally arrived in Australia in the mid-1960s (Donald Allen's book was banned for several years) they showed the local writers that there was a real and vigorous alternative to the world of Henry Lawson and A. D. Hope. (xvii)

This is the typical rhetoric of any (modernist) revolution in art—the clean break with a deadening past, the "overhauling of poetic method and function that seems to become necessary from time to time in any culture" (Tranter, *New Australian*

Poetry xxvi). In this instance the break with the local and national past is simultaneously an ecstatic conjunction with America to produce a revolutionary and internationalist Australian present. American poetry = freedom. In this equation, the new Australian poetry was both an expression of freedom *from* as well as freedom *to*. For Tranter, and the poets he is speaking for, the New American poetry offered an "anaesthetic," that is, an antidote to the stifling, conservative aesthetics of mid-century Australian literary culture. It generated a cultural and subjective space that was always already radical and emancipatory, an anti-imperialist practice and poetics. And it instigates the final moment in the lengthy collapse of humanism in modern Australia that had begun during the early 1940s. The first poem from Tranter's anthology, number 1 from Bruce Beaver's *Letters to Live Poets* volume (1969), is an address to, and an elegy for, Frank O'Hara. It announces exactly the project Tranter has described in his introduction:

> I make these words perform for you
> knowing though you are dead, that you 'historically
> belong to the enormous bliss of American death',
> that your talkative poems remain
> among the living things
> of the sad, embattled beach-head.
>
> Say that I am, as ever, the young—
> old fictor of communications.
> It's not that I wish to avoid
> talking to myself or singing
> the one-sided song.
> It's simply that I've come to be
> more conscious of the community
> world-wide, of live, mortal poets.
> Moving about the circumference
> I pause each day
> and speak to you and you.
> I haven't many answers, few
> enough; fewer questions left.
> Even when I'm challenged 'Who
> goes there?' I give ambiguous
> replies as though the self linking
> heart and mind had become a gap.
>
> . . .
>
> I have to live near this, if not quite with it.
> I realise there's an equivalent
> in every town and city in the world.

Writing to you keeps the local, intent
shark-watchers at bay
(who if they thought at all
would think *me* some kind of ghoul);
rings a bell for the gilded coin-slots
at the Gold Coast;
sends the president parliament's head on a platter;
writes Vietnam like a huge four-letter
word in blood and faeces on the walls
of government; reminds me when
the intricate machine stalls
there's a poet still living at this address. (2–3)

It also opened up the possibility of new and different social uses of poetry—as a discourse of subject formation and political protest:

> Poetry was not seen as a pastime by the new poets. It wasn't regarded as a hobby. It was not seen as a pleasant diversion from an academic routine, or a skill to be developed simply for its own sake. It was seen by many poets as an integral part of a wider struggle for freedom and individuality; freedom from conscription (Australia was at war with North Vietnam at the time, and conscription was part of that war), freedom from the censorship of imported books by the federal Customs department, freedom from police harassment, freedom to experiment with drugs, to develop a sexual ethic liberated from authoritarian restraints, and freedom from the handcuffs of rhyme and the critical strictures of the university English Departments. (Tranter, "Australian Poetry 1940–1980" 93)

The contradiction inherent in exchanging one imperialism for another, a limiting for an enabling one, a chosen for an imposed one, didn't escape the Generation of '68. They were well aware, at some level, of their involvement in a neo-colonial venture, appropriating and assimilating the New American poetry for their own political and expressive ends. Part of this tension, of course, was that the heterogeneity of the New American poetry included as much of the accusatory, wounded and corrosive outbursts of individual poets (from Olson to Ginsberg to LeRoi Jones) as it did of their celebrations or praise. The internal contradictions of the North American poetic tradition weren't lost in translation. External to that poetic tradition, the liberatory, utopian space of American poetry was (and is) in acute ironic tension with national and international movements of political dissidence that are rhetorically founded on resistance to the threat of colonising American values and U.S. global imperialism (Bernstein, *A Poetics* 212)—such as those generated by the Vietnam war, for instance. But from within a culture with a massive will-to-dominance emerges an oppositional discourse like the New American poetry, with a complex relation of its own to the whole, but with at least a rhetorical rejection of "General MacArthur's" America (Damon 21).

> The New American Poetry, by and large, rejected the grandiosity of scheme, of world-spirit, of progress, of avant-garde advance: the positivist, quasi-authoritarian assumptions of Futurism, Vorticism, or the tradition of Eliot. It rejected the heroic universalizing of poetic genius in favor of particularization, process, detail; extending the innovations of the 1910–1917 period, but giving them an entirely different psychic registration.[6] (Bernstein, *A Poetics* 204–5)

Part of the history of the New American poetry, then, involves its recontextualisation within a postcolonial cultural setting with its own contradictory relations to an imperial and discursive centre (England, English and English Literature). In a poem called "To the Bobbydazzlers," a younger member of the Generation of '68 puts this paradox of postcoloniality simply and directly:

> American poets!
> you have saved
> America from
> its reputation
> if not its fate
> & you saved me
> too, in 1970
> when I first
> breathed freely
> in Ted Berrigan's
> *Sonnets,* escaping
> the talented earache of Modern
> Poetry.
> Sitting
> on the beach I
> look towards you
> but the curve
> of the Pacific
> gets in the way
> & I see stars
> instead knocked
> out by your poems
> American poets,
> the Great Dead
> are smiling
> in your faces.
> I salute their
> luminous hum! (15)

This poem by John Forbes is a short-lined reformulation of O'Hara's "Ode:

Salute to the French Negro Poets." As a "salute" it represents perhaps the earliest and simplest gesture of poetic appropriation. It is disarming in its expression of the excitement and freedom of artistic revolution. As well as relatively open and naïve gestures such as Forbes's, Tranter's anthology represents a huge range of appropriations and engagements with the New American poetry broadly defined. Bruce Beaver's homage to O'Hara; Robert Adamson's reworking of Wallace Stevens; and Robert Duncan, Laurie Duggan and Alan Wearne's addresses to Dorn and Berrigan is all writing that, like the enzymes Stephen Greenblatt identifies as being at work in any politically uneven cultural exchange, change the ideological composition of a foreign poetry and poetics into one with an equivalent valency within Australian literary culture.

In late 1977 the academic journal *Australian Literary Studies* devoted an entire issue to an assessment of the cultural revolution in Australian writing in the late '60s and early '70s. This "New Writing in Australia" special issue covered fiction and little magazines but had also a significant emphasis on poetry. This was another contribution to the assessment of the new Australian writing that had emerged ten years earlier, but this time in the disciplinary field of Australian literary studies. The editorial explained that "the aim of this special issue has been to invite consideration of new writing that has grown up in Australia since the late 1960s by representing it primarily from the points of view of a range of writers themselves" (114). The issue included a review article, "Thoughts on Some Recent Poetry" by Dennis Haskell, about John Tranter, John Forbes and Robert Adamson's work to date, and Clive Faust's article "Careering Poetry." "Statements" by eight poets (as well as fiction writers and editors) in response to a questionnaire were included. More extended and idiosyncratic pieces by Tranter ("Four Notes on the Practice of Revolution"), Robert Kenny ("Living, Fighting and Sulking in the Seventies"), and Kris Hemensley ("'. . . The Wild Assertion of Vitality'") were also included.

This issue of *ALS* is another uneven sample of the state of critical discourse in Australia in the mid- to late-1970s. An obvious tension at the time, reflected in the various rhetorical gestures of the writers and even in the framing of the issue as a whole, is the problem of "academicism." Again, the defensiveness and confusions of this worthy attempt by *ALS* to respond critically to the new Australian writing is a function of the underdeveloped critical discourse on poetry and poetics that I have referred to above. The strongly (and understandably) anti-academic stance in many of the pieces reflects a particular relation of the new writing to then-current institutions of literary production and learning (universities and publishers). Thus, in Wilding's terms, which are socialist/libertarian, "academic" is synonymous with conservative-establishment:

As for academic objectivity, the development of the new writing in Australia coincides with the realisation of the fraud of 'academic objectivity'. 'Academic objectivity' was revealed as the ideology of conservatism, of the cold war, of the capitalist-industrial-military complex that got us into the war in Vietnam. *The Dialectics of Liberation* (ed. David Cooper), *Weapons of Criticism* (ed. Norman Rudich), *The Mythology of Imperialism* by Jonah Raskin, *The Politics of Literature* (ed. Louis Kampf and Paul Lauter) and *Ways of Seeing* by John Berger all demonstrate that case. This new vision of the way 'academic objectivity' was a fraud, has been a major component of the aesthetic of the new writing. (116–17)

And section 2 of Tranter's "Four Notes on the Practice of Revolution" is entitled "*Distrusting The Academy*." It identifies specifically "academic" writers: "the kind of cautious, earnest, correct, ironic and essentially reactionary writing done by McAuley, Buckley and the early Wallace-Crabbe (for example) . . . actively supported by critics in the English Departments of our universities. It had no support in the general community, and not much among writers under fifty" (130). This kind of position (along with Wilding's) was underwritten by what Donald Allen had articulated as *the* defining characteristic of the New American poetry: its "total rejection of all those qualities typical of academic verse" (xi).[7] The problem, though, was how to represent, critically, the writing and history these writers had been a part of. Tranter's piece, in some ways more sensitive to the tensions at work in the advent of the "new writing," ends up ventriloquising two positions in the debate about the importation of the American influence, energy/revolution/the U.S. vs. tradition/the academy:

Seeing the hegemony of English writing on the local scene, and the vitality of the Americans, we tried to bring some of that vitality into our own writing. It was manifestly obvious that the Americans had done wonderful things with poetry, and that the United States, from 1950 on, was the real centre of the poetry world. As Pope learnt from the Latin poets, as Baudelaire learnt from Poe, as Eliot learnt from Laforgue, so we learnt from the Americans.

You imported American cultural values here, they say. It's like rock'n'roll, it's a spreading disease with a cheap American accent, and you're responsible for sneaking it through quarantine. You're unwitting agents of American Cultural Imperialism. You can't even talk with an Australian accent any more. (134)

It is only in Hemensley's article, "'. . . The Wild Assertion of Vitality'", which is the most wide-ranging in its account of the relations of late-'60s developments in Australian new writing to cognate movements in the U.S. and the U.K. (and to a lesser extent Europe), that there is a conscious awareness of the problem of an underdeveloped critical discourse: "Having broken through the Oz Lit defences, having flamboyantly raised the banners of the new, there has been little or no analysis of the new works and their auguries; in fact there has been a stultification (which might in the future appear to be a period of consolidation?)" (232). He invokes Jean Ricardou of the *Tel Quel* group "of inventive writers, critics and theorists (founded in 1960)" (233) as an example of someone working within a more supportive and balanced scene of radical writing than the Australian one of the 1970s. Also, in the Hemensley piece, there are the elements of a theoretical analysis of the process of cultural exchange at work in the advent and development of the new Australian writing:

> . . . regarding the foreign imports (does one have to import initiative? Isn't development organic?): the foreign import dramatises the virtues as well as the lacks of the local scene. Often it isn't until the 'foreign' has been fêted that the 'foreign' within the local context is recognized; of course this is a mark of parochialism and cultural-political immaturity. . . . Although it is very true that there is no capital as such, at least not in the English-speaking world, where once London or New York or even Rapallo might have been the capital, English poets (for example) today do write out of a common prospect with American poets, and that goes for all genres and trends: 'Anglo-American' is a justifiable ascription. (235–6)

Hence the significance of a gathering like the "Assembling Alternatives" conference, where for the first time, really, radicality in contemporary writing is being negotiated critically and theoretically in a much richer and more flexible context than the "Anglo-American" one Hemensley is describing here in 1977.

Going back to Hemensley's essay after more than twenty years raises the question of the discursive and cultural relations between U.K. (also Irish and Canadian) and Australian contemporary radicalities in poetry and poetics. This was certainly a question highlighted by the "Assembling Alternatives" conference. In many ways, in the 1970s Kris Hemensley's was a lone voice, or at least a very locally restricted voice (Melbourne) in the context of the new Australian writing. The considerable amount of work of importation and relocation that Hemensley carried out in his own writing, in readings, and in magazines like *Earth Ship* (13 issues, 1970–72) and *The Ear in the Wheatfield* (1972–76), between the disparate universes of U.S., U.K., Australian, European and New Zealand radical traditions wasn't then, and hasn't been, as widely influential on *Australian* writing as it might have been. Or, at least, the strong and important ties that Hemensley represented to new writing in the U.K. were overridden by the American influence. More than twenty years later, in some of the work of John Kinsella, the potential of those specific exchanges of U.K. and Australian radical perspectives are only beginning to be realised. This situation may reflect a certain dominance of Sydney cultural power which has allowed its version of the "Generation of '68" to prevail. It may also be that, in the case of Australia at least, the postcolonial revolt, building on a history of national antipathy, cauterises the ability to read, for their linguistic and formal innovations, subsequent alternatives represented by the British Poetry Revival: Paladin's *The New British Poetry* (Gillian Allnutt, Fred D'Aguiar, Ken Edwards and Eric Mottram, eds., 1988) and other anthologies like *A Various Art* (Andrew Crozier & Tim Longville, eds., 1987); *Floating Capital: New Poets from London* (Robert Sheppard and Adrian Clarke, eds., 1991); or *Other: British & Irish Poetry Since 1970* (Richard Caddel and Peter Quartermain, eds., 1998). This is a highly fraught context, because it also includes the reverse appropriations of the old empire that we see so clearly in the rhetoric of the New Barbarians (Heaney, Walcott, Murray, etc.): the vigorous vernaculars of these ex-colonials, welcomed eagerly by the metropolitan centre, will revivify the sick heart of empire. In the brief discussion of John Kinsella's work later in this essay, I try to suggest a critical framework that might respond to those contemporary complexities.

Those are some of the ways in which the revolution in poetic praxis and theory in Australia, under the influence of the new American poetry, has been represented. Whatever the varying inflection of these narratives of influence, and however carefully encoded in terms of personal history, they are in fact invariably narratives of freedom or, the other way 'round, narratives of resistance to authority. If the pure products of American poetic experiment go crazy (at home), then that doesn't stop them—as in Bruce Beaver's exemplary narrative of political and formal freedom—being of revolutionary value when exported. They represent a facet of what has been, for Australia, probably its most important cultural encounter of the post-war period: the engagement with America. The story of the new Australian poetry is the story of the origins and entanglement of a (national) poetry and poetics in both the emancipatory and imperialist meanings of postmodern American culture. But it is an unfinished story.

Thirty years and more after 1968, the scene is very different. The history of Australia's relations to the U.S. cultural imperium is relevant to contemporary poetry and poetics, but in contemporary Australia the discourse of and on poetry now functions according to a very different paradigm of international exchange and influence. There are many historical, cultural and political factors in this shift and it would be difficult to list them here without seeming cursory, but crucial factors have been Australia's entry into global technologies of communication, the absorption of poststructuralist theory into all areas of Australian intellectual life—whether as appropriation or in opposition, whether institutionalised or not—and the local engagement with North American Language writing as a broadly defined movement in textual practice, poetic theory, critical discourse, modes of production and international communication. "Theory" was hardly available in the mid-'70s as a complementary discourse to the new Australian writing. The "poetics" that Tranter had called for in *The New Australian Poetry,* and that was obviously prompted by the influential

"Statements on Poetics" collected at the end of Allen's *The New American Poetry,* remained unarticulated, betrayed by the academic discourse of the time.[8] Now, as another wave of North American experiment has been appropriated and reterritorialised in Australia—not only as a discrete second-order revolution, but evolving out of the new Australian writing as well—there is a national and international context very different from that of the 1970s.[9] In the final section of this essay I want to look very briefly at two recent works produced in this environment.

Genre

In works like *Syzygy* (1993) and *The Radnoti Poems* (1996); in his critique of the national topos of the pastoral in *The Silo* (1995); in his essays in poetics, which include strong and articulate theorisings of the cultural and linguistic project of *Salt* magazine; and in the 1997 volume *Genre,* John Kinsella is working within the radical space opened up by Language writing over the past fifteen or so years. So far, *Genre* is perhaps the most powerful result of Kinsella's restless experimentation. It is a book-length piece of writing, arranged as a single, continuous, narrower-than-the-page column of text. Its structuration is complex. It begins with the overlaying of a Dadaesque "Theatre of the Imagination", with eight stages (9), onto a block of inner-city flats, a version of Perecian spatialisation of narrative: "The block is a Venn Diagram of fictions and exegeses" (11). A dominant and neurotic narrator, "The Renaissance man," in one flat is writing an essay for an art exhibition. This narrator's wife, a novelist, also lives in this flat with their children. There is a student in flat five, in another flat are "the girls" (10), there's a "steroid-hungry guy" and his girlfriend in flat six, an Indonesian couple in another flat, and one flat (or stage in the Theatre of the Imagination) is vacant. The text cuts, sweeps and dissolves between the various narratives and genres these "characters" suggest—although what is foregrounded in the writing is the *writing* rather than characterisation or setting. "There is no room for the author, and only through eavesdropping, surveying the contents, can the reader evolve within the text" (11). One dissolve:

> Writing poetry is a substitute for wealth, and Forbes knows he'll only be able to break free of his anxiety if he stops bluffing. Maybe the beach isn't such a relaxing place? Moving inland. It was a beautiful drive through the southern wheatbelt at that time of year. (113)

And sometimes—as the reader finds, disconcertingly—the whole block of flats is transposed, in the stream of consciousness of a narrator, to Jakarta or

Dhakar. Thus, *Genre* is a rich and layered assemblage of elements: first person interior monologues by the "characters," often with distinctive subgeneric styles (grunge-drug fiction and *noir,* for example); letters to Dennis Hopper, Julia Kristeva, Noam Chomsky, Simon Schama; research notes and drafts of an essay in aesthetics (the art exhibition work); porn, manifesto-poetics, theory, literary gossip, nature diary notes, tourist brochure speak, recipes (for *biscotti*); transcripts of Lynch's *Blue Velvet;* an extended and interspersed meditation on the poetry of John Forbes (as well as other literary critical interludes about Australian poetry, James Joyce, etc.); and much more. This heteroglossia, almost always "grammatical," has a kind of rapid readerly drive generated by both the fragmentary narrative elements and the conjunction of these with other (nonnarrative) elements. As one reviewer described it, it's "like channel surfing—are the narratives the serials and the bits about Australian poetry the commercials?" (Brooks 46).

McKenzie Wark is right to take the lead from Kinsella's title and to read *Genre* in terms of its "genre bending": "Genres are blocks in the sense that they put a boundary around a certain kind of relation between reading and writing, creating a kind of consistency to it, at the expense of marking it off as a type of experience. Genre blocks the movement of the reading and writing experience towards becoming something not consistent with the types of experience mandated in advance by genre" (32). Wark is alive to one of the main effects of Kinsella's new assemblage of generic and subgeneric elements: its sense that "writing can have a life outside of genre, outside of the conventions that police and constrain it" (32), and he might have zeroed in on a number of hints and clues as to how Kinsella produces these effects. One is alluded to, in one of the many moments that can be read as self-reflexive in this text, on pages 100–101. At this point the principal narrator, after another part of the meditation on Forbes, explicates the idea of literal and rhetorical levels to Donne's poetry (and metaphysical poetry more generally). He cites the New Historicist critic David Norbrook's distinction between the syllogistic markers of a poem and its enthymemes, "the merely approximate arguments of rhetorical proof" (100). Assertion and counter-assertion in Donne's poetry ("Loves Growth" is the example) appear as a grammatical string of strong argumentation and proof; but in fact the poem, *qua* poem, works with a "lower" level of proof: "Literal truth, for the rhetorician, is not the point: analogies are significant because they involve the emotional nuances which are more significant for exploring concrete human relations than metaphysical categories" (101). Like self-contradiction and lying. This has long been observed of Donne's and other metaphysical poetry and it amounts to the deconstructive point about the grammatical and rhetorical levels of any text, particularly the literary text. Kinsella's awareness of this theoretical point, though, is relevant to the kinds of reading *Genre* invites. The extraordinary thing about the overall assemblage is the way in which the grammatical level—so mercurial, hybrid and heteroglossic—both generates and undoes the tragedy of its rhetorical meanings. Substantiating this point would take much more space of reading, but as shorthand it can be said that *Genre* is not a piece of postmodern indulgence. It has a tragic story to tell, however allegorised, about the fate of the self in the contemporary world.

From Analogue to Digital

One of the notable effects of Language writing, both in North America and Australia, has been the paths back to earlier experimental writers of the modernist era—pre-eminently Gertrude Stein—it has allowed to be opened up. Language writing has often read back through the traditions of the historical avant-gardes, searching out and revalorising the proto-postmodern. It has also allowed readers to trace the complex filiations between the work of surrealists like Raymond Roussel, the Oulipo group and the more radical innovators of early modernism. John Tranter's *Different Hands: seven stories* (1998) owes much to this historical stranding of postmodern poetry and poetics, as it does to the recent imbrication of innovative writing in the electronic media. Computers, software and the internet are massively influencing the production and distribution of poetry and innovative writing, but the "new digital writing space" is also having profound effects on the genetics of contemporary writing. As Bernstein argues, it is poetry that continues "to be a crucial site to probe the possibilities of this new medium" ("Interview").

If there was space, it would be useful to delve back into the strange Saussurean (hypogrammatic) context for *Different Hands*; but given the complexity of the text, I need to use the space that's left here to give some idea of the work itself. The text is made up of seven "stories," each generated from two original pieces of writing. Analogous to Kinsella's aims in *Genre,* this is Tranter's experiment in creating a writer-free literary text—an "automatic" text in more than one sense of that word. As Tranter explains, he uses "BreakDown" software to analyse the letter and punctuation patterns of scanned-in text (not grammatical or syntactical patterns).

> 'BreakDown' is a text analysis and text generation program written for IBM-compatible personal computers, developed by many hands over the years. It was refined into a marketable product in 1985 by the San Francisco programmer Neil J. Rubenking. . . .
>
> To analyse a text, BreakDown looks at it in 'chunks' of a particular size—the 'chunk size' can be set from two to seven alphabetical and punctuation characters. BreakDown keeps a record—in the form of an index and a frequency table—of what character occurs immediately after a particular 'chunk'. . . .

> Once BreakDown has constructed an index and a frequency table for a sample text, it can generate a 'reconstruction' of that text by selecting at random a 'key chunk' that begins with a space (that is, one that doesn't start in the middle of a word). It then looks up the frequency array for that key and selects the next character at random from the characters with non-zero frequency, weighted by the frequencies listed in the table. . . . The program continues generating characters, words and lines of text until you ask it to stop. It could go on forever. ("'Dogs in the All the Unregarded Bales'" 636–37)

Rubenking's "documentation states that BreakDown was inspired by the 'Travesty' program in the November 1984 issue of *BYTE* magazine, by [Hugh] Kenner and Joseph O'Rourke," a computer scientist ("Unregarded Bales" 638). *Different Hands* is dedicated to "Professor Hugh Kenner": "Without his inspired investigations in the world of computer-assisted letter-group frequency analysis these texts could not have been written." Tranter is well aware, of course, of Kenner as one of the great critics and readers of modernism, and what he is acknowledging here is the connection between a deep readerly interest in modernism and the postmodern practice of digital writing.

Tranter says he then takes the letter-group analyses, "a heap of dreck" produced by BreakDown, and subjects them to a kind of jazz improvisation (*Different Hands,* "Author's Foreword"). The "raw material" for *Different Hands,* the "prior" texts subjected to Rubenking's BreakDown, were William Gibson's *Neuromancer* and Stein's *The Autobiography of Alice B. Toklas* ("Neuromancing Miss Stein"); Ginsberg's *Howl* and Laura Lee Hope's *The Bobbsey Twins on a Bicycle Trip* ("The Howling Twins"); Louisa M. Alcott's *Little Women* and Carlos Castaneda's *Tales of Power* ("Magic Women"); Radclyffe Hall's *The Well of Loneliness* and W. E. Johns's *Biggles Defies the Swastika* ("Lonely Chaps"); Edmund Wilson's essay on Paul Valéry in *Axel's Castle* and Charles Sales's *The Specialist,* a booklet about a handyman who builds outdoor lavatories ("Valéry's Room"); E. M. Forster's *A Room With a View* and advertisements for houses for sale in Sydney's eastern suburbs during June and July 1994 ("A Room With a View, Spa Bath, Many Extras"); and Henry Miller's *Tropic of Cancer* and Yasunari Kawabata's *The Master of Go* ("Carousel"). Tranter's half-joking way to describe his improvisatory writing practice with the dreck of electronically generated draft material is deliberately sly about the inhuman origins of these texts:

> I usually do maybe a dozen drafts of a piece of writing until it feels right, but these were each so scrambled when I began that I thought I'd never make them whole. The experience put me in mind of a bad dream about an accident in the Transporter Room of the *USS Enterprise*—the members of the exploration party have had their molecules mangled as they were being beamed up from the planet surface, and I'm Bones, the ship's doctor, charged with the job of making out of this mess something—not necessarily human—just something that can walk, speak English, and operate the phasers. (*Different Hands,* "Author's Foreword")

Unlike the meta-narrative drive of Kinsella's *Genre,* the experience of reading *Different Hands* is the experience of reading a text that could branch off in any direction with any given sentence. One effect of Tranter's improvisation is to dampen and frustrate, in favour of textual materiality and maximum suggestiveness, any overall narrative drive. This is the first paragraph of "Neuromancing Miss Stein":

> Hemingway looked in to see the great artist he really was, or could be if he tried hard, and instead found Janet Scudder and the Famous Writer there at the zinc bar at the front of the café, talking and drinking cassis. Miss Stein had a little book with her, something we all ought to know about, but know it too thoroughly would be a mistake. Janet was a little removed from herself, that is, from her own problems, per medium of cassis and white wine, and the transatlantic mail. Janet said that Hemingway wrote with colour and energy whole paragraphs that simply meant shit. His eyes reminded her of Minnesota. She was also reminded of sheep going to slaughter, and of her wish that Americans would leave America and then go back again. (9)

An experiment like this one of Tranter's is an instance of what is currently a massive number of dialectical interchanges between traditional ways of thinking about poetic form and the possibilities offered by e-poetry in its various individual and institutional manifestations. One way to think about these developments is along the rough analogy of analogue to digital: the extensive array of "traditional" poetic forms tends to be held captive to an ideology of organic (mimetic) essence—the idea of words as sensual objects, as intimately related to place and dialect, and owned by the poet-priest, who produces form as craft, etc. That's a cartoon version of a whole complex tradition and it ignores the alien invasion of the Mallarméan and, later, radical modernist gene that leads to the development of Language writing in recent decades. This alien element has a complex relation to any version of the traditional or mainstream and is not without profound influences on "official verse culture", at least at the level of poetics. But one could characterise it broadly as the *analogue* tradition (in its mimesis of word, sound, voice and Poet) in contrast to (postmodern, broadly speaking) *digital* practices.

Digital writing, then, could be said to work with an idea of the translatory, combinatory and permutatory possibilities of language, in a way that is aware of the mediation and difference between the poet/writer and the massively complex raw materials of an already up-and-running language. The fascination then with much of the Language work is in the text itself but simultaneously (in the act of reading) in the programs, protocols and scripts that went to produce it, and similarly in Tranter's BreakDown-generated, faux-Steinian texts in *Different Hands*. All this is happening in vigorous contention with what is understood as "traditional" poetic form. Take Ron Silliman, or Maria Damon, for example, working creatively and critically in what we could refer to as e-poetry: their writing and reading isn't dehistoricised or ignorant; they're always working with the whole array of poetics, because of course the "analogue" tradition isn't as homogeneous and unreflexive as I was characterising it as being. So the dialectic is definitely there. The analogue and digital networks overlap with each other; in some places reception is better on one network than the other.

Beyond Languagedome

What a cross-cultural reading of Language writing necessitates (from here at least) is a reformulation of the language in which we figure poetic and political practices. This time, the liberatory space opened up by American Language writing allows poetry to be rethought as a cultural practice. Most crucially it allows the question: what is the cultural work that poetry does? to be asked in a meaningful way. The poetics and practice of Language writing, in its reception and reinvention in Australia, underwrites above all a repoliticisation of poetry and the discourse on poetry—in theoretical terms (poetics), in institutional terms (pedagogical accommodations), and in terms of cultural production (magazines, writing communities, poetry publishing generally). The carapace of aestheticisation is always threatening to close over and to seal up the institutions of poetry. What work like John Kinsella's, and more recently Peter Minter in *Empty Texas* (1999), allows is the opening-up question of limits. One of the values of Language writing is the way it continues to keep the question of limits seriously in play: what are the limits of poetic language—what kind of address does poetic language make to the discourses of nation and identity? Nor is this recent history of Language writing in Australia irrelevant to the practices of everyday life; one of the discernible imperatives it has generated is the resistance to crudities of critical discourse that oversimplify the relationships between the contemporary political and poetic. It "disables the forms of universalism held by traditional aesthetics" (Frow 3) and thus effects all kinds of interpersonal and cultural relations. Meaghan Morris makes a similar point from the perspective of contemporary Cultural Studies:

> I [don't] think that poetry is just another form of cultural criticism (the other side of the "mirror" thesis). I have no idea how to talk about the relations between poetic and other kinds of writing, or other ways of thinking. . . . The practical point that I need to make is that I do not read these poems [John Forbes's 1988 collection, *The Stunned Mullet & Other Poems*], as a critic of literature might, by assembling a massive historical "context" from which to interpret the "text". On the contrary: I read the texts in order to learn more about the complex networks of living by which they are shaped, and in which, *as* poems (or "forms of life", in Deleuze and Guattari's terms), they participate. (10)

The appropriation of Language writing to the Australian context, part of the implementation and negotiation of postmodernity in Australia, seems to bear within it comparatively more powerful isotopes of critique than did the New American poetry (Frow 89). In the field of progressive Australian poetry and poetics, Language writing extends and develops the cultural work of the New Australian poetry, throwing the switch on poetic discourse such that it counters or critiques rather than transmits socially normative values (Damon 9), appropriating the liberatory space of American Language writing and assimilating its critique of closed forms, whether poetic or social.

Notes

1. For example, this is Andrew Taylor:

   > 'What is the main effect of being influenced by American models?' And the answer is quite simply that if I had not been, my notion of poetry would have been much poorer now than it is.
   >
   > The second effect could be described as a liberation from the influence of one's immediate environment, finding new parents. Oscar Wilde is surely right in saying that although nature gave us our parents, thank God we can choose our friends. But poets are fortunate in being able to choose other parents for themselves when they need them. And in being able, usually, to discard them when they've done their job. I've never wanted to be anything other than an Australian poet, but I didn't want James McAuley and Judith Wright for parents. Wallace Stevens and Emily Dickinson may seem strange foster-parents, but they—and many others—were most what I needed. (64)

   See also Wallace-Crabbe (47, 53).
2. The Geoffrey Moore *Penguin Book of Modern American Verse* also represented the influential *penguinisation* of American poetry in the U.K. and in the British publishing colonies. This anthology begins with Dickinson, not Whitman, and so the rediscovery of Whitman in the U.K. and its dominions in the '50s had to wait until the promptings of the various poets, particularly Ginsberg, in the Allen anthology. See Shapcott, "Beware of Broken Glass" 33.
3. Apart from one or two Americans published in *Angry Penguins*.
4. "In 1845, the Sydney *Weekly Register* published two unsigned articles titled 'American Poets.' The anonymous author (possibly Henry Parkes?) recommended the republican poetry of Longfellow, Lowell, Brant, Mrs Sigourney, and Nathaniel Parker Willis. . . . It would appear that Australian poets have been continually rediscovering America. In his review of *The American Model* . . . Douglas Stewart

finds it 'extraordinary' that 'there is virtually no reference [in this book] to the long and highly profitable tradition that preceded the American impact of recent times.' . . . Well, in fairness to the contributors to *The American Model,* it should be pointed out that they were talking about *their* American experience, and that was essentially a post-1960 phenomenon. On the other hand, we should all be grateful to Douglas Stewart for correcting our cultural myopia by pointing out the influence of Vachel Lindsay on Mary Gilmore and Furnley Maurice, of Emily Dickinson on Shaw Neilson, of Robert Frost on David Campbell" (Anderson 479–80).

5. In *Meanjin* for December 1976, there was a symposium of critical responses to Shapcott's anthology. Tranter's main objection is that the work of Australian poets like Hope, J.S. Harry, David Rowbotham, Malouf and Peter Skrzynecki looks amateurish in comparison with the Americans they appear alongside (Berryman, Berrigan, Bly, Strand, Schjeldahl) and that work by John Forbes, for example, that might have borne comparison with the Americans, is not included. So, "like a self-destructing post-art object, *Contemporary American Poetry* thrusts its bulk at the Australian reader, hoping—in Shapcott's words—to 'demonstrate . . . the variousness and diversity of their own [Australian] poetic heritage'. Its actual function, I hope, will be to demonstrate something quite different: that it's time Australian poetry grew up" (363).

Clive Faust, in his response, likens the anthology to an "Expo pavilion" (363). His persuasive point is that *The New American Poetry,* as a touchstone, was a *stylistically* coherent collection (despite its huge diversity) rather than a thematically or chronologically representative one. Thus Shapcott's collection is confusing because it represents American and Australian poets of very different styles. Ian Reid's objections were similar, if differently inflected. Is Shapcott's anthology actually pro-confessional (like Alvarez's *The New Poetry*) or anti-confessional (like Allen's)?

The fourth response in this symposium was from Robert Duncan. Duncan's excoriation of Shapcott's collection is almost eighteenth century in its scorn. As Duncan's outrage grows he even attacks Shapcott's organising, thematic categories:

> There remains one outstanding misconception that Shapcott seeks to leave with the reader. 'In Australia, for instance, the need to create a mythology of origin—a voyager ancestry—persists'—O.K., even the aboriginals, we realise from their mythopoetic culture, live deep in a mythology of origins—but then he goes on to say: 'Such a re-defining of origins, when it appears in recent American verse (for instance, George Keithley's *The Donner Party*) is more a sport, a challenge to the cliché of the Wild West tradition, than a major contribution to the mainstream of contemporary concern'. He can talk for safe about this George Keithley and his *Donner Party;* it does not happen to qualify for our consideration of poetry—it is, indeed, merely verse. But what is serious here in Shapcott's distortion is that the re-defining of origins has been a major concern in our new poetry in the United States—it is the grand theme and heroic task of the *Maximus* that Shapcott dismisses from his consideration, and it reappears in three of the most remarkable works of recent years: in Dorn's *Gunslinger* and his *Recollections*

> *of Gran Apacheria,* and in Jerome Rothenberg's *Poland/1931*. In each of these major works the insistent voice of the Indian is heard, as in Melville's *Clarel* in the nineteenth century he speaks. But there is another fact that Shapcott seems to be unaware of: today in the United States there is the beginning of the new Indians' presentation of that voice. The redefining of origins in the United States even as here in the Australian continent is not passed but lies ahead of us. (369)

The first *Meanjin* for 1977 published a reply from Shapcott ("Placing the Inheritors: A Reply to Critics"). Here Shapcott defends the project of *Contemporary American & Australian Poetry* from the point of view of the difficulties that "roping together two disparate verse traditions" presented (63). The most important single point Shapcott wanted to make in the anthology was "that younger writers, in both countries, are working in an 'inheritors' vein now," a "'digestive' rather than an innovative stage" (64–5). Shapcott goes on to defend his choice of apparently new academic poets like Kinnell against Olson: "Robert Duncan will hate me for it" (66).

6. Part of the point of this quotation is that it is about poetry and World War II ("The Second War and Postmodern Memory"): the historical moment of Australia's shift from the previously foremost alliance with Britain to Pacific and U.S. strategic relations.
7. Allen's "live" tradition followed "the practice and precepts of Ezra Pound and William Carlos Williams, it has built on their achievements and gone on to evolve new conceptions of the poem" (xi).
8. "The need to develop a new poetics appropriate to the age drew a different and highly individual response from each writer" (Tranter, *New Australian Poetry* xvii). Allen's collection of "Statements on Poetics" was in fact much longer than his rather brief introduction to the anthology.
9. We're talking about a process that has a focal moment in an edition of *Meanjin* for 1991 (50.1 Autumn 1991), which included a supplement of Language writing and related criticism.

Works Cited

Anderson, Don. "American Graffiti, or 'I'm Still Living in the Seventies'." *Meanjin* 41.4 (December 1982): 479–85.

Bail, Murray. "Imagining Australia." *Times Literary Supplement* 4 (417) (Nov 27–Dec 3, 1987): 1318+.

Bernstein, Charles. *A Poetics*. Cambridge and London: Harvard University Press, 1992.

———. "Charles Bernstein Interview." Seminary Co-Op Bookstore.

Brooks, Barbara. "Custodian of Seeing." *Australian Review of Books* 196 (November, 1997): 46.

Damon, Maria. *The Dark End of the Street: Margins in American Vanguard Poetry*. Minneapolis and London: University of Minnesota Press, 1993.

Dawe, Bruce. "Public Voices and Private Feelings." Joan Kirkby, ed. *The American Model: Influence & Independence in Australian Poetry*. Sydney: Hale & Iremonger, 1982, 160–72.

Derksen, Jeff. "Where Have All the Equal Signs Gone or Getting Ready to Have Been Canonized." Paper delivered at the "Assembling Alternatives" conference, University of New Hampshire, August 1996. See the revised version in this volume, p. 41.

Forbes, John. *New and Selected Poems*. Sydney: Angus & Robertson, 1992.

Frow, John. *Cultural Studies and Cultural Value*. Melbourne: Oxford University Press, 1995.

Gilbert, Roger. "The Dream of a Common Poetry." *American Literary History* 8.2 (Summer 1996): 350–63.

Greenblatt, Stephen. *Marvelous Possessions: The Wonder of the New World*. Chicago: University of Chicago Press, 1991.

Hemensley, Kris. ". . . 'The Wild Assertion of Vitality. . .'." *Australian Literary Studies* 8.2 (October, 1977): 226–39.

Kinsella, John. "Drafts, Place, and All Possible Meanings." *Westerly* (Autumn 1996): 33–38.

———. "Dialogues and Shifting Signifiers" [unpublished paper, 1996].

———. *Genre*. Fremantle: Fremantle Arts Centre Press, 1997.

———. *The Radnoti Poems*. Cambridge: Equipage, 1996.

———. *The Undertow: New and Selected Poems*. Todmorden, Lancashire: Arc, 1996.

———, ed. *Salt* since 1990.

Kirkby, Joan, ed. *The American Model: Influence & Independence in Australian Poetry*. Sydney: Hale & Iremonger, 1982. This collection published contributions to "The American Model" poetry conference held at Macquarie University in May 1979.

Moorhouse, Frank. *The Americans, Baby*. Sydney: Angus & Robertson, 1972.

———. *Forty-Seventeen*. Melbourne: Viking, 1988.

Morris, Meaghan. *Ecstasy and Economics: American Essays for John Forbes*. Sydney: EmPress, 1992.

Shapcott, Thomas, ed. *Contemporary American & Australian Poetry*. St Lucia: University of Queensland Press, 1976.

———. "Beware of Broken Glass: Models in a Room of Mirrors." Joan Kirkby, ed. *The American Model: Influence & Independence in Australian Poetry*. Sydney: Hale & Iremonger, 1982, 28–41.

Starobinski, Jean. *Words Upon Words: the Anagrams of Ferdinand de Saussure*. Trans. Olivia Emmet. New Haven and London: Yale University Press, 1979.

Taylor, Andrew. "The American Model: Penelope or Circe?" Joan Kirkby, ed. *The American Model: Influence & Independence in Australian Poetry*. Sydney: Hale & Iremonger, 1982, 54–68.

Tomlinson, John. *Cultural Imperialism: A Critical Introduction*. Baltimore: Johns Hopkins University Press, 1991.

Tranter, John. "Anaesthetics: Some Notes on the New Australian Poetry." Joan Kirkby, ed. *The American Model: Influence & Independence in Australian Poetry*. Sydney: Hale & Iremonger, 1982, 99–116.

——. "Australian Poetry 1940–1980: A Personal View." *Poetry* 169.1 (Oct–Nov 1996): 86–93.

——. *Different Hands: seven stories*. Fremantle: Folio/Fremantle Arts Centre Press, 1998.

——. "'Dogs in All the Unregarded Bales': Mr Rubenking's 'BreakDown'". *Meanjin* 50.4 (Summer, 1991): 635–38.

——. "Four Notes on the Practice of Revolution." *Australian Literary Studies* 8.2 (October, 1977): 127–35.

——. *The New Australian Poetry*. St Lucia: Makar, 1979.

Wallace-Crabbe, Chris. "The Quaker Graveyard in Carlton." Joan Kirkby, ed. *The American Model: Influence & Independence in Australian Poetry*. Sydney: Hale & Iremonger, 1982, 42–53.

Wark, McKenzie. "Genre Bender." *Australian* (Wednesday December 10, 1997): 32.

Wilding, Michael, "A Survey." *Australian Literary Studies* 8.2 (October, 1977): 115–26.

Part II

Intranational divides and intracultural differences

M. NourbeSe Philip

Interview with an Empire

Q: Why does a Black woman like yourself write the kind of poetry you do.
A: I'm not sure what you mean by the kind of "poetry you do."
Q: Your poetry has been described as "complex and abstract."[1] Do you care to comment on that.
A: No.
Q: Why?
A: Because the work is "complex and abstract." But so is jazz and that doesn't prevent anyone from listening, does it? A comment like that says more about the commentator than about the work.
Q: But doesn't being "complex and abstract" restrict your audience and doesn't that bother you?
A: Your question reminds me of one of the most difficult readings I have ever done which was to read after the Black British dub poet Linton Kwesi Johnson (LKJ) whose work I greatly admire. I had been asked as a last minute replacement to fill in for a Cuban poet who had not been able to obtain a visa to enter the United States. I arrived at the venue with very few minutes to spare and somewhat out of breath. LKJ, who was supposed to read second, offered to go first to allow me to catch my breath and collect myself. The audience loved him. His work is intended to be performed—he often works with a band; it is rhythmic, imbued with rhyme and carries an in-your-face political message.

My work on the other hand is page bound and far more in the modernist tradition which abandoned rhyme and rhythm, if not metre, a long time ago. Furthermore the audience had really come to hear LKJ and his was going to be the quintessentially hard act to follow. I found myself reading my more politically obvious poems—earlier works by and large—and avoiding those poems that challenged me as reader and them as audience.
Q: Were you envious of the audience response he got?
A: No. But I think it typifies one of the fundamental issues facing poets of African heritage who do not necessarily work within the context of performance.

Q: How so?

A: I believe some poets begin from a position where they take language as a given. Others, like myself, have a profound distrust of language. This may seem an extremely odd position—it's like an artist distrusting colour, a sculptor distrusting stone, or a musician distrusting sound. With one difference. Neither the painter, the sculptor or the musician needs his medium to function on a daily basis. We all need words and language to function. We are told it is what makes us human. But in its day to day use this very language is very much devalued coinage. This is the same medium that is used to sell us goods we don't want and, through political half-truths and lies, to convince us that what we know to be the truth is not really the truth. In general one of the most insidious uses of language is to separate us from a sense of integrity and wholeness. Essentially what I'm saying is that the potential seductiveness of language is dangerous. I believe many of those poets who are described as language poets begin from this premise. But for me there is another layer of distrust—historical distrust if you will. After all, this was a language that the European forced upon the African in the New World. So that the exploitative plantation machine could be more efficiently run. It was a language of commands, orders, and punishments. This language—english in my case, but it applies to all the languages of those European countries involved in the colonialist project—was never intended or developed with me or my kind in mind. It spoke of my non-being. It encapsulated my chattel status. And irony of all ironies it is the only language in which I can now function. And therein lies the conundrum—"english is my mother tongue," but it is also "my father tongue." *(She Tries Her Tongue; Her Silence Softly Breaks.)* I begin from a position of extreme distrust of language and do not believe that english—or any European language for that matter—can truly speak our truths without the language in question being put through some sort of transformative process. A decontaminating process is probably more accurate since a language as deeply implicated in imperialism as english has been cannot but be contaminated by such a history and experience.

Q: How are you able to write then, if you believe this to be the case?

A: With great difficulty. It is like having an abusive parent. You can't pretend you don't or didn't have the parent or the experience. First you have to find a way of healing—if that is at all possible—then a way of managing the memory of that experience. For me there is always a shadow around english and my use of english because this so-called mother tongue of mine is rooted in a very particular brutal and traumatic history—that of the four hundred year slave trade in which European peoples and nations kidnapped and traded African peoples to provide the labour force needed for the sugar and cotton plantations of the New World.

Even as I use the words "kidnap" and "trade" they in no way begin to convey the horror of it all. The murders, the rapes, the physical mutilation, the destruction of families, villages, cultures, languages are all neatly packaged and managed in the expression "slave trade." The exquisite challenge every writer faces is that language always stands in for the experience, the thought or feeling. The struggle is to reduce the gap between the experience and the expression of that experience. In my case there is a double standard if you will because of the history of the language in relation to me and my history. Essentially language represents a wound for me.

Q: Hasn't it healed by this time? After all it has been over a century?

A: A mother never forgets the birth of her child. Ask any woman who has given birth, no matter what her age, and she'll be able to tell you what the birth of each of her children was like.

Q: I'm not sure I get your point.

A: There are certain experiences that defy the passage of time is what I'm saying. The fact that the loss of a language didn't happen to me personally in no way means that I do not remember that loss. In fact, I remember it as if it happened yesterday.

Q: I'll have to take your word for it.

A: Yes, you will—in the same way we take a mother's word that she remembers the birth of her child. But to return to my earlier point. Because of this distrust that is lodged in the history of how I came to this part of the world, I handle language in a very self-conscious way—almost as a "foreign anguish" *(She Tries. . .)*. I hope in the way a painter approaches her paint, or a sculptor his marble. It is not me—it is outside of me—a foreign anguish. And yet it is me. As only language can be. The Heideggerian house of one's being, if you will. The only way I can then work with it is to fracture it, fragment it, dislocate it, doing with it what it did to me and my kind, before I can put it back together, hopefully better able to express some of my own small truths. And for me this is where form becomes so very important, because part of the transformative and decontaminating process is also to find the appropriate form for what I'm saying.

Q: What would you say then about poets who do not do this with their work—whose work is more accessible.

A: As in not being "complex and abstract"?

Q: If you wish.

A: Well, my role here is not to comment on their work—I believe that is more your function as critic. However, I would say that when a poet like LKJ uses a dub beat over his lyrics, I believe he is trying to accomplish the same thing I am trying to do when I fracture, fragment then put language back together again—trying to decontaminate it, perhaps. Refashioning it so that it can carry what you want it to say; managing the brutal history that casts a long and deep shadow around the language. The cultural practice which has survived most intact among Africans in the New World is music and I believe it offers another layer to the meaning and speaks of that shadowing—the wound if you will. One result of using music with words in that way, however, is that the work becomes far more capable of crossing over to non-African audiences. I doubt whether these audiences understand the context of the words any more with music, but they are entertained at least. The challenge for critics like yourself is to understand the cultural specificity of works like my own without the aid of music.

Q: Do you have any readership within Black communities—let me rephrase that—is it only white people—critics and students who can appreciate your work?

A: Poets and writers like myself who question and challenge the very ability of the language itself to speak the truth of their memories and engage in what I call practices of dislocation find themselves on the horns of a dilemma. Their poetry can be described as being language based and appears to share a great deal with those poets working within the European aesthetic of language poetry. The language based nature of poetry such as my own starts from a very different place. That of the wasteland between the terror of language and the horror of silence. White or European audiences who do not understand the matrix of this poetry miss what the poetry is all about. They see it as postmodern.

On the other hand there is a sense in which we have delegitimised ourselves to some degree in the eyes of our communities—who after all constitute our potential audience and market. Traditionally the Black poet has played a significant role in declaiming against the scourges that have plagued, and continue to plague, African people in the New World ever since their forced relocation. While wordplay is integral to certain African based musical forms like calypso, by and large language is taken as a given.[2] A daffodil is a daffodil is a daffodil. Although for those of us studying english literature in the colonies it would have been far more accurate to say: "A daffodil is not a hibiscus, poinsettia, croton or flamboyant."

Q: I'm not sure I quite understand what you mean.

A: If there is one central image that sums up english literature studies in the Caribbean for me it would be the daffodil. Every school child had to engage with Wordsworth's daffodils at some time, although we had never seen them, and most of us would probably never see them. And yet our very futures depended on being able to write about these bloody flowers.

Q: I see.

A: If I were to play around—riff on that image—I might turn out something like this:

Is not a daffodil
is
and not
is—

I'm far more interested in working with the structure of the language to destabilize the image of the daffodil.

It seems, however, that the urgency of all the ills we have to rail against as New World Africans appears to militate against this sort of play. But given that the universe is always in play, what else is there to do but play? I suspect, however, that the memory of the horror and terror of loss of tongue lies so heavily on us that playing with language appears almost frivolous.

There is as yet no parallel between the way in which New World Africans have used their language of music in the New World to create complex new forms like jazz and our literary use of english. This may have all to do with the fact that because we need language for everyday communication, unlike music, there is a powerful urge to approximate the standard use of language. Playing music, and in particular African based music, was never seen as a mark of being civilised. On the other hand speaking and writing english, french or spanish, properly—in the manner that whites did—was, indeed, a marker of being civilised. It put some distance between you and your more downtrodden African brothers and sisters. The recent controversy over the use of ebonics proves that very little has changed around issues of language marking acceptability by the white society.

Far too many of us still take language for granted—assuming its transparency. It is too seldom treated as raw material, no different than stone—to be cut, shaped, moulded, twisted, broken and put back together again in a new way.

Q: Would you describe your work as postmodernist.

A: It is if you say it is.

Q: What do you mean by that?

A: Many years ago I had a constitutional law professor who taught his classes according to the Socratic method. He never answered a question, but parried every query from us timid first-year law students with, "It is if you say it is." This phrase is the best response to those readers and critics who insist that *She Tries her Tongue; Her Silence Softly Breaks* is a postmodernist work. It is if you say it is. Postmodernist that is. But to see *She Tries* . . . as only or primarily a postmodernist work is to miss most of what the work is about. Unless, that is, one understands the Caribbean as a postmodernist space long before the term became current. Which is not that far-fetched.

Q: Code switching, bricolage, sampling, inventions—these are all significant markers of postmodernist work—

A: And of the Caribbean—but within a very different context. A context that is simultaneously African, European, Asian, creole and hybrid. However, I do understand that since the author, like history, is dead—my intentions as the humble author are dismissable.

Q: Not entirely—

A: My point is simply that while the work may look like a duck, walk like a duck and even talk like a duck, it is not a duck. The deep structure of the work is of and from the African Caribbean. I believe what happens is that the multicoded, multifaceted nature of the work which plays with quotations, engages with polyvocality and works almost as a sort of hypertext is what leads the reader to assume its postmodernity. I am saying that it both is. And is not postmodern. Simultaneously and disjunctively.

Modernism is understood to be a primarily Western, European phenomenon. This, despite the fact that what we now call the third world, or more euphemistically the developing world, was an integral aspect of it—if only in providing the savage Other against which the west could preen its civilised self. As you well know many of the ideas that influenced modernists like Picasso, Brancusi and company came from Africa and Oceania. And jazz, the creation of New World Africans, altered that most basic aspect of life itself—rhythm and timing. Yet when we think of modernism and its sibling and legatee postmodernism, we think primarily of European movements. Within that context work like my own is not postmodernist. However, if we understand modernism and postmodernism to embrace more than Europe, if we understand the postmodern reality of the African Caribbean, then and only then I think is anything gained by interpreting the work as postmodernist.

Q: How would you have me interpret the Caribbean then?

A: To understand the Caribbean one needs to understand it and the entire New World as a site of massive interruptions. Of Aboriginal life, for the most part fatally. In the traumatic and violent wrenching from Africa that slavery entailed, African life would also be ruptured, also often fatally. Indentureship of the Asian represented another interruption. And while the European tried to maintain continuity in the face of the Other there would be an interruption of another sort in that instance. The Caribbean is synonymous with rupture and break and hiatus and held breath. And death. And rebirth.

What I want you to do is hold the image of the woman's body—the Black woman's body—as central to all that is happening in the Caribbean. Because when we think of the Caribbean we have to think of cut—as in wound—and cunt into which Columbus, emissary of the Old World, would penetrate on behalf of his masters. You could call it a surrogate fuck, or a fuck by proxy, because the rapine and pillaging would truly begin in the english speaking world with the robber barons like Hawkins and Drake and others of their ilk wreaking havoc on the virginal space in rabid search of redemption, utopia and riches—whatever the anglo version of the fabled el dorado was—while bringing death, disease and pestilence.

Q: That is a very gendered reading of the Caribbean, isn't it.

A: How else can it be read? Consider that Columbus sails under Spanish flags on behalf of a country led by a woman, Queen Isabella of Spain, and that Hawkins receives his first commission for the importing of slaves from Queen Elizabeth I. Were these women men in drag, or were they merely powerful white women (how can you be merely powerful?) using men to do their dastardly acts? There's a lot of work to be done looking at the role of these kinds of powerful women in the colonialist project.

Q: How do you represent this in your work? Or do you even try to represent it?

A: Given the fragmentation, the ruptures, the discontinuities, it seemed to me that to force a work like *She Tries* . . . into a logical and linear way of reading—top to bottom, front to back—was to do the experience a second violence. The fragmented manner of representation was indeed a "truer" representation of the history. You can begin reading the work anywhere and within any poem—although certain poems like "Discourse on the Logic of Language" lend themselves more to this than others. Begin anywhere. Doesn't this sum up the colonialist project in one respect?

Q: How so?

A: So many peoples—in my case African—were forced to begin anywhere—to pretend and behave as if there had been no before and would be no after. Begin anywhere—I began with wanting to subvert—to destroy the lyric voice. I felt it could not bear the weight of my history. All this was presumptuous perhaps, but that was how I felt. I also questioned the tradition of the solitary voice of the poet—often a male, a white male, who embodied the wisdom of the society, and who spoke for, on behalf of and to *his* society or culture. In a voice of authority. Although he might be marginalized and he often was, his words were valued—he had a role to play even as outcast and had the authority to do so.

I would turn Eliot's objective correlative on its head—fog was supposed to be fog even in the Caribbean. And a little Black girl in the Caribbean was supposed to feel the same emotion as Prufrock.

Q: Did you succeed—in destroying the lyric voice?

A: I don't know. The certainties of youth appear to be just that now. I do know that what happened is that the work became impossible to read in the traditional sense—there were so many events happening on the page—not to mention the silences. In "Discourse. . ." for instance—the poem that most typifies this challenge—there are four different voices clamouring to be heard on the combined facing pages.

It seems to me that the work engages with one of the most significant African musical techniques—that of call and response. I also think that it encapsulates an African world view in which the ancestors become the call and we the response. In turn we humans call the ancestors into response, to act within our lives. It's like a snake doubling back on itself—eating its own tail. This call and response technique works both within poems and between poems. The contradiction in the centre refrain of "Discourse. . ."—"English is my mother tongue / is my father tongue. . ."—calls into response both the edicts against speaking in African tongues as well as the impulse to continuity of tongue, as in language, which the woman—in this case the Black woman—bears and expresses.

This does not—cannot—result in smoothly lyrical poetry. I saw the lyric voice as one of the tools used to further the ends of colonialism. And in upending the objective correlative I would immerse the poem once again in the mess and morass of history—not remove it out of its context as Eliot urged. History was not dead for me, as the postmodernists urged. I wanted a chance to rewrite it. According to *my* dictates—*my* memories. You may say this was presumptuous of me, but no more presumptuous than those who had written my history according to their dictates. And if the reader stumbled, stopped and started again. If s/he choked, and gagged on the words, then it was successful.

Q: I have some difficulty seeing how you equate success with—how do you put it?—the reader choking and gagging.

A: I once did a reading of "Discourse . . ." with two other women. One was a Canadian of European background, the other was a First Nations woman. When we were done the white woman said to me that she felt extremely uncomfortable reading the edicts forbidding Africans from speaking their languages. She understood, however, that the discomfort was an important lesson for her. The First Nations woman confessed to stumbling over the description of how the brain worked. This was also the section that spoke of the naming of certain parts of the brain after two nineteenth-century doctors who believed that Africans and other peoples of colour as well as women were inferior to white men. My answer to her was that as a First Nations woman she was intended to stumble over those words. The parts of the brain that controlled speech—our speech—were not named with her in mind. We—as Black and First Nations women—were never intended to be in control of our own lives.

I want to take this metaphor about eating further. So much of the so-called developing world has been/is being consumed—literally—slipping into the great maw of the west and slipping down its throat to its stomach, there to be digested and transformed into some imitation of the original. And bearing names and labels like "world music" that separate the product from its source. In such a world to be indigestible—to have the ability to make consumption difficult—is a quality to be valued.

Q: You've made reference on more than one occasion to history and memory. Would you care to talk about your history?

A: It's not only my history. It's also your history. Ours if you will.

Q: Talk to me of our history then. And how it influences your writing.

A: How does one write about the rupture that is Africa in the Caribbean? One doesn't. First one has to acknowledge the silence. Even after all the words, what remains is silence, because what happened demands silence. As a form of respect. But as a writer and poet the impulse is always to words. The question is do you—should you—turn the horror of a particular history into something beautiful, because of course it is that beauty which will make the work ultimately so digestible. I confess to being disturbed at texts which attempt to deal in this way with aspects of slavery—fictional works, poetry, which are so "beautifully" written that the horror is also beautifully managed. For me the more seductive the language, the more I distrust it—with a centuries-old distrust. Of course this leads to issues of marketability and audience. Most people appear to want anodynes.

Q: Aren't you shooting yourself in the foot—you did say you wanted a wide readership for your work.

A: Every writer wants that. The question is, I suppose, how much you are willing to give up for such an audience and market. The challenge for me is to mark within the structure of the language itself that which I am speaking about, but which I can't really speak about.

Q: Why do you say you can't speak about it? I assume that it is your—what you say is our history here in the New World. You have been speaking about it in works like "Discourse. . . ."

A: Because "it" didn't happen in english. Or french or spanish. It happened in another language—that I am a stranger to. So how do I (w)rite/right that? What happened, indeed, is happening/happened within the spaces between words, between clotted clumps of words, between letters even.

Q: Are you saying that you find it difficult to write your history.

A: Yes, in the traditional sense of history. What helps is memory.

Q: You see them as being in contradiction.

A: Don't you? There are many, many memories, some complete, some not so complete. But there is also only one memory. A single memory. Of loss. Loss, loss, and more loss. The challenge for me is to write from that place of loss. Of nothing if you will. To make poetry out of silence.

Q: I'm interested in how you read those poems that are speaking with more than one voice.

A: Over the years I had fallen into the habit of only reading certain poems—those that lent themselves most easily to the single voice. On one occasion a student asked me to read "Universal Grammar" *(She Tries. . .)* for her. Without thinking about it I replied: "I will, if you read it with me." It was then that I came to the realization that I had, indeed, succeeded in what I had set out to do, although not in quite the way I anticipated. I should confess at this point that most of the insights about *She Tries* . . . have come to me after completion of the work—in this instance substantially after completion. As I have said before, I wanted to destroy the lyric voice. As a Black, female, colonized subject, what was the source of my authority, and was such authority necessary—indispensable perhaps?—to speech, public speech. To poetry? Being neither male nor white and without an observable or tangible source of authority, could I even speak? Or would I only speak a silence?

What I hadn't realized until "I will, if you read it with me" was that in shifting the lyric voice, in at least forcing it to share the page with other voices, with other histories—moving it from centre stage and page; in clearing a space—I had allowed for other voices to be heard. A multivocal, polyvocal discourse could now be heard. It was the chorus of the unheard, the not-heard, the barely whispered. This to me was closer to the discourse of women. To the call and response of African speech. I saw the text now as a jazz text. If you look at "Discourse . . ." for instance, the centre refrain can be seen as the main musical theme and the linguistic events that are happening in english around this centre theme can be seen as riffs speaking into the silence around the "anguish that is English." Indeed the entire work can also be seen to be working around the central theme that "Discourse. . ." represents—the loss of language.

Q: I return to an earlier question—I assume you are writing about these issues—

A: I try not to write about issues when I write poetry.

Q: What are you trying to do then?

A: To get to the truth of certain experiences.

Q: The question remains—I assume that the audience you have in mind when you write is one which shares your context, but the issues—or rather your approach to them—appears—

A: You are back to the issue of "complex and abstract" aren't you? How do I bridge that gap? I confess that on completion of *She Tries* . . . I became very aware that while the work was complete on the page, there was another completion that was needed—the completion of performance. I believe that one very crucial aspect of the Caribbean aesthetic is performance, so it is interesting that the work contains within its structure that potential. When the poems are performed, even within the classroom, each 'reading' yields different information and new truths as occurred in the reading with the First Nations woman and the European woman.

Q: The body appears to have played a large part in this work.

A: Yes, the body erupted into the text of *She Tries . . .* in unexpected ways. There is a certain rightness to this given how the African body was inserted in the New World. Given that the African body—"black ivory", "pieces of the Indies" as they were euphemistically called—was the *sine qua non* of the development of the New World. Those early Africans came with nothing but the body which would become the repository of everything they would need to survive. The Body Memory if you will. For four hundred years those black bodies would withstand the onslaught of empire. Those black bodies are, in fact, the only thing standing between empire and a state of total annihilation. The erasure of memory in the face of history. Because to erase the body is to erase the memory.

Q: How is this work received in Canada?

A: I like to think of Canada as a space—the space that is Canada. What I should say right off the top is that works like *She Tries . . .* and *Looking for Livingstone* could only have been written in Canada.

Q: Why is that?

A: Had I lived in the U.S.A. the hegemonic weight of African American culture would have been so great that I would have had a great deal of difficulty—I doubt whether I would have been able to do it—speaking about the Caribbean—the wound that is the Caribbean. And had I lived in England, there would have been similar constraints of empire and its legacy—the Commonwealth. Only the space that is Canada allowed me the room I needed to work these ideas through. That space at times felt like a black hole in which everything was in danger of collapsing in and on itself. Both the U.S. and England have a long history of engaging with African culture in some way. Canada didn't, despite settlements in southern Ontario and the Maritimes that date back to the War of Independence. The deep cultural insecurity of Canada militates against the inclusion of African cultural practices except as they may fit under the rubric of multiculturalism. And the mantra of multiculturalism is repeated so often as to convince you of its talismanic properties. It is but a thin veneer which barely conceals a society as steeped in white supremacy as it is in hypocritical protestations to the contrary.

Having said that, however, the work is taught in some institutions and for that I am happy. As I said before, to erase the body is to erase the memory, and while this particular Black body is here in this white space called Canada, there is a memory.

Notes

1. Rhonda Cobham, "Women of the Islands," *The Women's Review of Books,* Vol.VII, Nos. 10–11, July 1990, 29.
2. Rastafarian language and speech contain many examples of unusual orthography and refashion words to reflect a certain world view. For instance, instead of "oppressed" they use "downpressed" and instead of system they use shitstem. For work in this area please see the work of Velma Pollard.

Bibliography

Philip, M. NourbeSe. *She Tries Her Tongue; Her Silence Softly Breaks.* Ragweed Press, 1988, and The Women's Press, 1993.

Philip, M. NourbeSe. *Looking for Livingstone: An Odyssey of Silence.* Mercury Press, 1991.

Don Wellman

Cultural Cannibalism and the Intercultural Text

An incommensurability of different realities is characteristic of the collisions that occur when the culture of corporate capitalism penetrates or undermines local cultures around the globe. Acknowledging that incommensurability and its role in the formation of subjectivities is crucial to reading world writing in its postcolonial, cross-cultural, or transgressive aspects. Examples of such texts include the works of Aimé Césaire, Wilson Harris, and Kamau Brathwaite—works that employ deconstructive intertextual strategies, most often a cross-weave of cultural referents and languages, to produce a space wherein normative notions of humanity appear fractured. What I choose to call "intercultural texts" come into being and deploy themselves on the margins between cultures. Marked by an opacity of hybrid forms, these texts defy translation, making access to "the global village" in Marshall McLuhan's utopian sense of the phrase impossible. Opacity screens the discourse from intrusions by the outsider and preserves the option of flight from inspection.

There is a lot to unpack in my opening paragraph. Jean-François Lyotard, for instance, seems to have insinuated himself among the words I have chosen to use. "Postmodern knowledge," he writes, "refines our sensitivity to differences and reinforces our ability to tolerate the incommensurable" (xxv). Let me say clearly then that I do not evoke "the desire for a return to terror" (82) that Lyotard associates with the postmodern take on the sublime; instead, I suggest that hybrid form "puts forward the unpresentable," Lyotard's phrase (81), in ways that compel attention to palpable realities. I do not desire to claim growth in my "ability to tolerate the incommensurable." Faced with the "unpresentable," I will admit to indigestion.

The poems that I will write about draw on everyday experiences that filter through the interstices between boundaries. Making distinctive use of hybrid forms, they inscribe what Mikhail Bakhtin, for one, has called "the active role of the other" (70). By way of illustration, let me turn to Kamau Brathwaite's *MiddlePassages,* where an insistence on local and material aspects of African-Caribbean culture maps some of those differences that are crucial to emergent subjectivity. In "Letter: Sycorax," he writes,

not fe dem / not fe dem
de way caliban

done

but fe we
fe a-we.
(*MiddlePassages,* 106)

The text of "Letter: Sycorax" is hybrid, giving visible form to spoken language, sometimes opaque, sometimes using puns to undercut standard English with the emergent language of an "a-we." In the first lines of "Letter: Sycorax," Brathwaite distinguishes between the role of the other assigned to the African by literary and political history and the active voice of the other. Addressing his mother, "Dear mamma," the language puns between the already hybrid reality of a creole language and the language and technology of global economic powers:

I writin yu dis letter / **wha?**
guess what! pun a computer o/kay?
like I jine de mercantilists! (95).

The language of the poem is transgressive or "thieving": "I mean de same way dem tief / in gun / power from sheena & taken we blues &" (96). Insistent orality, envisaged on the computer screen and reflected on the page in fonts familiar to those who have used Apple computers, conveys an urgency to speak for a people who know deeply that the discourse on individual freedom is incommensurable with their history.

Theorizing the intercultural text allows me to draw distinctions among forms of hybridity, different meldings of languages and cultural referents. For example, Ezra Pound's *Cantos* represent a polyglot intertextuality held together by a totalizing will, a thirst for order that is entirely consonant with the general shape of cultural imperialism. I also distinguish the intercultural text from other forms of multicultural production. For instance, in novels by Toni Morrison or Rudolfo Anaya, read as exempla of multiculturalism, an ethnic consciousness operating within a larger totality seeks to position itself so as to transform that totality or indeed redeem it (cf. James Baldwin, *The Fire Next Time*). The multicultural text compels recognition. Differences signify an irreducible integrity in their own right and bear witness to an irreducible factor with which the enunciating voice identifies. To refuse to acknowledge this "redemptive" ethos may well undermine the humanity of the reader. I am oversimplifying, but this to me at least seems accurate with respect to how the multicultural text is taught in "English B" (cf. Langston Hughes's poem of that title). By way of contrast, then, to now normative expectations for multicultural productions (especially in the United States), the intercultural text decenters the relation between subject and other. It often invokes carnivalesque or other anti-structural facts of social experience and posits no universals other than a cosmic void in which individual mortality, tradition (including tribal or oral heritages), and future civilization all founder or tilt maddeningly as a result of the by-play of incommensurable constructions of reality. Under this pressure language breaks down into experimental and polyglot forms; health and sanity take the figure of a flight along the margins—i.e., "dislodged" or "unhomely" subjectivities become shared positions.

Opacity of language is a feature of an incommensurability that is very real to Brathwaite as well as to the reader used to standard English. Edouard Glissant, in his discussion of "creolization," calls for texts that "in defiance of a universalizing and reductive humanism . . . [employ] specifically opaque structures," requiring the reader to accept "the irreducible density of the other." Glissant has developed a transphysical poetics of "the crosscultural imagination" ("Natural Poetics, Forced Poetics" 133–134). In "Letter: Sycorax," Brathwaite creates exactly such an "irreducible density" of language. His page, in its "raw feel" for the other, layers the tilted fields of ritual, history, and social fact upon the warp of a desiring subjectivity:

what is de bess way to say so/so it doan sounn
like

brigg
flatts or her. vokitz nor de

π.
san cantos nor de souf sea bible

nor like ink. le & yarico & de anglo saχon
chronicles

&
mamma!

a fine
a cyaan get nutten

write
a cyaan get nutten really

rite
while a stannin up hey in me years & like me
inside a me shadow (107–108)

At issue is not authenticity as in the recovery of a lost voice, but invention. In a Sisyphus-ean struggle, emergent desire cautions itself. Transparent language, language without shadows, is someone else's stone that the subject rolls uphill as "the man" watches you fail:

like de mahn still mekkin mwe walk up de
slope dat e slide
in black down de whole long curve a de arch (109)

Brathwaite's wail, "write / a cyann get nutten really // rite" employs creole and the subterfuge of pun to forge a connection between "write" (writing) and "rite"—those social practices including ritual that sustain the people, with whom he identifies, "mwe" closing the distance between "me" and "we."

Negotiating the rifts among incommensurable realities, Brathwaite's text inscribes a third sense of "w/rite"—"right." Reading against the grain, Brathwaite cites Basil Bunting's language, but that strong-stress Anglo-Saxon vibrancy of *Briggflatts* is not at home on his tongue. Brathwaite's reading of Pound's "I cannot make it cohere" (from the last pages of the *Cantos*) illuminates for me the disabling reality of the language and ideology of human rights. Pound's inability to assemble the fragments of his vision does not carry with it an admission of wrong-headedness with respect to his core beliefs. It does not atone. Individualism, read as an antidote to the gap between theory and practice, dissociates the right to believe from accountability for actions. That dissociation is at the root of liberal thought (and also at the root of Pound's *Jefferson and/or Mussolini*).

From the Caribbean perspective, nascent capitalism, by excluding the African from the grant of "human rights," undercut the new faith in rational coherence at the very moment of its inception (cf. C. L. R. James on the French Revolution in *The Black Jacobins*). As a result, emergent subjectivities have had to adapt strategies of resistance. To alien eyes (western eyes, eyes that have not experienced the rift between rights and practices), the face of the other may seem contorted by desire. Hybrid forms used to express desire may resemble dissociative disorders. We see the other then as Caliban, a near anagram for cannibal, even though we have been the agents of displacement and dismemberment. Brathwaite's digitized scrawl of an "X" (echoing the historical mark of indenture, used by owners to deny subjectivity to the possessed) joins "a countertradition of marronage, divergence, flight, fugitive tilt" (*Discrepant Engagement* 285), all subterfuges that according to Nathaniel Mackey turn "other" from a noun into a verb. The "X" becomes opaque inscription of a subjectivity that refuses identification with property and associated ideas of individuality.

Many of the intercultural texts that I identify with hybrid characteristics share an underlying topology: fluid boundaries shift as history overflows, inundates, or becomes the present to those who inhabit a "contact zone."[1] The intercultural text engages the ways desire bends or folds surface alignments, making boundaries amorphous, permeable. On the other hand, norms for mainstream reception tend to ignore the ways in which colonialism (in its various guises) has demonized (sometimes romanticized), exploited, and now markets "the other" as a global resource. Susan M. Schultz's paper, "Local Vocals: Hawai'i's Pidgin Literature, Performance, and Post-coloniality," presented at this conference, made a distinction between "aesthetic drama" and "social drama," a distinction that my reading habits tend to erase.* Her argument, like mine, puts into play not only the social drama of reception, but also contemporary resistances and adaptations with respect to aesthetic form (on the part of both ethnic authors and cultural institutions). My emphasis on hybridity and opacity embraces the forms of cultural solidarity embodied in a living pidgin like that used by Lois Ann Yamanaka in her "talk stories." Schultz writes, "They were hearing their own words in a language more often spoken than written." Her point is not dissimilar to that made by Trevor Joyce at the conference, when he asked in his inimitable way, "Where my language is disabled so am I?" Joyce and Schultz illustrate how, as Schultz put it in her paper, the literature of a contact zone "is almost inevitably in dialogue with the language and ideology of the dominant culture." However, using a focus on hybrid form in my approach to Brathwaite's work, I have also asked you to hear a new language, an emergent tongue insisting upon its relation to history, tradition, and evolving economic and social realities. Opacity and hybridity seem to me to be arts of an emergent subjectivity, drawing from a mix of cultural sources for purposes other than dialog or accommodation. They are instead ways of undermining the normative limits on discourse.

Although focused on Anglophone traditions of experimental writing, our conversations at the Assembling Alternatives conference revealed a rift between the institutionalization of the avant-garde and the imperative to acknowledge diverse subjectivities. The literary history addressed by the academy

*Editor's note: A version of Schultz's paper later appeared in *Close Listening: Poetry and the Performed Word,* edited by Charles Bernstein (New York and Oxford: Oxford University Press, 1998).

generally under the rubric of experimentalism must now include the intercultural text. One advantage of language-centered writing is that it warps experiment in the direction of social fact, although it also engages a specialized use of language, understood as artifice or game. Those poets here who are associated with "language writing" identify themselves with an avant-garde that just now, at the beginning of a new millennium, is negotiating the terms of its own institutionalization, wary of becoming displaced and unable to either write its own history or map its future with confidence. Under a gaze that has been trained to suspect authority, different "outrider" traditions (cited by Charles Cantalupo at the conference) have had cause to scrutinize the balance of integrity and privilege that underwrites the position of the avant-garde on the timeline that extends from this century to the next. These voices will find that they have more in common than they had imagined; but no one at Assembling Alternatives made a persuasive argument for bringing experimental language to bear on cultural revolution. Perhaps it is an inevitable property of institutionalization that the different revolutions in language represented at the conference exclude voices for whom "content" is political freedom. My argument is then that those of us from the States, especially, must learn to situate ourselves differently in the world—our preconceptions of what is at stake must alter.

"Your" and "my" poetry will gain (become more plastic or more resistant to ideological conditioning) as it becomes more familiar with the factual and situational uncertainties that threaten annihilation of "our" constructed selves. The experiential topology that I posit as characteristic of intercultural texts is one that motivates poetry in general—no matter who writes it or theorizes the desires that impel poetic utterance. Lacan for one, locates this topology outside and prior to language. On the other hand, language informs identity, including those unnamable prompts toward acknowledgment that censor our behavior, structuring, for instance, middle-class modes of seeking reaffirmation. All the same, language offers no antidote to difficult, unfamiliar things—whether personal things rooted in private desires or collective urgencies. Undercutting our best intentions, images of difficult and violent realities, now plugged into what Walter Benjamin calls the "optical unconscious,"[2] pursue, often seduce, even the most rational and moral among us. I am thinking here of the interplay of fantasy and virtual reality that conditions adolescence today. To play further upon what Bob Perelman said at the conference about marginalization of the poet within the academy, I am suggesting that even the most affluent among us lack sinecure or security—like children in front of computer screens, our constructed selves are not exempt from a loss of prepossessions.

Wilson Harris, the Guyanese author living in London, describes the effects of "extremity or marginality" in this way: "Extremity or marginality," writes Harris, " . . . lifts the medium or diverse experience to a new angle of possibility. . . . It involves us in a curiously tilted field in which spacial pre-possessions and our pre-possessions are dislodged . . . (*SE,* "In the Name of Liberty," 220).

The intercultural text has instructive value, even survival value. Presenting "a new angle of possibility," the knowledge of "human-kindness" inscribed on these pages models strategies for flight, containment, discipline. To read is to negotiate those "tilted fields" on which all of us engage difficult questions. Not mapping emergent realities in a Cartesian sense of discovering a workable grid of relations, the figure in flight along the margins discovers the distances produced by contact, a path perhaps more easily negotiated by an athlete in training than by a recursive reading, always looking back for an anchor, always up to attain a god's eye view, but feeling instead the sweat on the skin and the rush of air. Or is this only my "Planet Reebok" fantasy?

As an alternative to the media then (and its global reach), I argue that the postcolonial world provides a model for the experiential world of contingent realities. The modernist impulse employed separation and categorization so as to align aesthetics with moral imperatives. Instead, increasingly, experiences of "dispossessed man" without a history or language with which to identify (Edouard Glissant), experiences of the "dislodged self" (Wilson Harris) and of "the self-extinguishing I" (Nathaniel Mackey) are becoming commonplace. Like Homi Bhabha—at least this is the idea that I am playing with today—I take "the cultural and historical hybridity of the postcolonial world . . . as the paradigmatic place of departure" (21). It is a very different paradigm from the one that sought to articulate, after the horrors of World War II, a universal doctrine of human rights such as that enshrined in the UN charter.

Embodying the felt imperative for a paradigmatic shift, Charles Olson's "Projective Verse" has become the most frequently cited "place of departure" for American poetry [but I will skip over most of what I want to say about Olson—that is also where my references to cannibalism occur]. The first theorist perhaps of the postmodern condition, his push seems inexorably toward an alignment of interior space with outside realities—that is toward a resolution in modernist terms, aligning the individual with the cosmos, as though reality could, after a manner of speaking, be purified—just swallow enough of it. For instance, Olson's fetishization of the open-eyed, brown people that he comes into contact with among the Mayan might be thought laughable—a romantic quest for an untarnished reality. On the other hand, especially in the later work, Olson was keenly aware of the unwieldy proportions of his desire "to write a Republic / in gloom on Watch-House Point" (*Maximus* III.9). Demonic, phallic images of the sun that derive from Melville's Ahab (an alter-ego of Maximus), as well as from Memphite and Sumerian mythologies, exist in an unresolved tension with haunting images of loss or impotence. The size of *Maximus,* persona and book, are due to the immensity of Olson's transgressive ardor. In his determination to transform poetics by stripping back those layers of discourse that "estrange us from that with which we are most familiar," he seeks a knowledge that is sometimes associated with the body and its proprioceptive abilities, sometimes with "the face of God," figured as a wall or outer limit in *Special View of History.*

Both Olson and Bhabha identify humanism, understood as a set of inalienable rights, as a profound form of censorship, the primary means employed by the West to structure its relations with the world. It is not, in my reading, a naive or positivistic claim to internationalism that Olson ascribes to Melville, when he cites the following:

> "We are not a narrow tribe of men . . . we are not a
> nation, so much as a world."
>
> H. Melville
> Redburn (1849)
> (*Maximus Poems,* Vol. III, 599)

It is instead an ascription to Melville of a knowledge that Olson has appropriated: man must situate himself differently in his relation to geography than heretofore has been the case, whether among tribes or nations, among mapmakers or missionaries. Humanism is cooked (my third reference to cannibalism). My desire then is to enroll Olson among the ranks of those who practice a transgressive intercultural poetics. I will cite one instance, toward the end of *Maximus III* (609), and a second from the overleaf (610)—illustrating, for those who are unfamiliar with *The Maximus Poems,* I hope, Olson's ability to layer and fold the poetic field:

> Strod the water's edge & the
> land as though there were some reason to
> do such a thing   not going away any further
> to have his eggs than a rail does
>
> [Monday June 23rd

from the overleaf:

> Enyalion of
>   brown earth
>
> Strod the yellow earth
>
> with a long dry harsh call
>
> krk   krk   krk

Man, bird, resplendent war god, Enyalion/ Olson—forms a figure in flight along the margin, as recto and verso join to form an abstract space, dislocating Olson's prepossessions even as he clues in these fragments to his purpose of making a figure of "outward." What has become familiar is dislocation, an unhomely-ness of "un-homing" language—a language that when grasped ecstatically, embodies the "irreducible density of the other"—a phrase that I associate with our "human-kindness" as Victor Turner uses that phrase in *The Ritual Process* (128).

Nathaniel Mackey, an African-American poet with Caribbean roots, has acknowledged his debt to Olson, as well as to the intercultural theorists like Glissant and Harris that I have mentioned. In his work the loss of self or "prepossession" becomes a ritualized path or discipline, punctuated by deeply felt inadequacies. Sections of *School of Udhra* traverse layered fields of cultural referents. Narrative threads draw on memory, on local and immediate geosocial horizons, and on ritual (ranging among Voudun, Bedouin, Christian, Sikh and Hindu images) to create a textural density:

Unseizably

vast underbelly of

light

limb-letting thrust

Tread of

hoofs. Weighted udders of

dust . . .

His it their she

once they awake,

the

arisen one,

world

at her feet,

her feet

one with their

rapture,

ankle-deep in damage

though she

dances

(26)

The lines feel their way toward an ecstasy, in some ways reminiscent of Olson's Merry and the bull on Dogtown Common under the arch of Nut. What I want to highlight is the improvising, scat-like quality of the images, imposing a trance that submerges identity into a "his it their she." The speaker is not outside the lines but in them, marked by them, in a way that merges projective poetics with ritual:

And he with his
                    postures
  cramps the air,
                      bent
lotus-like, lips
                      part kiss,
                                  part
   pout

(27)

Part realization of an initial desire linked to consummation, part childlike and incomplete and unsatisfied, Mackey's lines seem always to feel their way toward resolution, never attaining a resolving phrase. In the surge and reflux of energy, similar in effect to the speaking among instruments and voices in blues or jazz, also similar to trance induced by shamanistic drumming, altering the listener's consciousness as the mind floats free of the pulse, I discover a means to address dislocation. Improvisatory response counters loss of prepossession by allowing the mind to seize and filter through restraints, engendering hybrid fusions that slide through the interstices of constructed identities.

Now, my conclusion sounds outlandish (or "outlantish" as Mackey has it), even to me. John Wilkinson, who read the final paper in the session at which I presented these ideas, aggressively pointed to the pragmatic and moral limitations of my position. Indeed, in his paper he suggested that "unhoming language . . . [does] violence on the readers." He insisted that "unhoming" language "does violence" because it disables the reader from participating in what he had earlier called the "reintegrative moment." To the contrary I have argued that "unhoming" language is not a language game or a fetishization of the primitive. It is instead an artful enactment of flight toward emergent subjectivity; it enables a feeling of freedom from structure that is crucial both for survival and for identity formation.

In *The Ritual Process* and elsewhere Victor Turner divides ritual into three phases. The first is separation from the structures associated with social position; the second is anti-structural or liminal; the third is reintegrative (allowing the subject to assume a new social position). I have drawn upon my understanding of the unstructured or liminal phase of ritual process as the site where we learn freedom (the very freedom necessary for realizing Wilkinson's "reintegrative moment"). Liminal spaces are being constantly compressed by the way we live, especially under media influence. Contrariwise I find that the practices of the intercultural or hybrid text expand our margins for learning "human-kindness." Do not then mistake my conclusion for a call for a renewal of the poet's role as shaman, as some at the concluding plenary session did. Instead, I seek to understand the ways in which diverse people enact desire, focusing on a use of language forms, whose value I think it perfectly essential for us to grasp.

Notes

1. cf. Mary Louise Pratt, "Arts of the Contact Zone." *Profession* 91. NY: MLA, 1991.
2. For an invaluable discussion of Benjamin and the "optical unconscious" see Michael Taussig, *Mimesis and Alterity.* New York: Routledge, 1993: 23 ff.

Works Cited

Bakhtin, Mikhail M. "The Problem of Speech Genres" in *Speech Genres and Other Late Essays.* Ed. Caryl Emerson and Michael Holquist. Austin: University of Texas Press, 1986: 60–102.

Bhabha, Homi K. *The Location of Culture.* London and New York: Routledge, 1994.

Brathwaite, Kamau. *MiddlePassages.* New York: New Directions, 1993.

Glissant, Edouard. *Caribbean Discourse: Selected Essays.* Charlottesville: Caraf, 1992.

Harris, Wilson. "The Writer in Society," in *Tradition, the Writer and Society.* London: New Beacon Books, 1967.

Harris, Wilson. *Selected Essays of Wilson Harris: The Unfinished Genesis of the Imagination.* Ed. A.J.M. Bundy. London: Routledge, 1999. Abbreviated in the text as *SE.*

James, C.L.R. *The Black Jacobins.* Second edition. NewYork: Vintage, 1989.

Lyotard, Jean-François. *The Postmodern Condition.* Minneapolis: University of Minnesota Press, 1984.

Mackey, Nathaniel. *Discrepant Engagement: Dissonance, Cross-Culturality, and Experimental Writing.* Cambridge: Cambridge University Press, 1993.

Mackey, Nathaniel. *School of Udhra.* San Francisco: City Lights, 1993.

Olson, Charles. *Selected Writings.* Ed. Robert Creeley. NewYork: New Directions, 1966.

Olson, Charles. *The Maximus Poems.* Ed. George Butterick. Berkeley: University of California Press, 1983.

Olson, Charles. Special View of History. Berkeley: Oyez, 1970.
Pratt, Mary Louise. "Arts of the Contact Zone." Profession 91. New York: MLA, 1991.
Taussig, Michael. *Mimesis and Alterity: A Particular History of the Senses.* New York: Routledge, 1993.
Turner, Victor. *The Ritual Process.* Ithaca: Cornell University Press, 1969.

Kathleen Crown

"Choice Voice Noise"

Soundings in Innovative African-American Poetry

the sound crumbs of the sea
that the delicate

reason   comes down to
feed on
—Ed Roberson

Swing the shoutout
Soundwaves loud.
Pushing the envelope
while moving through the crowd.
—Tracie Morris

choice voice noise
—Harryette Mullen

In recent years, discussions of linguistically innovative poetry have focused increasingly on "sound matters." As poets and critics have turned away from familiar critical concepts of poetic voice and vision, they have begun to theorize a "poetics of sound"[1] adequate to a range of contemporary language- and performance-based work, and they are reading or listening to poems as "sonic interventions"[2] capable of influencing social conditions outside the poem. This essay considers a notable development in formally innovative poetry—the convergence of sound games and sound technologies with a possessed lyric voice and an African-American aesthetic. I will suggest that in combining disjunctive sound play with a rhetoric of "possession," experimentalist black poets understand the human voice's capacity for dissociation and disarticulation as a reservoir for unclaimed experiences produced by the ruptures of the African diaspora. Developing compositional methods based on chance, coincidence, and physical contingency, these poets propose strategies for listening to the historical reverberations that can emanate from ways of speaking and "voicing" that follow from specifically African-American experience.

To think of lyric possession as a strategy for "sounding" this reservoir of unclaimed experiences raises questions about poetic agency and, ultimately, about poetic audience. What happens when poetic voice is constituted as "hearings"—when a poem allows for *heard sounds to speak the subject,* rather than for a subject who speaks through sounds? What are the effects of working at, or disrupting, this boundary between orality and aurality? These questions become even more difficult when we consider whether a possessed poetic voice can serve as an effective witness to traumatic historical events. Does an experimental poetry in which we can apprehend the voice's power of dissociation serve merely to textualize a crisis in witnessing, or does it actually erode any ground from which the witness can speak? This is the dilemma faced by poets who must find a way to reconcile the urgent need in our time for poetry to bear witness to traumatic historical events with their increasing sense of the instability of the witnessing "I," the erosion of the speaking subject's sovereignty. Harryette Mullen's *Muse & Drudge* neatly lays in place the elements of this quandary in a three-word line: "choice voice noise" (65). Embedding "voice" between "choice" and "noise," Mullen suggests that poetic voice in her work is complexly situated somewhere between agential practice and resistance (the exercise of individual and institutional choice) and the chaotic and disquieting off-rhyme of noise, that material or stuff of poetry that makes it possible for poetry finally to *matter.*

In addressing this dilemma, I will suggest that more is at stake than might appear in African-American poetry's recurrent scenes of what Susan Stewart has called "lyric possession." I argue that these haunted speakings and impossible utterances are acts of critical memory and history-making and do not represent, as some would claim, a nostalgic return to the Romantic ideal of poetry as transport or to an even older discourse of poetry as inspired utterance. Reading work by three very different experimental poets—Ed Roberson, Harryette Mullen, and Tracie Morris—I argue that each poet draws on and intervenes in a language-based poetics as well as in a speech-based African-American tradition to develop what I will call an "epistemology of sound," in which sound can be heard to perform its own knowledge. Despite the striking differences in their poetry, all three of these poets rework conceptions of lyric presence into a plural, mixed, possessed or "ecstatic" voice capable of developing new cultural literacies, new knowledges, and new audiences (rather than new meanings). Their work asks us to consider not merely the relation of sound to meaning but that of sound to knowledge and memory. To rethink poetry as epistemological practice refocuses our attention on the social location of the knower, whether that knower is poet or audience. The signal contribution of contemporary black avant-gardism in poetry, I argue, beyond the vernacular, musical, and vocal resources of the black aesthetic, is to challenge avant-gardist conceptions of audience. Located uneasily between disjunctive or "avant-garde" poetry's largely white readership and mainstream poetry's presuppositions of a black poet's accessibility, orality, and transparency (which often determine whose work will be published and anthologized), these poets cannot assume a homogeneous audience for whom they publish or perform their work. In reconfiguring poetic voice so that it verges on "noise" and seems at times to defer authorial "choice," these poets actively seek, cultivate, and create audiences that Roberson might term "unspeeched" and Mullen has called "unborn."

Possession and Trauma: Sound's Knowledge

Recent investigations of poetic sound have focused primarily on the tension between sound and meaning, or between sound and expression. In his introduction to *Close Listening: Poetry and the Performed Word,* Charles Bernstein asks, "What is the relation of sound to meaning?" and answers that "sound *enacts* meaning as much as designates something meant" (12, 17). Conversely, he also suggests that "meaning is rooted in the arationality of sound" (22). In a similar vein, Susan Stewart argues that "the dynamic tension between sound and semantic can at once both extend and diminish meaning" (34). In other words, while sounds do not necessarily have to "mean" anything, it is precisely their antidiscursive quality that can provide the foundation for meaning in poetry. Useful as such arguments are, we might benefit from considering the sonorous excess found in some recent poetry not only in terms of *semantics,* but in terms of its access to *knowledges* that have been subjugated or relegated to the realm of the unconscious. This is particularly true in the case of the poets under discussion here, for whom the ruptures produced by the African diaspora are a central concern of their work.

We might therefore productively extend Bernstein's questions to ask: What is the relation between sound and knowledge? Can knowledge be said to be rooted in sound? Or, as Susan Howe puts it, "How do sounds speak to memory?" (119). Indeed, Stewart proposes a relation between sound and memory that points us toward sound's ability to posit and retrieve knowledge:

> The sounds of the poem are not heard within the room of the poem, but they are heard within a memory of hearing that is the total auditory experience of the listener in response to what knowledge of the poem is extant at a given moment. (31)

This expansion of the poem's context away from "the room of the poem" to the larger space of the listening audience and its "memory of hearing" shifts our attention away from the poem's sound-language and toward its emergence in a material, performative, human, and embodied context.

This reconfigured relation between poet and audience depends in part on a recuperation and revitalization of the somewhat outmoded concept of poetic voice. Some avant-garde theorists have turned to sound as a means of dismissing "voice," which they see as irredeemably mired in humanism's illusions of a monologic, self-present lyric speaker.[3] Theorists who emphasize sound often do so in order to explode the poem's illusion of a speaking voice and thereby to separate "voice" from the human intentionality residing in a speaking body. Steve McCaffery, for example, celebrates the advent of audiotape because "it provided the revolutionary capability to finally transcend the biological limits on human bodily expression" (157). The most useful theories for thinking about the work of such poets as Roberson, Mullen, and Morris, however, do not reject the concept of the poem as an embodied human voice or deny it a spiritual dimension. Instead, they complicate, hybridize and pluralize the poetic voice, and challenge its status as a "rite of speaking truth" that ultimately produces the individual subject in conventional ways. For Nathaniel Mackey, there emerges in the poem as *cante moro* a "sound of trouble in the voice," which becomes "broken, problematic, self-problematizing" (195). The effect, he suggests, is like the "taking over of one's voice by another voice" (199), and he emphasizes the cross-culturality of this status in African-American poetry:

> To be possessed is to be mounted and ridden by a god. You find that imagery in *vodoun* in Haiti, in *candomblé* in Brazil, in *lucumí* or *santería* in Cuba. Possession means that something beyond your grasp of it grabs you, that something that gets away from you—another sense in which fugitivity comes in—gives you a voice. (203–4)

Jed Rasula points out that poetry's ancient function is to serve as a "voice-over" that "doubles the voice, splitting its allegiance in ways that can be *traumatizing* as well as *humanizing*" (275, emphasis added). But both Mackey's "*cante moro*" and Rasula's "voice-over" accentuate the traumatic component of lyric possession, and it is this sustained attention to the voice's troubled, split allegiances and to the operations of race and gender in the construction of knowledge that differentiates the work of these experimentalists from that of a Western tradition of lyric possession.

Harryette Mullen, for example, describes *Muse & Drudge* as a "'possessed' poem, full of different *voices,* a kind of chorus. But it is gendered," she says: "a group of women who have something in common but who are different and who are all speaking at the same time, or singing at the same time."[4] Situating the subjectivity and speech of the individual as the community and its ancestors speaking *through* the individual, Mullen reconfigures the concept of voice as plural, choral, and possessed. In thus depersonalizing the lyric speaker, she brings forward repressed elements of linguistic experience to assemble new audiences who share, across their cultural differences, varying modes of access to this new, hybrid, and syncretic literacy. Ed Roberson describes his poetics as a kind of "visual possession" that also relies on a sonic and rhythmic shift or catch: "When the possession occurs, there's a shift in the drumming, and sometimes a shift in the drummer. There is a shift that signals a possession."[5] In *Lucid Interval as Integral Music,* Roberson uses a strategy of "sound divination" to create a series of poems based on the sound correspondences found in the *New York Times* listings of "This Week's Concerts." For Roberson, possession involves reversible moments of catch, capture, and seizure, and the dynamic of possession can seem somewhat predatory—he describes "reason" as a "beak" that comes down to feed on "the sound crumbs of the sea" (58). Performer Tracie Morris describes her volatile poetic practice as allowing sounds to emerge and speak for themselves: "Stuff comes out that I am not prepared to utter. . . . Almost all the time, sounds come up that never have presented themselves before."[6] Exploiting the physical contingency and collaborative nature of performance—the open room, the microphone, and the audience response—Morris allows sounds to possess her voice in order to speak their own irruptive and precocious knowledge.

This idea that sound can "possess" the poetic speaker with its subjugated or repressed knowledge bears structural similarities to contemporary theories about traumatic experience. "To be traumatized," Cathy Caruth argues, "is precisely to be *possessed* by an image or event" (4–5). For Caruth, an extremely dislocating or traumatic experience presents itself as a pathology of history, in which historical knowledge possesses the unknowing speaking subject. Even those who have been subject to traumatic experience and seem to have survived unscathed are, apparently, doomed to repeat and reenact the event in strangely literal ways, inexorably "possessed" by latent knowledge or memories that seem unreliable, unwilled, and alien. Often the speaker who bears witness to trauma is possessed by voices of the dead; the reentry of these voices can be experienced as a reenactment of the trauma. Shoshana Felman, in a discussion of Paul Celan's poetry, argues that such traumatized vocal sounds are nonetheless capable of communication: "this breakdown of the word, this drift of music and of sound of the song which resists recuperation and which does not know, and cannot own, its meaning, nonetheless reaches a *you,* attains the hearing—and perhaps the question, or the answer of an Other" (37). These poems might be called "ecstatic" because they capture, formally and thematically, moments in which the psychic or bodily integrity of the speaking subject is threatened by boundary-rupturing experience. In the fundamentally dislocating experience of ecstasy (from *ex* + *stasis,* to be "beside oneself"), the boundary between self and other dissolves, whether in the invasive influx of an outside agency, or the projective transport of self into otherness. Such extreme and often traumatic experiences register the diasporic conditions of race and nation. In the poetry under consideration here, the dissociative, consciousness-splitting effects of trauma most often result from a specific racial violence that is understood as a disturbance in memory—the dis-memory or collective amnesia found both within and outside the African-American community.

Orality/Aurality

The work of re-memory requires that the poet enter into the shock of dissociation and thus establishes an ambiguous relation to lyric voice. "As hearings," Roberson writes in *Lucid Interval,* "the voice takes these unequalled stands / against an odds immense as sky" (72). Mullen's *Muse & Drudge* hyperbolically describes its material as "mongrel cyborg / mute and dubbed" (42), while Morris refers in her book *Intermission* to the "Mysterious backdraft" and "liquid consistency" of words as they "Fade black smack dab / in history" (51). None of these poets' works can be easily located on the spectrum between the aural and the oral. Ed Roberson, who has been described as a "representative postwar, postmodern African American poet [with] an intense obligation to art and history," is among the most writerly of experimentalists, despite the musicality and sound play of his work (Doreski 139). Influenced by the ethnopoetics movement, the Black Arts movement, and the "New American Poetry" (Spicer and Duncan in particular), Roberson describes his work in terms of "visual possession," and his poetic innovations are as visual and graphic as they are sonic.[7] Harryette Mullen's densely allusive writing embraces the pleasures and rigors of difficulty and disjunction, but her poetry is more performative than Roberson's, saturated as it is with the sounds and rhythms of popular culture and the electronic media. Whereas Roberson and Mullen are primarily identified with a writing-based poetic practice tied directly to the innovations of the "Language" movement, the spoken-word poet Tracie Morris (winner of the Nuyorican Grand Slam and the National Haiku Slam) works primarily out of an oral tradition. Her work is the least likely to be termed "experimental," despite her increasing involvement with sound poetry and her use of techniques often termed "postmodern," including syntactic disjunction, depersonalization, and disruption of speech rhythms.

The rigid binarism between speech and writing, orality and literacy, and vocal "expression" and written "experiment" has been particularly problematic for discussions of African-American poetry because, as Mullen argues, critics of African-American literature have tended to privilege a speech-based poetics, while excluding from consideration "more writerly texts" (Mullen 1996:

670). Aldon Nielsen makes a similar argument in *Black Chant: Languages of African-American Postmodernism,* demonstrating that there exists a set of "nearly hegemonic assumptions about the nature of the relationship between African-American oral traditions and writing, with a clear privilege given to the prevailing ideal of the oral" (18). In "Performing Blackness," Kimberly Benston argues that behind this opposition between oral and written poetry reside a "host of other, rather familiar, dualities" and he urges "that we shift the ground from underneath a criticism erected on such contraries" (166–67).

Houston Baker's concept of "supraliteracy" offers a way of escaping the insistence on such binaries as orality/literacy, colonizers/indigenous people, and self/other—divisions that Baker gives iconic shape in the relationship between Prospero and Caliban. Instead of promoting a "heroic" borderline status between the two worlds, Baker suggests that what is missing is "the *sound* of Caliban" (389) which is "monstrous and deformed only to the intruder" (391). He proposes *supraliteracy* as a "maroon or guerilla action carried out *within* linguistic territories of the erstwhile masters" and thereby "providing a space for poetry, a song, a *sound* rather than a sight, cite or site for further Western duels—and dualities" (395; emphasis added). The matter is not simply one of recalling the sounds of oral language into our visual practices of reading and writing, but of understanding how sound is already at work in both expanding and solidifying our present modes of literacy, which are most centrally our means of access to knowledge. Like Baker, I want to emphasize the activist dimension of poetic "soundings" as interventions capable of disturbing the conditions that enforce and promote conventional literacy.

To avoid describing the work of Morris, Roberson, and Mullen in oppositional terms, I propose to consider the ways that the work of African-American poets have increasingly come to defy these categories and, in effect, to stake out a new epistemological territory—not a middle ground but a "common ground"—one that refuses the dichotomizing of the voice poem and language writing as a racially and patriarchally constructed double bind. I find in the space between these conceptions of poetry, and despite their differences, a shared emphasis on the pressures that seemingly nonrational and nondiscursive elements of speech can bring to bear on rational public discourse.

"Soundwaves Loud" (Tracie Morris)

> *Sound poems challenge the notion of poetry, and one of the advantages—I don't want to affirm horrible racist conditions—but one of the advantages of having not had a good education in English is that my head is completely open in terms of what my English can do, what it's supposed to do, what it*

> *means. . . . Like what is a "word"? What is it, what is it, what is a word, really? What is a sound, really? What is a poem, really?*
>
> —Tracie Morris

Although Tracie Morris is a voice-based and community-based performance poet thoroughly of the Spoken Word movement,[8] her more recent work with sound poems or sonic improvisations has been described by some members of her audience as "more experimental" and "riskier." In these sound-poems, Morris blurs the boundaries between verbal and nonverbal through alteration of pitch and stress, shifts in tempo, breaking, riffing, rushing, scatting, bopping, gliding, and stuttering. Although vestiges of natural speech rhythms remain in the sound poems, the poet's "voice" is far more densely allusive, syntactically disjunctive, and depersonalized (so that natural speech rhythms, for example, are disrupted rather than imitated). The Spoken Word impulse to create "identification" between poet and listener is replaced by a desire to recover previously unheard voices and experiences through an "ecstatic" method that is open to contingency, chance, and seemingly alien influences. The ecstatic dimension of Morris's work, in which the poet seems possessed by "outside" voices and alien sounds, and seems to cultivate multiple voices, defies the conventional understanding of performance poetry and forces a more nuanced reading of the relation of performance poetry to avant-garde sound experimentation.

In an August 1999 performance at the Brooklyn Academy of Music's café in Fort Greene, Morris improvised her way through a brief "found" text—a familiar line taken from a Sam Cooke song:

> That's the sound of the men working on the chain gang.

Through extreme manipulations of her voice as a kind of musical instrument, Morris takes these recognizable words and disarticulates them into traumatized fragments, so that the hard "ch" and "g" sounds of "chain gang," for example, evoke the physical sounds of clanking chains and the grunts and heavy-breathing rhythms of physical labor. In a prolonged and visceral "working" of the line, Morris then allows the fragmented syllables to rearticulate themselves, improvisationally, as ecstatic, multivocal, and healing utterances, so that we hear, for example, the reconstituted words "Agun" and "Ogun," the names of West African deities. In this performance of trauma, political protest, and healing, the responsibility for the process of rearticulation falls somewhere between the improvising poet and the participatory audience—both collaborate in the recomposition of meaning as it is voiced or heard, but neither is in full control of how the inarticulate, improvised sounds become reconstituted or finally heard and understood.

As Morris has increasingly emphasized the disruptive sonic elements of her work, she has also increasingly composed poems that testify to trauma—to oppressive racial and gender practices. The audience experiences a voice that is wounded, dismembered, cut up and fragmented. At one level, Morris's sound performances enact the repetition of trauma, in which the poetic subject's possession by language takes the form of stuttering sounds, autonomic vocalizations, and enraptured speakings. In these sound poems, Morris conceives of "voice" as containing multiple potentialities that must be brought forward more or less violently by the poet, in order that they may undergo a collective hearing and verification. The performance poet is pure catalyst—she *permits* or conjures the appearance of what manifests in the unrepeatable performative moment, but does not command or control its presence. To understand this kind of ecstatic poetics as an ethical response to traumatic events, we need a view of poetic "voice" that goes beyond voice as the seat of personal expression of sincere emotion and individual will. Morris's poetry asks us to understand voice, instead, as a *medium*: a medium of being, a medium of history, and a medium through which language and personhood occur.

An example of a sound poem that seeks to bear witness to a local community's grief, loss, and trauma is Morris's poem of tribute to the memory of Anthony Baez,[9] a young man killed in 1994 by a New York City police officer under circumstances that provoked charges of police brutality. The poem consists solely of two words—the young man's first and last names—which Morris repeats over a long period of time, expressively shifting pitch, tempo, and tone. The live performance is profoundly moving, as the name "Baez," through the stuttering repetition, disintegration, and reintegration endemic to traumatic experience, comes to suggest an entirely other vocabulary, most notably the resonant word "bias" (meaning prejudice). In another poem, which Morris introduces by saying "this is about spousal abuse" and describes as being inspired by Doris Day movies, she riffs on the familiar song lyrics: "I'm in heaven, / I'm in heaven / And my heart beats / so that I / can hardly speak."[10] During the improvisation, Morris beats out time on her chest and throat, with increasing violence to the sound, as the audience becomes more and more uncomfortable listening to the prolonged stress to which she subjects her body and vocal cords. Finally, the word "speak" is squeaked out in a painful whisper that ends the poem. "[M]y voice takes a beating with those poems," says Morris in an interview, going on to emphasize her volatile poetic practice as one of allowing sounds to emerge and speak for themselves. "Stuff comes out that I am not prepared to utter, " she says. "Because the work is improvisational, I don't always know what the ending is going to be. . . . Almost all the time, sounds come up that never have presented themselves before." The unpredictability of the material context of the performance—stage, microphone, body, and café audience—is intimately involved in this poetic and spiritual strategy of "harnessing" external sounds and voices. As performance theorist Elin Diamond puts it, "performance is never only a voluntaristic or intentional act of making and communicating, but also, and simultaneously, an engagement with what constrains, limits, extends and distorts such acts" (4). For Morris, these limiting and extending factors include outside forces: not just the bodies of the audience as they give response and feedback, but also the surprising body of language as it presents itself in performance.

Morris suggests that it is the unpredictability and contingency of the performative moment that allow her to bear witness to inarticulate voices—whether enslaved African Americans or women trapped in abusive relationships—and she views this witnessing function of poetry as a "duty, because those voices were not allowed to be heard. They were completely cut off. The choking, the rushing of sounds to finally be articulated—I'm a descendant of that. That's my job." Morris's insistence that poets need to articulate previously unregistered experiences that were "not allowed to be heard" asks us to read the disintegrating language of Morris's sound poems not as pathological reenactments of trauma but as acts of critical re-memory.

This understanding of disarticulated language as a means of access to cultural memory and recovery participates in an African diasporic tradition. As Harryette Mullen suggests in her critical writing, much innovative African-American poetry draws on "the African diaspora's aesthetic and therapeutic use of disarticulation for the evocation of spiritual and emotional states of being" ("Phantom Pain," 39). Drawing on anthropological accounts of individuals possessed by Afro-Haitian spirits, in which possessed speakers are shown actually to heighten a sense of communal and collective possibilities for action, Mullen argues that such possessed speakers "may produce inarticulate sounds that nevertheless are subject to interpretation by other participants. The very openness of signification that such enigmatic expressions allow serves to generate the creative interpretive energies of the collectivity" (40). By these measures, the disarticulation of language into the uncommunicative babble or glossolalia of the alienated speaker can be an ethical poetic method capable of rearticulating lost connections and mobilizing collective energies. This is especially relevant to Morris's poetry, given the performative/stage context in which the poem is heard or witnessed collectively.

The convergence of a possessed voice with sound technologies and an African diasporaic aesthetic is evident in Morris's use of the microphone to capture a dynamic that she describes as being different from "just whispering or talking loud." For Morris, the acoustic technology allows her to bring out crucial "overtones and undertones that would definitely be missed because they are too subtle," a strategy evident in her "chain gang" poem. Here the microphone is crucial to her distortion of the words into a range of sounds (replicating grunts and clanking chains) that slip into and out of words taken from the West African Yoruba language. In composing this poem, Morris says that she was asking, "What is the sound that's going to physically work here?" In many cases, the words were not English words but Yoruba words, which Morris felt had the right "physical construct"—"a lot of very strong vowel sounds that are very bottom heavy, as musicians would say." The tinny, upper-register sounds of chains, for example, are balanced by the bass of words like "Agun" and "Ogun"—the names of West African deities—to give the sense of people moving and working, and the expiration of breath coming from the lower diaphragm. The microphone allows Morris to evoke not merely the sense of physical movement and dynamics that the sounds of the Yoruba language could provide, but also subjugated elements of an African spiritual tradition.

For Morris, harnessing the knowledge that sounds possess is a historical witnessing, which she views as a kind of "standing-beside-yourself work" that has an ecstatic, political, and even spiritual dimension. In seeking to reconnect her audience with lost reservoirs of knowledge, Morris refigures poetic voice so that it is no longer expressive of a deep, interior consciousness, or of a unique, personal, or original sensibility. Instead, voice is an intermediary—moving between body and language but situated finally in neither. Morris's ecstatic method, then, offers a poetic voice that is less concerned with self-expression than it is with re-memory and cultural re-integration after traumatic historical events. Although the sound poems—with their breakdown of language into fragments and violent vocal gestures—might seem difficult to grasp and less "accessible" to a general audience, it is evident from the enthusiastic audience response that the poems remain accessible and meaningful. In fact, Morris claims that they are "*too* accessible, in some cases" because the audience has to live in the moment, with the person who is re-experiencing trauma. The audience that watches Morris choking, beating her hand against her throat to simulate the silencing effects of domestic abuse, cannot escape into an intellectualizing, abstract contemplation of the poem's words or language. Instead, they are caught up in a visceral event whose final outcome in unpredictable.

The discomfort and violence of Morris's sound poems demonstrate that while Morris remains interested in shaping and building an audience for her work, she has become *less* concerned with pleasing the listener. She is less interested in making her poetry consumable—or at least less so than one might expect from a poet whose performance will be immediately judged according to an Olympics-style, number-based ratings form. In an article in *Ms.* magazine, Morris insists that "I don't want people to pressure me to compromise my aesthetic just to get over. They like the sassy black woman vibe, and that's just one aspect of my personality" (McDonnell 78). Without completely renouncing audience pleasure as a goal of her performance poetry, Morris challenges the idea that any easy or passive pleasure should be obtained from her work. The poem seeks audience *approval* less than the kind of pleasure that comes from active participation. It is this new relation with the audience—one that shuttles uncomfortably between critical distance and ecstatic identification with otherness—that will be the test of Morris's sonic improvisations.

"Enthusiastic Knowledge" (Harryette Mullen)

to deaden the shock
of enthusiastic knowledge
—*Muse & Drudge* (71)

Whereas Tracie Morris's sound poetry breaks down the human voice and builds it back up again, Harryette Mullen's 1995 volume *Muse & Drudge* sets the incoherencies of noise in a more uneasy tension with the expressive qualities of the lyric voice. Densely packed with obscure allusions that will not be fully accessible to any single audience, Mullen's improvisational sound play presents moments of decided, if pleasurable, incomprehension for many readers, with lines like "spaginzy spagades / splibbly splabibs" (65) among the poem's "blurred rubble slew of vowels" (46). The 80-page poem is composed entirely of blues-inspired quatrains[11] (four to a page) that splice together bits and pieces of overheard or secondhand language. A compendium of sly linguistic shifts and sleights of hand, the poem operates by means of homophones, riddles, jokes, puns, anagrams, and phoneme games such as the following:

divine sunrises
Osiris's irises
his splendid mistress
is his sis Isis (64)

Drawing on the linguistic resources of African-American culture (Mullen says the stanza above "alludes to Afrocentrism"[12]) and of the African diaspora, the book represents a kind of archaeological excavation of the strata of black language, exploring the continuities and discontinuities in its cultural transmission:

creole cocoa loca
crayon gumbo boca
crayfish crayola
jumbo mocha-cola (64)

Throughout the book, Mullen realigns sound and meaning to violently disrupt, "recycle," or signify on the detritus of popular culture—dead metaphors, familiar aphorisms, commercial jingles, street talk:

> it's rank it cranks you up
> crash you're fracked you suck
> shucks you're wack you be
> all you cracked up to be (24)

The book drifts between a glossolalia of private, enigmatic allusions (many of them expressions that Mullen heard from her mother and grandmother) and a heteroglossia where the multiple public languages of advertising, current events, and folk history collide. One quatrain, for example, alludes to the female rappers Salt N Pepa ("hip chicks ad glib / flip the script") who used rap as AIDS education, while another ("a strict sect's hystereotypist hypercorrects / the next vexed hex") refers to the Christian right.[13]

The poem is, above all, a performance of epistemological method—one with intensely personal, familial, regional, and cultural roots. At the most basic level, the book is a written performance of Mullen's research into her oral tradition, as she revealed in an interview with Calvin Bedient:

> Parts of that oral tradition were not accessible to me, coming from where I came from and being in a very religious household. There were aspects of the blues that I never got until I was an adult, because that was considered basically gut-bucket, lowdown music in our household. I collected my culture from books, from media, and to a certain extent from an actual oral tradition that I do participate in, but there were things missing that I have since gathered and collected. I have been collecting these virtual index cards for a long time. . . . This poem is a performance of that knowledge. It's a very hard-won knowledge that I treasure, because I did not want to be ignorant of my culture. (669)

Yet for a performance of knowledge, the poem seems vulnerable, foundationless, and mutable, as consonants shift and words slide into adjoining worlds—from "sunrises" and "irises" to "Isis." Even the arrangement of the quatrains on the page resists any kind of global or overarching order, and when Mullen reads from the book, she rearranges and shuffles the pages. Like Morris's improvisational poetics, Mullen's hypertextual compositional method leaves room for endless resequencing and variations in performance. It is as if "the shock / of enthusiastic knowledge" (71) ripples throughout the poem, unhinging words from their orthographies and meanings and destabilizing the lyric voice. The book's title, *Muse & Drudge,* points to the paradoxical nature of Mullen's project—her book's knowledge derived from a voice both ecstatic and ordinary, inspired and demeaned. Signifying on Zora Neale Hurston's observation that "the black woman is the mule of the world" by playfully shifting the word "mules" to "muse," Mullen's title deflates the lyric's claim to inspirational genius, suggesting the interchangeability, at almost any point, of the exalted "muse" with the menial poet or "drudge" that she possesses.

The use of the ampersand in the book's title—which gestures to the prominence of writing technologies or "hype-writer fonts" (42) in Mullen's aesthetic—points to a further tension in the book between orality and literacy. Mullen's work is affiliated with a writing-based avant-garde poetics, and she shares that movement's refusal of the supposedly "natural" or expressivist voices offered by media-saturated consumer culture and the culturally dominant voice-based lyric alike. *Muse & Drudge* was published by Singing Horse Press, which also publishes work by such language-affiliated writers as Charles Bernstein, Rachel Blau DuPlessis, and Rosmarie Waldrop. At the same time, Mullen cites such mainstream poets as Lucille Clifton, as well as speech-based poets Amiri Baraka and Bob Kaufman, as among her important influences. Thus Mullen's work is positioned uneasily between the avant-garde's wariness of the "voice poem" and the African-American tradition, which has been understood primarily in terms of orality and performance. The result of voice becoming a cultural prescription for African-American writers is that writers whose work is concerned, as Mullen's is, with the techniques and instruments of literacy might feel held hostage by the community's demand for a representative and transparent voice—and thereby forced into "silence, invisibility, or self-effacement" (Mullen 670).

Despite Mullen's deep concern with the visual practices of reading and writing, voice remains a key element in *Muse & Drudge*. One stanza evokes "voice" as having, in the past, taken its speaker "hostage," holding "a knife against my throat" (13):

> chained thus together
> voice held me hostage
> divided our separate ways
> with a knife against my throat. (13)

This violence done to the speaker by her own voice suggests both the possessed status of the speaker, who is alternately occupied by an alien agency ("divided our separate ways"), and the status of voice as cultural prescription imposed forcefully on the lyric poet ("chained thus together"). Voices in other sections, however, leap over these difficulties with bravado, claiming to be able to "sing it in my voice / put words in like I want them" (59). Elsewhere, another speaker points out that "you can sing their songs / with words your way / put it over to the people / know what you doing" (17). For Mullen, this singing or lyricism always involves mobile, shifting, and multiple voices: the entirely unpunctuated poem "spin[s] the mix fast forward," to quote one of her lines, quite likely itself a quotation—offering the poem as shortwave antenna for rapidly shifting fragments of "outside" language or voices. The voices are by turns streetwise, sassy, elegaic, and media-saturated, and the allusions range from Brancusi to the Baptist hymnal, from Miz Mary's mack truck to MOMA. Although this long poem—something of a "random diva nation of bedlam"—jump-cuts across an astounding range of cultural allusions, it is tuned in especially to linguistic constructions of race and gender, if only to implode them and leave the reader with the flotsam and jetsam that survives. There are few, if any, moments in the poem where the "I" can be said to refer to the poet herself, to provide some kind of "authentic" speaking voice, or to develop a self-present speaker who can claim to represent a particular identity.

So it is all the more striking that this type of gesture occurs, however briefly, in the final set of quatrains, on the last page of the book:

just as I am I come
knee bent and body bowed
this here's sorrow's home
my body's southern song

These lines powerfully ground and embody the speaker through the deictics "this" and "here," and by references to a regional, "southern," location (which Mullen has associated with her mother's voice) and to the geography closest in, "my body." The first line, "just as I am I come," quotes the classic Baptist invitational hymn, in another allusion to Mullen's own cultural background. The hymn, often used as a prolonged altar call, conjures up the patience of preacher and congregation as they wait for a response, so that we wonder who or what has called out this "I" in its posture of humility and authenticity. The doubling of the word "I," combined with the elimination of punctuation, playfully reveals the assertion of authenticity and symmetry—"I am I"—hidden in the lyrics. But for Mullen this supposedly "authentic" or personal Southern black voice, which had characterized her first book, *Tree Tall Woman,* is itself a construction, just as the black church no longer serves to guarantee an authentically black cultural identity or provide an automatically stabilizing force. Although Mullen is aware of how this coherent "I" might be able to call out into collective solidarity those readers who share similar experiences, it is to be trusted no more than the other voices—in part because of the hymn's professed desire for perfection, to "rid [the] soul of one dark blot." Mullen does not prolong this invitational call but quickly moves on to channel or invent other, no less authentic, voices as part of an extended series.

Mullen is more interested in composing for and developing an audience than one might expect from someone so closely affiliated with the poetic avant-garde. Whereas most language-oriented writing systematically refuses to provide poetry in which the reader (without disruption or fluctuation) identifies with the poem's speaker and the speaker's politics, Mullen does not push away that kind of identification so easily or reflexively. "It's not that I'm trying to please the reader," she has said, "but I do think of . . . how audiences are divided culturally and racially, and so forth, and of how there are particular cultural codes that are more comprehensible to some audiences than to others. *Muse & Drudge,*" she continues, "was particularly written to envision a diverse audience" (530). In an interview with Cynthia Hogue, she explains that she wanted the poem to provide moments of "familiarity and connection with the text as opposed to those moments of alienation, estrangement and feeling left out. I wanted there to be enough of those moments of inclusion for everyone so that they can tolerate the moments of feeling their exclusion" (22). In her interview with Calvin Bedient, Mullen says she is trying to move "beyond a fairly simple or reductive notion of what black culture is":

> I was trying to make a text that did address various audiences, and so the various registers and different lexicons and different allusive potentials had to do with that diverse audience that I want as my readers. So I address black audiences and audiences that are not black as well. . . . So for me the audience is made by the text. (664)

Moreover, Mullen thinks of her book as providing a shared "room" of hearing—she tells Kate Pearcy that she wrote *Muse & Drudge* "so that those audiences could sit in the same room together and they might not hear it in the same way but they would all get something they could relate to" (2).

At several points in *Muse & Drudge,* a speaker turns to address the audience—a series of readers/listeners who shift locations just about as rapidly as the speakers do. The poem addresses, for example, those who "pretend you don't understand . . . cant read my crooked hand" although "you were longing to belong / thoughts wander where have you gone" (69). Elsewhere, a speaker asks the reader archly, "am I your type / that latent lurid blurb"? (17). In many places, the poem appeals specifically to an audience of women (and black women) in order to call out or create that audience, in the traditions of call-and-response and feminist consciousness raising: "what you can do / is what women do / I know you know / what I mean, don't you" (38). Or elsewhere: "go on sister sing your song" (51). To invite and comfort a reader whose attention might stray during the more disjunctive moments, stanzas sometimes coalesce into brief "local" narratives, and the balladic stanzas periodically slip into regular rhymes and familiar syntax:

> no miss thing
> ain't exactly rude
> just exercising
> her right to bare attitude (55)

Where a traditional voice poem might find itself mired in the devitalized language of consumer culture, or trapped in a formulaic account of inspiration or deep feeling—and where an exemplary language poem might find itself risking an aesthetics of elitism and irrelevancy—the sonic fluidity of *Muse & Drudge* manages to escape these constraints. Ironically, it is the poem's status as a possessed, disjunctive work—its perpetual shifting between intentionality and randomness, between the self-determining voice "exercising her right" and the autonomic sounds that generate themselves—that allows it to gather up this new audience.

"Aural Rorschach" (Ed Roberson)

> *A poem is going to move from voice to voice inside you, as it's trying to deliver what happened, or deliver the story back to the village. It's going to say, I was afraid here, or I ran here. Or the tree was on fire. What do you mean, the tree was on fire? You just might mean it was in sunlight. Witness is much more beautiful than testimony, and I always assumed that that was the beauty of poetry.*
>
> —Ed Roberson

In the quotation above, Roberson differentiates between *testimony,* which consists of a narrative account delivered by a coherent, singular "I," and *witness,* in which the poet possesses a multiplicity of voices, among which the poem moves rapidly and incoherently. For Roberson, the work of witness is dominated by the "fragment"—created by an unending series of jumps, gaps, and leaps—and he built his long poem *Lucid Interval as Integral Music* (1995) as a series of pieced-together fragments resulting from interruptions, accidents, seizures, and coincidences. The book-length poem was a decade in the making, as the poet accumulated fragments during the years that he was caring for his young daughter, Lena, the poem's muse, who presides over the book as a figure of chance, interruption, and accident. *Lucid Interval* can be described as a birth poem, a meditation on the experience of the fragment, and a sustained act as bearing witness to traumatic events in African-American history. In interview, Roberson describes the poem's method as

> beginning to talk about words as divination, finding a deep meaning and emotional catch in words. But you have to stop even hunting for that, if you've got the baby to take care of. This business about [Lena] being chance—she *is* chance to deal with.

Lucid Interval is structured as a series of "readings" or "divinations" that depend almost entirely on coincidences of sound, as the poet plays with the language found in "This Week's Concerts," the *New York Times* listing of classical and jazz radio programs to be broadcast each week. The 72-page poem is divided into three sections: a prologue, "FORM"; the body, entitled "THIS WEEK'S CONCERTS"; and a coda, entitled "INTERVAL AND FINAL DAYS CONCERTS." Throughout the book, Roberson *reads into* the fascinatingly obscure and suggestive names of classical and jazz pieces, composers, performers, and conductors—"Pacific 231" and "November Steps." It is significant that these radio broadcasts cannot be heard by the poet, who is "five hundred miles inland and out / of signal range," who only wonders what the pieces might sound like (63). Playing with the sounds of these nearly nonsensical words as if they were an "aural rorschach," the poet hears "coarse air" in corsair, the seafaring "mariner" in Neville Mariner, and the sensual "caramel burr" in Carmina Burana (62). Some readers may remain unaware of the source of such exotic poem titles as "Simbi Petro Dambal-lah La Flambeau" or "The Seven Deltas of Shango's Wives" until they arrive, in the book's coda, at a poem entitled "12.b.obs.OED," which describes the poem's generative devices of associative logic, near homonyms, and other accidental connections based on sound and sight.

Examining the *Oxford English Dictionary*'s definition for the word "to read," the poet announces that instead of "reading in" law or history, he has been "reading in" the Sunday *Times* weekly concert listings. The poem thus draws attention to the multiple ways in which we "read" (know, understand, interpret) but gives special attention to two of its meanings: the first "obsolete" meaning "1.12b to know or to be read in" and the second meaning, "1.13," which is "to study   divination" (62). The first meaning holds in tension the reader's dual roles as active agent and passive text—one does not only read, or study, but one is alternately *read in*—with the effect of undoing that binary opposition.

The second meaning—divination—is the explicit method of another series of "readings" in *Lucid Interval,* which looks at the pictures made by the nine knots of a tie-dye rag. In these poems, Roberson says he wanted to explore "the magic of tying something, closing up, capturing a space, making your own kind of magic to make a poem." The magic is not external, but internal, conjured by the poet's ritualized injection of chance into the creative process: "the puzzle in bundles / is change" (53). The twisted cloth that the poet reads is itself a "body" and is compared with the twists of the umbilical cord and the DNA helix. It is also the skin—"There was a piece of brown material / out on the table. / I try everything against my skin / for whether it wears // right with my color   people." As the knots are "contracted," the speaker becomes "tied up with [his] skin somehow" (53). As the knots are opened up and read, the speaker says, "I have come unloosened" (56). The tongue loosens, too, so that in its last words the upper voice *sings* in a Caribbean dialect before it ceases:

day monkey eye
come open now.
who no know go know.
where day ah dreadness?

far here come (57)

The bottom voice, which had been silent, re-emerges along on the next page to close the second section of *Lucid Interval,* ending its long, double-voiced movement. This last poem suggests that there is something predatory about making meaning of fragments. Here the critical act of reading and writing is described as a "beak" of "delicate / reason" coming down to "feed on" the poem's "sound crumbs" (58). The empty beaks "are clear of meaning"—they are the "breaks," perhaps, that hold and create the fragments that the poet dives under and captures in order to bring them "back up into // the umbilicate ear":

out of the seizures of the organ tides,

out of the breaks.
out of the storm, the jazz. (58)

Reading this strategy of "sound divination" in the larger context of *Lucid Interval* as a whole, we can begin to understand it as an act of historical reclamation, in which the interruptions of the infant Lena parallel the ruptures of the African diaspora—and in which both of these fragmenting events (personal and historical) determine the poem's unusual visual structure.

Lucid Interval is, in fact, a birth poem, meditating on fathering and conception, the dislocation and trauma of childbirth. But it is equally a birth poem by virtue of its *form*—a self-described set of "doubling wombed // wave propagations" (37). Most pages are divided horizontally by a thin black line that serves as a kind of amniotic membrane separating the coherent, unbroken upper voice from the unbirthed or "unspeeched" bottom voice. The poem's lower voice evokes a range of "noises" that skirt the edges of music and speech, beginning with the infant's incoherent screams and ending, many pages later, with "the storm, the jazz." The poem-line of the "under-voice" includes blank pages and missing poems, whereas the Roman-numeral "upper-voice" is continuous and its series unbroken. Roberson describes the relationship of these voices in a way that emphasizes their independence of one another and suggests the poem's basis in the sounds and rhythms of an African-American community:

The upper voice is the poem, and the bottom voice is the one that's "singing over" or singing under in the sense that it's mumbling or that deep humming that you hear in church while the minister is preaching and somebody in the back is what they call "mourning." And the preacher is playing off that, is singing back and forth to that, to whoever is sitting up there on the mourner's bench. He's preaching to them, you see. That voice underneath doesn't go with the poem, it's got its own thing happening. In some of those Spanish songs, you get the soñero, the real high voice. If you were to structure it, the bottom voice would be the soñero, the voice that is leaping over top of everything. I would put the voice that is way over everything, the voice that knows more deeply than anything, at the bottom line.

The voices are not mere reflections kept in equipoise—they question, answer, and converse, while lines migrate from one half of the page to the other. The voices can be heard, in fact, as two separate, independent "lines," something like the two swiftly moving jump ropes of "Black children" playing "double-dutch" (37). The simultaneous rotation of the poem's two lines in opposite directions results, perhaps, in the other meaning of "double-dutch"—unintelligible language or gibberish. Yet the flux of the lines and the jumps and leaps of the voice, which refuse narrative or thematic progression and defy our conventional reading practices, are "unintelligible" only to hasty or overdetermined readings.

Lucid Interval's "double consciousness," to borrow W. E. B. DuBois's term, derives from having absorbed a history of racist violence. The "two jump ropes" mentioned above, for example, belong to "four little black kids" who were "lifted by powder" in the bombing at "Birmingham : Church : Double-dutch : Window" (39, 38). *Lucid Interval,* with its doubled and fragmented voice, full of gaps and hesitations, bears within its very structure the impact of such traumatic historical events. The gaps in the text contain the disappeared of history, the dead who are seized out of life: "people as air pocket" (46). Their ghosts have been absorbed into the "expensive white quiet," so that each one of the "silently white" pages that interrupts the poem (or appears in the place of a poem) gestures toward these absences (54, 24). Only traces remain, in a way that

> Makes   brilliant afterimages collect
> of the disappeared
> into inside   into nothing
> known
>
> And that is what they say. (31)

In trauma, Cathy Caruth argues, "the outside has gone inside without any mediation" (59). In *Lucid Interval,* this traumatic movement inward of people "into inside" leaves a collection of "afterimages" or ghost memories. But the poet insists that "no ghost or equation explains Birmingham," in which the four little girls disappear "by a speck like earth, / into the steps your government takes, // jumps. Blood rope" (38, 39). If institutionally taken "steps" have moved persons into the privatized space of individual memory, the poem picks up on the *fragment*—the memory fragment, or trauma fragment—as a device or empirical method for recovering these presences and reinserting them in public memory.

"Trauma fragment" is a term used by Dori Laub in *Testimony: Crises of Witnessing in Literature, Psychoanalysis, and History,* in which he demonstrates that "trauma returns in disjointed fragments in the memory of the survivor" (71). For his co-author Shoshana Felman, such fragments are derived from "accidents" of survival and location. She argues that the poet-witness is one who is both pursued by accident and willing to pursue it, "to actively pursue its path and its direction through obscurity, through darkness, and through fragmentation" (31). Texts produced out of violent, dissociating limit-experiences are often disarticulated, disjunctive, and esoteric; speech under these conditions often seems automatic, autonomic, or dictated from "outside." Stuttering rhythmically, the voice of trauma defies grammar and syntax, disintegrating into feverish fragments of syllable and sound. On entering the public sphere, such speech arouses cultural anxieties about the contagiousness of the traumatic experience—fears that listeners will be traumatized merely by the listening. But within the very contagion of trauma's memory-fragments lies the potential for the transmission of a new and healing historical knowledge.

The poet-witness must be vulnerable to "seizure by simple error" and able to absorb the "massive / shock of the body" (47). To witness—to take the imprint of these images or species—is akin to electrocution, which is described as fiery contagion:

> I know some electrocuted
>
> people who are fields
> blown like the sun
> on swaying configuration
> of spaces   their body holding
>
> their fires out to you   as what was charged. (30)

As the upper voice urges "you" to run forward and "touch the terror" of these people, the bottom voice ceases to speak, disappearing "into inside" (30, 31). The break in the bottom voice physicalizes, perhaps, the absence of a listener or respondent, especially if we think of the bottom voice as listening and testifying to the gaps that are only hinted at by the upper voice. What "they say" remains unheard, unwritten, for the space of a page—until the bottom voice picks up again.

The witnessing exchanges in *Lucid Interval* are neither chosen nor willed; instead, they result from accident, luck, or disaster. Witness is not something one can "work for" but "a moment that cannot be worked" (45). The value of these witnessing exchanges—as "specie"—depends on seemingly accidental correspondences that are in fact the fundamental elements of the poem's form as "lena" (a form based on interruption and named after the poet's daughter): "Chance is specie our daughter our mind" (63). Thus the book's reading strategy is deliberate openness to accident and error, and a willingness to tempt chaos and chance.

In tempting chance and courting interruption as a formal method, *Lucid Interval* entices readers into a new kind of reading practice that is attentive to the arational but knowledgeable sound fragment. Ultimately, he proposes a new literacy, in which we find

> the out of place-ment, the come up short cut-paste, the edges.
> the abruptness so familiar now as to be
> fluency . . . (62)

As Roberson puts it in the title of one of the poems in *Lucid Interval as Integral Music,* he is doing "Research at the Interstice" (89). In this poem, he describes his field experiences running marine biology experiments in terms that evoke the "darks disappeared" in the "Sargasso Sea":

> We are only running
>
> nitrogen fixation experiments
> a sample of each depth
> in a glass ball flask
> off the North American Coast's
>
> former slave states
> to see what the light
> reaching into the dark sea
> has made of this

By stepping deliberately, and with an experimental spirit, into the interval's opacity, illegibility, and noise, Roberson is seeking to make such historical interstices lucid—to bear witness to the breaks and gaps in our historical consciousness.

Refiguring Agency and Audience

> *I have fights with the poem. I learned to just stop fighting and get out of the way, or the poem be beating me up. It be beating me up, so I just leave it alone.*
>
> —Tracie Morris

There is a danger involved in this kind of sound-saturated poetics of possession. As Adalaide Morris points out, possession by an external force can encourage the possessed listener to surrender "values that we critique but nonetheless continue to endorse, among them, rationality, discrimination, and critical distance" (49–50). None of the three poets under discussion, however, is content with giving over to an external sound play that would completely short-circuit the intentionality, referentiality, and political responsibility of the speaking "I," despite the rhetoric of possession they use to describe their work with sound. Harryette Mullen emphasizes the deliberative and responsible act of "choice" that mediates between "voice" and "noise," while Ed Roberson insists on the lucidity of "reason," even when it does violence to the "sound crumbs" that fall on the "umbilicate ear." He argues in interview that "it isn't backing away from responsibility to think of something structurally or abstractly. Or spiritually." Even when Tracie Morris gets out of the poem's way, she says that it is "not so that I forget who I am. Because I have a responsibility to people there and to dealing with their energy. You can't just open people up and leave them there—that's irresponsible."

In her study of spirit possession among the Northern Sudanese *Zár* cult, *Wombs and Alien Spirits,* Janice Boddy considers possession less as a mystical experience than as an eminently social discourse that is neither frightening nor uncontrolled. As the young Sudanese woman Asia reports, the agential self is neither absent nor vacated:

> When it descends into you, you "go the limit" until the drumming stops, and then the person stops. When the drums are beating, beating, you hear nothing, you hear from far away, you feel far away. You have left the *mídán,* the place of the *zár*. And you see, you have a vision. . . . You see with the eyes of the spirit until the drumming stops. (350)

Although the radical detachment of the possessed from her spirit-text results in a performance that can appear semantically autonomous, suppressing or eliminating the signs of human or authorial motivation, Boddy finds that trance for the Hofriyati is a *participatory act* rather than a "depossession" of self, a "public idiom for the articulation and interpretation of experience" (138).

Rather than eliminate authorial agency, the paradigm of poetic creation as "possession" relocates agency in the poet's determined receptivity to the voice of another as it is projected across time. Stewart calls this complex negotiation of poetic agency a "willed dissociation" or "willed possession" (36). This tension between the poet's self-determination and his or her receptiveness to the autonomic capacities of languages gets played out most self-consciously in the relationship of poet to audience. The closing stanza of Mullen's *Muse & Drudge* contrasts the pleasure of abandon with the need to know "who you're playing for":

> proceed with abandon
> finding yourself where you are
> and who you're playing for
> what stray companion

Even though the poem courts a "stray companion" at every turn—one who, gathered in by a brief linguistic affiliation, might also be allowed to wander off—and even though the poet abandons herself to the pleasures of sonic improvisation, the poem insists, in its closing lines, on grounding, even if provisional: "finding yourself where you are." Roberson's *Lucid Interval* is less optimistic about the possibility of this balance between "hearings" and "voice," between irretrievable historical and personal experience (signified throughout the poem by white space between words and poems) and the need to hold on to an audience that is already, before the poem closes, "leaving":

> As hearings, the voice takes these unequalled stands
> Against an odds immense as sky like this were air.
> What is this?   What is the air   after?
> Only audience and cry leaving? Then everything goes? (72)

The unstated referent of Roberson's "this" might well be voice, or sound itself—an inarticulate "cry" that is finally produced by neither poet nor audience. Given the immense odds against bringing these intervals into voice, into lucidity, and into reason, the poet begins with a simple charge—he asks that we listen for the sound of departure.

Notes

1. Bernstein, quoted in Morris intro.
2. Charles Bernstein, ed. *Close Listening: Poetry and the Performed Word;* and Adalaide Morris, ed. *Sound States: Innovative Poetics and Acoustical Technologies.*

3. See Marjorie Perloff, "Language Poetry and the Lyric Subject: Ron Silliman's Albany, Susan Howe's Buffalo," *Critical Inquiry* 25 (1999): 405–434. Perloff points out that "One of the cardinal principles—perhaps *the* cardinal principle—of American Language poetics (as of the related current in England, usually labeled 'linguistically innovative poetries,') has been the dismissal of 'voice' as the foundational principle of lyric poetry" (405).
4. See Crown, "A Roundtable Conversation."
5. See Crown, "Down Break Drum: An Interview with Ed Roberson." October 10, 1997, and June 21, 1998. All quotations from Roberson are taken from the interview with the author, unless otherwise indicated.
6. Tracie Morris, interview with the author, Brooklyn, NY, August 14, 1999. All quotations from Morris are taken from the interview with the author, unless otherwise indicated.
7. In an essay in *Poetics Today,* I discuss the visual and graphic aspects of Roberson's poetry in detail.
8. Morris has held championship titles in the Nuyorican Grand Slam and the National Haiku Slam. Although her poems have appeared in magazines and anthologies, most notably Miguel Algarin's collection, *ALOUD: Voices from the Nuyorican Poets Café* and Bob Holman's *The United States of Poetry,* it was only recently that Morris took her poems fully from "stage" to "page," in the 1998 volume *Intermission,* published in New York by Soft Skull Press. This first full-length volume of Morris's poetry was preceded by a chapbook, *Chap-t-her Won: Some Poems by Tracie Morris* (Brooklyn: TM Ink, 1992).
9. Morris performed "Anthony Baez" at "Poetry and the Public Sphere: A Conference on Contemporary Poetry," held at Rutgers University, New Brunswick, NJ, on April 24, 1997.
10. Morris performed the "chain gang" and "heaven" poems at the People's Poetry Gathering in New York City, April 1999.
11. Elisabeth Frost discusses Mullen's participation in a blues aesthetic in "Lyric Hybridity."
12. Mullen, in an interview with Barbara Henning.
13. Mullen explains these allusions in her interview with Barbara Henning.

Works Cited

Baker, Houston. "Caliban's Triple Play." In *"Race," Writing and Difference.* Henry Louis Gates, ed. Chicago: University of Chicago Press, 1986.

Barthes, Roland. "The Grain of the Voice." In *Image, Music, Text,* trans. Stephen Heath. New York: Hill & Wang, 1977, 181.

Bedient, Calvin. "The Solo Mysterioso Blues: An Interview with Harryette Mullen." *Callaloo* 19.3 (1996): 651–669.

Benston, Kimberly. "Performing Blackness: Re/Placing Afro-American Poetry." In Baher and Redmond, eds. *Afro-American Literary Study in the 1990s*. Chicago: University of Chicago Press, 1989, 164–185.

Bernstein, Charles, ed. *Close Listening: Poetry and the Performed Word.* New York: Oxford University Press, 1998.

Boddy, Janice. *Wombs and Alien Spirits: Women, Men, and the Zár Cult in Northern Sudan.* New Directions in Anthropological Writing. Madison: University of Wisconsin Press, 1990.

Caruth, Cathy, ed. Introduction to *Trauma: Explorations in Memory.* Baltimore: Johns Hopkins University Press, 1995.

Crown, Kathleen, ed. "A Roundtable Conversation with Karen Brennan, Sharon Doubiago, Rachel Blau DuPlessis, Kathleen Fraser, Jenny Goodman, Donna Hollenberg, Jeanne Heuving, Laura Hinton, Susan Howe, Harryette Mullen, and Aldon Nielsen." *Women's Studies: An Interdisciplinary Journal* 28.5 (Sept 1998): 507–536.

———. "'Reading the Lucid Interval': Race, Trauma and Literacy in the Poetry of Ed Roberson." In "After-Shock: Poetry and Cultural Politics Since 1989." Ed., Jonathan Monroe. *Poetics Today* 21.1 (Spring 2000): 187–220.

———. "Down Break Drum: An Interview with Ed Roberson" [unpublished manuscript]. Spring 1998.

———. Interview with Tracie Morris, August 1999.

———. "'Sonic Revolutionaries': Voice and Experiment in the Spoken-Word Poetry of Tracie Morris," in Cynthia Hogue and Laura Hinton, eds. *We Who Love to Be Astonished: Experimental Feminist Poetics and Performance Art.* Tuscaloosa: University of Alabama Press, 2001.

Damon, Maria. "Was That 'Different,' 'Dissident' or 'Dissonant'? Poetry (n) the Public Spear: Slams, Open Readings, and Dissident Traditions," in Charles Bernstein, ed. *Close Listening,* 324–342.

Diamond, Elin. "Tight Spaces, Temporal Awakenings in Recent Feminist Performance." Paper delivered at the Women in the Public Sphere Seminar at Rutgers University, New Brunswick, NJ, April, 1998. A version of this paper appears in *Power, Practice, Agency: Working Papers from the Women in the Public Sphere Seminar,* ed. Marianne DeKoven. New Brunswick, NJ: Institute for Research on Women, 1999.

Doreski, C. K. Review of Roberson, *Just In: Word of Navigational Challenges: New and Selected Work. Harvard Review* 16 (1999): 138–140.

Felman, Shoshana, and Dori Laub. *Testimony: Crises of Witnessing in Literature, Psychoanalysis, and History*. New York: Routledge, 1992.

Frost, Beth. "Lyric Hybridity." *Women's Studies: An Interdisciplinary Journal* 28.5 (Sept 1998): 465–481.

Henning, Barbara. "An Interview with Harryette Mullen." *The Poetry Project Newsletter* 162 (Oct. /Nov. 1996): http://www.poetryproject.com/mullen.html

Hogue, Cynthia. Interview with Harryette Mullen. *Postmodern Culture* 19.2 (1999): 1–27.

Howe, Susan. "Ether Either," in Charles Bernstein, ed. *Close Listening,* 111–127.

Mackey, Nathaniel. "Cante Moro," in Adalaide Morris, ed. *Sound States,* 194–212.

McCaffery, Steve. "Voice in Extremis," in Charles Bernstein, ed. *Close Listening*, 162–177.
McDonnell, Evelyn. "Divas Declare a Spoken-Word Revolution." *Ms. Magazine* (Jan/Feb 1996): 78.
Morris, Adalaide. *Sound States: Innovative Poetics and Acoustical Technologies*. Chapel Hill: University of North Carolina Press, 1997.
Morris, Tracie. *Intermission*. New York: Soft Skull Press, 1998.
Mullen, Harryette. "African Signs and Spirit Writing." *Callaloo* 19, no. 3 (1996): 670–689.
———. *Muse & Drudge*. Singing Horse Press, 1995.
———. "Phantom Pain: Nathaniel Mackey's *Bedouin Hornbook*." *Talisman* 9 (1992): 37–43.
———. *S*PeRM**K*T.* Philadelphia: Singing Horse Press, 1992.
———. *Trimmings*. New York: Tender Buttons, 1991.
Nielsen, Aldon. *Black Chant: Languages of African-American Postmodernism*. Cambridge: Cambridge University Press, 1997.
Pearcy, Kate. "A Poetics of Opposition: Race and the Avant-Garde." Unpublished essay read at the "Poetry and the Public Sphere Conference on Contemporary Poetry," 24–27 April, 1998. Can be found at: http://english.rutgers.edu/pierce.html
Perloff, Marjorie. "Language Poetry and the Lyric Subject: Ron Silliman's Albany, Susan Howe's Buffalo." *Critical Inquiry* 25 (1999): 405–434.
Rasula, Jed. "Poetry's Voice-Over," in Adalaide Morris, ed. *Sound States*. 274–316.
Roberson, Ed. *Voices Cast Out to Talk Us In*. Iowa City: University of Iowa Press, 1995.
Stewart, Susan. "Letter on Sound," in Charles Bernstein, ed. *Close Listening*, 29–52.
———. "Lyric Possession." *Critical Inquiry* 22 (Autumn 1995): 34–63.

cris cheek

'giving tongue'

When I was four, my dad read me poems at bedtime. I heard a staple diet of Lewis Carroll and Edward Lear for two following years. It was the phonic logics of these poems that repeatedly drew me in; a hovering between song and poem. Their quirky iambic cadences which hinted at conventional meanings, without appearing to deliver them, snared me. They harboured senses that seemed to present a less policeable or graspable, flip-side of consensual meaning; although I wouldn't have thought about it like that then. These were poems that failed to deliver nonsense, remaining curiously tied in to my emergent experiences. Yet they are commonly referred to as 'nonsense' poems. This despite the ironic commentary that Carroll provides through Alice in the text that accompanies 'The Jabberwocky'.[1] I over-romanticise my childhood now, as lying awake in the gathering darkness, rapt in the sounds shaped by my father's mouth, rocked into sleep by the pleasure-giving movements of a kinship tongue; wrapped in Victorian sonolinguistic play.

Voices of authority inflect us, particularly when young of course, throughout our lives. Most habitually, in my case, a received sound of the predominantly European aspirational middle-classes, in the northeast London suburbs of post World War Two England. Teenwards I gravitated towards deliberately resisting this stiff-upper-lip-ish sound, increasingly attracted to various period oppositional speech attitudes: Mick Jagger's disdainful mid-sixties London scowl, later Johnny Rotten's rasping mangled mock-cockney disgust and Poly Styrene's siren wail 'Oh Bondage! Up Yours!'[2] My response was to the bad manners of the saying and the unkempt matters of the said. Aside from pop music, other widely available models for dissonant speech were to be found in comedy of that era.[3] Poetry though, still gave off the air of managing to remain largely unaffected by a decade of turmoil in other artforms. Perhaps it's hard to understand, outside the prevailing context of British poetries at that time, how startling it was, for a young Londoner, to hear Bill Griffiths read in 1975 a section of poetry such as:

> the buds brown, brutalized, at their gate out the state
> sub jugum
> in vulf-vault

in the gardens of Poknies and po-lice
coplines   teacher; breach
tongues out
mouths up clovery windows
Latchmere
solitary—no—lead-lifting
tongue
tight as tap

(Griffiths 6)

—but here, for me, was a brace of invigorating air, in a literary climate dominated by the well-turned (and too often slackly-tuned) phrase. It was part of a body of writing that helped to reawaken my interest in the potential for poetry against what was an otherwise drab diet of proper English verses, contracted in the service of petty-epiphanic niceties.[4] Griffiths' 'buds', brutalized at the prison gate, are far darker and more fiercely engaged with the machinations of a coercive state, than Larkin's comparatively tweely formulated suggestion that your mum and dad fuck you up. Griffiths writes a compacting sense, and consequently a crunched sound, of English, riven by implied erasure, targeted at social control, operated through the legislature. His 'tongues out' are committed to solitary, in a passage that links the silencing of speech to social violence within a British justice system, whose centres could no longer hold. Here are historically bitter ('vulf-vault') salival juices, leaking from beneath a battered body of linguistic decorum. Attention being turned, states of attention being retuned, onto the ruptured humours of colloquial ellision, in conflict with the official language and record of a post-modern Britain.

Writings published by Bill Griffiths, Ulli Freer, Glenda George, Barry MacSweeney, Jeremy Prynne and Allen Fisher, amongst many, in the mid- to late 1970s signal a shift of syntactical sensibility and subsequently of sonic shapings, away from the conservative sentiments offered by the Movement and they who had followed in its mostly dreary wake. Syntax, no longer the creation of a well-formed sentence, became an instrument with which to interrogate the ideologies of linguistic communication and its cadences of easy listening. The veil of Bourdieu's 'illusion of linguistic communism' (Bourdieu 43) was teased aside. Syntactical disruptions unloosened the conventions of meaning making, offering a critique of poetic rapture. Re-examinations of syntax went hand in mouth with rewriting the sonic terrains of poetries in these Englishes. But the monolithic block of literary English was subjected to other pressures at that time, signalled by writings which moved against the tum-tee-tum march of colonial parades, in a rhythmical revolution for writing and its reading, symbolized by the moment when Kamau Brathwaite took his measure from Calypso in the opening phrase of that eponymous poem; 'The stone had skidded arc'd and bloomed into islands' (Brathwaite 47). Not only a sensibility, but a strophe had also shifted.

The sounds of English today are the sounds of Englishes, both within the borders of that nation state which had exported the seeds through empire and trade, to beyond those borders in former commonwealths and world market-places. Resultant loss of monodirectional control, the hegemonic orders of top-down imposition, can be apprehended at every intersection between those Englishes, and throughout their linguistic diasporas. I celebrate that loss, as a positive sign that this is a language in a turmoil of great promise, opening, rather than resistant to, that vibrant plethora of influence and change which has enabled it to become so translocal. What seems undesirable is a language that mirrors the merely partially capacitated office body, chairbound, with relatively fixed view. These Englishes can now be heard as proliferating measures of dispossession and deterritorialisation, as re-patched versions, understood as a quilt conspicuously out of kilter with a body that it no longer covers. Its signature cadences continue to diversify, are entropically obliged. Harnesses on the geo-choreography of the English tongue have been undermined, often delightfully to my ears, by a roller-coaster of flips and spins and racinating tunes, such as this:

lang time
my song lock up tight
eena mi troat
like if a ever open mi mout
                                        jus to breathe
de roar would shake dis eart
an matterkine
                                  split
an microchip   cho   jus fly

(Jean 'Binta' Breeze, *Red Rebel Song*) [5]

Read as an expectant from imposed silence, this song-poem enacts disquiet at complicit post-colonial literary models of consumption. Breeze's advocacy, in a shift from 'my' to 'mi', is a re-verberation of a declining body of speakings and speakers, a reconnection of 'troat' to 'eart'; a vibration of sound between body and ground. The tongue, in being rewritten for strongly percussive representations and not pushing between her teeth to slacken through a repetitive 'th', is kept moving, and so identified as a site for the retaking of a measure of control. Her tongue is emphasised as an instrument for speaking out from under received self-restraint. Through the articulation of a palette of resistance to denial she repositions learning a 'lang' way from those classicisms exploited by a more conventionally celebrated Caribbean writer such as Derek Walcott. The projection of language as physical resonance, a toning of charged semantic particles in a rhythm that syncopates silent beats and sounded beats, energised by breath, is performed through a carefully re-weighted and spatially re-choreographed tongue. She reaffirms a purpose for language, for 'lang', to chime with song.[6]

. . .

Older binaries—between oralities and literacies and between the languages of mutating flux and of hegemonic standards—have reached a crisis point, more or less during the same period of time: the former through proliferating forms of indirect testimony, the latter intertwined with diasporic variegation. An entrenched defender of standard English, such as John Honey, depicts an over-reductive contest, fought to the death between absolute proprieties of 'good' usage and those who would accept all and sundry contributions to the English language, until the effective shape became utterly lost. But surely we need positions that acknowledge greater slippage between the seemingly intractable. Surely closure has a closer discourse with doubt than the stand-offs fostered by demarcating niche-market identities might allow, the survival of the one being implicated in the ongoing businesses of the other to such an extent that blankly oppositional positions seem redundant? Who, upon entering the Club of All Persuasions, could resist admitting usage to a term such as 'chopsy', referring to someone who has become over-'gabby' with the old 'north and south'?[7]

. . .

Throughout 'Assembling Alternatives', I listened to each speaker with multiple states of attention. I heard them as positioned among the many voices in the rooms into which they were speaking. That is, I didn't focus on dominant voices in exclusivity. I listened to them as multiple signals in a collaborative context. Furthermore, not a distant collaboration between discreet territories, but a close collaboration, involving intimacies that, at times, proved awkward to negotiate. In doing so, my attentions became partial subjects of distortion and distraction. I pursued listenings, orientated to the production of sound as an integral component of the production of meanings. Meanings, as a conversation between melody, rhythm and noise, with noise positively included, rather than edited out. Hearings, that struggled to retain the sense of paying attention to multiple voices and proliferating modes of address, in context, through time.

Both textual interpretations and their physical fixities are in various states of preservation and decay at any given time. I am not suggesting anything so silly as that the tongue is the chief source of play in language. I'm using it as a conceit in order to make some hopefully generative provocations. You might well ask, what about the lips, the teeth, the lungs, the pulse; the tongue being just one partner in linguistic communication (even if it's the silent tongue of a reader), why accord it so much privilege here? But the tongue is a more felicitously slippery and resonant term than the lips, the teeth and so forth. It is itself, for one thing, a sign for language. A tongue can be rendered as a dancing organ in the mouth. It is indexical of the body of language which it produces and of the body which produces it. A tongue is an organic site for projective reintegration between mind and body, between speaking and writing. It is an instrument of conscious and non-conscious, glossolalic articulations. The proposal in writing 'giving tongue' is to stimulate a tongue which has a generosity towards the appropriateness of influence, and has the ability to change and in doing so make a positive contribution back to those events with which it is primarily engaged. I'm arguing for a flexible tongue, that resists arrival at standards through stasis; a tongue that is too busy moving, playing, learning, to fall into the mores of fixation. No more than that. Such a tongue has much to offer contemporary poetics and poetries. It can teach us much, both positive and negative, about current constraints and habits within practice. It can reveal the terms of the violence of influence as much as the workings of thetic economy. It is the application of tonguing to the articulation of assemblage, through libinal play.

Speech has discourse with choreography, through habitus of stance and gesture in the given space of an informal or formally framed performance. Speaking is simultaneously chewing on both the programmatic and the more abstract communicative aspects of musical composition. Acts of speaking therefore have interdisciplinary resonance. Cross-artform terrains of linguistic communication ought to be taken into consideration more often. They are axiomatic to 'live' writing. But the more usual way of dealing with such evidences is to politely sideline their significance. Many writers still think of their work as that which only implicates the head, balanced panoptically on the top of the body. Boundaries between writing and other artforms can be subjected to forms of censorship, through reductive social consensus, as repressive as those operated against unwanted influence.[8]

Power no longer so clearly resides in autonomous, written traditions. Those aspects of knowledge, previously considered to be ephemeral, transient and of less value, which Foucault identifies as historically gendered female,[9] are back playing their full part in poetic discourses and the performances of situated writing. The ephemeral is once again a site for strategic intervention; the familiarly carnivalesque everyday tongue, a metaphorical site of slippage and control, of mis/takes and mis/understandings—as with the tongue in the ear, brings the pleasure and the disturbance of mis/hearings. We speak of tongues' furls and slips and lashes in the seas of meaning production;

we surf their catastrophic curves. My, often too-eager-to-please, tongue, sometimes begins to take on differing movements for subtly amending pronunciations in response to unfamiliar social contexts. It shapes, chameleonically into a paradoxical soundscape, appropriating a range of tonal colours that remind me of myself, but don't exactly sound like me. My jaw begins to ache a little as a result.

It recalls those discomforts when hearing one's own voice recorded onto tape, or, issuing from the radio, from a distance, effectively disembodied from an aural mirror. Writing isn't an echo of speech, but more an older form of indirect testimony; an echo of an echo or the skimming of Brathwaite's stone across a pond. My voice leaves me and returns to me, as though no longer so familiarly 'mine'. I am mediated, witnessing a production of defamiliarising, through a process of phonographic inscription. This is an awkwardness of becoming estranged from one's own meanings and one's own pronunciations, one's habituated manufacturing, that I find fascinating.

. . .

There's a cockney twang evidenced on recordings of my son's speech, when he was aged about five. We were living in East London then, and our neighbours from Pakistan, Turkey and Jamaica all spoke broad versions of the 'local'. After moving to north Suffolk, since 1994, he's developed another local burr, along with curious phraseology. He'll say 'now cummin!' in the place of 'I'm just coming', bringing an additional urgency to the summoning of a present. But both his lilt and his vocabulary changes subtly, dependent on which friends he's playing with; his speech is context responsive. The translocal opportunities offered by the diverse sounds of those Englishes, as spoken, in Suffolk in the extremely late twentieth century in dialogect with that of the urban Punjabi Scot are mouth-watering; prospective tongues, dancing in an abundance of influences.

Not that a diversity of dialect and locally specific vocabulary and regional terminology has been previously absent; simply that its presence has never before been so foregrounded on such a translocal scale. There are, though, no signs as yet of hybridity-fatigues. The fear is rather of yet another dumbed-down para-English being imposed as 'standard' to quell the incipient Babel, a meta-version for international diplomacy and all ordinary decent folk, leaving the routed rabble to chat amongst themselves on the multinational sidelines. Poets need to be more proactive in their advocacy for living tongues, reinvigorated from over-conventionalised coinages, secreting cunning billingsgates otherwise palimpsested onto the deadening palettes of coca-cola-ised business conference committee procedural utterances, policed street representations and inter-National news mediations; the debilitating standards taken so brilliantly to task by Tom Leonard:

I protest at this place
with no people in it
objects for reproducing images
people not actually present
from this wall to this wall
and this wall to this wall

(Tom Leonard, *Reports From the Present* 118; from 'Nora's Place')

or:

right inuff
ma language is disgraceful
ma maw tellt mi
ma teacher tellt mi
thi doactir tellt mi
thi priest tellt mi

ma boss tellt mi
ma landlady in carrington street tellt mi
thi lassie ah tried tay get aff way in 1969 tellt mi
sum wee smout thit thoat ah hudny read chomsky tellt mi
a calvinistic communist thit thoat ah wuz revisionist tellt mi
po-faced literati grimly kerryin thi burden a thi past tellt mi
po-faced literati grimly kerryin thi burden a thi future tellt mi
ma wife tellt mi jist-tay-get-inty-thi-poem tellt mi
ma wainz came hame fray school an tellt mi
jist aboot ivry book ah oapnd tellt mi
even thi introduction tay thi Scottish National Dictionary tellt mi

ach well
all livin language is sacred
fuck thi lohta thim

(Tom Leonard, *Ghostie Men*)

. . .

Consensual linguistic realities can be both local and translocal now. Adherence to specific instances can mean that Someone, charactered as a flashing light with fixated response, in reducing the idea of control to a seemingly mechanical interaction, will say 'Oh what a beautiful picture' when shown a 'beautiful' painting.[10] That is, that a given Someone's taste will be an orderly arbitration. It is equally possible, though not so likely, that this self-same Someone, might rather say—or find a way to so imply—'flattening wave leak teleofelt, rude, drastic, mail hoot, longer, swollen, final, coined matt, fog' in response to that same stimulus, and that Someone might really mean it. Someone could be thereby tendering a critique of consensual redundancy, or simply speaking errant nonsense, depending on one's energy and patience for engagement with the impact of messages whose syntactical density requires considerable efforts to decode. Such efforts can be linked to ideas of rewards gained through reading, that are complicit with knowledge as a bankable asset. The argument goes something like this: on what basis might efforts to glean meaning that offer personal advancement be invested, if such efforts are subsequently not found to have been worth it? In other words, why should I start trying to read something, or bother to listen to what Someone is saying, invest hope in finding something there, if I later discover that I have wasted my time? Such questions reveal an overwrought case of contracting the Protestant work ethic on the part of their posers. They overstate and reinforce values belonging to phallogocentric investiture.

Still, the pressure towards plain speech presides, particularly on the political left. This is a salutary admonition. To say what you mean and to mean what you say, is often interpreted as saying things simply, with simply meaning words of one syllable. This is harnessed to variously patronising opinions about what 'people' can and can't understand. Apart from being despairingly orientated towards a lowest common denominator (itself a patronising term) this attitude mitigates, partially, against the performative pleasure, the sheer fun[11] of giving tongues full rein and suggests that there are only certain things worth saying and certain ways in which they can be said. I should censure my dad, for indoctrinating me, and at such a susceptible age too, with pernicious sound-sense.

So I wonder how far we become shortchanged in our social relations by the exigencies of colloquial convention? With what frequencies do we converse, seeking approval along lines of least resistance, in the process revealing highly depoliticising mobilisations of attention away from the gritty specifics of local speech act engagements?

. . .

If, and only if, languages evolved to facilitate bonding within social groupings, they did so by foregrounding the encouragement of exchanges of socially relevant information. The noise within conversation was consequently subordinated to proprieties and formalities of such exchange. But this noise is more important than we think. A given conversation is about 65 to 75 percent devoted to social topics, broadly characterisable as gossip. Gossip goes further into the workings of consensus integral to human exchange than that which Aitchison after Malinovski's 'phatic communion' calls 'talking for the sake of talking' (Aitchison 21)[12] Communities of interest have context specific chitchats. These often circumscribe the territories upon which consensus might operate in each given situation or social transaction. Gossip thus lays the groundwork upon which conventions are built.

In over-privileging the conventional, the majority of gossip acts not as a radical focus for local engagements but as an agency of repression or control. Gossip fears becoming its own subject in much the same way as jokers dislike becoming the butt of their own jokes. The worry that 'tongues might wag' fosters cliquish agreement as to the dominant parameters of 'mature' or 'adult' or 'proper' (considered appropriate by others) workouts for the tongue, policing culturally acceptable shapes, sounds and manners of speech; both the moulds made by the mouth through which breath is poured and vibrated as well as the content of what's said. The effect is to promote those subjects which are considered to be fit for discussion and the modes of discursiveness that are considered proper. In such respects, gossip can be understood as a social fashioning, of language in the service of kinship formation and community-of-interest bonding. I wonder how much contemporary poetry then can also be seen to operate as gossip on these terms: fashionable subjects, fashionable cadences, fashionable methodologies? The adoption of modish movements of the tongue can be likened to forms of imitation born out of a desire to fit in, as I described my own adaptive tendencies earlier. Gossip, or what passes for it in conversation, the chit-chat, is therefore a key site for strategic syntactical interventions, for reinvestment with linguistic, socio-sonic imagination. Poetics can have at least that social application.

. . .

Better perhaps though to stick out one's tongue and openly display the transport of insult, than to try to ingratiate one's speech into its surroundings. For without doubt, the tongue has been treated through history as the root of insult, a dangerous weapon for the fermenting of social discord and an unreliable witness. Literatures are thick with admonitions to cut out an offender's tongue. Languages have been wiped from existence. But it's often struck me what a difficult thing that must be to do well. The awkwardness of opening the mouth and getting a decent grip on what is after all a slippery customer, inserting sharp instruments to hack at its poisonous base, or to edit its tip, to perform an injurious frenolotomy. Perhaps the most hideous of all hatreds is that which drives one to resort to biting Someone else's tongue out of their mouth. Well, how's that for live sampling!

. . .

Consider then a tongue as a sophisticated piece of sampling equipment; a mimic, a sponge, playing messages back to the messengers. A surprisingly large body–mind organ with five connection points into the nervous system, it is used in medicinal systems worldwide, for diagnosing the health of its host. The movements of the tongue during speech 'act naturally', as a means to extricate body–mind balance. Balance is approached through an interfusing series of intimately specific positions and through concomitant adjustments from position to position to position. Balance requires attention being paid to the details of the small dance, of the organs within the body; the tongue among them. Add the volubilities of the moments between those moments of closure, the pauses—the silences—and the spaces between the notes can be heard as being just as articulate as the notes themselves.

Silences born of declining to say, of witholding, differ significantly from the gaps that are parts of the saying in generative speech. These are the findings out of what one is trying to say whilst one is saying it; speaking as commentaries in the events of the speaking. The performances of language in a specific context, interpreted through our senses, constructed as an event. Each event and each staging of event, its tense, its process and its production, entangle. Process and product form a coil, mapping the slips of a giving tongue; during which, in a process of learning to speak, through constructions that deal up hot mouthfuls of birds, there comes a twittering, rapid interchange between previously held to be binary functions of receiver and transmitter. As one's skin on the palms of one's hands becomes heated when playing a drum; questioning whether it's one who is playing the drum or the drum playing the one. Apparent nonsense, such as this, embraced by critical curiosities, without fear, can be productive of interaction, further conversation. As much writing and reading is versional mulch . . . the mucusicalities of which, in a bordering onto hilarious exegesis . . . one lump . . . threw stale reasonings out. And kept what, the precious pieces in the attic, in a dusty box? No, rather sought the less easy comforts of writing as socially dispersive conversation.

The suggestion here is that the sounds of our languages and of our discourses can and do change radically, through a paying of attentions to the specific details of this buoyant twittering blur of the birds on the trees amongst us, or of the high-pitched chatter of microbes in mountain rock pools. That the tongue and the ear of a mimic is ever present in this process. That the sounds of a voice, dances in the bodies of both transmitters and receivers and that artfully tongued elisions, can falsify the masquerading sounds of ownership and confound the everyday syntaxes of dull control. That such dull control is very different from the sharply defined spaces articulated by conscious constraint. I'm referring here to logistics of oration, which negotiate patterns of connectedness through the regimes of the pro-verberal (a coinage indebted to Joan Retallack's slip of her tongue during a reading of her poetry at the Assembling Alternatives conference). A tongue acculturating its dances in a subtle acoustical chamber, the sonic architextures of our mouths, projects myriad moments of practiced closure. Perceptual pleasure, as dusk, the mouth of the cooking pot, is made available to both producer and consumer. Aural choreographies of discovery, through that tongue unseen, ulleiling[13] the veiled, by branching twists against skew. A process of ludic articulation, not intended as monument.

. . .

Flourishing in a border wetland, drenched with saliva, a tongue is literally a site of an embodiment of language, of the intercourse of a projection of a memory of a memory. These origins, these stains of plummage, 'tunge'—'tong'—'tonga', shaping breath, to enunciate vibrations of shared air. An excitation of molecules as sound; those molecules, or at least some of them, through conversation, taken into the body of another conversant on a following breath.

Giving tongue through discursion, as both a root and a source; both a one and an other. A site of seduction and persuasion and violation, of provocation and penetration. Where each and every shaping that a given tongue performs, impacts on that which follows that.

The speech of a giving tongue then, is here appreciated as a tool for a problematicised present of micropolitical positionalities; engaging its readers and its listeners decisively, assemblage by assemblage. Its every articulation an intersection between dance and sonic composition and syntactical invention, in the service of a revitalising social bond, based not around reductive consensus, but around that giving tongue. A platform through conclusion.

Notes

1. '". . . It's *rather* hard to understand!" (You see she didn't like to confess even to herself, that she couldn't make it out at all.) "Somehow it seems to fill my head with ideas—only I don't exactly know what they are! However, *somebody* killed *something*: that's clear, at any rate"' (Carroll, L. *Through the Looking-Glass*. London: Macmillan, 1962: 22).
2. Poly Styrene, born Marion Elliot, lead singer with the punk band 'X-Ray Spex'. Quoted by Jon Savage, she says, 'it was about being in bondage to material life. In other words it was a call for liberation. It was saying: "Bondage?—forget it! I am not going to be bound by the laws of consumerism or bound by my own senses"' (Savage, J. *England's Dreaming*. London: Faber and Faber, 1992: 327).
3. Johnny Speight's satirical character Alf Garnett, various reprehensible characterisations by Vivian Stanshall (formerly of the Bonzo Dog Doo Dah Band) and the class-parodic modes of speaking mobilised from time to time by Monty Python.
4. There had, of note, been the Albert Hall 'First International Poetry Incarnation' event, as it was called, in 1966, and various fringe activities organised by Michael Horowitz under the 'New Departures' banner, even some regional dialects taking the high ground. I'm thinking of Basil Bunting's sounding and writing of the sounding of 'Briggflatts', of Barry MacSweeney and Tom Pickard with their unabashed Newcastle and Durham intonations, even of Ted Hughes's thick Yorkshire drawl. Not a barren landscape, but a sparsely populated one.

5. Jean 'Binta' Breeze, from 'Red Rebel Song', a version printed in the anthology *The Popular Front of Contemporary Poetry,* published by the London-based performance poetry promotion organisation 'Apples & Snakes' (Apples & Snakes, 1992).
6. Breeze's nimble conflation of sound with sense is demonstrated by this use of 'lang' to read as long, in long time, and lang, as language time in relation to poetry and song. What I read in this passage leans towards Kristeva's espousal of 'oralization' (Kristeva, 153).
7. Someone who is 'chopsy', in the valleys of south Wales where people 'talk tidy', is somebody who talks a lot. If someone has the 'gift of the gab' they are skilful at putting their points across through speech, hence someone who is 'gabby' also talks a lot. 'North and South' is cockney rhyming slang for 'mouth'.
8. One example is provided by the treatment at the hands of Welsh language activists of a composer with whom I have collaborated for many years, Sianed Jones. Welsh is her mother tongue, her first language. She revisits Wales regularly, but doesn't live there now. About 8 years ago she was giving a performance in the mining caverns deep below Blaennau Festiniog in north Wales. She was singing settings of poems, written in Welsh by a Welsh poet, Gwyn Thomas, who lives in Bangor, north Wales. Yet she was criticised by language activists for singing Welsh with an outsider ('blues') inflection. Such are the thorny issues of influence on the tongues of nation languages. Such are the anxieties of those who would control language usage and development.
9. Foucault writes of the spoken word, through the taxonomic ambition of encyclopaedic projects around the turn of the of the late seventeenth century, as becoming downgraded and aligned with the passive intellect. Orality became associated with 'the female part of language', ephemerality, whilst writing was ensconced as the active male intellect, and the harbor of truth, longevity (Foucault, 38).
10. I'm obviously using Someone to designate an example unknown here. I've invented Someone, for argument's sake. They are as hypothetical as Anyone.
11. Barthes talks about this as 'writing aloud'. But he still wants to separate 'the articulation of the body, of the tongue' from 'that of meaning, of language' (Barthes, 66–67).
12. Who's doing what, who's doing what to who or doing what with who; what so and so says, this new such and such, that event and so forth.
13. The sounds produced by rhythmically singing the tip of the tongue against the front of the roof of the mouth. Used to signal joy or happiness, particularly produced by women under Muslim regimes, hiding the sight of the tongue moving in their mouths behind their veil and/or their hand.

Bibliography

Aitchison, J. *The Seeds of Speech.* Cambridge: Cambridge University Press, 1996.
Barthes, R. *The Pleasure of the Text.* New York: Hill and Wang, 1975.

Beasley, P. *The Popular Front of Contemporary Poetry.* London: Apples & Snakes, 1992.

Bourdieu, P. *Language & Symbolic Power.* London: Polity Press, 1991.

Brathwaite, E. (later publishing under the name of Kamau). *Rights of Passage.* New York: Oxford University Press, 1967.

Carroll, L. *Through the Looking-Glass.* London: MacMillan, 1962.

Foucault, M. *The Order of Things.* London: Routledge, 1974.

Griffiths, B. *War w/ Windsor.* London: Writers Forum & Pirate Press, 1974.

Kristeva, J. *Revolution in Poetic Language.* New York: Columbia University Press, 1984.

Leonard, T. *Ghostie Men.* Newcastle: Galloping Dog, 1980.

Leonard, T. *Reports From the Present.* London: Jonathan Cape, 1995.

Savage, J. *England's Dreaming.* London: Faber and Faber, 1992.

Nancy Gish

Complexities of Subjectivity

Scottish Poets and Multiplicity

She said she
woke up with him in
her head, in her bed
Her mother-tongue clung to her mouth's roof
in terror, dumbing her, and he came with a name
that was none of her making.
—Liz Lochhead, "Dreaming Frankenstein"

The cool black skin
of the Bible couldn't hold her,
nor the atlas green
on the kitchen table,
you stuck with thumbs
and split to fruity hemispheres—
yellow Yemen, Red Sea, *Ethiopia*. Stick in
with the homework and you'll be
cliver like yer faither.
But no too cliver,
no *above yersel.*
—Kathleen Jamie, "The Queen of Sheba"

Lately I make pictures of her
But I can see the smallness
she is tall and slim
of her hands, Yes
Her hair is loose curls
an opal stone on her middle finger
I reach out to catch her
Does she talk broad Glasgow?
But no matter how fast
Maybe they moved years ago
I run after
She is faceless. . .
—Jackie Kay, "The Adoption Papers"

Read out of context, these brief excerpts appear traditional: they retain standard syntax; they use Scots only in isolated words or references; they appear to be single speakers or dramatic voices. Placed back in the complete poems, however, each functions as a moment of switching, a sudden shift in which "self" is displaced or altered or made aware of an other within, or an other entering or penetrating—a different "tongue" or language or voice that is both self and not self. Given widespread current definitions of "experimental," the work of these contemporary Scottish poets can be read as conventional, yet the definitions themselves, while illuminating much recent work, can artificially contain its forms, excluding or erasing what I wish to argue are radical redefinitions of self and voice.

But the experimental is not containable. What is subjected to definition or limit ceases to be experiment and becomes a new dominant mode. As Lynn Keller pointed out at the conference, "Discussions of contemporary alternative or 'experimental poetry' in the U.S. tend to equate alternative writing with Language writing, a term that embraces diverse texts but denotes a fairly coherent category nonetheless."[1] When carried over to a "British" context, this definition can set up "experimental" versus "mainstream" as a binary that elides other innovative practices and relegates the work of many marginalized poets, however radical in their own terms, to the merely conventional. It is significant, for example, that the *Assembling Alternatives* conference had no Black participants and none from Scotland though there were several from Ireland and Wales. This absence raises questions about the further impact of subsuming diverse cultural sources and distinctive poetic traditions as well as different concepts of identity, voice, and language under either/or categories of "experimental" or "mainstream," especially when those categories have been structured in contexts they do not share. In the case of Scotland, generations of criticism focused on a notion of "British" that coincides with "English" hinder the ability even to recognize culturally specific forms.

In "Time Out of Motion" Charles Bernstein remarks that "even in the so-called British Isles the most imaginative poetries of this century, to my view, have staged a series of secessions from imperial English. Think of Bunting's Northumbrian or MacDiarmid's Scots . . . ," and he calls for "particularity and peculiarity of place and time and person acknowledged as such," and for "many arts, many poetries."[2] While MacDiarmid's Synthetic Scots[3] set off the most significant movement in twentieth-century Scotland, the reassertion of a distinctive linguistic and cultural history, contemporary Scottish experimentation both draws on his lexical innovations and forms a fresh set of disparate—if interconnected—secessions, not only from imperial English but from MacDiarmid's own reconstructed national language. Rather than focusing exclusively on disrupting Standard English through the opacity and complexity of a collage of Scots from all regions and times, contemporary poets more often use the Scots of their own region and their own speech forms—sometimes in opposition to English, sometimes in mixed forms of Scots, English, and localized speech that distinguish dialects of Scots. These usages, by disrupting or "seceding from" what is considered a norm in "Britain," allow a broad range of linguistic experiment.

In *Devolving English Literature,* for example, Robert Crawford argues that a key legacy of Modernism (which was created largely by Americans, Irish, Scots, and regional English writers) is reliance on the demotic: "Drawing so strongly on both anthropology and dialect and aiming to outflank the Anglo-centricity of established Englishness through a combination of the demotic and the multicultural, Modernism was an essentially provincial phenomenon."[4] This aspect of Modernism, he further argues, has its own legacy, a legacy he explicitly opposes to that of Post-Modernism and Language poetry.[5] This is not, however, to deny its focus on language. He devotes the final chapter of his book to a discussion of "Barbarians," writers he sees as engaged in alternative radical forms. These forms employ lexicons, pronunciations, rhythms, idioms, that are often incomprehensible, unrecognizable, or opaque, at least initially, to Standard English speakers. In a culture where oral forms remain more central to poetics, pronunciation, sound, and rhythm are cues to understanding and meaning. Whether non-English words or alternative sounds (Scots, for example, retains the Germanic umlauted "u" and the sounds of "hoch" and "ich"—all lost to English) or localized discourses, they assert distinctive linguistic possibilities: they "secede."

For such poets, "experiment" cannot be framed by opposing poles of Language writing or "mainstream." To see their genuinely distinct experimentation, we must start where it arises, start with its own formal structures and theoretical claims rather than attempt to place it by reference to claims constructed in relation to the Standard English it resists. If few Scots write Language poetry, it is because they write something else, and it might be asked why their poetics are not more used as a creative source. My interest in these forms lies both in their poetic effects and in their concomitant new forms of identity and subjectivity. The demotic, that is, *may* simply reenact traditional forms of the romantic "I"; but it carries the potential for multiple and fluid subjectivity in its defining polyphony, its play across borders of language and among internal differentiated voices—some in Scots, some in versions of English.

While modern Scots and modern English developed from separate Anglo-Saxon dialects—Northumbrian and Mercian respectively—and have thus been distinct from the earliest recorded texts, the effect of English political and cultural power since the Union of 1707 has been to displace any single standard Scots speech with many local vernaculars. MacDiarmid's synthesizing aimed to reconstruct a modern version of the language of Dunbar, a language no one speaks. His Scots has been succeeded by inscriptions of local speech, as in

Tom Leonard's phonetically transcribed Glaswegian, Sheena Blackhall's North-East Doric, Liz Lochhead's dramatic voices, W. N. Herbert's dictionary Scots—which, like MacDiarmid's, draws on the whole Scots lexicon but in which, as Edwin Morgan puts it, "the Dundonian is never lost"[6]—or Jackie Kay's individual fusions of Glaswegian, Highland-accented English, Anglo-Scots, and American Blues rhythms. These many dialects coexist as a disruptive potential within what may read as either Scots or English and, like a Creole, allow for variation, fluidity, and shifting perspectives quite different from standardized, ancient, national languages. Their lexicons are, for non-speakers, opaque, though for particular communities they are shared terms. While the vocabulary is not individually constructed, it displaces conventional expectations by the eruption of the unknown within the known, at borders where languages overlap and layer. Moreover, Scots are, of necessity, bilingual; they understand and can speak or write English. The choice to write in Scots or mixed forms—or English—is always a choice, not a given. Simply to write in English in forms considered experimental by English or American standards cannot function as it does for those to whom the dominant language is the mother tongue; to do so is to affirm what they reject: that Standard English is always already the center to be decentered. It is significant, moreover, that while Scots was for centuries a separate national language, and thus remains a distinct if mutually comprehensible sister language with English, Ireland and Wales as well as the Highlands of Scotland were originally Gaelic speaking, and their languages are thus totally separate. Their "English" is a second tongue in a way different from Scots. Irish English, nonetheless, contains a mixture of many sources. To experiment in these languages, then, depends on their origins and the forms they contain. Experimentation in Scots carries its own very distinctive implications about asserting a cultural history outside of what has been called "British."

My point is that American and English binaries of Language or mainstream poetry not only fail to account for Bernstein's "secessions from imperial English" but preclude recognition of their innovations. These secessions may construct new poetic and linguistic communities and critique dominant forms, or they may go further and inscribe new or distinct notions of subjectivity and identity. In the first case, the use of Scots as a poetic language, in itself, demands engagement with language play, though the focus is primarily on lexicon rather than syntax. If much experimental American or English poetry opens up words to new possibilities, creating multiple, complex potentialities of meaning through syntactical ambiguity, puns, neologisms, phonemic shifts, sound patterns,[7] those potentialities are already inseparable from Scots words themselves because the national literary language of the Middle Ages has been dispersed and fragmented into regional versions with distinct lexicons, spellings, sounds, and pronunciations. For example, "who" may be "wha," "fa," "qua," "whae"; "wha" may also be "what." "Quean" or "quine" (now North East) may be a maidservant, a sweetheart, a slut, a mistress. Scots as a single language is a concept existing only in a dictionary. But that means it is available for experimental use. Tom Paulin makes a comparable point in his description of Irish English words, which he claims "live in the careless richness of speech, but they rarely appear in print. When they do, many readers are unable to understand them and have no dictionary where they can discover their meaning."[8] Paulin bases his argument for a reconstructed Irish identity—a conscious use of contemporary language theory to create new cultural forms—on an "institutionalized existence," a dictionary, of Irish English. As Paulin further notes, "the platonic standard [Standard British English] has an actual location—it isn't simply free and transcendental—and that location is the British House of Commons."[9] MacDiarmid made a parallel argument, but for him that "institutionalized existence" was already available in *Jamieson's Etymological Dictionary,* which he likened to Joyce's *Ulysses* and raided for words that have no reified current meaning. He claimed that using a Scots word was like playing a chord rather than a note. Thus calling Christ a "byspale"—an example; a prodigy; a person or thing of rare and wonderful qualities, frequently used ironically; a by-word for anything remarkable; a term derived from proverb or a story; an illegitimate child—is to write what is already uncontainable by syntax because it has no recent history of usage to define its limits; it can serve as an already open field of meanings. Scots words often mean contradictory or seemingly incongruous things, as in "watergaw," which means "teeth," "the fragment of a rainbow," and an indication of bad weather. English words, of course, carry such histories and multiple layers. But to English speakers they also have current common significations that are assumed unless wrenched out of position by syntactic shifts or phonemic alterations. (No one, when reading "silly," immediately thinks, "innocent.") Or if they are archaic, that immediately stands out—as in Auden's "lonely as fell on chat." Because the bulk of specifically Scots words[10] have been largely lost to current use, their meanings lie hidden in the multiple disparate possibilities of the dictionary; to use them is to require the reader's participation in varying degrees.

Bernstein's "secessions from imperial English" include experimentations in alternative lexicons because they involve forms of linguistic opacity that call upon meaning-making and because they resist the notion of a single standard. Poets like Tom Leonard or Sheena Blackhall or W. N. Herbert carry this linguistic devolution further by eschewing any concept of a single reconstructed Scots language and phonetically transcribing their own vernacular: "Smeddum's a wird'll thole / thin hairsts"; "thi reason / a talk wia / BBC accent / is coz yi / widni wahnt / mi ti talk / aboot thi / trooth wia / voice lik / wanna yoo / scruff"; "O Howff, herein deid, hiddelt in broongrey shaddir."[11] While it is beyond the scope of this essay to explore these vernacular poems in detail, the languages they use demand new engagement with words, their cultural and political meanings, the construction of meanings as a shared experience. It may not read as obviously "experimental" to speakers of Standard English because the linguistic disruptions are lexical and the voices represented may appear as the lyric "I" rather than soundings of specific local discourses. Yet the words are often as opaque or intrinsically ambiguous as the broken phrasing or phonemic play of Language poetry, and the narrators speak out of "particularity and peculiarity of place and time and person . . ."—particularity and peculiarity hardly visible from the perspective of American and English culture and speech and in resistance to them. "Smeddum," for example, is difficult to translate into any single English word; Leonard's sounds of Glasgow carry very particularized urban class humor; "Howff" carries local Dundee associations: none of the poems are transparently readable even to Scots, who know the words, and very specifically not to speakers of Standard English despite the familiarity of the syntax and the many cognates. These poets are not writing in a separate, dominant, national language such as French or German; they are writing in alternate, marginalized "British" languages always coexisting with, overlapping, contesting the dialect of "Standard British English" that Paulin locates in the British House of Commons, languages recognizable to speakers of that privileged dialect but containing incomprehensible words or unknown sounds, or ambiguous meanings.

If one form of secession deploys particular historic conditions of Modern Scots, a second form more directly plays off against English. When Scots is employed in a dialogic relation with English, other possibilities open up, possibilities that go beyond the broad "secession from imperial English" to refiguring of self and identity in ways I see as radically critiquing traditional notions of "mainstream" expressive poetry. The politics of identity and the politics of language are interconnected in Scotland because every Scot lives in a world of English they have been trained to use, and yet they also have Scots or Gaelic—in varying degrees—as a mother tongue. So multiplicity of internal voices—and of selves—is a thematic focus and a structural device in much Scots literature. From James Hogg's *Confessions of a Justified Sinner* to Robert Louis Stevenson's *Dr. Jekyll and Mr. Hyde* to Hugh MacDiarmid's embrace of the "Caledonian Antisyzygy"[12] to Edwin Muir's argument in *Scot and Scotland* that every Scot feels in Scots but thinks in English (he concluded, somewhat confusingly, that they should therefore write poetry in English) to R. D. Laing's *The Divided Self* to the prominence of pseudonyms in William Sharp/ Fiona MacLeod, Leslie Mitchell/ Lewis Grassic Gibbon, Christopher Murray Grieve/ Hugh MacDiarmid, Scots have assumed and represented dual or multiple personalities and identities. So persistent is this conception of self or identity that Tom Nairn, in calling for a unified Scottish identity, could refer to the notion of divided or split or multiple identity as "joke dividedness" for which he could assume recognition.[13] He sees unity of identity for Scots as a political goal to claim or strive for, not a given. If subjectivity and identity are linguistically constructed, then a Scot works within an already divided and ruptured language—not only an English/ Scottish division but a multiple set of versions of Scots, what W. N. Herbert calls a "subject tongue, persecuted into rural corners."[14] For Scots, then, the very notion of a pre-existing, unified, central voice that "expresses" the experience of a traditional subject is extremely problematic. They have responded, however, in diverse ways: writing an easily accessible Scots-inflected English like that of most Burns poems, using English for prose and Scots for poetry, using Scots for rural or comic voices (as in Scott), writing separate Scots poems and English poems as Sheena Blackhall does, writing synthetic Scots in a deliberate construction of re-integrated Scottish identity as in MacDiarmid's early poetry or Herbert's contemporary Dundonian experiments, or deliberately using living, spoken regional Scots dialects and/or mixing such dialects with English to create dual or multiple voiced—polyphonic—texts. It is this last choice that I believe represents the initiation of a distinctive challenge to traditional concepts of subjectivity, a challenge drawing on Scottish theory and traditions, and differing from the fragmentation or erasure of a single constructing poetic voice.

Thus to multiply "I" in ways that critique both traditional expression and dominant public discourse may mean to orchestrate the tones and words of many selves and linguistic forms. To write in one of the many dialects of spoken Scots is to use language that is always a kind of presence within the dominant language and a self one might call beside one's self, another voice or voices speaking or writing another language yet one that is both recognizable and partially or wholely opaque in its vocabulary rather than its syntax. "Experiment" thus becomes not a form of play *in* English but a challenge to the very words, phrases, rhythms, and forms of discourse that make up Standard English by displacing them with the mixed forms of Scots and the "English" spoken in Scotland.

The poetry of Liz Lochhead, Kathleen Jamie, and Jackie Kay, for example, is focused less on breaking forms than in deploying interacting language forms. In the case of Lochhead, this becomes most apparent in her working class, female, urban personae in collections like *Bagpipe Muzak* or, in her drama, *Mary Queen of Scots Got Her Head Chopped Off,* in the mixed language forms of Mary and Elizabeth, both of whom merge into their ladies-in-waiting, Bess and Miriam, who speak Scots in one persona and English in the other—in Mary/Miriam's case, a French-accented Scots as Queen Mary. In each case a single actress shifts identity with a shift in speech, linguistically metamorphosing on stage. Robert Crawford has described this strategy in Lochhead's work as using language that is "explicitly heteroglossic in Bakhtin's terms; that is, it is explicitly composed of a variety of different languages and registers—demotic and literary, or (in the case of a few poems and several plays) Scots and English"; he quotes Lochhead's own description of the language of her *Tartuffe* as "a totally invented and, I hope, theatrical Scots . . . it's deliberately varied in register—most of the characters except Dorine are at least bilingual and consequently more or less 'two faced.'"[15] As Crawford has noted, Lochhead sees herself as "multiply divided":

> I guess I would say that the big split in Scotland is between the self and the other self. In many ways I think that the big theme in Scottish literature is the split, from *Justified Sinner* to *Jekyll and Hyde,* and I think that's natural if you're Scottish where you are half English, really. There's a bit of you who's internalized all of that, so you're English but you're Scots. So two different halves of you talk to each other which is very similar to the status of the male and the feminine with regard to Britain. You know the Celt, the other. Once again we split again—in Scotland, the Celt is the feminine, the Scot is the male, the standard. I don't know where that leaves Scottish Celts. They're split and split and split and split. It's probably between dominant cultures and undominant cultures I would like the split to become between self and other, but sometimes you're so busy defining self that you are talking to other halves of yourself.[16]

In the initial quotation from Lochhead, from *Dreaming Frankenstein,* the monster penetrates the writer and once inside is not easily ejected. This sense of a masculine "other" within a female persona is placed in the context of a kind of multiplication rather than division: it defines a moment of discovery when self ceases to be experienced as single and coherent. While her definitions of "splits" accord with the long discourse of Scottish duality and dividedness, they also suggest an alternative trope: not division but multiplication, the recognition of many selves, many voices internally coexisting and speaking not as a chorus but as a medley—sometimes in conversation, sometimes in debate, sometimes clashing, sometimes eerily dissonant or disturbing, but not as one and not as a central control constructing discourse or expressing an individual "personal" feeling.

In Lochhead's work, this multiplicity primarily takes the form of dramatis personae who may—as in her Glasgow characters—play on puns, demotic speech, varied rhythms, jokes or language shifts to create many voices in which, in Crawford's words, "the oral and literary language of the poems tend to infect one another."[17] The result is a mixture of ballads, literary speech, oral tradition, ancient and contemporary discourses interacting in ways that mingle self and other. But these forms of multiplicity retain a convention of externality; that is, the multiple registers of Scots allow for personae who are fluid, changing, linguistically disruptive. In Jamie and more intensively in Kay these mixes of language appear as poet and other, as voices that, in Jamie's words, are her own two languages and in Kay's account both are and are not her own. They become, that is, a poetry of self/not self or self beside the self. It is a key difference between the erasure or fragmentation of what is defined as "experimental" in American and English poetry and the multiplying and diversifying Lochhead finds in the specific histories and geographic conditions of Scotland. It goes beyond choosing to write in synthetic Scots or a particular Scots dialect to constructing multiple-voiced personae to speaking *as* multi-voiced.

In the case of Kathleen Jamie this is a recent development. Up to *The Queen of Sheba* her books were in English and conventionally "expressive" in the terms of the current binary. In the title poem, "The Queen of Sheba," Scots and English both alternate and merge, sometimes by voice shifts, sometimes by the emergence of internal alter voices, sometimes in individual words or phrases that create a specific class, gender, and location. The poem opens as an apostrophe to Scotland in an educated "English" voice ("Scotland, you have invoked her name / just once too often / in your presbyterian living rooms"), which switches without cue to include Scots words (come doun / the family like a lang neb, a thrawn streak, / a wally dug).[18] A second voice in a thicker, working class voice questions the first: "She's had enough. She's come. / Whit, tae this dump?" The narrator continues in the original voice but uses words like "keeks" (peeps) and "wee" and "kirk-yaird" (churchyard). The moment of shift appears as a Scots alter voice one carries inside and hears not only as a different sound but as a specific attitude of limit, caution, provincial containment:

. . . Stick in
with the homework and you'll be
cliver like your faither.
But no too cliver,
no *above yersel.*

There are a series of cues to shifts here. The pronoun change to "you" is the first displacement followed by the internalized cautionary voice to be "cliver like your faither" and the italicized voice (which returns later) as the voice of one kind of Scottish provincialism that calls for being narrow and closing off all that is strange or foreign or uncontrolled—everything assumed in the last voice (in capital letters) of the thousand laughing girls who want to "admire her hairy legs and / bonny wicked smile" and "take / Ph.Ds in Persian, be vice / to her president," and think they are "THE QUEEN OF SHEBA."

It might be argued that this is the same technique as Eliot's in "he do the police in different voices." Like *The Waste Land* this shifts voices over and over, sometimes with cue of typeface or grammar, sometimes not. But what I see as quite different here is the way language is deployed. These are not quoted phrases from German, Italian, or French; they are dual languages that are both Jamie's own speech. Moreover, the voices are dialogic in a way I think Eliot's are not—that is, there is genuine difference, contradiction, conflict in ideas and attitudes. And these voices are not externalized as dramatis personae but are, in one sense, all Jamie's own, and, in another, internalized voices, discourses, cultural attitudes—multiple voices of Jamie *and* of Scotland at once. Jamie has said that in 1989 her work changed:

> My life took a difficult turn, and I moved to Sheffield, and there I discovered I spoke Scots and English both, so then I got into a linguistic fankle, and couldn't write, couldn't find a voice, a language. (I'm beginning to understand that it's ok to have several, Scots do have several, people are beginning to talk about this, the babel, the Scots polyphony.)[19]

This polyphony is the focus of a specific kind of experimentation with subjectivity and voice. Lochhead, Jamie, and Kay all write in oral forms; Lochhead and Kay regularly perform their work and also write drama. But this speech is not the single voice speaking assumed in conventional definitions of mainstream poetry. It is, rather, the speech of many internal selves and voices constructed by a culture and history in which language is always an internal division, any voice always a political and cultural choice, and the division of English/Scots complicated by the dispersal of Scots into extremely diverse forms. (Glaswegian is, arguably, as different from Shetland speech or Aberdonian as it is from Standard English.) The inscription of these multiple voices that require knowledge of particular communities—along with the use of Scottish discourses such as the Glasgow working class ideology of Tom Leonard's characters or the cautionary "dour" convention of "cliver but no too cliver"—produces a poetry not only very different from the mainstream "expression" of American poetry workshops but one focused specifically on disrupting "imperial English" and constructing fluid, diverse linguistic texts. The difference is perhaps most explicit in the work of Jackie Kay, and this is so despite the fact that her work may appear—superficially—as what is called "mainstream." That is, *The Adoption Papers* might be read as traditionally expressive or narrative in its autobiographical focus and use of an "I" who remembers and speaks, and the narrators of *Other Lovers* and later poems may be read as dramatis personae resembling Lochhead's Glasgow characters. But Kay's self-conscious play on voices, dialects, and discourses destabilizes any notion of a consistent unified self; her "personae" are as often shifting voices or personae of Kay. Neither the unified constructing subject nor the fragmented or displaced subject of English and American experimentalism, Kay's voices are the dual or multiple selves of Scotland's "divided self" or dual personalities inscribed not as Muir's problem or Nairn's "joke dividedness" but as complexity and possibility. For Scottish poetry and poetics the lines of experimentation are differently configured than for contemporary English and American experimentalism: not the displacement of a traditional unified subject (which has not been so constituted for Scots) nor the rupture of English syntax (which is not where difference is located) but the freeing up of multiple subjectivities and the concomitant release of suppressed lexical and aural possibilities. Specifically, in the case of Jackie Kay, who is Scottish and Black as well as lesbian, "subject" is already multiple (one cannot say "the" subject). And lexical borders overlap, "infect" one another so that shifts among Glaswegian sounds, American Blues rhythms, Scots words and "English" speech allow a radical rupture of "imperial English" from within.

The link between assumptions about the subject and definitions of "experimental" can be clarified by reference to Marjorie Perloff's foundational discussion of Language poetry in *The Dance of the Intellect.* Quoting Ron Silliman's claim that "the words are never our own" but "our own usages of a determinate coding passed down to us like all other products of civilization," Perloff argues that "there are two ways of responding to this situation":

> One may, as do the bulk of "creative writing" teachers and students in workshops across the country, turn one's back on contemporary technology and write "personal" poems. . . . Or one can take on the very public discourses that seem so threatening and explore their poetic potential. To do this is to recognize that "I look straight into my heart and write the exact words that come from within. . ." is, strictly speaking, impossible, for the "exact words that come from within" are already coded by the historical and social context in which they function.[20]

This binary of totally constructing or constructed subject, of poetry as wholly private expression or as an exploration of the public discourses that are always already externally coded, is explanatory but not exhaustive. Recent theory has reconsidered the constructing/constructed opposition, and poetry may include multiple discourses chosen and inscribed in multiple forms. There are, that is, not two but many ways of responding to the recognition of public discourses and their relation to what is experienced as the self.

In *The Adoption Papers,* for example, an explicitly autobiographical and narrative poetic sequence, Kay constructs three voices—by graph and dialect—to represent her biological mother, her adoptive mother, and herself, but a "self" moving from child to adult and shifting from broad Glaswegian to English. The shifting from Glaswegian to Highland-accented English to a child's voice in Glasgow and an adult's in London sets multiple positions from which to speak. And though in one sense they are the dramatic voices of these women, in another they are all internal, imagined voices distanced both from the actual mothers and from any "I" that is an essential authorized voice. Yet each incorporates cultural sources impacting on the "I" who both recognizes herself in them and seeks to refigure "mother" in ways that include the few available images and voices of Blackness—a picture of Angela Davis, records of Bessie Smith, a child yelling "Sambo"—along with Scottishness—a bust of Burns, lines from the "Cherry Tree Carol," her "Grandmother's Highland number."

Kay has noted that while she was steeped in Scottish culture as a child, she had to go about finding and creating Black culture for herself. This precise awareness of the constructedness of Blackness and Scottishness, as well as Highland and Lowland as distinct linguistic and historic cultures, is played out in the "self-conscious multi-linguality"[21] of *The Adoption Papers* along with the sense of agency present in seeking out and creating reconstituted "selves" that are Black as well as Scot, Highland as well as Lowland. The speaking "I," when it appears in her work, is always under pressure to be unified and yet is always what she refers to in a poem entitled "Kail and Callalou" as many "strands":

> That poem was trying to explore different strands of identity. If you're brought up in a place, you get that identity very, very fixedly. And you don't necessarily get a sense of your being Black, because there's nothing around you affirming that you are. . . . So, although I was steeped in Scottish culture, of which I'm very appreciative, I never had any sense of Black culture at all, until I went about finding that and creating that for myself.[22]

There is no sense in which the "Kay" who speaks at any moment falls back on a stable individuality or occupies a mastery over meaning. Rather, her work serves as a negotiation among many intersecting selves, voices, discourses that can, in Susan Hekman's terms, be refigured, selected, and rearranged in a degree of self-creation. If there is not one transcendent self, neither is there no self or mere fragmentation.

Calling for an alternative to the constructing/constructed binary, Hekman argues for what she calls the "discursive subject." Rejecting both the "constituting, transcendent, essential subject" now associated with "mainstream" poetry and voice, and the "constituted subject" which, because it cannot be the knowing constituting center of the poem, is assumed to be displaced from "experimental" poetry by the discourse of which it is constructed, Hekman's definition of the discursive subject "does not entail reference to a prediscursive 'I' but, instead, entails that subjects find agency within the discursive spaces open to them in their historical period."[23] Subjectivity is thus created much as language is: "it is bounded by given discourses, but it can and does result in unique combinations."[24] In Kay's multiple discourses, subjectivity itself is not dissolved or fragmented but multiplied in unique ways. Her specific multiplication is at least in part a function of Scottish cultural and linguistic history. The presence of versions of Scots as suppressed languages within an imperial English imposed in schools and the continuous construction of "self" as, in Liz

Lochhead's formulation, not fully either English or Scots mean that "selves" and "voices" are always potentially in play. Many Scots, of course, have chosen and now choose to resolve this along Edwin Muir's lines by writing English or early MacDiarmid's by writing synthetic Scots: that is, to choose among selves for a poetic voice. And many Scots now choose Crawford's "Barbarian" stance of writing in the demotic of their own location or a more distanced stance of participating in the Language experimentation of American and English forms. The "English" spoken in Scotland is, after all, one of Scotland's three languages. But the choice to speak through many internal voices interacting and playing off one another constitutes a distinct form of language experiment central to much current Scottish work.[25] In *The Adoption Papers* Kay's particular reconfiguration is shaped by her sense of fluid borders of identity with the "mother" she knows and the one she does not.

In a passage from *The Adoption Papers,* "Chapter 8: Generations," the voice representing Kay and that of her birth mother, whom she had never met, are equally constructed and equally constructing voice(s) of "Kay":

> She was a waitress
> **My hair is grey**
> She wears no particular dress
> **The skin around my neck is wrinkling**
> **Does she imagine me this way?**
> Lately I make pictures of her
> But I can see the smallness
> **She is tall and slim**

The voice representing "Kay" thus imagines her mother imagining her: neither has any essential status. Cues to accent ("**her soft Highland voice,**" "**Does she talk broad Glasgow?**") intersperse the internal dialogue both to differentiate voices and to assert multilinguality not immediately apparent on the page. In the voice of the birth mother from the preceding section, this interpenetrating of self and "other" self is explicit:

> **She's lying in bed; I wake her up**
> **a pinch on her cheek is enough,**
> **then I make her think of me for hours.**
> **The best thing I can steal is sleep.**
> **I get right under the duvet and murmur**
> ***you'll never really know your mother.***
> **I know who she thinks I am — she's made a blunder.**

Like Lochhead's monster, the mother gets inside, speaks from within, yet is never not "Kay" or identical with "Kay." "Kay" is thus identified here as her own Highland ancestry, as in other places she identifies as Black or working class Glaswegian. She "is," in other words, all these, not in the sense of "aspects" of personality but as alter selves. She defines this "self-conscious multilinguality" as the voicing of multiplicity:

> It was as if when I was writing those voices in that book, that I contained the voices of those two mothers, that within me were both those mothers, and the voices just came very easily, flowing out of me, but the voice that you would expect to be the autobiographical voice, the "real" voice, didn't. And I think that that is a strange thing, but that can often happen. When we write we tap into other selves. . . . And so I think that if you write in that way you will find as you're writing that it is almost as if your self has got many layers, and every person has many, many different layers. When you write it's an effective way of scraping the top layer off and going to the layer underneath. That process, I suppose, I would describe as multiplicity, a finding a way to write about the other selves that we already contain. In a sense, I am my adopted mother, I am my birth mother, I am both these women, and am also myself, and I am also my son.[26]

In an interview for BBC radio, Kay described the many other selves and voices in her poems as someone else entirely and yet as retaining her voice also; she claims the narrators of her poems—whether speaking Glaswegian, Highland-accented English, a reconstructed eighteenth-century Scots, American Blues slang and rhythms, or the ostensibly "real" Scots-inflected "English" of Kay herself—are both her and not her.[27] When asked to explain this she responded that she does not "just think, 'Oh I'm creating this person; they're totally separate,' at all. They just become part of this multiplicity I was talking about."[28]

This multiplicity is in contrast with both unity and fragmentation of self, and its inscription has sources in specific Scottish theories of duality and multiplicity of self: forms of subjectivity and identity inseparable from the divisions of language and cultural forms inevitable in Scotland's domination by England and "English." "If you're Scottish . . . you are half English, really." But those halves are quite distinct, and if you are Scots and Black or Scots and Celt, there are many very distinct and overlapping selves from which writers were historically forced to choose or felt impelled to choose, to assimilate with English literature or to assert some form of Scots. Current experimentation covers a broad range, but among its most interesting forms is this play across borders or intermingling of multiple languages, cultural discourses, selves. Because the "strangeness" of tapping "other" internal selves in other internal languages, words, rhythms, discourses creates an opacity and displacement that estranges, it also creates a poetry in which language itself is at stake, as are speaking selves, in ways that challenge "imperial English."

If you are Scottish, to write in Standard English *or* to disrupt it in the ways of American and English poets may, of course, function as one form of experiment.

But if you have grown up speaking a variety of Scots yet learned "English" in school, to write in Standard English even to disrupt it is to buy into it rather than to secede from it. The poets who are complicating these linguistic borders are creating not something in between "mainstream" and "experimental" but culturally specific experimentation demanding of those who have internalized the dominant dialect the effort required to read genuinely different cultural work. To read the work of poets like Lochhead, Jamie, and Kay is to encounter complexities of subjectivity more fully accounted for in the particular context of their cultural and linguistic history than in theoretic dualisms of American and English poetics.

Notes

1. Lynn Keller, "The '*Then Some* In Between': Alice Fulton's Feminist Experimentalism," delivered at the *Assembling Alternatives* conference. Subsequently lengthened and published in *American Literature* 71:2 (June, 1999): 311–40.
2. Charles Bernstein, "Time Out of Motion," *A Poetics* (Cambridge, MA: Harvard University Press, 1992), 118–19.
3. Synthetic Scots is a constructed language using vocabulary from any period or region of Scotland. Because of the fragmentation of Scots into regional dialects after the Union of 1707, it is not a spoken language although much of the lexicon would be recognized by all Scots. MacDiarmid wished to recreate a "National" language which, like that of Dunbar, would serve all the purposes of literature, politics, and law but would also allow for modern usage.
4. Robert Crawford, *Devolving English Literature* (New York: Oxford University Press, 1992), 270.
5. Crawford, 271.
6. Edwin Morgan, "Lingua Scozzese," *New Generation Poets,* special issue of *Poetry Review* 84.1 (Spring 1994): 110. My comments on Herbert's Scots rely on Morgan's and Herbert's own description, as I am not sufficiently familiar with Dundonian to define its distinctive features.
7. Marjorie Perloff discusses these "syntactic and semantic difficulties" as characteristic of Language writing in her foundational essay in *The Dance of the Intellect* (Cambridge: Cambridge University Press, 1985), 234.
8. Tom Paulin, "A New Look at the Language Question" in *Ireland's Field Day,* ed. Seamus Deane et al. (South Bend: University of Notre Dame Press, 1986), 11.
9. Paulin, 16.
10. I mean here Scots words not existing in English—such as "watergaw"—as distinguished from cognates such as "mou" (mouth) or "stane" (stone).
11. "Gumption (or spirit or energy or common sense) is a word that will endure thin harvests"—Sheena Blackhall, North East Doric; "the reason I talk with a BBC

accent is because you wouldn't want me to talk about the truth with a voice like one of you scruff"—Tom Leonard, Glaswegian; "O Howff [old burial ground of Dundee], dead within, hidden in brown gray shadow"—W. N. Herbert, Dundonian enhanced by dictionary.

12. The "Caledonian Antisyzygy" is a term used by G. Gregory Smith to define what he considered the key characteristic of Scottish literature. It means "almost a zig-zag of contradictions . . . the very combinations of opposites . . . the contrasts which the Scot shows at every turn." G. Gregory Smith, *Scottish Literature: Character and Influence* (London: Macmillan, 1919), 4.
13. Tom Nairn, "Scottish Identity, a Cause Unwon," *Chapman* 67 (1991/92):2–12. Multiplicity is a problem or "joke," of course, only if one sustains the presumption of a prior idealized unity.
14. W. N. Herbert, "Author's Note," *Dundee Doldrums* (Edinburgh: Galliard, 1991), 4.
15. Robert Crawford, "The Two-faced Language of Lochhead's Poetry," *Liz Lochhead's Voices,* ed. Robert Crawford (Edinburgh: Edinburgh University Press, 1993), 68–69.
16. "Liz Lochhead," interview with Emily Todd, *Verse* 8.3 & 9.1 (Winter/ Spring 1992): 90.
17. Crawford, "Two-faced Language," 69.
18. Lang neb—long nose (or bird's beak or the whole face); thrawn—obstinate; wally dug—ornamental porcelain dog.
19. Richard Price, "Kathleen Jamie," *Verse* 8.3 & 9.1 (Winter 1991 / Spring 1992): 106.
20. Marjorie Perloff, *The Dance of the Intellect* (Cambridge: Cambridge University Press, 1985), 234.
21. At the conference, Bob Perelman quoted this apt phrase from Rachel Blau DuPlessis's *The Pink Guitar* as a way "to posit a wider democratic field of action for writing." It points to the language play of Kay's "Barbarian" positions. See his essay in this volume, on page 379.
22. Interview with Jackie Kay, *Sleeping with Monsters: Conversations with Scottish and Irish Women Poets,* R. Wilson and G. Sommerville-Arjat, eds. (Edinburgh: Polygon, 1990).
23. Susan Hekman, "Subjects and Agents: the Question for Feminism," *Provoking Agents,* ed. Judith Kegan Gardiner (Urbana: University of Illinois Press, 1995), 202.
24. Hekman, 204.
25. A similar point can be made about Black poets in Britain like Patience Agbabi, Grace Nichols, Merle Collins and David Dabydeen, whose use of English creates analogous possibilities, especially in cases were creole is also employed.
26. Jackie Kay, personal interview, Sept. 10, 1997.
27. Jackie Kay, interview with Brian Morton, *The Usual Suspects,* BBC Radio (Sept. 6, 1996).
28. Jackie Kay, personal interview, Sept. 10, 1997.

Linda A. Kinnahan

Feminist Experimentalism, Literary History, and Subjectivity

"this lyric forever error" of Kathleen Fraser and Denise Riley

Within the twentieth-century avant-garde, enacting the female signature and asserting a female-marked "I" have developed as contested performances, evoking questions of power within reading, writing, and critical communities linked to experimental or alternative poetries. These questions are intimately related to the production of literary histories that authorize lineages and writing practices. In a classic statement from 1986, Marianne DeKoven describes her perception of the relationship between an avant-garde reading/writing community and the writer who is female: "As long as an experimental writer whose 'signature' is female aligns herself with the language poets, for example, as many of them sometimes do, she has a place on the literary map. The price she pays, a price familiar to all of us, is twofold: the question of gender will be erased, declared a non-issue, and at the same time it is less likely than if her signature were male that she will become one of the stars, even in that tiny firmament" (13). In the decade that has followed, one might argue that the situation for women has improved; however, although women's writing is increasingly brought into the conversation (or anthology, etc.), the development of specifically feminist innovative practices and reading communities neither shapes nor fundamentally affects the masculine contours of the story of Language writing in America or of alternative writing in Britain.

In America, recent studies like Bob Perelman's *The Marginalization of Poetry: Language Writing and Literary History* or Jed Rasula's *The American Poetry Wax Museum* each provide valuable histories of innovative post-war American poetry while nonetheless joining the emerging production of mainstream venues that chart the contemporary history of language innovation through a primary focus upon men.[1] Although a few individual women writers, especially Lyn Hejinian and Susan Howe, garner critical attention, the history and analysis of a feminist avant-garde—an avant-garde richly informed by literary lineages and intellectual/philosophical infusions both distinct from and overlapping the masculine arena of innovative writing charted by Perelman or Rasula—has yet to be included in any full or significant way in considering the reading and writing practices of the current avant-garde. If one turns to British poetry, the attention recently being paid to alternative poetries developing since the 1960s charts the significance of American influence—both of contemporary poets interested in language and of earlier poets whose experimental works have remained important sources of formal innovation for poets of the British Revival and into the 1980s and 1990s. Reading such useful essays as those included in Barry and Hampson's *New British Poetries: The Scope of the Possible* and learning of the significant interactions of American and British experimental poetries, I am nonetheless struck again and again by the maleness of the litany of poets, past and present, who are foregrounded: Pound, Williams, Zukofsky, Oppen, Olson, Bunting, Jones, and on up into the present of Prynne, Bernstein, etc. Am I being unrealistic to yearn for a sense of female inclusion and recognition that the rich bounty of women's experimental work produced might/should/must warrant? Or to yearn for a more coherent picture of the impact of feminist theories and politics upon the developing language poetries of the last two decades?

This paper is a response to that yearning, one that intensified during the days of the Assembling Alternatives Conference. The role of poetry as social and cultural critique underpinned many of the panels and papers, and I gravitated (as can be expected) to those panels that focused upon women's writing as cultural intervention. Snatches of feminist histories and gendered aesthetics came my way: Nicole Markotic's paper on the prose poem as a feminist oppositional genre; Carla Harryman's "notes" on Gail Scott's *Main Brides*; Margy Sloan's comments on editing an anthology of experimental women's writing; Nancy Gish's paper on the Scottish black poet, Jackie Kay; Frances Presley's paper on Elaine Randell and Denise Riley; Alison Mark's talk on Veronica Forrest-Thomson; Kathleen Fraser's presentation of visual texts by women and their connection to Olson; Stephen Fredman's investigation of identity in the writings of Lyn Hejinian. I began trying to imagine a collection of essays only on women, focusing especially on feminist politics and poetics, as a counter-balance to the efforts of Barry and Hampson, Rasula, Perelman, and others—what would such a collection accomplish in informing our sense of language innovation, of poetic engagements with theory, politics, and subjectivity? I realized that I was imagining an extension, in many ways, of the project of *HOW(ever)*, an American journal founded by Kathleen Fraser in 1983, which ran for six volumes as a vehicle for the publication of works by and about women experimentalists. Each issue included contemporary poetry by women, authors' working notes, short essays on women writers or feminist theory/criticism, and correspondence. In a 1993 interview, after the journal's last volume, Kathleen Fraser claimed that the cultural intervention of such a project dedicated to women's writing is still necessary: a "principle of female editorship, choice, assertion of aesthetic pleasure and taste" that reflects a "need for women to have a place all theirs, where they feel they can make their choices and put these names forward" (9). In the 1990s, journals like *Big Allis, Motel, Black Bread,* and *6ix,* all descendants of *HOW(ever)*'s commitment to providing a place for the publication and discussion of women's innovative poetry, suggest a continuing perception "that there still isn't enough space given to female texts" (Fraser 9); certainly, the recent publication of *Out of Everywhere: Linguistically Innovative Poetry by Women in North America and the UK,* edited by Maggie O'Sullivan and published by Wendy Mulford and Ken Edwards at Reality Street Editions, responds to a similar need to foreground "the extraordinary range and diversity" of women writers and to "demonstrate that much of the most challenging, formally progressive and significant work over recent years . . . is being made by women," as O'Sullivan asserts in her introduction.*

Central to the projects Fraser and O'Sullivan describe is the urgency of developing a reading community that has some cohesion in terms of its apprehension of gender's centrality to modes of poetic practice, authority, and tradition, and of correcting a certain male focus within the broader reading community of linguistically innovative poetries. This extends into questions of lineage as well, as *HOW(ever)* devotes its pages to a reclamation of women writers like Lorine Niedecker, Marianne Moore, Gertrude Stein, Mina Loy, or H.D.; Fraser's editorial insistence upon naming the past and present in terms of female productivity becomes a necessary context for registering and revising the "I" or "self" within a theoretically informed writing and reading community skeptical of the self. In many works by women of the 1980s, writing without a sense of a reading community of scholars and poets open to the assertion of a gendered "I" in experimental terms, quite often that "I" is accompanied by a sense of fearing accusations of self-expression, of emotionalism, and of self-absorption that historically have been figured as female in our culture. Putting forth one's name, putting forth the "I" becomes risky within the experimental community if that name and that I are marked female: the feared consequences range from erasure to condemnation. I pull a representative example of this expressed anxiety from Kathleen Fraser's "re:searches" (*Notes Preceding Trust,* 1988):

*Editor's note: See the Contributors' List of Further Reading for collections on women's writing that have appeared since the present essay was revised for publication. See also the electronic continuation of *HOW(ever), HOW2,* which can be found on Bucknell University's website.

pink pearl eraser
erasing her face her
eee face ment
her face meant
.
he cut out
of her, her name
of each thing
she sang
each letter she
hung, on line
(divine)
.
this above
all to be who,
be nature's two,
and though heart
be pound-
ing at door
cloud   cuckoo
.
radial activ-
ity, who cow now,
who moo
.
not random, these
crystalline structures, these
non-reversible orders, this
camera forming tendencies, this
edge of greater length, this
lyric forever error, this
something embarrassingly clear, this
language we come up against (39–40)

Both the erasure of "her" face and its reconstitution in the opening stanza through linguistic restructuring are linked to the "he" who cuts out her name, her language, and, in the final stanza, attributes to "lyric" the status of "error," a gender-laden value judgment given the poem's movement to this point. Is the assertion of the female name, the female signature, the female face (erased and cut out by male hands) the mark of lyrical error? Is female subjectivity expressible in the arena of an anti-lyrical aesthetic dominant in this reading community? The poem's final lines insist upon an alternative notion of lyric, one that encounters rather than covers over the materiality of language—a lyric self both expressive and yet wary of an authentic realm of experience to call upon as source of expression, a wariness signaling an awareness of the mediative force of "this language we come up against" in configuring experience. And yet, the poem stubbornly reveals traces of the association of femaleness with lyric, and of the association of an assertion of female subjectivity as retrograde within the community interested in "this language."

For a project like *HOW(ever)*, the felt effects of a masculine "authority of historical privilege" underlies feminist practice involved in positioning and authorizing innovative women poets of this century (Fraser, "Line"155). In her essay describing the origin of *HOW(ever)*, Fraser discusses the need in the early eighties "to help in creating a community that has been waiting to come into view" ("Tradition" 26). The realization of a reading community receptive to gender as a "central category in their thinking on poetics" (Golding 151) took on high importance to many women feeling, in the late seventies and early eighties, isolated in their experimental fusings of linguistic innovation and feminist politics. In England, Wendy Mulford expresses a similar sentiment in "Notes on Writing: A Marxist/Feminist Viewpoint," published in *Red Letters* in 1979 and revised for republication in 1983.[2] Mulford traces some of the difficulties in writing a theoretically informed poetry attentive to questions of subjectivity, language, and capitalist ideology, but doing so as a woman within a male reading community centered in Cambridge: "The first problem is one of isolation. My writing is read and heard mainly by men engaged in poetic practices of differing kinds for whom my work has significance because of the attempt I have been making to work at the level of the production of meaning. But I want to join my voice with the voices of other women struggling to destruct the lie of culture" (31, 33). Reading and being read by men working from "the modernist or neo-modernist tradition within which I see my work as located," Mulford perceived that these writers "write from a clear sense of place defined by the work of previous writers in the modernist tradition . . . produced from a differently gendered place" than her own ("Notes" 34). She goes on to describe her gender-based sense of misplacement: "I have, as it were, only a colonial relationship to such texts inhabiting a language and a culture which I'm not quite at ease in, which doesn't quite fit. This problem is obviously keyed into . . . language, but it has a slightly different area of impact for it's particularly in reading that I'm made aware of it" ("Notes" 35). Publishing four women in the late 1970s (Veronica Forrest-Thomson, Alice Notley, Denise Riley, and herself) through her small press, Street Editions, Mulford as editor brought works to light that questioned the traditional relationship between poetic authority and maleness. These questions intensified, for women like herself and Riley, as readings of poststructural and feminist theories offered avenues for deconstructing the unified (male) self underlying such authority, and as exposure to American experimental writers increased. Still, in the late 1970s, Mulford identifies a necessary but then absent "cross-fertilization between women working in the theoretical field and those producing certain kinds of contemporary fiction and poetry" (33); later, discovering *HOW(ever),* where she published work, Mulford would be attracted to the cross-fertilization at the heart of the American journal's "peculiar hybrid of innovative poetry with feminist critical writing," as Fraser described the project's commitment to textually encouraging the interaction of poetic and theoretical/critical practices (*HOW(ever)* 2.1, 14).

Educated through *HOW(ever)* about poets in America pursuing feminist concerns through linguistic innovation, Mulford has sought to introduce to an English audience the poetically experimental work of American women writers whom she finds "useful" in considering "ideas about the questioning of the individual poetic voice" ("'Curved'" 264). This expansion of a reading community, developing out of cross-Atlantic connections between women, almost never receives mention in narratives of the interactive American and British experimental communities, unless as a side comment—as though there is the real (male) stuff under discussion and, oh yeah, here were these women doing something interesting over on the side but let's just keep that to the side. More attention has begun to be paid to individual poets in recent years (particularly in America), largely because of the efforts of women poets themselves to foreground discussion of their experiments and to consider both the gendered and feminist dimensions of language innovation.

Despite these efforts, the "I" in experimental women's writing continues to raise flags (or be ignored) within reading communities hostile to, indifferent to, or unaware of feminist concerns with language. Denise Riley's work is a case in point, exemplifying what Mulford describes as the questioning of individual voice typifying much work by women, or what Clair Wills (in a wonderful and useful essay on experimentalism and expressivity) argues is the reinterpretation of the speaking "I" and related "questions of interiority and emotional inwardness" within the historically specific pressures of mass media and culture (50). Riley's work represents, for Wills, an "investigation of the problem of articulating inwardness and emotion, and of gauging the "'authenticity' of feeling," meditating on the purpose of the lyric. Recognized by feminist critics like Wills or Rachel Blau DuPlessis as a textual engagement with the lyric, Riley's 1993 *Mop Mop Georgette* investigates the linguistic and discursive constructedness of self while searching for a means of expressivity of the gendered "I." Recognizing the lyric's cultural codes as part of a system preexisting and shaping the "I," one poem of Riley's queries: "I'd thought / to ask around, what's lyric poetry? / Its bee noise starts before I can: / You do that; love me; die alone" ("A Shortened Set," *Mop Mop Georgette,* 22). The poems in this volume, which insistently proclaim an "I" while inspecting the discursive determinations of subjectivity, interact with questions of female subjectivity that characterize Riley's intellectual background and work, including her theorization of the politics and history of feminine identity in *Am I That Name? Feminism and the Category of "Women" in History* (1988).

The treatment of the "I" in her poetry, however, has garnered criticism for Riley; and the insertion of female subjectivity has been linked to degraded and feminized aspects of privacy, emotion, narcissism—a critical reaction dramatizing Kathleen Fraser's poetic linkage between female authorship, masculine authority, and "this / lyric forever error." Interviewing Riley, Romana Huk observes that "It may be because you are considered by experimental poets to be experimental that your intense focus on the throes of the personal voice incurs such criticism" (20), referring to a series of essays debating what John Wilkinson calls a "curiously de-centered debate" over Riley's poetry, centered primarily around the use of the "I" pronoun and the status of the self. The debate occurs over the course of essays by Nigel Wheale (in *Parataxis,* 1993), James Keery (in *PN Review,* 1994), and Wilkinson (in *Parataxis,* 1994). The debate takes shape under the weighty history of negatively gendered associations clustered around women's expressions of (and experiments with) a lyric or speaking self. Riley's book *Mop Mop Georgette* (1993) stands accused by Wilkinson of an essential narcissism, a "reflexivity which is paraded" through a "working with the narcissistic grain which cannot divert or obstruct its pathological logic" (68). Nowhere does Wilkinson attribute such narcissism to gender, but the associations developed between self-reflexivity, narcissism, and pathology converge within the (unspoken) construction of Woman generalized in western metaphysical and philosophical thought and particularized, in psychological discourses, as deviant, undeveloped, narrow, self-involved. This deviance translates into "arch" feminism in James Keery's comments on Riley in a review of "British postmodernist poetry" (*PN Review,* 1994), to which Wilkinson's review is responding (11). For Keery, Riley's poetry is "hampered by a self-consciousness" tied clearly and negatively to feminism, leading to a "fatal reflexiveness: 'These sentences come fast, give me no grief. . . .' The quote feminism unquote ranges in tone from the arch—'I found some change in my trouser pocket, like / a man'—to the mordantly cynical—'and when her belly swells into an improbable curve / the she-husband will think Yes, it was me who caused that'—though there are some dignified images in between" (13). The opposition of a (familiar accusation of) feminist solipsism to "dignified images" is followed by the quoting of extremely tender, non-threatening lines to exemplify Riley's poetic potential. These critical reactions, formulated within masculinist ideologies of selfhood, suggest to a British readership, even if unwittingly, the danger to Poetry of the poetess turned feminist.

Such a reading of gender-marked subjectivity, practiced within a reading community attuned to the experimental, demonstrates an inattentiveness to the fusion of feminist politics and linguistic innovation that makes up a significant strain of contemporary experimental poetry in Britain and America. The history of the intellectual, theoretical, and poetic explorations enacted by such poetry has been ignored or barely acknowledged in the developing constructions of literary history that seek to establish avant-garde traditions that enable contemporary practice, that seek to map out innovative practices, and that seek to encourage a critical discourse around them. As with any reading community, the publication networks, projects, and attendant critical discourse affect the relative dominance or erasure of individuals, groups, etc. My questions have to do with why a feminist history is so often missing, and how this lack of history and community shapes readings of innovative women's poetry that engages a feminist politics, as well as readings of innovative poetries in general; my hope is that discussions and practices of innovative poetries register this history as a significant encounter between language, subjectivity, and gender.

Notes

1. Perelman's book includes a chapter on gender, which focuses upon both men and women. In a seventeen-page section, he surveys the poetry of Beverly Dahlen, Carla Harryman, Susan Howe, and Rae Armantrout. Rasula's study, while including a substantial discussion of Louise Bogan, maps a poetic and critical world primarily populated by men.
2. See my essay on Mulford, Denise Riley, and Geraldine Monk for a fuller discussion of each poet's feminist engagement with experimentalism and the lyric.

Works Cited

DeKoven, Marianne. "Gertrude's Granddaughters." *Women's Review of Books* 4.2 (1986): 13–14.

Fraser, Kathleen. "Editor's Note." *HOW(ever)* 2.1 (Jan. 1989): 14.

———. "How Error Pops Up: An Interview with Kathleen Fraser." With Robin Tremblay-McGaw. *Poetry Flash* 246 (Sept./Oct. 1993).

———. "Line. On the Line. Lining Up. Lined with. Between the Lines. Bottom Line." *The Line in Postmodern Poetry*. Ed. Robert Frank and Henry Sayre. Chicago: University of Illinois Press, 1988. 152–74.

———. *Notes Preceding Trust*. San Francisco: The Lapis Press, 1988.

———. "The Tradition of Marginality." *Frontiers* X.3 (1989): 22–27.

Golding, Alan. *From Outlaw to Classic: Canons in American Poetry*. Madison: University of Wisconsin Press, 1995.

Hampson, Robert, and Peter Barry, eds. *New British Poetries: The Scope of the Possible*. Manchester, U.K.: Manchester Universty Press, 1993.

Keery, James. "Well, There Was, and Wasn't, and There Is: The Third Cambridge Conference of Contemporary Poetry." *PN Review* 20.3 (1994): 11–15.

Kinnahan, Linda A. "Experimental Poetics and the Lyric in British Women's Poetry: Geraldine Monk, Wendy Mulford, and Denise Riley." *Contemporary Literature* 37.4 (1996): 620–670.

Mulford, Wendy. " 'Curved, Odd . . . Irregular'. A Vision of Contemporary Poetry by Women." *Women* 1.3 (Winter 1990): 261–274.

———. "Notes on Writing: A Marxist/Feminist Viewpoint." *On Gender and Writing*. Ed. Michelene Wandor. London: Pandora Press, 1983, 31–41.

O'Sullivan, Maggie, ed. *Out of Everywhere: An Anthology of Contemporary Linguistically Innovative Poetry by Women in North America and the UK*. London: Reality Street Editions, 1996.

Perelman, Bob. *The Marginalization of Poetry: Language Writing and Literary History*. Princeton, NJ: Princeton University Press, 1996.

Rasula, Jed. *The American Poetry Wax Museum: Reality Effects, 1940–1990*. Urbana, IL: NCTE, 1996.

Riley, Denise. *Am I That Name? Feminism and the Category of "Women" in History*. Minneapolis: University of Minnesota Press, 1988.

———. "Denise Riley in Conversation." With Romana Huk. *PN Review* 21.5 (1995): 17–22.

———. *Mop Mop Georgette: New and Selected Poems, 1986–1993*. London: Reality Street, 1993.

Wheale, Nigel. "Colours—Ethics—Lyric, Voice: Recent Poetry by Denise Riley." *Parataxis* 4 (1993): 70–77.

Wilkinson, John. "'Illyrian Places,' Review: Denise Riley, *Mop Mop Georgette: New and Selected Poems, 1986–1993*." *Parataxis* 6 (1994): 58–69.

Wills, Clair. "Contemporary Women's Poetry: Experimentalism and the Expressive Voice." *Critical Quarterly* 36.3 (1994): 34–52.

Susan Rudy

'& how else can i be here?'

Reading Cross-Wise through Some Poetries of Canada[1]

But these days I'm yearning not for a little outside to call my own, although I like good design as well and do feel that the proles can share a moment . . . after all it wasn't so long ago that I touched a spark plug or had a cute smudge of oil on my nose . . . but sure I'm wanting a little overdetermination with my contradictions. (Derksen, *JERK,* 5–6)	[I]f they [linguistic terms] are to become what they describe, become signifiers in their own right, then they must show themselves to be multiple, overdetermined,[2] and permanently available for new uses. To this end, which is that of a continually new beginning, an additional pair of crosswise relationships is created. (Bowie 130)

> *O the disparities*[3]*—how can i ever relate the two parts of myself? This life would have killed me—purdah, a woman in—the restrictions on movement, the confined reality. i can't stand it. i feel imprisoned in my class—my? This is what i came out of. & how else can i be here?*
>
> —Daphne Marlatt, "In the Month of Hungry Ghosts," 50

> *I've assumed a dull and ambiguous edge of difference in myself, the hyphen always seems to demand negotiation.*
>
> —Fred Wah, *Diamond Grill,* 137

Whether or not a title may be considered postmodern or poetry, this book's original, "working" title, merits close reading simply because *Assembling Alternatives: Essays on the Problems of Reading Postmodern Poetries Cross-Culturally* promises so much.* The word "cross-" in "cross-culturally" first catches my eye. Perhaps because so much feminist research has demonstrated the ways women are required to "cross" (to read, dress, talk, and act like men in order to be heard, paid, respected) and has begun to name what is lost in the crossing (the values, knowledges, skills and insights of women). Will these essays examine the ways that crossings differ from one another? Crossing from a place of relative power, as a white woman, for example, to a place of more power, by aligning oneself with white men, for example, is a common and indeed highly valued and rewarded form of crossing for both lesbians and heterosexual women. But crossing from a place of relative power, as a heterosexual woman, for example, to a place of much less power, indeed to a place of denigration and abuse, by making alliances with lesbians of colour, for example, is feared, avoided, and if at all possible, not done, or at least not seen to be done.[4]

Asked to guest edit an issue of *Diacritics* on gay and lesbian studies, Judith Butler and Biddy Martin "took the occasion to broaden the scope of that request." Their special issue, entitled "Critical Crossings," includes "work that interrogates the problem of cross-identifications within and across race and postcolonial studies, gender theory, and theories of sexuality" (3). I propose to extend and query the notion of reading "cross-culturally" by attending to alternative figurations of identity in analogous instances of crossing. Specifically, the chapter begins with an autobiographical investigation of crossing. I then consider class crossings in Jeff Derksen's *JERK* (1998) and *Dwell* (1993) before moving to a longer analysis (originally delivered at the conference) of Daphne Marlatt's *Zócalo* (1976), which investigates crossing sexualities. I conclude with a reading of racialized crossing in Fred Wah's *Diamond Grill* (1996).

Innovative writers in Canada, in crossing highly charged differences of class, race, and/or sexuality, have felt compelled to, in Fred Wah's words, reconfigure the "assumptions and confusions of identity" ("Half-Bred Poetics" 60), in ways Northrop Frye never imagined. In 1965, Frye was contemplating the impact new technologies would have on national borders when he wrote that "Canadian writers are, even now, still trying to assimilate a Canadian environment at a time when new techniques of communication . . . are annihilating the boundaries of that environment" (219–220). But he still imagined that Canadian sensibility was "less perplexed by the question 'Who am I?' than by some such riddle as 'Where is here?'" (220). By comparison, Derksen's long poem "Interface" (*Dwell* 1–17), which "at first glance appears to consist solely of a series of disjunctive sentences, mostly declarative, culled from a wide range of contexts, including personal reflection, economic statistics and various

*Editor's note: Please see the first pages of my Introduction to this volume for further commentary on the genesis of its present title.

news headlines" (Klobucar 19), includes the following quoted sentence: "'We can see a day when borders will mean nothing more than knowing where to cut your lawn'" (*Dwell* 2). Where, in the last months of the twentieth-century, is "here"? Butler and Martin remind us that

> "Crossing" may be conceived, on the one hand, as an appropriation, assimilation, or even a territorialization of another site or position, or it can be understood as a movement beyond the status attributed to "positions" located on a closed map of social power. In this second sense, then, crossing can be a movement that seeks to establish a connection or continuity. It can, of course, also constitute disavowal or defense and do all of this at once. (3)

The story on crossing that I wish to investigate comes from these three poets who have struggled to articulate the complexity, indeed the pain, of crossing. As Wah reminds us, "Maps don't have beginnings, just edges. Some frayed and hazy margin of possibility, absence, gap" (1). The "map" or social construction of identity, is known by its edges, by what it is not. In Derksen's lexicon, "here" is a little inside, "a little outside." The question of identity, indeed of poetry, cannot be asked without awareness of the homology of language and social order: "If I am alienated from the production of me, then I am in a commodity relation with myself, hence big bargains" (Derksen, *Dwell* 72). For Marlatt, "this self here" is disparate, "sieved through with other selves" (*Ghost Works* viii) and yet always desiring connection. For Wah, the "hyphen always seems to demand negotiation." Frye's "where is here?" has become Marlatt's, "& how else can i be here?" It has become a question about alternative relations between places and identities, a question of many crossings and many returns. "Interface of self and place passes me through a / translation machine," Derksen writes. "But when my left eye is jumping, I don't know where / I'm at" (*Dwell* 3). Not in crossing but in troubling the putative line—the interface—between white and Chinese, working and middle class, heterosexual and lesbian, for example, these writers challenge Butler and Martin's assumption that "every identification presumes a crossing of sorts" (3) and suggest other ways to be, here.

Susan Rudy: Being Seen to Be (T)here

Let me begin with an anecdote. For several years, I had been deeply drawn to and both excited and repelled by Daphne Marlatt's work since each time I sat down to write about it, I felt troubled by how much I could identify with it. How could I, a woman whose meaningful heterosexual life seemed likely to continue, so intimately identify with—indeed long for—the work of a lesbian writer? Would my reading be an illegal crossing? Perhaps Marlatt's work both moved and troubled me because like myself she too had married and had a child when she was very young and yet remained passionately committed to writing and reading. But because I saw her as having crossed over, from a heterosexual to a lesbian life, I didn't understand why or how her work spoke to my peculiar "dilemma," since I felt both a surprising and often unnerving capacity for lesbian desire and an ongoing pleasure in my heterosexual relationship. So who am I? Clearly, the difference between a fully realized heterosexual life and feeling the capacity for lesbian desire made it impossible for me to compare the two. Equally clearly, through reading Marlatt's work I had come to realizations about what I had not let myself feel or know or be with other women before and this knowledge too felt like an extraordinary gift. Nonetheless, being in the middle felt more like being on a very dangerous edge. The only way, I thought, to legitimately claim the knowledge I had come to was to cross, to stop being heterosexual. With some difficulty, I finally realized that such thinking depends upon a logic of sacrifice which sees "identity as a force of domination"—which sees "identity of the self as a repression of connection or of internal difference" (Weir 1).

The logic of sacrifice, "being on the cross," which underpins Western thought and language, depends on an interrelated system of binary oppositions. Take the seemingly innocuous prefix "cross-" for example. "Cross-" denotes "movement or position across something," "interaction" and, most intriguingly, a "passing from side to side" (*The Concise Oxford Dictionary*). "Crossing" thus carries a very strong message that I heard clearly and yet needed to resist. These poets offered models of resistance to the imperative to cross. Jeff Derksen's approach to language writing in this volume and his insistence on poetry's social role highlights the productive tension created by the interface between "inside," which he defines as "the reiterative act of a community," and "outside," a "powerful if mistakenly totalizing, value-defining discursive exterior." Daphne Marlatt's self is figured as a house which has been too narrowly constructed. Alternatives are available, she suggests, when crossers "[break] down its oh-so-edified walls" (*Ghost Works* viii). Wah's attention to the "hyphen" takes us directly to the middle of the road, what he calls the "ambivalences in hybridity" (60) that productively trouble our thinking about race.

But before I turn finally to the writers individually, let me name a final insight about crossing gained through my experience. Not once, in the years I struggled with Daphne Marlatt's work, did it occur to me that I was not asking the same questions of Fred Wah. In fact, I didn't seem to have any trouble at all identifying with a much older, male, heterosexual, Chinese-Canadian writer. A particularly revelatory moment occurred shortly after *Diamond Grill* was published. Wah read the following line at a book launch: "I want to be there but don't want to be seen being there" (136). Wah's narrator meant he wanted to be in the café of his Chinese-Canadian friend Lawrence but he didn't want his white friends to see him there. Ah ha! I said to myself. That's exactly how I feel. I identified. Wah had given me, by analogy, a way of thinking about what I wanted. I wanted to be in the company of lesbians. I wanted to be accepted in that community. But I didn't want to be seen—by either my heterosexual or my lesbian friends—to be there either. Because being seen by either group would put me on one side or the other when what I really wanted was to be in a middle place where no one knew for sure.

Jeff Derksen: "I" posed as a question

> *What happens to the poetics of place when your only "place" is your body and it's not moving?*
>
> —Jeff Derksen, *Dwell,* 63

The energy in Jeff Derksen's work comes from liminal spaces. Not from the desire to cross, but out of the realization that he does not want to cross, Derksen recognizes that "the potential adjectives for my body are in conflict with my class" (*Dwell* 69). Like several other members of the Kootenay School of Writing in Vancouver, Derksen's work emerges "from the ruins of privilege, from a marginalised position in society originating in language itself" (Klobucar 1). If his only "'place' is [his] body," he is determined to imagine dwelling, not moving, finding room.[5] For example, "[e]ntry into the reading space" of Derksen's University of Calgary website,[6] "is through a reproduction of Russian Constructivist Elena Semenova's design of a Worker's Club Lounge (1926)." Like this room, which was never built or put into use, Derksen's conception of dwelling has not been realized outside of poetry. But like the "French workers who visited the club in large numbers" and apparently said, "'This is how our club ought to be!'" Derksen offers alternative spaces for those of us interested in seeing labour as intellectual: "This reading room represents a conceptual reading space where reading was also ideologically imagined as work (and workers as readers)."

At Derksen's website you will also find his 1987 Tsunami editions chapbook *Until,* which begins with the following lines: "a cross / hatchet conferring / project it really is / what I / aluminum imprint / for form / fitting shirts." For Derksen, "a cross" is a potentially destructive and sacrificial tool, really a "hatchet conferring project," which limits the potentiality of the socially constructed yet determined body. Asking the question "& how else can I *be* here?" in relation to Derksen's work, the answer is: *Dwell,* participate in the social and discursive world in which you find an overdetermined self. Resist that "I" as "aluminum imprint / for form / fitting shirts." Aware of the body's circulation in and through "socially constructed space" (*Dwell* 61) and the contradictions produced thereby—the intersections which cross—Derksen at some moments imagines the possibility of open spaces, of potentiality. The last page, indeed the last lines, of *Dwell* look like this:

> from the body
>
> to the mind
>
> via (9)

But recently, while artist-in-residence at the Banff Centre for the Arts (in Banff, Alberta), Derksen completed a big (set in 18-point type), long poem called *JERK,* the first lines from which I quoted at the beginning of this chapter. As a "jerk," he grapples with the contradictory desire to have both an explicit and relentless politics *and* connections in the world as it has been given to him: "I'd like to see / the real relations / but you've Nikes / on and I like you so I have to / try and understand" (7).

In all of his work, Derksen aggressively, ironically, mischievously[7] inhabits the discourses of his moment in history: "My tropes peel off the landscape, moving in an apparently opposite direction to what I have to 'leave out.' Becomes body. Here is the closest place of social and beauty. The sentence that focuses attention" (*Dwell* 38). Derksen's "here" is very explicitly "the sentence," or rather sentences, on the page, what we are sentenced to. But the sentence is also that which "focusses attention" and so can be resisted by the subject. In "Central [Canada] Party Haus," a poem on *The East Village Poetry Web Site,* Derksen writes, "one can only negotiate / these contradictions textually / or risk a president's choice." In Canada, "president's choice" is a series of "choice" products available only at the "Real Canadian Superstore," and marked generically by the brand name "President's Choice." Negotiate the contradictory relation between lived experience and textuality or risk being commodified.

> My romantic belief is that historical
> consciousness may come. My sad
> cognitive mapping is that
> overdetermined contradictions
> don't lead to new social relations. (*JERK* 7)

In *JERK,*[8] while Derksen is explicit about the contradictions inherent in the discourses of "romantic belief" and of "cognitive mapping," the word "sad" appears, a word out of place in either discourse which suggests a longing for alternatives not yet, or perhaps no longer, available. Derksen poses the identity of the subject itself "as a question, poised between participant and observant" (*Dwell* 32). Observe and participate, be a subject, he seems to say. But although "participant" and "observant" look like words that carry equal semantic weight, "participant" is a noun, "observant" an adjective. Like Joseph Kosuth, whom he cites in his essay in this volume, Derksen sees poetry as a "liminal ground between commodity and experience, between public and private values" (196). In poetry, as in the unconscious, the overdetermination of signifiers makes them "permanently available for new uses," for new "crosswise relationships" (Bowie 130).

Daphne Marlatt: "crossing over / a (gap)"

> *i, first person, crossing over*
> *a (gap) i string out bridges of words to seek you there,*
> *perfectly composed. between us the rushing a-byss, a, not,*
> *undone, undoing all my bridges in itself a blue so clear*
> *fade into a, note, a single letter a*
>
> —Daphne Marlatt, *here & there,* n.p.

For Marlatt, the "i, first person," is in process, "crossing over / a (gap) ," as yet to be known, perhaps known only in that crossing. Born in Melbourne, Australia, Daphne Marlatt lived for several years in Penang, Malaysia before her family migrated to Vancouver, British Columbia, in 1951.[9] Her long poem "In the Month of Hungry Ghosts," an experimental rewriting of journal entries, letters and poems, records her return to Penang in 1976. Marlatt has come out of and returned to several communities, cultures, sexualities and poetics. Although she currently writes to and for women, her poetics continues to be shaped by Charles Olson, Robert Duncan, and Robert Creeley. She has returned to Malaysia and Britain and written out those pasts that continue to shape her in the present. She now identifies as lesbian; she has been married and has a son.

Marlatt has said that her preoccupation with "prob[ing] the house of the self, haunting its narrow construction, breaking down its oh-so-edified walls" is an "immigrant's preoccupation. Or a border-crosser's. Or a genre/gender crosser's (if autobiography can be seen as divorced from poetry—that muse again, or lesbianism divorced from heterosexuality—that haunting family). Heterogenous, this place here, so overlaid with other places: this self here sieved through with other selves" ("Preface," *Ghost Works* viii). In acknowledging the losses required for the presumption of a heterosexual identity, Marlatt comes to the same insights that Judith Butler does. We live "within a culture," Butler writes, "which can mourn the loss of homosexual attachment only with great difficulty" (*The Psychic Life of Power* 133). So difficult is it for us to mourn the loss of homosexual attachment that most of us are not even consciously aware that we have ever had homosexual attachment. Nonetheless, speaking of Freud's *Three Essays on the Theory of Sexuality* (1905), Butler reminds us that "'masculine' and 'feminine' . . . are understood as the effects of laborious and uncertain accomplishment, are established in part through prohibitions which *demand the loss* of certain sexual attachments, and demand as well that those losses *not* be avowed, and *not* be grieved" (135).

What happens to our notion of "crossing" when the losses are grieved, mourned, and alternatives imagined, articulated, even lived? Marlatt moves toward answering this question when she recognizes her disparate self and seeks alternatives to self-sacrifice. "& how else can i be here?" might be read as a rhetorical question which expects no answers. There may be no other way to be here. But the ampersand which begins the question signifies Marlatt's desire for—indeed her recognition of the inescapability of—continued connection *and* a desire for change, an alternative to "crossing" as moving from inside to outside, from here to there. She came from "here"—it is her history—*and* she wants to be here differently, to be, in the words of her 1981 chapbook, *here & there*.

Significantly, Marlatt focusses on the real political effects of formal experimentation. She has "whatever it is that gives us the courage to confront the actual conditions of our lives" (Marlatt review of Riis). Marlatt experiments with linguistic, generic, syntactic, and other formal aspects in order to bring to consciousness the potentiality of the present, "the pleasure of differentiation, the pleasure of signification, the pleasure of identification and interaction with others, the pleasure of learning to participate in a social world" (Weir 151). In the early, and infrequently discussed book *Zócalo,*[10] for example, the writing "experiments" not only in terms of genre, and an innovative use of the sentence and paragraph; but also in the sense that it moves tentatively, produces an unstable relation between "here" and "there." What can crossing mean in such a place? In Marlatt's words, *Zócalo* "struggles with the notion of here, what being here means, what it includes or excludes" (vii):

> que es r-e-y-l? Reyl? He says something in Spanish, something she doesn't understand . . . & staring at it suddenly she gets it, rail? . . . Si si, reyl, que es reyl? It is what a train runs along, a railroad, do you know that word? Reyl ro? please. . . . No, he insists, los Americanos gave him the word & they did not say it was a train. What else could it be? rail? railing? something you hold onto? she enquires, looking around for one, sees Yo a few yards away, pointing the camera at them, & calls, what could rail mean besides railroad & railing? Ranting & railing? he laughs, an impish laugh. That's too complicated. Oh well you know I don't know English . . . he tries again, reyl, REY-L. Oh! (the pronunciation) you mean REAL? Si si, his face breaks into that smile, & they are there,

they have hit it. Que es *reel?* he calls it into question (& is this real? any of it? their ground has fallen away & she is falling, how speak to that with her impoverished Spanish, his broken English?—help. (93–94)

This passage demonstrates the instability of our places, languages, selves, in the present, "the fact," in Marlatt's words, "that we're really restricted in all our perceptions to what's here." But "here" means what she can "hear," what only seems to be given, what only seems *to her* to be given. But who constitutes perception in the present—what is "here" and what is not—and for whom?

In *Zócalo,* the woman narrator is trying to understand her cross-cultural connection to her male, Japanese-Canadian, lover, Yo. But she is doing so with full awareness of the effects, not only of race, but of gender, what Marlatt calls "[t]he multiple nature of the real" ("Difference (em)bracing" 189). The question "& how else can I be here?" suggests one knows where one is. But the requirement in language that to speak the word "here" one must be elsewhere draws attention to the self-consciousness with which Marlatt approaches the question of presence, and indeed of essence. She does not want to watch, the way her partner, the photographer, watches, from a distance; she wants to act, enter in, "not to see but to be."

Since 1979 Marlatt has come to realize how difficult it is to represent "what you're actually experiencing" when your experience is not recognized or valued, when the very words and forms you are given will not accommodate your experience. In "Changing the Focus," Marlatt speaks of the anger she feels in the face of a culturally constructed invisibility. Here the adult lesbian confronted with the requirement to "fit in" to a heterosexual matrix reacts quite differently from the immigrant child who was eager to "enter in" to the culture she found in Vancouver in the 1950s. Speaking of "what it could be like for [women] to be acculturated otherwise," Marlatt says it would mean "mak[ing] present what has been erased—our bodies, our desire, our self-definition" (Carr, "Between Continuity and Difference" 105). As the journal writer/narrator of "In the Month of Hungry Ghosts" says, "Everyone we meet assumes another life for me than the one i actually live . . . I can't literally act on my own, i only act out a parody of myself" (105).

Like immigrants, women, lesbians, the tourist narrator in *Zócalo* finds—and indeed seeks—herself, within a culture not of her making. In "Entering In: The Immigrant Imagination" Marlatt writes, "the immigrant imagination embrace[s] the new place it enters. It seeks to enter into its mystery, its thisness, to penetrate it imaginatively even as it enters from outside" (219). But such entry, such crossing, has a cost; "for the sake of entry and acceptance" Marlatt often denied her own history, one different from the new place she found herself in. As early as 1979, in "Given This Body,"[11] Marlatt defined the "avant-garde" as "simply writing as close as you can to what you're actually experiencing at any given point. That's where the new forms arise" (33). Only when she came to recognize writing as a thorough investigation of the possibilities of language in a social context did she find a way to "knit the two places, two (at least) selves, somehow. . . . Now we make our exegesis of the difference using montage, using juxtaposition, knitting disparate and specific images from both places. Seeing the world as multidimensional as possible and ourselves present within it" ("Entering In" 223).

Fred Wah: "living in the hyphen"[12]

This silence that is a hyphen and the hyphen is the door.
—Fred Wah, *Diamond Grill,* 16

Poet, critic, editor, and teacher Fred Wah has lived on the edge or in the west of Canada for much of his life but in his more than fourteen books he takes his readers to middle spaces that are not at the centre.[13] "[H]alf Swede, quarter Chinese, and quarter Ontario Wasp" (*Diamond Grill* 36), Wah finds himself "languageless, mouth always a gauze, words locked behind tongue, stopped *in and out*" (*Diamond Grill* 5; emphasis mine). Here and there, white and Chinese, Wah examines the relation between the articulation of identity and the experience of sacrifice in his book *Diamond Grill* (1996). "Standing across the street from King's Family Restaurant," Wah's narrator reflects on his strained relationship with his childhood friend, Lawrence (who is Chinese-Canadian) by noting that they "always exchange greetings" when they meet "on the street" but that Wah "hardly ever" goes into "his café" (137).

On the street, Wah's mixed genetic inheritance allows him to pass as white, to say hello and realize he expects to be addressed in reply. But inside the café he knows he would be seen, and known, differently: "he would know me, he would have me clear in his sights, not Chinese but stained enough by genealogy to make a difference" (136). Although he hesitates before such knowledge, he decides, finally to "cross":

> When Lawrence and I work together, him just over from China, he's a boss's son and I'm a boss's son. His pure Chineseness and my impure Chineseness don't make any difference to us in the cafe. But I've assumed a dull and ambiguous edge of difference in myself; the hyphen always seems to demand negotiation.
>
> I decide, finally, to cross the street. (137)

Not white and "stained enough by genealogy to make a difference" but not Chinese, Wah in his epigraph to *Diamond Grill,* from *Waiting for Saskatchewan* writes, "You [his father] were part Chinese I tell them. / They look at me. I'm pulling their leg. So I'm Chinese too and that's why my name is Wah. / They don't really believe me. That's o.k. / When you're not 'pure'" you just make it up." Wah's self-deprecatory humour speaks directly to his dilemma. He is never seen in all his complexity and so is repeatedly accused of just "making it up."

Elaine Scarry argues that in order to be "made real," a poem, "having been made up," "must have gone on to a second stage of creation, where the initial work of invention was compounded by an additional process through which reality was conferred on, or discovered in it" (241). Since Wah claims that "Being there, in Lawrence's kitchen, seems one of the surest places I know" (138), the question is not whether that place is "real" for him, but whether he is "sure" what "pure" means. "[B]ack outside, on the street, all my ambivalence gets covered over, camouflaged by a safety net of class and colourlessness—the racism within me that makes and consumes that neutral (white) version of myself, that allows me the sad privilege of being, in this white white world, not the target but the gun" (138). Wah names his ambivalence about not being able to fulfill others' desires that he be either white or Chinese when he writes "I want to be there but don't want to be seen being there" (136). In crossing the street, he has seen the face of the white "other," the face of racism, as his own. In Lawrence's kitchen he is sure of what he has lost, an easy relation to community. But back outside on the street he is also sure that his privilege, his ability to pass as white, has produced ignorance, pain, disconnection. For Wah, then, "crossing" means more than simply moving from one side of the street to the other. "[T]he hyphen is the door" (*Diamond Grill* 16); his identity too is liminal, not spatial—about doors not streets:

> In the Diamond . . . are two large swinging wooden doors, each with a round hatch or face-sized window . . . looking through doors and languages, skin recalling its own reconnaissance . . . mouth saying can't forget, mouth saying what I want to know can feed me, what I don't can bleed me. (1)

Like the swinging doors that look both ways, Wah figures his hyphenated subjectivity as an ambiguous yet substantial middle where the door or the "mouth," the opening, tells him that what he wants to know can nourish a "me," can give him other ways to be there. But it also says that what he doesn't want to know can slowly drain the life out of that potential "me." The "face-sized window" looks both ways through "doors and languages." Such closely affiliated, even related, words, "feed" and "bleed" are examples of that "Stuttered inventive, invective process. The domain of this track is an ordered fiction, a serious intervention. Until we now know the only fiction here has to be the reader. You know, relative" (*Diamond Grill* 36). The "track" which determines what we can and cannot know is an "ordered fiction." But it is not real.

As the work of Derksen, Marlatt and Wah suggests, the "ordered fictions" in which we live both produce and negate the complexities of our desires and identities, make them possible and apparently impossible; produce differences and seem to require a dull edge. Or do they? Again we have returned to the seemingly inevitable either/or, to the cross as the site of sacrifice. Instead, in reading their work, let's note the ways that we begin to "experiment" too, when we are willing to relate to these issues, become a relative. To write experimentally is, for Marlatt, to recall the latent sense of the word "experiment" as in "based on experience, not on authority or conjecture" *(The Concise Oxford English Dictionary)*. To read experimentally might mean that we can begin to see that for us, as for Wah, what we want to know can feed us, and what we don't want to know can bleed us. "X" conventionally marks the place of error, the absence of language, the inability to write, or the intersection of lines going elsewhere, not resting at the interface. Another poet, Robert Kroetsch, writes that "x marks the known, the spot where she was / but isn't" (*The Sad Phoenician* 19). But Derksen, Wah, and Marlatt figure the potentiality, fullness, ambivalence, negotiation and ongoing desire in moments of intersection. In their work, the crossing, the hyphen, the interface, the ampersand, the swinging door, signify connection, difficulty, and pleasure. Derksen, Marlatt and Wah write in order to allow everything to be, for their readers as well as themselves. Their texts teach us to read cross-wise, to notice the intersections of the "real" and the "road" (the possible and the given), what Derksen calls "[t]he fleshy space where the hyphen was between work and place" (*Dwell* 14). These crosses, intersections, fleshy spaces are the bodies we inhabit, criss-crossed by history but still yearning. Reading at the hyphen thus allows us to, with Wah, "remain within an ambivalence without succumbing to the pull of any single culture" ("Half-Bred Poetics" 62). The hyphen connects us to ourselves, rather than crossing us, in all of our complexity, out.[14]

Notes

1. By inserting a hyphen between "cross" and "wise" I mean to emphasize both words, which separately are either prefix and suffix or words which mean quite differently on their own. Because they are carriers of unrecognized, lost, or repressed meanings which nonetheless have actual effects, words, as I argue, require thorough and attentive examination. My own process of examination begins here with the insertion of this hyphen which makes "crosswise" something else.

   For some other innovative writing in Canada, see the "POETRIES OF CANADA" issue of "The East Village Poetry Web Site": http://www.geocities.com/~theeastvillage/tc or email me at rudydors@ucalgary.ca.

2. Bowie offers the following useful definition of "overdetermination" from Laplanche and Pontalis' *The Language of Psychoanalysis:* "the fact that formations of the unconscious (symptoms, etc.) can be attributed to a plurality of determining factors" (130).
3. In *Periodics* in 1978, Marlatt echoes this desire for both difference and connection in her statement that the editor, "in acting as 'an agent of connection and association' is offering a new perception on what has been said—news in a truly contemporary sense. . . . Context: connection, the connection of disparate voices, what they have to say *to* each other, speaking out of their own particulars"; moreover, she goes on, the magazine represents "a space in which different voices can be heard in the context of each other, sounding their own disparities and particularities" (79).
4. I say this with full awareness that in the American academy, a handful of lesbians—Judith Butler and Biddy Martin among them, but Teresa de Lauretis and Diana Fuss as well—have attained a great deal of intellectual power. But lesbians are crossed by gender as well of course. As Martin reminds us, "the femme needs the butch in order to cross from her apparent normalcy to queer difference or to pass as a lesbian" and "the butch needs the femme" to avoid "femininity, lest she pass as a woman, and too literal a masculinity, lest she pass as a man" ("Sexualities and other Queer Utopias" 87).
5. For a full and useful discussion of the history, politics, and aesthetics of the Kootenay School of Writing, see Klobucar's introduction to the book *Writing Class: Collected Documents from the Kootenay School of Writing,* edited by Barnholden and Klobucar.
6. http://www.lot.at/mynewidea_com
7. I thank my friend and colleague Jeanne Perreault for suggesting these lovely adverbs.
8. *JERK* was written in the fall of 1998 while Derksen was artist-in-residence at the Banff Centre in Banff, Alberta, and can also be found at his website (see note 6 above).
9. Like Fred Wah, Marlatt has been active in the West Coast (of Canada) poetry movement of and since the 1960s; she has been an editor of *Tish Magazine* (1963), *The Capilano Review,* and *Periodics: a magazine devoted to prose.* She has published thirteen volumes of poetry, two novels, and collaborative work with both the feminist poet and editor Betsy Warland and the Québécois feminist experimental writer Nicole Brossard. For additional biographical and bibliographical information, including a list of books and articles by Marlatt and articles about Marlatt and her work, see the author profile at Northwest Passages, Canadian Literature On-Line: http://www.nwpassages.com/authors/marlatt.asp.
10. Published in 1977 by Coach House Press in Toronto, Ontario, Marlatt wrote *Zócalo* after a trip to Mexico with her then-partner, the late poet and painter Roy Kiyooka.
11. Daphne Marlatt's interview with poet and critic George Bowering (see Works Cited).
12. *Diamond Grill* 53.
13. See Wah's "Biobibliography" at his website: http://www.acs.ucalgary.ca/~wah/

biobib.html where you will learn that he was born in Swift Current, Saskatchewan in 1939, grew up in the West Kootenay region of British Columbia, studied music and English at the University of British Columbia. Was a founding editor of the poetry newsletter *TISH,* did graduate work in literature and linguistics at the University of New Mexico in Albuquerque, where he edited *Sum* magazine. Obtained an MA from SUNY at Buffalo in 1967 where he co-edited *Niagara Frontier Review* and *The Magazine of Further Studies*. Returned to the Kootenays in the late 1960s and edited *Scree* and taught at Selkirk College. Currently contributing editor to *Open Letter*. He was founding coordinator of the writing program at David Thompson University Centre in Nelson, B.C. In 1989 he and his wife Pauline Butling moved to Calgary where he teaches at the University of Calgary and she teaches at the Alberta College of Art.

14. I would like to thank my friends and colleagues Barbara Crow and Jeanne Perreault for reading several drafts of this essay and making essential suggestions for improvements. And thanks also to Fred Wah, Jeff Derksen, and Daphne Marlatt for many conversations, on and off the page.

Works Cited

Barnholden, Michael and Andrew Klobucar, eds. *Writing Class: Collected Documents from the Kootenay School of Writing*. Vancouver: New Star Books, 1999.

Bowering, George. "Given this body: an interview with Daphne Marlatt." *Open Letter* 4.3 (1979): 32–88.

Bowie, Malcolm. "Jacques Lacan." In *Structuralism and Since*. Ed. John Sturrock. Oxford: Oxford University Press, 1979, 116–153.

Butler, Judith. *The Psychic Life of Power: Theories in Subjection*. Stanford: Stanford University Press, 1997.

Butler, Judith and Biddy Martin. "Cross-Identifications." Introduction to "Critical Crossings." *Diacritics: a review of contemporary criticism*. 24.2–3 (Summer–Fall 1994): 3.

Carr, Brenda. "Between Continuity and Difference: An Interview with Daphne Marlatt." In *Beyond Tish*. Ed. Douglas Barbour. Edmonton: NeWest Press, 1991.

Derksen, Jeff. *Down Time*. Vancouver: Talonbooks, 1990.

———. *Dwell*. Vancouver: Talonbooks, 1993.

———. *JERK*. (1998; <http://www.lot.at/mynewidea_com/didactic.html>)

———. *Until*. Vancouver: Tsunami Editions, 1987.

East Village Poetry Web Site <http://www.geocities.com/~theeastvillage/tc>

Frye, Northrop. *The Bush Garden: Essays on the Canadian Imagination*. Toronto: Anansi, 1971.

Klobucar, Andrew. "Introduction" to Barnholden and Klobucar, *Writing Class*.

Kosuth, Joseph. *Art After Philosophy and After: Collected Writings 1966–1990*. Ed. Gabriele Guerioc. Boston: MIT Press, 1991.

Kroetsch, Robert. *The Sad Phoenician*. Toronto: Coach House Press, 1979.

Marlatt, Daphne. "Changing the Focus." In Warland, 127–134.
——. "Difference (em)bracing." In Scheier, Sheard & Wachtel, 188–193.
——. Editorial. *Periodics: a magazine devoted to prose* 4 (Fall 1978): 78–80.
——. "Entering In: The Immigrant Imagination." *Canadian Literature* 100 (1984): 219–223.
——. *here & there*. Victoria, British Columbia: Island Writing Series, 1981.
——. "In the Month of Hungry Ghosts." *The Capilano Review* 16/17 (1979): 45–95.
——. Rev. of The *True Story of Ida Johnson* by Sharon Riis. *Periodics: a magazine devoted to prose* 4 (Fall 1978): 74–75.
——. *Zócalo*. In *Ghost Works*. Edmonton: NeWest Press, 1993 (originally published in Toronto by Coach House Press, 1977).
Martin, Biddy. "Sexualities without Genders and other Queer Utopias." In *Femininity Played Straight: The Significance of Being Lesbian*. New York: Routledge, 1996, 71–96.
Scarry, Elaine. "The Made-Up and the Made-Real." *The Yale Journal of Criticism* 5.2 (1992): 239–249.
Scheier, Libby, Sarah Sheard & Eleanor Wachtel, eds. *Language in Her Eye: Writing and Gender* (Views by Canadian Women Writing in English). Toronto: Coach House, 1990.
Wah, Fred. *Diamond Grill*. Edmonton: NeWest Press, 1996.
——. "Half-Bred Poetics." *Absinthe* 9.2 (1996): 60–65.
——. *Waiting for Saskatchewan*. Winnipeg: Turnstone Press, 1985.
Warland, Betsy, ed. *InVersions: Writing by Dykes, Queers & Lesbians*. Vancouver: Press Gang, 1991.
Weir, Allison. *Sacrificial Logics: feminist theory and the critique of identity*. New York: Routledge, 1996.

Carla Harryman

The Nadja and Nanette of Gail Scott's *Main Brides (Against Ochre Pediment and Aztec Sky)*

We are surrounded by millennial discourses, both apocalyptic and utopian; medical science and technology promise us ever-greater control over birth, health, disease, and death, and promote an ethics of perfection reminiscent of late-nineteenth-century eugenic discourse. At the same time we are in the throes of confusion and conflict over what is often described in terms of plague as we watch the spread of AIDS both within and outside of what at first seem to be contained communities. While projective statistics (for 1991, for 2000) force us into fin-de-siècle *imagining, the churches, communities, and states struggle over how to support and maintain those already suffering. And this is to limit examples of millennial thinking to the sphere of the lived body—healthy or ill.*

—Frances Bartkowski, *Feminist Utopias*

. . . there is in young people and in erotic personalities throughout their lives a kind of intransitive mental feeling of being-in-love, which its objects only enter retrospectively; they were not given narcissistically in advance of this being-in-love either, that is, in their own body. Thus there is—not as a mental feeling, but rather as a state of mind—a light heartedness of character, even hope; it certainly does not only appear when it knows clearly what it is hoping for.

—Ernst Bloch, *The Principle of Hope*

In Gail Scott's *Main Brides,* the aesthetic is not perfect (it does not locate a millennial narrative as the site of utopian desire): "She thinks: 'it would be like reading a really embarrassing passage from my diary out loud. That one about

Shiny Genitals. Of course, it depends on how you handle it" (97). There is, however, a formulation of love, or desire, call it what one will, that in this work seeks the aesthetic and looks toward (*a forward feeling*—Bloch) a future *outside* the text.

The event of the novel, if one were to call it a novel (Scott originally wanted to call it "an installation"), occurs in a particular but not contained community, Montreal. The "characters" can be read as both aesthetic constructions (portraits written/drawn within the event of the novel) and hypothetical people, people who might exist and who might be able to affect the future as female subjects. In *Main Brides,* the anticipatory state is also a participatory state. Within its region are women subjects who individually and collectively practice becoming the subjects (even of their own participatory "self" objectifying) of a world in which the aesthetic signs of the culture, whether they created and instituted these signs/architectures or not, predominate as sites of engagement *for* them: "She glances up at the crookedly drawn 1904 pressed out of the metal ochre-colored roof-trim across the street. Remembering the time she let it unaesthetically hang out all over. Being too direct (example: in the portrait of Nanette)." In *Main Brides* the doing and undoing and redoing of the particular community is in an active relationship to the already given, the already known.

In this way, the particular community is the opposite of a contained community. The concept of a contained community negates the differences between people and what use they make of their habitat or how a face or skirt can call attention to an elsewhere: "it isn't a crime to make up portraits of patrons in a bar (eavesdrop a little). She looks around discreetly" (the middle-aged Lydia is a little femme); "the Portuguese woman in white blouse and dark skirt, like hers is getting up to try her phone call again" (97). Lydia's is a particular community—constitutive of gay, lesbian, bisexual, straight people, dark people, immigrant people—that certain fearful discourses, such as those promulgated in mass media targeting suburbanites who identify with cities as scary places—might construct as *contained* communities in a narrative that addresses itself to people it supposes not to live there. The narrative about the contained community (for example: scary urban environment with Queers and Québecois) is one that presumes itself to be outside that which it narrates: it tells a story that institutes a millennial state of mind and encourages fear, hatred, and violent attacks, such as those against the young women students at the University of Montreal in 1991, this event being an influence on Scott's novel.

. . .

It is frightening then when stories seem the same as empty duplications and reduplications of *Blade Runner* transposed onto nineteenth-century millennial thinking. The sexy technology of these films' "new" crazed-camera look and monumental tomb-like sound effects masks their parasitic attachment to residual nineteenth-century millennial narratives that have not been put to rest. As in the original aesthetically powerful *Blade Runner* with its depiction of the inventor Sebastian as a technological wizard with a degenerative disease, these weak replicant films characterize those with both "brains" and "bad" bodies as sickos. The body is an object that stands for the psyche; thus, as in the nineteenth-century novel, physical attributes of people and the objects that surround them signify states-of-mind or consciousness.

Breton and then later Robbe-Grillet hold in contempt what they identify in the nineteenth-century novel as a static and bankrupt literary psychology in which objects in rooms are both class markers and reflections of states of mind (Breton, *MOS,* 6–9). Breton wanted to transform this static state through a method that chose interiority turned inside-out into the world as the initiatory, not reflective, site of human transformation. Robbe-Grillet wanted to revolutionize the novel, using it as a kind of epistemological test by constructing a stringent division between things and human minds. Although the projects are quite distinct, both of these artists located a disease of narration that, among other things, circulates within the construction of millennial thought.

One wants to be taken out of millennial thinking, to be transported. Can't it, the utopian narrative, do something else? is a question that one of Bloch's "erotic personalities" would ask. After all, such a "personality" might see herself lusting after the anticipatory terrain that seems to be foreclosed on through the millennial narrative. The work of André Breton might serve as a site, analogous perhaps to some local architecture, that such a personality might situate herself in relation to . . . someplace else, a city, Montreal.

. . .

The dream of a dynamic urban life is severed from what lies outside the urban environment where AIDS is rarely mentioned but issues of cloning are easily debated. The millennial narrative could be *as if* a virus of abjection: its host would be the lassitude and hopelessness in those it inhabits. It really doesn't matter where any one of us lives. It feeds off perfection and plague, leaving a place, a stage, a contained community between what is said to be desired and said to be too frightening to think about. It speaks the truth in dishonesty by inventing the dynamics of the truth—between perfection and illness—and repeating these dynamics countless times so that one must think in terms of millennialism even in rejecting the construct.

Control and chaos. The millennial narrative seems entirely incommensurate with the blue sky above a building's ochre pediment, or the character in a novel, *Main Brides,* named Norma jean who can interpret the "novelist's" dream better than the novelist, or the round of light on the face, then the knee, of a cyclist who cycles toward another century: the twenty-first or the twentieth—they seem slightly mixed up. Aren't there any cars in this book? And what about the old-fashioned title? Ironically, it celebrates and eroticizes an eroded (im)"pediment."[1] This is the site in which Scott's female characters enlist their own libidinal energies to benefit themselves, however qualified (imperfect) the benefit might be. A millennial hopelessness is subverted by the novelist's courtship of pleasure and a certain "transposition of aesthetic categories into actual experience" (Nicholls, 279).

There is always more than one narrative, more than one possible outcome, and more than one possible impasse. If there is the splitting of men and women into class-designed reproductive functions,[2] there are other accounts in which women invent themselves with a certain tenacity in the face of prevalent dangers: the narrative of rape, violence, murder, control of the bodies of women can design the conditions for another form of narrative that entirely, and dangerously, ignores "victimage"; the stereotypical version of which goes something like this: "It's not going to happen to me/us, I/we're not like other women." A challenge, then, is to put "victimage" in the right place—by constructing a record of the liberating practice of self-invention without ignoring the dangers women face generically. One might entertain the utopic emotion, the desire "to know the ecstasy of the body's energy when it is not repressed by partriarchal rules and interdictions" (Brossard, 37). In *Main Brides:*

> She imagines them behind those sprouting orbs or sword points, rising from cornices and pediments in mock aggression toward the sky. It's true the mambo dancing woman stupidly spoiled pleasure on the trip to Cuba, by continually recalling she'd become (by proxy) an unfortunate statistic. Not that Lydia blames her. But she never focuses on statistics.
>
> She prefers another approach to History.
>
> She focuses on the music. Also keeping down (with a gesture of her hand) an inner voice saying: "things happen randomly to women no matter what they do." (98)

The connecting of those things that are typically kept separate such as erotic desire and rape, or aesthetic pleasures and statistics, with automatic/chance events is what brings Breton as a figure and a literary predecessor into Scott's novel in its beginning pages through the portrait of Nanette.[3] Scott's and Breton's writing practices can be associated in a reading of Scott's novel through their exploratory uses of autobiography. Scott is at pains to make us aware in the very structure of her book of the autobiographical impulse in her novel writing; in so doing, she displaces and critiques various notions of autobiography in literature, especially as they relate to clichés about women novelists. Bringing Breton into the biographical realm of her novel is a claim for a direct affiliation with a modernist male writer. Such an open acknowledgment can serve as a rebuke to those who either think that women should only tell their own stories or that it is women who have the weakness of only telling their own stories—since Breton, himself, subverts conventional novelistic practice by using various forms of narrative, including autobiography, in his writing of *Nadja*.

. . .

Main Brides is structured on a series of written portraits of women, and the first portrait is of a young woman, Nanette, who resembles Nadja. Like Nadja, Nanette enters the narrative reading Breton's manifestoes. Like Nadja, Nanette has exotic dark circles under her eyes and her clothes are the object of much attention: "hair now attached in wings atop her head; vaguely Slavic eyes looking oriental with the additional strokes of makeup; face white as a mask; lips cherry red; black décolleté leotard under her leather jacket" (30). She has a youthful revolutionary spirit characterized by an interior radicality and overt intellectualism qualified by a sense of damage. The possibility of things going entirely wrong for Nanette are not as great as for Nadja, for Nanette is the product of another era and loves her mother. She possesses what might be thought of as "an intransitive mental feeling of being in love," and she is inspired by Breton—her version of Breton: believing in nothing but chance and starting out from her own apartment "to see what chance would bring." In a sense, Nanette's agency is indicated by her innocent choice to identify with Breton while she is also identified with Nadja (to what degree, one might ask, can one separate the character from the author?) through the observations/portraiture of the narrator. She, the character Nanette, does not seem to make a distinction, really, between the author Breton and the figure of Nadja—one being the product of the other. Scott's novel questions the degree to which its character, Nanette, is well-served by her ability to play the parts of both Breton and Nadja. Can a woman constructively occupy or embody the position of philosopher and *femme savante*? Can she acquire the power of the philosopher within the discourses of this dual situation? Fuck whom she wants? Tap into unconscious resources of the imagination, court chance and survive? Does she, the hypothetically real young woman represented by the fictional Nanette, have as good a chance of surviving as André Breton, the man, did?

Behind the maskings, the portraiture, in Scott's book are questions that exceed the limits of the novel. We as readers are tempted into flirting with the notion that Nanette is based on a real person in Scott's life. Where does the real end and fiction begin? This question is too simple! Unless one also applies it to Breton. Scott's manipulation of the likeness between Nanette and Nadja is a kind of trick, a trick to ask the reader to question likenesses, the likenesses assigned women and therefore, also, Breton's likeness i.e. representation of Nadja. Subtly *Main Brides* interrogates the notion of transposing the aesthetic category (like novel) into actual experience—if a woman is writing the "novel" where would actual experience begin? If she were writing the "real" story of Nadja it would not be the same as Breton's version. Where would Nanette's romantic imitation of the Breton/Nadja dyad fit? The realism, dimensionality, complexity of Nanette lies not in her imitation but in her difference from those she imitates. She likes her mother. She is not mad. She acts fearless, because she wants to avoid fearful feelings and to reassure those around her; even though she is not entirely safe. Like Nadja, she is not careful. Unlike Nadja, she reserves for herself and not those men she might fear even a little more than she does (she is enamored of chance which brings with it, for a woman, danger) the philosophical position that placed Breton and Nadja in a profound power imbalance. Nanette's psychological victimage is related to physical power and separated from intellectual power. Yet her intellectual power and/or potential intellectual powers cannot be the only answer to the question: do the present and future Nanettes of the world have as good a chance of surviving as André Breton?

. . .

Lydia, the portraitist, is also identified with Breton. Lydia's attitude toward Nanette is both maternal and sexual just as Breton's relationship to Nadja is both paternalistic and sexual. Like Breton, the author of *Nadja,* Scott, the author of *Main Brides,* implicates herself as consequent to her character—posed as a hypothetically "real" person. Scott directs the reader's attention to this self-implication by indicating a subtle similarity of invasive, voyeuristic desire between her narrator, Lydia, and Breton. Lydia stands transparently for the author: the author's lusts and intellectual passions, including utopian emotion and transgressive desire, are mediated through Lydia. In constructing a fiction that tilts into autobiography, Scott challenges the autobiography that tilts into fiction. Scott assumes a more careful position in regard to Nanette than Breton assumed with the "real" Nadja. This position of care is exemplified in her looking for "possibility" in the figure of Nanette—a future-leaning and unknown promise, the anticipatory utopian emotion. What Breton did, through his literary use of his relationship with Nadja, is foreclose on his own utopian vision: for he sought the proof of his own great ideas in another, in effect canceling the openness of possibility that results in transformation for someone other than himself. Breton created a paradox and arrived at an impasse (remorse) with Nanette returned to her "prison" and Breton left with his "freedom."

The question of such complicity is no easy matter. The need to account for the emotional pain derived from the suffering of an other or others seems to be central to the motivation of both Breton's and Scott's works. Breton's remorse may be what decides that the book is written; and Scott's melancholic double, Lydia, forms her narrative, in part, around the difficulty of knowing that her own suffering and pleasures are the suffering and pleasures of other women. Also in this sense, Breton and Scott visit the problem of the part and the whole through self-implication without either turning against the self or condemning the other, willing as each is to suffer, celebrate, and know the unanswerable aspects of agency and causality; therefore, with great subtlety, Scott aligns herself with Breton's culpability while orchestrating a critique of the problem of *Nadja.* In this light, one might think of the Nanette chapter of *Main Brides* as a response to Breton's opening lines of *Nadja,* "Whom do I haunt?"

. . .

The transportation of art into life ought to be questioned, not because the association of "the real" with the aesthetic is wrong, but because powerful (hidden) ideologies can go along for the ride. Breton's normative patriarchal ideology of gender is neither one and the same as his revolutionary poetics nor is it entirely separate. More than acknowledging Breton as a predecessor, Scott has made use of him as a figure, a ghostly figure, to examine questions about the relationship between the aesthetic and lived experience. Breton's ghostliness is in part due to the question not resting, not being put to rest in the book.

Women assume powerful positions in the world by making their own desires and designs present and central to their projects, thereby unlinking their desires and energies from patriarchal repression. Irrespective of the alignment I have suggested, Scott does not make André Breton central to her feminist novel. She invents: he haunts. He is a part, a ghost, a residue of her epoch, and she makes use of his project for her own purposes. Those purposes are to refuse repression and to make imaginative investments in those things she has refused to repress, i.e. transgressive fantasies, voyeuristic pleasures, lesbian and heterosexual desires, and unregulated relationships to and appropriation of urban and public space.

Scott's novel enfolds, embraces, and critiques the possibility of Breton. This is carnivalesque. He is part of the parade. So is Scott, the author of *Main Brides.* The authorial clowns form alliances while representing contested ideologies in disparate yet overlapping epochs. If another formulation of a contained community is the separation of feminine (object) from masculine (subject), Scott's novel contests this history ("*Lydia prefers another approach to History*")—the traditional masculinist attitudes toward women artists of the avant-garde—and assumes authority over an array of sophisticated strategies in relationship to language, textuality, polemical positioning, the "uncanny." She also demonstrates the distance between the utopian desire of liberation and the real while positioning her very contemporary feminism to talk back to history without foreclosing the forward-looking, anticipatory possibilities of imaginative investments.

. . .

Thus we find Scott in public. The intellectual matter/s of the text exceed the tidiness of the story. Interiority is turned into the world and subverted by the world. And this world includes the carnivalesque ghost of André Breton. Through this figure, she links the novel to other literary and art projects that exceed any particular avant-garde history (the novel as installation for instance), and contaminates fiction with her own literary biography. The portraitist is always implicated in the portraits: they are processual and they rely on chance and habitat. The location for the portraits is always in public, in a bar. The portraitist Lydia/Scott sits in the bar and extrapolates from what she knows of the women who come and go from the bar, inventing their "fictional" lives. The bar in which Lydia, the character sits, is the same bar in which Scott writes her novel. The sense of the novel is that it is drawn from life *and* the life of the mind. This is the utopian trajectory of the book, for what is taken from life becomes the basis for an exploration of utopian emotion that does not know exactly what it is looking for. The not knowing how the portrait will turn out contributes to the overall open-endedness of the book and also to its provocative ending.

Whereas Breton placed the aesthetic within the real, Scott relies on degrees of displacement between notions of the aesthetic and the real in the construction of *Main Brides;* thus, she engages similar questions about the aesthetic and the real but to different ends. One can see this very clearly in her use of "background." The act of inventing women who both reflect the creative processes and energies of women and represent an open-ended possibility occupies the foreground of the novel. The background is occupied by two things: a singular image (that of a dead body in a park—eventually revealed as the body of a young woman) and an affect of male violence against women.[4] In placing male violence in the background, Scott effectively separates the erotic imaginations and desires of women from violent acts. Rape and other acts of violence deform and inhibit the desires of the women characters of her book, and she portrays them each as being in a struggle against allowing violence to intervene in their projections and projects—which include romantic adventuring, performance, running radio shows, entrepreneurship, and intellectual play.

The background omnipresence of violence is struggled against. It is difficult to hold it in mind. It is hard for the reader to hold it in mind as she is tricked into more optimistic versions of identification with the subjects. These women are all putting themselves together as fascinating and fascinated self-creations. They all seem to be part of a utopic construction: they precede their objects, and the urban environment is theirs to make of it what they will.

At the end of the book, the foreground and the background meet. A confrontation is devised. A man, who may have been stalking someone or no one all along, winds his way into the foreground of the narrative. Is he, is this one, really dangerous? It may be a matter of a judgment call. The woman in the radio station, working late at night, takes out her knife waiting for the male aggressor to appear. The novel enacts a kind of revenge against the fictional death of the young woman in the park—the displaced signifier of the young women murdered in a classroom in Montreal.

This woman is ready. She can defend herself, unlike the girl in the park, unlike the students. She has taken her own survival into account. But the novel also, if it is indeed engaging the struggle between utopian desire and violence, suggests that the struggle reaches a splitting point. Will all such energies be subsumed in combat and utopian emotion depleted? How far can the young women go? Before some version of a splitting millennial narrative takes its toll?

Notes

1. Architecture in Scott's novel is erotically charged. The concept of the bride and the architectural ornament are artifacts of the past (and impediments to change) on the one hand; but on the other hand, in so far as they are dynamically interconnected in a process of decay and change, they register Scott's interpretation of Québecois *modernité*. This particular cultural *modernité* roughly lies between American Modernism and Postmodernism. The Québecoise avant-garde does not separate the concept of modernism and postmodernism into competing terrains. Thus traditional gender roles and architecture serve metaphorically as aspects of the structure of Scott's novel, which observes that the nineteenth-century (arcane) novel and the novel of the twenty-first are coextensive.
2. Margaret Atwood's *The Handmaid's Tale* would fill the slot of this kind of millennial narrative.
3. A metatextual connection involves Scott's invention of Nanette as derived from Breton's invention of *Nadja:* the lesbian writer takes over the project of the heterosexual author.
4. In her article "Writing from the Border," Barbara Goddard discusses the murders in the context of Scott's novel. *Trois* II nos. 1–2 (10th Anniversary Issue, 1996).

Works Cited

Bartkowski, Frances. *Feminist Utopias* (University of Nebraska Press, 1989).
Bloch, Ernst. *The Principle of Hope* vol. 1, trans. Neville Plaice, Stephen Plaice and Paul Knight (MIT Press, 1995).

Breton, André. *Manifestoes of Surrealism,* trans. Richard Seaver and Helen R. Lane (1972; University of Michigan Press, 1993).
Breton, André. *Nadja,* trans. Richard Howard (1960; Grove, 1988).
Brossard, Nicole. *The Aerial Letter,* trans. Marlene Wildeman (1988; Women's Press, 1998).
Nicholls, Peter. *Modernisms* (University of California Press, 1995).
Robbe-Grillet, Alain. *For a New Novel: Essays on Fiction,* trans. Richard Howard (1960; Northwestern University Press, 1989).
Scott, Gail. *Main Brides* (Toronto: Coach House Press, 1993).

Part III

In practice / polemics

John Cayley

Hypertext/Cybertext/Poetext

I

1. Reading, hearing, writing, performing the linguistically innovative poetries and swept up in the enthusiasms of their deep, but lo-tech, engagements with new textualities through formal experiment and in their play of significations, there is a temptation to say to its practising writers and readers, "I/you/we/they don't *need* 'new' technologies or 'new' media." There is so much left to be explored, that *is being* explored, in both codexspace and performancespace, as to suggest that it would be a waste of time to buy into some novel textgadgetry; to risk an expense of spirit in the wastes of techno-narcissism; or to subject poetics ". . . to the trade of a calculation that dominates most tenaciously in those areas where there is no need of numbers."[1]

2. No need of *numbers?* This essential term, read as enclosing a contradiction, is at once the sign of art-less "calculation" and the basis of all artistic formalism. Unresolved, it becomes a necessary reminder of the romanticized dissociation of "writing" (or, more broadly, verbal creativity) from its techniques and technologies, and the elevation of the former over the latter, as if certain privileged spheres of rhetoric—literacy and its codexspace being the examples necessary here—were transparent to the content they selflessly bear, whereas other "newer" varieties are branded forever with their technological origins.[2]

X [1]

the formless formations of
kno**w**ing that is debarred
from ever entering
into the realm of t**h**e
realm of culture and
civilization
modern science **a**nd the
total state as necessary
consequences of the
nature of **t**echnology let
alone retracing in f**a**ct that
we today
in all seriousness discern
possibilities of
demonstrating human
freedom
and of numbe**r**s by
building up the world
technologically
as an object human
b**e**ings must stand out for

3. The machineries of hypertext, cybertext and poetext are still often confused with the potential rhetorics they adumbrate. Even if these transient terms (as likely to fade and die out as to thrive within a short space of years or months) referred to physical delivery media, such as those associated with the cinema, there would still be no need in critical discourse to confuse the equivalent of camera or projection device with, for example, the grammar of montage. In fact, these technologically overdetermined textualities are realized in formal engineering which is itself "authored" and this fact provides such textualities with many of the qualities which most clearly distinguish them from other, previous and still dominant, technologies of literary culture.

4. "It is important to make it clear that literary developments in cybertext are not constrained by hardware technologies themselves; they are constrained only by software, which is an authored delivery medium." (Although "[a]part from these constraints which are surmountable through engineering, there are those produced by, as it were, a 'false consciousness' generated by the 'ideology' surrounding the current use of computer-based systems.")[3]

5. ". . . these agents [active, co-creative functions of cybertextual media] are themselves constructed, and they may be authored by the writer or designer of both given text and its modulated form (in any particular reading or performance) as an integral part of the entire 'work.' Writers may also write 'with and against and amongst' the code."[4]

6. [Thus,] the advocacy of hypertextual or cybertextual technologies in the context of innovative poetics is not the same thing as promoting a new and better word processor. It is a continuity with the development of form-in-content or indeed the creation of new forms which has always been characteristic of the ancient and various tradition of innovative linguistic art. The writer may choose to inscribe new form itself in the work, proposing a novel poetext with each new publication. (Versions of the present essay revisited simple, hypertextual reformations of the linear exposition, using an indexing metaphor which is both familiar and internalized in Western codexspace.) The point is, whereas I am severely constrained in my re-engineering of an essay which will appear in a bound paper collection, in software the potential is much

everybody and happy in
all respects what is
objective
conversely an eye that
looks upon the integral
whole of production
can be ventured without
any danger as long as the
nonobjective character of
its raw materials even this
that man becomes
subject and of
establishing a new value
theory
is a sign of the
predominance of
technological ideas
whose development has
long since been removed
beyond the nature of
production can be
ventured without any
danger
consists in the threat that
assaults human beings'
nature
in modern science and the
total organization
but above all technology
itself over the earth
ever more quickly
ruthlessly and gives what
levels every *ordo*
every rank down to the
uniformity of technology
shows itself further in
place of all the market
value of a consequence of
full it develops in the

greater, the forms are more plastic, such that the creation of the form becomes an integral and appreciable part of the creation of the work, if not a *necessary* part.

7. [For] there is no *requirement* to engineer a form for each new text, no necessity to take up the (programming) skills which are the tools of a conception of writing extended into the technologies of its production. Form—even the conceptual poetic form and certainly not the (material) delivery medium—does not necessarily, in itself, determine the nature of the textuality instantiated in a particular work.

II

8. Apart from the advocacy of textual technologies to poetics as a continuation of its own practices, there is a growing literature which represents hypertext in particular as the instantiation or embodiment of modern and post-modern critical theory.[5] However, while this literature acknowledges a quantity of previous (chiefly prose) work, especially modernist exemplars and criticism associated with, for example, the poetics of Barthes and *Tel Quel,* and (to a limited extent, writers associated with) Fluxus, the OuLiPo, post-structuralist schools, etc., and while it has engaged radical textualities in "traditional" delivery media (codexspace), it has not, especially in its more polemical moments or when focused on pedagogical methodology, given the same degree of attention to radical poetries *per se*—for instance those of Cage, Mac Low, L=A=N=G=U=A=G=E, and so on. Even these new critics of hypertext are occasionally caught as the uncertainty as to whether they should promote a new projection device—the "new" delivery media of electronic hypertext—or continue to develop a radical cultural critique. It is as if the supposed representation of post-modern critical theory attracts special privilege when set against its representation as a function of, say, the writerly *(scriptible)* text of codexspace; as a function, that is, of the writer's proposal of new textualities, *regardless of delivery media,* and the reader's disposal of interpretative, intertextual engagements.[6]

9. The underlying metaphors of critical theory's instantiation or embodiment in "new media" are seductively rich, redolent of

rea**l**m of the m**a**nufacture
of machines is no**t** yet
technology w**i**th the help
of traditional values but
in these efforts
technological means of
numbers by building up
the world of human
beings must be mortals
who reach sooner into
the abyss
the daring that is
s**u**pposed to yield itself to
master technology
where**b**y the inh**e**rent
natural power of cultu**r**e
and civilization
modern science and the
individual'**s** personal
vie**ws** and t**h**e object-
ch**a**racter of technological
dominion spreads i**t**self
over the earth
ever more quickly
ruthlessly and completely
block their path
already obstructed into
the h**a**nds of total
o**r**ganization
but abov**e** all res**p**ects
what threatens human
c**o**ndition
tol**e**rable for everybody
and happy in all **t**he
world-content of
demon**s**trating human
freedom and of
establishing itsel**f** when

notions of (historical) originality, novelty, incarnation. If hypertextuality is the signal of a paradigm shift in verbal culture, then better ways of representing its significance may be found in analyses of the previous shift from orality to literacy. Here, Ong's notion of the "internalization" of literacy is useful.[7] It was not that codexspace (especially books and printing) embodied or instantiated a latent literacy in verbal cultures which had acquired writing technologies; rather, they allowed the internalization of literacy, its elevation to the invisible, all-pervasive "ground" of verbal culture, such that today, to take two examples, in high critical discussion, papers are read out loud in a pseudo-oration which has little, sometimes nothing, to do with orality, or, in the performance of poetry, where the reading of hyper-literate production is a norm (even amongst many poets for whom spontaneous "voiced" expression is an ideal).

10. Hypertext, [then,] does not instantiate, but it may well *allow the internalization* of textualities or modes of verbal culture which have been characterized in recent critical theory. And, with the World Wide Web growing daily, massively, in accessibility and popularity—while remaining no more or less socially or politically marked than was the printed codex—this does seem increasingly likely.

III

[Not all of the characteristics of hypertext receive equal attention in this essay. Brief remarks will be made about many aspects of machine-modulated textuality before concentrating on its engagement with the reader's participation in the construction of meaning.]

11. Intertextuality is often cited as the modern critical term most clearly associated with and "embodied in" hypertext; but, just as clearly, intertextuality predates, even as critical concept, its cybernetic representations by a period of time which, some might argue, is equal to the entire history of literature. Going outside a text to other texts as a way of reading and understanding is not a notion which is dependent on a particular technology or is even, for that matter, confined to literacy (if, for these purposes, the assumption of the priority of writing in the term

the utilizati**o**n of **r**ising
technology wi**t**h the
thingn**e**ss of things
dissolve into the
calculated market
value of physi**c**al nature
establis**h**ing a new value
theory
is a sign of the
predominance of
tech**n**ology
are n**o**t mere external
forms for generally
the utilization of
machinery and the
manufacture of machines
is not yet technology
itself when the poet
experiences the open
as the nonobjective
character of full nature
the ca**l**culated market
value of a market
which not only spans the
whole earth as a world **of**
technolo**gy** begin to **y**ield
itself to te**c**hnical
production
the object-ch**a**racter of
technological dominion
spreads itself it estab**l**ish
all things as producible
in the process of
production
can be vent**u**red without

"text" is bracketed). In contemporary writing, intertextuality seems to me a "done deal," an accepted and necessary part of writing practice across a wide range of discourses and genres. Beyond the promise of extreme convenience which is granted by hypertextual systems like the World Wide Web, the existence of hypertext does not add, conceptually, to our understanding of intertextuality as a strategy of reading and understanding.

12. Insofar as intertextuality has problematized the notion of closure, however, the situation is more complex. Despite the priority of intertextuality as a concept, the physicality of the textual object (in codexspace) contributes to a sense of closure, and the related notions of, for example, "author"ization/ity, integrity, position in the textual hierarchies of aesthetic/critical value, "primary" vs. "secondary" material, and so on. Since hypertextual forms may bracket or disrupt the physical closure of the text, they clearly have potential to "open" the text to these underlying critical problems, and to popularize, or at least make familiar, literary works which are already predicated, for many of their effects, on this field of openness. The obvious examples here are from the (intrinsically) non-closed serial poem, stemming from *The Cantos,* Zukofsky's *"A",* Olson's *The Maximus Poems,* Blaser's *Image-Nations* . . .

13. While strategies for representing nonlinear forms in codexspace can and have been devised, cyberspace provides an environment in which a non-linear poetics—perhaps even one generalized to encompass linear and time-based varieties—should find room to grow and thrive.[8]

14. The problematization of the (unitary) identity, intentionality, presence or, indeed, existence of author(ity) is already addressed in the disruption of closure which hypertext proposes, although the composition of the elements (lexia) of most currently existing hypertextual work follows, for the most part, a conventional, "authoritarian" model. The construction of procedural, generative work in cybertext does, however, help to represent and generalize a disrupted, mediated, undermined authorship, or, as some critics have recognized, a notion of "cyborg authorship," meaning one in which engineered reading or text-generation procedures are recognized as jointly "responsible" for the work and in which the human participant acknowledges ar-

any danger consists in a**ll**
beings
deliber**a**tely and
completely no**t** only does
it establish all techn**o**logy
itself i**n** the abyss the
huma**n** beings' nature
in tho**u**ght that **m**an
becomes subject and the
world in order
while in fact this
ordering is precisely what
levels every *ordo*
every rank down to
Being **e**mployed that are
not mere external forms
fo**r** generally the
utilization of machinery
and
the manufacture of
machines i**s** not yet
technology itself
it is **w**illing creates a
secureness for **h**er
in contrast and in **a**ll **t**he
world-content of **a**ll
beings as othe**r** interests
b**e**sides such as perhaps
the interests besides
such as perhaps the
interests of a faith
retain their currency
what threatens human
beings deliberately and
completely
block their path already
obstructed into the hands
of **p**roduction
it **o**ut there must be
v**e**ntured without any

bitrary and procedural elements of cultural (self-)construction as aspects of her manifest identity(ies).[9]

IV

15. [Before returning to the reader's participation in the construction of meaning,] there are certain aspects of (potential) textuality which are more or less specific to work which is realized as software—procedures and figures which it would be very difficult to realize in other media. Unsurprisingly, these potentialities are associated chiefly with the production and presentation of the work, rather than with the literary substance of what is produced and presented, although this distinction is more useful in outlining these figures than it is in understanding them, where it instances the same problematized relationship between "writing" and its media.

16. The permutational "power" of the computer allows an approach to process-based work in which the adjective "experimental" takes on a sense closer to that which it carries in the laboratory. The time and effort involved in producing a text through procedural or chance operations by hand can be considerable. Software can be used to generate these texts relatively quickly, such that judgements may be made both concerning the results of the procedures and the procedures themselves. The implications of these judgements can then be fed back into the cocreative process. Alterations can be made both to the given texts and to the procedures used to generate the final work. All this can be done quickly enough to give rise to a fruitful feedback loop, to experiments in the creation of meaning which even a scientist might recognize as such.

17. As delivery media, computer systems also allow the realtime presentation of aleatory and procedural work, which may be both complex and radically indeterminate to a degree which is very difficult to realize in codexspace. Not that the presentation of such work is impossible in more familiar media. Even as books *The Classic of Change* (Yi Jing), Raymond Queneau's *Cent Mille Milliards de Poèmes,* Mark Saporta's *Composition no. 1,* for example, allow their readers to become the producers of their texts, to such an extent that these works properly should not be

danger
consis**t**s in the threat that
is debarred from ever
entering
into the realm o**f** the
essential nature of
technology
let alone retracing in
thought that nature's
origin
the danger consists in the
threat that assaults
human beings' nature
fo**r** while i**t** is developing
its natur**e**
could render t**h**e human
condition tolerable for
everybody and happy i**n**
all respects what
threatens human
freed**o**m and of
establishing a new va**l**ue
theory is a sign of
traditi**o**nal values
but in thou**g**ht that
nature's origin the
uniformit**y** of production
this willed view is even
now delivered
into the hands of
ma**c**hinery and the
manufacture of tot**a**l state
as **l**ong as other interests
besides such as perhaps
the interests of
technological dominion
spreads itself f**u**rther in

considered as fixed texts at all—neither the static record of, for example, many throws of the dice, nor the application of, say, diastic rules (as with certain of Mac Low's *printed* works), nor a function of some set of specific readings by particular readers. The work in these and other cases is the entire conception and the whole process of its reading. Literary objects engineered through software (especially where the software is immediately accessible to or manipulable by the "reader") allow a more thorough realization of works with similar textual characteristics (see ¶28 below), potentially works which may exist *only* as the literary performance of the object itself (where, for example, there is no static or persistent inscription, only a writing which is presented in a particular duration).

18. This type of work also reveals the explicit introduction of a third term into the writer/reader probability space. The programmer or engineer of the procedures takes on a role that is much more than that of facilitator/technician in an unusual form of publication. As the procedural manipulation of literary texts becomes more sophisticated, the role of the designer of processes approaches that of the writer.

19. "Each term of the writer/reader/programmer triangle is a shifter. Just as writer may be reader, and reader, writer in current (post-modern) critical perspectives, so either of these absent agents may be programmers: systematic manipulators of text and intertext, making use of software which has become intimate with poetics. Poets and readers must become intimate with software."[10] At the present juncture, the distinctions between the identities or positions represented by these three terms have been subverted (rightly so) by critical thinking; they remain in place more as a function of established or preferred cultural practice (actions and behaviours associated culturally with readers, writers and programmers). Yet without even invoking the current disruptions of programmable media, it can be seen, for example, that the roles of writer and reader are constructed within particular cultures, and even within the microcultures of particular groups of reader/writers (mainstream/avant-garde; British Poetry/US poetry/Irish poetry), and that "programming" a text, in the sense of designing it for a suggested mode of reading, has always been at least partly within the gift of the writer, and since the advent of desk-top publishing, has progressively

a**ll** respects
what thre**a**tens human
beings in **t**he threat
that assaults human
be**i**ngs must be m**o**rtals
who reach soo**n**er into
material huma**n** beings
become h**u**man material
which is disposed of with
a view to proposed goals
only in modern times
does
this hidden nature of
hu**m**an beings **b**y th**e**
peaceful **r**elease
transformation **s**torage
and channeling of
kno**w**ing t**h**at is debarred
from ever entering
into m**a**terial for self-
assertive production **t**he
humanness of
technologic**a**l ideas
whose development has
long as other interests
besides
such as pe**r**haps the
interests of a faith
r**e**tain their **p**ath already
obstructed into th**e** realm
of the essential na**t**ure of
technology let alone
retracing in thought that
nature's origin
the danger consists in it**s**
fullness what it has l**o**ng
since been removed
beyond the realm of

involved both writers and readers in acts of what I'd be happy to call "textual programming."

20. If, through hypertext or any other delivery technology, literary objects are constructed as "open," then this permeability of writer/programmer is extended to reader/programmer, as readers configure or radically change the literary objects of their attention.

21. [Finally,] the potential media represented by networked computing systems offer novel metaphors and models for some of the crucial subjects of poetic writing. To take just one simple example, in the world of networks, multi-user systems—those sharing information-processing resources across several terminals—are a commonplace. The popularization of this new metaphoric vehicle may make it easier to conceive of multiplicity or decentralization as applying to the mind(s) or body(ies) of person(s) seen as multi-user system(s), but without the usual associations of such multiplicity with personality disorder, (mental) illness or (harmful, anti-social) disjunctions. For, in networked computing, plurality, multiple/parallel processing, and decentralization are signs of robustness and efficiency in our attempts to represent, manipulate and create meaning from complex inputs and interactions.

V

22. [Briefly,] how might the existence of these systems and literary objects lead to the internalization of a shifted paradigm of language art? The usual way to answer this would be to say that it would arise out of the popularization of new forms of textuality and as a function of perceived homologies between those forms and the new structures of understanding represented by developments in critical theory. Forms which demonstrate these homologies would tend to be privileged over more traditional forms, where the new forms matched ascendant (albeit subversive) modes of thought, as formal exemplars of that thought.

23. [However,] perhaps it would be as well not to attempt to ascribe any sort of priority to forms of thought and simply to see the popularization of alternative textualities as the development

culture and civilization
modern science and the
total state as necessary
consequences of the
nature of rising
technology directing it
toward those realms
from which there could
perhaps emerge a
surpassing that would be
primordially formative
the formless formations
of technological
production
the earth and its own self
to proposed goals
only in accidental perils
the predominance of
technology's nature for
while it is only an object
human material
which is disposed of with
a view to proposed goals
only in modern times
does this hidden nature
of technology
directing it out there
must be mortals who
reach sooner into the
world technologically as
an object human
material
which is disposed of
technological dominion
spreads itself over the
earth
ever more quickly

of "new forms of life"—and as hard evidence of realizable potentialities—not, necessarily, as homologous with supportive theoretical structures, but evolving and proliferating themselves along with other cultural and technological developments until they finally allow the internalization of strategies for the creation of meaning which are currently difficult or rare.[11]

VI

24. Interactivity is, on the face of it, one of the most attractive and compelling promises held out by the new technotextuality, as also by the entire multimedia thrust of networked infotainment. Apart from their more directly venal ambitions, these would-be producer/broadcasters dream of replacing passive televisual half-life with "a fully interactive experience." Meanwhile the makers of interactive texts promise real-time reader interactivity with the substance and sense of literary creation itself, as an (obvious) improvement over the (passive) consumption of the printed word, locked into lines and bound into the structure of the codex.

25. [But] interaction is a term which sits happily in the phrase "complex interaction" and it implies reciprocity and mutual influence, between persons and/or things. It is too rich a term for the programmed stimulus and response, or configurational controls which are currently offered over the limited channels of today's electronic publishing systems—keyboard, pointing device, screen; less commonly simple voice recognition and speech-generation; full-motion video or virtual reality if you are lucky. Doubtless, the technology will improve and improve quickly. In the meantime it is strange that there is so much willingness to apply the term interaction to simple human-machine exchanges when in face-to-face encounters with other persons (or animals or things for that matter) we have experiences which are truly interactive, to an extent which might make us wary of applying the term when dealing with software.

26. Transactional might be more like it, as in the phrase "a simple transaction" or the sense of transaction as "a piece of business," not only because it would be more consonant with current systems' capabilities, but also because it points to the

ruthlessly and completely
not o**nl**y does it establish
all things tech**n**ically
objectivated the essence
of life is supposed
to yield itself to technical
production p**u**ts the
world **m**arket **b**ut abov**e**
all technology a**r**e also its
attendants
not only are living thing**s**
technically objectivated
the **w**hole earth as a fait**h**
retain their currency
wh**a**t threatens human
condi**t**ion tolerable for
self-**a**ssertive production
inte**r**pose th**e**mselves
before the open as
perhaps the interests of a
faith retain their relati**o**n
to Being **e**mployed
that are not mere
external forms for
generally
the utilization of
machinery and the
manufacture of machines
is not yet technology
direc**t**ing it toward those
realm**s**
from which there could
perhaps emerge a
surpassing of the
technical
a w**o**rld market which

underlying intentionality of many developers of so-called interactive technologies, for they will be quite happy to develop televisual culture up to a point where certain economically "essential" transactions may be carried out, but then, suddenly, have little inclination for taking things further, pending some return on their investment in R&D.

27. Interactivity might well be one of the *goals* of an extended textuality, but it is not enough to be content with or to fetishize a model of interactivity which is simply the arts-pages equivalent of handing over electronic credits in the virtual intermall as a (self-) expression of "choice."

28. The question of interactivity is, however, a useful tool in the interrogation of the "writerly" text, and its reader's participation in the creation of meaning. Espen Aarseth, in the course of his work on textuality in its new domains, has attempted to outline a method for categorizing different varieties of textuality, regardless of delivery medium.[12] Interactivity *per se* does not enter into his discussion. To radically simplify his scheme, he assesses texts on the basis of their Dynamics (static or alterable); Determinability; Transience (does the text reveal itself with the passing of time or must it be looked over/worked at); Perspective (allowing role playing by the reader or not); Access (random or controlled); Linking (explicit or conditional or no linking); and (the most complex scale) "User" function (interpretative or explorative or configurative or "textonic," which implies the ability of readers to co-author the text). Such a scheme allows him not only to characterize and analyse the widest range of textual phenomena, including the extraordinary, more genuinely interactive textuality of MUD and MOO spaces, but also to make some useful broader categorizations, elaborating on those represented by hypertext and cybertext, or ergodic and non-ergodic literature.[13]

29. For Aarseth, cybertext is a more inclusive term capable of encompassing most of the currently conceivable aspects of what we might call interactivity—text generation (dynamics), indeterminacy, animation (transience), role-playing perspective, configurative and authorship-sharing "user" functions, and so on. Hypertext is reserved for the normally static, but linked and randomly accessible texts which are now familiar to us through the World Wide Web. "Ergodic" texts are those which demand

not only a**r**e no**t** mere
external forms
for generally the
utilization of machinery
and
the manufacture of
machines is not yet
technology itself
wh**e**n the poet
experiences the essen**c**e of
life is t**h**e view that
domi**n**ates most
tenaciously in m**o**dern
times does
this wi**ll** view is
disp**o**sed of risin**g**
technolog**y**

"work" from the reader above and beyond the work of interpretation (the "success" of which is bracketed pending authoritative critical judgement), or in Aarseth's more considered terms, "The ergodic work of art is one that in a material sense includes the rules for its own use, a work that has certain requirements built in that automatically distinguishes [*sic*] between successful and unsuccessful users."[14]

30. Clearly, schemes such as Aarseth's are useful for the better understanding of textual technologies, and this is entirely within the scope of every poet's concerns. However, poets, even the innovative variety, seem to have been primarily interested in the construction of highly sophisticated texts which nonetheless remain conservative in their exploitation of the potential of textuality itself as a *plastic* medium. There are good reasons for this. The "interpretative user function" in Aarseth's scheme is, after all, the doorway to the writerly universe. While the manifest textuality of a poem may be limited in its "technology," it may nonetheless open out into endless readings, ramifications, inspirations, linkings, intertextualities, not only in the mind of the reader, but in her library, her own writing, her life. There is nothing *stopping* a reader from extending the meaning-creation of any text of any kind outside itself into radically new and indeterminate (literary) situations. Returning to the spirit in which this essay set out: what more do you want?

VII

31. [However,] poets, even the most codextextual, have also been concerned with the notion of performance, if not of the work itself in ritual, vocalized utterance, then at least in the performance of their texts within the world of letters. So I want to examine those types of performance which are accessible to some basic varieties of language art, while bearing in mind the potential for interactivity which is presented by these various performance modes, aiming to arrive at a point in which the mode of performance offered by a cybertextual poetics may be perceived more clearly.[15]

32. Strangely, in the performance of "purely oral" language art (as Ong makes clear) there is room for indeterminacy and true listener ("reader") interaction. The bard never (or only in the most exceptional circumstances) performs the same work in the same words; the bard is always responsive to the mood and demands of the audience, to a degree which is typically far greater than that offered by the reading poet. This is strange, because the sound of the work is all there is—it is a transient shape as language in time and space which, instantaneously, returns to absolute physical nothingness the moment the performer's voice ceases (unlike this essay, for example, which *seems* to persist because your reader's eyes constantly, without *attending* to it, refresh its image in the mind and because you may return to it in a different time and place). There is no "text" or recording in pure orality from which to to recover the shape of the work. Moreover, when that shape is realized again, by the same or by another performer, it is significantly different. Despite these disjunctions, listeners have no difficulty in identifying and distinguishing particular works.

33. In the "pure literacy" of codexspace—I mean the, perhaps, unobtainable ideal of applied grammatology—the text performs silently, without necessary reference to a prior or an anticipated voice.

What interaction there is takes place not in relation to an author, but with the text itself, or rather with impressions of the text which are transferred into the textual life of the reader. The text itself does not change, although the way it is constructed and printed may indicate alternate reading strategies, and the random or indexed reordering of sub-elements may be possible. However, the most meaningful extension of the text occurs through the (unlimited) interpretative function of the reader (see above ¶30), who may even experience the indication of alternate strategies (where they are enforced by the writer, designer or programmer) as an unwarranted attempt to control or contain the reader's self-liberated pleasures of the text.

34. [But] pure literacy is an unrealized state in a culture which, although it can hardly (re)conceive of pure orality (despite its continued existence on the planet and despite the fact that it precedes our own internalized literacy), is nonetheless logocentric. Typically, written texts, where they do not explicitly transcribe (as in the earliest form of text-based performance, namely plays, or in novelistic dialogue), imply speech or verbal performance. Paradoxically, such texts, which indicate a voice and often pretend to realize their (full) potential in ritual, voiced readings, are those which seem to preserve their authorial integrity, as their readers-turned-listeners maintain absolute decorum and silence in the auditorium (which may also be an imaginary auditorium, faithfully constructed by a silent reader for the poet's voice). In poetry, the impetus to perform is strong and, in contemporary culture, it grows stronger as we hear some of the most innovative writers turning to forms which, while based on experimental literacy, nonetheless achieve their most faithful representation in oral realizations. Thus, the fruitful, suggestive oxymoron of "performance writing" swims into view, recast and partially resolved in the strongly indicative phrase, "writing as performance."

35. [Finally, in this brief and partial sketch,] cybertextual technologies offer a potential form of pure literacy with a (currently limited) capacity to, itself, perform. The performance of literary objects may be read back into both the pure literacy of the silent text and also into text-based performance writing, but cybertextual technologies already exist which, as mentioned above, animate the generation of procedural and chance modulated work in "real time." Although there is a long way to go before such literary objects display any depth in their appropriation of, say, the less exploited terms in Aarseth's analysis of textuality, existing works have invoked dynamics, indeterminability, transience, random access, linking, reader configuration and reader co-creation of textual elements.[16] The potential for the interaction of literary objects with both readers and also the third term, programmers, is not closed, and will continue to problematize the role of the author, who may also be an interactive reader or programmer. In the last analysis, the meaning-creation of the work is provided by the performance of the literary object itself.

36. While the instances of interactivity offered by existing texts are *currently* extremely limited, it is important to remember that this need not always be the case, and remark that the type of interactivity offered is different from that offered by, in particular, the (pure) literary art of codexspace and of text-based performance. The interactivity offered by pure orality was *both* what I will call catastrophic/judgmental (limited to the dismissal of the work, its rejection or forcible suppression—e.g.

stopping a speaker, "putting down" a book) and *also* cooperative/critical/co-creative. Bard and audience were able to develop a relationship—not one in which skill (even mastery) was necessarily in doubt, nor a sense of the "priority" of the impetus to produce verbal art, but one, nonetheless, which allowed the work to be significantly, meaningfully changed and, in exceptional circumstances, co-created. These possibilities, which are not typically or *materially* available to pure literary or text-based performance (where interaction is too often consigned to its catastrophic/judgmental mode) are not only accessible but, arguably, extended and radicalized in a cybertextuality where literary objects themselves both perform to their readers and are worked with by these readers as co-authors and co-programmers.

37. In this "late age of print" writers are tantalized by the potentiality of programming (pro-writing) which may allow cooperative, co-creational interaction with their own works.[17] This is a potentiality which is already some part of the experience of all readers and writers, but it has typically been seen as allied with the (radical, subversive, occasional) practices of writers who are, at times, characterized as "innovative." If the language-based textualities of cyberspace are not drowned out in the coming audio-visual deluge, they promise to internalize a new, but (strangely, theoretically) familiar form of literacy for a much broader community of reader-writer-programmers.[18]

Notes

1. Martin Heidegger, "What are poets for?" in *Poetry, Language, Thought,* trans. Albert Hofstadter (New York: Harper & Row, 1975), p. 115. The parallel "X" text of this essay is based on an edited sequence from the same Heidegger piece, extracted from pp. 111–20. The text has then been collocationally transformed, using a procedure I have described elsewhere (in John Cayley, "Beyond Codexspace: potentialities of literary cybertext," *Visible Language,* 30.2 (Oct. 1996), 164–83, hereafter cited as BC). "This transformation can proceed beginning with any word in the given text, which we then may call 'the word last chosen'. Any other word—occurring at any point in the base text—which follows (collocates with) the word last chosen may then follow it and so become in turn the word last chosen. // Clearly, in this type of transformation, at the very least, each pair of successive words are two-word segments of natural English. However, the text will wander within itself, branching at any point where a word that is repeated in the base text is chosen, and this will most often occur when common, grammatical words are encountered." In addition, words at the end of collocational jumps have, where possible, been chosen to spell out the mesostic message (in outline) "what are poets for: technology calculation numbers." The text printed is one possible rendition of a quasi-aleatory procedure which produces indeterminate results. It has not been edited. Heidegger's text is cited and subverted as, in this context, an arch-conservative counter-current, one apotheosis of the view of "writing" which claims that it can (in exceptional instances) transcend (even) its (traditional) technologies (see ¶2), and (the evil of) technology itself.
2. See also the discussion of related issues in John Cayley, "Pressing the 'Reveal Code'

Key," *EJournal,* 6.1 (Mar. 1996), hereafter cited as PR. [*EJournal* is an e-mail delivered, peer-reviewed, academic periodical—to subscribe, send 'sub ejrnl' to: list serv@albany.edu; to get vol. 6, no. 1, send 'get ejrnl v6n1' to the same address, or visit the journal's web site: http://www.hanover.edu/philos/ejournal/home.html.]

3. BC, op. cit., p. 168.
4. PR, op. cit., lines 237 ff. This, in turn, was written in response to remarks of Jim Rosenberg, remarks posted to the (majordomo) discussion list "ht_lit" (hypertext literature: ht_lit@journal.biology.carleton.ca), 9 June 1995.
5. George P. Landow, *Hypertext: The Convergence of Contemporary Critical Theory and Technology* (Baltimore: John Hopkins University Press, 1992); Jay D. Bolter, *Writing Space: The Computer, HyperText, and the History of Writing* (Hillsdale: L. Erlbaum Associates, 1991); George P. Landow, ed., *Hyper/text/theory* (Baltimore: John Hopkins University Press, 1994); Michael Joyce, *Of Two Minds: hypertext pedagogy and poetics* (Ann Arbor: University of Michigan Press, 1995).
6. Perhaps it would be clearer to use Barthes' original terms, since the standard translation of *scriptible,* "writerly," must also be understood as "reader-centred." Roland Barthes, *S/Z* (translation by Richard Miller, Oxford: Blackwell Publishers, 1990; orig. French ed. Paris: Edition du Seuil, 1973), pp. 3–6.
7. Walter J. Ong, *Orality and Literacy: the technologizing of the word* (London & New York: Routledge, 1988; orig., Methuen, 1982), pp. 78 ff. and p. 81: " . . . intelligence is relentlessly reflexive, so that even the external tools that it uses to implement its workings become 'internalized', that is, part of its own reflexive process."
8. See, in particular, Jim Rosenberg's introductory essay to: *Intergrams* (Boston: Eastgate Systems, 1993, published as part of *The Eastgate Quarterly Review of Hypertext,* 1.1). He has also posted a draft discussion of these issues to ht_lit (see note 4), 26 Mar. 1995. See also the discussions of non-linearity in the various works cited in note 5.
9. Espen Aarseth has discussed a "cyborg aesthetics" of literature in *Cybertext: perspectives on ergodic literature* (Baltimore: John Hopkins University Press, 1997), p. 51 ff.
10. Op. cit., PR, lines 243 ff. I pursue the programmer/writer relation briefly in "Of Programmatology," *Mute* 11 (Fall 1998), pp. 72–75; and, more substantially, in a paper for the conference of Digital Arts and Culture, Bergen, 1998, "Performances of Writing in the Age of Digital Transliteration." An abstract of this paper is on the Web at: http://cmc.uib.no/dac/, and is being prepared for full publication in due course.
11. For ¶22–23 I must acknowledge both the discussion of a "logic of [formal] exemplification" derived from Cage, in a paper presented at the Assembling Alternatives conference by Tyrus Miller, "Paragram as participation: anarchist poetics in John Cage and Jackson Mac Low," and especially Joan Retallack's challenge to this suggestion, namely her preference for the "experience of a possible form of life" in questions afterward.
12. Aarseth has developed this in a number of places, firstly, in his essay, "Nonlinearity and literary theory" in Landow ed., op. cit., p. 51 ff., then in more detail in "Text, Hypertext or Cybertext: a typology of textual modes using correspondence analysis," *Research in Humanities Computing, 5,* ed. Giorgio Perissinotto, Susan Hockey, and Nancy Ide (Oxford: Oxford University Press, 1996), pp. 1–16; and also in his *Cybertext,* op. cit., p. 58 ff.

13. MUDs (Multi-User Dungeons) and MOOs (MUD Object Orientated) are recast by Aarseth as Multi-User Discourses (*Cybertext,* op. cit., p. 142 ff.) and they represent what is perhaps the most radical form of textuality currently implemented beyond codexspace. Despite their origins in game playing, these textual spaces require just the sort of analysis which Aarseth has pioneered, an analysis capable of treating them as "potential literature." As a practical experiment, hypertext researchers at Brown University have established "Hypertext Hotel," a MOO space with explicitly literary inclinations.
14. Aarseth, *Cybertext,* op. cit., p. 179. Much as it concerns many of the questions raised, it is impossible to discuss ergodic art further within the scope of this essay. It is an analytical concept well worth pursuing.
15. In her contribution to this volume, "In the Place of Writing," Caroline Bergvall has made a strong case for "performance" as a model of practice bringing together innovative poetic engagements and cross-art experimentation which invoke "non-literary" media or sites—contexts "contained by and *specifying the intertextual*" (her emphasis). Performance is an intertextual (or hypertextual) path out of codexspace into anyspace. Performance ("to carry through in due form," *OED)* may also be seen as the realization or publication of writing and text-making, where the latter becomes *more properly* a "programming" (rhyming with the cybertechnical usage), a "pre-writing" or a "prior indication" of what and how to read. Bergvall hints at this: ". . . each publication . . . announces the text prior to our reading it, deciphers the text as we read it . . . rewrites to an extent the text." However, I am suggesting that the text here is itself the prior thing, the program, while any publication of the text and each subsequent reading in anyspace and by whomever, is a performance.
16. Here is a brief list of examples (with no attempt on my part at "catastrophic/judgmental interaction," see ¶36). Linking is everywhere, especially on the World Wide Web but also in work published by pioneers of "serious, literary" hypertext such as Eastgate Systems in Cambridge, MA, publishers of Michael Joyce's landmark hypertext *Afternoon: a story,* which employs the sophisticated local hypertext authoring software "Storyspace." The work of Robert Kendall, for example his most recent, *A Life Set for Two* (published by Eastgate, 1996), exhibits transience (it is kinetic), conditional linking and user configuration. Jim Rosenberg's *Intergrams* and *Barrier Frames* (also Eastgate) can only be read if the reader intervenes (it is ergodic in Aarseth's sense), revealing (tone-like) clusters of word-"simultaneities" arranged in spatially represented (diagrammatic) syntactic relations. Charles O. Hartman has produced a body of generative, quasi-aleatory work, sometimes with other writers, including Jackson Mac Low and Hugh Kenner, accessible through his books, *Sentences* (with Hugh Kenner, Los Angeles: Sun and Moon, 1995), and most recently, *Virtual Muse* (Middletown, Conn.: Wesleyan University Press, 1996). My own disk- and Web-published "Indra's Net" series, described (up to Indra's Net VII) in BC, op. cit., exemplifies all the textual characteristics mentioned. As World Wide Web works extend their abilities to processing as well as linking, they too will exhibit a wider range of cybertextual features, although aleatory linking or linking which is reader-determined is already a powerful, if anarchic, technology which can be easily exploited. See Chris Funkhouser's remarks in his Web essay and its links to relevant

resources in "A proto-anthology of hypermedia poetry" at http://cnsvax.albany.edu/~poetry/hyperpo.html.

17. "Late age of print" is a much-discussed phrase of Jay Bolter, op. cit.
18. The possible effect of the rise of audio-visual channels on the development of literary cybertext is also discussed in BC, op. cit., pp. 166–67.

Caroline Bergvall

In the Place of Writing

The French poet Francis Ponge's book of drafts, *Comment une figue de paroles et pourquoi* ("How a fig of utterance and why"), starts with the poem's first scrawl (in 1951) and follows through the two years (1958–59) of intense reworkings, rethinking, researching, writing and rewriting which led to the text's precarious point of rest, its "final" word, Ponge signing off, quite inappropriately as it would turn out: "Ainsi soit-il", so be it. Sixty-nine drafts for one text.

In 1977, at the fourth publication of the text, it is the entirety of the drafts themselves (including the three previously published versions) that he decides to turn in for publication. Doodles, false starts, crossing-outs, hesitations over titles, over vocabulary, associations dropped or pushed, research notes, publishing contract, unclear progressions from hand- to typewritten to typeset pages, visible erasures, scribbled additions; in short, the entire portfolio of every single traceable sheet relating to his work in-progress would now make up the poem itself. One text of sixty-nine drafts. Or, as Ponge called them, with an explicit ear to the musical art of the fugue, "variations".

From then on, it's the messy actuality of writing's visible quarry, its hands-on environment, that the reader is asked to handle as text: a rough, repetitive, even fastidious, process of extrication and explication. Reading becomes the memory ground of composition, and writing, caught in the making, is primarily seen to be generative of processes of intellectual as much as psychosocial investment: "Poetry is not to be found in chapbooks . . . it is in the enraged/incarnated drafts of those who wish for, who militate in favour of, a new embrace with reality" (my translation).[1]

As Ponge's declared ars poetica the entirety of *How a Fig* defines the act and impact of writing not at any one, finite, point of completion but rather at its many instances of production. While it still is, literally, "dans tous ses états", roughly "all over the place". Indeed, by the time the reader gets to the final version of the text first intended for publication, which Ponge had interestingly enough entitled "La figue (sèche)" [(dried) fig], so many detailed alterations and buried cues have been absorbed and read then read again with slight alteration, that it is as though the dense, compacted language-matter of the poem could not be fully appreciated outside of this slowed-down masticatory behaviour.

To Ponge, who munches on a word, "sans fin comme on fait de bons proverbes", endlessly as one does good sayings, as one sucks a nipple,[2] as one eats a fig, this confirms the very raison d'être of the compiling of the drafts as text. Tellingly, he had already, a few years previously, stressed his interest in the notion of the draft as a poetic form in its own right, with the publication of *La fabrique du pré* (as in: constructing the meadow or rather, the field), translated into English as *The making of the Pré* (as in: filing, compiling the fielded text "Le Pré"). Or, as Genette has discussed it: the making of the pre (-text) (Genette, 1997:398).

Indeed, for Genette, the collections of drafts, notebooks, loose leaves, torn pages, which varyingly define a manuscript and locate it in a private sphere of composition where it is only indirectly affected by the contingencies of publishing—for Genette then, a manuscript—will invariably be seen as preceding the text. The book of the text, that is.

Thus by giving his drafts up for publication, his pre-texts to read, one could say that Ponge chooses to situate his writing at the level of the page (site of production) rather than at that of the book (site of consumption). He hands on a private site of ruminatory events to public reading. Asks the reader to find the text as much in its semantic and stylistic manipulations as in the exhibition of the many non-verbal fissures, hesitations and "undecipherable" marks (the term is Ponge's editor's) which it is customary to remove from a book.

An early example of published marks that do not merely complement but are an inescapable part of the textual matter are the rough graphic notes and hand-drawn map sketches that so fascinatingly keep on interrupting the already digressive course of Stendhal's autobiographical *La Vie de Henri Brulard*. Writing inscribing itself backwards, "jusqu'à la tache", from studious printed signs to the thickening line, the accidental inkblot, a coexistence of structured language and the physical stain of the mark of writing. Such a practice inevitably signals what is becoming an increasingly pressing preoccupation, that of the sharp divide maintained by literary textuality between process and product and of the hierarchy of literacy which opposes verbal and non-verbal elements. In a short essay, the philosopher Didi-Huberman discusses Victor Hugo's use of the pen as both a writing and a drawing tool and sees in this contradictory dual practice an awareness of the liminalities of the inscriptive tool in that it confuses the experience of reading with the unexpected experience of revealing unstable Rorschach-like figures (Didi-Huberman, 1998:154). The point made is not so much that of transforming the manuscript into a drawing as that of acknowledging the range of perceptual fields which stretch our experience of reading.

Of course, there are innumerable books which straddle the line between literary and artist books, and texts that play the format and know that they're manuscripts passing for books. Since Mallarmé's idea that the paper intervenes each time an image, of its own accord, ceases or withdraws went via dada and

Concrete to and beyond Smithson's "all language becomes an alphabet of sites" (95), much poetic and text-based performative work acknowledges broad as well as discrete materialities, tools and support systems as part of its textual apparatus and stages, rather than elides some of the dynamic tensions, relays and conventions at play between the verbal and non-verbal dimensions of writing. "What is the interpretive stance to be toward a work which unmasks its own discontinuities, flaunts its core ideas as candy coating, and insists throughout not on its deferred meaning but its enacted meaning?" (Bernstein, 1986: 380). Hesitations, erasures, the accidental details left in become a formal decision which calls up the elusiveness of writing's corporeal (individuated) and material (instrumental) base. In this sense, a joint exploration of the semantic materialities and processual sitings of writing would lead to a heightened sense of its many levels of mediation and, in turn, would allow the reader to view the conventions which structure our perception (and construction) of the places through which writing, as literarity, is seen to occur (there are many places in which writing occurs that are not seen as writing).

Take for instance that most archetypal of writing sets: the page. De Certeau discusses the writer's page as blank: a self-contained and transitional site of writing: "an autonomous surface . . . put before the eye of the subject who thus accords himself [sic] the field of an operation of his [sic] own" (de Certeau, 1988: 134). This operation is, he continues, the preparation and recreation of language into text, from the processual stage's messy, near-corporeal jostling and intertextual sweating out of information, to the product of a writing which (re)turns these to literary culture. The page set up as autonomous, voire neutral, is of course as questionable a claim as the Modernist myth of the "non-place" of art. To consider the page, not as an actual sheet of space, loaded with particular socio-historical properties, but as a surface-zero, remains in this sense highly symptomatic of the many dissociative operations linked to the genesis of a literary text. In fact, this deep-rooted notion of the blank, amnesiac page, this material void which supposedly faces and blocks the writer, who writes only ever at the risk of knowing that some day they will be losing themselves to the terrifying white (whale) of the page, has played a critical role in the way writers and poets such as (or inspired by) Gysin, Burroughs, the OuLiPo, the Language Poets, Mac Low, Acker, and Tom Phillips have formally sought to wrench their work from the clean slate of the page: through procedural writings, systemic projects, explicit intertextual structures, plagiaristic methodologies, cross-arts and collaborative frictions which all situate the beginnings of writing not in the white silence of the page but in the noise of written language, in the business of its cultural machines, in the lifted pages of existing books and documents. They exemplify in this an artistic and critical distancing from the page as tabula rasa, still frequently assumed to be at the root of literary activity. Like the much debated frame of the artistic canvas, the writerly page can become an available, rather than unavoidable, constraint and format. As Marjorie Perloff writes, referring to statements by bp Nichol and Steve McCaffery in her discussion of their collaboration: "A page . . . is not just a blank sheet, waiting for 'meaningful' print to be affixed to it, but a kind of trellis upon which words and letters are fastened visually as well as semantically" (Perloff, 1991: 175).

This said, de Certeau's concomitant emphasis on the page as a middle-ground, threshold, passage, or in Genette's term, "zone", which signals a traffic, a walking through, between private and public, written and spoken uses of language, sets up fascinating metaphors between the act of writing and the strategic apparition of the text, between the act of marking, inscribing the page and that of the inscripted or legalised (readerly) body. Similarly, by choosing to maintain his project at the transitional and transactional, less coded site of the page, rather than at the more socially prescriptive, financially led place of the book, Ponge attempts to break away from the reified text and make available the writerly traces and humours which litter, as much as make up, sign for, retain the authorial physical presence in the text. Indeed, both excitement and regret can be gleaned from his exclamation that "once the machine is done, the author means nothing. It all works of its own accord!" (Ponge, 1997: 279).[3]

This close to the chest (Ponge talks of body posture in relation to the act of writing) while ambiguously at the threshold between conceptual demands and public placing, the intimate yet publishable, hence repeatable, status of these drafts seems akin to the contradictory nature of the signature's performative aura, its encroaching materiality, famously mused on by Derrida. As Elizabeth Grosz also remarks: "The trace of the signature cannot simply be identified with the proprietary mark of the author; instead, it is an effect of the text's mode of materiality, the fact that as a product the text is an effect of a *labor,* a work on and with signs, a collaborative (even if hostile) labor of writing and reading" (Grosz, 1995: 20). Importantly, she continues: "The signature cannot authenticate, it cannot prove, it cannot make present the personage of the author; but it is a remnant, a remainder of and a testimony to both a living past and a set of irreducible and ineliminable corporeal traces" (Grosz, 1995: 21). The visual artist Bracha Lichtenberg Ettinger's disturbing use of the photocopy with which she interrogates visual and linguistic "memory machines" and the fabrication and dissipation of loss highlights this: "The same image-photo, the same plate-text can pass again and again by different circuits of inscription and effacement, so that there are only traces and even 'arch-traces'" (Buci-Glucksmann, 1996: 285).

A text being, according to Ponge, "cette façon de mordre dans la vérité, . . . ", this way of biting into the most obscure thing of truth "(qui est . . . le fond obscur des choses)", some of the writer's material bulk (or trace) needs to be retained, materialised in the product of the text. Ponge's sensuous, eroticised rapport with poetry as a specifically structured corporeality and to singular poems as objects or verbal things in the world, exhibits this need for his work to challenge the depersonified, customised consumption associated with the infinitely reproducible (erasable) text. Ironically, for Marcel Duchamp, whose drafts and manuscripts had ended up similarly turning writing itself into a text-object: the multicoloured, manuscripted loose-leaf boxset of the *Green Box,* the point had been the reverse. To forward writing and textual sketches as a way of eluding, bypassing, quite simply reducing as much as possible, the unique, physically locatable, art-object of *The Large Glass* (and sublimate the existing gender matrix of his erotic machinery [rather he confirmed it]). Still, Duchamp's known attention to the detail of his multiples (later taken to extremes with his *Boite-Valise*), shows, as it does for Ponge, a critical need to enter the art and publication machine by dissociating himself from their immediate commodification and to assert the value of artistic activity as opposed to collectability (was he not in fact in the end only pushing the frontiers of collectability?). In both the Duchamp and the Ponge examples, one could say that writing is treated as a process which demands and occupies local, contextual, as much as conceptual, space. A space for the book, yet from and beyond the literary book, which values and locates as text the making of a writing which with hindsight might be seen to come out of an "acceptance of a multiplicity of means and ways to reorganise those energy patterns we perceive as literature" (McCaffery, 1992).

It is therefore not remarkable that the publishers of these two projects should have chosen to lift the writings so far from their construction-site that the work itself would find itself reduced to pocket formats which retain little more than a documentary evidence of text. As Jean Ristat, the editor of the 1977 edition of Ponge's manuscripts, says: "I have attempted to *describe* the manuscript every time the typography did not allow us to show for the complexity of the creative work: encircled or erased words, discarded sentences that I have tried to decipher, sometimes unsuccessfully" (Ponge, 1997: 55). The same emphasis on the descriptive rather than on Ponge's "demonstrative" applies to the *Duchamp Du Signe* pocket-book edition of the *Green Box.* In fact, in both books, the legibility question which characterises the presentation format of the pieces is replaced by heavily annotated editions which indicate that texts need to be customised to become readable. Indeed, the editors' notes are all descriptions of the dematerialisation, or despatialisation needed to downsize the texts in order to fit the condensed space of black and white mass production.

Quite simply, the perversion of this kind of readability is that it ends up editing out most of the text while the notes are all descriptions of the notes themselves. For instance, the footnotes, p.100, *Duchamp Du Signe,* describe 1) erasures made by Duchamp, are unerased in the text of the edition and subsequently footnoted as erased, "biffé" (beefed out); 2) words superscripted by Duchamp that do not appear as superscripted in the edition and get footnoted as "superscripted"; 3) coloured sections or circled words, unreadable in black-and-white, that get footnoted as "red" or "blue". And so on and so on. By contrast, Richard Hamilton's long out-of-print translation/publishing of the *Green Box* as book replica of the perforated *The Bride Stripped Bare* is a compromise between the abatoir of process and the wrapped meat of paperbacks. It insists on retaining some of Duchamp's randomised boxmaterial while packing it in bookform. He translates verbal doodles, decides that a red circle around a French word will also circle red in English, folds sheets, alters paper weight, all in all responds as pro-actively as possible to the limitations of moving from box to book and to the demands of publishing an affordable edition which has long since been replaced in English by the absurdly mistitled *Collected Writings of Marcel Duchamp*.

This is also the difference between reading and raiding, between bungling and handling texts and perhaps why the frequently hands-on, flexible, less customised, and usually author-friendly world of small press publishing has had such a fundamental role to play beyond providing "unpublishable" poets with a publishing platform: taking the book into the writing and ensuring an explosion in reading habits. The demands of small press work and its frequent coexistence with interdisciplinary and performic forms has developed a keen understanding of the performance of writing as specific textualised and contingent occurrences. It is the paradox of Barthes' degree-zero that it can be read as seeking to both historicise and over-motivate the arbitrary sign. Yet, in a sense, it is still largely clear that writers don't write books, they write "books" or Books. As a rule, publishers (and their editors) write the books. As Susan Howe reminds us regarding the Emily Dickinson manuscripts: "Johnson breaks the lines into four per stanza, as Dickinson must have known would happen if they were ever printed. In her own handwriting the line-breaks are somewhat different. Although I have used the Johnson numbering for convenience, it should be remembered that she never numbered her poems" (Howe, 1985: 35). There are countless examples of poets whose work gets manipulated into inappropriate, unthought-through page standards and house styles. Which might explain why performative poetics and the currently blooming world of net-writing are playing such a decisive part, if still marginalised, in making the book's textual materiality be taken as written.

Discussing early twentieth-century typographical experimentation, Johanna Drucker explicates the ambient resistance to it as one rooted in a resistance to conceptualising textual manipulation beyond literary considerations of verbal and semiotic production: "The threat to linguistic authority made by the manipulation of the words on the page was that it returned the written language to the specific place, instance, conditions of production—it became a highly marked text" (Drucker, 1994: 46). Johanna Drucker's own choice of writing her texts at a high production level means that her books have a very small run, and are mainly on view in specialist libraries.

Each publication of the quote unquote exact same text does bring out certain aspects, erases some, enables or disables others. Each announces the text prior to our reading it, deciphers the text as we read it through the social codes of what Genette has called its paratexts. Furthermore, any publishing of a text, whether in a magazine, a catalogue or a bookform, rewrites to an extent the text. Ultimately, whether for a book or for a gallery, the liabilities and practicalities of writing's material and contextual condition plays an intrinsic, yet still largely unrecognised part in its composition and in the ulterior composition of its reading. By extension/implication, some writers will aim to localise their text into a number of discrete performances, customising, staging each publication to measure, by commission. This is close to Ponge's "variations" and cris cheek's cross-disciplinary idea of "versionings".

This exploration of differential contexts and environments of writing as part of the work's formal and conceptual methodology, turns the text into an event. This is more or less intrinsically linked to the workings of much installation and performance art, which owing to their frequently ephemeral and interactive nature determine and mark the artwork (the text), not as a singular object, but as a spatio-temporal event (of reading). Steve Benson's comment on his poetry performances illustrates this in a nutshell: "I hope that my performances, involving improvisatory oral generation of texts, intermedia real-time relations, site-specific engagements of circumstances proper to the social and physical properties of the event setting, dramatic inflections of the presentation, and interpersonal collaborations with other writers, have called attention to a performance as a constructive, constitutive act". Gary Hill, whose early text-based video installations can be seen as an activation of different physicalities of reading, remarks on his use of time that "there are really so many folds in time involving media, feedback, delay, writing, speaking, and the body. Time becomes more like a Mobius band or Klein bottle without an absolutely 'real' side" (Hill, 1998: 3).

The notion of real-time enters Literature, and Borges' allegory of the book of sand which one can never read back, must always read on, turning one page after another describes quite accurately the mixture of excitement and horror this kind of practice generates from the point of literary practice. The evolving environment of kinetic writing and performative poetics might be seen to rest on some of the time-based and space-surround actualisations of such immersive reading experiences. Unavoidably, this leads to articulating the question of writing not only from within literature but also and perhaps fundamentally at the breaking point between literary discourse and the way textual strategies are developed in other artforms. To presenting textuality and textual practice "in the context of other media, other cultural and social institutions and their practices" (Prinz, 1991: 174). Unavoidably too, the writer as text-based practitioner becomes engaged in explicating the relationality of the writing process, a relationality which can be informed by collaborative work and/or by localised use of one's chosen media. cris cheek's recent project, the compact-book-disc, *Songs from Navigation,* a collaboration with Sianed Jones, in which each collaborator informs the continued progression of the other, toing and froing back and forth between recorded/treated voice and the inscriptual and verbal work on the page, each process having become co-dependent, to "maximise the interplay between materials, structures and formats" (cheek & Jones, 1998: unnumbered preface) and where the reader is provided with a rough-and-ready environment of pages to wade through. A relationality, then, which involves commitment to the embodiment of process: a formal and conscious grappling with the tools and locale of the particular project, an interrogation of the textual base. Sophie Calle's *Absence* project (1989) is very significative of this mood for methodological public writing of private readings. She asked staff at the museums she was intervening in to describe from memory the paintings on loan or stolen or under restoration. She inscribed their partial descriptions/impressions/anecdotes at the exact location and size of the missing piece: "I replaced the absent painting with these recollections" (Calle, 1990: 25). Kosuth's *Investigations* project during which he presented thesaurus entries in newspaper advertising spaces demonstrates similarly an interest in an arts practice which takes place within a clearly flagged context "without generating any residual, collectible object" (Spector, 1994: 7). The critic Katherine Hayles' observation that there is an overall "shift of emphasis from ownership to access" (Hayles, 1996: 270) seems increasingly pertinent to ideas of textuality which do not exclusively or singularly rely on verbal or even literary styles.

This relationality lets up through varying entourages of skills, predetermined genres or writing modes and investigates conceptual/contextual platforms (the book, the page, the room, the screen, the newspaper, the physical body . . .) in order to implement noisy, polluted, syncretic traffics of clips, quacks, quotation circuits and trails of spit as writing. John Cayley talks in his essay for this volume of such "disrupted, mediated, undermined authorship" as "cyborg authorship" in which "engineered reading or text-generation procedures are recognized as partly 'responsible' for the work and in which the human participant acknowledges the procedural itself as an aspect of her identity". This argument is paralleled by Donna Haraway's slightly technofrantic view of the "etched surfaces" of writing as "preeminently the technology of cyborgs": "the struggle for language and against perfect communication . . . the illegitimate fusions of animal and machine" (Haraway, 1990: 218).

By extension, this does mean that the blurring of style with slot-machines, of identity with access, of sexuality with prosthesis, of writing with transience, of memory with faction, plays out figures of place and behaviour as so many localised and changing occupancies of social, cultural and emotional relations. This also means that narratives of identity (constitutive of readability) become partly channeled into narratives of locationality and its technologies. Indeed, for Gayatri Spivak the dynamic implications of a writer's sense of context, what she calls the "clearing space" of the writer,[4] provide a way of questioning the negative dislocations brought about by essentialist notions of identity and the "native tongue" embedded in the status quo of literary and literate conventions. The Asian-American writer-artist Theresa Cha's complex, and heavily cross-genre multi-lingual book DICTEE or Gómez-Peña's borderspeak performances have, for instance, each found their work subsumed to issues of community, migrancy, etc., where in fact their range of formal and performic strategies quite clearly questions the inadequacy of the essentialist and literary frames given to their work: "Cha's formal practices throw into relief the ways in which Asian-American women writers are caught up within the politics of genre. In working outside of genres such as the autobiography or the bildungsroman, which are predicated on developmental narratives, Cha writes against interpellative narratives of assimilation and incorporation" (Wong, 1994: 45).

If the ways we explore textual forms and investigate methods of reading emerge partly in response to the ways in which we have access or not to certain spaces—physical, technological, emotional, sexual as much as conceptual spaces—then to over-internalise our responses to these spaces by explicating neither material situation nor contextual conditioning can stultify, if not altogether sublimate, their impact on the writing process and on the regeneration of contextual and representational fields. For this reason, content does not take care of itself, and cannot be accounted for by form alone. In fact, it is insufficient to maintain that form is only ever an extension of content. Form and content are in very different ways subject to ideological status-quos, do's and don'ts. One can explode forms while leaving social conventions and prejudices unchallenged. Jeff Derksen's remark in this book that we ought "to move towards a cultural poetics that is able to accomodate both text and context without reducing historical particulars to a mere backdrop for the production of literature" provides a useful stepping-stone.

Indeed, there is a need for a text-based community which can outgrow conventionalised modes and views of writing as exclusively verbal. Modes which hold that writing takes place mainly as textual spread, on the transparency of the page, in the absence of the writer(& their machines)'s particulars. There is a need to be personally implicated in the making and taking of text into processual and/or contextual events. All in all these are party to or originate from wider socio-cultural and artistic contexts of exchange as experimentation.

Notes

1. "La poésie n'est pas dans les recueils poétiques, . . . elle est dans les brouillons acharnés de . . . ceux qui espèrent, qui militent pour une nouvelle étreinte de la réalité" (Ponge, 1997): 279.
2. "Une tétine qui, par chance deviendrait tout . . . fait comestible".
3. "Une fois que la machine est faite, l'auteur n'a plus aucun intérêt. Ça marche tout seul!" [my translation].
4. Spivak brings in the notion of space and stepping out as against that of an experience of spatial territory which is confirmed by self-contained identity and voice. Ironically, a few lines later she resorts to the physical analogy when describing how such a stepping out is like "clearing one's throat". Inevitable persistence of the body in one's experience of space and language. . . .

Indicative Bibliography

Kathy Acker, 1994. "Dead doll prophecy" in *The Subversive Imagination* ed. by Carol Becker (London & NY: Routledge).

Steve Benson, 1996. Introduction to his pieces "The Birds" and "Between Seasons" in *Language aLive* 2, n.p.

Charles Bernstein, 1986. *Content's Dream: Essays 1975–1984* (Los Angeles: Sun & Moon).

Benjamin H. D. Buchloh, ed. 1988. *Broodthaers: Writings, Interviews, Photographs* (Cambridge, Mass.: MIT Press).

Christine Buci-Glucksmann, 1996. "Bracha Lichtenberg Ettinger: Images of absence in the inner space of painting" in *Inside the Visible: an elliptical traverse of 20th century art: in, of, from the feminine,* ed. by M. Catherine de Zegher (Cambridge, Mass: MIT Press).

Sophie Calle, 1990. *Absence* (catalogue published by Museum Boymans Van Beuningen, Rotterdam, 1994).

Michel de Certeau, 1988. *The practice of everyday life* (Berkeley: University of California Press).

cris cheek & Sianed Jones, 1998. *Songs from Navigation* (London: Reality Street Editions).

Jacques Derrida, 1992. *Acts of Literature,* ed. by Derek Attridge (London & NY: Routledge).

Georges Didi-Huberman, 1998. "Don e la page, don du visage" in *Phasmes: essais sur l'apparition* (Paris: Ed. de Minuit).

Johanna Drucker, 1994. *The Visible Word: Experimental Typography and Modern Art, 1909–1923* (Chicago: University of Chicago Press).

Gérard Genette, 1997. *Paratexts: Thresholds of interpretation* (Cambridge: Cambridge University Press).

Elizabeth Grosz, 1995. *Space, Time, Perversion: essays on the politics of bodies* (London & NY: Routledge).

Donna Haraway, 1990. "A manifesto for cyborgs: science, technology and socialist feminism in the 1980s" in *Feminism/Postmodernism,* ed. by Linda Nicholson (London & NY: Routledge).

N. Katherine Hayles, 1996. "Virtual Bodies and Flickering Signifiers" in *Electronic Culture: Technology and Visual Representation,* ed. by T. Druckrey (NY: Aperture).

Gary Hill, 1998. "Liminal Performance: Gary Hill in conversation with George Quasha and Charles Stein", *PAJ* (*Performing Arts Journal*) vol. 20 (January 1998): 1–25.

Susan Howe, 1985. *My Emily Dickinson* (Berkeley: North Atlantic Books).

Steve McCaffery, ed. 1992. *Rational Geomancy: The Kids of the Book Machine: The Collected Research Reports of the Toronto Research Group 1973–1982* (Vancouver: Talonbooks).

Marjorie Perloff, 1991. "'Inner tension / In attention', Steve McCaffery's Book Art" in *The Artist's Book: The text and its rivals, Visible Language*, vol 25 2/3 (Spring 1991): 173–192.

Francis Ponge, 1997. *Comment une figue de paroles et pourquoi,* ed. by Jean-Marie Gleize (Paris: GF Flammarion).

Jessica Prinz, 1991. *Art Discourse/Discourse in Art* (New Brunswick: Rutgers University Press).

Robert Smithson, 1996. "A Thing is a Hole in a Thing it is Not" in *The Collected Writings,* ed. by Jack Flam (Berkeley: University of California Press).

Nancy Spector, 1994. "Negativity, purity and the clearness of ambiguity: Ad Reinhardt, Joseph Kosuth, Felix Gonzalez-Torres" in *Ad Reinhardt, Joseph Kosuth, Felix Gonzalez-Torres: symptoms of interference, conditions of possibility* (London: Art & Design).

Gayatri Chakravorty Spivak, 1996. *The Spivak Reader,* Donna Landry and Gerald MacLean, eds. (New York and London: Routledge). See p. 21 of her interview with Alfred Arteaga, "Bonding in Difference".

Shelley Sunn Wong, 1994. "Unnaming the Same: Theresa Hak Kyung Cha's DICTEE" in *Feminist Measures: Soundings in Poetry and Theory,* ed. by Lynn Keller and Cristanne Miller (Ann Arbor: University of Michigan Press).

David Marriott

Signs Taken for Signifiers

Language Writing, Fetishism and Disavowal[1]

It will be the argument of this chapter that Language writing, in its systematic attempt to empty the linguistic sign of its referential function, replaces representation with a fetishistic substitute, that of the signifier. The process of signification in these texts offers a signifier which does not let itself be recognised as a signifier and allows neither address nor the pragmatics of communication. However, what is nevertheless instituted by this disavowal of heteronomous speaking subjects, is a fetishist logic of the subject as a pure function of signification, pure occurrence, which tirelessly refers to itself as a figure of pure representation. That is, through Language writing poetic signifiers are designified and enigmatic, gestural signals whose affect recalls Kristeva's account of the way in which language itself, based on fetishist denial ('the sign is not the thing, but just the same') can be understood as a 'counterphobic object'.[2] Kristeva elaborates the characteristics of adult phobic speech: 'extreme nimbleness', 'vertiginous skill', 'travelling at top speed over an untouched and untouchable abyss . . . giving not a sign but a signal'.[3] These characteristics and their affects bear witness to the fact that this type of counterphobic language use is no longer capable of 'revealing the anguish of original want'.[4] Instead this anguish is demetaphorised, incorporated—the fetishisation of the signifier intrinsic to this 'strongly barricaded discourse'[5] swallows and commemorates rather than speaks a loss. To put this another way, rather than a fetishisation, what Language writing is presenting us with is a theorisation of symbolic investment and representation via a symptomatic reading of consumer culture, language and world. But in this fascination with reference and consumption language is fetishistically turned into a counterphobic object in a way that covers over the phobic beginnings of speech. The specular intensity of the signifier in Language writing occupies the phanstasmatic space of the fetish, masking the site of abjection via the signifier's own seductive and enigmatic figure or sheen. In the connection between signification as spectacle and counterphobia as disavowal, the projected affect of Language writing is that of an intensified form of commodification in language. It is precisely this 'ideology of the signifer'[6] which I wish to question.

The links I'm drawing attention to here between consumption and representation are obviously not restricted to Language writing. For many political aesthetics of the 1970s,[7] the critique of realist representation as fetishistically imbricated in referential theories of language and signification was felt to be liberating precisely because this critique of realism and representation drew attention to how mobilities and instabilities of meaning undermined the naturalising tendencies of dominant ideologies and the aesthetics of realism generally. Language theories, in drawing attention to the connection between reference and commodity fetishism, must be seen as part of this wider movement.

Language's political aesthetic has argued, drawing heavily on Marx's notion of fetishism[8] and not, noticeably, on Freud's theory of fetishism, that realist paradigms in contemporary poetries and poetics replicate the commodity forms of industrial capitalism. The central analogy being between the inscription of commodity values through generalised exchange processes and the abstracted representational values attached to referents in language as an imaginary investment in the real. It has been claimed—by Marjorie Perloff, Ron Silliman, Bruce Andrews, Steve McCaffery, Michael Davidson and Charles Bernstein[9]—that Language writing, by breaking down the semantic and syntactical codes of discourse and representation at the level of poetic form, makes manifest the ideological workings of realist discourses and representations. In order to make these claims these critics and poets have had recourse to linguistics in its Saussurean version, i.e. language as a system of differential relations which precedes and makes possible the speech of an individual speaking subject, consigning speech to a secondary consideration. Or as Robert Grenier has said, rather loudly, I HATE SPEECH.[10] My problem with this strategy, as an oppositional political aesthetics, is that it elides the oppositions between referential speech and a poetics that could make the symbolic disavowals of the former manifest, precisely by forgetting the question of address and citationality. Marginalised voices—black women and men writers for example—have traditionally had their claims to representation, their positions of performativity, silenced, ignored, and oppressed.[11] Grenier's dismissal of speech has a different ring entirely if one's speech has not been a privileged source of positionality and individuation but has been the source of an agonised attempt to make oneself HEARD. The ideological structures of disavowal that have race as their symptomatic structure present a different problematic of reference to the ideological process of commodification which requires a different critical axis. Whereas these noncanonical writings are striving to reinscribe marginalised histories and collectivities onto contemporary cultural signs, Language writing reads these selfsame cultural signs as markers of semiotic difference and fails to address either its own process of disavowal or the historical dimensions of its construction.[12]

For me the problem of referentiality in capitalistic culture can no longer be understood solely in terms of Marx's theory of commodity fetishism. Money, which is a symbolic representation of value, in terms of currency speculation and financial markets, no longer represents either commodities or their production. The speed of financial speculation, which has transformed the world into a single global day, is fundamentally based on communication and not on production. The indexical relations between labour producer and value, model and copy, must now be cognitively mapped in terms of nonidentitical categories of culture and value. The shifting economic signifiers of capital read symptomatically as a simulated real have no 'depth structures' that can be simply referred to as such. The intense overinscribed nature of the commodity as spectacle foregrounds its own constructedness and infinite repeatability in a masquerade of value infinitely nonrecuperable. The disavowal of production processes in Marxist notions of the fetish does not allow us to address this dissociation of cause and effect in the allure of culture as spectacle. The immanentist claims of poetic works as directly embodying the experience of value in authorial 'presence' work precisely because they disavow this dissociation. The relation between value and exchange in symbolic economies of the lyric, say, where the source and origin of value is located in the synthetic activity of the prehending mind, can only present itself as a moment of intense personal experience because of the overinvested cultural values placed on a simulated rhetoric of sincerity. Even objectivist claims to a form of radically empiricist presentation or denotative enactment in the objective structure of facts as a politics of representation reenact a form of radical subjectivism that serves to reaffirm the dissociation between acts of perception and historical reality, between the sign as spectacle and the structures of disavowal in postwar American culture. This worldwide dominance of information technology and mass culture as spectacle has made the poetic work, whether conceived as a discrete record of personal experience or as an ongoing postmodern performativity or negative dialectic, extremely antiquated. Technologies of the word which allow marginal or medium publishing houses to continue circulating radical poetries and poetics seem almost quaint—quaint being the exact word for postmodern conceptions of nonreferential extremity.

Of course poetry, as a therapeutic means of mass confession, remains extremely popular, judging by the number of annual entries submitted to national competitions in the U.K. alone. I do not think this spectacle represents a mass fetishism of poetic form, but rather the use of poetry to address disavowal, which, in psychoanalytic terms, refers to the primary processes of displacement as a mechanism of the unconscious. The psychic process of disavowal was first elaborated by Freud in his discussion of fetishism. Through disavowal, the fetish allows access to its own cause, acknowledging a traumatic event. The spectacle of reference in popular poetic forms—the narrative lyric, ubiquitous use of first-person pronouns, the affected naturalism of the realist lyric—can be read symptomatically from this point of view as precisely blocking out the fear and anxiety occasioned by the proliferation of referents, as a defense against reference, rather than a transcendence of it leading to the real. In critiquing these differing genres of discourse, what Language theory leaves unexplored is how these genres represent and present an originary and paradigmatic affect of traumatic symbolisation which is, in turn, a cathected process of sublimation. It is precisely because attempts at grasping originary, prereflexive, lived sensible experience show the limitations of language that the phantasmatic space of the fetish and its disavowal of difference occurs, and not the other way 'round. The dimensions specific to language in use bear witness to an unbridgeable hiatus between language and world, between the phenomenal opacity of 'figural' desire, signification and sense. According to J.-F. Lyotard, in *Discours, figure,* the figure is the name of an unspeakable other necessarily at work *within* and *against* discourse.[13] It is not in opposition to discourse in any unproblematic sense, but is the point in which discursive oppositions open to a radical incommensurability, or unresolvable conflict in the psychical apparatus and the origination of the unconscious. Better put, the entry into language should be seen as a traumatic event, a primal repression which establishes an irrecoverable fantasy in the social unconscious: this fantasy seeks to reveal itself through a disruption and overturning of the order of language, or, alternatively, seeks to disavow this original traumatic entry in terms of a defense against the radically heterogeneous. The irreducibility of this unconscious affect in the psychical apparatus cannot be reduced by representation and results in a splitting of the subject between recognition and disavowal.[14] This 'something' in psychical reality which cannot be reduced and around which the real is constructed, is a problematic of signifieds and reference across which speech emerges *in addition to* a notion of language as a closed system of signifiers.

In contemporary American culture it is precisely because of the traumatic excess associated with referential markers of sexual and racial difference that this aesthetics of disavowal has moved considerably away from any realist aesthetic of reference. What I think we are faced with here is a phobic inability to face up to the symbolic exhaustion of the social and psychic spheres. Symbolic exhaustion results when the reader is sent messages he cannot understand or present to himself, which he cannot *symbolise*. The exhaustion stems from the fact that this nonsymbolisation repeats an originary 'gap' between trauma and fantasy which, in turn, is structured around the foreclosure of a key signifier by the speaking subject.[15] Which brings me back finally to Language writing. Literally reading a Language poem is, for me, to be confronted with an inability to inscribe signs of value to poetic progression, which, in turn, induces exhaustion—I feel literally screened out by the overdetermined, excessive, and phantasmatic inscriptions of the poetic signifiers. According to the theory, however, this indeterminacy is meant to be enabling as a noncommodified basis for communication (even though the theorists reject this term). The logic of this argument is of course circular, especially in its system of dependencies whereby indeterminacy induces helplessness which in turn induces knowledge (of ideological mechanisms at work in language) which in turn allows the reader to grasp the circumstances of indeterminacy (reference and its relationship to commodity capitalism). I'm afraid I don't buy that, not for a moment.[16] This exhaustion I'm talking about results from an excess which presents a fantasy of a lack which substitutes for something missing in a presence-absence contestation. This nonreferential opacity of the signifer (which I term fetishistic) is a negative projection of referential loss onto the reader constituted as an affect without ideational autonomy. This violence can only write readerly difference as absence of affect, i.e. it is a refusal to acknowledge the *nonrepresentative* status of the subject's traumatic entry into language and fantasy. Language writing's fetishism of signification is a disavowal of this threat and also a memorial to this process. Semantic, lexical, phonematic values are over-inscribed on the poetic surface as the site of lack through a substitution of meanings. This phantasmatic over-inscription relates directly to Freud's psychoanalytic account of the fetish in his short essay "Fetishism". The fetish object acts as a 'sign' in that it substitutes for something thought to be missing.[17] The substitute also functions as a mask, covering over and disavowing the traumatic sight of nothing, and thus constructing a phantasmatic space, a surface and what the surface might conceal. In reading Language poetry, what attracts the gaze is not the making manifest of the ideological operations of language, nor the nonreferential complexity of idiolects in the social sphere; but rather, the gaze is drawn back to a symbolic and excessive process of spectacle and disavowal—'I know very well, but all the same . . . '. What I am saying is that there is a fetishism of the signifier in Language writing which serves to conceal and guard against something else, and that something else is the encroachment of nameless anxieties and displacements associated with knowledge, power and agency. In this presence-absence process of disavowal the signifier is emptied out of its representational function, leaving nothing but the sheen of substitution; i.e., the poetic signifiers hide and cover up what is missed, leaving phantasies and symptoms. This overly symbolic investment in signification excludes its own historical-political inscription—that is, the pure nonreferential signifiers of Language poetry represent in a representation which is not a reference but a nonreferential 'enigma' as phrased by Alan Davies. 'These disintegrative moments ensure the preservation of what Alan Davies calls the "enigma", which must *not* be distributed, dispersed or otherwise extended: "When the integer is serialised, or valued, when it is perceived through horizontal or vertical loci, it achieves a rhetorical or narrative function; it relaxes"'.[18] These enigmatic signifiers interrogate the reader but do not allow him or her to respond. The phrase 'enigmatic signifier' is taken from the work on originary repression by the French psychoanalyst, Jean Laplanche.[19] The enigmatic signifier is a designified signifier that has no signification for the subject to whom it is signified. The enigmatic signification of Language poetry interrogates the reader without placing the reader on any axis of referentiality or address (that is, without allowing the reader to represent or respond). To offer signifiers *to* the reader without offering signification *for* the reader results in the surface enigma of poetic form being a seduction in itself. That is, rather than making manifest the connotational values of linguistic reference as commodified, the enigmatic signifier reifies cultural signs whilst simultaneously detaching them from the content of social relations, thereby mimetically reproducing the fetishistic attitude required of postwar consumers. The traumatic and symbolic exhaustion described above results from the fact that the enigmatic signifier is de-signified (it is not the signifier of any signified) of any mediation between particularities and the state, of any ethical or principled notion of human autonomy, because of the confused relations between language's metadiscursive claims and the poetry's processed and technologically repeated rationality of disruption—this traumatic event results in a reification of representation which is consequently fetishised. Language poetry is a poetry of *fascinare*[20] rather than *détournement*.

My problems with this are manifold. Can this fetishism of the signifier be itself political? To recreate a resistant consciousness of individuation from a nonreferential theory of communication strikes me as an oddly regressive retreat into bourgeois aesthetics, especially in its oppositional notion of practices theorised as determinate negation.[21] In other words, Language theory makes the *formal* heterogeneity of aesthetic experience look unitary and universal in its reduction of language to material inscriptions (which, in turn, are irreducible) and in its claims that such a reduction has an ideological significance. Rather, Language writing should be seen as a fetishistic poetics of embodiment, a failed articulation between aesthetic and propositional judgement, and a willing suspension of imaginative adequacy in its disablement of meaning, response and agency. This, at a time when representation and historical events are becoming increasingly dislocated, if not segregated.

Notes

1. An earlier version of this paper was given to a conference on the theme, 'Writing at the Limits: The Poetics and Politics of Recent American Poetries', University of Southampton, May 20–22, 1994; thanks to Peter Nicholls and Peter Middleton for

the opportunity of presenting these ideas. I would also like to thank Richard Godden, Romana Huk, Marjorie Welish, Vicky Lebeau and Charles Bernstein for their comments and criticism.

2. Julia Kristeva, *Pouvoirs de l'horreur; Powers of Horror: An Essay on Abjection* (New York: Columbia University Press, 1982), 38.
3. Ibid., 41.
4. Ibid.
5. Ibid.
6. Andrew Lawson, 'The Short Revolution? Reassessing Language Writing', in *fragmente,* no.2 (Autumn, 1990), p.77.
7. I am thinking in particular of the work of Victor Burgin, Art & Language, Barbara Kruger, Mary Kelly, John Hilliard, Robert Smithson, as artists whose political aesthetics is heavily implicated in the discourses of semiotics, psychoanalysis and 'poststructuralism'.
8. The central passage occurs in *Capital,* Volume 1: 'In order, therefore, to find an analogy, we must have recourse to the misty realm of religion. There the products of the human brain appear as autonomous figures endowed with a life of their own, which enter into relations both with each other and with the human race. So it is in the world of commodities with the products of men's hands. I call this the fetishism which attaches itself to the products of labour as soon as they are produced as commodities, and is therefore inseparable from the production of commodities'. [trans. B. Fowkes (London, 1982), p.165]. Marx's anthropological notion of fetishism refers to the disavowal of the origins of value and the processes of work and symbolisation that has brought it into being. The commodity fetish 'presents the logic of symbolic exchange as an imaginary investment in objects as such'. [Laura Mulvey, 'Fetishism in the Context of Contemporary Culture', *October* 65 (Summer, 1993), 11.] But while the symbolic system of money value is essential to the appearance of the commodity fetish as spectacle, the Freudian fetish is constructed precisely to disavow the symbolic system at stake in racial and sexual difference. The phantasmatic and excessive visibility of the scopic drive *vis à vis* racial recognition testifies to how disavowal and difference may not be assimilable to the diacritical relations between linguistic terms. In the important positional essay, 'Disappearance of the Word, Appearance of the World', Ron Silliman argues that 'the perceptible presence of the signifier', as a purely gestural inscription connecting product and maker, is symptomatic of 'tribal poetry' (*The New Sentence,* Roof Books, 1987, pp. 10–11). This argument is based on a mythopoetic notion of origin and anthropological sense of language—that is, the connection between referent and thing in 'tribal' societies is assumed to have been more integral and visible without the symbolic and abstractly representational economies of investment and exchange. This position is anthropologicaly and philologically incorrect. See Émile Boisacq, *Dictionaire Étymologique de la Langue Grecque* (Paris-Heidelberg, 1938); Hugh Hencken, *Indo-European Languages and Archaeology,* American Anthroplogical Association, LVIII, No.6, Pt.3, Memoir 84 (December, 1955); Jan de Vries, *Altnordisches Etymologisches Worterbuch* (Leiden, 1961); and H.B. Woolf, *The Old Germanic Principles of Name-Giving* (Baltimore, 1939), for a cross-cultural reading of early European societies.

9. See Marjorie Perloff, *The Dance of the Intellect; Studies in the Poetry of the Pound Tradition* (Cambridge: Cambridge University Press, 1985), especially chapter 10 for a highly formalist account of language poetries and poetics; Ron Silliman, *The New Sentence* (New York: Roof Books, 1987); Bruce Andrews and Charles Bernstein, eds., *The L=A=N=G=U=A=G=E Book* (Carbondale: Southern Illinois University Press, 1984); Steve McCaffery, *North of Intention: Critical Writings 1973–1986* (New York and Toronto: Roof Books, 1986); Michael Davidson, 'Skewed by Design: from Act to Speech in Language Writing', in *fragmente,* no.2 (Autumn, 1990), 44–49; and Charles Bernstein, *Content's Dream, Essays 1975–1984* (Los Angeles: Sun & Moon Press, 1986).
10. Robert Grenier, 'On Speech', in Ron Silliman, ed., *In the American Tree* (Orono, Maine: National Poetry Foundation, 1986), 496–98.
11. For an excellent critique of white feminist misrecognition of the politics and language of black feminism, see bell hooks, 'Critical Interrogation: Talking Race, Resistance, Racism,' *Inscriptions* 5 (1989): 41–43; *Talking Back: Thinking Feminist, Thinking Black* (Boston: South End Press, 1989); and Hazel V. Carby, *Reconstructing Womanhood: The Emergence of the Afro-American Woman Novelist* (New York: Oxford University Press, 1987). And for a critique of the politics of deconstructionist readings of race see Joyce A. Joyce, 'The Black Canon: Reconstructing Black American Literary Criticism,' *New Literary History* 18 (Winter, 1987): 335–44.
12. The formal aesthetics of Afro-American poetic expressivity cannot be simply reified as gestural immediacy; rather, it involves a dialectical engagement with social and canonic forms of address and meaning. Contextual reflexivity is always already implicated in the political project of black poetry in its engagement with the social construction of race, fantasy, and subjectivity. See Homi Bhabha, *The Location of Culture* (London and New York: Routledge, 1993) and Abdul Jan Mohammed, *Manichean Aesthetics: The Politics of Literature in Colonial Africa* (Amherst: University of Massachusetts Press, 1983).
13. 'The dream-work is not a language; it is the effect on language of the force exerted by the figural'. *Discours, figure* (Paris: Editions Klinksieck, 1971), p.270.
14. Even Nick Piombino's attempt to frame a formal analogy between normative grammar and the psychic processes of repression and displacement depends on a simple phenomenology of reading which, properly speaking, is not psychoanalytical, but linguistic. If the subjective cannot be translated into social mediation without originary repression, what is the epistemological status of poetic claims that nonreferentiality makes this foreclosure manifest?
15. In *Les Psychoses,* Jacques Lacan writes: 'In the unconscious, it is not that everything is repressed, that is, misrecognised by the subject after having been verbalised, but one also has to acknowledge that there is, behind the process of verbalisation, an admission into symbolic meaning, which can be missing' (*Seminar III: Les psychoses,* p.21).
16. Similar critical reservations about the positioning of the reader in Language theory have been voiced by Rod Mengham, in *Textual Practice* Vol.3, no.1 (Spring, 1989), 115–24, and J. H. Prynne, in *Language Issue,* no.1. [See Editor's Note, p. 141.)
17. Julia Kristeva has pointed out the connection between the signifier and fetishism.

Kristeva argues that the traumatic origin of symbolisation remains as a trace in language use. Very schematically, Kristeva has suggested that language always and necessarily retains the traces of its own traumatic origin in that moment when the subject first detaches itself from the body of the mother. In the gap which opens up between the maternal body and the subject at the point of its constitution—the gap which ensures that the subject can become a user of words—Kristeva locates the simultaneous origin of the phobic object against which the subject attempts to defend itself *through* language: 'any practice of speech, in as much as it involves writing, is a language of fear'. [*Pouvoirs de l'horreur; Powers of Horror; An Essay on Abjection* (New York, 1982), 38.] In this sense, the counter-phobic mechanism of disavowal makes possible language, speech, as such—including, of course, aesthetic discourse. Further, in 'The True-Real', Kristeva seems to suggest that 'a separate place must be set aside for so-called artistic discourse. If there is any disavowal, it is introduced in the minutiae of such a practice (in each word, sound, colour, rhythm . . .) such that these are never "pure signifiers" but always "word" and "flesh" . . . ' [in *The Kristeva Reader,* ed. Toril Moi (New York: Columbia University Press, 1986), 227]. From this I would suggest that the specificity of the aesthetic discourse of Language writing is its fetishisation of language as pure signification, pure systemic relation, which disavows the phobic and anxious origin of language use in speech.

18. Cited in Mengham, *Textual Practice,* p.123.
19. Jean Laplanche, *Nouveaux fondements de la psychoanalyse* (Paris, 1987); *Problématiques IV: L'inconscient et le ça* (Paris, 1981); and *Vie et mort en psychanalyse* (Paris, 1970).
20. *Fascinare* is the Latin word for laying under a spell, to enchant, to effect by witchcraft. Or, according to the *O.E.D.,* 'to deprive (victim) of power of escape or resistance by one's look or presence (esp. of serpents); attract irresistibly, enchant, charm'. The symbolic process of investment and disavowal is here uncannily encrypted.
21. For an interesting and sharp critique of a similar and not unrelated regression into bourgeois aesthetics by a British neo-avant-garde group of poets, see Anthony Mellors, 'Resistance and Representation', in *Parataxis: Modernism and Modern Writing,* no.6 (Spring/Summer, 1994): 49–57.

Barrett Watten

What Is Literature?

From Material Text to Cultural Poetics

The text will be as wonderful as the falling star of its original, the world.[1]

My intention here is polemical: to suggest that an overly narrow focus on material textual effects in recent experimental writing has had the effect of effacing cultural motives and meanings from this work. If, for interventionist purposes, or as an opening for discussion, one may at least propose such a denial of cultural reference as leading to a "lingua franca" of decontextualized textuality, two aspects of recent writing, in its production and reception, support this characterization. A great deal of work by recent innovative writers, it seems to me, is willing to reproduce an unstated and normative hierarchy of formal values derived from previous avant-gardes. Such a reproduction depends, in turn, on a culturally centrist reception of the avant-garde framed in denial of its historically specific politics at almost every moment of its formation and reinterpretation. As both claims are polemical, it is not my intention to support either with specific examples; rather, I will refer to the degree of truth the reader may recognize in either statement.

In the American context, the Language School's rejection of expressivist poetics—from Robert Grenier's famous dictum "I hate speech" to Ron Silliman's interpretation of it as a move toward the textual horizons of "writing"[2]—was a specific response to the cultural context of the period of its emergence, the 1960s. The politics of the 1960s were, of course, chaotic rather than univocal, and include the Vietnam War and its negative effect on national narratives; the Civil Rights movement and the ensuing crisis of urban life; the emergence of broad critiques of patriarchal cultural assumptions and the rise of alternative gender politics; and a broad challenge to cultural hegemony in the name of the democratization of everyday life—as well as the frustrations of the era's politics that echoed throughout the 1970s. This may seem an overly pessimistic view of the utopian horizons of the 1960s, but it is impossible to read the work of the Language School in the period of its emergence, or in its horizons of possibility, apart from that history. This is not an innocent claim, as Jeff Derksen points out in seeing the American *reaction* to political domination as a hegemonic narrative itself that precluded identification by Canadians, just north of the border but noncombatants in the Vietnam War, in its assumptions.[3]

If there ever was a literary movement that rejected a transparent internationalism (perhaps the Achilles' heel of French Surrealism), it is the Language School. Compared to the way Surrealism aligned the transparency of French with the transcendent horizons of desire (reproducing one of the Enlightenment's most rigidly nonrelativist cultural assumptions), the Language School has insisted on the immanence, particularity, and even obduracy of language.[4] In a recent attempt to find a common ground between diverse cultural motives for language-centered writing, Charles Bernstein, in a more provisional way than the Surrealists, tries to construct an internationalist avant-garde "poetics of the Americas" that is based on shared assumptions of linguistic differences from national norms.[5] It may be, after Derksen's remark on American and Canadian politics, that any commonly shared poetics of difference must assume an unquestioned linguistic or contextual norm; in this case, hegemonic Anglo-American English as the international standard language from which poetic differences will be measured; it seems an inescapable conclusion that the specific politics of given national or international language will qualify a poetics of difference from that language. Anglo-American English, in this sense, is a language that aims at global universality and is shared by some hundreds of millions of native speakers, as well as an even greater number who speak English as anything but a universal second language. Domination is inscribed in English, and not just as a word. In the spirit of ending bad history, I don't want to further reproduce such a politics, however elided they may be from ahistorical accounts of the Language School or the Canadian 4 x 100 Relay Team.[6] Rather, I want to move from "language" as the horizon of the work to a generally more unexamined category, the "literary"—specifically the Russian Formalist concept of *literaturnost*—as a point of departure for discussing the politics of aesthetic alternatives.

Literaturnost is, of course, at once historical and atemporal. So is Detroit, seen as the context for a work of art based on its mode of production—which is, of course, the best way to see Detroit. Looking for a computer rental company that would supply the laptop on which I wrote the initial version of this essay, I found myself in the industrial suburb of Sterling Heights, where the Sterling Stamping Plant of the Chrysler Motor Company, a shiny blue box of unimaginable interior dimensions, is positioned axially within a square mile bounded by Jeffersonian township lines, on the north and south, Fifteen Mile and Sixteen Mile roads; on the east and west, Ryan and Van Dyke. Metro Detroit is laid out, partly, on mile roads numbered on the abscissa and named on the ordinate; the Sterling Stamping Plant, then, is built on a square mile bounded by the coordinates (15, 16; Ryan, Van Dyke), each a four-way intersection with traffic lights. Having obtained my machine (from a low cement building of two office suites off an unpaved dirt road next to the plant), I drove home. Rather than take the faster but more circuitous route (15 Mile to I-75, I-75 to I-696, I-696 to Telegraph, Telegraph to 15 Mile and into the square-mile quadrant in which I live), I chose to drive straight across Fifteen Mile for about, it turned out, fifteen miles (thirty minutes). Along Fifteen Mile, one intersects in crossing an imaginary line at a fifteen-mile distance from a point of origin with Cartesian coordinates (0, 0) that takes the place of an evacuated downtown (which I imagined as the "place where all the traffic comes from" as I drove along, surrounded by millions of cars). The resulting tour of suburban Detroit had all the aesthetic and epistemological interest of one of Richard Long's hikes in Snowdonia, though I didn't think of that.

Rather, I thought about Roland Barthes. In a genealogy of *literaturnost* that begins with the Russian Formalists and ends in the cautionary moral of *Writing Degree Zero,* "Literature becomes the utopia of language."[7] Barthes's essay, of course, is cannily split between a skeptical assessment of literature's "horizon of language" and a historical optimism that language may become a site for political agency as it translates cultural referents into literary style. Beginning with Shklovsky's work on "transrational language" in the poetry of Velimir Khlebnikov, the Russian Formalists likewise saw language as interpreting specific cultural referents, initially from the work of the avant-garde, as the basis for a "scientific" approach to the nature of *literaturnost.* The alliance between science and the avant-garde, a specifically modernist cultural moment, arrives at a crucial definition in Roman Jakobson's formulation: "The object of literary science is not literature but literariness *[literaturnost],* what makes a given work a literary work."[8] In a subtle shift of emphasis, Jakobson's position constructs literature as an object of knowledge, one that leads to normative institutions, which may be compared to Shklovsky's earlier, more historical and contextualist, motives. For Shklovsky, while "every art has its own organization—that which transforms its material into something artistically experienced," the total effect of this organization is "to transform the extra-aesthetic material of the work by providing it with form."[9] The work of art reconstitutes materials given to it by the world in the organization of form, while for Jakobson, more abstractly, "The function of poetry is to point out that the sign is not identical to the referent." What now becomes important, for one historian of Formalism, is "not the reader's attitude toward reality [or cultural context], but the poet's attitude toward language [identified with poetic form]."[10] This shift of emphasis extends to the nature of the work of art's "material," its cultural or linguistic sources.[11] The materiality of language, mediating between culture and art for the Formalists, turns into a preexisting set of cultural codes in Jakobson—and we are well on the way to Barthes's worry about literature becoming merely a "utopia of language."[12]

I want to speak of a move from the material text, the "writing degree zero" that has been misunderstood as the point of origin (0, 0) of Language School *literaturnost,* to a cultural poetics that takes into account the specific historical and cultural environment that produces it (just as the violently historical and abstractly rationalist grid of Detroit facilitates the production of cars). Peter Middleton calls for a comparable cultural poetics in his discussion of a specific British mode of reproduction of the form of individual authorship (the cult of the singular poet without claims to historical motives or group identity) that resists any democratization of the social in the name of a "higher" cultural destiny, even at the risk of canceling authorship itself.[13] When authors like Philip Larkin or Ted Hughes retreat to the isolation of rural life, far from the prestige and commerce of literary London, it is clear that they are reproducing a resolutely British hierarchy of cultural values even as they threaten (but never quite manage) to disappear from view. If this privileged withdrawal from "society" has often been seen as the hallmark of the "literary" in the British context, a different practice of self-canceling literary agency may be described in the context of the American avant-garde. Recent examples would include the "writing degree zero" of some of the Language School's inaugural moments—the self-undoing speech act of Robert Grenier's "I hate speech," certainly,[14] but also the textual immanence of early works of Clark Coolidge like "A Page That Is Nothing But Words Written By Itself," an exemplary American instance of Barthes's writing at zero degree.[15] At this late moment, however, many followers of the Language School remain trapped at a location some fifteen miles (or years) from a "point of origin" without any sense of how to comprehend the cultural moment of its "original" determining grid. A static concept of *literaturnost* keeps writing at the level of a material production that endlessly reproduces a literary version of what the Ford Motor Company would like to think of as the advent of the "world car"[16]—a universal product that is potentially able to be assembled anywhere, marketable in all national contexts, if only because it is *un*regulated in all of them.

What I am arguing against is a misattribution of universality to Language School techniques such that they become the sole bases for its cultural intervention. As a result, contextual motives, both historical reference and utopian prospectus, often appear in the work as conflicted aftereffects, ghosts of vocabulary or even thematic content presumed immanent in a mode of signification that amounts to the "carrier frequency" of the work. Context becomes a matter of overtones, consonances or dissonances, resident in the materials from which the text is constructed; but it must remain incompletely thematized at the level of total form. If we return to the Russian Formalists' notions of *ostranenie* (defamiliarization) and semantic shift, we may understand them as specifically designed to bridge a gap between literary and contextual series. In the 1920s, for example, Shklovsky explicitly saw the literary modernism he was constructing as a dialogue between language and culture, toward a horizon in which both are transformed in poetic language:

> Russian literary language, which was originally foreign to Russia, has so permeated the language of the people that it has blended with their conversation. On the other hand, literature has now begun to show a tendency toward the use of dialects [and] barbarisms. . . . Maxim Gorky is changing his diction from the old literary language to the new literary colloquialism of Leskov. Ordinary speech and literary language have thereby changed places. [Finally,] a strong tendency, led by Khlebnikov, to create a new and properly poetic language has emerged, [so that] we can define poetry [as opposed to prose] as *attenuated, tortuous* speech.[17]

Toward the democratization of the national language, Shklovsky's reserved a specific task for the difficulty and opacity of the avant-garde in its foregrounding of linguistic innovation; even so, the avant-garde simply highlights processes of cultural change that also occur in other genres. Both historical motive and cultural context, then, are specific in such apparently abstract and universal notions as *defamiliarization* and the *semantic shift*.

For Shklovsky, when a literary form, seen within its historical horizon, runs out of work to do, it turns to what he calls "peripheral forms"—in one of Shklovsky's examples, the "penny-dreadful" detective novel for Dickens and Dostoyevsky; for Joyce, advertising and cheap romances, newspapers and bar talk; for the French Surrealists, the spectacle in popular films such as *King Kong* and the desiring machines of department store window displays; for the New York School, a cup of coffee at Horn and Hardart's, the songs of Billie Holiday at the Five Spot. Such a negotiation of expanded cultural contexts—in the "many languages" of myth, history, and dream in the expansive work of Charles Olson, or in the opening to urban mass culture in the aesthetics of the New York School, or in the countercultural moment of the 1960s itself—must be seen as the central motivating assumption of the Language School and of the American avant-garde in general. By virtue of the tradition of recondite authorship Middleton describes, it may at first appear that modern and contemporary instances of the "canonization of peripheral forms" in postwar writing in the United Kingdom will be more difficult to find. We may note, for example, as a specifically English index of *literaturnost,* a general horror of mass culture in the tradition of regressive pastoralism as it aligns with post-Eliotic modernism.[18] Innovative writing in the United Kingdom, in this sense, may be seen as emerging in a space triangulated by three intersecting failures—of the genteel tradition; of high modernism; and finally of the mainstream "oppositional" literature of the Left—to the extent that they converge in a stultifying official poetics of cultural monologue.[19]

The perceived irrelevance of the "official verse tradition" in England (or the U.K.) has offered, in fact, a space of aesthetic freedom for a wide range of counterexamples to a poetics of linguistic monologue, leading to the canonization of many "peripheral forms." This cultural openness may be seen in the inclusion of mass-cultural icons such as Bovril and Marmite in Tom Raworth's poetic vocabulary; the use of dance tunes such as "Boogie Breakdown" in the Allen Fisher's *Brixton Fractals,* as well as his inclusion of popular culture in his comprehensive epistemology; the interdisciplinary poetics of cris cheek's breaking apart of literary boundaries, as in his performance piece/sound poem "Skin Upon Skin"; and Linton Kwesi Johnson's use of Caribbean dialect in "dub" poetry. The demands of a Marxist cultural criticism based in an attack on commodity reification and its cultural consequences can also be seen as leading to a wider range of cultural referents for formal innovation in poets such as J. H. Prynne, Gavin Selerie, and Tony Lopez. Finally, the recent anthology of experimental poetry by U.K. (and North American) women writers challenges the great divide between literature and culture as it proposes multiple sites of linguistic engagement—including an expanded reference to the poetics of everyday life and the exploration of psychoanalytic processes—in the work of Glenda George, Wendy Mulford, Denise Riley, Maggie O'Sullivan, and Grace Lake. As a site for cultural critique, United Kingdom poetry is in the process of moving from a monologic, high modernist *literaturnost* toward a dialogic poetics that offers an expanded register of "many languages," particularly those that were previously rejected as the opposite of "poetic."[20]

In raising the issue of "cultural poetics," I am calling not simply for an undoing of static *literaturnost* in the name of popular discourses—that has long since taken place—but for an expanded account of cultural motivations. What kind of cultural work is a literary text doing? is a question that should be more frequently, and more complexly, asked of writers and critics of experimental writing. And perhaps it should be asked as well of fundamental assumptions of the nature of the literary—from the Formalists' *literaturnost* to Barthes's notion of the "text" to our contemporary "horizon of language." As we have seen, for the Formalists *literaturnost* is a species of agency—the notion of "foregrounding" that led to what Jakobson later called the structural "dominant" of the literary work—that is motivated as much culturally as in terms of ahistorical categories of perception and cognition (Shklovsky's desire for the "stony" stone). As a consequence, we may move quickly from an abstract relation between cognition and agency to seeing Russian modernism as identifying its cognitively transformative agency with its revolutionary context while at the same time preserving the relative autonomy of art—and in so doing, giving a central example of what may be called "cultural work." An analogous example of a more recent return to cultural motives is given by John Mowitt's rereading of Roland Barthes's 1971 essay "From Work to Text,"[21] which seeks to situate the "literariness" of Barthes's notion of the "Text" (following the problematic of *Writing Degree Zero* by almost twenty years) in specific debates after 1968 and the tensions, to say the least, of the horizons of revolutionary politics within institutions controlled by the Communist Party. Such a specifically contextual intervention is what the Text *is* and *does,* for Mowitt—it is not a matter of merely adequating text to context (as New Historicist or Cultural Materialist methods often do) but of seeing the Text itself as a cultural construction that is simultaneously productive of the new meaning it represents. So where theories of literary production, from Pierre Macherey to Terry Eagleton, often founder on dilemmas of base and superstructure, Mowitt reads the Barthesian Text not merely as a material entity (as in, say, the New Critics' fixity of poetic form) but as a set of differential relations.

For Mowitt, the central concept of the Text "underscores [its own limits] as a unit or event of actualization, both by disclosing the presuppositions about language that support such a notion and by establishing the irreducible character of the processes exterior to language as a system that nevertheless take place within language as a means of communication" (8). The Barthesian notion of the Text, then, is not reducible to "language," even as it is informed by the substitution of language as a mode of signification (in the sense of preexisting codes) for an embodied act of speech. Moving from Barthes's notion of the Text to concrete instances of it in the work of the Language School, in this sense, reveals these works to be, not reduced to instances of significatory practice, but enacted in their own constitutive limits as relations to processes "outside the text"—namely those of history and culture. In my previous examples, as Robert Grenier cancels himself out in saying, "I hate speech," Clark Coolidge, in "A Page That Is Nothing But Words Written By Itself," raises the question of authorial coherence in a mode of writing that cancels an immanent horizon of "language" in favor of exterior motives that, to begin with, provide evidence of the subjectivating fissures of labor and desire, work and affect that give the early texts of the Language School their transformative charge. Here, context and work are mutually activated in the form of a theoretical object—as in either Barthes's abstract notion of text or Coolidge's concrete example of it—identified with social and cultural agency: for Barthes and *Tel Quel,* the Text offers a move away from the literary work toward a transformative practice; for Coolidge, it is a move from expression to a work of literary "assembling" (if not on the assembly line) that is at once "to fit or put together" and "to translate by using an assembler" one language to another:

Even the sky will characterized by causes in place. Writing a sort of bark in a certain wind. Cemetery drop. To go all told to first impressions, shirking the car. Makes the line into a starving place, can emit only what goes to the loss column, a sky on straws. Says basketball players pounding down to lower the brass floor. At slouching speed and in stripes assigning sport. The water has loosened in the last century, opposing deuterium. Writers will now have to focus from a greater distance still subject to everything. Come to a bird, what is said? Fill the tube up with seed, turn it a notch and type again. Nothing, a variant. And the sky did all but rise and vanishing filled its void of words. Though being today skywriters were not meant.[22]

In Coolidge's text, the limits of authorship meet the horizon of language at a liminal point of constructed relations that are both distanced and "still subject to everything."

In my view, and practice, a cultural poetics may begin with a retooled notion of "author," but it certainly does not need to end there. For Mowitt, the "productivity" of the Text, rather than the "agency" of the author, is central to its capacity to enact a critique of disciplines (in a post-1968 context, those institutions Louis Althusser saw as delivering the ideology, particularly those of the Left, and centrally but not exclusively the university). By positioning itself in the public sphere between literature and revolution, the Text, when it finds itself in the university, is therefore for Mowitt necessarily between disciplines—to begin with, those of linguistics and literature—and in so doing becomes not an easy form of hybrid discourse but what he calls an "antidisciplinary object." In other words, for Mowitt the notion of the Text that Barthes calls for in "From Work to Text" exceeds the boundaries of disciplines precisely as it makes new meaning in the absence of the Work (a canonical category that, in fact, remains cannily unchallenged in what may seem to be the anticipation of a subsequent "call to order"). So for Barthes,

Interdisciplinarity is not the calm of an easy security; it begins *effectively* (as opposed to the mere expression of a pious wish) when the solidarity of the old disciplines breaks down—perhaps even violently, via the jolts of fashion—in the interests of a new object and a new language neither of which has a place in the field of the sciences that were to be brought peacefully together. [The] mutation in which the idea of the work seems to be gripped must not, however, be overestimated: it is more in the nature of an epistemological slide than a real break. (155)

This instability and mutability leads, in Barthes's essay, to a notion of *literaturnost* that seems close to some of the original and reiterated motives of the Language School, particularly insofar as its utopian agency may be identified with deferred action—either self-canceling speech or writing as the "horizon of language." Barthes's notion of the Text, in fact, seems precisely to be one addressed to the political needs of bourgeois intellectuals negotiating May 1968 (if not the more agonized politics of the contemporary American context in the Vietnam War, with its ongoing war and real body count): "The Text . . . practices the infinite deferment of the signified, is dilatory; its field is that of the signifier and the signifier must not be conceived of as 'the first stage of meaning', its material vestibule, but, in complete opposition to this, as its *deferred action*" (158). At the same time, the Text has agency, or better, "productivity," precisely in the way it assembles alternatives, namely for Barthes the disciplinary perspectives whose incompleteness it negates as an "*irreducible* plural" (159). The Text is a network that is also a signifying practice, not bound by generic limits but one where "no language has a hold over any other, where languages circulate"; "a social space that leaves no language safe, outside, nor any subject of the enunciation in position as judge, master, analyst, confessor, decoder" (164).

The point of Barthes's essay is that the Text is not to be seen as confined within the boundaries of a literary work; in being "*experienced only in an activity of production*" (just as I find myself in Detroit), the Text "can cut across the work, several works" (157) even as it dismantles and reforms disciplinary knowledge. The Text, in other words, acts to destablibilize disciplinary categories, and certainly that of Literature, as it continues to defer stability in interpreting the horizon of language as one of pure "productivity." What can we make, then, of the many writers in the Language School whose *works* themselves, clearly as enactments of the kind of political practice Barthes called for, seem to adhere to the generic properties—deferred action, irreducible plurality, foregrounding of signification—Barthes reserves for the "antidisciplinary" object itself, the Text even as they become materially concretized as "works"? The Text, we may recall, is social and cuts across individual works in Barthes's utopian and impossible sense of it. Can a viable notion of *literaturnost,* in other words, be founded on an analogy of literary work to Text, as it seems clearly to have been in the Language School? As examples of such an analogy, one need only think of the capacious textuality of originary works such as Clark Coolidge's *The Maintains* and *Polaroid,* his subsequent and as yet unnamed "long work" and others; Ron Silliman's *Ketjak, Tjanting,* and compendious *Alphabet*; Lyn Hejinian's *The Cell, Oxota,* and *A Border Comedy*; my own *Progress, Under Erasure,* and *Bad History*; Bernadette Mayer's *Memory*; Bruce Andrews's *I Don't Have Any Paper So Shut Up (or, Social Romanticism)*; Steve McCaffery's *The Black Debt*; and Steve Benson's *Blue Book* as works that, if translated and available at the time, might have extracted a share of "theory blackmail"—a demand for recognition of a work as example of a theoretical object—from Barthes had he not been so concerned to separate the Text from any enactment in a work (especially one in a language other than French!).[23]

I want to propose an expanded notion of text as work that takes seriously the constitutive nature of an act of production *between* languages, discourses, and already existing works, one that would complete Barthes's deferral of agency from work to Text. Such a move returns the space between texts to its cultural and historical moment—for Barthes, after 1968; for the Language School, in the aporia created after the Vietnam War and with the subsequent call to order in the name of economic rationalization in the 1980s. As a counter, then, to Bob Perelman's nomination of the authorial undoing of Grenier's "I hate speech" as candidate for founding moment of the Language School, I want to propose, from the same "prepoetic" number of *This* that contained the critical pieces that Grenier would place under erasure in his subsequent practice (in the Chinese box of *Sentences* or the handwritten poems), the following poem by Clark Coolidge:

MADE THOUGHT

made thought which of it
all of which a kind yet
best it in and on should must
whatever it is often once to do

in a while once is there and in
as it like it but often ever that it is
in which in separate that
often only very not in which way

all of this but this which as are alike
or in an only not what made as for
it in its well as made open as in
that which it once all but made but
for all as it is[24]

This poem is nothing less than a call for an identification of *literaturnost* with agency, a phenomenological assembling of linguistic alternatives if not yet Barthes's more global and encompassing notion of "productivity." The kind of act it is—proposing the poem itself as having "made thought" from the disjunct particles of language, reconstituted within the percussive metrics of Coolidge's exploration of lyric form—establishes a pure moment of coincidence (0, 0) between the Russian Formalist notion of the literary device (foregrounding the materials of the poem, in this case the words themselves, in order to create an effect of defamiliarization, *ostranenie*) and what might later be seen as the horizon of language. A kind of metalinguistic continuum is proposed in which this assembly of alternatives (many possible constructions of meaning) is arrayed on a time line (not yet an Assembly Line), opening the way to speculation on the relation between such hybrid languages and the predicative mode of cognition the Russian psychologist L. S. Vygotsky called "inner speech."[25] Inner speech is, following Joyce and in direct refutation of Althusser's atemporal and ahistorical moment of "hailing" as interpellating ideological effects, one of the privileged but unexamined modes of assembly of ideological meanings.[26] Here, I am beginning to indicate, I hope, what kind of cultural work this poem was doing—anything *but* the kind of zero-degree *literaturnost* of "A Page That Is Nothing But Words Written by Themselves."

The constructivist phase of Coolidge's work hit a kind of apogee with the 1974 publication of *The Maintains,* the inaugural book of This Press. This work, which has all the properties of the Barthesian Text (even in its concrete form), struck me like an adrenaline thunderbolt from God: Coolidge's staging of a multivocal reading of *The Maintains* at Franconia College, New Hampshire, where Robert Grenier was then teaching, opened the way for a consideration of poetic language that could be organized on a different temporal axis than the more painterly formal disjunctions of Ashbery's *The Tennis Court Oath,* the then-competing disjunctive work. Coolidge's temporalization of language was anything but a simple demonstration of the productivity of the material Text:

blunt sun it is used quartz
by and by some in charge
tile like quatrain malaria
ask doubt of a mark doubt
landing a tree small but long pit
for an in or of an in
also behalfs having foils
pare to board one roll no brim
ore pierrot

taker sharer connected kept
thing item in character fraction
heliocentrics fond
the glebe and house and graduate but parole
gourd favors stand loud odds the brave
to assume to facing a still
one may any cited
lyre class rockrose of a bar
crinoid bass plinth
pan splints an octave letter
thermoplastic all

up to alphabetic
converter pierce memorating
moraine and delivers
yacht audible opal
xylic mopboard
wulfenite the parent
yard word extent christ
yet thickening which in somehow
answer other acts in soon [. . .][27]

As Louis Zukofsky might say, "Thanks to the dictionary." Coolidge's constructivism, clearly a poetics of material signification sited toward a reconfigured horizon of meaning, foregrounds as well the material basis of these effects as the act of language as it assembled a preconstituted vocabulary taken from a standard American dictionary, moving between *definiens* and *definienda* to create the unit values of the work's assembly of lines. As Text, however, *The Maintains* is doing more than that; it bases its "degree zero" of writing on the social act of the construction of the dictionary itself, which has a material history of its own. J. A. H. Murray's *New English Dictionary,* as we know, was constructed by means of a nationwide network of scribes who read canonical literary texts, parsed meanings, wrote the individual citations down on slips of paper, and forwarded them, through a widely dispersed network of local committees, to Murray (who was so slow in assembling them, dying in fact at about the letter *T,* that rats and mice ate their way into the bags of citations, potentially destroying meanings as they built their nests).[28] As an act of national narration, Murray's dictionary was one of the Victorian wonders of the world; it was seen by its editor as competing with other national dictionaries in terms of size, complexity, and literary pedigree, establishing not only a national standard but claiming an imperial right. Anticipating its vast bulk, Noah Webster's *American Dictionary of the English Language,* first published 1828, sought out differences in spelling, pronunciation, and meaning from English exemplars in a Protestant-inflected act of national narration as a form of textual dissent. Two values of dictionaries, then—the positive assemblage of the national edifice, the negative differentiation of competing national languages—may be educed in the constitution of an Anglo-American English language as a Text that, in a Barthesian sense, traverses both national dictionaries as works. This is the Text that *The Maintains* partakes of, whose values it assimilates and transforms as *its* work.[29]

Let us fast forward through thousands of days, as in the movie *Koyaanisqatsi,* through the writing of millions of pages of material text.[30] The Navajo Nation has built a large, coal-burning power-generating plant on their reservation in the meantime; the social context of national narration has changed. In looking at Coolidge's *The Maintains* in relation to the social text of the dictionary, I want to suggest a wider horizon of "cultural poetics" based on the productive effects of the material text. Such a cultural poetics has a dialogic, rather than apocalyptic, horizon; it is predicated on the temporal unfolding of meanings held as "strands in the culture" it has assembled, according to the "demands of the present," as Shklovsky would say. How does the later work of the Language School, which I have described on analogy to Detroit as either fifteen years or fifteen miles from its point of origin at writing degree zero, hold up to such a demand for a cultural poetics? One may say, as I am of Coolidge, that the multivocality of a specific cultural horizon was booted onto language's hard drive at the outset—only we had never heard of hard drives then. The "Twenty Languages" of the Text are, simply, there to be discerned in the work as a form of critical account of the notion of *literaturnost* with which I began.[31] And how does subsequent work, over the last fifteen or thirty years, imagine its assembly of alternatives as a culturally specific form of *literaturnost*? It should be obvious by this point that I think that much work of the preceding period, however intelligently constructed as material text, addresses an absurdly over-narrow horizon of cultural meanings. This is not to say that I think Language Writers should give up poetry and become social workers—far from it. I think they should be writing in a wider and more truly innovative array of forms, and I am criticizing the range of cultural meanings that I see in the work. What do I mean by cultural meanings? Different languages and genres, incorporations of popular or noncanonical culture, gendered alternatives, historical engagements, social topographies, modes of subject formation, productive encounters with the world in all the forms in which it is presented—not a narrow window of textual effects that founds its community in a mutual commitment to deferred action in the horizon of language.

What's wrong with a lot of recent writing that wants to enact discrepancies of vocabulary, of formal procedure, of national context, of gendered cathexis, is that it merely hints in the direction of doing so; it is not fully engaged. When I listen to Detroit techno on the car radio driving the freeway downtown to work, I am really listening (watch out for traffic); perhaps I am listening to Björk. Here I would argue, as an act of cultural as well as literary criticism, for a synthesis, a syncretic assemblage, or even a reflection on the relation of cultural interest and literary form. Where writers often possess highly informed, nuanced registers of cultural information, I often do not see that knowledge interpreted in higher levels of organization than the horizon of the material text. Here, cris cheek's interpretation of the foundational English narrative of Robinson Crusoe in the linguistically disjunct performance text "Skin Upon Skin" is exemplary; the form of the work itself demands a processing of the themes of knowledge and discovery in a way that does not reinforce the empire's purview of the *tabula rasa* of colonial history. Robert Sheppard's use of sources from World War II, identifiable as such and conveying their unique cultural resistances, is another example of the construction of textual effects in ways that are richly informed by actual historical experience. Such complex motivations and critiques demand forms that are not simply reduced to monovalent textual effects. I would like to see the development of genres of writing in which cultural materials become more than signifying practices, in examples that enact a reconfiguration of literary form—a new sense of the "work"—specific to an engagement with their materials.

Where do I see such a reconfigured notion of the work? Often in writing that comes out of dialogues between collaborators, as in Lyn Hejinian and Carla Harryman's *The Wide Road* or the multiauthored collaboration that produced *Leningrad.* Often in works that rethink conventions of genre, particularly in relation to a politics of gender as in Robert Glück's *Jack the Modernist* and *Margery Kempe,* or in Kevin Killian's novels as well as in his often unbearable theatrical spectacles. Often in work that refuses to grant a national language a normative horizon, as with many U.K. writers, or that integrates dialectal differences in its unfolding cultural text, as in the work of Nathaniel Mackey and Harryette Mullen. Or in work that addresses itself to spaces between the literary and other arts, as in the performance-based work of Jackson Mac Low, Fiona Templeton, and Steve Benson. Often in writing that foregrounds the particular interests of the social codes it reconstructs, as in Rod Smith's *CIA Sentences* or Chris Tysh's "Dead Letters." Or in writing that calls into question the mode of visual display, as most recently in Ann Lauterbach's intervention in *American Poetry Review,* "The Night Sky" or Lisa Samuel's multitrack lyricism in some of the visual forms of *The Seven Veils.*[32] These projects are mentioned to support the specificity of what I am advocating: I want to see prospects for the "work" in a wider horizon, one not limited by the normative values of a universally defamiliarizing affect.

And I am not Georg Lukács; his moment of antagonism has been so thoroughly rewritten in postmodern critiques of modernism and its relation to modernity that it even has charm as a kind of historical relic, much like the display of defunct statues of Lenin and Stalin that open that piece of popular culture trash, *Goldeneye.*[33] I am simply asking that the range of a work's *literaturnost* be expanded to include more of the world as we know it. This work, as in the formal experiments of the Language School of an earlier period, should define a new location for cultural practice in the spaces abandoned between subject positions, disciplines, vocabularies, languages. We have been alternative in our ways of assembling texts; we should now assemble more cultural alternatives.

Notes

1. Barrett Watten, "Conduit," in *Frame (1971–1990)* (Los Angeles: Sun & Moon Press, 1997), 169.
2. Silliman discusses the cultural moment of "I hate speech" in Ron Silliman, "The Dysfunction of Criticism: Poets and the Tradition of the Anti-Academy," *Poetics Journal* 10 (June 1998): 179–94.
3. Jeff Derksen, "Where Have All the Equal Signs Gone: Inside/Outside the Language Site," in the present volume.
4. See, for example, André Breton's notion of the universal translatability of the Surrealist image/object, "Surrealist Situation of the Object," in *Manifestos of Surrealism,* trans. Richard Seaver and Helen R. Lane (Ann Arbor: University of Michigan Press, 1972), 255–78.
5. Charles Bernstein, "Poetics of the Americas," *Modernism/Modernity* 3, no. 3 (1996): 1–23; reprinted in Bernstein's *My Way: Speeches and Poems* (Chicago and London: University of Chicago Press, 1999), pp. 113–137. For a response, see Barrett Watten, "The Bride of the Assembly Line: From Material Text to Cultural Poetics," *Impercipient Lecture Series* 1, no. 8 (October 1997).
6. In August 1996, this team, led by [Derrick] Bailey, had just upset the American 4 x 100 relay team, led by [Carl] Lewis, in the Olympics.
7. Roland Barthes, *Writing Degree Zero,* trans. Annette Lavers and Colin Smith (New York: Hill and Wang, 1968), 88.
8. Cited in Peter Steiner, *Russian Formalism: A Metapoetics* (Ithaca, N.Y.: Cornell University Press, 1984), 23. See also Lee T. Lemon and Marion J. Reis, ed. and trans., *Russian Formalist Criticism: Four Essays* (Lincoln: University of Nebraska Press, 1965); and Victor Erlich, *Russian Formalism: History—Doctrine,* 3d ed. (New Haven: Yale University Press, 1981).
9. Steiner, *Russian Formalism,* 50.
10. Erlich, *Russian Formalism,* 181.
11. In Yury Tynyanov's 1929 statement, "The boundaries of literature and life are fluid," implying that genres previously considered as nonliterary in relation to cultural context may be seen as literary. This statement may be compared to the marked relativism of, even an indifference toward, context in Roman Jakobson's 1941 claim that "today anything can serve as material for a poem"—and so literature, by virtue of its independence from context, becomes a more static and fixed concept; ibid., 183.
12. Perhaps the importance of Jakobson's codification of Formalist insights was, not so much the "structure-in-dominance" of the autonomous work of art, but his extension of the material organization of art to the forms of a given culture. It is this reciprocity, on the one hand, that allows for a notion of "language" to emerge as the central concern of the "human sciences" in French Structuralism, and, on the other, that will eventually permit the work of art to be seen as the site for a cultural reflexivity.
13. Peter Middleton, "Imagined Readerships and Poetic Innovation in U.K. Poetry," in the present volume.

14. Robert Grenier, "On Speech," *This* 1 (1971): n.p.
15. Clark Coolidge, "A Page That Is Nothing But Words Written By Itself," *This* 8 (1977): 21–26.
16. A "world car" is transparent to all contexts: it can be produced at an assembly point in any country and satisfy all the regulatory and import/export requirements of that country. The literary obverse of a "world car" would be opaque in all contexts and thus generalize all forms of regulation in its univocal denial of them.
17. Lemon and Reis, *Russian Formalist Criticism,* 23.
18. It is unclear whether Eliot had arrived at the necessity of renouncing American citizenship when he portrayed his "young man carbuncular" as fumbling through a sex act whose degradation is precisely indicated when "she puts another record on the gramophone." Thematically, however, Eliot continued to be a firm upholder of the great divide between modernism and mass culture in both of his national identities.
19. For a wide-ranging account of the postwar politics of innovative writing in the United Kingdom, see Keith Tuma's review of *Out of Dissent: A Study of Five Contemporary British Poets,* by Clive Bush, and *Contemporary British Poetry: Essays in Theory and Criticism,* ed. James Acheson and Romana Huk in *Criticism* 40, no. 2 (1998): 313–22.
20. See particularly the recent anthologies, *Conductors of Chaos: A Poetry Anthology,* Iain Sinclair, ed. (London: Picador, 1996); and *Out of Everywhere: Linguistically Innovative Poetry by Women in North America and the UK,* Maggie O'Sullivan, ed. (London: Reality Street Editions, 1996). [Editor's Note: Grace Lake now publishes under the name Anna Mendelssohn.]
21. In John Mowitt, *Text: The Genealogy of an Anti-Disciplinary Object* (Durham, N.C.: Duke University Press, 1992), 117–40.
22. Coolidge, "A Page That Is Nothing," 21.
23. Clark Coolidge, *The Maintains* (San Francisco: This Press, 1974); Coolidge, *Polaroid* (Bolinas, Calif.: Big Sky Books, 1975); Ron Silliman, *Ketjak* (San Francisco: This Press, 1978); Silliman, *Tjanting* (Berkeley, Calif.: The Figures, 1981); Lyn Hejinian, *The Cell* (Los Angeles: Sun & Moon Press, 1992); Hejinian, *Oxota: A Short Russian Novel* (Great Barrington, Mass.: The Figures, 1991); Hejinian, *A Border Comedy* (New York: Granary Books, 2001); Barrett Watten, *Progress* (New York: Roof Books, 1985); Watten, *Under Erasure* (La Laguna, Sp.: Zasterle Press, 1991); Watten, *Bad History* (Berkeley, Calif.: Atelos Press, 1998); Bernadette Mayer, *Memory* (Berkeley, Calif.: North Atlantic Books, 1975); Bruce Andrews, *I Don't Have Any Paper So Shut Up (or, Social Romanticism)* (Los Angeles: Sun & Moon Press, 1992); Steve McCaffery, *The Black Debt* (London, Ont.: Nightwood Editions, 1989); Steve Benson, *Blue Book* (New York and Great Barrington, Mass.: Roof/The Figures, 1988).
24. Clark Coolidge, "Made Thought," *This* 1 (1971), n.p. The poem has not been reprinted in any collection of Coolidge's, to my knowledge.
25. While this cannot be developed further here, there is an important relation between the internal continuity of Vygotskian "inner speech" and the kind of continuity established by the authorial default to exterior language in poetry such as Coolidge's;

see L. S. Vygotsky, *Thought and Language,* ed. and trans Eugenia Hanfmann and Gertrude Vakar (Cambridge, Mass.: MIT Press, 1962).

26. A form of organization Raymond Williams was noticing, based on a close reading of the segmented form of a TV news program in his book *Television* at about the same time Coolidge wrote this poem and I published it; *Television: Technology and Cultural Form* (New York: Schocken, 1975).
27. Coolidge, *The Maintains,* 86.
28. Katharine M. E. Murray, *Caught in the Web of Words: James A. H. Murray and the Oxford English Dictionary* (Oxford: Oxford University Press, 1977).
29. Coolidge's jazz-based percussive drive may, in this sense, reinterpret Webster's dissenting monomania in making the dead letter of the national language come alive.
30. *Koyaanisqatsi* (1983), dir. Godfrey Reggio, uses time-lapse photography to give the impression of rapidly changing processes of a long duration, accompanied by a score by Philip Glass. In one scene, a power plant on the Navajo Reservation in Arizona seems to be devouring huge quantities of coal as it emits billows of ecologically unsound smoke.
31. "Twenty Languages" was the name of a boat anchored at a San Francisco waterfront tavern (the Mission Rock Resort) that many writers frequented in the 1970s and 1980s.
32. Michael Davidson et al., *Leningrad: American Poets in the Soviet Union* (San Francisco: Mercury House, 1991); Robert Glück, *Jack the Modernist* (San Francisco: Gay Men's Press, 1985); Glück, *Margery Kempe* (New York: High Risk Books, 1994); Nathaniel Mackey, *Djbot Bhaghostus's Run* (Los Angeles: Sun & Moon Press, 1993); Harryette Mullen, *Muse & Drudge* (New York: Tender Buttons; Philadelphia: Singing Horse Press, 1995); Fiona Templeton, *You—the City* (New York: Roof Books, 1990); and work by Rod Smith, Chris Tysh, and Lisa Samuels in *Poetics Journal* 10.
33. *Goldeneye* (1995), dir. Martin Campbell. The end of the Cold War provokes a textual crisis in the James Bond canon, indexed by the motif of statues of defunct Communists.

John Wilkinson

Too-Close Reading

Poetry and Schizophrenia

My opening discussion of two poems by John Wieners aims to identify some of the contradictions inherent in the term 'schizophrenic poetry', and to distinguish his writing from modernist and postmodernist verse which exhibits schizoid mannerisms. This will form the basis for some thoughts on the conduct of poetry.

Billie

He was as a god,
stepped out of eternal dream
along the boardwalk.

He looked at my girl,
a dream to herself and
that was the end of them.

They disappeared beside the sea
at Revere Beach as
I aint seen them since.

If you find anyone
answering their description
please let me know. I need them

to carry the weight of my life
The old gods are gone. What lives on
in my heart

is their flesh
like a wound,
a tomb, a bomb.

The poem starts in the theatre of memory, that 'eternal dream' which is repetition, where at last to forget is to make loss possible and real and to be restored to the flesh. This poet's reverie has spun him off as a god, promoted him as a girl, but while each has ontological priority over the residual self we know they are cultural archetypes too—the god may have his feet on the ground but the ground is symbolic language. Who is it says 'my girl'? Because the boardwalk, the ground on which the god steps, has been appropriated from popular song where such gods live, we can hear 'my girl' as another fragment ('Talkin' bout my girl')—the first person is inauthentic, the speaker insecurely located, in god and girl or nowhere.

Both god and girl become dreams to themselves in the look, in the stare; in meeting together they encounter their own inauthenticity and indeed their destiny, since 'that was the end of them' means not only their disappearance but the end to which boy-meets-girl always tends in this story. They are indeed the parents as well as the products of that speaking voice marked in the vernacular of 'I aint seen them since', the bridge line of the poem in its return to the poet's self whilst still shadowed by the typicality of what goes before. 'I' is born of the disappearance of the eternal figures which had conveyed it forth and time is restored.

This is why the final stanza of the poem has its uncanny effect, where the speaking voice is enucleated from the body in a rush, and the flesh which is contemplated from outside is the flesh of the dream-creatures. The dream-creatures are the matrix from which the self has been born, but that recognition is made through the violence of its repression—what is missing and denied and undeniably present in 'a wound, / a tomb, a bomb' is none other than the womb.

The poem courts and resists and flirts with schizophrenia, and in that lies its uncanniness; the poet's later schizophrenia might have been an identity-choice. The force of the poem arises from the tension between the exercise of an insistent control and the workings of its productive genera; what makes the poem could also unmake it as a poem, requiring such resourcefulness to keep it within bounds.

How well do I listen? The uncanniness I sense through close reading relies on my reading practice for its completion. Doesn't the poem's care depend on a pre-detachment, a camp displacing of affect into exemplary figures of suffering open to this linguistic investment and for which the title—which probably alludes to Billie Holliday—should sign an alert? Can I take the 'eternal dream' seriously? To read a poem in English from another culture and time facilitates my own projections; it may be I enact a paranoid apprehension of the poem as holy writ. But the poem is a gift, and if I am re-made by it I re-make it and its giver too; it answers my description.

. . .

What would a schizophrenic poem look like?

February
Cornhill Life
Art News

Textual exercises are examples to
reward proof that theatre pieces pertain to
human growth. Like for instance jewelry
in German jewry contain erotic imagery, see

Causeways provoke plantagenet gripes
as Richard the Lion-hearted's New York Times
in Londonderry Commonwealth bureau Town
from the Fire-escape to opera stars Boers.

How does this measure against the technical attributes of schizophrenic language as identified by Louis A. Sass—desocialization, automization and impoverishment? Desocialization is apposite to the second stanza: '. . . . language may sound telegraphic, as if a great deal of meaning were being condensed into words or phrases that remain obscure because the speaker does not provide the background information and sense of context the listener needs to understand'. The string of nouns and proper names following the verb 'provoke' is telegraphic. Automization is as strongly present in those '. . . tendencies for language to lose its transparent and subordinate status and to emerge instead as an independent focus of attention or autonomous source of control over speech or understanding'. 'Jewelry' produces or by its variant spelling anticipates 'jewry', and it is hard to account for 'Boers' except by association from jewellery to De Beers, the world's largest diamond dealers. The poem in its entirety might be a paste brooch, remembered out of February's theatrical experiences. Finally impoverishment, 'the single most distinctive feature of schizophrenic language, often manifest[ing] itself in utterances that sound, to many listeners, like "empty philosophizing", "fruitless intellectualizing", or "pseudo-abstract reasoning"' is marked in the poem's opening flourish, which for all its grandiosity might say little more than 'this poem shows what the theatre has meant to me'.

But 'pseudo-abstract' reasoning may be hard to distinguish from abstract reasoning; Freud granted as much at the close of his essay 'The Unconscious', writing ' . . . it must be confessed that the expression and content of our philosophizing . . . begins to acquire an unwelcome resemblance to the mode of operation of schizophrenics'. Returning with this in mind, I note how 'proof' and 'pieces' prepare for jewellery, and that the apposition of 'textual exercises' and the cold hardness of jewels gives poignancy to the assertion of their significance for 'human growth'.

So it may be legitimate to read the pell-mell names of the second stanza, a plain instance of words attaining a priority over their signifying function, as not so much a pathological symptom as indicative of the difficult relationship between 'textual exercises' and 'human growth'. Epithets such as 'plantagenet' and 'Lion-hearted' are adornments directing human growth—they must be lived up to, as must a commonwealth. These are the causeways of development. The relationship is ambiguous, for human growth may also be thwarted or compromised by names; after all the poem arrives under the sponsorship of the assurance company Cornhill Life and the journal of the fine art industry, *Art News*. Names may be erotically productive or sterile, as indeed 'human growth' may be reified as an objective of artistic practice or psychotherapy, or assume the dynamics of a political project. Or the poem may be making sardonic play with the pretensions that surround artistic products such as a Shakespearean drama or grand opera, with the opening clauses being deliberately pompous in their claim for art and the second stanza providing an example of the brilliant tawdriness of memory's constructs; what is retained may not be so spiritually improving as incidental to a social milieu—a gala evening reported in the *New York Times*; bejewelled dowagers. Such emphasis on what straight bourgeois culture regards as incidental is seriously camp; seriously so because it occasions the art of this poem and because in its love of illusion it is radically disillusioned, clear-sighted as to the commercial and social sponsorship. Even eroticism is subordinate as imagery in this scheme of things.

If nothing were known of the writer would this poem appear pathological or as a modernist literary work? Or is this a false binarism; could it be both? And what does it mean to describe language as 'an autonomous source of control over speech or understanding' when what is being considered is a poem rather than speech? Is it not true that to make a poem and to see it into print is to assert control over language? And how does the language of this poem sit with the preoccupations of Wieners' earlier verse?

Schizophrenia names a pathological process rather than a state of being; and just as in any act of poetical writing different levels of consciousness are involved, it is possible that in 'February' Wieners is deploying the language of his madness under conscious control, and for calculated literary purpose. There is evidence this may be so in the history of his extraordinary book *Behind The State Capitol: Or Cincinnati Pike* (1975) where poems as formally achieved as 'Billie' in their earlier magazine publication are flooded and swathed in schizoid language revelatory of the political, cultural and sexual matrix in which the poems had been conceived, disturbing irrevocably the originatory lyric self. But this visible process of massive decompensation—if that is what it is—may constitute evidence of schizophrenia's inconsistency and the ability of the poet to call on other resources to put any materials to effective poetic use; might not such late poems as 'February' be merely pathological and my reading an instance of misguided ingenuity? For the intentionalist fallacy has been succeeded by the intentionless fallacy, where any textual shard becomes grist to the critic's own hermeneutic compulsion.

What is striking about the late poems is their formal wit. In the poem examined, both vacuous orotundity and telegraphese, those first-rank linguistic symptoms, are reconciled in brief compass. What of the formal control, the stanzaic patterning, the skilled sound-fabric? Are these to be regarded as the the sad relics of the decades of previous work, behavioural automatism carrying away evacuated pathological matter in neat parcels? Or to turn away from the positive markers of schizophrenic language, what do the late poems of Wieners lack by comparison with 'Billie'?

In schizophrenia speech is textualised, and in text the written word disjoined from speech and the situated body. A similar disjunction is evident in the languages of business and bureaucracy. Competence in a formulaic language erasing the situatedness of the writer is a core skill for manager and academic alike; anyone who has worked for a large business organisation will know the expenditure of time on checking and revising written communication to expunge all trace of individual origin. The divorce of language from bodily speech leads to a flattening in tonal range as characteristic of the informational universe generally as of mandarin artistic practices. This applies also to the amateur and popular practice of poetry, where the formulaic determinants of what constitutes poetry tend to overcome the felt necessity for personal expression which impels people to write poetry. The irony is that play with a formulaic repertoire by a person with schizophrenia may be more controlled by intention than the formulaic verse of the amateur poet.

What is striking in 'February' is its poetically non-formulaic quality. The Wieners poem is the unmistakable product of a particular gay literary milieu, the Boston of John Wheelwright and Steve Jonas as well as Wieners; and what would appear to mark the poem as schizophrenic could be referred to as an idiolect—the poem could be 'transparent' to some readers, playing off shared cultural referents. The perils of mis-diagnosis of schizophrenia through ignorance of a patient's cultural and linguistic matrix are well-known, as is the ingenuity of the oppressed in linguistic resistance.

Poems which are demonstrative of schizophrenic language may be written by poets who, like Wieners, have suffered a psychotic illness, but by virtue of their individual artistry cannot therefore be considered schizophrenic products. This would not apply to transcribed speech as with some sections of *Behind the State Capitol*; but the control exercised by the poet over the selection of passages of transcribed speech and their disposition within the book as a whole, introduces an artistic purposiveness which also cannot be called schizophrenic.

Hence, the language of schizophrenia in poetic use could be consistent with the absence of schizophrenic process, whilst the absence of the language of schizophrenia and the deployment of an excessively conventional—which is to say, an anachronistic—repertoire of poetic phraseology may indicate active psychosis. The empty phrases into which the amateur poet invests his or her feeling are difficult to distinguish from the machine poems of the psychotic—except by their relative linguistic inertia, the dearth of twist or pun.

There is a possible diagnostic explanation for Wieners' manipulation of schizophrenic language and its alliance with camp, in the choice of a schizophrenic career by some severely hysterical individuals, especially men. Wieners works amidst the detritus of popular culture, the film and gossip journals which are exhausted before publication, a formulaic flux of a kind that the conventions of high art—such as the white page—simply disavow. To invest serious feeling into such material may be camp if it holds to the mythological figures; once the investment is made into names, identity may become distributed; the prosthetic star dissolves into the warp of the star-map.

Those sophisticated writers who are romantically inclined towards madness as a patent of excessive feeling are mistaken; rather, a hypertrophic self-consciousness characterises the language-games the schizophrenic plays at more than one remove with the conventional signifiers of excessive feeling. Those who would be dissolute in their language are not writing on the edge of madness but within a secure genre, either flirting with what is no more likely to harm them than ecstasy or following a strictly literary programme with conscious designs to 'subvert' the assumptions of ordinary speech or text. As ever with such designs, they tend to be more complicit with the culture with which they take adversarial issue than is apparent to their authors or their readership.[1] The eradication of the author in the mass media or in commercial texts is so far normative that the assertion of strongly marked personality in newspaper columns has become another factitious construct which the readership knows to be no more expressive of an individual than intimate lifestyle features on the famous. Commerce killed the author long ago: who writes Joan Collins?

The further paradox is that what may touch most fully is that writing which does not presume to share, which like the Wieners poem 'Billie' is of so perilous and personal an anticipation of dissolution. In the informational universe, communication starts with resistance. The impersonality of such poems is achieved by way of an almost unreachable innerness, become impersonal in the reader's connection with it. It does not set out to be unconventional or subversive, but is driven by a need as much for self-preservation as for expression, and in seeking self-preservation makes unbearable pain or joy impersonal and poetic. Such poetry is always stepping back from madness, and bringing away from madness the materials it requires and which it struggles to accommodate to the uses of a poem, seeking to make them less harmful. This is a very different motive from the gleeful wish to do harm to the reader (a sadistic fantasy which yearns for forgiveness and reconstitution) or to enjoin the reader in a giddy *folie à deux,* where the readers are connoisseurs of such strategies and subsume the text readily into the categories of those literary theories they espouse.

After Ashbery, much accomplished American poetry of the eighties sounded and looked like the epic of hypertrophic consciousness. It was schizoid in its blank control, but also relaxed, sampling and processing its own vagaries with amusement and relish of its extraordinary skill, its look-at-me negotiations; it had access to all areas and consumed indifferently. Revelling in the detachment of consciousness from the body and from coherent subjectivity, its tonal range from touristic to hedonistic was notably restricted. Like commerce talking to itself it was radically unsituated, but like commerce again required niche-marketing to make its readers feel special: there were variants for race, geography, sexual orientation but these were textual hooks; readers were reminded repeatedly and ingeniously that bodies and their activities are linguistically constructed, but did not the advertising industry know that long before poets? Because the 'I' is nowhere situated it is absolutely everywhere, not so much solipsistic as all-inclusive. Consider these recent lines by Charles Bernstein:

My bread has some nerve. No
sooner does it come out of the oven
than I have to slap it for being
so fresh. My head has some
curve. No sooner does it run for
the patio than the lights begin
to jam, the commotion dies down
in the corridor outside the
farm administration building.
Randy & Billy & Bob grab a Diet
Lite with a side of slope,
the nerve doctors convene for
an all-night session on breaking
the self-help habit. I'm okay
you're not worth the paper you're
printed on, or I'm in deep
trouble but you never came up
to the surface after that dive,
lo these many years ago.
—Boy that makes me mad. Madder
than a scratched eel at a
Crossing-Guard kettle-shoot, tireder
than a Bel Paese cheese at a
[. . . etc.]

Where to stop quoting when each line lends itself to a purpose so willing, whilst feigning to disavow purposiveness? Its skippiness is adorable, how jaunty phrase launches jaunty phrase, and its piling-on, its circling round the constellation of slap and slope and curve and dive and nerve, bright and breezy and laughing in the shallows. This Saussurian playground of difference where every phrase is of equivalent value—the same in weight, the same in infra-referentiality—recalls Freud's anticipation of Saussure in his essay on 'The Unconscious': 'Moreover, by being linked with words, cathexes can be provided with quality even when they represent only *relations* between presentations of objects and are thus unable to derive any quality from perceptions'. What is the poem about but to demonstrate this in a *healthy* way, dissolving the self-construct in an aerobic linguistic workout. There is something of the programmatic schizoid poem about this passage with its head running away and curving; as Freud writes, 'Here the schizophrenic utterance exhibits a hypochondriac trait: it has become "*organ-speech*"'.

Bernstein's poem is notable for its all-over affective investment, steady tone, and the paradoxical foregrounding of the authorial or the reading self inevitable when referentiality is lifted and attention rests on the self-constitutive operations of language. Everything is then referred back to the constitutive and constituted writer and reader—the first person and the last person, whose pronouns are batted from phrase to phrase in a ping-pong set of reassignments.[2]

There is a long way between what I discover or conceive as the identity perils of Wieners' 'Billie' and the teasing, laid-back lines of Bernstein. 'Billie' is an envelope of semantic anxiety radiating from a point of unbearable tension, torn between concession to 'the predominance of what has to do with words over what has to do with things', a catastrophic decompensation, an unhoming which beckons in the final stanza and is resisted in suppression of the word 'womb'; and on the other hand the saving knot of experience, however linguistically transformed, which must be integrated and contained so the poem—and the poet—should be at all.

For me Wieners anticipates a poetry which does not set out with programmatic design but negotiates the torn halves, seeking to mobilise the lyric voice both inaccessibly personal and beyond individuality in full apprehension of the near-fatal fouling of the lyric source by self-consciousness, the felt knowledge of the linguistic constitution of the self, the felt necessity for accepting and making positive a defamed social identity. Writing a determinedly gay, transvestite poetry, publishing in gay journals as well as in the canonical journals and anthologies of postmodernist poetry, Wieners' poetic practice has wrested from the disintegrative attacks of schizophrenia poems of exquisite poise. Lyric poetry unhomes and yearns for home.

But there is no home to which to return; indeed, once to have left home is to see home razed, and to travel linguistically as the gaseous plasma from which physical form is but an evanescent and reactive precipitate. Mass is disposed evenly in linguistic space, cathected into provisional selfhoods, drifting towards coherent texture. The texture of 'the real' is now one of unassimilated knowledge, an overabundance made coherent by the ever-emergent individual's restlessly connective activity across promiscuously assorted domains. Bernstein's poem reminds us by its access to all areas—as does a truly great poem, Stephen Rodefer's *Four Lectures*—that everything does return home to the land of the free. Such poetry may be gold, of a density impenetrable to all but the adept, and script also, of a vapidity unfiltered by intention or for practical use. For if merely contingent and self-replicatory, poetry reduces to exemplars of the act of poeticizing, to the flutterings of the linguistic fabric as it passes through one node, one consciousness, and asserts its ceaseless coming into being. Are the only effective skills management and counselling, both of them heedless of the specifics of experience and substituting for conversation and memory—but drained of content and positivistic? Out of unbearable complexity and quantity can one but focus on inputs, activity levels or outcomes? Making gold from air: that is schizophrenic if you like.

Poetry must refuse to acquiesce in this dis-valency. Wieners' poetic practice in despite of schizophrenia has something to teach all who write with and against a schizo-saturated culture. There is a pulse in his arresting lyric poetry between a linguistic productivity, with its straining away from object-perception, and a reintegrative movement which returns to situated identity in the body. The hypertensiveness is registered in a language breathing and physical, which must stay close to the rhythm of exchange in order to not buckle into self-referential incoherence, an extreme of attention to its own processes which would yield to madness.

Identity has become distributed through metaphor. What makes the matter of poetry is connectivity rather than reference; but what charges the connectivity, what cathects the links other than forms of identification secured to powerful objects whether of love or of broader social construction? Indeed poetic identity increasingly is composed of multiple pronouns, of part-people whose intersection and interaction develop a populace, deposing both the regal author and the puppet persona. But these figures are not the only alternatives to dissolution; a situated if transcursive reintegration can allow us the sense of a possible instrumentality amongst others.

To read such work is to become entrammelled as though the white noise of information stopped, acquired weight, and it were possible to inhabit it a while and for that to be bearing and bearable and even beautiful. Weltering particularity is reknit like a bolus, a catch in the throat, restarting the intersubjectivity which produces the world and the traveller through it as preciously, temporarily coherent and inseparable. If unhoming language in its yearning for home tends to be accompanied by sadistic fantasies seeking restoration of belief in the full being of the other, much postmodernist writing could be taken as poignant in its violence on the reader.

I have used these poems unfairly as stalking horses for my self-reproaching and hopes; and just as my close reading of Wieners is facilitated by a studied dyslexia, my reading of Bernstein takes the rhetoric which announced his verse at its word and ignores, for instance, a different filiation from O'Hara which would preclude my typically British moralising.[3] I think my rhetorical hopes describe what has been called identity poetics in the writing of Lyn Hejinian and Lisa Robertson; and Stephen Rodefer's poems are charged with a consciousness of the absurd wager of lyric poetry after the dissolution of the subject, and make it notwithstanding. These are poets who know both lyric control and lyric abandon, the necessary systole and diastole, to be anachronistic, but work nonetheless by such means in the informational miasma—as programmers say, making choices among local destinies. Being well-spoken I'm hardly one to talk.

Notes

1. See Bob Perelman's contribution to this volume for a more developed distinction between writing as institutionalised 'subversion' and writing of social power.
2. Barrett Watten took this reading of Bernstein as exemplary of British snobbery in the face of mass culture; cf. his contribution to the present volume: 'One notes, as an English index to *literaturnost,* a generally unutterable horror of mass culture in the British context'. 'One notes' tends to announce an unsupported statement in academic discourse; one did note however that the earlier discussion of Wieners and popular culture preceded Mr Watten's arrival in the seminar room.*
3. In her contribution to this volume Lisa Robertson implies by way of rejoinder to an essay of mine that moral considerations are inimical to thought. In order to do so she converts moral questions (as cited) into moralising. In her essay the questions have prompted thought more interesting and instructive than such strictures.

Acknowledgments

This paper is particularly indebted to Sass, L., *Madness and Modernism,* Harvard University Press 1994, and benefited also from comments by Drew Milne and D.S. Marriott on an earlier version.

* Editor's note: The wording has changed slightly in Watten's essay, which now reads "We may note . . . " (351).

Other references

Bernstein, C., from 'The Manufacture of Negative Experience', *Salt* 8, Applecross: Western Australia, 1996, pp. 106–112.

Freud, S., tr. Strachey, 'The Unconscious' in Freud, *On Metapsychology,* Harmondsworth: Penguin Freud Library vol.11, 1984, pp. 159–222.

Freud, S., tr. Strachey, 'The "Uncanny"', in Freud, *Art and Literature,* Harmondsworth: The Penguin Freud Library vol. 14, 1985, pp. 335–376.

Wieners, J., ed. Foye, R., *Selected Poems 1958–1984,* Santa Barbara: Black Sparrow, 1986.

Bob Perelman

Polemic Greeting to the Inhabitants of Utopia

[Since I gave this paper in New Hampshire in 1996 I have been surprised at the reactions it provoked. I was taken to be advocating a return to conventional writing and to be dismissing any value for innovation. I hope that such reactions are injudicious and that when this is read I will be heard to be urging consideration of the social aspects of our materials at all levels of composition. Such considerations don't make the need for innovative writing any less urgent.]

. . .

I want to make a case for syntactic and rhetoric effects which have been systematically denigrated in Language writing and poststructuralist contexts over the past few decades. Or—since the terms for these effects are finally little more than crude generalizations that have assumed dogmatic profiles—perhaps I simply want to make a case against the case against them. Among these dogmatic terms are transparency; habit; coherence of person, subject, voice; narrative; grammaticalness: the case against such things has assumed foundational status for a whole range of antifoundational writing and critique. These real sources of social—and hence poetic—relevance are being overlooked—at least, in our poetics; in practice we use them all the time.

Instantly I need to make clear what I am not saying. I am not arguing for anything like the status quo in poetry—I have not suddenly lost faith in the range of innovative work that has shaped and spurred my writing mind. Stein remains more interesting than Housman. I am not saying that innovative writing is no longer necessary. But there is now a great deal of fractured reference and syntactic displacement that, to me at least, does not seem particularly innovative.

What I want to say is suspended between the specific and provisional (attackable) and the theoretical (impervious). I mean more than that these effects can be useful in specific poems. That kind of ad hoc advice can be subsumed under fashion tips: disjunction and opacity are getting a little long in the tooth;

try connectedness. Such a cynical view can be derived from a reading of Paul Mann's *The Theory-Death of the Avant-Garde.*[1] Mann notes that there is a market in Dada items, and that the mainstream sooner or later picks out some incomprehensibilities of the avant-garde to make provocative taste-treats in normative salads; he concludes that the avant-garde can be described as the design research laboratory for the taste-factories of advanced capitalism. If this is so, then the twists and turns necessary to stay ahead of the consuming maw of the mainstream may well push writing that wants to stay innovative back near older modes and effects, with whatever novel aspects and adjustments. Examples would be Pound and Eliot turning back to rhymed quatrains in "Hugh Selwyn Mauberley" and *Ara Vos Prec;* Ashbery's use of conversation-tones after the disjunction of *The Tennis Court Oath,* etc.

To move things a little closer to the present, one could note a decrease in fragmentation, and an increase in complete sentences and discernible narrative structures or gestures in the recent work of Language writers. This is arguable, depending on the examples picked; nor do I mean it in a crudely statistical way. But compare Lyn Hejinian's *Oxota* with her *Writing is an Aid to Memory* or Barrett Watten's *Bad History* with his *1–10*. In the later works, the person of the author exists without raising any epistemological blister; description, narrative, unproblematized turns of phrase are fully in evidence. These do not delimit the range of the writing, but they are there and, in fact, allow a wider range of effects to exist. At a glance, the immediate surface of the writing may look more stable, but the social variety of the writing is greater. The writing is not tamer. I am not making the circular argument that Language writers are being absorbed into the mainstream and that their work reflects this. I am opposing the standard (and circular) poststructuralist celebrations of subversion; I want to make the case that contact with familiar social structures in language is a crucial element for politically and poetically ambitious writing. That's "contact with," not "slavish reproduction of," these (extremely complex) social structures.

This equation of social power (which involves social intelligibility—the familiar) with poetic value challenges much of our poetics. We are used to the equation going the other way, with evidence of social adaptation and prestige equaling enslavement to ruling ideologies. The equation is less clear in any positive sense, i.e., that social marginality produces good poetry, though Maria Damon's *The Dark End of the Street*[2] argues this fairly explicitly. She studies vanguard writing that has emerged from the social margins, and it is, to compress her assumptions, more valuable.

But this argument, if it is pursued in too logical a vacuum, can get problematic quickly. Damon argues passionately and convincingly for an unusual collection of specific writers who are almost never linked, from Robert Lowell to Jack Spicer to Bob Kaufman to literarily anonymous teenage girls from a

Southie housing project in Boston. The perspective of her book is not purely sociological and its point is not to level literary evaluation. Spicer's and Kaufman's poems are good because of their verbal capacities to bear witness to a wide variety of social conditions. The housing project poetry offers the greatest challenge to literary evaluation of whatever stripe, since these poems seem at first glance to be cobbled together out of the clichés of mass culture. But Damon argues that the particular poems are good—i.e., that they are witty and socially perspicacious acts of critique in dialogue with their immediate contexts, and that if we enlarge our reading habits, what at first reads as compulsive ideological repetition can be read as poetic work against it.

The positive side of the equation, then, is tricky, and quickly bumps into assumptions of individual talent, communal talent, flexibility, adroitness, heroism, genius—exemplariness at whatever level we want to posit it. But usually the equation is expressed in the negative: socially valorized communication is, as far as poetry is concerned, regressive reinforcement of the status quo. What the mystified liberal or smug conservative reader sees as engrossing content purveyed through transparent and powerfully harmonic, undissonant language, radical critique sees as the naked balls and chains of ideology, elastic and insidiously self-reproductive.

Against this globalized enemy we have wielded and celebrated various avant-garde, anti-instrumental anti-tools that have been justified by claims for readerly freedom, perceptual reinvigoration, making it new, defamiliarization; justified also by senses that there are fresher strata in language less contaminated by complicities with master narratives. Again, the negative proscriptions are more particular than the positive prescriptions. It is easier to specify the workings of the material-textual, paralogical, cross-generic explosives to be thrown into the citadels filled with naive, overly compliant, ideologically hypnotized readers—so many! I had not thought false consciousness had beguiled so many!—than it is to specify the invigorating effects of making it new, making it strange and how such effects will come to pass, either within the individual, or in society. Are increased readerly perception, toned-up ethics, strengthened sympathies, more accurate cognitive and social mapping all future benefits? Do they involve mediation: teaching, criticism? Or is writing considered straightforward social information available to a general public, a literal map, a specific set of ethical or political guidelines? Unless the effect of writing is considered to be immediate, a position I find ultimately mystificatory—after all, every reader was once illiterate and every reader's taste has undergone changes—then even the most uncompromising shock tactics need civic planning to effect lasting results.

These are hard times to believe in a future that won't be sheer social entropy. But the material difficulties aren't spread out evenly; there are degrees of insulation and relative autonomy. Many innovative writers write in those privileged interstices; but if the writing stays there, it withers. Outside the poetic fields, language matters, too, as specifically as it does within poetry polemics. And the results of these conflicts are of course more brutal. Witness a recent picture in the paper: a restaurateur tangled in barbed wire separating Turks and Cypriots, being kicked to death, while some UN police, in the random, instantaneous parataxis of photography, stood nearby behind shields bearing the insignia "POLIS."

"Polis / is this" ends one of Charles Olson's most ecstatic poems with a cry that claims private poetic realization gives simultaneous birth to community (polis).[3] For those who know the poem, the pun is brutal. In the *New York Times* photograph, polis is this: foundational, identitarian, rigid with solidarity, silenced, exploited, enraged, mediated, photographed, edited, produced, paginated, collaged with other stories. Our poetic pages, wrinkled and creased as they are, are calibrated if not constituted by their distance from the *Times*. Our poetry is new, but is it news? And to whom?

The future is crucial in any act of writing, and yet the future may be exceedingly indifferent to any given poem, single body of work, or literary tendency. The butterfly effect—that the one flap of a butterfly's wings in China may cause a tornado in New York—is a convenient daydream for writers. At any rate, it posits a relation to the future that is in complete contrast to the one I am worrying over here. According to it, intention has no effect on the future. And it's clearly true that even the most intention-driven writer is working if not worshipping quite near such a shrine since the difference in scale between page and world is so huge, and intention can only stretch so far. Perhaps this is why criticism has such power: criticism is implicitly about the future of a given poem or way of writing. All of our works are written on future pages. No one wants the words he or she is writing to remain on the particular screen or page of their birth. They should appear on other pages or screens. Criticism addresses the fact of these other pages.

I'll cite a few examples that are well-known—at least in our circles. The first is from Charles Bernstein's "Living Tissue / Dead Ideas," an essay that attacks the "rule of always-already formulated concepts, habits of agreement running roughshod over newly formulating vistas. Call it a *necroidiocracy,* ideas stiffened by rigor mortis wounding flesh with their rigidity and technorationality: the arrogance of logic and the perniciousness of the 'common-sense' stereotype, each disguising its biases in the shadows of its neutrality."[4] Here the living flesh of writing is set against the killing-field file cabinets of intellectual bureaucracies. This is in the present. As for the future: "Perhaps we can reinterpret Pound's remark that poets are the antennae of the race to mean ideas embodied in poetry construct a new polis in the site of the old: no longer postponed, *enacted*. Then poetry's pealing would be a toll from that 'other' world calling for its truth to be established in *this* one" (379). There is a tension here between "a new polis" and an "enacted" one, between future and present. A reader has to already believe in the new polis to hear those peals as "truth"; and perhaps has to have read Olson and to know what "polis" refers to in order to want to believe.

In the following excerpt from Rachel Blau DuPlessis's *The Pink Guitar,* the present and the future are mixed. What DuPlessis sees as an emergent literary matrix is a blueprint for a creolized cultural and social future that is more equitable and active.

> And the language? Nathaniel Mackey . . . has proposed . . . "calibanization": . . . a . . . self-conscious multi-linguality, choice of patois, dialect, neologisms, puns, technical jargon of specific work-based groups (teachers, dancers, mothers), all mingled in a kind of macaronic or pastiche—both of these terms reanimated with the most serious and aggressive concern, and losing their clownish, motley, implications. I see a language broken into. One whose capacities to represent "transparently" can no longer be credited, but whose connotive, denotive and textural powers must be engaged. . . . [A] multi-poly-mishuganah set of discourses is set into play to explore and enact our crossings. The language of poetry is the language of anything: taboo words, grunts, babytalk, "French."[5]

Language as material, sonic utopia; and language as privileged site of coalition-building; saying no to hierarchies of taste and correctness; positing cosmopolitan and multicultural mixes: these hopes and positions are influential for good reason. They posit a wider democratic field of action for writing, and certainly they open up more intriguing compositional possibilities for the writer. But these possibilities are not endless, nor are they autonomous with respect to our positions in the contemporary social multiverse. The wide social field that is so often traversed *within* our writings, via sound, word, phrase, collage, does not mean that our writings circulate through anything like that same wide field. There is—and has long been—a rather circumscribed place set aside for utopic embodiments, ideological demolition-derbies: the poetry corner, a large, seemingly infinite place with room for tremendous vistas of activity, ecstatic certainty, alienation and resentment, but where, all too often, as Bourdieu points out, one's competitors are one's only customers.[6]

David Simpson, in *The Academic Postmodern and the Rule of Literature,*[7] makes a convincing demonstration of how pervasive the trope of "poetry" is across a wide spectrum of academic disciplines. Not poetry as a specific practice, exactly, and certainly not the kinds of poetry that go under the name of innovative writing. It is a more generalized sense of "poetry" as authentic local detail, where difference can exist without being crushed under the weight of panoptical totality. It is a generalized but utterly contained utopianism that is similar to the tropes I'm saying we shouldn't be relying on so automatically. A few representative examples: Laclau and Mouffe argue against the "Jacobin imaginary" of master theoretical narratives and for "the infinite intertextuality of emancipatory discourses in which the plurality of the social takes shape"; Judith Butler speaks of gender as "a complexity whose totality is permanently deferred" and calls for "an open coalition . . . without obedience to a normative telos of definitional closure"; Richard Rorty's ideal of conversation is most embodied in the poet, whom we should see as "the maker of new words, the shaper of new languages, as the vanguard of the species" (97–8); Clifford Geertz describes anthropology as literary, "like trying to read [a manuscript] full of ellipses, incoherences" (122). Stephen Tyler calls for an ethnography that returns "to the original context and function of poetry which, by means of its performative break with everyday speech, evoke[s] memories of the *ethos* of the community." The ethnographer takes part in the "cooperative story making" of a "polyphonic text," which must be fragmentary; it "creates its own objects in its unfolding and the reader supplies the rest."

This sounds close to much of our poetics. Simpson comments that "the superficially anarchistic poetic paradigm" is "not so far removed from the liberal poetic paradigm." Both offer the "traditional release and return cycle by way of the somatic, cathartic, and figurative resources of the aesthetic experience" (130–31). Such appeals to a socially open textuality are imaginary solutions to real problems.

In the contemporary world where our writing has its *unheimlich* home, there are specific poetry venues, watersheds of prestige; the universities; poets who hate universities; professors who may read the occasional poem—a complex, contradictory social terrain. Any kind of poetry has to contend against the contemporary visual and aural entertainment-political climate where speed is the dominant value. Movie previews cutting-to-the-chase-and-whiting-out-the-context; sound bites; half-second fashion slashes, whether of cars, bodies, fashion goods, or food. This climate is profoundly hostile—or worse, indifferent—to the complex layerings of verbal work, to writing. In the worlds of art, poetry has a minor spot, in which, too often, it erects bite-size monuments to beauty and sententiousness. We fight against these with our work, our anger and our boredom, which can flash up furiously in less than a second when the wrong tone is privileged.

Along with an almost animistic celebration of the natural world, Mr. Heaney has consistently emphasized the physicality of English words. In "The Spirit Level" he asks us to *Hoard and praise the verity of gravel. / Gems for the undeluded. Milt of earth. / Its plain, champing sound against the shovel / Soundtests and sandblasts words like "honest worth."*

The Anglo-Saxon pith of "gravel" and "milt" rubs shoulders with the biblical and Latinate "verity." And notice the satisfying consonant rhyme of "gravel" and "shovel," and the elegant music of the feminine half-rhymes "soundtests" and "sandblasts" tucked into the last line. If you can't hear the "champing song" when shovel digs into gravel, you don't have ears.

The transcendence the reviewer wants to grant here is actually the site of Seamus Heaney's conflicted conscience. The impulse toward universalism troubles Heaney at many violent border crossings. How to differentiate such universalisms from the social intelligibility I am advocating here? Does all intelligibility that extends beyond aesthetically homogeneous local poetry contexts have to involve compromise, and then, slippery-slope-wise, bad faith and other ethical slurs? How to speak across aesthetic, linguistic and economic borders is the crucial issue which undoes any mastery that may be claimed for any specific poetics.

I have ears, and I hear "soundtests" and "soundblasts" as evidence of modernity, big machines, sound studios, endlessly propagating media that completely undercut the homely, autonomous labor of the shoveler. The "verity" and "milt" that the reviewer points out make sonic claims on two standbys of cultural authority: race and the Bible. I looked up "milt": it's fish sperm. No real surprise there: like capers and lemon, sperm combines flawlessly with "Anglo-Saxon," that racialized noise where a ruling class has for centuries seen history and nature marry producing hegemony out of a predestined past. The review of Heaney ends: "Anyone who reads poetry has reason to rejoice at living in the age when Seamus Heaney is writing."[8]

The reviewer's degree of sycophancy is painful; I've picked on it because it is representative of much of what I couldn't take when I was learning to write: coercion, mystification. But it will not finally be useful to simply other it. Angry, irritated, alienated registration of social power and prestige is common to all our literary activities—reviewing, syllabus-making, bookstore choices, writing. There is no aspect of writing or of poetics that is not saturated with instantaneous social thinking. Whether it's a question of reputation (Arnoldian or transgressive); whether the writing reinforces ideological solidarities or prefaces the most distant utopias, readers are acted on, allegiances are proposed, both between social groups and within warring or pacified selves of individual readers.

At any point, writing acts through complex species of identification. If identification is taken to imply a striving for an unassailable identity then it can be endlessly derided, and has been in innovative poetics—voice, mystification, false consciousness, the Oedipal/Lacanian shaggydog joke "That's me." But a more provisional kind of identification—or a quickly shifting series of provisional identifications—is crucial for any act of reading. No transformation of the reader takes place except through identification with the temporal priority of the writer. The new (which needs to be socially enacted, argued with) emerges from the familiar. The emergence itself need not be coercively or blandly familial. Call this social intelligibility. Any new condition needs to be made out of the conventional materials of the old. These materials have to be utterly conventional or they would not be linguistic. The writer's materials involve stretching habits of agreement: letters, words, speech genres, rhythms that touch on groups, classes. Disruptive gestures, if they are too autocratic in ignoring these habits, can too easily be swept into preexisting poetry corners all too instantaneously.

I have heard paradise within words and I have read utopia in language. To many, paradise and utopia are idealist, or at least evanescent, unavailable, displaced into future or past by the blare and drone of ideology coating all our words and their couplings, sunderings, rearrangements. But both perfections lie within language and can be grasped, can be specified. They are historical geographies, inhabited by speakers and writers. Traffic signs, quite like ours, are in use there, though they are not always obeyed. Cars drive down roads, transforming fuel to smoke. Territories are fenced, and the boundaries are in dispute. Reports of paradise being inhabited by a single naked couple or utopia by a rapt individual or communal consciousness are delusive. They have newspapers there, weather, sports and propaganda. It is quite crowded, overcrowded in fact. There are huge populations; the numbers are stuporous. Fantastic masses, liberal and fanatic, starving and indolent, make an environment that is overwhelmingly present. Restaurateurs momentarily tangled in barbed wire strung along political boundaries are kicked to death because of their accent or their grandparents' accent. Lessons in violence, waste, systematic consequence and systematic chaos abound. Desire reflects and refracts endlessly, welling up in each locally wedged person, making walls that are often quickly shared, walls and malls, toll roads, cities, airports; the plastic possibilities seem endless, though in all cases they are utterly enlaced in properties of matter: iron can float, cotton can kill. Language there is a shortcut to the infinite, often forming slogans in reaction, and forming social bonds strong beyond belief.

Notes

1. Paul Mann, *The Theory-Death of the Avant-Garde* (Bloomington: Indiana University Press, 1991).
2. Maria Damon, *The Dark End of the Street* (Minneapolis: University of Minnesota Press, 1993).
3. Charles Olson, *The Maximus Poems* (Berkeley: University of California Press, 1983), 185.

4. Charles Bernstein, *Content's Dream* (Los Angeles: Sun & Moon Press, 1986), 364. Subsequently cited in the text.
5. Rachel Blau DuPlessis, *The Pink Guitar* (New York: Routledge, 1990), 155.
6. See Pierre Bourdieu, *The Field of Cultural Production* (New York: Columbia University Press, 1993), especially the first chapter.
7. David Simpson, *The Academic Postmodern and the Rule of Literature* (Chicago: University of Chicago Press, 1995). Subsequent page references given in the text.
8. Richard Tillinghast, "Poems Into Ploughshares," *New York Times Book Review,* July 21, 1996, 6.

Rod Mengham

After Avant-gardism

Her Weasels Wild Returning

Her Weasels Wild Returning (Equipage, 1994) has a texture that is subtly different from that of J. H. Prynne's earlier work. Perhaps the most prominent feature of this new writing is its powerful cohesiveness. As expected, there is a complicated array of registers, but this complication does not present the reader with an experience of jarring unevenness, with the problem of a lack of fit between different vocabularies and conceptual frameworks. Discrepancies of this sort were central to the experience of reading Prynne in the '70s and '80s, but with *Weasels* the case seems quite otherwise. Two of the most important words in the text are in fact 'even' and 'evenly', and it seems that the further the reader progresses with the poem, the more she or he is likely to acquire the sense that the poetry is trying to 'even out' the differences between separate discursive formations and their specific agendas.

In the '70s and '80s, a collision of registers had been used to relativize individual cognition and the individual apprehension of data in respect of those macro- and micro-processes determining the various levels at which individual subjectivity gets formed. Moreover, discursive heterogeneity had always been posed with reference to at least the last remaining traces of an ebullient colloquialism, drawing into itself and illuminating with an extraordinary vividness the vectors of a social politics. In other words, the organizing strategies of individual consciousness, lodged in the routines of a speaking voice, were all there, overlapping with, or competing with, or being side-lined by, or being controlled by, the interests of various discursive projects. One crucial point was that, despite the constant threat of being pulverised, it was nonetheless a challenged individualism that remained somewhere near the centre of attention. The range of tones and rhythms encountered in reading were ultimately orientated towards the speaking voice, towards the resonance of lyric, towards a proverbial roundness of phrase, towards a gleefully impacted slang.

This just is not so with *Weasels.* With the exception of one or two fragments, it is composed in a language which resolutely and systematically excludes any phrasing that retains the balances and tensions we would normally be able to detect in the manner of a speaking voice. What we get instead is not a discursive free-for-all filling the vacuum—not an intensifying of fracture and dispersal—but, off-puttingly, a weirdly concerted texture, that works hard to make the separate parts of the whole comply with one another. The language is more bizarre than ever, but it is also more heavily synthesised, more systematically correlated, simply more commensurable.

As a rule, cohesion figures in Prynne's work either in terms of its ideological shortcomings, or in terms of an intimated comprehensiveness that cannot be grasped cognitively but which is alluded to in an approach to a renewed version of the sublime (which is what I assume is at stake in *The Oval Window*). In *Weasels,* comprehensiveness is completely earth-bound and incorporated by means of technique, although that technique pivots around the cultivation of routines that concentrate on deranging the usual relations of the most ideologically neutral words such as prepositions.

In Tarkovsky's science fiction film *Solaris,* the scientists left on the deep space research station are driven mad by having to cope with a life form that simulates in material form their own desires and fears. It is a near perfect mimicry, but it differs from terrestrial life forms in its underlying structure, which is not nuclear but neutrinal. I draw this analogy to try to find a way into *Weasels,* because it is a text which in a sense replicates the concerns of Prynne's other works, but which diverges crucially from them in terms of its fundamental language structures.

Many of Prynne's texts have returned repeatedly to the conceptual alternatives that stem from the conditions of settlement and nomadism in order to reflect on the origins of those social relations that arise with the creation of money economies and the establishment of property relations. Certain texts, like *Aristeas* and *News of Warring Clans,* have taken as their scenario the nomad community, or have imagined the nomad's attitude towards community. Others, while not going that far, have worked with the relevant verbal collocations, in trying out, or borrowing for tactical purposes, the nomadic point of view in order to reap the advantages of an estranged, displaced perspective on the systems of values that derive ultimately from settlement.

In *Weasels,* there is the same basic tension that lies behind the alternatives of settlement and nomadism, but it is not imprinted with the same pattern of validation, with the same distribution of gains and losses. Settlement is figured in intensely domesticated terms, while the nobility of transit, the enhancement of spirit formerly almost guaranteed by the nomadic option, is now jettisoned and replaced by stark alternatives, both equally dispiriting. One is the enforced flight of the refugee, for whom transit represents painful uprooting, for whom wandering is figured as a compulsion to 'escape', for whom being unsettled is seen as nothing more positive than a movement *between* conditions of safety and protection. And the other is an inauthentic form of transculturalism figured in the poem by international air travel as a social ritual with its own symbolic language. The sarcastically drawn parallels and contrasts between these two forms of 'flight' are introduced on the first page in the notion of the 'escape drill', that little pantomime performed by the air steward at the start of the flight. The drill encodes the idea of survival into a routine whose repetition works almost to ensure indifference to the meaning of 'escape', and which can even be thought of as providing a peculiar form of reassurance.

There are references throughout the poem to aviation, to flight calls, to the departure lounge, but it is on the final page that these references are most obviously insistent. Appropriately enough, they help to create the conditions of a 'return flight' for a poem which announces in its title the necessity to reflect on the ambiguities of return, on flight to and from a wild, uninvested, unhoused condition. In the poem as a whole, movement outwards is repeatedly conceived of in terms of impulsive, precipitate, even rash, behaviour. Movement away from base involves a 'dash' outwards, while movements of return involve connotations of reluctance, of aimlessness. Coming 'back' is what you do for want of anything better; return involves a form of 'straying'.

Of course, it is the other reference in the title—or rather, one of the other references—to female agency, which allows me to question the motivation for choosing to create such a strangely synthetic language for the purposes of this text. The most obvious thing about *Weasels* is the avidness of the attention it pays to the feminine pronoun and its politics. The sense of extreme urgency and anxiety that pervades the whole poem really hinges on the obstacles to comprehension that characterize the attempt to find out what 'she' really sees, hears, thinks, feels and knows, and whether she grasps what he sees, hears, thinks, feels and knows. These inquiries are typically intensified by modifiers, such as 'really', 'exactly': 'what did she *really* see', 'what . . . for her was / it *exactly'* [my emphases]: and by signs of the speaker yielding to impatience: '*can't* she see', '*won't* she notice' [my emphases].

The focus for this problematic, the one most consistently worried at, is the status of 'observation', perception, vantage, which should come as no surprise to readers of Prynne's earlier works, which question so profoundly the nature of vantage in various contexts. In synthesising his language around an apparent barrier of mutual incomprehension between masculine and feminine, and around the conditions of what the poem itself refers to as that particular kind of 'self difference', Prynne provides a paradoxical means of approach towards something like an authentically 'synoptic' account of contemporary experience. (The word 'synoptic' occurs on p. 5.)

The poem's figuring of social relations is almost entirely devoted to the symbiosis of masculine and feminine agents. Larger units are referred to, but are represented as fundamentally unstable and evanescent, even oxymoronically self-cancelling: movement of the symbiotic pair towards the larger unit is characteristically an approach 'towards / the rally diminished'. Going in the other direction, the disengagement of the symbiotic pair only shows up on the scale at the level of the construction of the single cell: 'Pick your own cell for mean / further'. Between these two extremes, the symbiotic pair is at the centre of a host of transactions, a full variety of predications of social maintenance involving the dividing and combining of various kinds of resources, mapping the relation in economic and cultural terms, and not least in terms of the history of literature (there's a series of multilingual puns on the idea of 'letters', splitting it up into masculine and feminine traditions).

So what I am suggesting is that the peculiarly powerful abstractness of the language in *Weasels* represents an attempt to deterritorialize both masculine and feminine, not by neutralizing their differences, but by at least proposing to equalize them; by demonstrating how the only viable *terra nullius,* previously unoccupied, unsettled, unowned, is one that can be projected in a synoptic language that shows remarkably little interest in either *écriture feminine* or the masculine tradition.

But it is precisely the stylistic uniformity this entails that readers of Prynne will find disconcerting. The earlier work provided an encounter with radically uneven velocities, where the movement of verse performed by the reading voice would part company with the speed of thought, or with the velocity of those macro- and micro-processes whose rate of movement is either infinitesimal or instantaneous. The experience of reading was defined by a form of syncopation, by the sensation of gearing up and gearing down. In *Weasels,* the average velocity is completely unrelated to the speaking voice; it does not operate in terms of what the poem calls 'rational earshot'. When a time signature, *alla breve,* is provided, there is nothing that the reader can usefully relate it to. There is rather a weightless, gravityless, uniformity of tones, rhythms, velocities and syntactical habits.

If the defining characteristic of avant-garde formalism is the use of montage, enabling the irruption of aesthetic discourse into the discourses of everyday life, then *Weasels* seems to point in a direction beyond avant-gardism. With montage, the threshold between the aesthetic and the everyday is encountered with a shock that produces fragmentation and discontinuity. In *Weasels,* all those discourses participating in the language of the text are subjected to a total reconfiguration that allows them to be systematically imbricated with each other in every aspect of the structure and according to every measure. Thoroughly informed by the concerns of the public sphere, evidently constrained by the historical moment, *Weasels* is couched in a language that provides a new kind of gauge for the formation of the subject. Linguistic conventions are broken and re-set in unprecedented shapes that record the impact of concatenating discourses at every point. It is an unique textuality in which the politics of gender genuinely infuses, rather than predominates over, a poetry whose projected centre of gravity is what adjusts the scale of contemporary discursive relations to the scope of the literary text.

Lisa Robertson

My Eighteenth Century

Draft towards a Cabinet

> *I know a young person who learned to write before learning how to read, and who began to write with the needle before writing with the quill. Of all the letters, she first wanted only to make O's. She incessantly made big and little O's, O's of all sizes, O's inside one another, and always drawn backward. Unfortunately, one day when she was busy with this useful exercise, she saw herself in a mirror; and finding that this constrained attitude was not graceful for her, like another Minerva she threw away the pen and no longer wanted to make O's. Her brother did not like to write any more than she did, but what irritated him was the discomfort and not the appearance it gave him. Another tack was taken to bring her back to writing. The little girl was refined and vain. She did not stand for her linen being used by her sisters. Others marked it for her; they no longer wanted to mark it. She had to learn how to mark it herself. The rest of her progress can easily be conceived.*

The suchness or quiddity of the print on the page, the phoneme on the air, the paratactic fragment, stand in current "innovative" poetries as material metaphors for the radical outer limits of language as a social medium. I want to consider how this linguistic figure of radical materiality may buttress the foundational opacities which also encrypt symbolically maintained metaphysics of difference. I'm speaking here of gendered difference, that political fiction which apparently finds its mark and its guarantee in the phenomenal opacity of the flesh. I'm beginning to think that current avant-garde poetry practise, with its tendency to defend a narrow range of primarily paratactic method at the expense of a richly figured field of rhetorical techniques, might methodologically entrench deeply banal structures and pedagogies of gender. Perhaps the materially radical outer limit is a frontier myth, with attendant wild heroisms and sheriffs.

I want to consider materiality as a construction of the political imaginary. By "political imaginary" I mean a symbolic figuration which motivates and underwrites the production of public meaning. It's gendered. I pose the opening vignette as an index to materiality's ground in the pedagogical production of girls and boys.

The story is from Rousseau's educational treatise *Émile* (Rousseau, p. 369). A charming allegory of feminine narcissism prescribes a style of moral conduct for the young Sophie, who is destined by design to be the wife for citizen Émile. We see how, for Sophie, to write is first a girlish material pleasure; her maturing feminine self-consciousness converts this pleasure first to silence and then to domestic economy, in a gesture which curiously foreshadows Freud's theory of the translation of the site of mature female pleasure from a useless, narcissistic little tissue to the socially useful reproductive site. The conversion or translation is what figures Sophie as feminine icon, a pedagogical success. Rousseau shifts the negative reflexivity of narcissism to the site of womanly domestic economy, and it is this gendered site which provides an inalienable, natural, moral foundation for the liberty of the revolutionary citizen-father. In the Rousseauian political imaginary, public rights are a male perogative and derive their authenticity from the natural enclave of the family. Women are moral conduits for the radical economy of masculine citizenship. From vain girls, Rousseau invents mothers to suckle the Nation. As for the girl who shirks such lessons: she's stuck in a pathological zero, needs translating, as Charcot and Freud would dramatically demonstrate.

And so Rousseau invokes a familiar female subject: a narcissistic beauty pathologically embroidering O's: little dumb pocket mirrors reflecting origin, other, for the paternal theorist. Correctly socialized, she is fit to oversee the laundering of the theorist's linens. Through Rousseauian pedagogy, an ambiguous figure of feminine materiality is established—she is both the threshold or limit separating nature from culture, and the degree zero which lends itself pliantly to the transformational will of political, familial, and psychoanalytic techniques. Sophie serves as pathological ground and material proof of methodological efficacy.

Judith Butler has explored the philosophical construction of the concept of materiality in relation to the cultural construction "woman." She proposes that the two ideas meet at an enforced irreducibility. I'd like to join Butler in asking, "What does it mean to have recourse to materiality, since it is clear from the start that matter has a history (indeed, more than one) and that the history of matter is in part determined by the negotiation of sexual difference?" (Butler, p. 29). Reading Rousseau we may find, like Butler, that "matter itself is founded through a set of violations." The therapeutic or pedagogical motivation for the fractured, paratactic methodologies of avant-garde materialist practice—expressed so succinctly in Walter Benjamin's recommendation that while in the cultural bordello, the historical materialist "remains in control of his powers, man enough to blast open the continuum of history" (Benjamin, p. 262)—can be a difference-producing mechanism whose matter is often not only sexually, but racially inscribed. Rey Chow has discussed the colonialism of Benjamin's violent isolation of cultural tropes and artifacts. In *Writing Diaspora* she insists that "the violent concept that is often quoted by Benjamin lovers as a way to read against 'progress' . . . is as much a precise description of imperialism's relentless destruction of local cultures as it is a 'politically correct' metaphor for redeeming the history of the repressed" (Chow, p. 44). From this perspective, the material fragment of language is an anthropological souvenir which represents the successful colonization and administration of a differential symbolic. From another point of view, it's one of gender's holy relics.

So a second interpretation of Rousseau's vignette might articulate how an historical movement has naturalized itself, and assumed an ideological veracity. Eighteenth century revolutionary romanticism, with its heightened gothic sensibility for the fragment, its nationalist passions for etymologies and folk origins and sublime contrasts, not only dramatized a mythic image of a maternal Nation with fraternal citizenry of (breast-fed) heroic subjects; it demonstrated how aesthetic metaphors contribute efficiently to the construction of a political imaginary. Rousseau theoretically stigmatized a feminized ancien regime theatricality, discursive reflexivity, salon culture and women's political agency. A spectrum of public agencies, sexualities, ambivalences and rhetorics once available to male and female ancien regime writers became, in Rousseau's mirror, morally tainted, dangerous to the fraternal civitas. The distance from aesthetic moral to punitive surveillance was brief. Bad mother Marie Antoinette, political theorist and theatrical impresario Olympe de Gouge, public rhetorician Madame Roland, receive the quick therapy of the guillotine. A feminized theatricality is excised from the revolutionary republic. In Rousseauian romanticism, while both polis and subject are cleansed of "feminine" inauthenticities and insincerities, "woman" is constrained to a symbolic materiality: Liberty and the Nation can be allegorized as female only when women themselves are political ciphers framed by the patriarchal family, and trained to receive the methodological stamp of Father's will. Women provide a material source and mute symbol for the political state and revolutionary pedagogies and methods.

To claim for a material paratactic method an originary potency, a fractal radicality, a political veracity, as do Language Poetry's originating agents, is to align the aesthetic allegory of material limits with a pedagogy of the polis. In this avant-garde, the place of identification becomes depersonified; that is, the traditional mimetic identification of reader with text is disengaged, replaced with an *a priori* identification of fractal method with radical political pedagogy or critique. Rather than experiencing textuality affectively, the reader of the paratactic work is directed towards an allegorized critical engagement with method. Both method and material are implicitly gendered. What a defensively conceived practise promotes as politically viable depends on the concurrent demotion of apparently antithetical figures. Compositional parataxis accrues social and aesthetic value to the extent that it is posed in contradiction to narrative or other rhetorics of identification. The paratactic writer or reader can indeed remain in control of those mannish fractal powers celebrated by Benjamin, to the extent that she imagines the surrounding culture in terms of narrative decadence, false consciousness, and proliferative equivalencies. Oppositional ideology pathologizes popular and historical identificatory rhetorics. Consumer surfaces are loaded with the immoral whiff and tang of Benjamin's bordello. The moral of the story is clear: The good poet enters the bordello for research purposes only, retaining her gloves. She's a social worker.

I don't mean to suggest that we simply repudiate an avant-garde aesthetic which displays such abundant velocities and felicities. (As if we ever could abolish aleatory contingencies, as if the structure of our language had no apparent effect on the structure of the polis, as if we should not permit ourselves to risk our most flamboyantly anti-narrative desires.) I do want to show how some proliferative tropes that have acquired the taint of feminized false consciousness, insincerity, might contribute to a political imaginary which with nuanced skepticism dispenses with the need to defend oppositionally conceived limits or origins. We might come to see how certain avant-garde methodological precepts—paratactic disunity, aleatory composition, the multiple or decentred subject—need not be repeatedly promoted as continuum-blasting militarisms, but could be more fruitfully considered in a rhetorical register, as tropes of style dispersed among a much broader spectrum of social dictions.

So I propose to catalogue the backwards O's of Sophie, Rousseau's quintessential Girl. "Big and little," "inside one another," "always drawn backwards," these are pleasure's proliferating vowels, reduced by the therapeutic glove to ciphers of feminine narcissism and material origin. And it doesn't surprise me that they should lean backwards, directing my attention to a pre-romantic eighteenth century, where the aesthetics of origins were complicated by the practise of skepticism, dissimulation, duplicity, wit. In my eighteenth century, language is a theatre. Identifications are mutual, temporary; pleasures and poems are funny, fast, mawkish, biting, and public. Sophie's O's.

Item: O is for rhetoric. Pleasure and power meet here. The rhetor's practise shapes the gestural, communicative, expressive artifice of the speaking body, the public body addressing itself to someone it wishes to persuade, to love, to fight. Rhetoric is the performed milieu of the living relation between persons—simply, of politics. Butler's notion of gender as performative is based on such a rhetorical model. Her reevaluation of performativity in *Bodies that Matter* helps ground the notion of persuasive artifice in a critique of power. In her discussion of identification, she develops the idea that we are compelled by constraint to iterate or echo an engendering behaviour, that the agency of self-fashioning is perhaps not so much a metaphor for the unchastened production of gendered identity as a fantasized best-case scenario. But even given this qualification, Butler's idea that gender is not only a passive structure imposed by institutional surveillance, in Foucault's terms, but an active, processual identification produced and constantly modified by its social practise, gives me the will to counter the dominance of overarching concepts such as materiality. The deployment of rhetoric, of language's social appearing, lends a provisional autonomy which could meet or deflect the adjudicating compulsions of gendered, institutional power. Foregrounding the enunciative rhetorics and artifices of language does not dismantle or blast apart structures of authority, nor does it solidify the identity of an extra-ideological margin. But by presenting identity in language as a social artifice, as always already for the joy or judgement of both speaker and auditor, we structure multiply affective identificatory sites, emotive spaces that frame knowledges for only the duration of our mimetic contracts. We don't need to eradicate identities or methods. They reveal themselves textually as unnatural, available, mercurial. We should move among them together.

Item: O is for narcissist. *Looking in pools to see things flick* (Riley, *Mop Mop,* p. 25; all subsequent italicized passages are from Riley's *Dry Air* and *Mop Mop Georgette*). With whom does the narcissist identify, bent over that sultry pond, the smudged zero of the compact? The dual Freudian account of narcissism enfolds its own ambiguities. In Freud's first account narcissism is configured as a formative cathexis of the subject with an outer milieu. Libidinal drives, a nexus of recognitions and desires, both structure the ego and animate it. In this account, the self is no unity, no bedrock, but the enacted site of shifting agencies and perceptions and identifications. The narcissistic identification constitutes the subject as always already multiple. Narcissism can be considered as the presentation of the supple sociality of a self produced by its own desire for, and in, the world. Leo Bersani puts it this way: "The ego, at its origin, would be nothing more than a kind of passionate interference necessitated by the anticipated pleasure of its own dismantling" (Bersani, p. 39). Narcissism is an actively prepositional technology: It constellates consciousness. It's tactical, not foundational.

Denise Riley's poems have been accused of the pathological *faux pas*. In a review of *Mop Mop Georgette* published in the British journal *Parataxis,* John Wilkinson has aligned himself with Freud's second, intransitive discussion of the Narcissist. In Freud's revised account, narcissism is a pathologically regressive self-reflexivity that shirks ethical and civic maturity. It's interpreted as a symptom of jejune posturing, or in Wilkinson's symptomology, as a turning away, a turning from a poetics of psychological and cultural healing to a flaunting of sardony. *I. neglect. the. house* Denise Riley replies (*Dry Air,* p. 27) in the grand tradition of the Bad Mother. Riley doesn't need me to defend her. But the finally sad accusation of Wilkinson's "Sardony does prevail" (Wilkinson, p. 69)—sardony as a method of *managing* narcissism—reaches for the same social pedagogy Riley succinctly chucks. *say no to sociology always* (*Dry Air,* p. 53). Is it the poet's role to heal, placate, nurture, feed—must the ethical poet nurse? Who wants to be that Rousseauian goddess? Riley's narcissism frustrates the expectation of nurturance. But it is active in the sense that her reflexivities pose a series of transitive spaces from which we can think and judge otherwise, tentative spaces which disturb foundational unities. *It is called feeling but is its real name thought?* (*Mop Mop,* p. 20). If we can't, among other reflexivities, bring skepticism to bear on our constitution as female subjects, what other lens is there? I want to underline Bersani's premise here: the intense pleasure in dismantling one's own constitution as a subject, in interfering with one's own gendered social positioning as essential ground, sexual cipher—indeed, the insistent disintegration of the self as ground—cannot be over-stressed nor should its political import be disregarded. The reflexivities of Riley's poems index variant identificatory economies, economies vigilant in their enacted critique of the enculturation of femininity as a signifier for nature, managerial adeptness, familial morality and material availability. Riley's sardony preserves the duplicity, the neitherness, the *not-me* of the narcissistic identification. It's the skeptic's tool for deflecting the trajectory to well-socialized femininity. *inside a designation there are people permanently startled to bear it, the not-me against sociology* (*Dry Air,* p. 26). I get the feeling Wilkinson is horrified by the apparition of this ambivalence on her sleeve. "It becomes necessary to ask," he claims, "whether the knowingness, the reflexivity which is paraded throughout this poem, is any kind of saving grace" (Wilkinson, p. 68). Wilkinson's critical repudiation of narcissism is moralistic: Riley's gaze averts high moral ground and saving graces to invent some rhetorical genders, some prepositional ethics, for thought. Doubt's a mobile tool; narcissists slip. Must the ethical proceed from a solid ground, rather than from "narcissistic fidgeting" as Wilkinson puts it? Who shall consolidate this ground from a prepositional variousness? What is it then named? In the symbiology of origins that underwrites the social ethos, what persons, what practises, are consigned to a mutely redemptive role? Riley replies: *Aha we are frozen* (*Mop Mop,* p. 21). Why shouldn't the O in her ethos be glazed with ice? We like to slip and fidget. Our frigidity's tactical. We ask for enunciative mobility not therapeutic redemption. *By these snow graphics* (*Mop Mop,* p. 18) she's in my century.

Item: O's a cipher for irony's apolitical triviality. In Barrett Watten's estimation that is. In his essay "The Conduit of Communication in Everyday Life," he sets the figures of irony and fragmentation in politically charged methodological opposition. His argument functions analogically: to wrest language from a pseudo-context of capitalist hegemony, from a false everyday, is to fragment the structures of authority which motivate the temporal surface of the hegemonic. Irony on the other hand is a signifier for cultural dread. In Watten's argument, irony's a rhetorical reproduction of consumerist proliferations of postmodern equivalencies. It remains tied to the spurious surface of temporal experience while Watten's fragmenting strategy is a topological practise aligned to adeptly blast into material depths. Irony's affect and surface are demon others, pseudo productions of the pseudo everyday. Watten wants "to take language out of the everyday, and put it back into circulation as a 'new and improved' fragment. This strategy is a formal one and uses language at the limits of its possibilities rather than simply as an ironization of an already received cultural content . . . " (Watten, p. 34). Here is the symbolic of heroic limits in counterpoint to devalued dailiness. Frank O'Hara is enthroned at the centre of the demonology, a dupe to the spurious and habitual, a foil, a ghostly Marie Antoinette to the revolutionary ardour of strategic iconoclasm. His urbane dailiness, his Gene-Kellyesque annotations of street-time are diagnosed as hysteria. This pathologizing of irony complements the heroic poesis of limits and fragments. Yet considered differently, this odd couple, decadent Queen Mother and philosopher hero, could yield a different interpretation.

Watten's prescription to use "language at the limits of its possibilities" reveals its own historical romance, its own topological frontierism. And bad mother O'Hara's manipulation of ironic ambivalence, pleasure, could shine the light on those gothic glooms and shades, the fragments and rugged limits—in short the swashbuckling epic of thwarted origins and fractal audacity that informs Watten's rhetoric. I can't resist quoting O'Hara's "Lexington Avenue, an eclogue": " . . . your penis is showing. Put that bunch of grapes back on your lap. Just for dignity" (O'Hara, p. 91). In O'Hara's eighteenth century, irony's a humorous tool picked up to deflect the adjudicating compulsions of cultural authority. I want to defend a use for irony that constructs ambiguities as speculative follies, doubled economies whose blatant inutility shows a potentiality, a threshold of counter-hegemonic agency, or play, more simply put. In other words, it's a misuse—it diddles intention to say what can't be said. I mean misuse in the sense that de Certeau suggests in *The Practise of Everyday Life,* or in the sense that the Situationists practiced "la détourne"—"Everyday life invents itself by poaching in countless ways on the property of others" states de Certeau (xii), and here we read an interpretation of the everyday in which users are cast as agents whose consumption of capital's products is in fact a translation, a production of itinerant economies in the interstices of social space. The trope of irony, with its *both* and *neitherness,* does turn the site of daily life into something more amusing, more critical, more engaged than a duped false consciousness, by moving against the grain of cultural intention, by doubling spaces and foundations, naming as it negates, yet refusing the stasis of names and pathologies, and translating the anxiety of power to the erotics of doubt. Like de Certeau's notion of poaching, irony is an enunciative "logic articulated on situations" (de Certeau, xx). It's a simultaneous appropriation and demotion of dominant cultural logics. Irony doesn't simply contribute to the infinite equivalencies of postmodernity's invisible museum; it throws curatorial rhetoric into relief, makes it visible. Rhetorical figurations do function as agencies. Irony may mirror power's artifice, double it. In the long frieze of revolution we could think now of irony as the rigorously homeopathic treatment of the symptom of mastery. Sure, O'Hara's crown's paste. But so's Watten's sword. Each flaunts its charms.

Item: O is for humour. Didn't Benjamin know that the bordello was really good *trompe d'oeil*?

I've been suggesting that the means by which materiality has been defended as a dominant critical trope of avant-garde practise are similar to those symbolic structures of authority which circumscribe and limit the performative site of gender as an enunciative rhetoric. That is, feminized, devalued, identificatory tropes figured as decadent, insincere, pathological, or neurotic, receive the therapeutic or pedagogical or revolutionary stamp of radically corrective materialist method. Value—ethical, aesthetic, moral, political—and gendered—coins itself according to such delimitations and proprieties. But the currency's worn out.

Method, whether paratactic, ironic, fragmented, aleatory, or reflexive, must remain open for use. The specific uses or skeptical misuses and tactical negotiations of such techniques on their enunciative stages, configure and produce a political imaginary. The assumption that social change can only proceed from the cohesion of a defended, guarded method, finally entrenches certain identity pictures in deeply confining oppositional ideologies. The political imaginary needs to present itself as irreparably multiple, mobile, simultaneous to both doubt and pleasure. Discourse is many-tongued. Change is unquantifiable. The new is not a limit, but a transitive agency. To greet the flicker of becoming, we need skeptical suppleness, a tactical shimmering.

Sources Cited

Benjamin, Walter. "Theses on the Philosophy of History" in *Illuminations,* ed. Hannah Arendt, New York: Schocken Books, 1969.

Bersani, Leo. *The Culture of Redemption,* Cambridge and London: Harvard University Press, 1990.

Butler, Judith. *Bodies that Matter: On the Discursive Limits of "Sex,"* New York and London: Routledge, 1993.

Certeau, Michel de. *The Practice of Everyday Life,* Berkeley, Los Angeles, London: University of California Press, 1984.

Chow, Rey. *Writing Diaspora: Tactics of Intervention in Contemporary Cultural Studies,* Bloomington: Indiana University Press, 1993.

O'Hara, Frank. *Selected Plays,* Full Court Press, 1978.

Riley, Denise. *Dry Air,* London: Virago, 1985.

Riley, Denise. *Mop Mop Georgette,* London and Cambridge: Reality Street Editions, 1993. (Riley's seminal work on irony as a political figuration, *The Words of Selves: Identification, Solidarity, Irony,* published by Stanford in 2000, was not available when this essay was written in 1996. The reader would be well advised to follow Riley's bracing argument.)

Rousseau, Jean-Jacques. *Émile,* trans. Allen Bloom, New York: Basic Books, 1979.

Watten, Barrett. "The Conduit of Communication in Everyday Life," *Aerial 8: Contemporary Poetics as Critical Theory,* ed. Rod Smith, Washington DC: Edge Books, 1995.

Wilkinson, John. "Illyrian Places" (review of Denise Riley, *Mop Mop Georgette*), *Parataxis* 6 (1994): 58–69.

Contributors' List of Further Readings

Aarseth, Espen. *Cybertext: Perspectives on Ergodic Literature.* Baltimore and London: Johns Hopkins University Press, 1997.

Acheson, James, and Romana Huk, eds. *Contemporary British Poetry: Essays in Theory and Criticism.* Albany: State University of New York Press, 1996.

Alderman, Nigel, and C.D. Blanton, eds. "Pocket Epics: British Poetry after Modernism." Special Issue of *The Yale Journal of Criticism* 13.1 (Spring 2001).

Algarín, Miguel, and Bob Holman, eds. *ALOUD: Voices from the Nuyorican Poets Cafe*. New York: Owl Books, 1994.

Apter, Emily. *Continental Drift: From National Characters to Virtual Subjects.* Chicago: University of Chicago Press, 1999.

Apter, Emily, ed. "Translation in a Global Market." *Public Culture* 13.1 (Winter 2001).

Barrett, Lindon. *Blackness and Value: Seeing Double*. Cambridge: Cambridge University Press, 1999.

Beach, Christopher. *Poetic Culture: Contemporary American Poetry Between Community and Institution.* Evanston, IL: Northwestern University Press, 1999.

Bernstein, Charles, ed. *Close Listening: Poetry and the Performed Word.* New York: Oxford University Press, 1998.

Bertram, Vicki, ed. *Kicking Daffodils: Twentieth-Century Women Poets*. Edinburgh: Edinburgh University Press, 1997.

Boyarin, Jonathan, ed. *The Ethnography of Reading*. Berkeley: University of California Press, 1993.

Brathwaite, Kamau. *ConVERSations with Nathaniel Mackey.* New York and Minneapolis: We Press & Xcp: Cross-Cultural Poetics, 1999.

Brown, Fahamisha Patricia. *Performing the Word: African American Poetry as Vernacular Culture*. New Brunswick, NJ: Rutgers University Press, 1999.

Brown, Lee Ann. *The Sleep that Changed Everything*. Middletown, CT: Wesleyan University Press, forthcoming [2003].

Bruce, Susan. " 'My Only Frame of Reference': Anthologising the Scottish Woman Writer." *Verse* 9.2 (Summer 1992): 98–109.

Cayley, John. "Between Here and Nowhere." *Gravitational Intrigue, The Little Magazine* Volume 22 cd-rom (Spring 1999) and also on the Web at http://www.shadoof.net/in/translit/transl.html

Cayley, John. "Of Programmatology." *Mute* (Fall 1998): 72–75.

Cayley, John. "Writing (under-)Sky: On Xu Bing's 'Tianshu'." *A Book of the Book: Some Work and Projections About the Book and Writing*. Jerome Rothenberg and Stephen Clay, eds. New York: Granary Books, 2000, 497–503.

Cobbing, Bob and Lawrence Upton, eds. *Word Score Utterance Choreography*. London: Writers Forum, 1998.

Crawford, Robert and Anne Varty, eds. *Liz Lochhead's Voices*. Edinburgh: Edinburgh University Press, 1993.

Damon, Maria. *The Dark End of the Street: Margins in American Vanguard Poetry.* Minneapolis: University of Minnesota Press, 1993.

Damon, Maria. "When the NuYoricans Came to Town: (Ex)Changing Poetics." *Xcp: Cross-cultural Poetics* 1 (1997): 16–40.

dANDelion: prose poetry image text. 26.1 (Spring 2000).

Davis, Alex, and Lee M. Jenkins, eds. *Locations of Literary Modernism: Region and Nation in British and American Modernist Poetry.* Cambridge: Cambridge University Press, 2000.

Davies, Kevin. *Comp.* Washington D.C.: Edge, 2000.

Devlin, Paul (director). *Slamnation* [film]. Cinema Guild, 1998.

Doris, Stacy. *Conference.* Massachusetts: Potes and Poets, 2001.

Doris, Stacy. *Paramour.* San Francisco: Krupskaya, 1999.

DuPlessis, Rachel Blau. *Genders, Races, and Religious Cultures in Modern American Poetry, 1908–1934.* Cambridge: Cambridge University Press, 2001.

DuPlessis, Rachel Blau, and Peter Quartermain, eds. *The Objectivist Nexus: Essays in Cultural Poetics.* Tuscaloosa: University of Alabama Press, 1999.

Fisher, Allen. *Brixton Fractals.* Vancouver: Tsunami Editions, 1999.

Fisher, Allen. *The Topological Shovel: Four Essays.* Toronto: The Gig Editions, 1999.

Forrest-Thomson, Veronica. *Selected Poems.* Anthony Barnett, ed., with Postscript by Alison Mark. London: Invisible Books, 1999.

Forrest-Thomson, Veronica. *Poetic Artifice: A Theory of Twentieth-Century Poetry.* Alison Mark, ed. Manchester: Manchester University Press, forthcoming.

Fraser, Kathleen. *Translating the Unspeakable: Poetry and the Innovative Necessity.* Tuscaloosa: University of Alabama Press, 2000.

Gish, Nancy K. "Adoption, Identity, and Voice: Jackie Kay's Inventions of Self." *Imagining Adoption.* Marianne Novi, ed. Ann Arbor: University of Michigan Press, 2001.

Grossberg, Lawrence. "Speculations and Articulations of Globalization." *Polygraph* 11 (1999): 11–48.

Guest, Barbara. *If So Tell Me.* London: Reality Street, 1999.

Hardt, Michael, and Antonio Negri. *Empire.* Cambridge: Harvard University Press, 2000.

Harper, Glenn, ed. *Interventions and Provocations: Conversations on Art, Culture and Resistance.* Albany: State University of New York Press, 1998.

Harris, Wilson. *Selected Essays of Wilson Harris: The Unfinished Genesis of the Imagination.* Andrew Bundy, ed. London and New York: Routledge, 1999.

Hayles, N. Katherine. *How We Became Posthuman: Virtual Bodies in Cybernetics, Literature, and Informatics.* Chicago: University of Chicago Press, 1999.

Heathfield, Adrian. *Small Acts: Performance, the Millennium and the Marking of Time.* London: Black Dog Publishing, 2000.

Hejinian, Lyn. *The Language of Inquiry.* Berkeley: University of California Press, 2000.

Hinton, Laura, and Cynthia Hogue, eds. *We Who Love to Be Astonished: Experimental Women's Writing and Performance Poetics.* Tuscaloosa: University of Alabama Press, 2001.

Hitchcock, Peter. "The World According to Bakhtin." *Materializing Bakhtin: The Bakhtin Circle and Social Theory.* Craig Brandist and Galin Tahanov, eds. Houndmills, Basingstoke: Macmillan, 1999, 3–19.

Huk, Romana. "On foreign-national locations of the place and/or non-place of the(ir) unpronounceable *idir eatortha:* Returns of nationalism in/as disguise undisguised, or: Ironies inherent in current descriptions of Irish experiment in American and British avant-garde circles." *the Journal* 2 (1999): n.p.

Jarnot, Lisa. *Ring of Fire*. Cambridge: Zoland, 2001.

Johansson, Birgitta. *The Engineering of Being: An Ontological Approach to J. H. Prynne*. Umea, Sweden: Swedish Science Press, 1997.

Kennedy, David, and Keith Tuma, eds. "Additional Apparitions: Poetry, Performance and Site Specificity." *The Paper* 3/4 Special Double Issue (March 2002).

Kim, Elaine H., and Norma Alarcon, eds. *Writing Self, Writing Nation: Essays on Theresa Hak Kyung Cha's Dictee*. Berkeley: Third Woman's Press, 1994.

Kinsella, John. "A New Lyricism: Some Early Thoughts on Linguistic Disobedience." *Angelaki* 6.3 (December 2001): 85–100.

Kittler, Friedrich A., trans. by Geoffrey Winthrop-Young and Michael Wutz. *Gramophone, Film, Typewriter*. Stanford: Stanford University Press, 1999.

Kumar, Amitava. *Passport Photos*. Berkeley: University of California Press, 1999.

LaBelle, Brandon, and Cristof Migone, eds. *Writing Aloud: The Sonics of Language*. Los Angeles: Errant Bodies Press/Ground Fault Recordings, 2001.

Lakoff, George, and Mark Johnson. *Philosophy in the Flesh: The Embodied Mind and Its Challenge to Western Thought*. New York: Basic Books, 1999.

Lorca, Federico Garcia, trans. by Michael Smith. *The Tamarit Poems*. Dublin: The Dedalus Press, 2002.

Lyon, Janet. *Manifestoes: Provocations of the Modern*. Ithaca, N.Y.: Cornell University Press, 1999.

Mackey, Nathaniel. *ATET A.D.,* Vol. 3 of *From a Broken Bottle Traces of Perfume Still Emanate*. San Francisco: City Lights, 2001.

Mackey, Nathaniel. *Whatsaid Serif*. San Francisco: City Lights, 1998.

Mark, Alison, and Deryn Rees-Jones, eds. *Contemporary Women's Poetry: Reading/Writing/Practice*. London and New York: Macmillan/St. Martin's Press, 2000.

Mark, Alison. *Veronica Forrest-Thomson & Language Poetry*. Tavistock, Devon: Northcote House, 2001.

Marriott, David, and Vicky Lebeau, eds. *Psychoanalysis and Poetics*. Special issue of *fragmente,* 1998.

Matthias, John, ed. *23 Modern British Poets*. Chicago: The Swallow Press, 1971.

Meanjin magazine. "Poetics" issue 60.2 (2001).

Mellors, Anthony, and Robert Smith, eds. "Poets on the Verge." *Angelaki* 5.1 (April 2000).

Mengham, Rod, and Glen Phillips, eds. *Fairly Obsessive: Essays on the Works of John Kinsella*. Fremantle: Fremantle Arts Centre Press, 2000.

Middleton, Peter. " 'Particulars of Time and Space of Which One is a Given Instance': Poetry, Science and Politics in the Sixties." *Open Letter* 11.1 (Spring 2001): 42–65.

Middleton, Peter. "The Transitive Poetics of Jerome Rothenberg's Transnational Anthologies." *West Coast Line* 34.2 (Fall 2000): 90–104.

Morris, Adelaide, ed. *Sound States: Innovative Poetics and Acoustical Technologies.* Chapel Hill: University of North Carolina Press, 1997.

Mottram, Eric. *The Triumph of the Mobile: The Structure of Information, the Language of Computers and Contemporary Poetry*. First published in *Intrepid* 23/24 (Summer-Fall 1972). Allen De Loach, ed. Buffalo, NY; London: Writers Forum, 2000.

Mowitt, John. *Text: The Genealogy of an Antidisciplinary Object*. Durham, N.C.: Duke University Press, 1992.

Moxley, Jennifer. *The Sense Record*. Washington D.C.: Edge, 2002.

Nelson, Theodor Holm. *Literary Machines 93.1*. First published 1981. Sausalito: Mindful Press, 1993.

Noland, Carrie. *Poetry at Stake: Lyric Aesthetics and the Challenge of Technology*. Princeton, N.J.: Princteon University Press, 1999.

North, Michael. *Reading 1922: A Return to the Scene of the Modern*. Oxford: Oxford University Press, 1999.

North American Centre for Interdisciplinary Poetics, www.poetics.yorku.ca

Open Letter: A Canadian Journal of Writing and Theory, "the 'open letter' issue." 11.3 (Fall 2001).

O'Sullivan, Maggie. *In the House of the Shaman*. London: Reality Street, 1993.

O'Sullivan, Maggie, ed. *Out of Everywhere: Linguistically Innovative Poetry by Women in North America and the UK*. London: Reality Street Editions, 1996.

Patterson, Ian. "'the medium itself, rabbit by proxy': some thoughts about reading J.H. Prynne." Denise Riley, ed. *Poets on Writing*. Basingstoke: Macmillan, 1992: 234–246.

Perelman, Bob. *The Marginalization of Poetry*. Princeton, N.J.: Princeton University Press, 1996.

See the panel discussion of the above book involving Steve Evans, Ann Lauterbach, Kate Lilley, Ron Silliman, and Juliana Spahr with counter-response by Bob Perelman, in *Jacket* 2 (http://www. jacket.zip.com.au/jacket02/index.html).

Philip, M. NourbeSe. *She Tries Her Tongue; Her Silence Softly Breaks*. Toronto: Mercury Press, 1988, and the Women's Press, 1993.

Philip, M. NourbeSe. *Looking for Livingstone: An Odyssey of Silence*. Toronto: Mercury Press, 1991.

PhillyTalks Online. www.english.upenn.edu/~wh/phillytalks/

Prynne, J.H. *Poems*. Newcastle upon Tyne: Bloodaxe Books, 1999.

Raworth, Tom. *Tottering State*. O Books, 2000.

Reeve, N.H., and Richard Kerridge. *Nearly Too Much: The Poetry of J. H. Prynne*. Liverpool: Liverpool University Press, 1995.

Riley, Denise. *The Words of Selves: Identification, Solidarity, Irony*. Stanford: Stanford University Press, 2000.

Riley, Denise. *Selected Poems*. Reality Street Editions, 2000.

Rothenberg, Jerome, and Pierre Joris, eds. *Poems for the Millennium*. 2 Vols. Berkeley: University of California Press, 1995, 1998.

Schwerner, Armand. *Selected Shorter Poems*. Junction Press, 1999.

Searle, Chris. *The Forsaken Lover: White Words and Black People*. Harmondsworth: Penguin, 1973.

Sklair, Leslie. *The Transnational Capitalist Class*. London: Blackwell, 2001.

Simpson, Megan. *Poetic Epistemologies: Gender and Knowing in Women's Language-Oriented Writing*. Albany: State University of New York Press, 2000.

Smith, Rod. *Protective Immediacy*. New York: Roof, 1999.

Spahr, Juliana. *Everybody's Autonomy: Connective Reading and Collective Identity*. Tuscaloosa: University of Alabama Press, 2001.

Strathern, Marilyn. *The Gender of the Gift*. Berkeley: University of California Press, 1988.

Thiong'o, Ngugi wa. *Decolonising the Mind: The Politics of Language in African Literature*. London: James Currey, 1986.

Tuma, Keith. "Criticism and Warships." *Búllan* [forthcoming].

Tuma, Keith. "Ed Dorn and England." *The Gig* 6 (July 2000): 41–54.

Tuma, Keith. *Fishing by Obstinate Isles: Modern and Postmodern British Poetry and American Readers*. Evanston, Ill.: Northwestern University Press, 1998.

Tuma, Keith. "Whatever Irish Poetry: Some Musings." *the Journal* 2 (1999): n.p.

Tuma, Keith, ed. *Anthology of Twentieth-Century British and Irish Poetry*. Oxford: Oxford University Press, 2001.

Venuti, Lawrence, ed. *Rethinking Translation: Discourse, Subjectivity, Ideology*. London and New York: Routledge, 1992.

Vickery, Ann. *Leaving Lines of Gender: A Feminist Genealogy of Language Writing*. Middletown, CT: Wesleyan University Press, 2000.

Wallace, Mark, and Stephen Marks. *Telling it Slant: Avant-Garde Poetics of the 1990s*. Tuscaloosa and London: University of Alabama Press, 2001.

Ward, Geoff. "Nothing but Mortality: Prynne and Celan." In *Contemporary Poetry Meets Modern Theory,* Antony Easthope and John O. Thompson, eds. London: Harvester, 1991, 139–152.

Ward, Geoff. *Language Poetry and the American Avant-garde*. British Association for American Studies, 1993.

Watten, Barrett. *The Constructivist Moment: From Material Text to Cultural Poetics*. Middletown, CT: Wesleyan University Press, forthcoming 2003.

West Coast Line. "reZonings 2": writing images criticism. 34/2 (Fall 2000).

Notes on Contributors

Caroline Bergvall

Caroline Bergvall's work as a poet includes the books *Eclat* (Sound & Language, 1996), *Jets-Poupee* (RemPress, 1999), and *Goan Atom I* (Kruspkaya, 2001). She has performed her texts widely and has developed a number of mixed-arts performance and installation projects, frequently in collaboration with other artists: *Ambient Fish* (Hull Time Based Art, 1999), *About Face* (Berlin, 2000 & Bard College, New York, 2001), and *Say Parsley* (Exeter, 2001). Her critical work is increasingly concerned with plurilingual writing and sited textwork. She was the Director of Performance Writing, Dartington College of Arts in Devon, England (1994–2000) and is currently Associate Fellow in Performance Writing at Dartington, Associate Lecturer in Creative Writing at the University of Cardiff and Honorary Research Fellow in English at Birkbeck College, University of London.

John Cayley

John Cayley is a London-based poet, translator, sinologist and publisher, born in Ottawa, Canada. He is the founding editor of Wellsweep, a small press which has specialized in literary translation from Chinese, and he is known internationally for his writing in networked and programmable media (www.shadoof.net/in). Cayley is the recent winner of the Electronic Literature Organization's Award for Poetry 2001 (www.eliterature.org). Wellsweep has published pioneering selections from individual Chinese poets and the first ever English translation of a Chinese martial arts and fantasy novel. His last book of poems, adaptations and translations is *Ink Bamboo* (London: Agenda & Belew, 1996). Cayley has lectured in the writing program at the University of California, San Diego, where he was also a Research Associate of the Center for Research in Computing and the Arts (CRCA). He is now an Honorary Research Associate in the Department of English, Royal Holloway College, University of London, and an Honorary Fellow of Dartington College of Arts, in close association with their degree-level course on Performance Writing.

cris cheek

cris cheek is a writer, artist and sound composer interested in intradisciplinary and hybrid poetic textualities/performances. Much of his recent work has been on co-authorship and models of creative collaboration. He lives in Lowestoft and currently works with Kirsten Lavers as Things Not Worth Keeping. He has an interest in the boundaries between poetry and song, gathering a Sony Gold Award for broadcast work on song-poems used for healing in south-west Madagascar as well as working on ghazal form with Samia Malik in the group Garam Masala. He works as a freelance research consultant and lecturer in writing poetics as a cultural practice.

Kathleen Crown

Kathleen Crown teaches and writes on modern and contemporary poetry at Kalamazoo College in Michigan. She is currently at work on a study of performance poetry, having completed a book manuscript entitled *Possessed by History: Trauma and Vision in American Poetry Since World War II.* She has edited a special issue of *Women's Studies: An Interdisciplinary Journal* on American women poets and the long poem. Her essays on modern and contemporary poetry have appeared in *Poetics Today, Contemporary Literature, Sagetrieb, H.D. and Poets After,* and other books and journals.

Jeff Derksen

Jeff Derksen is the author of seven books of poetry, including *Down Time, Dwell,* and the forthcoming *Transnational Muscle Cars* (Talonbooks), and his work is anthologized in *The New Canadian Long Poem Anthology.* His critical writing on literature, art, and architecture appears in *hunch, C* magazine, *Xcp, West Coast Line, Architektur Aktuel, Springerin* and *Tripwire.* He edited *Disgust & Overdetermination:* a poetics issue for *Open Letter* (10:1, 1998). For 2001–2002, he is a research fellow at the Center for Place, Culture and Poetics at the City University of New York Graduate Center.

Steve Evans

Steve Evans teaches poetry and critical theory at the University of Maine, where he is also the co-editor of *Sagetrieb: Poetry and Poetics after Modernism.* He recently edited *After Patriarchal Poetry: Feminism and the Contemporary Avant-Garde,* a special issue of the journal *differences* 12.2 (2001). His work has also appeared in *Qui Parle* and in the collection *Telling it Slant: Avant Garde Poetics of the 1990s* (Tuscaloosa and London: University of Alabama Press, 2001).

Nancy Gish

Nancy K. Gish is Professor of English and Women's Studies at the University of Southern Maine. She is the author of *Time in the Poetry of T.S. Eliot* (London: Macmillan, 1981); *Hugh MacDiarmid: The Man and His Work* (London: Macmillan, 1984); and *The Waste Land: A Poem of Memory and Desire* (New York: Twayne, 1988). She edited *Hugh MacDiarmid: Man and Poet* (National Poetry Foundation and Edinburgh University Press, 1992) and is currently co-editing a collection of essays provisionally entitled *Gender, Sexuality and Desire in T.S. Eliot.* She has also published articles on Marianne Moore, Denise

Levertov and contemporary Scottish women poets; her current research includes issues of Scottish literature and language.

Carla Harryman

Known for her genre experiments and gender irreverence, Carla Harryman, a native Californian who has spent much of her life in the San Francisco Bay area, now lives in Detroit where she teaches Women's Studies, Creative Writing and Literature at Wayne State University. Her most recent book, *Gardener of Stars* (Atelos, 2001), is an experimental novel that explores the paradise and wastelands of utopian desire. Other works include two volumes of selected writing, *There Never Was a Rose Without a Thorn* (San Francisco: City Lights, 1995) and *Animal Instincts: Prose, Plays, Essays* (Oakland, CA: This, 1989). Her most recent play, "Performing Objects Stationed in the Sub World," premiered last year in a staged reading at Oxford Brookes University, England, and will be staged in San Francisco and Detroit in 2002–2003.

Romana Huk

Romana Huk is an Associate Professor of English at the University of Notre Dame. She taught at the University of New Hampshire from 1987 to 2002 and owes her thanks to that institution for their support of the conference that gave rise to this book. Her other books are *Contemporary British Poetry: Essays in Theory and Criticism,* edited with James Acheson (University of Canterbury, New Zealand) (Albany: State University of New York, 1996), and *Stevie Smith: Between the Lines,* forthcoming from Palgrave Books. Her essays on innovative forms of twentieth-century writing have appeared in numerous collections and journals, and her activities as Research Fellow 2000–2002 in the Centre for Modern and Contemporary Poetry, Oxford Brookes University, Oxford, England, included organizing a series of seminars and colloquia on the relations between poetry, performance writing and public art.

Trevor Joyce

Trevor Joyce was born in 1947 in Dublin, Ireland, where in 1967 he co-founded New Writers' Press with Michael Smith. NWP published a wide range of Irish and international exploratory poetries, and was largely responsible for the rediscovery of the neglected Irish poets of the 1930s, such as Thomas MacGreevy, Brian Coffey and Denis Devlin. NWP's initial publication was Joyce's first book. His later volumes included a working of a classic middle-Irish text in *The Poems of Sweeny, Peregrine.* This, along with later volumes from NWP and Wild Honey Press are collected in *with the first dream of fire they hunt the cold: A Body of Work 1966/2000* (NWP/Shearsman Books, 2001), distributed in the United States by Small Press Distribution.

Linda Kinnahan

Linda Kinnahan is an Associate Professor at Duquesne University, in Pittsburgh. She is the author of *Poetics of the Feminine: Literary Tradition & Authority in William Carlos Williams, Mina Loy, Denise Levertov, and Kathleen Fraser* (Cambridge: Cambridge University Press, 1994). She has published on a variety of 20th-century poets, including Denise Riley, Wendy Mulford, Geraldine Monk, Carol Ann Duffy, Erica Hunt, and Barbara Guest. She has recently completed a study of feminist experimental poets in Britain and America, and she is working on a study of modernist women poets and economics.

Alison Mark

Alison Mark is the author of *Veronica Forrest-Thomson & Language Poetry* (Horndon, Tavistock, Devon: Northcote House, in association with the British Council, Writers and Their Work, 2001); co-editor (with Deryn Rees-Jones) of *Contemporary Women's Poetry: Reading/Writing/Practice* (London: Macmillan and New York: St. Martin's Press, 2000); and is an editor of the journal *Women: a cultural review.* She is an Honorary Research Fellow at Birkbeck College, University of London.

David Marriott

David Marriott is a lecturer in English at Queen Mary College, University of London. He is the author of *On Black Men* (Edinburgh and Columbia University Press, 2000) and has published several chapbooks of poetry, including *Lative* (Equipage, 1992) and *Dogma* (Barque Press, 2001). *Letters to Langston,* a book on African-American modernism, is forthcoming from Rutgers University Press.

Philip Mead

Philip Mead was born in Brisbane in 1953 and educated in Queensland, the U.K. and in the United States. He has been associated with poetry publishing, particularly in little magazines, since 1972. From 1987 to 1994 he was Poetry Editor of *Meanjin Quarterly* magazine and Lockie Lecturer in Australian Writing at the University of Melbourne. He reviews poetry for various magazines and newspapers and has edited, with John Tranter, the new *Penguin Book of Modern Australian Poetry* (1992). His last volume of poetry, *This River is in the South* (1984), was published by University of Queensland Press. His edited collection of essays, *Kenneth Slessor—Critical Readings,* appeared with University of Queensland Press in 1997; and *Frank Wilmot: Selected Poetry and Prose* was published by Melbourne University Press in 1997. He is currently editing a collection of Australian poetics with John Kinsella. He is a Senior Lecturer in English at the University of Tasmania.

Rod Mengham

Rod Mengham is a Senior Lecturer in the Faculty of English at Cambridge University where he is also Director of Studies in English at Jesus College. He has written *The Idiom of the Time: the Writings of Henry Green* (Cambridge: Cambridge University Press, 1983); *"Wuthering Heights": a Critical Study* (Penguin, 1988); *The Descent of Language: Writing in Praise of Babel* (Bloomsbury, 1993); and *Charles Dickens* (Writers and their Work, 2001). He has also edited the short stories of E. M. Forster and *An Introduction to Contemporary Fiction* (Polity, 1999); and has co-edited with Jana Howlett *The Violent Muse: Violence and the Artistic Imagination in Europe 1910–1939* (Manchester: Manchester University Press, 1994) and with Neil Reeve *Fiction of the 1940s: Stories of Survival* (Palgrave, 2001). He is currently working on *Upward Spiral: Edward Upward and the Politics of Writing* for Oxford University Press. He is the editor of the Equipage series of poetry pamphlets and is co-organizer of the Cambridge Conference of Contemporary Poetry; his own poems have been published under the title *Unsung: New and Selected Poems* (Folio/Salt, 1996; 2nd edition 2001).

Peter Middleton

Peter Middleton is the author of *The Inward Gaze: Masculinity and Subjectivity in Modern Culture* (New York and London: Routledge, 1992) and (with Tim Woods) *Literatures of Memory: History, Time and Space in Postwar Writing* (Manchester: University of Manchester Press, 2000). He has published many articles on contemporary poetry and culture, most recently articles on the lyric self, parental elegies, the Titanic, and J. H. Prynne. His poems appear in small magazines and in Robert Archambeau ed., *Vectors: New Poetries* (Chicago: Samizdat, 2002). He is Reader in English at the University of Southampton, UK.

Miriam Nichols

Miriam Nichols teaches contemporary literature and theory at the University College of the Fraser Valley and edits *West Coast Line,* a journal of the contemporary arts. Her recent work includes *Even on Sunday: Essays, Readings and Archival Materials on the Poetry and Poetics of Robin Blaser,* forthcoming from the National Poetry Foundation at Orono, Maine, and essays on contemporary poetics in *Open Letter, Studies in Canadian Literature, Tessera,* and *Public*. She is currently editing the *Collected Essays of Robin Blaser.*

Bob Perelman

Bob Perelman is the author of a number of books of poetry, most recently *Ten to One: Selected Poems* (Middletown, CT: Wesleyan University Press, 1999) and *The Future of Memory* (Roof/Segue Foundation, 1998); and two critical books, *The Marginalization of Poetry: Language Writing and Literary History* (Princeton: Princeton University Press, 1996) and *The Trouble with Genius: Reading Pound, Joyce, Stein, and Zukofsky* (Berkeley, Los Angeles and London: University of California Press, 1994). He is Professor of English at the University of Pennsylvania.

M. NourbeSe Philip

M. NourbeSe Philip is a poet, essayist, novelist and playwright who lives in the space-time of the City of Toronto. She practiced law in the City of Toronto for seven years before taking up her vocation as a poet and writer. She has published four books of poetry, one novel and three collections of essays. She was awarded a Pushcart Prize (USA) in 1981; the Casa de las Americas Prize (Cuba) in 1988; the Tradewinds Collective Prize in 1988; and was made a Guggenheim Fellow in Poetry (USA) in 1990. In 1994 she was awarded the Lawrence Foundation Prize (USA) for short fiction and her work was recognized in 1995 by the Arts Foundation of Toronto by its Writing and Publishing Award. In 1999 her play *Coups and Calypsos* was a Dora Award finalist.

Lisa Robertson

Lisa Robertson has published three books of poetry: *XEclogue* (Tsunami Editions, 1993, reissued by New Star, 1999); *Debbie: An Epic* (1997; nominated for the Governor-General's Award for Poetry); and *The Weather* (2001) (both co-published by New Star in Canada and Reality Street in the UK). A past member of the Kootenay School of Writing, she lives in Vancouver, Canada, and works as a freelance writer and teacher. Current projects include *Soft Architecture,* a linked series of prose talks on city space, architectural history, and decorative design, which will be collected and published by Clear Cut (Astoria), and a book of lyric poems, *The Men.*

Susan Rudy

Susan Rudy is a Professor of English at the University of Calgary where she teaches contemporary poetry. She has recently completed a co-authored book with Pauline Butling entitled *At the Moment: Alternative Poetries and Communities in English Canada Since 1960.* Current research projects include preparing an annotated bibliography of and critical introduction to the work of Fred Wah and working with Nicole Brossard to publish a (possibly bilingual) edition of her uncollected essays.

Keith Tuma

Keith Tuma is the author of *Fishing by Obstinate Isles: Modern and Postmodern British Poetry and American Readers* (Evanston: Northwestern University

Press, 1998); editor of the *Anthology of Twentieth-Century British and Irish Poetry* (New York: Oxford University Press, 2001); and co-editor of *Mina Loy: Woman and Poet* (Orono, Maine: National Poetry Foundation, 1998). His essays, reviews, notes, interviews, and a scattering of poems and collaborations have appeared in a variety of journals and books. His most recent work includes a special issue of *The Paper,* co-edited with David Kennedy, on poetry and site-specific performance. He is Chair of English at Miami University in Oxford, Ohio.

Barrett Watten

Barrett Watten is Associate Professor of English at Wayne State University and author of two forthcoming volumes of criticism: *The Constructivist Moment: From Material Text to Cultural Poetics* (Middletown, CT: Wesleyan University Press, forthcoming 2003), and *Horizon Shift: Progress and Negativity in American Modernism.* Among his recently published work is a special issue of *Qui Parle* (University of California Press), featuring the writing of emerging poet/critics. His critical articles have appeared in *Genre, Poetics Today, Modernism/Modernity, Qui Parle, The Impercipient Lecture Series, Postmodern Culture, Textual Practice* and *Cultural Studies. Total Syntax,* essays on modern and contemporary poetics, was published in 1984. His most recent creative work is *Bad History* (Atelos Press, 1998); *Frame: 1971–1990* came out in 1997 from Sun and Moon Press. He has also published two book-length poems, *Progress* (1985) and *Under Erasure* (1992), and is co-author of *Leningrad: American Poets in the Soviet Union* (1992). As editor, he brought out two landmark journals of poetry and poetics, *This* (1971–82) and *Poetics Journal* (1982–98); he has also served as associate editor of *Representations,* as corresponding editor of *Artweek* (1989–95) and is on the editorial board of *Criticism.* A recent edition of *Aerial* is devoted to his work.

Don Wellman

Donald Wellman is Professor of Humanities and Writing at Daniel Webster College in Nashua, New Hampshire. His publications and conference papers include work on Ezra Pound, William Carlos Williams, Charles Olson, and Charles Bernstein. For ten years he edited *O.ARS,* a series of anthologies presenting various postmodern poetics and poetries. His "A Complex Realism: Reading *Spring and All* As Seminal For Postmodern Poetry" is forthcoming in *Sagetrieb.* His most recent collection of poetry is *Fields* (Kenosha: Light and Dust, 1995).

John Wilkinson

Many of John Wilkinson's poems are collected in the volumes *Oort's Cloud, Earlier poems* (Barque/subpress, 1999), *Flung Clear, Poems in six books*

(Parataxis Editions, 1994), and *Effigies Against the Light* (Salt Publishing, 2001). He is Head of Mental Health, North East London Strategic Health Authority, and lives in Cambridge with his wife Maud Ellmann. He is the recipient of a Fulbright Distinguished Scholar Award to work on mental health and urban ecology in New York in 2003/04.